LEMON-AID

USED CARS
1999

LEMON-AID

USED CARS
1999

Phil Edmonston

Stoddart

Published in 1998 by
Stoddart Publishing Co. Limited
180 Varick Street, 9th Floor, New York, New York 10014
Email gdsinc@ccmailgw.genpub.com

Distributed by
General Distribution Services Inc.
85 River Rock Drive, Suite 202, Buffalo, New York 14207
Toll-free tel.: 1-800-805-1083   Toll-free fax: 1-800-481-6207

ISBN 0-7737-6022-9

Cover design: Bill Douglas @ The Bang
Typesetting and text design: Wordstyle Productions
Editing: Greg Ioannou/Colborne Communications Centre

Printed and bound in Canada

CONTENTS

Introduction/NO MORE SECRETS!
1

Part One/USED BUT NOT ABUSED
2

Five Reasons to Buy Used 5
Safety Features............................8
Choosing the Right Seller 16
Paying the Right Price 25
Financing Choices...................29
Dealer Scams 30

Private Scams.........................32
Choosing the
Right Kind of Vehicle 34
Other Buying
Considerations 44
Summary 51

Part Two/THE ART OF COMPLAINING
53

Invest in Protest.......................54
Getting Your Money Back.......54
Warranties................................55
Three Steps to a
Settlement................................67
Lemon Laws.............................75
Involving Other Agencies.......79
Launching a Lawsuit...............81

Key Court Decisions 87
Defects (Safety Related) 87
Defects (Body/
Performance Related) 90
Getting a Settlement.............97
Illegal/Unfair Insurance
Company Practices 105

Part Three/CAR AND MINIVAN RATINGS
106

SMALL CARS
112

Chrysler/Eagle
Charger, Horizon,
Omni, Shelby 114
Colt, Expo, Mirage,
Summit, Vista, Wagon 115
Neon 118
Ford
Aspire....................................122
Escort, EXP, Lynx, Tracer...124
General Motors
Cavalier, Sunbird, Sunfire ...129

General Motors/Suzuki
Metro, Swift..........................135
Honda
Civic, CRX, del Sol 137
Hyundai
Accent...................................142
Excel 143
Elantra 145
Mazda
323, GLC, Protegé 148

Nissan/Datsun
Classic, Sentra 151
Pulsar/NX 154
Saturn
SL, SL1, SL2, SC 156
Subaru
Justy.......................................162
Chaser, DL, GL,
Loyale, Impreza, XT 163

Suzuki
Esteem 166
Toyota
Paseo....................................167
Tercel....................................168
Corolla, Prizm 171
Volkswagen
Fox 174
Cabrio, Golf, Jetta................175

MEDIUM CARS
180

Acura
Integra 181
2.2 CL, 3.0 CL 184
Vigor 186
Chrysler/Eagle
Aries, Reliant.......................187
Acclaim, LeBaron, Spirit.....188
Lancer, LeBaron GTS..........192
Duster, Shadow, Sundance ...193
Breeze, Cirrus, Stratus.........196
Ford
Tempo, Topaz 200
Contour, Mystique 203
Sable, SHO, Taurus 206
General Motors
6000, Celebrity,
Century, Ciera......................216
Bonneville, Cutlass Supreme,
Delta 88, Grand Prix,
LeSabre, Lumina,
Monte Carlo, Regal 221
Beretta, Corsica,...................229

Achieva, Calais,
Grand AM, Skylark 233
Honda
Accord 240
Hyundai
Sonata...................................245
Mazda
626, Cronos,
MX-6, Mystère 248
Mitsubishi
Galant 251
Nissan
Altima 253
Stanza....................................255
Subaru
Legacy...................................257
Toyota
Camry 260
Volkswagen
Corrado 265
Passat 266
Volvo
240 269

LARGE CARS/WAGONS
271

Chrysler
Caravelle Salon, Diplomat,
N.Y. Fifth Avenue (RWD) ...273
Dynasty, Fifth Avenue,
Imperial, New Yorker 275

Concorde, Intrepid, LHS,
New Yorker, Vision 277
Ford
Crown Victoria,
Grand Marquis......................284

Cougar, Thunderbird..........288
General Motors
Olds 98/Regency,
Park Avenue........................291

Caprice, Custom Cruiser,
Impala SS, Roadmaster,
Wagon 294

LUXURY CARS
300

Acura
Legend 302
Audi
80, 90, 100, 200,
5000, Coupe, Quattro,
V8 Series, A4, A6, S6 305
BMW
3 Series, 5 Series..................310
General Motors
Aurora, Riviera,
Toronado, Trofeo 315
Allanté, Catera, Eldorado,
Seville 319
Concours, DeVille,
Fleetwood (FWD) 324
Brougham,
Fleetwood (RWD).................328
Infiniti
G20, I30, J30, Q45 330
Lexus
ES 250, ES 300,
LS 400, SC 400......................334

Lincoln
Continental, Mark VII,
Mark VIII, Town Car 338
Mazda
929 345
Millenia 347
Mercedes-Benz
190 Series, C-Class 348
300, 400, 500 Series.............350
Mitsubishi
Diamante................................352
Nissan
Maxima...................................354
Saab
900, 9000 357
Toyota
Avalon.....................................361
Cressida 362
Volvo
700 Series 363
850 Series 365
900 Series 368

SPORTS CARS
370

Chrysler
Daytona, Laser, Shelby 372
Avenger, Sebring...................374
Chrysler/Mitsubishi
Eclipse, Laser, Talon, 4X4...376
3000GT, Stealth 379
Ford
Mustang, Cobra 382
Probe 386

General Motors
Camaro, Firebird, IROC-Z,
Trans Am, Z28 390
Corvette.................................396
Honda
Prelude 400
Hyundai
Scoupe...................................403
Tiburon 405

Mazda
MX-3, Precidia 406
MX-5, Miata 408
RX-7.................................410
Nissan
200SX 412

240SX 413
300ZX...............................415
Toyota
Celica...............................417
MR2 419
Supra 420

MINIVANS
423

Chrysler
Caravan, Town &
Country, Voyager 425
Ford
Aerostar..............................440
Mercury Villager,
Nissan Quest 446
Windstar.............................451
General Motors
Astro, Safari.........................453
Lumina APV, Silhouette,
Trans Sport 457

Honda
Odyssey, Oasis 460
Mazda
MPV.................................462
Toyota
LE, Previa...........................465
Volkswagen
Camper, EuroVan,
Vanagon 468

Appendix I/LEMON-PROOFING BEFORE YOU BUY
471

Safety Check.........................471
Exterior Check......................472

Interior Check 474
Road Test 474

Appendix II/21 BEST INTERNET GRIPE SITES
477

Appendix III/1995–97 MODEL NHTSA CRASH-TEST SUMMARY
481

Appendix IV/INDEX OF KEY DOCUMENTS
490

Appendix V/SURVEY AND BULLETIN SEARCH
493

Introduction
NO MORE SECRETS!

Lemon-Aid Used Cars 1999 is unlike any other auto book on the market. Its main objective, to inform and protect consumers in an industry known for its dishonesty and exaggerated claims. This guide also focuses on secret warranties and confidential service bulletins that automakers swear don't exist. That's why you'll be interested in the "Index of Key Documents" found at the end of the book. There you'll find the exact bulletin, memo, or news clipping reproduced from the original so neither the dealer nor the automaker can weasel out of its obligations.

Lemon-Aid guides have been popular in Canada for 26 years. *Lemon-Aid*'s information is culled mostly from U.S. and Canadian sources and is gathered throughout the year from owner complaints, whistle blowers, lawsuits, and judgments, as well as from confidential manufacturer service bulletins.

Each year, we target abusive auto industry practices and lobby for changes. For example, in last year's Canadian guide, we highlighted the Chrysler minivan's automatic transmission, paint, and brake problems, in addition to calling for airbag on-off switches to protect women and seniors from severe injuries caused by airbag deployment during fender-bender accidents. Following *Lemon-Aid*'s urging, the federal government and automakers agreed to make the switches available and published the names of cooperating garages on the National Highway Traffic and Safety Administration's (NHTSA) Internet site. Chrysler set up a special review committee (see Part Two, "Invest in Protest") to compensate owners even if their warranty had expired or they had been refused a refund in the past. This year, we take Ford to task over its failure-prone automatic transmissions and air conditioners (afflicted by what experts call the "Black Death"), in addition to defective head gaskets on its 3.8L engines.

This guide makes a critical comparison of 1990–97 cars and minivans, and safer, cheaper, and more reliable alternatives are given for each vehicle.

Lemon-Aid combines test results with owner complaints, Internet postings, and surveys to determine its ratings. Please fill out the questionnaire found at the end of this guide and list the degree of satisfaction or dissatisfaction you've experienced with your vehicle. Your information will be compiled and used in the next edition of *Lemon-Aid Used Cars.*

I wouldn't dare keep it a secret.

Phil Edmonston
October 1998

Part One
USED BUT NOT ABUSED

"Out of 100 vehicles, we're apt to build 10 that are as good as any that Toyota has ever built, 80 that are okay and 10 that cause repeated problems for our customers."

Robert Lutz, President
Chrysler U.S.
Chrysler Times, 17 July 1995

That's right, Robert, and it's *Lemon-Aid*'s job to warn buyers to steer clear of that last 10 percent and even reconsider that 80 percent you consider "okay."

It's hard to believe I've been writing *Lemon-Aid* guides for almost 27 years. Imagine, when the first guides were written, Volkswagen had a monopoly on cold, slow, and unsold Beetles and minivans, Ford was selling biodegradable pickups (and denying it had a J-67 secret warranty to cover rust repairs), and a good, three-year-old used car could be found for less than $2,000. The average price now tops $15,000.

Chrysler owners' protest against paint peeling led to the creation of CLOG (Chrysler Lemon Owners' Group). Chrysler cars and minivans are examples of a good idea gone bad. Although they're reasonably priced, spacious, and loaded with convenience features, chronic automatic transmission, brake, electrical, and paint defects can easily put a $5,000–$7,000 dent in your wallet. When faced with paint peeling or discoloring claims, Chrysler usually blames its workers, bird droppings, or the sun and then settles out of court.

Throughout the 1980s, the quality of imports improved dramatically, with Toyota, Nissan, and Honda leading the pack. American quality, on the other hand, improved at a snail's pace over the same period because there was no Japanese competition. Today, the Big Three automakers' quality control is about where the Japanese automakers' was in the mid-'80s. Where the gap hasn't narrowed (and a case can be made that it's actually gotten wider) is in powertrain reliability and fit and finish.

For example, take a look at the following three confidential internal service bulletins depicting serious powertrain defects affecting Chrysler, Ford, and GM cars, minivans, and trucks.

Chrysler's "Radar" Stalling

NO: 18-16-96
GROUP: Vehicle Performance
DATE: May 3, 1996
SUBJECT:
Intermittent Driveability Problems When Driving Near Radar
MODELS:
1996 (NS) Town & Country/Caravan/Voyager
SYMPTOM/CONDITION:
Some vehicles may experience intermittent driveability concerns or problems when driven in close proximity to military or air traffic control radar installations.
REPAIR PROCEDURE:
This bulletin involves installing a new "hardened" crankshaft position sensor and/or reprogramming (flashing) the PCM with new software calibrations.
POLICY: Reimbursable within the provisions of the warranty.
TIME ALLOWANCE:
Labor Operation No: 08-19-43-94   0.5 hrs.
FAILURE CODE: FM – Flash Module

A Chrysler official tells me that "driveability" is a euphemism for engine stumbling and stalling. CLOG (Chrysler Lemon Owners Group) members tell me this is a common problem.

Ford's "Aluminum" Transmission

Article No.
94-24-7
11/28/94
TRANSAXLE – AXOD, AXOD-E, AX4S – FORWARD/REVERSE ENGAGEMENT CONCERN – REVISED FORWARD CLUTCH PISTON
FORD:
1986-95 TAURUS; 1993-95 TAURUS SHO
LINCOLN-MERCURY:
1986-95 SABLE; 1988-94 CONTINENTAL
LIGHT TRUCK:
1995 WINDSTAR
ISSUE:
The forward clutch piston may crack on its outside diameter, seal groove or apply wall (bottom of piston). This condition could allow internal clutch leakage resulting in engagement concerns.
ACTION:
Use the chart for proper application if replacement of the forward clutch piston is necessary.
NOTE:
Use a magnet to verify the forward clutch piston being installed is the new steel piston. The magnet will adhere to the steel piston and not to the aluminum piston.
Do not use any service stock of aluminum forward clutch pistons. Return stock to parts depot for credit.

Imagine, this failure-prone aluminum piston was used in the 1986–95 Taurus, Sable, Continental, and Windstar models.

GM's "Clunking" Transmission

File In Section 4 — Drive Axle
Bulletin No.: 56-44-01A
Date: October 1996
INFORMATION
Subject:
Driveline Clunk
Models:
1997 and Prior Light Duty Trucks
This bulletin is being revised to include 1996 and 1997 models. Please discard Corporate Bulletin Number 56-44-01
(Section 4-Drive Axle). GMC recommends that a copy of this bulletin also be placed in Section 7 — Transmission.
**Some owners of light duty trucks equipped with automatic transmissions may comment that their truck
exhibits a clunk noise when shifting between park and drive, park and reverse or drive and reverse.
Similarly, owners of trucks equipped with automatic or manual transmissions may comment that their
truck exhibits a clunk noise while driving when the accelerator is quickly depressed and then released.**
Whenever there are two or more gears interacting with one another, there must be a certain amount of clearance
between those gears in order for them to operate properly. That clearance or free play (also known as lash) can translate into a clunk noise whenever the gear is loaded and unloaded quickly, or whenever the direction of rotation is
reversed. The more gears you have in a system, the more freeplay the total system will have.
The clunk noise that customers sometimes hear is believed to be the result of a buildup of freeplay (lash) between components in the driveline.
For example, the potential for a driveline clunk would be greater in a 4-wheel drive or all-wheel drive vehicle than a 2-
wheel drive vehicle. This is because in addition to the freeplay from the rear axle gears, the universal joints, and the
transmission (common to both vehicles), the 4-wheel drive transfer case gears (and their associated clearances) add
additional freeplay to the driveline.
In service, dealers are discouraged from attempting to repair driveline clunk conditions for two reasons:
1.   Comments of driveline clunk are almost never the result of one individual component with excessive lash, but rather
     a result of the additive effect of the freeplay (or lash) present in all the driveline components.
     Since all components in the driveline have a certain amount of lash by design, changing driveline components may
     not result in a satisfactory lash reduction.
2.   **While some customers may find the clunk noise objectionable, it will not adversely affect durability
     or performance.**
Important:
The condition described in this bulletin should not be confused with Driveline Stop Clunk, described in corporate bulletin
number 964101R (Chevrolet 92-265-71, GMC Truck 91-4A-77, Oldsmobile 47-71-20A, GM of Canada 93-4A-100).

*GM's transmission "clunks" affect only its rear-drive Astro/Safari mini-
vans and pickups. Surprisingly, unlike Ford, GM still hasn't worked out a
fix for these clunky transmissions.*

Good buys are out there

This is an excellent year to buy a used car or minivan. Most vehicles
are now equipped with many of the essential safety features that
were ignored by automakers two decades ago; overall reliability
and durability have improved and are backed by longer warranties
that are still in force; and millions of reasonably priced leased
vehicles are now entering the used car market. Right now, for example, Ford's popular Crown Victoria, Mercury Grand Marquis, and
Windstar minivans are coming off two- and three-year leases and are
in abundant supply both from dealers and private parties.

You can reduce your risk of buying a lemon by getting a recommended vehicle that has some of the original warranty in effect.
Not only will this protect you from some of the costly defects that
are bound to crop up shortly after your purchase, but the warranty
allows you to make one final inspection before it expires and

requires both the dealer and automaker to compensate you for all warrantable defects found at that time. The ultimate irony is that because Chrysler dropped its seven-year warranty on its 1995 models, your used '93 Chrysler will be under warranty until the year 2000—surpassing the 1996 models' three-year guarantee.

Five Reasons to Buy Used

How popular are used vehicles in North America? Estimated private U.S. car sales in 1996 were 11.5 million vehicles valued at $50.2 billion, according to CNW Marketing Research. Why are people buying used? Mostly to save money, but there are other important reasons as well:

1. Less initial cash outlay, slower vehicle depreciation, and better and cheaper parts availability.
New vehicle prices that hover around an average $18,000 payout are priced out of reach for many first-time purchasers. Insurance for young drivers runs about $4,000 a year—probably more than the monthly payment. And once you add financing costs, maintenance, taxes, and a host of other expenses, expect to shell out about $3,000–$5,000 annually in overall operating costs. Minivans are a bit cheaper to own and operate due to their slower rate of depreciation—the biggest expense for most vehicles.

Be practical. In buying a used car or minivan, keep in mind you're simply buying transportation and function: principally, no-surprise handling, a comfortable ride, reliable performance, and interior, cargo, and passenger capacity. Because you only need about one-half the cash or credit required for a new vehicle, it's easy to see that you won't have to invest as much money in a depreciating investment and may be fortunate enough to forgo a loan.

Depreciation savings
If someone were to ask you to invest in stocks or bonds guaranteed to be worth about one-half of their initial purchase value after three to four years, you'd probably head for the door. But this is exactly the trap you're falling into when you buy a new vehicle, which may depreciate 20 percent in the first year and 15 percent each year thereafter (minivans and other specialty vehicles like trucks and sport-utilities depreciate about 10 percent each subsequent year). Here's how a new car adds up without a trade-in:

Cost (New)

Purchase price	$20,000
Combined sales tax (5%)	$1,000
Total price	**$21,000**

Now, the motorist buying a new vehicle is certain that the warranty and status far outweigh any inconvenience. If he or she had a trade-in, its value would be subtracted from the negotiated price of the new vehicle and sales tax would be paid on the reduced amount. He or she forks over $21,000 and takes possession of a new car or minivan.

When you buy used, the situation is altogether different. That same vehicle can be purchased three years later, in good condition and with much of the manufacturer's warranty remaining, for about one-half of its original cost (in the red-hot truck and sport-utility market, depreciation may be much less).

Cost (Used)

Purchase price (3 years old, 60,000 miles)	$10,000
Combined sales tax (5%)	$500
Total price	**$10,500**

In this conservative example (some savings exceed 50 percent), the used-vehicle buyer saves $500 in sales tax and gets a reliable, guaranteed "set of wheels" for about one-half of the vehicle's original price. Furthermore, the depreciation "hit" will be much less in the ensuing years.

Cheap parts
Generally, a new gasoline-powered vehicle can be expected to run at least 125,000 miles to 200,000 miles in its lifetime and a diesel-powered vehicle can easily double those figures. Some repairs will crop up at regular intervals and, along with preventive maintenance, your yearly running costs should average about $500. Buttressing the argument that vehicles get cheaper to operate the longer you keep them, the U.S. Department of Transportation points out that the average vehicle requires one or more major repairs after every five years of use. However, once these repairs are done, it can then be run relatively trouble-free for another five years or more.

Time is on your side in other ways, too. Three years after a model's launching, the replacement parts market catches up to consumer demand due to dealers stocking larger inventories and parts wholesalers and independent parts manufacturers expanding their output. Used replacement parts are unquestionably easier to come by, through bargaining with local garages or through a careful search of auto wreckers' yards. A reconditioned or used part goes for one-third to one-half the cost of a new part. There's generally no difference in the quality of reconditioned parts and they're often guaranteed as long as new ones. Also, shopping at discount outlets, independent garages, or through mail order houses can save you big bucks (30–35 percent) on the cost of new parts and another 15 percent on labor.

There are generally no problems with parts distribution for American vehicles, unless a particular unit has been off the market for some time or a specific component has experienced a high failure rate (such as electronic control units that regulate engine, transmission, and braking performance). In these cases, though, there are many independent suppliers who can find the missing parts and price them far below dealer cost. Components can also be more easily interchanged on American and Japanese vehicles than on European models.

Hard-to-find body panels ("crash parts") are frequently replaced with metal or fiberglass panels made by independent manufacturers. According to tests carried out by consumer groups and government agencies, these less-expensive parts are just as durable and carry guarantees against premature rust-out and poor fits. Nevertheless, carmakers oppose their use and trot out dubious safety, durability, and depreciation advantages to using original-equipment body parts.

Auto clubs are often helpful sources for parts that are otherwise unobtainable. Club members trade and sell specialty parts, keep a list of where rare parts can be found, and are usually well informed as to where independent parts suppliers are located. The Internet and most car enthusiast magazines will put you in touch with auto clubs and suppliers of hard-to-find parts.

2. Lower insurance rates.

The difference in annual insurance costs between a new and used car or minivan can be considerable, and by increasing the deductible, smart shoppers can further reduce the annual premium by hundreds of dollars. For example, as an automobile gets older, the amount of the deductible should be increased. It may reach a maximum of $500 per collision. As the amount of the deductible increases, the annual premium for collision coverage decreases.

By agreeing to a higher deductible, the motorist agrees to pay for damage repairs where the cost doesn't exceed the deductible amount. Generally, by purchasing used parts (remember, you bought a used vehicle) from a local auto wrecker and having the work done by small, specialized garages, the total amount of your repair losses can be controlled. What may have been an estimated loss of $500 may be significantly reduced by sharp repair bargaining.

3. Fewer "hidden" defects.

Have your choice checked out by an independent mechanic (for $50–$75) before paying for a used vehicle. This examination before purchase protects you against any hidden defects the vehicle may have. It's also a tremendous negotiating tool, since it allows you to use the cost of any needed repairs to bargain down the purchase price.

If you can't get permission to have the vehicle inspected elsewhere, walk away from the deal, no matter how tempting the selling price. The seller is obviously trying to put something over on you. Ignore the standard excuses that the vehicle isn't insured, the license plates have expired, or the vehicle has a dead battery.

4. You know the vehicle's history.
Smart customers will want to get answers to the following questions before paying a penny for any used vehicle: What did it first sell for and what is its present value? How much of the original warranty is left? How many times has the vehicle been recalled for safety-related defects? Are parts easily available? Does the vehicle have a history of costly performance-related defects that can be corrected under a secret warranty, a safety recall campaign, or with an upgraded part? (See "Service Tips" in Part Three.)

5. Litigation is quick, easy, and relatively inexpensive.
A multitude of federal and state consumer protection laws go far beyond whatever protection may be offered by the standard new vehicle warranty. Furthermore, buyers of used vehicles don't usually have to conform to any arbitrary rules or service guidelines to get this protection.

Let's say you do get stuck with a lemon. Most small claims courts have a jurisdiction limit of $3,000–$10,000, which should cover the cost of most used cars or minivans. Therefore, any dispute between buyer and seller can be settled within a few months, without lawyers or excessive court costs. Furthermore, you're not likely to face a battery of lawyers standing in for the automaker and dealer. Actually, you may not have to face a judge either, since many cases are settled through court-imposed mediators.

Safety Features

Before buying any used "bargain," determine what degree of active and passive safety the vehicle provides. Passive safety assumes that you will be involved in life-threatening situations and should be warned in time to avoid injury. Daytime running lights and third, center-mounted brake lights are two passive safety features that do this job extremely well. In fact, the NHTSA, an arm of the U.S. Department of Transportation, estimates that center brake lights—a required safety feature since 1986—reduce the number of rear-impact crashes by 4.3 percent, thereby preventing 92,000 crashes, 58,000 injuries, and $655 million in property damage annually. The annual cost to the consumer of the brake lights is about $13.60 per car and about $20 for vans, pickups, and sport-utilities.

Passive safety also assumes that some accidents aren't avoidable and that when such an accident occurs, the vehicle should provide as much protection as possible to the driver, the vehicle's occupants, and other vehicles that may be struck—without depending on the driver's reactions. Passive safety components that have consistently been proven to reduce vehicular deaths and injuries are safety belts and vehicle structures that absorb or deflect crash forces away from the vehicle's occupants.

Advocates of active safety stress that accidents are caused by the proverbial "nut behind the wheel" and believe that safe driving can best be taught through schools or private driving courses. Active safety components are generally those mechanical systems that may help avoid accidents, such as high-performance tires and traction control, if the driver is skillful and mature.

The theory of active safety has several drawbacks. First, there's no independent proof that safe driving can be taught successfully. Even if a new driver learns how to master defensive-driving techniques, there's still no assurance that this training will be of any use in an emergency. Second, 40 to 50 percent of all fatal accidents are caused by drivers who are under the influence of alcohol or drugs. Surely all the high-performance options and specialized driving courses in the world will not provide much protection from impaired drivers who take a bead on your vehicle. Finally, because active safety components get a lot of use—you're likely to need anti-lock brakes 99 times more often than an airbag—they have to be well maintained to remain effective.

Safety features that kill
In the late '70s, Washington forced automakers to include essential safety features like collapsing steering columns and safety windshields in their cars. As the years have passed, the number of mandatory safety features has increased to include seatbelts, airbags, and crashworthy construction. These improvements met with public approval—until two years ago, when reports of deaths and injuries induced by anti-lock brakes (ABS) and airbags showed that defective components and poor engineering negated the potential life-saving benefits associated with these devices.

For example, one out of every five ongoing NHTSA investigations into possible defects in cars and light trucks concerns inadvertent airbag deployment, failure to deploy, or injuries suffered when the bag did go off. In fact, airbags are the agency's single largest cause of current investigations, exceeding even the full range of brake problems, which runs second.

Anti-lock brake system (ABS)
ABS pumps the brakes automatically, many times a second, to prevent wheel lockup and enable the driver to maintain steering control. This can mean substantially shorter stopping distances on wet and slippery roads but not on dry roads. If you anticipate driving a lot on slick roads, anti-lock brakes might be worthwhile. Remember,

they're more about steering control than about stopping on a dime. Finally, if you do decide to buy a vehicle with ABS, make sure you can adapt to the excessive pulsation and noise that often occur when the brakes are applied.

Despite impressive test track performance, the on-the-road safety benefits of car anti-locks are disappointing—they haven't cut the frequency of crashes or the cost of insurance claims for vehicle damage. Studies by the government, the Insurance Institute for Highway Safety (IIHS), and automakers find that vehicles with anti-locks are in more single-vehicle crashes than those with conventional brakes. It's not clear why this is so, but it is apparent that many drivers don't know how to use anti-locks.

And then there are the hardware and software shortcomings. Sold as a $500–$600 option on most new vehicles, used ABS-equipped models are risky buys because their brakes were rushed to production in the mid-'80s without sufficient testing. This has resulted in owners reporting thousands of incidents of brake failure attributable to poor design and defective components (see "Safety Summary" for the Dodge Caravan, for example). In fact, *AutoWeek* magazine reports that General Motors has secretly bought back hundreds of vehicles equipped with failure-prone Kelsey-Hayes anti-lock brakes.

General buyback. While publicly blaming drivers for problems with the antilock braking systems on millions of pickup trucks and sport/utility vehicles, General Motors was quietly buying some trucks back from consumers whose dealers could not repair the systems, according to documents filed with the National Highway Traffic Safety Administration.

NHTSA has been investigating ABS defects on 1991-94 Chevy Blazer, GMC Jimmy and Typhoon, and Olds Bravada sport/utes, as well as on Chevy S-10 and GMC Sonoma and Syclone pickups for three years. The agency has received more than 15,000 consumer complaints. In late 1995, NHTSA added 1992-94 Chevy/GMC Suburbans to the probe. In dozens of cases, when owners threatened to contact attorneys or file lemon law claims, GM either bought vehicles back or offered vehicle trade-in assistance to get customers into new vehicles. NHTSA officials are expected to meet soon with GM to discuss a possible recall. A GM spokesman did not respond to requests for comments before presstime. ▶

Since NHTSA began investigating GM ABS failures in 1994, over 9,000 complaints involving 2,401 crashes have been lodged against GM's 1991–94 pickups, which include the S-10, Sonoma, Blazer, Bravada, and Jimmy. Recently, the 1992–95 Suburban was added to the list.

Furthermore, the replacement of aging ABS components, usually around the fifth year of use, can easily cost $700 or more because mechanics can't troubleshoot them very well and many replacement parts are no longer manufactured. Not surprisingly, mechanics will often junk the old design and put in a new assembly to make sure you don't come back with other failures. If you were trained to brake gently on slippery roads or pump your brakes to avoid a skid, you now have to "unlearn" these old habits and use hard, continuous brake pressure to activate the anti-lock feature.

Airbags
If you're female, a senior, someone of slight stature, or unable to sit at least 10 inches away from the airbag housing, don't buy an airbag-equipped used vehicle—unless it has a cut-off switch, can be retrofitted for one, or you know where to go to deactivate the system (hint: try the Internet at *airbags.com*). Another option is to keep well back from the dashboard with pedal extenders; call 819-932-8566 for info. Granted, airbag-equipped used cars and minivans are lifesavers in high-speed collisions but they're also life takers and mutilators in low-speed, "fender-bender" collisions of 7–10 mph, according to the following Transport Canada research study, "Airbag Deployment Crashes in Canada." (Paper number 96SI-0-05, presented by Dainius J. Dalmotas of Transport Canada and Kennerly Digges of George Washington University to the Fifteenth International Technical Conference on the Enhanced Safety of Vehicles, Melbourne, Australia, May 13–16, 1996.)

Air Bag Deployment Crashes in Canada

ABSTRACT

In the fall of 1993 Transport Canada initiated a major field accident study to examine the injury experience of occupants protected by supplementary air bag systems. While the initial findings of this study confirm that belted drivers are afforded added protection against head and facial fracture injury in moderated to severe frontal collisions, **the findings also suggest that these benefits are being negated by a high incidence of bag-induced injury.** Most bag-related injuries consist of AIS 1 facial injuries and AIS 1 to 3 upper extremity injuries. However, they can include AIS ≥ 3 injuries to other body regions if the occupant is close to the deploying air bag. **The incidence of bag-induced injury was greatest among female drivers.**

To further quantify the benefits and drawbacks afforded by air bag systems particularly as a function of collision severity, additional analyses were carried out using U.S. field accident data. Both Canadian and U.S. data examined suggest the protection afforded belted drivers by air bag systems would be greatly enhanced if the deployment thresholds were increased. **Far greater attention to the protection requirements of female drivers needs to be given in federal regulations addressing restraint system performance.**

http://www.nhtsa.dot.gov/ *is a particularly informative U.S. Department of Transportation web site that answers frequently asked questions concerning airbags and keeps a current listing of repair facilities willing to install airbag disabling devices.*

Federal legislation makes it a crime to disable an airbag without government permission, and automakers won't sell you a shut-off switch without NHTSA approval. To get that approval (a three to

eight week process), owners have to show that they meet the following criteria:
• They cannot sit at least 10 inches away from the airbag housing.
• They have a medical condition that would put them at risk (such as osteoporosis).
• They have a rear-facing child safety seat that must be used in the front passenger seat.
• They must routinely place children in the front seat (as with car pools).

Adding insult to potential injury, cut-off switches are estimated to cost $200–$300 (an Alabama class action lawsuit winding its way through the courts says automakers should pay for the switch installation) and won't be installed by most independent garages. Some import automakers like BMW, Mercedes-Benz, and Volvo won't provide the switches and other importers don't expect to have them for sale before late 1999. In the meantime, don't be surprised to find dealers reluctant to touch the devices until they get clear instruction from automakers and insurers. In fact, the American Automobile Association (AAA) estimates that 84 percent of the repair facilities it has surveyed won't install cut-off switches. The NHTSA's web site (see Appendix II) has an extensive listing of garages/dealers willing to install switches in the United States.

Crashworthiness
The most important safety features are those that reduce the risk of death or serious injury when a crash occurs. This aspect of vehicle design is referred to as crashworthiness. Purchasing a used vehicle with the idea that you'll be involved in an accident is not unreasonable—according to the IIHS, the average car will likely be involved in two accidents before ending up as scrap.

The vehicle's structural design is the starting point for protecting you during a serious crash. A good structural design should have a strong occupant compartment, or safety cage, and front and rear ends designed to buckle and bend to absorb crash forces during serious crashes. It's important for these crush zones to keep damage away from the safety cage because the likelihood of injury increases rapidly once this cage begins to collapse. If effectively designed, a longer crush zone lowers both the likelihood of damage to the occupant compartment and the crash forces inside it.

Not all vehicles are equally well designed. Some have crush zones that are too stiff and/or too short and safety cages that aren't strong enough. Such poorly designed crush zones can contribute to the collapse of the occupant compartment in serious crashes. Crash tests demonstrate differences in structural design among vehicles in the same weight class.

The NHTSA has determined that some larger vehicles like the Dodge B-series van, shown above, give excellent protection to their occupants during an accident while "aggressively" endangering the lives of smaller vehicles' passengers. Other, more recent, studies dispute these findings.

Top "Killer" Vehicles That Endanger Others in Crashes

1. Dodge B-series van
2. Chevrolet S10 pickup
3. Chevrolet Blazer
4. Toyota 4Runner
5. Mazda MPV
6. GMC Jimmy
7. Ford F-series pickup
8. Ford E-series van
9. Ford Explorer/Bronco II
10. Chevrolet/GMC G-series van
11. Dodge Dakota
12. Dodge D50/Colt pickup/Ram
13. Chevrolet Astro van
14. Ford Ranger
15. Chevrolet C, K, R, and V-series

Occupants of large vehicles have fewer severe injury claims than do occupants of small vehicles. This was proven conclusively in a 1996 NHTSA study that showed collisions between light trucks or vans with small cars resulted in an 81 percent fatality rate for the occupants of the small cars.

Vehicle weight protects you, principally, in two-vehicle crashes. In a head-on crash, for example, the heavier vehicle drives the lighter one backwards, which decreases forces inside the heavy vehicle and increases forces in the lighter one. All heavy vehicles, even poorly designed ones, offer this advantage in two-vehicle collisions but may not offer good protection in single-vehicle crashes.

Interestingly, a vehicle's size or past crashworthiness rating doesn't always guarantee that you won't be injured in an accident. U.S. government crash tests show, for example, that a 1991 Ford Escort small car gives better full-front collision protection than a 1994 Mercury Villager or Nissan Quest, two large minivans that could have been easily engineered to crash safely at moderate speeds of 35 mph. Also, different years of the same model or size variation can produce startlingly different scores. For example, Chrysler's 1995 Caravan and Voyager minivans earned better driver crash protection scores than did the 1996 and 1997 Grand Caravan and Grand Voyager.

Two Washington-based agencies monitor how vehicle design affects crash safety. They are the U.S. National Highway Traffic and Safety Administration (NHTSA) and the Insurance Institute for Highway Safety (IIHS), an insurance research group that collects and analyzes insurance claims data. Crash information from these two groups doesn't always agree because, while the insurance research group's results incorporate all kinds of accidents, the NHTSA figures relate only to 35 mph frontal and some side collisions. The frontal tests are equivalent to two vehicles of equal weight hitting each other head-on while traveling at 35 mph or to a car slamming into a parked car at 70 mph. Bear in mind that a car providing good injury protection often produces the highest damage claims because its structure, not the occupants, absorbs most of the force of the collision.

Unsafe designs
Although it sounds hard to believe, automakers will deliberately manufacture a vehicle that will kill or maim simply because, in the long run, it costs less to pay off victims than to make a safer vehicle. I learned this lesson after reading the court transcripts of *Grimshaw v. Ford* and listening to court testimony of GM engineers who deliberately placed fire-prone "side-saddle" gas tanks in millions of pickups to save $2.20 per vehicle. In the Grimshaw case, tried in the late '70s, a teenager riding in a Ford Pinto was rear-ended by another car and suffered burns to over 90 percent of his body. Subpoenaed Ford internal documents showed that the automaker had known about the defect for years. In fact, Ford accountants had made a cost comparison of the price of recalling and redesigning the defective fuel tanks ($128 million) with what they'd likely have to spend in lawsuits to compensate those injured or killed if they continued to stonewall victims and accident investigators ($69 million). Ford had chosen to stonewall and litigate.

More recent examples of corporate greed triumphing over public safety: airbag designs that maim or kill women, children, and seniors; anti-lock brake systems that don't brake (a major problem with GM minivans, trucks, and sport-utilities and Chrysler sport-utilities and minivans); flimsy front seats; the absence of rear head restraints; and fire-prone GM pickup fuel tanks and Ford ignition switches. All of these are examples of hazardous engineering designs that put profit ahead of safety. Incidentally, State Farm Insurance has filed a lawsuit against Ford to recoup the millions of dollars in claims it paid out for fire damage caused by Ford's fire-prone ignition switches.

Recalls

Vehicles are recalled for one of two reasons: they may be unsafe or they may not conform to federal and state pollution control regulations. Whatever the reason, though, recalls are a great way to get free repairs—if you know which ones apply to you.

On average, about 800,000 motor vehicles are recalled each year because of safety problems. More than 200 million unsafe vehicles have been recalled by automakers for the free correction of safety-related defects since American recall legislation was passed in 1966. During that time, about one third of the recalled vehicles never made it back to the dealership for repairs. Auto Service Monitor, an American firm that tracks recalls, estimates this means there are close to 20 million vehicles, still on North American roads, that could suddenly career out of control, catch fire, or fail to brake. Surprisingly, motorists aren't generally motivated to bring in their recalled vehicles—even when the result of the defect is as life-threatening as fire. For example, NHTSA figures show that Ford's recall of 1.4 million Pinto and Bobcat small cars in the late '70s to correct the much-publicized exploding gas tank defect received a response rate of just 52 percent. According to the NHTSA, the average completion rate is 68 percent. This lack of public concern can be blamed partly on apathy, but carmakers must also bear much of the blame because they downplay the defect's safety implications (see the "Safety Summary" for the Chrysler Caravan in Part Three) and send out only one recall letter to the first recorded owner of the vehicle. If the owner has moved or leased the vehicle, he or she likely won't be notified.

Auto thefts and automaker thievery

Automakers are making bundles of money on stolen vehicles. They manufacture products like the Caravan (a kid using a pair of scissors can easily break into the vehicle and then override the ignition), then make money repairing them if they're recovered or replacing them if they're not found. Insurance companies get to raise their rates and it's the average consumer who gets screwed.

The Caravan heads the list of the most stolen vehicles not because of its popularity but simply because it's so easy to steal. I have received dozens of letters from *Lemon-Aid* readers imploring me to warn 1984–96 Chrysler minivan owners to invest in an ignition kill switch or risk the very real probability that their minivans will be heisted. Chrysler is aware of the problem but prefers to blame the victims rather than make their vehicles more theft proof.

General Motors is worse. Throughout the 1980s and early '90s, its trucks and vans were ranked among those easiest to steal because GM's Saginaw steering column had a cheap, plastic protective covering for the ignition switch instead of a metal plate (used by Ford, for example). This cost-cutting measure was an open invitation to amateur thieves using nothing more than household tools to "rip and ride."

The company began embedding a computer chip in the ignition key in the late '80s and thefts declined dramatically.

Less than a decade ago, Honda and Toyota had similar reputations for building easy-to-steal vehicles. Their doorlock tumblers and switches used bearings made of low-grade metal that wore down over time. Once worn, any thief using a blank key bought from the local hardware store could easily bypass the lock and ignition switch and rip off any 1982–89 Honda or Toyota truck in 30 seconds or less. Unlike GM, the two Asian automakers quickly changed their design and thefts became less of a problem.

Break-ins and thefts cost motorists billions of dollars annually; there is a 1 in 130 chance your vehicle will be stolen and only a 60 percent chance you'll ever get it back. No wonder over one-third of new vehicles are equipped with standard or optional security systems. These include fuel cut-off devices, electronic alarms, active and passive units that are armed by the driver or are self-arming, ignition disablers, parts identification, and security keys.

The most effective theft-deterrent systems are not always the most expensive ones. Don't waste your money on expensive anti-theft devices that depend mainly on your vehicle's horn or lights to scare thieves away. They often go off at the wrong time and can be deactivated easily. Furthermore, they frighten the thief away only after the vehicle has been damaged. When it comes to protecting a vehicle's contents, no alarm system can resist a brick through a side window. It takes just 12 minutes for thieves to strip a vehicle's seat, radio, and body parts. As well, few citizens are brave enough to personally stop a theft or testify in court. Your best protection is discretion: take your radio with you or lock it in the trunk, particularly if you own a sport-utility with an upgraded sound system.

Since most cars and minivans are stolen by amateurs, the best theft deterrent is a visible device that complicates the job while immobilizing the vehicle and sounding an alarm. For less than $100 you can install both a steering wheel lock and a hidden ignition disabler. The club-like steering wheel locks cost about $50 and deter thieves by forcing them to carry a hacksaw and adding about a half minute to the time it takes to steal the average vehicle (they have to cut through the steering wheel or bust the lock). Ignition disablers are also inexpensive and very effective. They sell for $25–$75, depending on their sophistication.

Choosing the Right Seller

When to buy

Used car sales are seasonal, depending where you live. In the northern and western states, fewer used vehicles are sold in the winter months of December through March than in the spring or summer. Dealers see few customers and used vehicles generally show their worst characteristics: they won't start, have defective heating and defrosting systems, poor suspensions, etc. On the other hand, in fall and spring, dealer stocks of good quality trade-ins and off-lease returns are at their highest level and private sellers are more active. It's precisely for these reasons that smart consumers shop during these months for real bargains.

Should you use a broker?

My answer is a qualified yes. Even with my thirty years' experience as a consumer advocate and automotive expert, I have used brokers and found them to be well worth the money spent for their services when I considered the runaround time they saved me.

Brokers are independent agents who try to find the new or used vehicle you want at a price below what you'd pay at a dealership, including the extra cost of the broker's services. Broker services appeal to buyers who want to save time and money while avoiding most of the stress and hassle associated with the dealership experience, which for many people is like a swim in shark-infested waters.

According to *Automotive News*, automobile brokers represent only about 5 percent of new and used car transactions even though their numbers have grown perceptibly in the past few years. Because their services aren't effectively regulated throughout the country, it's difficult to determine how many brokers are operating in any one area.

Brokers get new vehicles only through dealers, while used vehicles may come from dealers, auctions, private sellers, and leasing companies. Basically, a broker finds an appropriate vehicle that meets the client's expressed needs and then negotiates the purchase (or lease) on behalf of the client. The majority of brokers tend to deal exclusively in new cars, trucks, or vans, with a small percentage dealing in both new and used vehicles. Ancillary services vary among brokers and may include such things as comparative vehicle analysis, price research, and battling dealers and insurance adjusters to ensure their clients are treated fairly.

The cost of hiring a broker ranges anywhere from a flat fee of a few hundred dollars to a percentage of the value of the vehicle. Sometimes a broker may offer his services for a nominal fee, or even tell the buyer that the service is "free." In such cases, it's best to remember that nothing is free in the car business. If the customer isn't paying the fee directly, then the broker's fee is being paid by the dealer, who simply buries that commission in the total price of the vehicle. Ultimately, the customer pays, either way. While it's not impossible to get a reasonable deal under such an arrangement, beware: the broker may be unduly biased towards a certain dealer or manufacturer. Reputable brokers are not beholden to any particular dealership or make and will disclose their flat fee up front or tell the buyer the percentage amount they charge on a specific vehicle.

There are both advantages and disadvantages to using a broker. The advantages follow:

• Brokers can save you lots of time. This is particularly true with used vehicles, because each one is unique and must be approached accordingly. A responsible broker may check out and reject a number of used vehicles before finally recommending one to the buyer.
• Brokers work full time at buying vehicles. Since they deal in volume, they have access to new vehicle fleet rates. This "fleet price" can translate into thousands of dollars off the manufacturer's suggested list price.
• Brokers know how to haggle. A recent survey of over 2,700 used car transactions in the U.S. found that dealerships that permitted price haggling generally gave buyers a better deal. Savings ranged from $481 to $937, depending on the vehicle chosen. Most brokers also have had experience working in dealerships, so they understand the rhythm and ploys of negotiations. As negotiators, they have the distinct advantage of being emotionally detached from the purchase in a way the actual purchaser rarely is. They also tend to know current wholesale values of vehicles, so the buyer doesn't get shortchanged on a trade-in or pay too much for a used vehicle.

Finding the right broker

Buyers who are looking for a broker should first ask friends and acquaintances if they can recommend one. Word-of-mouth referrals are often the best, because people won't refer others to a dissatisfying service provider. If a referral isn't an option, try a broker that's used by your local AAA, Costco, or Price Club store. This will give you some important leverage if you aren't treated fairly.

Obviously, buyers should use a broker they trust, but trust must be earned. Ask about the benefits of the buying service above and beyond the usual "locate and negotiate." Does the broker have industry experience? Is the broker well informed? Impartial? Sympathetic to your needs? The broker should provide full disclosure of all charges related to the service at the time of your first interview. If the broker seems vague or evasive on this point, you should probably choose someone else.

Private sellers

Private sellers are your best source for a cheap and reliable used vehicle, because you're on an equal bargaining level with a vendor who isn't trying to profit from your inexperience. This translates into a golden opportunity to negotiate a fair price, which isn't common in many dealer transactions.

Apart from newspaper classified ads, you can track down good private deals and get a good idea of prices through the following:
• word of mouth
• grocery store bulletin boards

- specialty publications (e.g., *Auto Trader, Auto Mart,* or *Buy and Sell Bargain Hunter*)
- The *NADA Official Used Car Guide,* the *Kelley Blue Book* and *Edmund's Price Guide:* these are three of the most popular guides used throughout the States, offering comprehensive ratings and prices. They are sold at newsstands and bookstores for less than $10, are available from the reference section of your local library, and can be consulted, gratis, through the Internet: *Kelley Blue Book* at *http://www.kbb.com* and *Edmund's* at *http://www.edmunds.com*

The best way to determine the price range for a particular model is to read the publications listed above before you buy the vehicle. This will give you a reasonably good idea of the top asking price. Remember, nobody expects to get his or her asking price, be it a dealer or private party. A 10 to 20 percent reduction from the advertised price is common. The fact is that these values are very volatile and no one source can be considered completely accurate. For example, I find the *Kelley Blue Book*'s prices more accurate than the other two guides and I especially like its listing of the MSRP (Manufacturer's Suggested Retail Price) for each model year going back to 1983. *Edmund's,* on the other hand, only goes back ten years; it gives vehicles the lowest values, and includes a short summary of what's was new each year, in addition to a bar graph rating safety, reliability, performance, and comfort. The *NADA Guide* is sanctioned by the National Automobile Dealers Association, covers ten years, and lists values comparable to those in the *Kelley.*

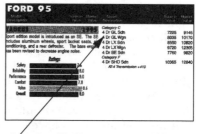

1995 FORD				
Body Type	VIN	List	Retail Good	Retail Excellent
CONTOUR—4-Cyl.—Equipment Schedule 5 W.B. 106.5"; 2.0 Liter.				
GL Sedan 4D	P653	15470	8150	9450
LX Sedan 4D	P663	16665	8575	9900
V6 2.5 Liter	L		435	438
CONTOUR—V6—Equipment Schedule 5 W.B. 106.5"; 2.5 Liter.				
SE Sedan 4D	P67L	18355	9450	10850
MUSTANG—V6—Equipment Schedule 4 W.B. 101.3"; 3.8 Liter.				
Coupe 2D	P404	17550	10750	12250
Convertible 2D	P444	23610	12350	15050
Hard Top (Conv)			665	665
Manual Trans			(765)	(765)
MUSTANG—V8—Equipment Schedule 4 W.B. 101.3"; 5.0 Liter.				
GTS Coupe 2D	P42T	19080	11450	13450
GT Coupe 2D	P42T	20710	12500	14600
GT Convertible 2D	P45T	25400	15100	17600
Cobra Coupe 2D	P42D	23060	17100	19500
Cobra Convertible 2D	P45D	27365	20100	22700
Hard Top (Conv)			665	665
PROBE—4-Cyl.—Equipment Schedule 5 W.B. 102.8"; 2.0 Liter.				
Hatchback 3D	T20A	15890	9650	10900
SE Pkg			200	200
PROBE—V6—Equipment Schedule 5 W.B. 102.8"; 2.5 Liter.				
GT Hatchback 3D	T22B	19485	11050	12400
TAURUS—V6—Equipment Schedule 4 W.B. 106.0"; 3.0 Liter, 3.2 Liter.				
GL Sedan 4D	P52U	18295	10100	11550
GL Wagon 4D	P57U	19390	11400	12950
SE Sedan 4D	P53U	19185	10200	11700
LX Sedan 4D	P53U	20290	10900	12350
LX Wagon 4D	P58U	22090	12100	13800
SHO Sedan 4D	P64Y	26465	12350	14500
Manual Trans			(765)	(765)
V6 3.0L Flexible Fuel	1		0	0
V6 3.8 Liter	4		435	435
THUNDERBIRD—V6—Equipment Schedule 4 W.B. 113.0"; 3.8 Liter.				
LX Coupe 2D	P624	17895	10250	11700
V8 4.6 Liter	W		565	565
THUNDERBIRD—V6 Supercharged—Equipment Schedule 4 W.B. 113.0"; 3.8 Liter.				
Super Coupe 2D	P64R	24195	13100	14750
CROWN VICTORIA—V8—Equipment Schedule 4 W.B. 114.4"; 4.6 Liter.				
Sedan 4D	P73W	21315	12750	14600
LX Sedan 4D	P74W	23365	13250	15100

Imagine, Kelley *says your '95 Taurus GL is worth between $10,100 and $11,550 but* Edmund's *says don't pay a penny more than $9,145. My suggestion: use* Kelley *if you're selling, and* Edmund's *if you're buying.*

Don't be surprised to find that many price guides have a north-
eastern bias that often results in unrealistically low price quotes for
buyers in the southern and western states or residents in rural
areas, where good used cars are often sold for outrageously high
prices or simply passed down through the family.

Some price guides have three prices listed, from left to right: the
MSRP, showing what the vehicle sold for new; the wholesale price
negotiated between dealers; and the retail price charged by dealers
to walk-in customers. Used vehicles purchased from dealers over
the Internet or from private sellers will sell for somewhere between
the wholesale and resale prices.

When you compare dealer ads with the price guides, you'll see
the dealers have added incredible markups that ensnare unsuspecting buyers. Take the *Lemon-Aid* guide along and bargain down
the markup by about one-third.

Protect yourself

As a buyer, you should get a printed sales agreement, even if it's just
handwritten, that includes a clause stating there are no outstanding
traffic violations or liens against the vehicle (a lien is a debt for which
the vehicle is used as collateral). It doesn't make a great deal of difference whether the vehicle will be purchased "as is" or as certified
under state regulation. A vehicle sold as safety "certified" can still be
dangerous to drive or turn into a lemon. The certification process
can be sabotaged by incompetent mechanics or poorly calibrated
instruments, or if a minimal number of components were checked.
"Certified" is not the same as having a warranty to protect you from
engine seizure or transmission failure. Certified means only that the
vehicle has met minimum safety standards on the day tested.

Make sure the vehicle is lien-free and hasn't been written off
after an accident. Some states with lax reporting laws are dumping
grounds for rebuilt wrecks and write-offs shipped from states where
there are stringent disclosure regulations.

In most states, you can do a lien and registration search yourself.
If a lien does exist, you should contact the creditor(s) listed to find
out whether any debts have been paid. If a debt is outstanding, you
should arrange with the vendor to pay the creditor the outstanding
balance. If the debt is larger than the purchase price of the vehicle,
it's up to you to decide whether or not you wish to complete the
deal. If the seller agrees to clear the title personally, make sure that
you receive a written relinquishment of title from the creditor
before paying any money to the vendor. Also, make sure the title
doesn't show an "R" for "restored."

Even if all documents are in order, ask the seller to show you the
vehicle's original sales contract and a few repair bills in order to
ascertain how well it was maintained. The bills will show you if the
odometer was turned back and will also indicate which repairs are
still guaranteed. If none of these can be found—*run, don't walk,*

away. If the contract shows that the vehicle was financed, verify that the loan was paid. If you're still not sure that the vehicle is free of liens, ask your bank or credit union manager to make a check for you. If no clear answer is forthcoming, look for another vehicle.

Repossessed vehicles
Repossessed vehicles are usually found at auctions but they're sometimes sold by finance companies or banks—institutions that have been held by the courts to be as legally responsible as dealers for the defects found in the vehicles they sell. The biggest problem with repossessed vans, sport-utilities, and pickups, in particular, is that they're likely to have been abused by their financially troubled owners. The full extent of the abuse can't always be ascertained in one brief examination by a mechanic. Before buying a repossessed vehicle, try to find out something about the previous owner and what care the vehicle received. A visit to the local dealer for that particular make, with the vehicle's identification number and a small gratuity in hand, will get you a vehicle history printout from the dealer's PC link with the manufacturer.

Cross-border shopping
In spite of the plummeting value of the Canadian dollar (65¢ U.S.), there's no iron-clad guarantee that you'll save money by purchasing a used vehicle in Canada and bringing it into the States. Safety and pollution control regulations differ considerably between the two countries and it may be impossible to upgrade your used vehicle to American standards. Find out which ones pass muster by accessing the NHTSA's web site.

Buyers of used Canadian vehicles should also be wary of the following: the odometer registers in kilometers instead of miles; safety-related defects may not have been corrected because Canada doesn't have a cross-border owner notification system; and engine calibrations may not be set for American emission control standards, thereby putting you in violation of some state pollution control regulations. Furthermore, vehicles that are exported to the United States may have rolled-back odometers; as a buyer, you will have no legal recourse worth pursuing, once you add up the cost of civil litigation.

If you do decide to import a used vehicle from Canada, be careful to check for liens and make sure the vehicle wasn't stolen. Unfortunately, there's little cooperation among provincial registrars and no effectual link-up between U.S. and Canadian registrars, so your chances of getting the required information are pretty slim.

Rental and leased vehicles
The second-best choice for getting a good used vehicle is a rental company. Budget, Hertz, Avis, and National sell cars, minivans, vans, and sport-utilities that have one to two years of service and

approximately 50,000 to 60,000 miles. These rental companies will gladly provide a vehicle's complete history and allow an independent inspection by a qualified mechanic of the buyer's choice, as well as arrange competitive financing, without "boosting" the price.

Rental vehicles are generally well maintained, sell for a few thousand dollars more than a privately sold vehicle, and come with a strong guarantee. Rental car companies also usually settle customer complaints without much of a hassle so as not to tarnish their image with rental customers.

Vehicles that have just come off a three- or five-year lease are much more competitively priced, generally have less mileage, and are usually as well maintained as rental vehicles. You're also likely to get a better price if you buy directly from the lessee rather than going through the dealership, but remember, you won't have the dealer's leverage to extract post-warranty "goodwill" repairs from the automaker.

New car dealers
Although going to a new car dealer is the most expensive way to get a used vehicle (prices are 20–30 percent higher than those for vehicles sold privately), they aren't a bad place to pick up a good used car or minivan if you don't mind paying top dollar. For example, new car dealers are insured against selling stolen vehicles or vehicles with finance owing or other liens. New car dealers offer financing, occasionally allow a prospective buyer to have a used vehicle inspected by an independent garage, and offer a much wider choice of models. Repair facilities are also available for warranty work, and if there's a possibility of getting post-warranty "goodwill" compensation from the manufacturer, your dealer can provide additional leverage. Plus, if you have to take the dealership to court, dealers have deeper pockets than private sellers, so there's a better chance that you'll get paid should the judge rule in your favour.

Automaker "certified" vehicles
Try to get a vehicle that the dealer's had certified by an auto association or an automaker. Buying one of these independently certified vehicles allows you to sue both the dealer and certifier if things go wrong.

The Big Three American automakers and some importers have begun to refurbish and certify used vehicles sold by their dealers. They guarantee the vehicle's mechanical fitness and provide a warranty where length depends on the age of the vehicle. Remember that dealers get their used vehicles as trade-ins, from auto auctions and rental car sales, and off the street. They then have to recondition them, add a warranty, and pay advertising and sales commissions. This means you won't find low-priced used vehicles sold through the automakers' certification programs.

Automaker and dealer leasing

Automakers like Mercedes-Benz, Ford, Chrysler, GM, and Nissan/Infiniti, as well as some dealers, are now leasing three-year-old cars, trucks, sport-utilities, vans, and minivans for additional two- to three-year periods. For a relatively low monthly payment (relative to leasing new), you can get a better-equipped vehicle with some of the automaker's original warranty in effect and a used warranty that kicks in afterwards.

Leasing has been touted as a method of making the high cost of vehicle ownership more affordable but, for most people, the pitfalls (whether you lease new or used) far outweigh any advantages. Keep in mind that leasing is costlier than an outright purchase. If you must lease, do it for the shortest time possible and make sure the lease is closed-ended (meaning that you walk away from the vehicle when the lease period ends). Also, make sure there's maximum mileage allowance of at least 15,000 miles a year and that the charge per excess mile is no higher than 6¢.

Used car dealers

Used car dealers usually sell their vehicles for a bit less than what new car dealers charge but their vehicles may be worth a lot less, too. They're usually marginal operations that can't invest much money in reconditioning their vehicles, which are often collected from auctions and new car dealers reluctant to sell the vehicles to their own customers. And they don't always have repair facilities to honor what warranties they do provide. Often, however, they may offer easier (but more expensive) credit terms than franchised new car dealers.

Used car dealers operating in small towns are an entirely different breed. These small, often family-run businesses recondition and resell cars and trucks that usually come from within their community. Routine servicing is often done in-house and more complicated repairs are subcontracted out to specialized garages nearby. These small outlets survive by word-of-mouth advertising and would never last long if they didn't deal fairly with local townfolk. On the other hand, their prices will likely be higher than elsewhere due to the better quality of used vehicles they offer and the cost of reconditioning and repairing under warranty what they sell.

Superstores

Used car "superstores" like Car Max are nationally franchised operations backed by Circuit City and other investors. Although for the past three years they have been expanding slowly, they are expected to pick up steam, once differences with automakers have been ironed out.

These aren't the places to find "super" bargains when compared with what's offered by traditional new or used car dealers. The December 1995 issue of *Smart Money* magazine, for example, found that Car Max prices and warranties came up short 25 out of 26 times when compared to used vehicles sold by local dealers. Furthermore, *Automotive News* reports that studies show used car superstores tend to drive up prices in the regions where they are established. On the plus side, however, their emergence makes existing dealers more consumer sensitive when it comes to warranties and disclosure. In fact, Car Max's 5-day/250 mile money back guarantee and 99-day warranty puts most dealers to shame.

	CarMax Price	NADA Value	SAVE	
'95 FORD EXPLORER XLT 4D 2WD, BLK, 40K mi, AUTO, #3286,	$17,998	$20,475	$2,477	FT
'96 FORD EXPLORER XLT 4D 2WD, GRN, 26K mi, AUTO, #3518,	$17,598	$21,625	$4,027	FT
'96 FORD EXPLORER XLT 4D 2WD, GLD, 35K mi, AUTO, #3488,	$18,998	$22,375	$3,377	FT
'96 FORD RANGER XLT STYLSDE, BLU, 26K mi, AUTO, #13759,	$10,598	$12,550	$1,952	BB
'95 JEEP CHEROKEE COUNTRY 4D 2WD, WHT, 50K mi, AUTO, #3387,	$13,598	$14,950	$1,352	FT
'97 PONTIAC GRAND AM SE 4D SDN, RED, 25K mi, AUTO, #3618,	$11,598	$13,375	$1,777	FT
'94 SATURN SC2 2D CPE, BLU, 49K mi, MANUAL, #3478,	$7,998	$9,800	$1,802	FT
'96 VOLKSWAGEN GOLF GL 4D H'BCK, WHT, 26K mi, MANUAL, #3424,	$11,598	$13,275	$1,677	FT

High prices and good warranties characterize many used car superstores. Stung by the high-price charge, this Miami-based Car Max dealer (above) claims lower prices than those listed by NADA's price guide (below). I don't agree. NADA says a '95 Explorer XLT has a $13,200 to $17,225 value, plus $900 for the XLT trim, for a total value of $14,100 to $18,125— NOT $20,475 as advertised by Car Max.

Auctions

You need patience and smarts to pick up anything worthwhile at an auction. Government auctions— places where the mythical $50 Jeep is sold—are fun to attend, but are risky ventures because you can't determine the condition of the vehicles put up for bid and government employees often pick over the stock before you.

You swim with the piranha, however, at commercial auctions. They are frequented by "ringers" who bid up the price and professional dealers who pick up cheap, worn-out vehicles unloaded by new car dealers and independents who are afraid to sell them to their own customers. There are no guarantees, cash is required, and quality is apt to be as low as the price. Remember, too, that auction purchases are subject to state sales taxes and the auction's sales commission (3–5 percent), and an administrative fee of $25–$50 may also be charged.

Say what? This Chicago Times *ad promises there's no need to purchase anything in order to win one of three $1,000 prizes—to be used ONLY with the purchase of an auctioned vehicle. Watch out! Like phony carpet "Customs auction" scams, there are many false auto auctions run by used car dealers and independent brokers. Make sure you're dealing with a legitimate auctioneer.*

If you are interested in shopping at an auto auction, remember that certain days are reserved for dealers only, so call ahead. You'll find the vehicles locked in a compound but you should have ample opportunity to inspect them and, in some cases, take them for a short drive around the property before the auction begins.

Paying the Right Price

Get ready for "sticker shock" when pricing popular used cars and minivans—most of these vehicles don't depreciate very much and it's easy to get stuck with a cheap one that's been abused through lack of care. Furthermore, it's such a seller's market out there that even those vehicles with worse-than-average reliability ratings, like early GM Cavaliers, Ford Tauruses, and Chrysler minivans, still command ridiculously high resale prices simply because they're popular.

If you don't want to pay too much when buying used, you've got the following four alternatives:

• Buy an older vehicle. Choose one that's five-years-old or more and has a good reliability and durability record and buy extra protection with an extended warranty. The money you save from the extra years' depreciation and lower insurance premiums will more than make up for the extra warranty cost.

• Look for off-lease vehicles sold privately by owners who want more than their dealer is offering. If you can't find what you're looking for in the local classified ads, put in your own ad asking for lessees to contact you if they're not satisfied with their dealer's offer.

• Buy a vehicle that's depreciated more than average simply because of its bland styling, lack of high-performance features, or its discontinuation by one of its distributors. For example, many of the Japanese pickups cost less to own than their American-made counterparts yet are more reliable and more than adequate for most driving chores. And, now that the Dodge Stealth has been dropped by Chrysler, used versions can be picked up for a song and servicing is easily found at Mitsubishi dealerships who sell the Stealth's twin, the 3000GT.

• Buy a twin or re-badged model. Listed below are some of the better-known cars, minivans, vans, sport-utilities, and trucks that are nearly identical but sold under other nameplates. They usually share the same basic design, appearance, dimensions, and mechanical components but their resale values may differ considerably.

"Twin" Savings

Chrysler

Chrysler Cirrus, Dodge Stratus, Plymouth Breeze
Dodge Omni, Plymouth Horizon
Dodge Dart, Duster, Plymouth Valiant, Duster
Dodge Colt, Eagle Summit
Chrysler Concorde, LHS, New Yorker, Dodge Intrepid, Eagle Vision
Dodge Spirit, Plymouth Acclaim
Dodge Volaré, Plymouth Aspen

Chrysler Sebring, Dodge Avenger, Mitsubishi Galant
Dodge Colt Wagon, Eagle Summit Wagon
Dodge Caravan, Plymouth Voyager
Chrysler Town & Country, Dodge Grand Caravan, Plymouth Grand Voyager
Dodge Stealth, Mitsubishi 3000GT
Eagle Talon, Mitsubishi Eclipse, Plymouth Laser

Ford

Ford Pinto, Mercury Bobcat
Ford Escort, ZX2, Mercury
   Tracer, Lynx, Mazda 323
Ford Tempo, Mercury Topaz
Ford Contour, Mercury
   Mystique
Ford Taurus, Mercury Sable
Ford Mustang, Mercury Capri
Ford Probe, Mazda MX-6

Ford Thunderbird, Mercury
   Cougar
Ford Crown Victoria, Lincoln
   Town Car, Mercury Grand
   Marquis
Ford Explorer, Mazda Navajo,
   Mercury Mountaineer
Ford Ranger, Mazda B-Series
Mercury Villager, Nissan Quest

General Motors

Buick Park Avenue, Riviera,
   Cadillac Seville, Olds Aurora
Buick LeSabre, Olds 88,
   Pontiac Bonneville
Buick Century, Regal, Olds
   Intrigue, Pontiac Grand Prix

Olds Achieva, Pontiac Grand
   Am
Chevrolet Metro, Pontiac
   Firefly, Suzuki Swift, Sprint
Chevrolet Prizm, Toyota
   Corolla

The Cavalier (shown above), Sunbird, and Sunfire: identical cars, different prices.

Chevrolet Cavalier, Pontiac
   Sunbird, Sunfire
Chevrolet Corsica, Beretta,
   Pontiac Tempest
Chevrolet Lumina, Monte
   Carlo
Chevrolet Malibu, Olds
   Cutlass

Chevrolet Camaro, Pontiac
   Firebird
Chevrolet Astro, GMC Safari
Chevrolet Express, GMC
   Savana
Chevrolet Lumina APV
   minivan, Olds Silhouette,
   Pontiac Trans Sport

Chevrolet Venture, Olds
  Silhouette, Pontiac Trans
  Sport
Chevrolet S-10 pickup, GMC
  Sonoma pickup
Chevrolet Blazer, GMC Jimmy,
  Olds Bravada

Chevrolet Blazer, Tahoe, GMC
  Yukon
Chevrolet C/K pickup, GMC
  Sierra pickup
Geo Tracker, Pontiac
  Sunrunner, Suzuki Sidekick
Saturn SC, Sl

Imports

Acura Integra, Honda Civic
Acura CL, Honda Accord
Acura SLX, Isuzu Trooper
Infiniti I30, Nissan Maxima
Honda Odyssey, Isuzu Oasis
Honda Passport, Isuzu Rodeo
Lexus ES 300, Toyota Camry

Hyundai Elantra, Tiburon
Infiniti QX4, Nissan
  Pathfinder
Toyota Paseo, Tercel
Lexus LX 450, Toyota Land
  Cruiser
VW Golf, Jetta

Prices will vary

In spite of the many guide books (including *Lemon-Aid*), cars and minivans have no "official" selling price. Most dealers will charge as much as the market will bear and use any pretext they can to boost prices—if you let them. Although they pretend to have abandoned negotiated prices and high-pressure sales tactics in favour of "no haggle prices," dealers will negotiate and it's in your best interest to make sure they do.

Consumer Reports, for example, found that its expert shopper saved hundreds of dollars buying from a conventional dealership as opposed to one which displayed the dealer's invoice cost and a "no haggle" selling price.

There are several price guidelines, however, and dealers use the one that will make the most profit on each transaction. The most common quoted price is from the *NADA Price Guide*, which shows the full retail price (similar to the Manufacturer's Suggested Retail Price, or MSRP). The wholesale price, thousands of dollars less, is more likely what the dealer paid. Never mind that few people ever pay that price. The fact that it's there is sufficient enough reason for most dealers to charge the higher rate. Both price indicators leave considerable room for the dealer's profit margin and some extra padding—inflated preparation charges and administration fees that shouldn't exist for a used vehicle.

Just as with new cars, dealers know that last-minute add-on charges to used cars are their last chance to stick it to you before the contract is signed. They, therefore, try to extort extra profits through so-called preparation and documentation fees and charge extra handling costs that give you nothing in return. These charges should have no place in a used vehicle transaction—but wait until the opportune moment before objecting. Patiently await management's approval of the vehicle's bottom-line price and then reject these add-on charges; otherwise, the dealer may try to pad the price to get its normal add-on profit.

Financing Choices

No one should spend more than 30 percent of his or her annual gross income on the purchase of a used vehicle. By keeping the initial cost of a used vehicle low, the purchaser may be able to pay in cash, a key bargaining tool to use with private individuals selling vehicles directly. Used car dealers are not all that impressed by cash sales because they lose their kickback from the finance companies, which is based on the volume and amount of finance business they write up. Furthermore, a portion of the life insurance premium may also be remitted to the dealer as part of the sales commission.

In spite of the lower costs involved (as compared to a new vehicle purchase), not everyone can pay cash for a used car or minivan. If you need a loan, consider the advantages and disadvantages of going through the following lending institutions.

Credit unions. A credit union is the preferred place to borrow money at low interest rates and with easy repayment terms. You'll have to join the union or have an account with them before the loan is approved. You'll also probably have to come up with a larger down payment relative to what other lending institutions require.

Banks. Banks want to make small loans to consumers who have average incomes and appear to be financially responsible. Their interest rates are very attractive and can be negotiated downwards if you have a good credit history or agree to give them other business. Auto club members can benefit from lower interest rates at banking institutions recommended by the association. Bank loans are seldom made for more than 36–48 months.

Dealer financing. Dealers can finance the cost of a used vehicle at rates that compete with those of banks and finance companies because they get substantial rebates from lenders and agree to take back the vehicle if the creditor defaults on the loan. Some dealers mislead their customers into thinking they can get financing at rates 3 or 4 percentage points below the prime rate. Actually, the dealer jacks up the base price of the vehicle to compensate for the lower interest charges.

Finance companies. With their excessive interest rates, finance companies should be the last place to go for a small, short-term loan but the fact remains that these lenders fill a consumer need created by the restrictive policies of other institutions. The advantages of relaxed credit restrictions and quick loans appeal to many people who can't get financing elsewhere or who may wish to extend their payments for up to 60 months.

Dealer Scams

Used vehicles are subject to the same deceptive sales practices that are deployed by dealers who sell new vehicles. One of the more common tricks is to not identify the previous owner, either because the vehicle was used commercially or had been written off as a total loss from an accident. It's also not uncommon to discover that the mileage has been turned back, particularly if the vehicle was part of a company's fleet. These scams can be thwarted if you demand the name of the vehicle's previous owner as a prerequisite to purchasing the vehicle.

It would be impossible to list all the dishonest tricks employed in used vehicle sales. As soon as the public is alerted to one scheme, other, more elaborate, frauds are used by crooked sellers.

Here are some of the more common fraudulent practices you're likely to encounter.

Failing to declare full purchase price. This tactic, used almost exclusively by small, independent dealers, involves the buyer being told by the salesperson that he or she can save on sales tax by listing a lower selling price on the contract. But what if the vehicle turns out to be a lemon or the sales agent has falsified the model year or mileage? The hapless buyer will usually be offered a refund on the fictitious purchase price indicated on the contract only. If the buyer wanted to take the dealer to court, it's quite unlikely that he or she would get any more than the contract price. Moreover, both the buyer and dealer could be prosecuted for making a false declaration to avoid paying sales tax.

Sales agents posing as private parties ("curbsiders"). Independent scam artists and some crooked dealers get agents to pose as private sellers in order to get a better price for their vehicles and avoid giving a warranty. Once again, this scam is easy to detect if the seller can't produce the original sales contract or if few repair bills are made out in his or her own name. You can also identify a dealer in the want ads section of the newspaper by checking to see if their telephone number is repeated in different ads.

Most new car dealers get very angry when one of these scamming teams hits town. Unfortunately, they don't get angry enough, because they continue to sell used vehicles at wholesale prices to curbsiders who they know are stealing their business and cheating consumers and tax authorities in their communities.

If you get taken by one of these scam artists, don't hesitate to sue, through small claims court, both the newspaper carrying the ad (the papers know these are scammers from the volume of ads placed each week) and the state agency responsible for dealer registration and consumer protection. These parties could be considered negligent for allowing these rip-off artists to operate.

"Free-exchange" privilege. Dealers get a lot of sales mileage out of this deceptive offer. The dealer offers to exchange any defective vehicle for any other vehicle in stock. What really happens, though, is that the dealer won't have any other vehicles selling for the same price and thus will demand a cash bonus for the exchange or he or she may have nothing but lemons in stock.

"Money-back" guarantee. Once again, the purchaser feels safe in buying a used car with this kind of guarantee, because what could be more honest than a money-back guarantee? Dealers using this technique often charge exorbitant handling charges, rental fees, or mechanical repair costs to the customer who's bought one of these vehicles and then returned it.

"50/50" guarantee. This means that the dealer will pay half the repair costs over a limited period of time. It's a fair offer if the repairs can be done by an independent garage. If not, the dealer can always inflate the repair costs to double their actual worth and write up a bill for that amount. The buyer winds up paying the full price of repairs that would probably have been much cheaper at an independent garage. The best kind of used vehicle warranty is 100 percent with full coverage for a fixed term.

"As is." Buying a vehicle "as is" means that you're aware of mechanical defects, are prepared to accept the responsibility for any damage or injuries caused by the vehicle, and that all costs to fix it shall be paid by you. The courts have held that the "as is" clause is not a blank check to cheat buyers and, therefore, must be interpreted in light of the seller's true intent. That is, was there an attempt to deceive the buyer by including this clause? Did the buyer really know what the "as is" clause could do to his or her future legal rights? It's also been held that the courts may consider verbal representations ("parole evidence") made by the seller as to the fine quality of the used vehicle but never written into the formal contract. Courts generally ignore "as is" clauses when the vehicle has been misrepresented, when the dealer is the seller, or when the defects are so serious that the seller is presumed to have known of their existence.

Odometer tampering. It's often too dangerous for the dealer or "curbsider" to turn back the mileage, so independent outfits are hired to pick up the vehicle or visit the dealership and "fix" the odometer. Still, the seller is taking a big risk since this scam can lead to jail time for fraud and consumer protection statutes allow citizens to sue for triple damages, plus lawyer and court costs, if they find their odometer has been rigged. Nevertheless, the best protection is prevention and that can be achieved by simply demanding that the seller (dealer or private party) put the mileage figure on the contract and give you the name and address of the previous owner as well as all repair receipts.

Misrepresentation. Used vehicles can be misrepresented in a variety of ways. A used airport commuter minivan may be represented as having been used by a Sunday school class. A mechanically defective pickup that's been rebuilt after several major accidents may have sawdust in its transmission to muffle the "clunks," heavy oil in the motor to stifle the "clanks," and cheap retread tires to eliminate the "thumps." These fraudulent practices may lead to the seller being charged with civil or criminal fraud. The best protection against these dirty tricks is to have the vehicle's quality completely verified by an independent mechanic before completing the sale.

Private Scams

A lot of space in this guide has been used to describe how used car dealers and scam artists cheat uninformed buyers. Of course, private individuals can be dishonest, too, so in either case protect yourself at the outset by keeping your deposit small and getting as much information as possible about the vehicle you're considering buying. Then, after a test drive, you may sign a written agreement to purchase the vehicle and give a deposit of sufficient value to cover the seller's advertising costs, subject to cancellation if the automobile fails its inspection.

After you've taken these precautions, watch out for these private sellers' tricks.

Used vehicles that are stolen or have finance owing. A lot of used vehicles are sold without free title because the original auto loan was never repaid. Here's where car dealers have a net advantage over private parties. Dealers aren't easily fooled and they have insurance to compensate buyers if they do inadvertently sell a stolen vehicle. When buying from a private party, you have to contact the state agency that registers property and pay a small fee for a computer printout that may or may not be accurate. You'll be asked for the current owner's name and the vehicle's 17-character identification number (VIN), which is usually found on the driver's side of the dashboard and on title or insurance documents.

There are two other high-tech ways to get the goods on the seller: have a "vehicle history" check done by a dealer of that particular marque through a computer link-up with the automaker's main frame. That check will tell you who the previous owners and dealers were, what warranty and recall repairs were carried out, and what other free repair programs may still apply.

Secondly, you could use Carfax (*www.carfax.com* Tel.: 888-422-7329) to carry out a background check to see if the vehicle has been wrecked, had flood damage, is stolen, or shows incorrect mileage on the odometer. The $20 fee by telephone is cut to $12 if the order is placed via the Internet. A typical search takes only a few minutes.

Both amateur and professional crooks sell vehicles that haven't been paid for because it's so easy to do and the profits are enormous. They skip town after sticking you with the finance payments and, by the time the lender tracks you down, most legal recourse is ineffective. Your best bet may be to buy the car again from the lender at a discount and take a tax loss.

This racket can be avoided by asking for proof of purchase and payment from any individual who offers to sell a used vehicle for an incredibly low price. Check the sales contract to determine who granted the original loan and call the lender to see if it's been repaid. Place a call to the Department of Motor Vehicles to ascertain whether the vehicle is registered in the seller's name. Also, find out if a finance company is named as a beneficiary on the auto insurance policy. Finally, call up the original dealer to determine whether there are any outstanding claims.

Misrepresentation (wrong model year). That bargain-priced import you just bought may be a year older that you think. That's why you should check its true age by looking at the date-of-manufacture plate found on the driver's side door pillar. If the date of manufacture is 7/96, it was one of the last 1996 models made before the September changeover to the 1997 models. Exceptions to this rule are those vehicles that are redesigned or relatively new to the market, which arrive at dealerships in early spring or mid-summer. They're considered to be next year's models but depreciate more quickly due to their earlier launching (a difference that narrows over time). If you have any doubts, look up the tenth character in the vehicle identification number (VIN) which identifies the model year.

MODEL YEAR INDICATOR (10th VIN POSITION)			
Code	Model Year	Code	Model Year
A	1980	S	1995
B	1981	T	1996
C	1982	V	1997
D	1983	W	1998
E	1984	X	1999
F	1985	Y	2000
G	1986	1	2001
H	1987	2	2002
J	1988	3	2003
K	1989	4	2004
L	1990	5	2005
M	1991	6	2006
N	1992	7	2007
P	1993	8	2008
R	1994	9	2009

During the '70s, Nissan and Ford conspired with their dealers to sell previous years' cars and trucks as the latest models. Private sellers may continue the fraud unwittingly because the actual model year was never disclosed to them. By the way, 02/01/91 indicates that this is a '91 model Ford.

Now, one last word on protecting yourself from legal liability if you are selling a vehicle to a private individual. Normally, once you take the tags and give the buyer a bill of sale, you're no longer the registered owner. Unfortunately, though, if you don't personally go down to the registry office and make sure the title has changed, you could be sued by an insurance company for damages arising from an accident if you're still the owner of record.

Choosing the Right Kind of Vehicle

The "Buy American" quality myth

Forget all the popular mythology about what is "North American-made" and what is "foreign-made." The seesaw value of the dollar and yen has led to a rush of foreign automakers moving production facilities to the U.S., Canada, and Mexico, in addition to importing major components from offshore. Surprisingly, this has been accomplished without a corresponding drop in quality control. On the other hand, it has made it practically impossible to designate many vehicles as American-made.

As far as reliability and dependability are concerned, sport-utilities, vans, and pickups are more problem-prone than cars, simply because there are more things that can go wrong. Nevertheless, they often cost less to repair because key components are easily accessible—many vehicles are actually modified trucks, parts have been around for years and can be purchased from independent jobbers, and knowledgeable do-it-yourself manuals abound. Furthermore, reliability and durability have improved considerably during the past decade. In a 1995 J. D. Power study ranking customer satisfaction after the first year of ownership, multipurpose vehicles had a 29 percent improvement in owner satisfaction since the study was first done, in 1988. Dealer servicing improved 30 percent, compared to a reported 12 percent improvement in product quality over the same period.

As a rule, 4X4s, minivans, vans, and pickups have more squeaks and rattles and engine, transmission, electrical system, brake, and paint problems than automobiles. Separated into vehicle classes, owners of small pickups and compact sport-utilities submitted the best customer satisfaction evaluations, according to the Power survey.

Take the phrase "car-like handling" with a large grain of salt. Since many rear-drive models are built on a modified truck chassis and use steering and suspension components from their truck divisions, they tend to handle more like trucks than cars, in spite of automakers' claims to the contrary. What you see is not necessarily what you get when you buy or lease a new 4X4, minivan, van, or pickup, because multipurpose vehicles seldom come with enough standard features to fully exploit their versatility.

Additional options are usually a prerequisite to making them safe and comfortable to drive. Consequently, the term "multipurpose" is a misnomer unless you are prepared to spend multi-bucks to outfit your 4X4, van, or pickup. Even fully equipped, these vehicles don't always provide the performance touted by automakers.

Front-drives handle better than rear-drives, but the size and weight of multipurpose vehicles still require a whole new set of driving skills when cornering under moderate speeds, parking, or turning. A moment's inattention can easily lead to a deadly rollover when driving a sport-utility or pickup—vehicles that are two to three times more likely to roll over than passenger cars.

Bear in mind that off-roading requires suspension, engine, and drivetrain packages and other components, such as off-road tires and a skid plate, that may not come as standard equipment on the vehicle.

The following is a summary of *Lemon-Aid*'s ratings of sport-utilities, vans, and trucks. Cars and minivans are rated in Part 3 of this guide.

SPORT-UTILITIES

Recommended

Acura SLX
Ford Expedition/
  Lincoln Navigator
Ford Explorer (1995–97)
Honda CR-V

Infiniti QX4
Isuzu Trooper
Lexus LX 450
Toyota 4Runner (1996–97)
Toyota RAV4 (1997)

Above Average

Chevrolet Blazer, Jimmy, Tahoe,
  Yukon (1995–97)
Ford Explorer (1993–94)

Toyota 4Runner (1988–95)
Toyota RAV4 (1996)

Average

Dodge Ramcharger (1990–93)
Ford Bronco (1994–96)
GM Tracker/Suzuki Sidekick
  (1994–97)
Honda Passport/Isuzu Rodeo,
  Trooper (1993–97)
Jeep CJ, YJ, Wrangler (1997)

Jeep Cherokee (1995–97)
Jeep Grand Cherokee (1995–97)
Nissan Pathfinder
Subaru Outback
Suzuki Samurai (1992–94)
Toyota Land Cruiser

Below Average

Chevrolet Blazer, GMC Jimmy,
  Bravada (1995–97)
Dodge Ramcharger (1987–89)
Ford Bronco (1988–93)
GM Blazer, Jimmy, Tahoe, Yukon
  (1990–94)

GM S-10, Jimmy, Bravada
GM Tracker/Suzuki Sidekick
  (1989–93)
GMC Suburban (1995–97)
Honda Passport/Isuzu Rodeo,
  Trooper (1990–92)

Not Recommended

AM Hummer
Ford Bronco II
Ford Explorer (1991–92)
GM Blazer, GMC Jimmy/
  Bravada (1988–94)
GMC Suburban (1985–94)
Jeep CJ, YJ, Wrangler (1988–96)

Jeep Cherokee (1985–94)
Jeep Grand Cherokee (1992–94)
Jeep Wagoneer, Grand Wagoneer
Land Rover Discovery
Suzuki Samurai (1986–91)
Suzuki X-90

FULL-SIZE VANS

Recommended

Ford Econoline, Club Wagon
  (1993–97)

GM Chevy Van, Vandura
  (1996–97)

Above Average

Chrysler Ram Van, Wagon
  (1993–97)

GM Express, Chevy Cargo Van,
  GMC Savana (1997)

Average

Chrysler Ram Van, Wagon
  (1987–92)

Ford Econoline, Club Wagon
  (1991–92)
GM Chevy Van, Vandura (1995)

Below Average

GM Chevy Van, Vandura (1990–94)

Not Recommended

Ford Econoline, Club Wagon (1985–90)

TRUCKS
Recommended

Ford F-series (1997)   Nissan Pickup (1990–97)
Ford Ranger (1993–97)   Toyota Pickup, Tacoma (1995–97)
Mazda B-series (1993–97)

Above Average

Ford F-series (1993–96)   Toyota Pickup, Tacoma (1989–94)
Mazda B-series (1990–92)   Toyota T100 (1997)

Average

Dodge Dakota (1995–97)   GM C/K, GMC Sierra (1994–97)
Dodge Ram D-150, 1500 (1997) Isuzu/Passport Pickup (1992–94)
Ford F-series (1990–92)   Toyota T100 (1995–96)

Below Average

Dodge Dakota (1990–94)   GM S-Series, GMC Sonoma
Dodge Ram 50 (1991–93)   (1996–97)
D-150, 1500 (1990–96)   Isuzu/Passport Pickup (1989–91)
Ford Ranger (1985–92)   Toyota T100 (1993–94)
GM C/K, GMC Sierra (1990–93)

Not Recommended

Dodge Ram 50 (1985–90)
GM S-series, GMC Sonoma (1987–95)

Import or domestic model?
Whether you buy domestic or imported, overall vehicle quality has improved a great deal during the past decade. Premature rusting is less of a problem and factory-related defects aren't as numerous as they once were. But problems remain. Owners of American-made vehicles still report serious deficiencies, often during the first three years in service. These include electrical system failures caused by faulty computer modules, malfunctioning ABS, failure-prone air conditioning and automatic transmissions, and defective powertrains,

fuel systems, suspensions, steering, and paint. Further evidence that American cars are more failure-prone than their Japanese-made counterparts can be seen by the service bulletins sent out each month by the automakers. For this guide, I've compared the bulletins of the Toyota Camry to those of the Ford Taurus and Mercury Sable.

1994 Ford Taurus V6
DSB SUMMARY

1. SEP-89 20 STEPS TO SUCCESSFUL AUTO TRANSMISSION REPAIR
2. JAN-94 A/C - BLOWER MOTOR INOPERATIVE IN AUTOMATIC MODE
3. JAN-94 A/C - MANIFOLD AND TUBE ASSEMBLY REPLACEMENT
4. JUL-95 A/C EVAPORATOR CORE-ON VEHICLE-LEAK TEST
5. OCT-94 A/C SERVICE TIP - OIL VISIBLE AT SPRING LOCK COUPLERS
6. JUL-96 A/C SYSTEM SERVICE TSB LIST
7. MAR-94 A/T (AX4N) - SERVICE PROCEDURE FOR ORANGE TAGGED UNITS
8. MAR-94 A/T (AXOD/AXODE/AX4S) - LEAK AT TORQUE CONVERTER
9. JAN-96 ACCELERATOR CABLE - DIAGNOSTIC PROCEDURE
10. JAN-95 ACCUMULATOR SPRINGS - IDENTIFICATION
11. MAR-96 ADDING REFRIGERANT OIL PROCEDURE
12. MAR-96 AIR BAG - DIAGNOSTIC FAULT CODE 51
13. OCT-95 AIR BAG MODULES - DISCOLORED/MARRED COVERS
14. AUG-97 AIR COMPRESSOR MOAN
15. SEP-95 AIR CONDITIONING - FORD APPROVED FLUSHING
16. FEB-98 AIR CONDITIONING MUSTY AND MILDEW TYPE ODORS
17. SEP-96 AIR CONDITIONING O-RING AVAILABILITY AND APPLICATIONS
18. JAN-95 AIR CONDITIONING O-RING REMOVAL - SERVICE TIP
19. SEP-96 AIR CONDITIONING THICK O-RING APPLICATIONS
20. DEC-93 AIR IN POWER STEERING SYSTEM
21. SEP-87 ALL AUTOMATICS - FRONT BUSHING WEAR
22. MAY-95 ANTENNA - BOWED CONDITION ONLY - WARRANTY REVISION
23. MAR-94 ANTI-LOCK BRAKES - PEDAL FEELS LIKE IT HAS EXTRA TRAVEL
24. OCT-95 ANTI-LOCK BRAKES CYCLING ON ROUGH ROADS
25. JAN-94 AUTOMATIC TRANSMISSION - AX4S - DO NOT SERVICE TAG
26. FEB-90 AUTOMATIC TRANSMISSION FLUID
27. AUG-89 AUTOMATIC TRANSMISSION MATH FORMULAS
28. OCT-89 AUTOMATIC TRANSMISSION MATH PART 2
29. AUG-96 AX4S TRANSAXLE - NEW MAIN CONTROL COVER AND PAN GASKET
30. NOV-94 AX4S TRANSAXLE EXCHANGE PROGRAM
31. FEB-98 AX4S/AX4N NEW TRANSAXLE FLUID
32. NOV-97 AX4S/AX4N, TROUBLE CODES STORED AFTER TRANSAXLE REPLACED
33. JAN-96 AXLE NUT/LUG NUT TIGHTENING SPECIFICATIONS
34. SEP-92 BATTERY REPLACEMENT 72AH TO 84AH
35. MAR-95 BLOWER MOTOR - CHIRP/SQUEAK FROM BLOWER MOTOR
36. NOV-93 BLOWER SPEED CONTROL - AUTOMATIC TEMPERATURE CONTROL
37. SEP-97 BRAKE AND ROTOR SERVICE TIPS
38. DEC-94 BRAKE ROTOR MACHINING EQUIPMENT AND WARRANTY INFORMATION
39. OCT-95 BRAKES - PETROLEUM BASED LUBRICANT CAUSES SWELLING
40. MAR-96 BRAKES - REAR BRAKES NOISE/SQUEAL
41. MAR-95 BRAKES - ROUGHNESS DURING BRAKE APPLICATION
42. NOV-93 BUMPER COVER REPAIR MATERIALS
43. APR-94 BUMPERS - ISOLATOR AND BRACKET ASSEMBLY REPLACEMENT
44. MAY-96 CALIFORNIA REFORMULATED GASOLINE (CARFG) SERVICE TIP
45. JAN-96 CASE BREAKAGE AT REAR PLANET SUPPORT

Look at this service bulletin summary for the '94 Ford Taurus and Mercury Sable. Out of a total of 162 bulletins, 53 bulletins concerned a factory-related defect.

46. DEC-97 CHIRPING/SQUEAKING FROM BLOWER MOTOR AT LOW SPEEDS
47. JAN-98 CODES 327, 332, MIL LAMP ON, 32 DEGREES F OR BELOW, 3.0L
48. JUL-94 COOLING SYSTEM BY-PASS HOSE LEAK
49. FEB-98 CUSTOMER ASSISTANCE-TELEPHONE NUMBERS FOR TIRE COMPANIES
50. JAN-95 DELAYED ENGAGEMENT, SHIFT ERRORS, POSSIBLE MLPS CODES
51. NOV-93 DRIVEABILITY CONCERNS - DAMAGED FUEL PUMP
52. MAY-94 DRIVER'S SEAT SENSOR CAUSES DOORS TO LOCK WHEN EXITING
53. NOV-93 EGO SENSORS - SILICONE CONTAMINATION
54. NOV-96 ELECTRICAL DIODE IDENTIFICATION AND REPLACEMENT
55. JUN-93 ELECTRICAL INFORMATION - AXOD/E
56. AUG-95 ELECTRONIC SHIFT SOLENOID APPLICATIONS
57. OCT-96 ELIMINATION OF SANDING BRAKE ROTORS AND DRUMS
58. MAY-97 ENGINE COOLING FAN MODULE SERVICE INFORMATION
59. OCT-90 ENGINE TESTING WITH A VACUUM GAUGE - AUTO TRANS.
60. JAN-95 ERRATIC/HIGH LINE PRESSURE
61. OCT-93 FAILSAFE MODES - COMPUTER SHIFTED TRANSMISSIONS
62. JUL-96 FILTERING REFRIGERANT AFTER REPLACING A/C COMPRESSOR
63. OCT-96 FOG/FILM ON WINDSHIELD/INTERIOR GLASS
64. JUL-96 FORD'S POSITION ON PROPYLENE GLYCOL COOLANT
65. JAN-95 FORWARD PISTON CHANGE
66. JAN-94 FORWARD SPRAG UPGRADE
67. NOV-94 FORWARD/REVERSE ENGAGEMENT CONCERN - AXOD, AXOD-E, AX4S
68. DEC-97 FRONT END ACCESSORY DRIVE BELT SLIP, 3.0L 2-VALVE
69. FEB-96 FUEL INFORMATION OF GASOLINE - SERVICE TIP
70. MAR-97 FUEL ECONOMY - CUSTOMER EXPECTATIONS VS. VEHICLE USAGE
71. JAN-96 FUEL PUMP BUZZ/WHINE THROUGH RADIO SPEAKER
72. OCT-97 FUEL SYSTEM - FUEL ODOR INSIDE PASSENGER COMPARTMENT
73. OCT-94 FUEL TANK - FUEL SLOSH NOISE
74. OCT-93 GLASS - IRIDESCENCE OR MOTTLING IN TEMPERED GLASS
75. OCT-95 GROANING NOISE FROM POWER WINDOWS
76. JAN-94 HARSH SHIFTS, NO 3-4 SHIFT, ERRATIC SHIFTS
77. JUL-97 HEADLAMPS OPERATE INTERMITTENTLY
78. AUG-94 HEATED EXHAUST GAS OXYGEN SENSOR APPLICATION CHART
79. JAN-95 HEATER TO ENGINE COOLANT BYPASS HOSE REPLACEMENT
80. JUN-94 HEATER/ A/C - COLD ENGINE LOCKOUT OPERATION
81. MAR-96 HESITATION/NO START/STALLING - INTERMITTENT (HOT)
82. NOV-91 HOW TO USE A PRESSURE GAUGE - AUTOMATIC TRANS.
83. JAN-98 HUB-MOUNT BRAKE ROTOR MACHINING EQUIPMENT AVAILABILITY
84. SEP-97 IDENTIFICATION OF NON-FORD APPROVED REFRIGERANTS
85. APR-94 IGNITION CONTROL MODULE CONNECTOR UPDATE
86. MAR-95 INCORRECT PCM USAGE WILL CAUSE TRANSAXLE DAMAGE
87. FEB-98 INTERMITTENT NEUTRAL CONDITION, NO FORWARD/REVERSE, AX4N
88. AUG-97 LOOSE CATALYST OR MUFFLER HEAT SHIELDS
89. DEC-94 LOW TRANSAXLE FLUID LEVEL IMPROPERLY SETTING DTC
90. AUG-87 METAL SEALING RINGS - AUTOMATIC TRANSMISSIONS
91. JAN-94 MODIFICATION TO IMPROVE GEAR LUBRICATION
92. AUG-95 NEW ROTUNDA FLUID CHANGER - SERVICE TIP
93. JAN-96 NEW TORQUE SPECS FOR INSTALLING NEW DESIGN TIE RODS
94. DEC-94 NO CRANK - POSSIBLE CORROSION AT STARTER SOLENOID
95. FEB-96 NOISE - CLICK FROM TRANSAXLE DURING REVERSE ENGAGEMENT
96. JUL-96 NOISE - FUEL PUMP GURGLING AFTER HOT RESTART
97. DEC-96 NOISE FROM REAR TENSION START - WAGONS ONLY
98. SEP-94 NON-MATING CONDITION - HARNESS CONNECTOR/IGNITION SWITCH
99. SEP-97 ON-VEHICLE HEATER CORE PRESSURE TEST FOR WARRANTY CLAIM
100. NOV-93 PAINT - REGULAR PRODUCTION OPTION PAINT CODES
101. MAR-95 PAINT - IRON PARTICLE REMOVAL
102. NOV-93 PAINT CODES AND SUPPLIER STOCK NUMBERS
103. NOV-94 PAINT PREPARATION PROCEDURE AND MSDS INFORMATION
104. JUL-94 PASSENGER SEAT BACK RATTLES WHEN UNOCCUPIED
105. JUL-94 POWER DOOR LOCK ACTUATORS
106. AUG-97 PREVENTING BRAKE VIBRATION SERVICE TIP

107. JUN-94 PROGRAM 94B48 - FUEL TANK CONTAMINATION
108. JAN-95 RADIATOR - NEW MANUFACTURING PROCESS
109. SEP-97 RADIO AM BAND STATIC WHILE DRIVING
110. MAR-95 REAR SUN GEAR AND DRUM BEARING SERVICE - TRANSAXLE
111. JAN-96 REAR SUN GEAR BEARING - UPDATE
112. DEC-96 REAR TIRE INNER EDGE WEAR
113. AUG-94 REAR VIEW MIRROR - DETACHES FROM WINDSHIELD
114. AUG-97 REAR VIEW MIRROR REATTACHMENT
115. DEC-95 RECALL 95S22 ENGINE COOLING FAN
116. SEP-95 RECYCLED ENGINE COOLANT - SERVICE TIPS
117. DEC-94 RELEASE OF R-134A FLUORESCENT DYE
118. NOV-97 REMOTE KEYLESS ENTRY (RKE) DIAGNOSTIC SERVICE TIPS
119. NOV-93 REMOTE KEYLESS ENTRY SYSTEM
120. FEB-94 REMOTE KEYLESS ENTRY SYSTEM - SERVICE TIPS
121. JAN-95 REMOTE KEYLESS ENTRY SYSTEM TRANSMITTERS
122. OCT-96 REPLACEMENT OF THE MASS AIR FLOW SENSOR AS AN ASSEMBLY
123. NOV-94 REPLACEMENT PROCEDURE FOR FRONT DOOR MOULDING
124. DEC-93 RETURN OF OBSOLETE STARTER SOLENOIDS AND STARTER DRIVES
125. JAN-96 REVISED FORWARD SPRAG RACE
126. JAN-96 REVISED SPLINE DRIVE JOINT - OVERDRIVE DRUM
127. JUL-95 REVISED TORQUE CONVERTER IDENTIFICATION CODES
128. AUG-95 REVISED TRANSAXLE CLUTCH CLEARANCES
129. SEP-94 ROUGH IDLE, HESITATION/STUMBLE, BUCKS/JERKS ON COAST
130. NOV-93 ROUGH IDLE/HESITATION/ POOR HEATER OUTPUT
131. MAR-97 SAFETY REGAL 97S66 ENGINE COOLING FAN MOTOR CIRCUIT
132. JUL-97 SEAT LEATHER CLEANING PROCEDURE
133. JAN-94 SERVICE PARTS RETURN OF OBSOLETE FUEL PRESSURE
134. JUN-94 SERVICE PARTS RETURN OF OBSOLETE FUEL TANKS
135. MAY-97 SERVICE TIP - REFRIGERANT OIL REFILL CAPACITY
136. NOV-96 SERVICE TIP - TORQUE CONVERTER LEAK TEST PROCEDURE
137. APR-97 SERVICE TIPS - ELECTRONIC AUTOMATIC TEMPERATURE CONTROL
138. JUL-97 SERVICE TIPS - WINDNOISE AROUND DOORS
139. AUG-94 SHIFT CONCERNS OR TRANSAXLE DAMAGE - INCORRECT PCM
140. JUN-97 SPEEDOMETER NEEDLE WAVERS AND STICKS
141. NOV-95 SQUEAKS FROM REAR WINDOW AREA
142. SEP-96 SUSPENSION RIDE HEIGHT MEASUREMENT AND ADJUSTMENT
143. SEP-95 TEMPERATURE GAUGE - FLUCTUATION/INACCURATE
144. JUL-95 TEMPERATURE GAUGE READS LOW/ERRATIC
145. DEC-94 THROTTLE POSITION SENSOR - FUNCTION AND DIAGNOSTIC II
146. NOV-94 THUMPING/CLACKING NOISE WHILE BRAKING
147. FEB-94 TORQUE CONVERTER - CHANGE FROM 23 TO 25 TEETH
148. DEC-94 TORQUE CONVERTER CLEANING AND REPLACEMENT GUIDELINES
149. OCT-94 TRANSAXLE - AX4S/AXOD - NEW LUBE TUBES
150. OCT-94 TRANSAXLE (AXOD, AXODE, AX4S) - RETAINING RING ORIENTATION
151. OCT-94 TRANSAXLE LUBE TUBE BRACKET
152. JUL-94 TRANSAXLE - AX4N - FLUID PAN EMBOSSED WITH SHO
153. APR-96 TRANSAXLE - AX4S/AX4N DRIVELINE NOISES
154. DEC-95 TRANSAXLE - BONDED MAIN CONTROL SEPARATOR PLATE GASKETS
155. FEB-96 TRANSAXLE - REVISED GROB SPLINE DRIVE JOINT
156. JUL-95 TRANSAXLE REAR PLANET SUPPORT RETAINING RING I.D
157. JAN-95 TRANSMISSION CONTROLLED CLUTCH PULSING ON/OFF
158. MAR-97 TRANSMISSION FLUID USAGE CHARTS
159. FEB-96 TURBINE SHAFT SPEED AIR GAP MEASUREMENTS CHANGE
160. JUL-95 WHEEL COVER DISTORTED OR MELTED
161. JUN-95 WINDSHIELD, URETHANE MOUNTED, MATERIAL USAGE TIP
162. NOV-97 WIRE HARNESS TERMINAL REPAIR KIT AND WIRE SPLICE REPAIR

Japanese vehicles hold up fairly well, until their fifth year. Then the engine head gasket will probably have to be replaced, the front brakes will need reconditioning, and the rack-and-pinion steering system will likely have to be overhauled. Furthermore, the front-wheel-drive constant-velocity joints will probably need replacing— at a cost of about $200 each. Unfortunately, used Japanese-built vehicles are seldom priced reasonably, because their owners paid inflated prices when they were new and want to get some of their money back when they're resold.

1994 Toyota Camry Sedan 4-Door V-6
DSB SUMMARY

1. APR-94 1994 TOYOTA SPECIAL SERVICE TOOLS
2. JAN-95 1995 TSB BINDERS
3. SEP-89 20 STEPS TO SUCCESSFUL AUTO TRANSMISSION REPAIR
4. MAY-96 A/C COMPRESSOR MAINTENANCE FOR STORED VEHICLES
5. OCT-93 A/C COMPRESSOR OIL APPLICATION
6. NOV-94 A540E SECONDARY REGULATOR MODIFICATION
7. MAY-97 AIR CONDITIONING EVAPORATOR ODOR
8. MAR-95 AIRBAG ASSEMBLY REPLACEMENT PROCEDURE
9. SEP-93 ALIGNMENT SPECS - 94 YEAR MODELS
10. SEP-87 ALL AUTOMATICS - FRONT BUSHING WEAR
11. NOV-96 ALTERNATIVE REFRIGERANTS AND RETROFITS
12. JUN-93 APPLYING CAUTION LABEL TO R-12 AIR CONDITIONING SYSTEMS
13. MAY-95 ATM TRANSMISSION FLUID SEEPAGE
14. FEB-90 AUTOMATIC TRANSMISSION FLUID
15. AUG-89 AUTOMATIC TRANSMISSION MATH FORMULAS
16. OCT-89 AUTOMATIC TRANSMISSION MATH PART 2
17. DEC-96 AUTOMATIC TRANSMISSION SERIAL NUMBERS
18. JAN-95 AXLE NUT/LUG NUT TIGHTENING SPECIFICATIONS
19. FEB-95 BATTERY MAINTENANCE FOR IN-STOCK VEHICLES
20. SEP-97 BRAKE BOOSTER PUSH ROD GAUGE
21. JUN-94 BRAKE PAD KITS - NOW AVAILABLE WITHOUT HARDWARE
22. OCT-94 BRAKE REPAIR
23. FEB-94 BRAKES - CAUSE AND REPAIR OF VIBRATION AND PULSATION
24. DEC-96 CARPET CLEANING PROCEDURES
25. JAN-96 CHECKBALL WEAR
26. JUN-95 EMISSION CONTROL LABEL ORDER FORM
27. JUN-94 EMISSION CONTROL LABELS - ORDERING FORM
28. OCT-95 ENGINE SUPPORT BAR IMPROVEMENTS
29. OCT-90 ENGINE TESTING WITH A VACUUM GAUGE - AUTO TRANS
30. JUN-96 EXHAUST PIPE HEAT SHIELD
31. MAR-96 FRONT BRAKE GROAN NOISE
32. SEP-93 FRONT STABLIZER - NEW LINK NUTS
33. AUG-95 GROOVED B CLUTCH DISC ON AS4OE ATM
34. NOV-91 HOW TO USE A PRESSURE GAUGE - AUTOMATIC TRANS.
35. JAN-96 IMPROVED POWER WINDOW REGULATOR ASSEMBLY INSTALLATION
36. AUG-95 INTRODUCTION OF BRAKE SHIM/FITTING KITS
37. JAN-97 MAIN BEARING CHANGES
38. AUG-87 METAL SEALING RINGS - AUTOMATIC TRANSMISSIONS
39. APR-96 MOONROOF PANEL WIND NOISE
40. SEP-93 NEW PDS FOR 1994 MODEL YEAR VEHICLES
41. AUG-94 NEW WIRE HARNESS REPAIR KIT AVAILABLE
42. SEP-94 OVERDRIVE CLUTCH BEARING - IMPROVED DURABILITY

Look at this service bulletin summary for the '94 Toyota Camry. Out of a total of 79 bulletins, only 13 covered a manufacturing defect.

43. DEC-93 PAINT AND REFINISHING FORMULA CODES
44. SEP-95 PAINT REPAIRS ON POLYURETHANE BUMPER
45. OCT-94 POWER WINDOW REGULATOR - NEW PARTS OPTIONS AVAILABLE
46. SEP-93 PRE-DELIVERY SERVICE - SHORT PIN INSTALLATION (NON USA)
47. JUN-94 PRE-DELIVERY SERVICE - SPRING SPACER REMOVAL
48. NOV-94 PROTECTIVE FILM REMOVAL PROCEDURES
49. APR-96 PUBLICATION CORRECTION - GENERAL INFORMATION
50. MAY-95 PUBLICATION CORRECTION INFORMATION
51. JUN-93 R-12 CAUTION LABEL - APPLICATION INSTRUCTIONS
52. MAR-97 REAR BRAKE SQUEAK
53. SEP-93 REAR SUSPENSION - NEW MEMBER NUT
54. MAR-96 REFRIGERANT LEAK DETECTION - SERVICE HINTS
55. JUL-94 REPLACEMENT BATTERY PART NUMBERS
56. JUL-97 REPLACEMENT CERTIFICATION LABELS
57. MAR-94 REPLACEMENT REFRIGERANTS DAMAGE TO SYSTEM
58. JUL-97 REPLACEMENT VIN PLATES
59. OCT-96 SEAT BELT EXTENDER
60. APR-94 SEAT BELT EXTENDER - AVAILABILITY
61. NOV-95 SEAT BELT EXTENDERS
62. OCT-97 SEAT BELT EXTENDERS.
63. NOV-94 SPOILER LAMP SENSOR REPLACEMENT
64. AUG-96 STAIN ON PAINT
65. JUL-95 STANDARD BOLT TORQUE SPECIFICATIONS
66. SEP-94 STEERING COLUMN CLICKING NOISE - CORRECTION PROCEDURE
67. MAY-96 STEERING GEAR/WHEEL REMOVAL WITH SRS
68. APR-95 SUSPENSION SQUEAK/GROAN NOISES
69. JAN-94 TIRES CHANCE IN ORIGINAL EQUIPMENT
70. AUG-94 TOYOTA CHECKER APPLICATIONS (REFERENCE GUIDE)
71. DEC-94 TRUNK FINISH PLATE LOOSE
72. OCT-95 TRUNK LID TORSION ROD ADJUSTMENT
73. NOV-93 WATER LEAKAGE - NEW SEALS
74. MAY-95 WATER PUMP SEAL IMPROVEMENTS
75. MAR-96 WHEEL BALANCE ADAPTER KIT
76. SEP-96 WHEEL BALANCE ADAPTER KIT UPDATE

Japanese vehicles are redesigned every three to four years, while American carmakers often wait a decade or longer. The Big Three American automobile manufacturers know that the Japanese and their dealers build, market, and service vehicles to a higher standard than the Americans do. That's why the Big Three gave up much of the small car market to Asian producers in the late 1980s; it was easier and more profitable for them to buy high-quality Asian products and market them as homegrown. Today, the small, compact, and luxury car markets have been literally conquered by Japanese imports and homegrown offerings.

Don't buy the myth that parts for imports aren't easily found. It's actually easier to find parts for used Japanese or domestic vehicles than for new vehicles due to the large number of units produced, the presence of hundreds of independent suppliers, the ease with which relatively simple parts can be interchanged from one model to another, and the large reservoir of used parts stocked by junkyards. Incidentally, when a part is hard to find, the *Mitchell Manual* is a useful guide to substitute parts that can be used for many different models. It's available in some libraries, most auto parts stores, and practically all junkyards.

The most reliable and durable new vehicles are Japanese makes, some European imports, and American co-ventures (such as the Chevrolet Metro, which is actually a re-badged Suzuki). But where used vehicles are concerned, the following American-made rear-drive cars are better choices than many imports: Chrysler's V8 New Yorker; Ford's Mustang, T-Bird, Cougar, Crown Victoria, and Mercury Grand Marquis; the Lincoln Town Car; and GM's Camaro, Caprice, and Cadillac Fleetwood. Their depreciated prices are more competitive than the inflated values of Asian and European imports, they're cheap and easy to service almost anywhere, they can support lots of power-hungry accessories, and they sustain high mileage with fewer major breakdowns. The only problem is that American rear-drives have become an endangered species, with Ford being the only automaker still churning them out in large numbers.

South Korean cars are poor imitations of Japanese vehicles. They start to fall apart after their third year due to poor-quality body construction, cheap and unreliable electrical components, and parts suppliers who put low prices ahead of reliability and durability. This is particularly evident when one looks at the failure-prone Hyundai Excel.

Hyundai's Sonata—you know Hyundai has serious quality-control problems when late-night talk show host David Letterman likens Hyundai reliability to the Russian space station Mir.

European cars and minivans deserve much of the bad-mouthing they've received over high parts costs and limited parts availability. With some European models, you can count on lots of aggravation and expense due to the unacceptably slow distribution of parts and their high markup. Because these companies have a quasi-monopoly on replacement parts, there are few independent suppliers you can turn to for help. And auto wreckers, the last-chance repository for inexpensive car parts, are unlikely to carry foreign parts for vehicles older than three years or manufactured in small numbers.

Other Buying Considerations

Front-wheel drive

Front-wheel drives direct engine power to the front wheels, which *pull* the vehicle forward, while the rear wheels simply support the rear. The biggest benefit of front-wheel drive (FWD) is foul-weather traction. With the engine and transmission up front, there's lots of extra weight pressing down on the front-drive wheels, increasing tire grip in snow and on wet pavement. However, when driving up a steep hill or towing a boat or trailer, the weight shifts and there's no longer a traction advantage.

Although I recommend a number of FWD vehicles in this guide, I don't feel comfortable driving them. Granted, front-drives give a bit more interior room (no transmission hump), provide more car-like handling, and provide better fuel economy than rear-drives, but damage from potholes and fender-benders is usually more extensive and maintenance costs (premature front tire and brake wear, in particular) are much higher than with rear-wheel drives.

Servicing front-wheel drives can be a real nightmare. Entire steering, suspension, and drivetrain assemblies must be replaced when just one component is defective. Downtime is considerable, the cost of parts is far too high, and the drivetrain and its components are not designed for the do-it-yourself mechanic. A new front-wheel drive transmission assembly, called a transaxle, can cost about $2,000 to repair, compared to $700 for a rear-drive transmission.

Accident repairs are a unique problem. Front-wheel drive transmissions and steering and suspension components are easily damaged and alignment difficulties abound. Repair shops need expensive, specialized equipment to align all four wheels and square up a badly smashed unibody chassis. Even if you can get all four wheels tracking true, the clutch and transaxle can still be misaligned. No wonder many insurance companies prefer to write off a FWD car than repair it. And when that happens, you wind up eating the difference between what you paid for the vehicle and what the insurance company says your vehicle is worth—minus your deductible, of course.

I also feel front-drives are unsafe because braking requires a whole new set of reflexes than what we've developed over the years with rear-wheel drive vehicles. You remember the routine from driving school: *when in a skid, pump the brakes lightly and turn into the direction of the skid.* Well, if you pump the brakes of a front-drive in a skid, you've bought the farm.

Rear-wheel drive
Rear-wheel drives direct engine power to the rear wheels, which *push* the vehicle forward. The front wheels steer and support the front of the vehicle. With the engine up front, the transmission in the middle, and the drive axle in the rear, there's plenty of room for larger and more durable drivetrain components. This makes for less crash damage, lower maintenance costs, and higher towing capacities than front-drives.

On the other hand, rear-drives don't have as much weight over the rear wheels as front-drives do (and putting cement blocks in the bed or trunk will only void your transmission warranty). As such, they can't provide as much traction on wet and icy roads unless equipped with an expensive traction-control system.

Four-wheel drive
Four-wheel drives direct engine power through a transfer case to all four wheels, which *pull* and *push* the vehicle forward, giving you twice as much traction. The system is activated with a floor-mounted shift lever or a dashboard button. When 4X4 drive isn't engaged, the vehicle is essentially a rear-drive truck. The large transfer case housing makes the vehicle sit higher, giving you additional ground clearance. Two-wheel RWD vehicles have some of the highest payload and towing capabilities, usually slightly more than four-wheel drives.

Many 4X4 customers have been turned off by the typically rough and noisy driveline; a tendency for the vehicle to tip over when cornering at moderate speeds (a Bronco specialty); vague, truck-like handling; high repair costs; and poor fuel economy. Also, extended driving over dry pavement with 4X4 drive engaged will cause the driveline to bind and result in serious damage. Some buyers are turning instead to rear-drive pickups equipped with winches and large, deep-lugged rear tires.

All-wheel drive
Essentially, this is four-wheel drive *all* the time. Used mostly in sedans and minivans, AWD never needs to be deactivated when running over dry pavement and doesn't require the heavy transfer case (although some sport-utilities and pickups do use a special transfer case) that raises ground clearance and cuts fuel economy. AWD-equipped vehicles aren't recommended for off-roading because of their lower ground clearance and fragile driveline parts, which aren't as rugged as four-wheel drive components.

Diesels
Diesel engines become more efficient as the engine load increases, whereas gasoline engines become less so. This is the main reason diesels are best used where the driving cycle includes a lot of city driving, with its slow speeds, frequent stops, and long idling times.

At full throttle, both engines are essentially equal from a fuel-efficiency standpoint. The gasoline engine, however, leaves the diesel in the dust when it comes to high-speed performance. Many owners of diesel-equipped vehicles are frustrated by excessive repair costs and poor road performance on vehicles that lack turbo. (Ford truck diesels often self-destruct after 100,000 miles due to a problem called "cativation.")

Fuel economy fantasies

Fuel economy figures are supplied by the federal government and are based on data supplied by the automakers following U.S. Environmental Protection Administration (EPA) testing guidelines. These figures are often off by 10 to 20 percent due to the testing method chosen. In fact, a recent Ford bulletin warns dealers that "Very few people will drive in a way that is identical to the EPA tests....These [fuel economy] numbers are the result of test procedures that were originally developed to test emissions, not fuel economy."

Rustproofing

Even though automakers have extended their own rust warranties up to seven, in some cases ten, years, it's a good idea to get your car or minivan undercoated each year and keep it in an unheated garage. A full rustproofing job isn't really needed. In fact, you have a greater chance of seeing your rustproofer go belly-up before he makes good on your warranty than having your untreated vehicle ravaged by premature rusting. Even if the rustproofer stays in business, you're likely to get a song-and-dance about why the warranty won't cover so-called "internal" rusting or why repairs will be delayed until the sheet metal is actually rusted through. If you live in an area where roads are heavily salted in winter, or in a coastal region, or if you own a Toyota truck or Ford sport-utility, make sure you regularly have undercoating sprayed on the rocker panels (door bottoms), the rear hatch's bottom edge, and the wheel wells.

"Beaters" and collectibles

If an independent mechanic says that the more common and costly defects have been repaired, and if you have the time, knowledge, and parts suppliers to do your own maintenance and repairs, you may find an old, beat-up-looking vehicle that runs well (most of the time) in the $500–$1,000 range. Look for one of the following recommended vehicles, avoid the non-recommended ones, take your time, and insist upon an independent check-up. Be wary of the trouble areas listed in parentheses.

If you have a bit more money to spend and want to take less of a risk, look up the recommended vehicles found at the beginning of each vehicle category in Part Three.

Recommended Beaters

Checker—Last made in 1982, the Checker is the poor man's Bentley. Its rear-drive configuration, sturdy, off-the-shelf mechanicals, and thick body panels all add up to bulletproof reliability. Beware of corrosion along door rocker panels and wheel wells.

Chrysler—Dart, Valiant, Duster, Scamp, Diplomat, Caravelle, Newport, rear-drive New Yorker, Fifth Avenue, and Gran Fury (engine, electrical system, suspension, brakes, body and frame rust, plus constant stalling when humidity is high).

If you can get by the two-tone paint job, Chrysler's 5.7L V8-equipped, rear-drive Fifth Avenue (shown above), Caravelle Salon, and Diplomat Salon are excellent buys. They have high performance, reliable powertrains and lots of room. (Weak spots: brakes, electrical shorts, and ignition glitches.)

Ford—Maverick, Comet, Fairmont, Zephyr, Tracer, Mustang, Capri, Cougar, Thunderbird V6, Torino, Marquis, Grand Marquis, LTD, and LTD Crown Victoria (trunk, wheel well, and rocker panel rusting, brakes, steering, and electrical system).

General Motors—Chevette (steering and brakes you have to stand on to stop); rear-drive Nova, Ventura, Skylark, and Phoenix (suspension); front-drive Nova and Spectrum; Camaro, Firebird, Malibu, LeMans, Century, Regal, Cutlass, Monte Carlo, and Grand Prix (suspension and brakes); Bel Air, Impala, Caprice, Catalina, LeSabre, Bonneville, and Delta 88 (suspension and brakes).

Nissan—The Micra is a small commuter car that was sold 1985–91. It uses generic Nissan parts that are fairly reliable and not difficult to find, except for body panels that are more problematic (electrical shorts, premature front brake wear, and body rusting along the door rocker panels and wheel wells are the more common deficiencies).

Toyota —All models, except the LE van (brakes, chassis, and body rusting).

Beaters to Avoid

American Motors—Hornet, Concord, Spirit, Pacer, and Eagle 4X4 (faulty engines, transmissions, and steering).

Audi—Fox and 4000 (engine, transmission, and fuel system).

British Leyland—Austin Marina, MG, MGB, and Triumph (electrical system, engine, transmission, clutch, and chassis rusting).

Chrysler—Cricket, Omni, Horizon, Volaré/Aspen—all years—(engine, brakes, steering, and chassis rusting); Charger, Cordoba, and Mirada (brakes, body, and electrical system).

Datsun/Nissan—210, 310, 510, 810, F-10, and 240Z (electrical system, brakes, and rusting).

Eagle—Medallion and Premier. These bargain-priced French imports—$700–$900 for the Medallion and $1,000–$2,500 for the Premier—had a model run 1988–92. Sold through Chrysler's Renault connection, they are two of the most failure-prone imports ever to hit our shores. (Note: powertrain, fuel system, electrical system, AC, suspension, and brakes are the worst offenders.)

Fiat—All Fiat models and years are known for temperamental fuel and electrical systems and biodegradable bodies. Alfa Romeos have similar problems.

Ford—Cortina, Pinto, Bobcat, and Mustang II (electrical system, engine, and chassis rusting); the fire-prone Pintos/Bobcats are mobile Molotov cocktails.

The Cortina was the first and last "redated" car sold by Ford. Redating—selling unsold previous year's cars as the following year's model—involved Ford trucks, Datsun 510, Toyota Corolla, and Mazda cars and trucks. The practice was discontinued in the late '70s.

The 1988–93 Festiva, another import (this time, from South Korea), is a subcompact that's two feet shorter than the Escort and weighs about 1,700 lbs. Acceleration is slow but the manual transmission is precise and easy to use. The Festiva is only adequate for city use and with one passenger, at best. Parts are hard to find, floorboards, body panels, and exhaust components quickly rust out, brakes and electrical components frequently need replacing, and the tall body and tiny tires make highway cruising a scream.

A Cadillac "lemon"? Sure, just think of the Cimarron and Allanté (above). Can the Catera be far behind?

General Motors—Vega, Astre, Monza, and Firenza (engine, transmission, body, and brakes); Cadillac Cimarron and Allanté (poor-quality components and overpriced); all front-drives (engine, automatic transmission, electronic modules, steering, brakes, and rust/paint peeling); Citation, Skylark, Omega, and Phoenix (engine, brakes, electronic modules, and severe rust canker).

The Pontiac Fiero, sold 1984–88, snares lots of unsuspecting first-time buyers through its attractive, sports-car styling, high-performance pretensions, and $700–$1,500 price. However, the hapless buyer quickly learns to both fear and hate the Fiero as it shows off its fiery disposition (several safety recalls) and "I'll start when I want to" character.

Buick's Reatta, a luxury two-seater sold only 1988–91 (present value: $6,500–$10,000 for the convertible), has higher-than-average maintenance costs, although repairs aren't that dealer dependent, except for the electronically controlled fuel system. The Reatta also has higher-than-average parts costs and body parts are tough to find. This front-wheel drive luxury coupe and convertible combines lots of luxury with a checkered repair history. GM improved the quality somewhat with its 1991 models but then discontinued production. The 1988–89 cars were replete with the same low level of quality control that affected the Riviera.

Design and manufacturing defects include chronic problems with fuel injection, the engine computer, and the electrical system. The electronic cathode ray tube on the instrument panel, which the driver touches to operate the accessories, was taken from the Riviera and is awkward to use and dangerously distracting. The automatic transmission is subject to costly failures, shock absorbers wear out quickly, and the front brakes aren't very durable and perform poorly. Surface rust and poor paint quality are the most common body complaints on all years.

Geo—The 1990–93 Isuzu-built Storm is a fun-to-drive small coupe that's attractively styled, easy to handle, and is fuel-thrifty. So why isn't it recommended? Because practically all if its body and drive-train components are prone to premature failure. Servicing is prob-lematic, too: both servicing and parts are hard to find.

Jaguar—All models (poor body assembly/paint, electrical system, and service).

Lincoln—Versailles (electrical system, suspension, and rusting) and early front-drive Continentals (transmission, electrical system, brakes, and fuel system).

Renault—All models (fuel and electrical systems, CV joints and brakes, no parts, and few mechanics).

Saab—All models (electrical fires, short-circuits, hard-to-find parts, and few competent mechanics).

VW's Camper minivan: all the comforts of home during those long road-side waits for Helmut and Franz to come along with a tow truck.

Volkswagen—Beetle (unsafe front seats, heater that never worked, hazardous fuel tank placement, wheels, and seat tracks); Camper minivan (engine, transmission, fuel system, and heater); Rabbit/Dasher and 411/412: these cars are full of surprises, parts are rare, and the slow and expensive dealer servicing would give anyone nightmares (engine, electrical system, front brakes, and cooling system).

Collectibles?
Be wary of investing in recent high-performance American and Japanese sports cars. For example, GM took the Corvette ZR-1 off the market due to poor sales after only four years of production. Although 3,000 vehicles were to be produced annually, that figure dropped to fewer than 500 units. Owners who paid $59,555 for a new 1990 ZR-1 now own a car worth about $23,000.

Discontinued Japanese sports cars have fared no better, with the possible exception of the limited-production 1965–70 Toyota 2000 GT. Datsun's 1961–69 1500/1600/2000 sports cars, for example, were better made, more reliable, and better equipped than the MGBs and MGAs, yet the English roadsters sell for about $15,000, while Nissan's barely go for a third of that price. The 240Z/260Z/280ZX used values decreased in direct proportion to their increased heft. What's the outlook on the just-axed 1990–96 300ZX? More of the same.

If you're seriously interested in collecting cars remember that most vehicles jump in value after their 20th birthdays. So you probably won't lose money if you buy a car of this vintage, especially if it's a convertible (trucks, sport-utilities, and vans are riskier investments). Shop the Internet and car shows—they're good places to contact wholesalers and restorers. Car clubs also offer a wealth of information and are regularly listed in major auto magazines like *AutoWeek, Car and Driver, Motor Trend,* and *Road and Track. Hemmings' Motor News* and *Old Cars Weekly* out of Iola, Wisconsin, are two other excellent sources of collector news.

Saving Money and Keeping Safe

You can get a good used vehicle at a reasonable price—it just takes lots of patience and homework. You can further protect yourself by becoming thoroughly familiar with your legal rights as outlined in Part Two and buying a vehicle recommended in Part Three. Following is a summary of the steps to take to keep your risk to a minimum.

Summary

1. Keep your vehicle for at least ten years.
2. Trade in your vehicle if the dealer's sales tax reduction is more than the potential profit selling privately.
3. Sell to a private party (10 percent premium).
4. Buy from a private party (10 percent savings).
5. Use an auto broker to save time and money.
6. Buy a *Lemon-Aid* recommended vehicle for depreciation, parts, and service savings.
7. Buy a three- or four-year-old vehicle with lots of original warranty that can be transferred (35–50 percent savings over a new vehicle).
8. Choose a vehicle that's crashworthy and cheap to insure.
9. Carefully inspect Japanese-built vehicles that have reached their fifth year (weak spots: engine head gasket, CV joints, steering box, and front brakes).
10. Don't buy an extended warranty ($500–$1,000 savings) unless it's recommended in this guide or you've bought a vehicle five years old or older.

11. Have non-warranty repairs done by independent garages (50 percent savings).
12. Install used or reconditioned parts (30–50 percent savings).
13. Keep all the previous owners' repair bills to facilitate warranty claims and to help mechanics know what's already been replaced or repaired.
14. Upon delivery, adjust mirrors to eliminate blind spots and adjust the head restraints to prevent your head from snapping back in the event of a collision. On airbag-equipped vehicles, move the seat backwards more than half its travel distance and sit at least a foot away from the airbag housing. Make sure the spare tire and tire jack haven't been removed from the trunk.
15. Make sure the dealer and automaker have your name in their computer as the new owner of record. Ask for a copy of your vehicle's history, stored in the same computer.

Even Japanese vehicles that have a reputation for bulletproof reliability, like the '96 Honda Civic shown above, can require expensive powertrain (engines and constant-velocity joints), brake, and steering repairs around the five-year mark. And they have secret warranties, too (see page 62).

Part Two
THE ART OF COMPLAINING

Chrysler Battles Paint Blemishes by Banning Deodorant

"Paint-line workers at Chrysler Corp.'s Jeep plant were asked to stop using antiperspirant after the company discovered that falling flakes left costly blemishes on the new Jeep...General Motors officials contacted late yesterday said they didn't believe they had a similar problem....

One woman filed a grievance last year after her supervisor asked to check her armpits...."

Newsday, 1991

Ford Admits Its Paint Mistake

"...In June 1990, a field survey of about 1,000 F-series trucks (1985–1990 models) was conducted in three locations by Body and Chassis Engineering to assess paint durability. Results showed that about 13% of the F-series trucks displayed peeling paint, which would represent about 90,000 vehicles annually..."

Memo to Members of the Finance Committee from
A. J. Trottman, Executive Vice President
Ford North American Automotive Operations

Nick Verburg, a West Coast hauler, in front of his problem-plagued 1991 Dodge Ram truck. His protests succeeded in getting five Getrag transmission replacements—one almost lasted 23 miles.

Invest in Protest

Few people really like to complain and even less are willing to make their dissatisfaction public. However, with 10 percent of cars estimated by Runzheimer International to be "lemons" and automakers promising more quality than they deliver and then cutting back on warranty coverage, consumers have discovered that they must either act up or get shut out—even if this means carrying signs or going to court to get compensation.

Getting Your Money Back

When letter writing and public protests fail to elicit a satisfactory response, your only recourse is to sue or, at least, to threaten to sue. Yet, we all know that you can win in court and still end up losing your shirt. That's why this section of the book is dedicated to helping you get your money back without having to go to court or getting frazzled by the seller's broken promises and "benign neglect." But if going to court is your only recourse, you'll find here the jurisprudence you need to get an out-of-court settlement or to win your case without spending a fortune on lawyers or research.

First of all, forget about the seller's claim that "there's no warranty" or "because it was sold 'as is' you can't claim a refund." This is all hogwash. Any sales contract for a used vehicle can be canceled for one or more of the following reasons:
• It was misrepresented.
• It's unfit for the purpose for which it was purchased.
• It wasn't reasonably durable considering its selling price, how well it was maintained, the mileage driven, and the type of driving it was used for.
• It was seriously defective at the time of purchase.

For example, if the seller claims that a minivan can pull a 2,000-pound trailer and you discover that it can barely tow half that weight, you can cancel the contract for misrepresentation. The same principle applies to a seller's exaggerated claims concerning a vehicle's off-road capability, fuel economy, and reliability; and to "demonstrators" that are, in fact, used cars with false (rolled back) odometer readings.

It's essential that printed evidence and/or witnesses (relatives are not excluded) be available to confirm that the false representation actually occurred. These misrepresentations must also concern an important fact that substantially affects the vehicle's performance, reliability, or value.

Some vehicles are meant to be driven hard, but when they fail to live up to the advertised hype, sellers often blame the owner for having pushed the vehicle beyond its limits. Therefore, when you attempt to set aside the contract, the testimony of an independent mechanic is essential to prove that the vehicle's poor performance wasn't caused by negligent maintenance or abusive driving.

Another hurdle to overcome is the "reasonable diligence" rule that requires one to file suit within a reasonable time after purchase or after the defect is discovered. This delay must not exceed a few months if there have been no negotiations with the seller. The delay for filing the lawsuit can be extended if the seller has been promising to correct the defects for some time or has done some minor repairs while negotiating a final settlement.

Warranties

Unscrupulous dealers and con artists won't tell you this, but it's true: *every vehicle sold has some kind of warranty that can be enforced in court.* In fact, every new or used vehicle sold is covered by both state and federal warranties that protect you from misrepresentation and a host of other evils. Furthermore, American law and jurisprudence presume that car dealers, unlike private sellers, are aware of the defects present in the vehicles they sell. That's why dealers are paid a commission. The vehicles they sell are expected to be reasonably durable and merchantable. What is reasonably durable depends on the price paid, miles driven, the purchaser's driving habits, and how well the vehicle was maintained by the owner. Judges carefully weigh all these factors in awarding compensation or canceling a sale.

There is no standard warranty period, however, and some states require that dealers provide only minimal warranty coverage. Safety restraints like airbags and seatbelts often have coverage extended for the lifetime of the vehicle. On the other hand, you can lose warranty coverage through abusive driving, inadequate maintenance, or by purchasing after-market products and services such as gas-saving gadgets, rustproofing, paint protectors, air conditioning, and van conversions.

The manufacturer or dealer's warranty is a legal promise that the product it sells will perform in the normal and customary manner for which it was designed. This promise remains in force regardless of the number of subsequent owners as long as the warranty's original time/mileage limits haven't expired.

Some dealers tell customers that they need to have original equipment parts installed in order to maintain their warranty. A variation on this theme: a dealer requires that routine servicing, including tune-ups and oil changes (with a certain brand of oil), be done by the selling dealer or the warranty is invalid.

Nothing could be further from the truth.

Congress passed the Magnuson-Moss Warranty Improvement Act (under the Federal Trade Commission) years ago to protect motorists from this kind of abuse. The Act says that whoever issues a warranty cannot make that warranty conditional on the use of any specific brand of motor oil, oil filter, or any other component,

unless it's provided to the customer free of charge. If it is not provided for free, the customer should ask the issuer of the warranty to
produce a copy of the FTC waiver. If the waiver isn't forthcoming,
the repair is free, and the repairer can be fined for violating a federal statute.

Sometimes dealers will do all sorts of minor repairs that don't correct the problem and then after the warranty runs out, they'll tell you
that major repairs are needed. You can avoid this nasty surprise by
repeatedly bringing in your vehicle to the dealership before the warranty ends. During each visit, insist that a written work order include
the specific nature of the problem as you see it and that it carries the
notation that this is the second, third, or fourth time the same problem has been brought to the dealer's attention. Write it down yourself, if need be. This allows you to show a pattern of non-performance
by the dealer during the warranty period and establishes that it's a
serious and chronic problem. When the warranty expires, you have
the legal right to demand that it be extended on those items that consistently reappear on your handful of work orders.

Extended (supplementary) warranties

Extended warranties provide extended coverage, may be sold by
the manufacturer, dealer, or an independent third party, and are
automatically transferred when the vehicle is sold. They cost
$500–$1,500 and should be purchased only if the vehicle you're
buying is off its original warranty, has a poor repair history (see Part
Three), or if you're reluctant to use the small claims courts when
trouble arises that is factory related. Don't let the dealer pressure
you into deciding right away. Generally, you can purchase an
extended warranty anytime during the period the manufacturer's
warranty is still in effect.

Dealers love to sell extended warranties because about one-third
to one-half of this warranty's cost represents dealer markup. Out of
the remainder comes the sponsor's administration costs and profit
margin, calculated at another 25 percent. What's left is a minuscule
25 percent of the original amount paid to the dealer. It's estimated
that of the car buyers who purchase an extended service contract,
fewer than half actually use it.

It's often difficult to collect on supplementary warranties
because independent companies not tied to the automakers frequently go out of business. When this happens, and the company's
insurance policy won't cover your claim, take the dealer to small
claims court and ask for the repair cost and the refund of the original warranty payment. Your argument for holding the dealer
responsible is a simple one: by accepting a commission for acting as
an agent of the defunct company, the selling dealer took on the
obligations of the company as well.

Emission control warranties

These little-publicized warranties come with all new vehicles and cover the emission control system for up to 8 years/100,000 miles (California residents will find they may have longer warranties for these same emission components). Unfortunately, although owner manuals vaguely mention the emissions warranty, most don't specify which parts are guaranteed. Fortunately, the federal Environmental Protection Agency (EPA) has intervened on several occasions with hefty fines against Chrysler and Ford and ruled that all major motor and fuel-system components are covered. These include fuel metering, ignition spark advance, restart, evaporative emissions, positive crankcase ventilation, engine electronics (computer modules), and catalytic converters, as well as hoses, clamps, brackets, pipes, gaskets, belts, seals, and connectors. Many of the dealer service bulletins listed in Part Three under "Service Tips" show which parts failures are covered under the emissions warranty.

Secret warranties

Secret warranties have been around since automobiles were first mass-produced. They're set up to provide free repairs to fix performance-related defects caused by substandard materials, faulty design, or assembly-line errors. In 1974, *Lemon-Aid* exposed Ford's J-67 secret seven-year rust warranty, which covered the company's 1970–74 models. After first denying that it had such a warranty, Ford admitted two years later that it was indeed in place and negotiated a $2.8-million settlement with this author to compensate owners of rust-cankered Fords who had formed the Rusty Ford Owners Association. And you know what? Twenty-five years later, hundreds of secret warranties continue to exist among most automakers and *Lemon-Aid* is still the only consumer publication blowing the whistle on hundreds of current programs that secretly allocate funds for the repair of engine, transmission, fuel pump, and paint defects on cars, sport-utilities, trucks, minivans, and vans.

Even mundane little repairs that can still cost you a hundred bucks or more are covered. Take, for example, the elimination of foul, musty, or mildew odors emitted by your air conditioning unit. Despite what the dealer may say, it's covered by the base warranty. In fact, as you can see from the following GM, Ford, and Chrysler service bulletins, automakers have secret warranty policies that pay for AC service adjustments.

File In Section: 1 - HVAC
Bulletin No.: 53-12-12A
Date: December, 1996
Subject:
Air Conditioning Odor at Start Up in Humid Climates
(Disinfect Evaporator Core, Install Delayed Blower Control Package)

Models:
1993-96 Passenger Cars (Except GEO)
1993-96 Light Duty Models (Except Tracker)

Condition
Some owners may comment on odors emitted from the air conditioning system, primarily at start up in hot, humid climates.

Cause
This odor may be the result of microbial growth on the evaporator core. When the blower motor fan is turned on, the microbial growth may release an unpleasant musty odor into the passenger compartment.

Correction
To remove odors of this type, it is necessary to eliminate the microbial growth and prevent its recurrence- To accomplish this, these two procedures must be completed.
• Deodorize the evaporator core using Deodorizing Aerosol Kit, P/N 12377951 (AC Delco 15-102).
• Install the new A/C Delayed Blower Control Package, P/N 12370470, (AC Delco 15-8632).

GM's AC warranty service will take about an hour.

Article No.
98-2-7
02/02/98
AIR CONDITIONING - MUSTY AND MILDEW TYPE ODORS - SERVICE PROCEDURE
FORD:
1992-93 FESTIVA
1992-94 TEMPO
1992-97 CROWN VICTORIA, ESCORT MUSTANG, PROBE, TAURUS, THUNDERBIRD
1994-96 ASPIRE
1995-97 CONTOUR
LINCOLN-MERCURY:
1992-94 TOPAZ
1992-97 CONTINENTAL, COUGAR, GRAND MARQUIS, SABLE, TOWN CAR, TRACER
1993-97 MARK VIII
1995-97 MYSTIQUE
LIGHT TRUCK:
1992-95 BRONCO
1992-97 AEROSTAR, ECONOLINE, EXPLORER, F SUPER DUTY F-I50, F-250 HD, F-250 LD, F-350, RANGER
1995-98 WINDSTAR
1997 MOUNTAINEER
1997-98 EXPEDITION
1998 NAVIGATOR
MEDIUM/HEAVY TRUCK:
1992-97 F & B SERIES

This TSB article is being republished in its entirety to include the Expedition, Navigator and 1998 Windstar.

ISSUE: Musty and mildew type odors may come from the air conditioner and heater system. This odor is caused by mildew-type fungi growth in the A/C evaporator. It is most noticeable when the A/C is first turned on.

ACTION: A new Disodorizer(R) which encapsulates the mildew is now available to reduce these odors. This is a seasonal repair. Engineering effort to provide a long term repair for A/C odors will continue. Apply the Ford A/C Disodorizer(R) product (F6AZ-19G210-AA or YN-18) to the A/C system as directed in the following A/C Odor Treatment Procedure.

WARRANTY STATUS: Eligible Under The Provisions Of Bumper To Bumper Warranty Coverage

Ford's AC warranty service is a 20-minute job.

```
NO: 24-11-97
GROUP: Heater & A/C
DATE: Jul. 11. 1997
SUBJECT:
A/C Evaporator Odor

MODELS:
1992 - 1995 (AA) Spirit/Acclaim/LeBaron Sedan
1994 - 1998 (AB) Ram Van/Wagon
1992 - 1993 (AC) Dynasty/New Yorker/New Yorker Salon
1992 - 1993 (AG) Daytona
1992 - 1995 (AJ) LeBaron Coupe/LeBaron Convertible
1992 - 1998 (AN) Dakota
1992 - 1994 (AP) Shadow/Shadow Convertible/Sundance
1992 - 1995 (AS) Town & Country/Caravan/Voyager
1992 - 1993 (AY) Imperial/New Yorker Fifth Avenue
1994 - 1998 (BR) Ram Pickup
1993 - 1995 (ES) Chrysler Voyager (European Market)
1996 - 1998 (GS) Chrysler Voyager (International Market)
1995 - 1998 (JA) Cirrus/Stratus/Breeze
1996 - 1998 (JX) Sebring Convertible
1993 - 1998 (LH) Concorde/Intrepid/LHS/New Yorker/Vision
1996 - 1998 (NS) Town & Country/Caravan/Voyager
1995 - 1998 (PL) Neon
1997 - 1998 (TJ) Wrangler
1992 - 1998 (XJ) Cherokee
1994 - 1998 (ZG) Grand Cherokee (International Market)
1993 - 1998 (ZJ) Grand Cherokee/Grand Wagoneer

SYMPTOM/CONDITION:
Some vehicle operators may experience a musty odor from the A/C system, primarily at start up in hot and humid climates.
This odor may be the result of microbial growth on the evaporator core. During normal A/C system operation, condensa-
tion forms in and around the A/C evaporator. When airborne pollutants mix with this condensation, bacteria and fungi
growth begins and odor results.

DIAGNOSIS:
Operate the A/C system, if a musty odor is experienced, perform the Repair Procedure.

PARTS REQUIRED:
1  04897625AA Cleaner, Aerosol Evaporator
POLICY: Reimbursable within the provisions of the warranty.
```

*Chrysler's AC warranty service may take from 30 to 90 minutes and is
classed: "Failure Code: XX–Service Adjustment."*

Automakers are reluctant to make secret warranty extensions
public because they feel it would weaken confidence in their product and increase their legal liability. The closest they come to an
admission is sending a "goodwill policy," "product improvement
program," or "special policy" service bulletin to dealers or first owners of record. Consequently, the only motorists who get compensated for repairs to defective parts are the ones who are the original
owners, haven't moved or leased their vehicle, or yell the loudest
and present automaker service bulletins (see Appendix V to order
your own bulletins). Connecticut, Massachusetts, New York,
Maryland, Texas, and California have enacted laws prohibiting
secret auto warranties under penalty of a $2,000 fine, but they're

seldom enforced because it's hard to get written proof they exist.

If you're refused compensation, keep in mind that secret warranty extensions are an admission of manufacturing negligence. Try to compromise with a pro rata adjustment from the manufacturer. If polite negotiations fail, challenge the refusal in court on the grounds that you should not be penalized for failing to make a reimbursement claim under a secret warranty you never knew existed!

Here are a few examples of the latest and most comprehensive secret warranties that have come across my desk this year. Keep in mind that an up-to-date listing of other secret warranties and service programs can be found in Part Three under the heading "Secret Warranties/ Service Tips."

Ford/Nissan
• **1995–96 Villager and Quest minivans equipped with 3.0L engines.** **Problem**: Excessive engine noise is caused by a poorly designed connecting rod that's insufficiently lubricated. The design on the VG30E was changed in January 1996 to provide a quieter operation; the new design should have worked its way into production by March of that same year (check the month of production on the doorplate). **Warranty coverage**: Ford will replace at no charge any 3.0L V6 engine block if customers complain of engine knock following a cold start. Ford is replacing the entire engine, including the cylinder head, and says it will issue an owner notification (not a recall) or set up a warranty extension program. Nissan, on the other hand, doesn't plan to notify customers of this free replacement program.

Automotive News   JUNE 24, 1996

Gripers get new Nissan engines

MARY CONNELLY
Staff Reporter

Nissan and Mercury are replacing engine blocks or entire engines in up to 125,000 1995 and 1996 vehicles because of engine knock in Nissan's 3.0-liter V-6.

Vehicles involved are the Nissan Quest, Pathfinder and pickup plus the Mercury Villager. The affected vehicles were built between May 1995 and January 1996. As many as 80,000 Nissans and 45,000 Villagers are susceptible to engine knock after a cold start in cold climates.

Ford Motor Co. is replacing the entire Villager engine; Nissan is replacing the engine block, but not the cylinder head.

The engine noise results from a connecting rod design that fails to provide sufficient lubrication. Nissan changed the design in the VG30E V-6 engine in January 1996 to produce quieter operation.

The engine knock does not affect engine durability, Nissan and Ford said. "The noise itself will not cause a mechanical engine failure," Mercury told its dealers in a service bulletin. "Customers may drive the vehicles without causing damage to the engine."

Engines are being replaced because connecting rod designs are not interchangeable. Ford routinely replaces — rather than repairs — engines in new, low-mileage vehicles to increase customer satisfaction and to avoid creating new engine troubles.

"If the customer has a concern, the engine is being replaced under warranty," said spokeswoman Francine Romine.

The company is investigating to determine the scope of the problem, she said. Based on those findings, Ford expects to determine soon if it will order an owner notification or warranty extension program, she said. Whether engines in unsold models will be replaced depends on the outcome of the investigation, she said.

Nissan is replacing engine blocks only if a customer complains. Nissan is not notifying owners of the possible flaw and is not replacing engines in unsold vehicles. **AN**

Staff Reporter Mark Rechtin in Los Angeles contributed to this report.

Both Ford and Nissan also have a serious problem with engine exhaust manifold studs breaking and costing over $3,000 to repair. Both companies will offer "goodwill" compensation, if pressed, particularly if owners show up with service bulletins in hand (see Part 3).

General Motors

• **1992–93 Cavalier/Sunbird with 2.2L 4-cylinder engines. Problem**: Faulty head gaskets may cause loss of engine coolant, engine overheating, or destruction of the engine. **Warranty coverage**: GM will replace the faulty head gasket or repair the engine damage caused by head gasket failure at no charge up to 7 years/160,000 km, as set out in its March 1996 letter to first owners. Second owners and repairs done by independent garages are included in this program. This warranty extension sets the benchmark at a new high for engine durability and can be used in claims against all automakers with similar engine problems.

Dear General Motors Customer:

As the owner of a 1992 or 1993 Chevrolet Cavalier equipped with a 2.2L engine, your satisfaction with our product is of the utmost concern to us. Your vehicle was provided with a new vehicle warranty, which covers certain parts of your vehicle for a specified period. These warranties are of considerable value to you if you should experience problems with your vehicle.

This letter is intended to make you aware that some 1992 and 1993 Chevrolet Cavalier models with 2.2L engines may develop a failure of the cylinder head gasket that allows coolant to leak from the cylinder head gasket to engine block joint. Early evidence of this would be a loss of coolant in the coolant reservoir and an odor of coolant from the engine compartment, or a low coolant lamp. There may also be visible coolant deposits at the cylinder head to engine block joint.

General Motors of Canada Limited is, therefore, taking the following action:

We are providing owners with special coverage. If the above-mentioned condition occurs within seven (7) years of the date your vehicle was originally placed in service or 160,000 km, whichever occurs first, your vehicle will be repaired for you at no charge.

This special policy applies only to repairs requiring cylinder head gasket replacement as a result of cylinder head gasket failure that results in an engine coolant leak. It does not cover engine damage from continuing to operate the engine in an overheated condition after loss of coolant.

This is not a recall campaign. Do not take your vehicle to your GM dealer as a result of this letter unless you believe that your vehicle has the condition as described above. Keep this letter with your other important glovebox literature for future reference.

If you have already paid for some or all of the cost to have the cylinder head gasket replaced and in-service time was less than seven (7) years and 160,000 km, you should contact your GM dealer. You may be eligible for partial or complete reimbursement of costs if genuine GM parts were used in the repair. If the work was done by someone other than a GM dealership the amount of reimbursement may be limited to the amount the repair would have cost GM to have it completed by a GM dealership. Please provide your dealer with your original paid receipts or invoices verifying the repair, the amount charged, proof of payment, and the date of payment of those charges by March 1, 1997.

Repairs and adjustments qualifying under this Special Policy coverage must be performed by your GM dealer.

Honda/Acura
• **1995–97 Civic, 1996–97 Accord, Prelude, and Odyssey. Problem**:
Engine malfunctions cause emissions to exceed the federal norm.
Warranty coverage: In a settlement with the Environmental
Protection Agency, Honda extended its emissions warranty to 14
years or 150,000 miles. The automaker has agreed to the EPA's
demand that it provide a full engine check and emissions-related
repairs at 50,000 to 75,000 miles and give free tune-ups at 75,000
to 150,000 miles. Judging by Honda's past actions in denying its
responsibility for these kinds of problems, don't hesitate to complain to the EPA if you encounter a scintilla of evidence that the
company won't keep its promise.

Toyota
• **1988–94 compact pickups, T100 pickups, and 4Runner sport-utilities with 3.0L and 3.6L 6-cylinder engines. Problem**: Defective
head gaskets may cause loss of engine coolant, engine overheating, or destruction of the engine's short block. **Warranty coverage**:
Toyota will replace the defective components at no charge up to
8 years/100,000 miles (*Automotive News*, February 10, 1997).

Although some repairs have been attempted, it's recommended that the entire short block be replaced and new head bolts be
installed. This has resulted in warranty claims as high as $6,000
among the 36,000 vehicles repaired up to February 1997.
Although Toyota doesn't mention it, jurisprudence, as well as similar warranty extensions set up by other automakers, lead one to
assume that second owners and repairs done by independent
garages are included in this program.

Incidentally, there have been a lot of 1995–96 model head gasket
failures reported to the National Highway Traffic and Safety
Administration (NHTSA); Toyota will likely extend the warranty
again.

```
WARD-005                                                    February 10, 1998


TO:            ALL TOYOTA DEALER PRINCIPALS
               ALL TOYOTA DEALER GENERAL MANAGERS
               ALL TOYOTA DEALER SERVICE MANAGERS

SUBJECT:       3VZ-E ENGINE CYLINDER HEAD GASKETS -
               CUSTOMER SATISFACTION PROGRAMS

As advised in my preliminary announcement of December 23, 1997, we are proceeding to announce a major customer
satisfaction program involving 3VZ-E V6 engine equipped Trucks, T100, and 4Runners.

The attached information kit provides all detailed information for your staff and replaces all previous bulletins.

For reference, I will again briefly outline the components of this program:

3VZ-E Cylinder Head Gasket Special Policy Adjustment (S.P.A.)

Affects 3VZ-E equipped Trucks and 4Runners produced from June 1987 to December 1989.
Policy extends the warranty coverage on the engine cylinder head gaskets to 8 years/160,000 km from the original reg-
istration date or 12 months from the policy announcement (February 28th, 1999) for vehicles which have already exceed-
ed 8 years/160,000 km.
As there is less durability concern with these vehicles, the gaskets are to be replaced under this policy only if they are leak-
ing.

The mailing to advise all approx. 8,600 vehicle owners will proceed prior to February 28th, 1998.

3VZ-E Cylinder Head Gasket Special Service Campaign (S.S.C.)

Affects 3VZ-E equipped Trucks, T100, and 4Runners produced from January 1990 to October 1994.
Due to greater durability concerns, the cylinder head gaskets installed in these vehicles will be replaced whether or not
they are currently leaking, regardless of vehicle age or km. Vehicles which have already been replaced by a Toyota Dealer
using modified gaskets will be excluded.

The initial mailing to approx. 4,000 owners will proceed prior to February 28th, 1998, with all owners to be contacted via
subsequent mailings by August.

Please ensure all related staff review the attached material and are prepared to assist owners who contact your dealer-
ship. This is an excellent opportunity to maximize customer satisfaction and retention among these owners.

R.P. Daniels
```

Toyota, much to its credit, hasn't tried to keep this Special Warranty secret and, in fact, gave me a copy of the above notice to dealers when I requested it.

Confidential service bulletins

These are special warranties confirmed by technical service bulletins (confidential, for the most part) sent to dealers by automakers to advise them of special warranties and to help them quickly diagnose and correct factory defects. These bulletins also disclose how much of the repair the dealer can charge back to the manufacturer and which parts are available free of charge. Armed with these bulletins, motorists can use less expensive, independent garages to diagnose and repair their vehicles or to negotiate compensation for defects that the bulletins point out are the manufacturer's fault.

The major problem with these bulletins is that they're difficult to get. Dealers and automakers are reluctant to provide this kind of detailed technical information because it allows customers to second-guess a mechanic's work or to buttress their demands for compensation. However, as long as their involvement isn't disclosed, some dealers will discreetly provide copies of service bulletins to help their customers fight for compensation from the auto manufacturer.

If needed, you can always order service bulletins from the author for $5 each (see Appendix V for ordering instructions).

How long should parts/repairs last?

Let's say you can't find a service bulletin that says your problem is factory related or covered by a special compensation program. Or a part lasts just a little longer than its guarantee, but not as long as is generally expected. Can you get a refund if the same problem reappears shortly after it has been repaired? The answer is yes if you can prove the part failed prematurely.

Automakers, mechanics, and the courts have their own benchmarks as to what's the reasonable period of time or amount of mileage one should expect a part or adjustment to last. The following table shows what most automakers consider to be reasonable durability as expressed by their original warranties and secret warranties that are often called "goodwill" or "special policy" programs.

Estimated Part Durability

ACCESSORIES
Air conditioner	5 years
Cellular phone	5 years
Cruise control	5 years/ 100,000 miles
Power antenna	5 years
Power doors, windows	5 years
Radio	5 years

BODY
Paint peeling	7 years
Rust (perforations)	7 years
Rust (surface)	5 years
Vinyl roof	5 years
Water/wind/air leaks	5 years

BRAKE SYSTEM
Brake drum	100,000 miles
Brake drum, turn	35,000 miles
Brake drum linings	25,000 miles
Disc brake calipers	20,000 miles
Disc brake pads	25,000 miles
Master cylinder, rebuild	100,000 miles
Wheel cylinder, rebuild	80,000 miles

ENGINE AND DRIVETRAIN
Constant velocity joint	5 years/ 100,000 miles
Differential	7 years/ 140,000 miles
Engine (gas)	7 years/ 140,000 miles
Radiator	4 years/ 80,000 miles
Transfer case	7 years/ 140,000 miles
Transmission (auto.)	7 years/ 140,000 miles
Transmission (man.)	7 years/ 140,000 miles
Transmission oil cooler	5 years/ 100,000 miles
Universal joint	5 years/ 100,000 miles

EXHAUST SYSTEM
Catalytic converter	5 years/ 100,000 miles or more
Muffler	2 years/ 40,000 miles
Tailpipe	3 years/ 60,000 miles

FUEL SYSTEM

Carburetor	5 years/ 100,000 miles
Fuel filter	2 years/ 40,000 miles
Fuel pump	5 years/ 100,000 miles
Injectors	5 years/ 100,000 miles

IGNITION SYSTEM

Cable set	60,000 miles
Electronic module	5 years/ 100,000 miles
Spark plugs	40,000 miles
Tune-up	20,000 miles

SAFETY COMPONENTS

Airbags	life of vehicle
ABS brakes	7 years/ 140,000 miles
ABS computer	7 years/ 140,000 miles
Seatbelts	life of vehicle

STEERING AND SUSPENSION

Alignment	1 year/20,000 miles
Ball joints	80,000 miles
Power steering	5 years/ 100,000 miles
Shock absorber	2 years/ 40,000 miles
Struts	5 years/ 100,000 miles
Tires (radial)	4 years/ 80,000 miles
Wheel bearing	3 years/ 60,000 miles

VISIBILITY

Aim headlights	20,000 miles
Halogen/fog lights	3 years/ 60,000 miles
Sealed beam	2 years/ 40,000 miles
Windshield wiper motor	4 years/ 80,000 miles

The guidelines on pages 64–65 were extrapolated from Chrysler's payout to dozens of Chrysler Lemon Owner Group (CLOG) members from December 1997 through March 1998, in addition to Chrysler's original 7-year powertrain warranty applicable from 1991–95. Other sources for this chart were the Ford and GM transmission warranties outlined in their secret warranties (page 3) and GM, Toyota, and Mercury engine "special programs" laid out in their internal service bulletins (pages 61, 63, and 210, respectively).

Safety features generally have a lifetime warranty, with the exception of ABS brakes, which are a wear item. Nevertheless, the ten-year "free service program" portion of Chrysler's ABS recall announced several years ago can serve as a handy benchmark as to how long one can expect these components to last.

Airbags are a different matter. Those that are deployed in an accident and the personal injury and interior damage their deployment will likely have caused are covered by your accident insurance policy. However, if there is a sudden deployment for no apparent reason, the automaker and dealer should be held jointly responsible for all injuries and damages caused by the airbag. This will likely lead to a more generous settlement from the two parties and prevent your insurance premiums from being jacked up. Inadvertent deployment may occur after passing over a bump in the road, slamming the car door, having wet carpets in your Cadillac (no kidding), or, in some Chrysler minivans, simply putting the key in the ignition. This happens more often than you would imagine, judging by the hundreds of recalls and thousands of complaints recorded on the NHTSA's web site (for recalls and complaints addresses, see "Safety defect information").

Finally, the manufacturers' emission warranty serves as the primary guideline governing how long a vast array of electronic and mechanical components should last. Look first at your owner's manual for an indication of which parts are covered on your vehicle. If you come up with few specifics, use the EPA's guidelines along with GM's bulletins on the matter. Keep in mind that these durability benchmarks, secret warranties, and emissions warranties all apply to subsequent owners.

Recall repairs
Let the automaker know who and where you are. If you've moved or bought a used vehicle, it's a smart idea to pay a visit to your local dealer and get a "report card" on which recalls, free service campaigns, and warranties apply to it. Simply give the service advisor your vehicle identification number (VIN), found on your insurance card or on the dashboard just below the windshield on the driver's side, and have it run through the automaker's computer system ("Function 70" for Chrysler, "OASIS" for Ford, and "CRIS" for GM). Ask for a computer printout of the vehicle's history (have it faxed to you, if you're so equipped) and make sure you're listed in the automaker's computer as the new owner. This ensures that you'll receive notices of warranty extensions and emission and safety recalls.

Still, don't expect to be welcomed with open arms when your vehicle develops a safety- or emissions-related problem that's not yet part of a recall campaign. Automakers and dealers generally take a restrictive view of what constitutes a safety or emissions defect and frequently charge for repairs which should be free under federal safety or emissions legislation. To counter this tendency, look at the following list of typical defects that are clearly safety-related, and if you experience similar problems, tell the dealer you expect your repair to be paid by the manufacturer:
• airbag malfunctions
• corrosion affecting safe operation
• disconnected or stuck accelerators
• electrical shorts
• faulty windshield wipers
• fuel leaks
• problems with original axles, drive shafts, seats, seat recliners, or defrosters
• seatbelt problems
• stalling or sudden acceleration
• sudden steering or brake loss
• suspension failures
• trailer coupling failures

Recall campaigns force automakers to pay the entire cost of fixing a vehicle's safety-related defect. They may be voluntary or ordered by the U.S. Department of Transportation. Voluntary recall campaigns are a real problem, though; they aren't as rigorously monitored as government-ordered recalls, and dealers and automakers routinely deny they exist. Also, the company's so-called "fix" may not correct the hazard, and the company may take its own sweet time in notifying owners. Take, for example, Chrysler's voluntary "service program" to strengthen the rear latches on as many as 4.5 million 1984–95 minivans. Almost 50 percent of affected owners were still waiting for Chrysler to fix their minivans nearly two years after the company volunteered to correct the defect without the government's involvement.

Safety defect information
If you wish to report a safety defect or want recall information, you can access the NHTSA web site and recall/complaint database. You can search the database for your vehicle specifically and be thoroughly briefed on recalls, crash ratings, safety defects reported by other car owners, and a host of other safety-related items. The web address is *http://www.nhtsa.dot.gov/cars/problems/recalls/* for recalls and *http://www.nhtsa.dot.gov/cars/problems/complain/* to access the complaint database.

For those of us not fortunate enough to have a computer or who cannot access the Internet, the NHTSA's fax-back service provides the same free recall information through its toll-free line (most calls take five to ten minutes to complete). For calls placed within the U.S., the toll-free hot line is 1-800-424-9393 (1-800-424-9153 for the hearing impaired). If you find the 800 number busy, try the regular long-distance number: 202-366-0123 (202-366-7800 for the hearing impaired). It will get you into the automatic response service just as quickly and can be reached 24 hours a day.

Searches and printouts are available free of charge. Unless your request is complex, you can get the data you need within an hour by calling the hot line. An operator will conduct a search while you're still on the phone and a printout will be faxed or mailed to you within 24 hours.

Office hours are 8:00 a.m.–10:00 p.m. (EST) and an answering machine is available 24 hours a day so that you can leave your name and number for a return call.

Three Steps to a Settlement

Step 1: Informal negotiations
If your vehicle was misrepresented, has major defects, or wasn't properly repaired under warranty, the first thing you should do is give the seller (the dealer and automaker or a private party) a written summary (by registered mail or fax) of the outstanding

problems and stipulate a time period in which they must make the repairs or refund your money. Keep a copy of the letter for yourself along with all your repair records. Be sure to check all of the sales and warranty documents you were given to see if they conform to state laws. Any errors, omissions, or violations can be used to get a settlement with the dealer in lieu of making a formal complaint.

At the beginning, try to work things out informally. In your attempt to reach a settlement, keep in mind that the cardinal rule is: ask only for what is fair and don't try to make anyone look bad.

- Listen. The really tough part of negotiating is listening. Listen to the automaker's rep or the dealership principal and try to understand their problem while thinking of a cooperative solution. This means frequently restating the other side's position so they realize you understand their offer.
- Line up evidence and allies. Be sure to line up your proof (work orders, service bulletins, and independent garage reports) and allies before making your claim.
- Be reasonable and give as well as take. Consumers are frequently given a "Let's Make a Deal" spiel where the initial offer of 50 percent is often boosted to 75 percent compensation if the customer will agree—at that very moment—to pay 25 percent of the repair.
- Keep your demands reasonable but add a request for consequential damages (frustration, inconvenience, rental cars, missed work/vacation, etc.) and keep it as a throwaway claim to be used at a critical juncture in the talks. You should allege the maximum possible damages in your complaint, so remember to add up all your repair and rental bills. Also, hit them for days you couldn't use the vehicle even if you didn't rent one (the reference for this is *Gent v. Collinsville*, 451 NE2d).
- Don't set up an unrealistic timetable.
- Know when to shut up.

Furthermore, take a close look at the following confidential GM bulletin which outlines for dealers the strategy they should follow and questions they should ask before offering their clients any goodwill warranty consideration.

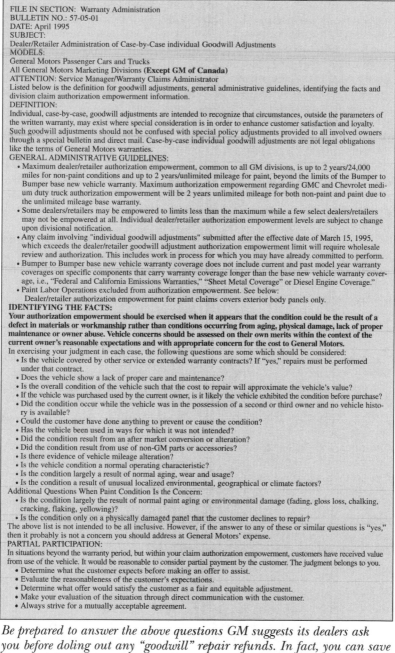

FILE IN SECTION: Warranty Administration
BULLETIN NO.: 57-05-01
DATE: April 1995
SUBJECT:
Dealer/Retailer Administration of Case-by-Case individual Goodwill Adjustments
MODELS:
General Motors Passenger Cars and Trucks
All General Motors Marketing Divisions **(Except GM of Canada)**
ATTENTION: Service Manager/Warranty Claims Administrator
Listed below is the definition for goodwill adjustments, general administrative guidelines, identifying the facts and
division claim authorization empowerment information.
DEFINITION:
Individual, case-by-case, goodwill adjustments are intended to recognize that circumstances, outside the parameters of
the written warranty, may exist where special consideration is in order to enhance customer satisfaction and loyalty.
Such goodwill adjustments should not be confused with special policy adjustments provided to all involved owners
through a special bulletin and direct mail. Case-by-case individual goodwill adjustments are not legal obligations
like the terms of General Motors warranties.
GENERAL ADMINISTRATIVE GUIDELINES:
 • Maximum dealer/retailer authorization empowerment, common to all GM divisions, is up to 2 years/24,000
   miles for non-paint conditions and up to 2 years/unlimited mileage for paint, beyond the limits of the Bumper to
   Bumper base new vehicle warranty. Maximum authorization empowerment regarding GMC and Chevrolet medium duty truck authorization empowerment will be 2 years unlimited mileage for both non-paint and paint due to
   the unlimited mileage base warranty.
 • Some dealers/retailers may be empowered to limits less than the maximum while a few select dealers/retailers
   may not be empowered at all. Individual dealer/retailer authorization empowerment levels are subject to change
   upon divisional notification.
 • Any claim involving "individual goodwill adjustments" submitted after the effective date of March 15, 1995,
   which exceeds the dealer/retailer goodwill adjustment authorization empowerment limit will require wholesale
   review and authorization. This includes work in process for which you may have already committed to perform.
 • Bumper to Bumper base new vehicle warranty coverage does not include current and past model year warranty
   coverages on specific components that carry warranty coverage longer than the base new vehicle warranty coverage, i.e., "Federal and California Emissions Warranties," "Sheet Metal Coverage" or Diesel Engine Coverage."
 • Paint Labor Operations excluded from authorization empowerment. See below:
   Dealer/retailer authorization empowerment for paint claims covers exterior body panels only.
IDENTIFYING THE FACTS:
**Your authorization empowerment should be exercised when it appears that the condition could be the result of a
defect in materials or workmanship rather than conditions occurring from aging, physical damage, lack of proper
maintenance or owner abuse. Vehicle concerns should be assessed on their own merits within the context of the
current owner's reasonable expectations and with appropriate concern for the cost to General Motors.**
In exercising your judgment in each case, the following questions are some which should be considered:
 • Is the vehicle covered by other service or extended warranty contracts? If "yes," repairs must be performed
   under that contract.
 • Does the vehicle show a lack of proper care and maintenance?
 • Is the overall condition of the vehicle such that the cost to repair will approximate the vehicle's value?
 • If the vehicle was purchased used by the current owner, is it likely the vehicle exhibited the condition before purchase?
 • Did the condition occur while the vehicle was in the possession of a second or third owner and no vehicle histo-
   ry is available?
 • Could the customer have done anything to prevent or cause the condition?
 • Has the vehicle been used in ways for which it was not intended?
 • Did the condition result from an after market conversion or alteration?
 • Did the condition result from use of non-GM parts or accessories?
 • Is there evidence of vehicle mileage alteration?
 • Is the vehicle condition a normal operating characteristic?
 • Is the condition largely a result of normal aging, wear and usage?
 • Is the condition a result of unusual localized environmental, geographical or climate factors?
Additional Questions When Paint Condition Is the Concern:
 • Is the condition largely the result of normal paint aging or environmental damage (fading, gloss loss, chalking,
   cracking, flaking, yellowing)?
 • Is the condition only on a physically damaged panel that the customer declines to repair?
The above list is not intended to be all inclusive. However, if the answer to any of these or similar questions is "yes,"
then it probably is not a concern you should address at General Motors' expense.
PARTIAL PARTICIPATION:
In situations beyond the warranty period, but within your claim authorization empowerment, customers have received value
from use of the vehicle. It would be reasonable to consider partial payment by the customer. The judgment belongs to you.
 • Determine what the customer expects before making an offer to assist.
 • Evaluate the reasonableness of the customer's expectations.
 • Determine what offer would satisfy the customer as a fair and equitable adjustment.
 • Make your evaluation of the situation through direct communication with the customer.
 • Always strive for a mutually acceptable agreement.

*Be prepared to answer the above questions GM suggests its dealers ask
you before doling out any "goodwill" repair refunds. In fact, you can save
time and improve your chances for getting compensation by incorporating
some of the questions and answers in a fact sheet accompanying your
complaint letter.*

Finally, when negotiating, speak in a calm, polite manner and try to avoid polarizing the issue. Talk about how "we can work together" on the problem. Let a compromise slowly emerge—don't come in with a hardline set of demands. Don't demand the settlement offer in writing, but make sure that you're accompanied by a friend who can confirm the offer in court if it isn't honored (relatives can testify in court). Be prepared to act upon the offer without delay so that you won't be blamed for its withdrawal.

Dealer/service manager
If you bought a used vehicle from a dealer who sells the same make new, you stand a good chance of getting free repairs, particularly if the vehicle is still under warranty, is covered by a "goodwill" program, or you intend to plead premature failure of a specific part based upon the parameters listed in the Estimated Part Durability chart found on pages 64–65.

The service manager is directly responsible to the dealer and manufacturer and makes the first determination of what work is covered under warranty. He or she is paid to save the dealer and automaker money and to mollify irate clients—almost an impossible balancing act. When a service manager agrees to warranty coverage, it's because you've convinced him he must. This can be done by getting them to access the vehicle's history from the manufacturer's computer and by presenting the facts of your case in a confident, forthright manner with as many supporting dealer service bulletins and NHTSA owner complaint printouts as you can find.

Don't use your salesperson as a runner, since the sales staff are generally quite distant from the service staff and usually have less pull than you do. If the service manager can't or won't set things right, your next step is to convene a mini summit with the service manager, the dealership principal, and the automaker's rep. By getting the automaker involved, you run less risk of having the dealer fob you off on the manufacturer and can often get an agreement where the seller and automaker pay two-thirds of the repair cost.

Dealers selling a different brand of vehicle and independent dealers give you less latitude. You have to make the case that the vehicle's defects were present at the time of purchase and should have been known to the seller, or that the vehicle doesn't conform to the representations made when it was purchased. Emphasize that you intend to use the courts if necessary to obtain a refund—most independent sellers would rather settle than risk a lawsuit with all the attendant publicity. An independent estimate of the vehicle's defects and cost of repairs is essential if you want to convince the seller that you're serious in your claim and stand a good chance of winning your case in court. The estimated cost of repairs is also useful in challenging a dealer who agrees to pay half the repair costs and then jacks up the costs one hundred percent so that you wind up paying the whole shot.

Step 2: Send a registered letter or fax

This is the next step to take if your claim is refused. Send the dealer and manufacturer a polite registered letter or a fax that asks for compensation for repairs that have been done or need to be done, insurance costs while the vehicle is being repaired, towing charges, supplementary transportation costs like taxis and rented cars, and damages for inconvenience.

Specify that either party has five days (but allow ten) to respond. If neither the dealer nor the manufacturer makes a satisfactory offer, file suit in small claims court. Make the manufacturer a party to the lawsuit, especially if the emissions warranty, a secret warranty extension, a safety-recall campaign, or extensive chassis rusting is involved. The two sample claim letters and fact sheet on the following pages can be useful in getting compensation for a defective used vehicle or for unsatisfactory repairs. Include in your letter references to any court decisions you find in this section of the book that support your claim and add a fact sheet if you're seeking a "goodwill" payout from the automaker and dealer.

Used Car Complaint Letter/Fax

WITHOUT PREJUDICE

Date: _____
Name: _____

Gentlemen,

Please be advised that I am dissatisfied with my used vehicle,
a_____, bought from you for_____ on_____.

The vehicle has not been reasonably durable and is, therefore, not
as represented to me. You have been given repeated opportunities,
to no avail, to fix the following recurring problems:

1. _____
2. _____
3. _____

In compliance with the federal *Magnuson-Moss Warranty
Improvement Act*, state consumer protection statutes and the lemon
law, I formally put you on notice to repair the above defects without charge or refund the purchase price. A summary of the facts
relating to this claim is included on a separate sheet.

Should you fail to repair these defects in a satisfactory manner and
within a reasonable period of time, I may choose to get an estimate
of the needed repairs from an independent source and claim that
amount, plus consequential damages, in court, without further
delay.

A response by fax or phone within the next five (5) days would be
appreciated.

Sincerely,

_____
(signed with telephone or fax number)

Secret Warranty Claim Letter/Fax

WITHOUT PREJUDICE

Date: _____
Name:_____

Gentlemen,

Please be advised that I am dissatisfied with my vehicle,
a_____, bought from you on_____.
It has had the following recurring problems that I believe are
factory-related defects as confirmed by internal service bulletins
sent to dealers and covered by your "goodwill" policies:

1. _____
2. _____
3. _____

If your "goodwill" program has ended, I ask that my claim be
accepted, nevertheless, inasmuch as I was never informed of your
policy while it was in effect and should not be penalized for not
knowing it existed.

I hereby put you formally on notice under the federal *Magnuson-
Moss Warranty Improvement Act* and state consumer protection
statutes that your refusal to apply this extended warranty coverage
in my case would be an unfair warranty practice within the purview
of the above cited laws.

I have enclosed several estimates (my bill) showing that this problem is factory related and will (has) cost $_____to correct.
I would appreciate you refunding me the estimated (paid) amount,
failing which, I reserve the right to have the repair done elsewhere
and claim reimbursement, plus consequential and punitive damage
from you in court, without further delay.

A response by fax or phone within the next five (5) days would be
appreciated.

Sincerely,

_____
(signed with telephone or fax number)

Claim Fact Sheet

Claimant: _____ Date: _____

Reference: Failure of _____ to last a reasonable period of time.

Dealer/Automaker: Request for "Goodwill" repair/refund for the following reasons:

VEHICLE
- Vehicle has NOT performed as represented by seller
- Vehicle isn't covered by any other warranty/service contract
- Vehicle shows no signs of mileage alteration or accident damage
- Vehicle has been properly maintained and driven
- Vehicle was NOT used for purposes for which it was not intended

PROBLEM
- Problem is recurring and seller has been given ample opportunity to fix it
- Problem NOT a normal operating condition or part of normal maintenance
- Problem NOT caused or worsened by owner's actions
- Problem NOT caused by after-market conversion, use of accessories, or servicing
- Problem NOT the result of normal aging, wear, usage, or environmental factors
- Problem likely existed at the time of purchase

_____
(signed with telephone or fax number)

Step 3: Mediation and arbitration
If the formality of a courtroom puts you off or if you're not sure that your claim is all that solid and don't want to pay legal costs to find out, consider using mediation or arbitration sponsored by the Better Business Bureau, the American Automobile Association, or state courts (often a prerequisite before a small claims trial is convened or lemon law provisions are applied). Understand, too, that BBB efficacy and fairness in arbitration is spotty at best (the Miami BBB is bankrupt and under investigation for corrupt practices), and that arbitration may not be suitable if previous decisions are silenced through gag orders or you are barred from using the courts though you consider the decision to be unfair.

Mandatory arbitration clauses
Automakers and car dealers are inserting mandatory arbitration clauses into their new and used car contracts as a means to override

federal and state legislation that protect buyers. Unfortunately, most consumers miss the significance of binding arbitration clauses and never realize they are renouncing their legal right to use the courts and apply state lemon laws, which give them special protections such as the right to a replacement when their vehicle comes with serious defects, and the federal Magnuson-Moss Act, which establishes strict requirements for consumer warranties.

One recent Supreme Court decision (*Allied-Bruce Terminex Cos. v. Dobson*) has held that these arbitration clauses are valid provisions of consumer contracts and can't be prohibited by state law. In other words, if you sign a sales contract that requires binding arbitration, you may be agreeing to undisclosed costs, such as high per-hour arbitrator fees, risky loser-pays provisions for attorneys, and the requirement that the dealer gets to choose the arbitrator.

Lemon Laws

Lemon laws protect consumers with warranties for consumer goods. They most often are used when a consumer buys a defective new or used car, and the manufacturer or dealer refuses to buy the car back or give the buyer a replacement vehicle. Although there are different lemon laws in almost every state, they are all quite similar, as you can see from the sampling below. There's also a federal lemon law which applies to all fifty states; therefore, even if your state doesn't have a separate lemon law, you can still enforce your warranty rights under federal statutes.

Here's a listing of some states with lemon laws. Since these laws are updated continually, contact the state Attorney-General's office for a copy of the latest law.

California
Qualify: Four unsuccessful repairs or 30 business days out of service within shorter of 1 year/12,000 miles. **Notification:** Certified mail notice to automaker and delivery of vehicle to repair facility for repair attempt within 30 days. Leased vehicles included. California-certified arbitration is available. Call 916-322-3360.

Florida
Qualify: Three unsuccessful repairs or 20 days out of service within shorter of 1 year/12,000 miles. **Notification:** Written notice by certified or express mail to automaker which has 14 days (10 if vehicle has been out of service 20 cumulative days) for a final repair attempt after delivery of vehicle to a designated dealer. Leased vehicles included. State-run arbitration is available. Call 800-321-5366.

Illinois
Qualify: Four repair attempts or 30 business days out of service within shorter of 1 year/12,000 miles. **Notification:** Written notice to automaker and opportunity to repair. Call 217-782-9011.

New York
Qualify: Four unsuccessful repairs or 30 days out of service after notice within shorter of 2 years/18,000 miles. **Notification**: Certified mail notice to automaker, agent, or dealer. Leased vehicles included. State-run arbitration is available. Call 518-474-5481.

Pennsylvania
Qualify: Three unsuccessful repairs or 30 days out of service within shorter of 1 year/12,000 miles or warranty. **Notification**: Delivery to authorized dealer. If delivery can't be done, written notice to manufacturer or dealer obligates it to pay for delivery. Call 215-560-2414.

Texas
Qualify: Four unsuccessful repairs, with two occurring within shorter of 1 year/12,000 miles and other two occurring within shorter of 1 year/12,000 miles from date of second repair attempt; or two unsuccessful repairs of a serious safety defect with 1 occurring within shorter of 1 year/12,000 miles and other occurring within shorter of 1 year/12,000 miles from date of first repair; or 30 days out of service within the shorter of 2 years/24,000 miles and at least two repair attempts made within shorter of 1 year/12,000 miles. **Notification**: Written notice to automaker. Leased vehicles included. State-run arbitration is available. Call 512-476-3618.

Do lemon laws apply to used cars?
Yes, if the buyer has bought the vehicle with a warranty. As with new cars, the defect must exist within the warranty period. So, if a used car has a 30-day warranty, and a defect doesn't appear until one year later, one may not be able to get help through a lemon law suit.

However, if the defect was a concealed defect, such as undisclosed accident damage, a problem covered by a secret warranty, or the dealer drags his feet in correcting the problem until the warranty is over, the buyer may yet have rights under the lemon laws. This is because the defect existed at the time of sale, the dealer was advised of the problem during the warranty period and failed to make the necessary repairs, or he attempted to defraud the buyer.

Robert F. Brennan, a Hollywood, California consumer fraud attorney (tel: 213-463-2547; fax: 213-463-5527; email: *rbrennan@direct-net.com*) gives the following advice to attorneys faced with a used car fraud:

> Most automotive consumer fraud occurs in the sale of used cars. There can be fraud in any aspect of the buying transaction. The two which we see the most are undisclosed accident damage and rolled-back odometers. Sometimes we see both in the same car. If you have a client who has purchased a used car and is having particular difficulties with it, you can direct appropriate inspections to determine if your client has been defrauded in either of these ways:

Undisclosed Accident Damage: Often, this shows up as severe alignment problems, premature tire wear and a lot of unexplained noise while the car is executing turns or braking. To determine if your client has been defrauded in this manner, have your client take the car to a certified auto body shop for a complete inspection, along with a complete photographic history if any signs of damage are found during the inspection.

Rolled-Back Odometers: This is indicated by premature wear and failure in brake drums, belts, hoses, transmission and drivetrain components. To check this out, a mechanical inspection is useful, but it is better to order the complete ownership history of the vehicle from the Department of Motor Vehicles. By federal law, any time a car is sold the seller must fill out and sign, under penalty of perjury, the "Odometer Disclosure Statement" that provides the amount of miles on the car at the time of sale.

In odometer cases, you will often find, upon ordering the vehicle's history, that the "vehicle sold two years ago with 78,000 miles on it, and then (was) sold to your client with only 21,000 miles on it." In this case you have a rolled-back odometer on your hands.

Tampering with odometers is specifically prohibited by federal and California law, and tampering with odometers also implicates theories of fraud, breach of warranty and California's Consumer Legal Remedies Act...

Do lemon laws apply to minor defects?

Ordinarily, no, unless the consumer specifically bought the vehicle for a particular feature which is found to be defective. For instance, you would not normally be entitled to a refund or replacement vehicle because, say, the radio antenna is bent. However, if you buy a vehicle for a specific feature—say, air conditioning—and the dealer and manufacturer cannot make it work properly, you could well have an enforceable lemon law claim.

As a general principle, lemon laws apply to more serious defects, such as brakes, transmission, suspension, serious engine problems (oil burning, stalling, and hard starting), and the like. However, many consumers have enforced their lemon law rights for paint defects (excessive paint peeling which could not be remedied), for repeated instances of the engine light coming on, for unusual noises and rattles in the vehicle, and for other defects which do not quite rise to the level of a serious brake or transmission problem, but just the same, produce stress and anxiety due to their repeated failure or cumulative effect.

How does it work?

A lemon law gives the buyer of a defective vehicle an opportunity to get either a refund or a replacement car, plus up to triple damages (a $15,000 used car could result in a $45,000 award). However, the defect must have existed within the warranty period.

For example, if a consumer buys a car with a one-year warranty, a defect which does not manifest until two years after purchase is probably not covered by the lemon laws, although it can be still be covered under other state consumer protection laws or the federal Magnuson-Moss Act.

However, any defect which arises during the warranty period (keep those old work orders) will entitle the buyer to lemon law rights, if the dealer and manufacturer cannot fix the defect after a reasonable number of repair attempts (usually two or three tries).

How do you get "lemon law" protection?
When it's obvious the vehicle is defective, the buyer must promptly bring the vehicle back to an authorized dealership for warranty repairs and give the dealership and manufacturer a reasonable opportunity to correct the problem—one repair attempt will not bring the lemon law into play. However, where the dealership and manufacturer have multiple repair attempts and cannot fix the defect, then the lemon law comes into force.

After the dealership and manufacturer have failed to repair the defect, demand a refund or a replacement vehicle. Do this in writing and send a copy to both the dealer and the manufacturer. If you're lucky, they may give you a refund or replacement. Or, they may request that you go through the manufacturer's private arbitration system. You may do so if you wish, but do not be disappointed or surprised if you encounter a "kangaroo court" where the arbitrators are all-too-chummy with the dealer or automaker.

If you still do not get any remedy and it looks like everyone is dragging their feet, then it's time to seek out the assistance of an attorney for advice as to your overall strategy and which other state or federal statutes you should use.

Are there any lemon law traps that can catch me?
There sure are. Foremost is the service manager's reluctance to write the same problem on subsequent work orders so you can't prove the dealership had multiple opportunities to correct the same defect. You can counter this little trick by adding your own comments on the work order or appending a separate list (keep a copy).

Another trap is where the dealer or the manufacturer offer a newer car for a bit more money. Unfortunately, the buyer is stuck with paying additional sales tax, depreciation loss on the returned vehicle, another sales commission, and registration and licensing fees—costs that would not be applicable under most lemon laws.

Finally, the dealer may try to delay servicing until you're no longer under the warranty or the lemon law's protection. Protect yourself by giving a written deadline for the defect to be corrected and stating that legal action will commence if that deadline isn't respected.

Do I have to pay a lot of money to enforce my rights under lemon laws?
Not usually. Most lawyers will take such cases on a contingency or a semi-contingency basis, because a dealer or manufacturer who loses a lemon law claim must pay attorney's fees to the prevailing plaintiff. Generally, a consumer who loses a lemon law case pays minimal costs. However, verify this, because some states, like California for instance, may require that the losing plaintiff pay more substantial court costs.

Involving Other Agencies

Groups like the Ralph Nader-founded Center for Auto Safety (202-328-7700), your state bar association, and Legal Aid can often refer you to local members who specialize in "consumer rights" or "lemon laws." For both automotive cases and consumer fraud cases, the National Association of Consumer Advocates in Boston has a referral panel of consumer attorneys working throughout the United States; their number is 617-723-1239. Chances are these groups won't refer you to either a turkey or a weasel attorney. If they do, you can hold them responsible for their reference, if you believe they were negligent.

To save money when seeing a lawyer, remember that the first interview is free, and you may buy an hour of the lawyer's time for more research or more detailed instruction, or you may hire a lawyer on a contingency basis (nothing up front—about one-third of the settlement or award if you're successful).

Government consumer affairs offices
Investigation, mediation, and some litigation are the primary areas in which state and federal consumer affairs offices can be helpful. Despite severe budget restraints, consumer protection legislation has been left standing in most states and resourceful consumers can use these laws along with media coverage to prod state consumer affairs offices into action. Furthermore, state bureaucrats aren't as well shielded from criticism as are their federal counterparts. A call to your state representative or senator's executive assistant can often get things rolling.

Online services/Internet/web sites
America Online and CompuServe are two online service providers with active consumer forums that use experts to answer consumer queries and to provide legal as well as technical advice. The Internet offers the same information but uses a worldwide database. If you or someone you know is able to create a web site, you might consider using this site to attract attention to your plight and arm yourself for arbitration or court.

Several years ago, Debra and Edward Goldgehn's 1985 Ford Ranger caught fire and burned completely. The couple's suspicions

that it was a factory-related defect were later confirmed by a TV
show that reported a series of similar Ford fires. The couple created their own web site called "Flaming Fords" and began amassing
an incredible database containing reports of similar fires, class
action lawsuits, expert witnesses, and actions taken in other countries. (For example, Ford had already recalled a number of its vehicles in order to fix the problem in Canada.) Shortly thereafter, Ford
USA recalled 8.7 million cars and trucks, representing the largest
recall ever announced by a single auto manufacturer. Ford says that
the Internet pressure was coincidental and not a factor in its decision to recall the vehicles in the States.

Right, and Elvis is building Cadillacs in Detroit.

Michael Hos, a dissatisfied Acura owner, became fed up with
what he felt was Acura's stonewalling of his complaints. Rather than
get angry, he got organized and set up a web site called "1997 Acura
CL 3.0L: My Lemon" to collect other owners' comments and list
some of the most common Acura problem areas. Within six
months, Acura settled. Here's what Hos has to say:

Phil,
Hi, remember me? I'm the guy that had the 1997 Acura CL lemon.
Well, as it turns out Acura settled with me. I got payoff on the car, my
attorney fees taken care of, and I'm walking away with $4000 in my
pocket after the experience. I was so glad to get rid of this car you
have no idea.

I have pulled down my "anti-Acura" website and washed my
hands clean of the entire ordeal. I turned in the CL about 2 weeks
ago, and my checks should be here next week...

At any rate, I wanted to say thanks for all your input into the case
and the encouragement to continue on. The last few months of driving the car were horrible, I'm glad it's done.

In a follow-up posting:

As far as my website goes, I think it was a major part of them settling
early. I had a counter placed on it which showed them how many
people had visited the site. Anyone can set up a web page like mine
pretty easily. I have web space on my university's computer, so it was
free for me to use. Folks without space should expect to spend about
$20 a month for space, or if they have their own email account, web
space is usually provided for free. If they don't know how to set up
their web page, paying someone to do it will be kinda pricey, a few
hundred bucks should cover it. The main thing it needs to have is the
counter, and it also needs to be libel free. I had only facts on my web
page as I didn't want to get involved in a libel suit. They also need to
register the site with all the major search engines so it comes up
when looking for the manufacturer. Submitit.com offers such services for free. Putting in a <Meta> tag into the page also helps move
it up the search engines' list of hits. Posting to newsgroups also is
helpful. I also wrote to JD Power, NHTSA, *Consumer Reports*, and any
other consumer oriented agency I could think of.

When we settled before going to court, I had to sign the settlement papers saying I would pull down my site. They would not settle with me until I did that. This shows how much power the site can have. I would also put the manufacture's phone number and address on it so viewers of the site can contact the manufacturer.

For the most part, everyone who read my site took my side of the story and agreed that Acura should pay up. I did have a few folks that were mad I was slamming Acura, but I wasn't concerned with them. I have about 200 email responses that people have mailed to me over the last few months.

As a side note, I think the only real reason they settled with me, in addition to the page being up, was my attorney. I had 7 charges filed against them in Superior Court. Also keep in mind that I paid nothing for my attorney until after we settled. My bill for him is $1,500, but that's included in the settlement. Also, I'm only 23, so anyone can do this if they are persistent.

Classified ads

Use your local paper's "Personals" column to pressure the seller and to gather data from others who may have experienced a problem similar to your own. This alerts others to the potential problem, helps build a core base for a class action or group meeting with the automaker, and puts pressure on the dealer or manufacturer to settle.

PROJECTS AND CAUSES

A BAD FIRE occured in our 1994 Jeep Cherokee because of driving with a compact spare tire while in 4WD (could not get out of 4WD). Compact spare is standard equipment but appropriate warning not in Owners Manual. No appropriate answers from Chrysler Canada yet. Seeking others with similar experience. R. Richards 416-481-4117.

Launching a Lawsuit

When to sue

If the seller agrees to make things right, give him or her a deadline and then have an independent garage check the repairs. If no offer is made within ten working days, file suit in small claims court. Make the manufacturer a party to the lawsuit only if the original, unexpired warranty was transferred to you, your claim includes extensive chassis rusting, or it falls under the emissions warranty, a secret warranty extension, or a safety recall campaign.

Choosing the right court

You must decide upon the remedy to pursue; that is, whether you want the cost of repairs, a partial refund, or a cancellation of the sale. To determine the refund amount, add the estimated cost of repairing existing mechanical defects to the cost of prior repairs. Don't exaggerate your losses or claim for repairs that are considered routine maintenance.

There are practical problems involved in a suit for cancellation of sale. The court requires that the vehicle be "tendered" back to the seller at the time the lawsuit is filed. This means that you are without transportation for as long as the case continues, unless you purchase another car in the interim. If you lose the case, you must then take back the old car and pay storage fees. You could go from having no car to having two, one of which is a clunker.

Generally, if the cost of repairs or the sales contract falls within the small claims court limit, the case should be filed there to keep costs to a minimum and to obtain a speedy hearing. Small claims court judgments aren't easily appealed, lawyers aren't necessary, filing fees are minimal ($50–$100), and trials are usually heard within a few months.

If the damages exceed the small claims court limit and there's no way to reduce them, you'll have to go to a higher court—where costs quickly add up and lengthy delays of a few years or more are commonplace.

Small claims court

Before getting into the details of launching a small claims action, read the following letter from Steve Wheeler and Eleanor Crawley, which describes how they got almost $4,000 (Cdn.) refunded after following *Lemon-Aid*'s court tips:

> We purchased an 88 Tempo….Within six days $1,700 had been spent on repairs (on an emergency trip to Cleveland). The head gasket, a tension pulley, and an axle all had to be replaced during the first few days. The car never made it to Cleveland and my wife was stranded in motels or stuck sitting beside the interstate or in garages waiting for repairs….The dealer said he would only reimburse us if we signed an agreement which gave up any future legal claims on repair on the Tempo. We wouldn't sign and negotiations ended….
>
> We filed in small claims court for the refund of $2,800, the car's price with tax, $737 we paid for repairs while the car was under warranty (dealer had already paid $1,000 using his credit card over the phone), and expenses incurred while my wife was stranded for a total of $3,796 plus $50 for the small claim. On the advice of the lawyer, we named the company, the dealer (who also owned the company), and the mechanic as defendants.
>
> We had written the dealer using the example of the Used Car Letter in *Lemon-Aid Used Car Guide 1996* during the negotiations, and had cited the Sale of Goods Act and several sample cases from the book.
>
> In the preliminary hearing, the dealer's defence was that my wife had misunderstood the warranty and that he didn't warranty any work not done at his mechanic's garage.
>
> Yesterday, our day in court came. We got there at 9:30 a.m. and left at 5 p.m. We were awarded $3,800 and the dealer had to take the car back. The judge based his decision on the Sale of Goods Act and found that the Tempo was "not fit for the purpose for which it was sold."(…)

Without the first few chapters of *Lemon-Aid Used Car Guide 1996*, we wouldn't have known where to start or how to proceed.

A few things we noticed which might help someone else stuck with a lemon: Get inspections done as quickly as possible after you realize you don't want the car. Park it and don't drive it as soon as possible. Get a mechanic to accompany you to court to back up his inspection; the judges seem to be more impressed by a personal appearance than a written report. Keep good records of all meetings and communications for the recounting of events in court. We found that the dealer who was trying to confuse the issue had no answers when we itemized clearly the negotiations and attempts at agreement....

I hope that this letter and the case will encourage anyone else who gets stuck with a lemon.

There are small claims courts in every state and territory, and you can make a claim in the county or parish where the problem happened or where the defendant lives and conducts business. The first step is to make sure that your claim doesn't exceed the dollar limit of the court (the limits differ from state to state). Then you should go to the small claims court office and ask for a claim form. Instructions on how to fill it out properly accompany the form. Remember, you must identify the defendant correctly. It's a practice of some dishonest firms to change a company's name to escape liability; for example, it would be impossible to sue Joe's Garage (1998) if your contract is with Joe's Garage Inc. (1984).

At this point, it would be a smart idea to hire a lawyer or a paralegal for a half-hour walk-through of small claims procedures to ensure that you've prepared your case properly and that you know what objections will likely be raised by the other side. If you'd like a lawyer to do all the work for you, there are a number of inexpensive law firms around the country that are experienced in small claims litigations. Get a reference from the state bar association and call the firm to get an estimate of their hourly charges and fees.

Remember, you're entitled to bring any evidence to court that's relevant to the case, including written documents such as a bill of sale or receipt, a contract, or your claim letter. For severe paint or rust problems, take a photograph to court. Have the photographer sign and date the photo. You may also have witnesses testify in court (a family member may act as a witness). It's important to discuss a witness's testimony prior to the court date. If a witness can't attend the court date, he or she can write a report and sign it for representation in court. This situation usually applies to an expert witness, such as an independent mechanic who has evaluated your car's problems.

If you lose your case in spite of all the foregoing preparation and research, some small claims court statutes allow cases to be retried at a nominal cost in exceptional circumstances—if a new witness has come forward, additional evidence has been discovered, or key documents, formerly not available, have become accessible.

Class actions

Class action suits allow a single individual to sue a company, government, or other entity on behalf of hundreds or even thousands of others with similar claims. They have been used successfully for three decades in the United States.

Class actions allow contingency fees where consumers can enter into no-win-no-pay agreements with lawyers. Usually, if you lose, you pay your expenses and move on. However, in some jurisdictions, judges can require losing class-action plaintiffs to pay the defendant's fees as well. Another pitfall is the tendency of some plaintiff lawyers to sell out their client's interests in exchange for hefty lawyer's fees.

How to file a class action
• Like any other lawsuit, a lawyer files the plaintiff's statement of claim against the defendant and the plaintiff applies to the court to certify the lawsuit as a class action.
• The presiding judge will then decide whether there is an "identifiable class of two or more persons," whether a class action is the "preferable procedure," and whether the plaintiff truly represents the class. If you meet all the above criteria, the judge will issue a certification order and designate you as the Class Representative.
• Other class members must be notified of the lawsuit. Small groups can be contacted by mail, but larger groups may require notification through newspaper ads backed up by a toll-free telephone line. Members of the class must then be given an opportunity to opt out of the lawsuit. If they don't, they remain part of the class.

If the class wins, individual cases may then be heard to assess damages or a notification will be sent to each member to apply for their part of the settlement or award.

It may take from three to five years before a final judgment is rendered. However, appeals may double that time. Lawyers typically charge the class one-third of the amount obtained.

Presenting your case

As plaintiff, you will get the first opportunity to rise and state your case to the judge. You should ask for the exclusion of witnesses from the courtroom (this increases the chance that the other side will give contradictory testimony) and then proceed to lay out your proof, concluding within five to ten minutes. Hang your narrative on the documents that you produce (you can call them "P-1," "P-2," as "Proof 1," "Proof 2," and so on) and let them serve as note cards.

The first three documents should be the sales contract, all work orders relative to the problems you've had, and your registered complaint letter or fax. After that, you may wish to produce the dealer or automaker's response, a report or work orders from an independent garage supporting your position, and copies of your maintenance records and dealer service bulletins in order to show that the problems are factory related and not maintenance items. Conclude your presentation by simply restating the claim as it's written on your court complaint.

On the day of the trial, bring in a mechanic to confirm that the defects exist and to provide an estimate of repair costs. If the repairs have already been carried out, he can explain what caused the defects and justify his bill for repairing them. This should be done by presenting the defective parts, if possible. He must convince the judge that the defects were present at the time the vehicle was sold and not caused by poor maintenance or abusive driving habits.

When the dealer gets on the stand, ask for the exclusion of all witnesses and try to ferret out the following facts:

- When and from whom was the used vehicle last purchased?
- How much was it bought for?
- What was done to recondition the vehicle and at what cost?
- What was the *Edmund's Book* value of the vehicle when first bought from the previous owner and when sold to the plaintiff?

This line of questioning should show the judge the considerable profits the dealer made by buying the vehicle below the market value, by not spending much to recondition it, and by reselling it far above the *Edmund's Book* value.

Before the dealer leaves the stand, get him to confirm whether he or his salespeople made any representations, either verbally or through a newspaper ad, extolling the vehicle's qualities. With the witnesses excluded, it's quite likely that they will contradict the dealer when their turn comes to testify.

Other witnesses who can help your case are the vehicle's previous owner (who can testify as to its deficiencies when sold), and any of your co-workers or friends who can testify as to how well you maintained your vehicle, how you drove it, and the seriousness of the defects.

Dos and don'ts

- Don't sue a car dealer if he has no money, isn't bonded, is bankrupt, has changed his company, or is willing to negotiate a settlement.
- Don't sign a false sales tax receipt. Crooked car dealers try to get their customers to take a receipt that indicates a selling price far below the price paid.
- Don't threaten or insult the dealer. This will only gain sympathy for him and hurt your own credibility.
- Do complain to the state Motor Vehicle Bureau and consumer affairs about possible violations of state laws.
- Do bring in the police fraud squad if you suspect the odometer has been tampered with.

- Do contact local consumer groups for used vehicle jurisprudence and help in mediating the complaint.
- Do publicize any favorable court judgment as a warning to other dealers and as encouragement for other consumers.

Settlements
You may be asked to sign a document, called a release, which proves that a final settlement has been made. Generally, once you sign the release, you can't sue the other person for that particular debt or injury. If you're the debtor, it's very important that you make sure the other person signs the release when you pay him or her. If you're the creditor collecting on the debt, you must sign the release, but don't do so until you've received the money. Release the debtor from that particular debt, but don't release him or her from all future debts.

Sample settlement form

> I, John Doe, hereby acknowledge the payment of $300 by Jane Smith to compensate me for the defects in the vehicle I bought from her on _____. In accepting this payment, I hereby drop all present and future claims against Ms. Smith arising from the purchase of this vehicle.

_____   _____
Date   **John Doe**

                                 _____
                                 Jane Smith

Deadbeat defendants
If you're dealing with a professional crook, the real work begins once you win your case. You may have to garnish (seize) part of the defendant's bank account or wages or ask the sheriff to serve a writ of execution. This writ allows the sheriff to demand full settlement plus court costs and, failing that, to seize the defendant's goods to cover the amount of the judgment. But here's the catch: property that's needed to earn a living (car, tools, machinery, etc.), household goods, and anything encumbered by a lien are exempt from seizure.

Professional deadbeats can tell the sheriff that practically everything they own is exempt—and it will take another action before the regular courts, at the plaintiff's expense, can have the defendant questioned under oath. If he's found to be lying, he can then be sent to jail for perjury or contempt of court. And the small claims court judgment will remain unpaid.

Key Court Decisions

The following lawsuits and judgments cover typical problems that are likely to arise. Use them as leverage when negotiating a settlement or as a reference should your claim go to trial. Additional court judgments can be found in the legal reference section of your city's main public library or at a nearby university law library. Ask the librarian for help in choosing the legal phrases that best describe your claim.

There is a lot you can find out on your own, beginning with West's *Causes of Action*, an encyclopedia for lawyers preparing lawsuits, particularly Volume 11 on Consumer Protection. You will find information there on how to sue a car company for selling you a defective car, references to relevant cases listed by state, and even a sample complaint. Another useful reference is *Blashfield's Automobile Law*, a 15-volume encyclopedia exclusive to automobile-related lawsuits. Sections 485 and 487 are especially helpful in providing jurisprudence. *Automobile Design Liability* by Goodman and the Center for Auto Safety is a four-volume legal reference that is essential for proving that a safety defect is design or factory related. Finally, you'll want to read the "rules of civil procedure" for your state to find out how lawsuits are filed and argued and to make sure that you won't be tossed out of court on a technicality.

Using an Expert (Whistleblower)

GM v. Elwell. U.S. Supreme Court, January 1998. Auto industry whistleblowers have gained an ally: the U.S. Supreme Court ruled that they are free to testify against their former employers in other states, despite having signed an employee agreement not to help plaintiffs in litigation against their employer. Justice Ruth Bader Ginsburg wrote the majority opinion that the employee-employer agreements were valid only in the state where they were signed. Elwell, a former GM engineer active in assessing product liability lawsuits for the automaker over a 15-year period, has been particularly effective, since he retired, in helping plaintiffs win against GM in cases involving fire-prone fuel tanks in pickups.

Defects (Safety Related)

Airbags

Although safety experts agree that you are likely to need anti-lock brakes 99 times more often than an airbag, the bag's advantage is that it doesn't depend upon driver skill or reaction time, and it deploys when it's too late for braking. Nevertheless, there have been some reports of airbags accidentally deploying and causing injuries. In fact, General Motors has just recalled almost a million Cadillacs, Cavaliers, and Sunfires for airbags activated by wet carpeting in Cadillacs and passing over a bump in the road for the other vehicles.

NHTSA staff estimates that 25,000 people were injured by airbags between 1988 and 1991. Sixty lawsuits have been filed that claim a malfunctioning device or aggravated injuries after deploying as designed; however, there is scant information as to how these claims were adjudicated. Chrysler is the target of most of these lawsuits because it was the first company to install airbags as a standard feature and used a Thiokol airbag whose escaping gases allegedly cause first- or second-degree burns to the hands. Used on Chrysler's 1988–91 models, these airbags have vent holes that direct hot gases at the three o'clock and nine o'clock hand positions. In late 1990, the vent holes were relocated to the 12 o'clock position. A class action lawsuit asking for damages arising from the earlier Thiokol design has been filed in the Court of Common Pleas in Philadelphia County. Coincidentally, a U.S. national auto safety group, the Insurance Institute for Highway Safety (IIHS), has launched an exhaustive investigation into reports that inflating airbags have seriously injured motorists.

Brakes (ABS)
Chrysler has come under fire over the past several years for installing defective anti-lock brakes in its minivans. The judgment below is the first of a series of lawsuits (filed but not yet judged) alleging that the company's base braking system is also faulty.

Santos v. Chrysler Corporation, Suffolk County Superior Court, February 1996. The plaintiff's wife and three children were killed when his 1988 Caravan's rear brakes locked as he applied them to avoid rear-ending another vehicle. The jury award for $19.2 million followed Paul Santos's pleadings that Chrysler "knowingly built the vehicle with a deadly defect that caused the rear brakes to lock before the front brakes." Chrysler's defense was that Santos drove the Caravan 100 miles with a broken windshield wiper and steered directly into oncoming traffic.

Fires
Delage vs. Saab, San Francisco Superior Court, November 1997. A jury awarded Jean Delage $1.4 million for damages caused by an electrical fire in his 1988 Saab 9000 even though the car was never examined. After hearing testimony from eight other Saab owners whose cars had caught on fire, the jury concluded that a defective fuse box caused the fire. The *San Francisco Chronicle* had also published a Saab internal memo that indicated a main connection in the 9000 box (located behind the glove compartment) could loosen, overheat, and ignite the insulation.

Seatbelt design/defects
Door-mounted seatbelts, motorized seatbelts, and lapbelts have come under fire during the past decade from safety advocates and

the courts after insurance studies and trauma specialists showed that they increase the severity of accident injuries.

Door-mounted seatbelts
Federal safety agencies are currently looking at the reliability and safety of door-mounted seatbelts in light of accident reports showing a high failure rate and increased severity of injuries. GM, for example, has been sued for $33 million over the inadequate performance of the driver's door-mounted seatbelt on a 1990 Pontiac Sunbird, according to the Washington-based Center for Auto Safety. The driver was killed when the car door opened, rendering the seatbelt inoperative. The suit claims that GM was negligent in the design that caused the belt to be undone, leaving the driver unprotected and unrestrained.

Motorized seatbelts
These front seat restraints run along a channel and cross the shoulder when the ignition is turned on. A lapbelt has to be fastened separately. These automatic belts are set so high above the door frame that they're uncomfortable to wear and a nightmare to adjust. Their most serious shortcoming, however, is that they give the driver a false sense of security and the separate lapbelt often goes unfastened (the U.S. government says that only 29 percent of people with motorized seatbelts use the lap portion). This has resulted in a number of accidents where the driver or front passenger has been decapitated or paralyzed by the shoulder belt. Ford was sued for $1.3 million in Akron, Ohio, where the driver of a 1990 Escort was paralyzed in an accident in which only the automatic shoulder belt was fastened (*Pflum v. Ford*). Nissan faces a $10-million suit in Newnan, Georgia, from the father of a woman who didn't have the lapbelt fastened and was decapitated by her 1989 Sentra's motorized shoulder harness (*Smith v. Nissan*).

Three-point seatbelts, failure to provide
In *Garrett v. Ford*, a Baltimore, Maryland, Federal Court jury rendered a $3.2-million verdict against Ford for installing a dangerously designed lapbelt and for not including back seat shoulder harnesses in a 1985 Escort. The lapbelts were designed to cross at the waist instead of the pelvis, an error that contributed to the passengers' paralysis. If shoulder harnesses had been installed, the lapbelts would not have aggravated the injuries, according to the Center for Auto Safety. Ford is involved in another ongoing trial, under appeal, where the company is being sued for compensatory and punitive damages arising from the death of a 72-year-old nun, Sister Mary Margaret LeGlise. She was riding in the rear seat of a 1987 Ford Tempo with her lapbelt fastened when the accident occurred. At trial, California Superior Court judge Jeffrey Miller attacked Ford for keeping its settlements in other cases secret

(referring to a $6-million payout to settle a San Diego case) in order to avoid embarrassment and other lawsuits. Judge Miller noted further that Ford could not claim that the technology to install three-point belts had not been perfected when the company had, for years, put the safer three-point belts in its European models. Judge Miller concluded:

> Ford knew that the rear seat lapbelt not only did not provide adequate protection but actually caused injury to its users. Ford also knew through its own internal engineering analysis and experimentation that the three-point restraint system was vastly superior and would save many lives.

Defects (Body/Performance Related)

When a used vehicle no longer falls within the limits of the warranty expressed by the manufacturer or dealer, it doesn't necessarily mean that the manufacturer can't be held liable for damages caused by defective design. As mentioned before, the manufacturer is always liable for the replacement or repair of defective parts if independent testimony can show that the part was incorrectly manufactured or designed. The existence of a secret warranty extension or service bulletins will usually help to prove that the part has a high failure rate.

Paint delamination/peeling

A defect that first appeared on Ford sport-utilities, vans, and pickups in the '80s, paint delamination occurs when the top coat of paint separates from the primer coat or turns a chalky color, mostly along horizontal surfaces and often as a result of intense sunlight. When the paint peels, the entire vehicle must be repainted after a new primer resurfacer has been added. For some vehicles, the labor alone can run about 20 hours at a cost of $75 an hour.

The same paint problem affects mostly 1986–97 Chrysler, Ford, and GM vehicles equally; however, each company has responded differently to owners' requests for compensation. To help you prepare the best arguments for negotiations or court, each automaker is profiled separately, beginning with an analysis of the problem and a web site reference, followed by copies of lawsuits, judgments, or dealer service bulletins that will help your claim. Pay particular attention to GM's "Goodwill Administration" service bulletin (see page 69). It gives you a peek into how all the automakers play mind games with their customers in order to keep their warranty payout as low as possible.

Chrysler

Chrysler's paint deficiencies include paint delamination, cracking, and fading between the third and fifth year of ownership. One Chrysler service bulletin that can serve as a guide for paint claims is Bulletin 23-11-90, "Base Clearcoat Paint Damage Resulting from Alkaline Spotting, Industrial Fallout, or Chemical Etching," issued September 10, 1990. It contains a number of illustrations relating to the kinds of paint problems that Chrysler will repair under its base warranty on all 1990 model year vehicles; it puts Chrysler on record as accepting so-called environmental paint damage.

That bulletin and other helpful documents can be downloaded from the Internet at: *http://www.glue.umd.edu/~kaustin/Chrysler.html* (Chrysler); *http://home.earthlink.net/~robkeane/jeep.htm* (Jeep).

There is also a class action lawsuit recently filed in the state of Washington which seeks damages for all Chrysler owners who have owned or leased paint-delaminated 1986–97 models. The case is *Schurk, Chanes, Jansen, and Ricker v. Chrysler*, No. 97-2-04113-9-SEA, filed in the Superior Court of King County, Washington on October 2, 1997 (contact Steve Berman or Clyde Platt with the Seattle, Washington law firm of Hagens and Berman at 206-623-7292).

The 29-page Statement of Claim uses many photos, internal bulletins, and memos to show that Chrysler engaged in the following:

> ...unlawful, unfair, and fraudulent business practices and unfair competition by treating different members of the class differently with respect to repairs it agrees to perform as "goodwill gestures," and by effecting partial repairs that do not address the true nature and extent of the delamination defect.
>
> In explaining the delamination defect, plaintiffs' lawyers maintain that Chrysler knew the defect also subjects the paint to softening, chipping, and other damage well before the delamination is detected.
>
> Chrysler did not, however, disclose the defect to potential or actual purchasers, and has until recently denied the existence of any defect, blaming the problem on "acid rain," "the environment," or other factors that are beyond Chrysler's control.
>
> Instead, Chrysler has pursued the practice of only selectively repainting vehicles for a few customers. In doing so, the company has turned away many more customers with the same problem explaining that Chrysler bears no responsibility for the condition. It has not notified purchasers or lessors of the defect, or offered them a refund for the difference between what these damaged cars were worth and the actual purchase or leased price. Rather, it has engaged in a uniform course of conduct designed to deceive class members, who have asked about the cause of the delamination, by falsely stating that it was caused by "environmental factors, road conditions, the age of the car, normal wear and tear, and other similar false and misleading responses."
>
> Only a few customers who have repeatedly complained about their defective paint have received offers from Chrysler to pay for repainting their vehicles. Chrysler also sometimes offers "patch" paint jobs, temporary cosmetic cures that don't halt progressive damage. Even then, Chrysler offers to pay for only a portion of the

expense of such partial repairs and offers different amounts to different consumers, even though all vehicles concerned show the same extent of damage.

In researching the root cause of Chrysler's delamination defect, the *Schurk, Chanes, Jansen, and Ricker v. Chrysler* lawsuit quotes Chrysler's Northwest Division Customer Sales Manager, Mr. Michael Mackey.

Mackey identified the cause of the delamination as an "incompatibility between the primer and the paint" that prevented adhesion between the two. He also said that Chrysler had known about the problem for "quite some time." Mackey further stated that Chrysler encountered the problem when it was forced to begin using water-based paints due to a ban on the use of leaded paints. In order to rectify the problem, Mackey said it would be necessary to strip the existing paint and primer and to put on a new primer coat using a process known as "etching."

This 1992 Chrysler minivan's paint peeling typifies Chrysler's peeling problem, while the 1988 Dodge Ram (over) shows the effects of paint delamination. Both problems are common to Ford and GM vehicles.

The cause of the delamination and its widespread nature

Beginning in the early 1980s, Chrysler changed the constituents of its exterior car paints in order to enhance corrosion resistance, reduce the expense of the painting process using the new, corrosion-resistant paint, and comply with environmental regulations. In doing so, Chrysler streamlined the painting process for its vehicles. Up to that time, Chrysler painted its vehicles using a three-coat process: a bottom-layer electrocoat, applied directly to the sheet metal; a spray primer; and a color coat. Chrysler then changed to a two-coat process. It substituted Uniprime ("HBEC" or "Ecoat"), a "high-build electrocoat" manufactured by PPG industries and other paint manufacturers, for the bottom coat and spray primer. By eliminating the intermediate layer of paint, Chrysler partly offset the cost increase of using Uniprime by reducing the time and expense required for its painting processes and by reducing chemical emissions. One of its competitors, Ford Motor Company, which had also begun to use Uniprime, estimated a savings of $6–$16 per vehicle by eliminating the middle layer of paint. Chrysler made the change without thoroughly testing the process or the integrity of the vehicle finishes it produced.

Contrary to Chrysler's claim that the problem is not widespread, a memo to "Members of the Finance Committee" from A. J. Trottman, Executive Vice President, Ford North American Automotive Operations, indicates what others in the automotive industry experienced on one model vehicle made with the same two-step system as on Chrysler vehicles:

> ...In June 1990, a field survey of about 1,000 F-series trucks (1985–1990 models) was conducted in three locations by Body and Chassis Engineering to assess paint durability. Results showed that

about 13% of the F-series trucks displayed peeling paint, which would represent about 90,000 vehicles annually.

In or about 1983–85, Chrysler began to use the new two-stage "enamel electrocoat" process at its plants in Newark, Delaware, Belvedere, Illinois, and Windsor, Ontario; in or about January 1985, the company announced that it intended to coat all of its products with Uniprime.

The new enamel electrocoat process was flawed. Uniprime is typically applied electrostatically, with the result that the topmost (or color) coat did not adhere properly. The Uniprime was further defective because its use rendered the bond with the finish coat subject to progressive deterioration when exposed to ultraviolet radiation produced even in climates with less-than-average sunlight conditions. Ultraviolet light causes the Uniprime to oxidize, which weakens its bond with the color coat of paint. In addition, the painting process was subject to a number of variables, including timing of application and thickness of the topcoat, temperature fluctuations during the painting process, and humidity inside the paint booth: variables which are critical to producing a durable finish, but which were not properly controlled. These conditions added to the progressive bonding failure inherent in the use of Uniprime as the primer and undercoat.

Chrysler knew that its new painting process was flawed almost as soon as it was used in production. The experience of car manufacturers like Ford illustrates that people in the automobile industry knew of the existence and cause of the paint peeling problem.

Chrysler's 1992 Warranty Manual provided that it covered "the cost of all parts and labor needed to repair or adjust any Chrysler supplied item...that proves defective in material, workmanship or factory preparation."

Chrysler's actions and knowledge, as alleged above, constituted a breach of these warranty conditions.

Ford
Louisiana attorney Danny Becknel, along with other lawyers, have filed three separate class action lawsuits against Chrysler, Ford, and GM. He's also filed suit against PPG Industries, a company out of Pittsburgh that he says sold defective car paint to the three companies.

Becknel claims in his suits that in the late '80s to the early '90s, the Big Three bought Uniprime from PPG Industries without thoroughly testing it. He says when the companies bought Uniprime, they switched from a three-coat car painting process (bottom coat, spray primer, color coat) to a two-coat process eliminating the middle coat, the spray primer. Mr. Becknel claims eliminating that middle layer, the spray primer, saved from $6 to $16 a car. States Bucknel: "This paint seems to be a minor cost but when you multiply it by 10 to 15 million times a year, it's a big number."

Faced with an estimated 13 percent failure rate, Ford repainted its delaminated 1983–93 cars, minivans, vans, F-series trucks, Explorers, Rangers, and Broncos free of charge for five years under a secret "Owner Dialogue" program. Ford whistleblowers say the company discontinued the program in January 1995 because it was proving to be too costly. Nevertheless, owners who cry foul and threaten small claims action are still routinely given initial offers of 50 percent compensation, and, eventually, if they press further, complete refunds.

In your negotiations with Ford, be sure to refer to Ford's admission of the delamination problem found in Ford's service bulletin and in the Washington state Chrysler class action.

Apart from the Becknel class action, Ford hasn't been a party to many lawsuits as it prefers to settle before cases come to trial. You can get the latest information and internal documents relating to Ford's secret warranty for repainting by logging onto the following site set up by dissatisfied Ford owners: *http://www.ihs2000.com/~peel*.

General Motors
Confidential U.S. dealer service bulletins and memos confirm the 6-year/unlimited mileage benchmark that GM uses to accept or reject secret warranty paint claims. Of course, GM wants its customers to jump through hoops to benefit from its secret paint warranty, hence the line of questioning contained in its service bulletin reproduced on the following page.

The dealer service bulletin that GM put out several years ago guides dealers in determining whether paint delamination is a factory defect and not due to other external causes like acid rain, stone chips, etc. Pay particular attention to GM's explanation of the cause of the delamination problem. In effect, the automaker admits that it didn't apply sufficient primer to protect the clearcoat from ultraviolet light. Also, look at the masking tape test GM recommends in its "Problem Identification" section to diagnose clearcoat delamination; it's the same test used by Ford and Chrysler.

Preliminary Information
FILE IN SECTION: 10-Body
BULLETIN NO.: 23-10-54
DATE: June 1995
SUBJECT:
Service Procedures for the Repair of Paint Colorcoat Delamination from ELPO Primer (Repair Surfaces Above the Body Side Moldings)
MODELS:
1988-91 Buick Century (Plant Code 6)
1988-92 Buick LeSabre (Plant Code H), Skylark
1988-90 Chevrolet Celebrity
1988-92 Chevrolet Beretta, Corsica, Skylark
1988-90 Oldsmobile Cutlass Supreme
1988-91 Oldsmobile Calais, Ciera (Plant Code 6)
1988-92 Oldsmobile Achieva, Eighty Eight (Plant Code H)
1988-90 Pontiac Grand Prix
1988-91 Pontiac 6000 (Plant Code 6)
1988-92 Pontiac Firebird, Grand Am, Tempest
1988-92 Chevrolet and GMC Truck C/K, R/V, S/T M/L, G Models
1991-92 Oldsmobile Bravada
This bulletin is being revised to provide a process change for the repair of paint delamination from ELPO primer. Please discard previous publications:

Buick	92-10-57
Chevrolet	92-300A-10
GM of Canada	93-10-100
GMC Truck	92-10-134A
Oldsmobile	93-T-05
Pontiac	93-10-59

EFFECTIVE DATE:
THE REVISED REPAIR PROCEDURES, NEW LABOR OPERATION NUMBERS AND REVISED TIME AND MATERIAL ALLOWANCES CONTAINED IN THIS BULLETIN ARE EFFECTIVE WITH REPAIR ORDERS WRITTEN ON OR AFTER JUNE 20, 1995.
CONDITION:
This bulletin is being issued to assure that the correct procedure is followed to repair a condition known as delamination. Some of the listed passenger cars, light duty trucks, and vans may have DELAMINATION (peeling) of the paint colorcoat from the ELPO primer depending upon variable factors including prolonged exposure to sunlight and humidity.
Blues, Grays, Silvers and Black Metallics are the colors that have the highest potential for this condition. On rare occasions, other colors may be involved.
Important:
Delamination is different than other paint conditions and/or damage. A proper problem identification is necessary, and the service procedure that follows is specific to the proper repair of delamination and must be followed. The information in this bulletin covers paint delamination of the colorcoat from the ELPO primer ONLY. It does not address any other paint conditions. Procedures for the repair of other paint conditions (stone chips, scratches, environmental damage, clearcoat peeling, runs, dirt, fading, etc.) will not effectively repair delamination and customer dissatisfaction will result.
CAUSE:
*This condition may occur on vehicles produced in plants where the paint process did not call for application of a primer surfacer. Under certain conditions, ultraviolet light can penetrate the colorcoat, sometimes causing a reaction and separation of portions of the colorcoat from the ELPO (electrocoat) primer.
PROBLEM IDENTIFICATION:
On a clean surface, at or above room temperature, firmly apply a 2" wide piece of masking tape and pull upward quickly. DO NOT USE duct tape, cloth backed tape or other aggressive tapes. If the colorcoat flakes or peels away from the ELPO (leaving the ELPO intact) the colorcoat is delaminating and the vehicle should be repaired.

Before settling your paint claim with GM or any other American automaker, download whatever info you can find from dissatisfied customers who've banded together and set up their own self-help web sites on the Internet.

Getting a Settlement

The following settlement advice applies mainly to paint defects, but you can use these tips for any other vehicle defect that you believe is the automaker's/dealer's responsibility. If you're not sure that the problem is a factory-related deficiency or a maintenance item, have it checked out by an independent garage or a dealer service bulletin summary for your vehicle. The summary may include specific bulletins relating to the diagnosis, correction, and ordering of upgraded parts needed to fix your problem.

1. If you know the problem is factory related, take your vehicle to the dealer and ask for a written, signed estimate. When you're handed the estimate, ask that the paint job be done for free under the manufacturer's "goodwill" program. (Ford's euphemism for this secret warranty is "Owner Dialogue Program," GM's term is "Special Policy," and Chrysler just calls it "goodwill." Don't use the term "secret warranty" yet; you'll just make the dealer and automaker angry and evasive.)
2. Your request will probably be met with a refusal, an offer to repaint the vehicle for half the cost, or, if you're lucky, an agreement to repaint the vehicle free of charge. If you accept half-cost, make sure that it's based on the original estimate you have in hand, since some dealers jack up their estimates so that your 50 percent is really 100 percent of the true cost.
3. If the dealer/automaker has already refused your claim and the repair hasn't been done yet, get an additional estimate from an independent garage that shows the problem is factory related.
4. Again, if the repair has yet to be done, mail or fax a registered claim to the automaker (send a copy to the dealer) claiming the average of both estimates. If the repair has been done at your expense, mail or fax a registered claim with a copy of your bill. A sample letter/fax can be found on page 72.
5. If you don't receive a satisfactory response within a week, deposit a copy of the estimate or paid bill and claim letter/fax before the small claims court and await a trial date. This means that the automaker/dealer will have to appear, no lawyer is required, costs should be minimal (under $100), and a mediation hearing or trial will be scheduled in a few months followed by a judgment a few weeks later (the time varies among different regions).

Things that you can do to help your case: collect photographs, maintenance work orders, previous work orders dealing with your problem, dealer service bulletins, and an independent expert (the garage or body shop that did the estimate or repair is best, but you can also use a local teacher who teaches automotive repair).

Other situations

- If the vehicle has just been repainted but the dealer says that "goodwill" coverage was denied by the automaker, pay for the repair with a certified check and write "under protest" on the check. Remember, though, if the dealer does the repair, you won't have an independent expert who can affirm that the problem was factory related or that it was a result of premature wear out. Plus, the dealer can say that you or the environment caused the paint problem. In these cases, internal service bulletins can make or break your case.
- If the dealer/automaker offers a partial repair or refund, take it. Then sue for the rest. Remember, if a partial repair has been done under warranty, it counts as an admission of responsibility, no matter what "goodwill" euphemism is used. Also, the repaired component/body panel should be just as durable as if it were new. Hence, the clock starts ticking again until you reach the original warranty parameter, again, no matter what the dealer's repair warranty limit says.
- It's a lot easier to get the automaker to pay to replace a defective part than it is to be compensated for a missed day of work or a ruined vacation. Manufacturers hate to pay for consequential expenses apart from towing bills because they can't control the amount of the refund. Fortunately, the courts have taken the position that all expenses (damages) flowing from a problem covered by a warranty or service bulletin are the manufacturer's/dealer's responsibility under both state and federal law. Nevertheless, don't risk a fair settlement for some outlandish claim of "emotional distress," "pain and suffering," etc. If you have invoices to prove actual consequential damages, then use them. If not, don't be greedy.

Very seldom do automakers contest these paint claims before small claims court, opting instead to settle once the court claim is bounced from their customer relations people to Legal Affairs. At that time, you'll probably be offered an out-of-court settlement for 50–75 percent of your claim.

Stand fast and make reference to the service bulletins you intend to subpoena in order to publicly contest in court the unfair nature of this "secret warranty" program (automaker lawyers cringe at the idea of trying to explain why consumers aren't made aware of these bulletins). One hundred percent restitution will probably follow.

A good example is *Shields v. General Motors of Canada*, No. 1398/96, Ontario Court (General Division), Oshawa Small Claims Court, 33 King Street West, Oshawa, Ontario L1H1A1, July 24, 1997, Robert Zochodne, Deputy Judge. Judgment rendered January 6, 1998.

Reasons for Judgment

The Plaintiff owns a 1991 Pontiac Grand Prix. This car was manufactured by General Motors. The Plaintiff did not buy the car new but purchased it about one year after it was built and when it had over 100,000 kilometres [62,000 miles] on its odometer.

Commencing in 1995 the paint on this car began to bubble and then flake and eventually peel off. Exhibit 1 shows that the problem is most evident on the front hood of the vehicle.

After the Plaintiff encountered this problem, he approached General Motors of Canada Limited. After significant debate, General Motors agreed to pay for one-half the cost of repairing the three affected panels. The Plaintiff asked General Motors if the rest of the car would peel and he advised that General Motors' response was that they could not guarantee that that would not occur. The Plaintiff rejected the proposal on the basis that he believed that if the work was done, the car would look like a "checkerboard."

The Plaintiff claims that there are thousands of people with the same problem with General Motors' cars. In particular, however, the Plaintiff filed as Exhibit 5 a letter dated May 5, 1997, from Aldina Moniz, identifying the problem she experienced with her 1988 metallic gray Pontiac Grand Prix. The Plaintiff contends that the only solution to his problem is to strip this motor vehicle to the bare metal and repaint it. As Exhibit 6 are two estimates, one from Fixation R.M. Services and the other from Yorkdale Auto Body Repair. Both estimates state that the vehicle should be stripped and refinished completely. In his letter dated July 31, 1996, Mr. Masini states, "partial repairs are not the solution, as eventually the balance of the unrepaired panels will also begin to flake due to faulty factory primer." The Yorkdale Auto Body Repair contains the following words, "It is my professional recommendation that Mrs. Shields' car should be completely stripped and repainted. Painting only the presently affected areas will likely leave the car with two (2) different shades of white. As well, since the car was originally painted at the General Motors plant at one time, and there is already paint peeling off of multiple panels, it is extremely likely that the paint will soon peel off of all of the panels." The Plaintiff also presented repair estimates from Dean Myers Chevrolet Oldsmobile and Roy Foss.

The Roy Foss estimate contains the following words, "Only way to ensure proper adhesion of paint to metal and prevent peeling, is to strip all panels to bare metal and re-coat with 2 stage epoxy primer and refinish." The signature below that phrase is that of Sean McCarthy. Interestingly, as Exhibit 9, the Defendant filed a statement from Mr. McCarthy. Mr. McCarthy stated in part as follows: "I explained to Mr. Shields that paint was delaminating from the primed surface and that it was best to leave the primer intact and that after market primers could not duplicate the protection of factory e-coat primers." He went on to state that the Plaintiff insisted that the car be stripped. He went on to state that the Plaintiff insisted that he get a guarantee that the paint would not again peel. That is why the estimate was written in the way it was.

The amount of the estimates range from $2,450.00 to $3,800.00.

As Exhibit 7 is a letter from Mr. Masini from Fixation R. M. Services Ltd. which states: "This Auto Body Shop has been in operation for over 20 years, and is not the first time we have seen this problem with General Motor Vehicles."

What was the cause of the Plaintiff's difficulty?

Grant Greenwood is an engineer with General Motors. He has worked for General Motors since 1963 and carries the title of Senior Product Investigator. He testified that he checked the vehicle history and confirmed that it went into service in November 1990. He advised that the warranty on this vehicle is three years or eighty thousand kilometers, whichever occurs first. Exhibit 13 is a copy of the warranty booklet.

He testified that the paint warranty was against defects and workmanship. He also testified that the warranty excluded consequential losses. He also stated that General Motors has not extended the warranty for paint.

Mr. Greenwood inspected the vehicle in March 1997 at Plaza Pontiac Buick. He stated that paint was coming off in three areas. He said that the cause was that the colorcoat, that is the coat visible to you and I, was separating from the primer. The cause of this was, in Mr. Greenwood's view, ultraviolet rays in the atmosphere. He stated that the ultraviolet rays were going through the colorcoat, attacking the primer and breaking down the bond between the primer and the colorcoat.

He said that ultraviolet rays have been increasing over the past decade and that since General Motors has become aware of this, they have been working on new paints that are more retardant to the effects of ultraviolet rays. He emphasized that the problem was not caused by the primer, which has been used by General Motors for decades, but rather by the ultraviolet rays. He stated that waxing a vehicle helps prevent delamination as well as storing the vehicle inside.

He said that light gray and light blue vehicles are more susceptible to this problem and appeared to be somewhat skeptical about the fact that this condition appeared with a white vehicle. At the time of his inspection the vehicle had traveled 156,000 kilometres. He noticed a scratch on the left front fender and chipping on the front hood.

As I indicated previously, he identified three areas on the vehicle where the paint was coming off. There is an extensive area on the hood as well as the trunk and left rear quarter-panel. He said that this was not typical paint delamination. He also found it odd that there was no paint peeling off of the roof of the car. He stated that if the vehicle was repaired and repainted, it would be difficult to tell that it had been repainted.

Paint Should Last Six Years, Says GM!

PONTIAC

PONTIAC DIVISION
General Motors Corporation
One Pontiac Plaza
Pontiac, Michigan 48340-2952

October 16, 1992

TO: All Pontiac Dealers

SUBJECT: Partners in Satisfaction (PICS)
Dealer Authorization

Pontiac continually reviews the Warranty Management System to ensure that Warranty Administration achieves its purposes, including high levels of customer satisfaction with after sale treatment.

Following a recent review, Pontiac has decided to provide dealers authorization for cases involving paint repairs for vehicles up to six (6) years from the date of delivery, without regard for mileage. This is a change from the current PICS dealer self-authorization which allows paint repair goodwill adjustments to be made up to 6 years/60,000 miles. Dealers who have a deductible override capabilities may also waive deductibles as they see appropriate on this type of repair.

Paint repairs are only to be authorized beyond the warranty period by the Dealership Service Manager on a case-by-case basis as with any other goodwill policy adjustment.

Assistance should only be considered for cases involving evidence of a defect in materials or workmanship by the manufacturer. Assistance should not be considered for conditions related to wear and tear and/or lack of maintenance (such as fading, stone chips, scratches, environmental damage, etc.).

Please contact your Zone representative if you have specific questions.

Perry S. White

Perry S. White
Director of Service/
Customer Satisfaction

This confidential memo to Pontiac dealers applies to all of GM's vehicles, and can be used as a benchmark for what the automaker considers its obligation when faced with paint claims. Note GM doesn't use any "weasel" words, like "acid rain" or "UV ray deterioration," to duck its responsibility.

Exhibit 2 is a memo to all Pontiac dealers dated October 16, 1992, from Perry White, Director of Service/Customer Satisfaction with Pontiac Division of General Motors (U.S.). This letter states in part as:

Following a recent review, Pontiac has decided to provide dealers' authorization for cases involving paint repairs for vehicles up to six years from the date of delivery, without regard to mileage.

Mr. Greenwood stated that this bulletin was not sent in Canada but only in the United States. He also stated that it did not deal with paint delamination, which was the Plaintiff's problem in this case.

Mr. Greenwood indicated that insofar as damages were concerned that the answer to the problem did not lie in removing the primer. He stated that the primer gives very good protection against rust and that if the primer was removed, the vehicle was more likely to rust even if it was replaced with primer.

Mr. Greenwood arranged for an estimate to be completed to strip the colorcoat and repaint the vehicle from the lower molding up. That repair estimate was marked as Exhibit 12 and is in the sum of $1,305.72.

In cross examination, Mr. Greenwood stated that delamination is a common condition. He also acknowledged that there were no warnings given to customers of such a problem.

Exhibit 8 is a Product Service Bulletin issued by General Motors of Canada. It is entitled "Service Procedures for Identification and Repair of Paint Colorcoat Delamination from ELPO Primer." Mr. Greenwood identified this document as being a valid Product Service Bulletin issued October 31, 1992 and revised on December 15, 1992.

The bulletin states as follows:

This bulletin is being issued to assure that the correct procedure is followed to repair a condition known as DELAMINATION.

This condition may occur on vehicles produced in plants where the paint process does not call for application of a primer surfacer. Under certain conditions, ultraviolet light can penetrate the colorcoat, sometimes causing a reaction and separation of portions of the colorcoat from the ELPO (electrocoat) primer.

CORRECTION:

Refinish the ENTIRE BODY ABOVE THE BODY SIDE MOULDINGS using the following repair procedure...

[Author's note: The original GM bulletin is found on page 96.]

Mr. Greenwood did not offer any explanation of this issue during his examination and chief or cross examination. However, I asked Mr. Greenwood about primer surfacers at the conclusion of his evidence. He stated that it is a layer between the primer and the colorcoat. He stated that he was not aware whether this vehicle was manufactured in a plant that had a primer surfacer at the time but confirmed that virtually all of General Motors' plants now have primer surfacers. He said that the reason for the primer surfacer was to prevent the very problem complained of the Plaintiff. He also stated that General Motors has moved to new primer surfacers, which are polyester based as opposed to epoxy based.

In assessing the evidence, I would start from the proposition that I believe that the Plaintiff and his wife overstated their case. The husband described General Motors as having "lied to them" and talked about being "bullied." The Plaintiff's definition of bullying is that General Motors told him that if he did not like their offer, he could take them to court.

I also thought that Mrs. Shields greatly exaggerated the problem by calling it a safety issue and described problems in relation to pieces of paint coming off of the hood and sticking to the front windshield. She said that since that time, she checks the car before she drives it to ensure that this would not occur.

Frankly, the zeal demonstrated by the Plaintiff and his wife is also consistent with the Defendant's submission in relation to the quantum of damages claimed by the Plaintiff. After assessing all of the evidence, it is my conclusion that if General Motors is held to be liable to the Plaintiff, the proper measure of damages is $1,305.72, that being the cost to strip and repaint the colorcoat from the lower body side moldings up.

Beyond what I have already stated, I do not accept that the purpose of this exercise is to prevent the Plaintiff from ever having a paint peeling problem in the future. I accept Mr. Greenwood's evidence that the problem is not in relation to the primer and that the problem can be effectively repaired without removing that primer and, more to the point, that removal of the primer might put the Plaintiff in a worse position in the sense that the car might be more likely to rust.

Given the evidence that was presented in relation to the Plaintiff's dealings with Sean McCarthy, I have no doubt that he aggressively sought opinions which stated that the primer would have to be removed, and I am sure that there were repairers who were willing to accommodate the Plaintiff in his request.

Given that the proper measure of damages includes painting from the lower body side moldings up, I do not see that matching of paint will be a problem at all and I accept the evidence of Mr. Greenwood in that regard.

Is the Defendant liable to the Plaintiff?

As the Plaintiff did not purchase this vehicle from General Motors, the Sale of Goods Act does not apply. In order to succeed, the Plaintiff must establish that General Motors of Canada's warranty covers this problem.

That warranty provides in part as follows:

REPAIRS COVERED

This warranty covers repairs or adjustments to correct any vehicle defect related to material or workmanship occurring during the WARRANTY PERIOD. New or remanufactured parts will be used. Adjustments refer to minor repairs not usually associated with the replacement of parts.

The warranty also provides as follows:

The complete vehicle is covered for 3 years or 80,000 kilometers, whichever comes first.

It also states as follows:

Warranty repairs and adjustments, including Towing, Parts and Labor, will be made at NO CHARGE (except for $100 deductible per repair visit after the first 12 months or 20,000 kilometers, whichever comes first).

The warranty also provided:

This warranty is for GM vehicles registered in Canada and normally operated in Canada or the United States and is provided to the original and any subsequent owners of the vehicle during the WARRANTY PERIOD.

The Defendant did not seek to rely upon any exclusion within the warranty.

The questions to be decided therefore are as follows:

1. Did the vehicle have a "defect"?
2. If so, did the defect occur during the warranty period?

In my view, the vehicle did have a defect. While I acknowledge and accept Mr. Greenwood's evidence that the increase in ultraviolet rays has caused delamination, it is my view that the presence of ultraviolet light is an environmental condition to which the vehicle is subject. If it cannot withstand this environmental condition, it is defective, in my view. This is no different from a situation where a vehicle does not start in weather below 0 Celsius (32^0 F). Since motor vehicles are operated in such conditions on a regular basis, the failure of the vehicle to adequately operate in such temperatures is a defect, in my view. To be precise, the defect is the failure to ensure proper bonding between the colorcoat and primer. In reviewing the Product Service Bulletin and hearing the evidence of Mr. Greenwood, it is clear to me that the lack of a primer surfacer was a defect as defined by the warranty.

2. Did this defect occur during the warranty period?

The answer to this question is yes. General Motors contended that the problem was caused by ultraviolet light. A logical inference is that they contend that the problem did not arise until sufficient exposure to ultraviolet light, the result being that the warranty period would have expired.

I do not accept this contention.

The defect, which I have found, that is the lack of primer surfacer, occurred at the time that the vehicle was manufactured. At that point, however, the defect was latent. The defect became patent when the paint began to bubble, flake, and then peel off of the vehicle.

Having decided that the warranty responds to this loss, I grant judgment in favor of the Plaintiff in the amount of $1,205.72 plus costs.

Illegal/Unfair Insurance Company Practices

Inadequate compensation

The following two lawsuits may be helpful in any disputes you may have with an insurance company over its failure to pay a claim or use quality replacement parts in repairs. Don't get the impression that this is just a State Farm problem. These abuses are widespread.

Campbell v. State Farm Mutual Insurance Automobile Insurance Co. This Utah case saw a $147.6 million jury award against State Farm cut to $26 million by the presiding judge who didn't want the case over-turned on appeal because the original award may have been considered excessive.

In his December 19, 1997, verdict, Judge William B. Bohling called State Farm "greedy, callous, clandestine, fraudulent, and dishonest" after evidence showed the company refused to pay off a claim until its own policyholder sued State Farm for bad-faith dealings.

The Campbell attorneys successfully asserted that State Farm had a national plan to cheat policyholders that included using inferior car parts in repairs, low-balling settlements, and misleading consumers about policy benefits.

This evidence led the judge to conclude that State Farm "appeared to have preyed on the weakest of the herd" in cheating "the most vulnerable" policyholders with its "calculated and callous attitude towards settling valid claims." He concluded:

> It became a matter of plain evidence that State Farm has sold as its product, peace of mind, and has used as its advertising slogan, 'like a good neighbor.' State Farm's action amounts to betraying the trust that it invites its policyholders to place in it.

Poor quality replacement parts

In a $2 billion Illinois class action, State Farm has been accused of breaching its promise to restore policyholders' autos to their "pre-loss condition," after it was found the company used aftermarket bumpers, door panels, and other parts that failed to meet automakers' specifications for fit, finish, corrosion protection, and safety. If the suit is successful, over 20 million car owners whose vehicles were repaired since 1980 would be eligible for refunds or repairs. The trial is set for February 1999.

State Farm has settled similar lawsuits in Cook County, Illinois, and San Diego.

Part Three
CAR AND MINIVAN RATINGS

"In the early '60s boomers grew up believing the Establishment, including the U.S. car industry, was no good, and in the '70s, we proved them right, we taught them that we build junk."
— James C. Bulin
Ford Motor Company
Generational Studies Manager

A used car or minivan must first live up to the promises made by the manufacturer and dealer. Ideally, it should be crashworthy, reasonably durable (lasting at least 10 years), cost no more than $500 a year to maintain, and provide you with a fair resale value a few years down the road. Parts should be reasonably priced and easily available, and servicing prompt, efficient and friendly. We also factor into the rating the relative availability of a particular vehicle, those models and years that are the best buys, the estimated annual maintenance and repair costs averaged over five years, and alternative vehicles that will give you as much or more for less money.

Models are rated on a scale from Recommended to Not Recommended. Recommended vehicles are those which are an excellent choice in their class, and promise their owners relatively trouble-free service (like post-'91 Ford Escorts). Vehicles that are given an Above Average or Average rating are good second choices if a Recommended vehicle isn't your first choice or is too expensive. Vehicles given a Not Recommended rating are best avoided no matter how low the price, even though they may be attractively styled and loaded with convenience features (Chrysler minivans, for example); they're likely to suffer from a variety of durability and performance problems that will make them expensive and frustrating to own. Sometimes, however, a Not Recommended model will improve over several model years and garner a better rating (as recent Ford Aerostar and GM Astro and Safari minivans have done). Keep in mind, too, that the reliability and quality averages are rising, so that a newer vehicle rated Average is a far better buy than an older model with an Average rating.

A '96 or later GM Cavalier/Sunbird is a better-than-average buy. Prior model years should be shunned.

Reliability data is compiled from a number of sources: confidential service bulletins; owner complaints sent to the author by the 2,000-plus readers who filled out the readers' survey in Appendix V; vehicle-owner comments posted on the Internet; and survey reports and tests done by auto associations, consumer groups, and government organizations. Some car columnists feel this isn't a scientific sampling and they're quite right. Nevertheless, it seems to have been right on the mark over the past 27 years. Not all vehicles sold during the last decade are profiled; those which are newer to the market or relatively rare may only receive an abbreviated mention until sufficient owner or service bulletin information becomes available. Best and worst buys over the past 26 years for each model category (e.g., "Small" or "Medium") are listed at the beginning of each rating section. They are further profiled in the "beaters" section on pages 46–50.

Strengths and weaknesses
Unlike other auto guides, we pinpoint potential parts failures as well as why those parts fail. Complementing the "Secret Warranties/Service Tips" and vehicle "Profile" tables, we look at a vehicle's overall road performance and reliability, providing details as to which specific mechanical, electrical or body part fails repeatedly. This helps an independent mechanic check out the likely trouble spots before you make your purchase.

Dealer service bulletins
Imagine spearing your service manager with a confidential bulletin, detailing that pesky defect your car has which he always claimed was your fault. Here we summarize problem areas addressed by confidential dealer service bulletins for more recent models. Important bulletins offering substantial repair refunds are reproduced in the "Secret Warranties/Service Tips" section.

108

Lemon-Aid

Safety summary/recalls

Data from independent crash tests, insurance claims statistics, ongoing NHTSA safety investigations, owner safety-related complaints, and safety recalls make up this section. Vehicles are rated according to how well they performed in U.S. government 35 mph frontal crash tests (the impact is the same as if two identical vehicles, each traveling at 35 mph, collided head-on). Information recorded during the crash tests measures the likelihood of serious injury and vehicles are classified by the estimated chance of injury for the driver or passenger. For the past several years vehicles have been given a one- to five-star rating by the NHTSA, with five stars indicating the best protection. Cars and minivans that are identical but carry different nameplates from the same manufacturer can be expected to perform similarly in these crash tests. On the other hand, sometimes the same vehicle tested from one year to the next will post dramatically different results even though the model has remained relatively unchanged. Safety experts admit that this happens occasionally and that consumers should look at the trend established over several model years.

Lemon-Aid is unique in that it includes estimated head, chest, and leg trauma as life-threatening factors in determining a model's safety rating. This explains why the crash rating scores shown below are often lower in *Lemon-Aid*. Also, this guide's safety rating applies only to the driver.

❶	❷	③	④	⑤
Multiple injuries	One injury	Average protection	Above average protection	Excellent protection

Both safety and emissions recalls are listed in chronological order. If your vehicle is listed and hasn't been fixed, the dealer and manufacturer must pay for the inspection and correction of the defect regardless of the vehicle's mileage, model year, or number of previous owners. It's not the law, but it's general practice.

Keep in mind that recalls affecting only a few hundred vehicles haven't been listed, and be watchful for the cut-off years. Even if your model year isn't listed it may be currently under investigation or may have been recalled since this year's guide was published. Also, safety probes may be upgraded or dropped; download NHTSA's data files from the Internet for an update (*http://www. nhtsa.dot.gov/cars/problems/recalls/recmmy1.cfm*).

Secret warranties/service tips

It's not enough to know which parts on your vehicle are likely to fail. You should also know which repairs will be done for free by the dealer and automaker even though you aren't the original owner and the manufacturer's warranty has long since expired.

Welcome to the hidden world of secret warranties found in confidential dealer service bulletins (DSBs) or gleaned from owner feedback. A summary of all the important DSBs for each model year

is listed along with selected diagrams. These bulletins target defects
related to safety, emissions, and performance that service managers
would have you believe don't exist or are your responsibility. They
also list the upgraded parts that will best repair the vehicle you plan
to buy or have just bought.

Service bulletins cover repairs that may be eligible for warranty
coverage in one or more of the following five categories:
• Emissions warranty (5–8 years)
• Safety component warranty (this covers seatbelts and airbags and
  usually lasts the lifetime of the vehicle)
• Body warranty (paint: six years; rust perforations: seven years)
• Secret warranty (coverage varies)
• Factory defects (depends on mileage, use, and repair cost)

Use these bulletins to get free repairs—even if the vehicle has
changed hands several times—and to alert an independent mechanic
about which defects to look for. They're also great tools for getting
compensation from automakers and dealer service managers after the
warranty has expired, since they prove that a failure is factory-related
and, therefore, not part of routine maintenance or the effect of an
environmental anomaly (like bird droppings and acid rain).

Their diagnostic shortcuts and lists of upgraded parts make these
bulletins invaluable in helping mechanics and do-it-yourselfers
troubleshoot problems inexpensively and replace the right part the
first time. Auto owners can also use the DSBs listed here to verify
that a repair was diagnosed correctly, the right upgraded replacement part was used, and the labor costs were fair.

Getting your own bulletins
If you want a personalized DSB summary for your vehicle, fill out
the "Bulletin Search/Survey" order form in the Appendix. For a
$15 fee (this includes my computer time and fax or mailing costs),
you'll receive an exhaustive summary of all DSBs that concern your
vehicle. For $5 for each bulletin thereafter (no fax charge), you can
then order every DSB listed in the summary that addresses your
concerns.

Vehicle profiles
These tables cover the various aspects of vehicle ownership at a
glance. Included for each model year are details on crashworthiness,
repair histories for major mechanical and body components (specific
defective parts are listed in the "Strengths and Weaknesses" section
for each vehicle rated), and which model years have secret, "goodwill," warranties or should be bought with an extended warranty.

Prices
Dealer profit margins on used cars vary considerably—giving lots of
room to negotiate a fair price if you take the time to know what the

vehicle is really worth. Three prices are given for each model year: the vehicle's selling price when new as suggested by the manufacturer, its maximum price used (↑), followed by its lowest price used (↓).

Used prices are based on private sales as of October 1998. Prices are for the lowest-priced standard model in each category that is in good condition with 20,000 miles for each calendar year. The original selling price (manufacturer's suggested retail price) is also given as a helpful reference point. Sellers overprice some vehicles (mostly Japanese imports, minivans, and sport-utilities) in order to get back some of the money *they* overpaid in the first place.

Why are many of *Lemon-Aid's* prices lower than the prices found in dealer guides? The answer is simple: dealer guides inflate their prices so that you can bargain the price down and wind up convinced that you made a great deal. I print a top and bottom price to give the buyer some margin for negotiation, as well as to account for regional differences in prices, the sudden popularity of certain models or vehicle classes (sport-utilities, trucks, minivans, etc.), and the appreciated value of used cars, generally.

Don't forget to bargain down the price if the odometer shows a cumulative reading of more than 15,000-20,000 miles per calendar year. Since no evaluation method is foolproof, check dealer prices with local private classified ads and add the option values listed below to come up with a fairly representative offer. Remember, these options are priced as individually ordered. If they were standard features with a pricier model, their combined value is included within that model's price range.

Model Year	1997	1996	1995	1994	1993	1992
Air conditioning	$900	$600	$500	$400	$300	$300
AM-FM-CD	300	200	175	150	100	100
Anti-lock brakes	300	175	150	125	100	50
Automatic transmission	500	400	300	275	250	200
Cruise control	225	125	100	75	50	50
Electric 6-way seat	300	175	150	125	100	50
Leather upholstery	700	400	325	225	200	100
Level control (suspension)	250	150	125	100	75	50
Paint protector	0	0	0	0	0	0
Power antenna	125	75	50	50	25	0
Power door locks	300	175	150	125	100	50
Power windows	325	175	150	125	100	50
Rustproofing	50	25	25	0	0	0
Sunroof	300	150	125	75	50	50
T-top roof	900	700	500	400	300	200
Tilt steering	175	100	75	75	50	50
Tinted windows	50	50	25	0	0	0
Traction control	400	275	175	150	125	100
Wire wheels/locks	275	175	150	125	100	75

It will be easier for you to match the lower used prices if you buy privately. Dealers rarely sell much below the maximum prices. They inflate their prices to cover the costs of reconditioning and paying future warranty claims and to make you feel better. If you can come within 5–10 percent of this guide's price, you'll have done well.

Extended warranties and secret warranties
Usually, but not always, an extended warranty is advised for those model years that aren't rated Recommended. Model years that are eligible for free repairs under a secret warranty are listed in the Profile and further detailed in the "Secret Warranties/Service Tips" section. A **Y** signifies that one or more secret warranties exist or that an extended warranty is needed. An **N** means that no secret warranty applies or that there's no need to buy an extended warranty.

Reliability
The older a vehicle, the greater the chance that a major component like the engine or transmission will fail as a result of high mileage and environmental wear and tear. Surprisingly, there's a host of other expensive-to-repair failures that are just as likely to occur in a new vehicle as in an older one. Air conditioners, electronic computer modules, electrical systems, and brakes are the most troublesome components, manifesting problems early in a vehicle's life. Other deficiencies that will appear early, due to sloppy manufacturing and a harsh environment, include failure-prone body hardware (trim, finish, locks, doors, and windows), water leaks, wind noise, and paint peeling/discoloration.

The following legend shows a vehicle's relative degree of overall reliability and which mechanical and body parts are subject to premature failure. Note that the numbers lighten progressively as the rating becomes more positive.

❶	❷	③	④	⑤
Unacceptable	Below Average	Average	Above Average	Excellent

SMALL CARS

The proverbial "econobox," this size of car is for city dwellers who want economy at any price. Small cars offer excellent gas economy, easy maneuverability in urban areas, and a low retail price.

One of the more alarming characteristics of a small car's highway performance is its extreme vulnerability to strong lateral winds, which may make the car difficult to keep on course. Most of these cars can carry only two passengers in comfort—rear seating is limited—and there is insufficient luggage capacity. As well, engine and road noise are fairly excessive.

Crash safety may be compromised by the small size and light weight of these vehicles. Nevertheless, engineering measures that direct crash forces away from occupants and the addition of airbags have made many small cars safer in collisions than some larger cars.

Recommended

Chrysler Colt, Summit, Vista (1993–96)
Ford Escort, EXP, Tracer (1992–97)
Geo Prizm (1993–97)
Honda Civic (1993–97)
Mazda 323, Protegé (1996–97)
Mitsubishi Expo (1993–95)
Mitsubishi Mirage (1993–96)
Subaru Impreza, Loyale (1996–97)
Suzuki Esteem (1996–97)
Toyota Corolla (1993–97)
Toyota Paseo (1994–97)
Toyota Tercel (1993–97)
Nissan Sentra (1995–97)

Above Average

Geo Metro (1995–97)
Geo Prizm (1991–92)
Honda Civic (1992)
Hyundai Accent
Hyundai Elantra (1996–97)
Mazda 323, Protegé (1991–95)
Nissan Sentra (1991–94)
Nissan Pulsar, NX (1991–93)
Suzuki Swift (1995–97)
Toyota Corolla (1991–92)
Toyota Paseo (1992–93)
Toyota Tercel (1991–92)
VW Golf, Jetta (1993–97)

Average

Chrysler Colt, Summit, Vista (1989–92)
Ford Aspire (1994–97)
Ford Escort, EXP, Tracer (1991)
Geo Metro (1990–94)
Geo Prizm (1990)
GM Cavalier, Sunbird, Sunfire (1996–97)
Honda Civic (1989–91)
Hyundai Elantra (1991–95)
Mazda 323, GLC, Protegé (1985–90)
Mitsubishi Mirage (1989–92)
Nissan Sentra (1988–90)
Nissan Pulsar, NX (1987–90)
Saturn (1997)
Subaru Impreza, Loyale (1993–95)
Subaru Justy (1991–95)
Suzuki Swift (1990–94)
Toyota Corolla (1988–90)
Toyota Tercel (1987–90)

Below Average

Chrysler Colt, Summit, Vista (1985–88)
Geo Metro (1987–89)
Honda Civic (1984–88)
Hyundai Excel (1992–94)

Saturn (1992–96)
Subaru DL, GL, Loyale (1987–92)
Suzuki Swift (1987–89)
VW Fox (1990–93)

Not Recommended

Chrysler Charger, Horizon, Omni, Neon, Turismo
Ford Escort, EXP, Tracer (1981–90)
GM Cavalier, Sunbird (1984–95)

Hyundai Excel (1986–91)
Saturn (1992–96)
Subaru Justy (1988–90)
VW Golf, Jetta (1988–92)
VW Fox (1987–89)

Ford's '96 Escort is a best buy due to its improved reliability and reasonable purchase price. This wasn't always the case, though. Pre–'91 models were a nightmare.

Chrysler's '96 Neon isn't recommended due to its poor quality drivetrain and body components. Yet it was rated a "Best Buy" and "Car of the Year" by auto journalists.

CHRYSLER/EAGLE

Charger, Horizon, Omni, Shelby

Rating: Not Recommended (1983–90). The Shelby is a high performance variant of the Charger. All of these cars are virtually identical and have been off the market for almost a decade. **Maintenance/Repair costs**: Inexpensive; can be done by independents. **Parts**: Easily found and relatively cheap.

Technical Data

ENGINES	Liters/CID	HP	MPG	Model Years
OHV I-4 2 bbl.	1.6/98	64	25–31	1985–86
OHC I-4 2 bbl.	2.2/135	96	23–27	1985–87
OHC I-4 FI	2.2/135	93–96	23–27	1988–90
OHC I-4 2 bbl.	2.2/135	110	22–26	1985–86
OHC I-4T FI	2.2/135	146–148	20–26	1985–87

Strengths and weaknesses: Gone and best forgotten, these cars are relatively roomy for subcompacts (except for rear seating and an awkward driving position); they give good, but not spectacular, fuel economy; they perform well with the 2.2L powerplant; and they can be repaired almost anywhere—which is good, because they tend to break down almost everywhere. Expect serious problems with the 2.2L engine (see "Service Tips"), in addition to fuel, electrical, and ignition system problems that are difficult to diagnose and even harder to repair due to the poor quality of components. The power-steering rack develops leaks and the exhaust system rusts quickly. Other problems include rapid brake wear and unreliable electronic components. Air conditioners and turbochargers often malfunction and are expensive to troubleshoot and repair.

All 1978–90 models suffer from extensive surface rust, with perforations found around rear wheels and the rear hatch. Many owners also complain of severe underbody rusting that affects safety. All years have such poor body assembly that doors are constantly sticking shut (some owners have had to climb out the windows), locks fall off, handles detach, and water and air leaks are legion.

Safety summary/recalls: **Recalls**: **1985–87 Turbo**—The fuel hose connection may leak. **1986**—The rear suspension may partially separate from the vehicle, causing a sudden loss of control. **1987**—A faulty pressure regulator may leak fuel. **1989–90**—2.2L and 2.5L engines leak oil at the valve cover; this can be corrected with a new cylinder head cover kit.

Secret Warranties/Service Tips

1988–90—2.2L and 2.5L EFI engines that run roughly at idle may require a new EGR valve. **1989–90**—2.2L EFI engines with a spark knock during hot engine idle in drive may need a new engine controller. **All models/years**— 2.2L, 2.5L, and 3.0L V6 engines that surge and buck at 35–55 mph with A413 and A670 transmissions may require driveability kit #4419447. • All front-drives with automatic transmissions that have delayed engagement and no Drive or Reverse after start-up should have the front transmission pump replaced.

Charger, Horizon, Omni, Shelby Profile

	1983	1984	1985	1986	1987	1988	1989	1990
Cost Price ($)								
Omni/Horizon	6,675	6,690	6,871	7,146	6,895	7,116	7,719	8,689
Charger	7,213	7,420	7,522	7,790	7,585	—	—	—
Charger Shelby	8,602	9,354	9,391	9,747	10,226	—	—	—
Used Values ($)								
Omni/Horizon ↑	1,200	1,300	1,400	1,600	1,800	2,300	2,700	3,000
Omni/Horizon ↓	900	1,000	1,200	1,300	1,400	1,800	2,300	2,500
Charger ↑	1,200	1,400	1,600	1,800	2,000	—	—	—
Charger ↓	1,000	1,200	1,400	1,600	1,600	—	—	—
Charger Shelby ↑	1,300	1,500	1,700	1,900	2,100	—	—	—
Charger Shelby ↓	1,100	1,300	1,500	1,700	1,800	—	—	—
Extended Warranty	Y	Y	Y	Y	Y	Y	Y	Y
Secret Warranty	N	N	N	N	N	N	N	N
Reliability	❶	❶	❶	❶	❶	❶	❶	❶
Crash Safety	❷	❷	❷	❷	❷	❷	❷	❷

Colt, Expo, Mirage, Summit, Vista, Wagon

Rating: Recommended (1993–97); Average (1989–92); Below Average (1985–88). The '97 Mirage is the standout among these small cars and "mini" minivans. **Maintenance/Repair costs**: Repairs aren't difficult to perform and can be done by cheaper independent garages or Mitsubishi dealers. **Parts**: Easily found and relatively inexpensive, although Summit and Colt wagon body panels may be in short supply.

Technical Data

ENGINES	Liters/CID	HP	MPG	Model Years
OHV I-4 2 bbl.	1.5/90	68	26–36	1985–88
OHC I-4 FI	1.5/90	75	26–35	1988
OHC I-4 FI	1.5/90	81	24–30	1989–90
OHC I-4 FI	1.5/90	92	23–29	1991–98
OHC I-4T FI	1.6/97	102–105	24–27	1984–88
DOHC I-4T FI	1.6/97	135	21–25	1989
DOHC I-4 FI	1.6/97	113	22–26	1990

DOHC I-4 FI	1.6/97	123	21–25	1991–92
OHC I-4 FI	1.8/112	87–113	24–30	1993–98
OHV I-4 2 bbl.	2.0/122	88	23–27	1985–87
OHC I-4 FI	2.0/122	96	22–26	1988–91
OHC I-4 FI	2.4/144	116–136	22–25	1992–96
OHC I-4 FI	2.4/155	136	22–25	1993–94

Strengths and weaknesses: Some of the best small cars and wagons that Chrysler doesn't make (they're all Mitsubishi imports). Although the E and DL models aren't sparkling performers, they remain competitive in the subcompact arena and can be purchased for a lot less than their Japanese cousins. The 1985–88 Colts don't handle as well or offer as much rear leg room and cargo space as the more rounded, aero-styled, contemporary 1993–96 Colts and Mirages. The 1989–92 versions got a small horsepower boost that gives them a more spirited performance; however, passenger and cargo room are still at a premium.

This well-proven design has accumulated few problems over the years, due primarily to good quality control. Body construction and assembly are also quite good, although inadequate soundproofing allows the intrusion of lots of engine and road noise. Early models tend to have some front-brake, electrical-system, and engine problems, while the later '89–96 versions are mostly beset with fuel supply, electrical system, and brake malfunctions.

A troublesome turbocharged 1.6L motor was first offered in 1984. The engines on high-mileage cars often burn oil because of worn piston rings. Models equipped with automatic transmissions vibrate badly when idling in gear. Air conditioners are unreliable and expensive to repair. Carburetors can be finicky, too. Front brakes wear rapidly. There are many reports of ignition troubles for the 1984–85 models. Problems carried over to the 1986–92 models are premature engine and exhaust system wear. Since then, Colts and Mirages have shown few serious defects. In fact, the redesigned '97 Mirage (the Colt was dropped in '94) carries an upgraded automatic transmission, uses a stiffer body, and is much quieter and better appointed than its predecessor. Post-'86 LX, Vista, and 4X4 models are plagued by similar defects, with the addition of transmission and fuel-system malfunctions.

The Expo, Vista, and Summit Wagon were small minivans with 5- to 7-passenger seating. They are more reasonably priced, practical, and fuel efficient than many other small wagons. The five-passenger Colt wagon is similar to the Summit and Nissan Axxess in that it offers the extra versatility of a third seat in back and a tall body. As such, it makes a great car for a small family, while being able to haul small loads to the cottage or wherever. The wagon series is available in four-wheel drive and uses practically the same mechanical components as the other Colt models. If the wagon's price is too steep, check out the Nissan Axxess, which offers similar advantages. The Summit wagon is essentially a wagon version of the Colt 200 and sells at a premium. The 1.8L or 2.4L engine goes best with the 5-speed manual transmission. With an automatic, there is a significant fuel penalty and the 2.4L takes a while to change gears, particularly when going uphill.

On post-'90 Colts and Summits, the 2.4L head gasket may fail prematurely. Shocks aren't very durable, braking isn't impressive, and the front brakes have a short life span. Emission components like the oxygen sensor often fail after two years of use. A few owners have reported automatic transmission failures. Be especially wary of the troublesome 4X4 powertrain on 1989–91 wagons and the 16-valve turbo dropped in 1990. Owners of the 1993 wagon complain of poor heating and defrosting. Surface rust is common, as are rust perforations on door bottoms, the front edge of the hood, and the rear hatch.

Owners of 1992–97 models report premature piston ring wear and excessive engine noise caused by carbon buildup on the top of the piston. Front brakes and shock absorbers continue to have a short life span.

Safety summary/recalls: NHTSA probes: 1989–93 Colts and Summits—Automatic shoulder belts malfunction. • The wagon's sliding doors have childproof door locks. Unfortunately, some Summit wagons may have defective sliding door latches. • 1994 Mirage and Summit inadvertent airbag deployment killed driver. **Recalls: 1986–1991 Colts and 1989–1991 Summits**—Takata seatbelts need replacing. **1992–93 Colts and Summits**—Automatic seatbelts may not move into place. **1993 Colts and Summits**—Shoulder-belt-guide rail cable may jam.

Secret Warranties/Service Tips

1989–90—Cold start driveability problems can be fixed by cleaning the engine of carbon deposits and putting in an upgraded valve cover (#MD 118-125). • Squeaky front suspension: replace both stabilizer bar bushings. **1991**—Hard shifting or gear clashing can be corrected by installing an improved 1–2 synchronizer hub and sleeve, a 1–2 synchronizer spring, and a 3–4 synchronizer spring on cars equipped with manual transaxles. **1992**—Wagon fuel tanks may be slow to fill because the in-tank baffle impedes fuel flow. • Wagons may have excessive wind noise around the upper front door frame. **1992–93**—A front-end popping noise means the stabilizer ball joint grease has deteriorated. Add new grease and install an upgraded dust cover. **1992–94**—Carbon buildup on the piston top can be reduced by adding a bottle of Mopar Fuel Injector Cleaner to a full tank of gas. • The sliding door may not open from inside due to a faulty connecting door latch rod clip. **1993**—Wagons with poor heating/defrosting require upgraded distribution ducts. **All models/years**—A common problem with the 1.6L engine is that the exhaust manifold can come loose, causing an exhaust leak. When you first spot the trouble, simply tighten the exhaust manifold bolts. Chrysler may cover costs related to premature engine-head-gasket, ring, and valve wear if the five-year emissions warranty is applicable.

Colt, Expo, Mirage, Summit, Vista, Wagon Profile

	1990	1991	1992	1993	1994	1995	1996	1997
Cost Price ($)								
Colt/Summit	8,331	8,247	8,640	9,260	10,779	—	—	—
Mirage	8,310	8,508	8,823	8,822	10,548	11,563	12,422	11,962
Colt Wagon	10,935	13,695	—	—	—	—	—	—
Summit Wagon	—	—	12,806	12,926	14,565	15,799	16,347	—
Expo Wagon	—	—	12,639	12,988	14,627	17,894	—	—
Used Values ($)								
Colt/Summit ↑	3,900	4,400	5,000	6,300	7,100	—	—	—
Colt/Summit ↓	3,100	3,600	4,000	5,200	6,000	—	—	—
Mirage ↑	3,900	4,400	4,900	7,100	8,000	9,000	10,000	11,000
Mirage ↓	3,100	3,500	3,900	6,000	6,900	7,800	8,800	9,500
Colt Wagon ↑	4,200	5,700	—	—	—	—	—	—
Colt Wagon ↓	3,300	4,700	—	—	—	—	—	—
Summit Wagon ↑	—	—	8,000	—	—	—	—	—
Summit Wagon ↓	—	—	6,800	—	—	—	—	—
Expo Wagon ↑	—	—	12,639	12,988	14,627	17,894	—	—
Expo Wagon ↓	—	—	12,639	12,988	14,627	17,894	—	—
Extended Warranty	N	N	N	N	N	N	N	N
Secret Warranty	N	N	N	N	Y	N	N	Y
Reliability	②	②	②	②	③	③	③	④
Air conditioning	②	②	②	②	③	③	③	④
Body integrity	②	②	②	②	②	②	②	③
Braking system	②	②	②	②	②	②	②	②
Electrical system	②	②	③	③	④	④	ε	⑤
Engines	②	②	③	④	④	④	④	④
Exhaust/Converter	③	③	③	④	④	⑤	⑤	⑤
Fuel system	③	③	④	④	④	⑤	⑤	⑤
Ignition system	③	③	⑤	⑤	⑤	⑤	⑤	⑤
Manual transmission	④	④	⑤	⑤	⑤	⑤	⑤	⑤
- automatic	③	③	③	③	❷	❷	③	③
Rust/Paint	②	③	③	③	③	④	④	⑤
Steering	④	④	④	④	⑤	⑤	⑤	⑤
Suspension	②	②	③	③	③	④	③	③
Crash Safety								
Colt Sedan	❷	❶	❶	❶	❶	❶	❶	—
Colt Wagon	❷	❷	❷	❷	❷	❷	❷	—
Vista Wagon	❷	❷	❷	❷	⑤	—	—	—

Neon

Rating: Not Recommended (1995–97). A high-priced, low-quality econobox that promises more than it delivers. Chrysler cut the '96 Neon Sport's MSRP price, leading to a lower resale value. Choose a model with touring suspension for the best ride. The Highline and Sport versions are more feature laden. **Maintenance/Repair costs**: Higher than average; repairs must be done by dealers. **Parts**: Easily found and relatively inexpensive.

Technical Data

ENGINES	Liters/CID	HP	MPG	Model Years
OHC I-4 FI	2.0L/122	132	27–35	1995–98
DOHC I-4 FI	2.0L/122	150	27–35	1995–98

Strengths and weaknesses: A small, noisy car with big quality problems, the Neon does offer a spacious interior and responsive steering and handling. Nevertheless, it uses an antiquated 3-speed automatic gearbox, a DOHC engine that has to be pushed hard to do as well as the SOHC engine, and a mushy base suspension. Furthermore, a perusal of service bulletins and owner comments clearly shows that these cars have a plethora of serious factory-related defects, including a raucous engine, an abrupt-shifting and unreliable automatic transmission, an air conditioning system that often requires expensive servicing, lots of interior noise and leaks, uneven fit and finish, and poor-quality trim items that break or fall off easily. The finish is not as good as on most other subcompacts; Chrysler uses only two coats of paint versus the Japanese practice of applying three coats. Furthermore, the thickness of the coat varies considerably and can chip easily.

Except for the addition of a cast aluminum oil pan to reduce engine vibrations, redesigned wheel covers, improved sound system, and a center console with armrest, the 1997 Neon is basically unchanged from previous years. A redesign is planned for 1999.

Dealer service bulletins: **1995**—Engine sags, hesitates, shudders, and surges. • Rough idle especially bad during cold start-up. • Oil leaks at the cam position sensor. • Buzzy manual and automatic gearshift lever, and harsh-shifting, erratic automatic transmission. • Noisy clutch pedal and wheel cover. • Rear suspension bottoms out. • Steering wheel shakes and accelerator pedal vibrates. • Premature front brake pad wear. • AC freeze-up, poor performance, and evaporator odors. • Inaccurate fuel gauge readings, instrument panel glare, and water leaks. • Water leaks into the passenger compartment on left-hand turns. • Flickering headlights. (Chrysler Neons are so cheap that the electrical system can't take the AC load and often the headlights will flicker annoyingly. DSB 08-25-95, issued June 3, 1994, says too bad; it's operating as designed.) • Discharged battery. • Intermittent wiper operation. • Excessive engine noise in passenger compartment, exhaust noise/hiss, B-pillar wind noise, power-steering rattles, steering column and right engine-mount click, and chattering steering column tilt lever. • More noise: front seat rattle and front seatback squeak, hood prop-rod rattle, idle air control motor whistle, front brake moan, poorly fitted deck-lid rattle, and poor AM reception (static). • Glue oozes out at backlight/windshield molding and backlight molding lifts off. **1996**—Cold start hesitation, engine misfiring, and erratic idling. •

Excessive engine vibration and exhaust noise. • Transmission slippage from second to third gear during light acceleration. • Speed control overshoots or undershoots. • Rear brake chirps or howls. • AC evaporator produces a high-pitched whistle. • Fuel tank won't fill or is slow to fill. • Delayed windshield washer fluid output. • Interior-window film buildup. • Water leaks at cowl cover seam. **1997**—Rear brake howl. • Front foot well creak/rattle. • Scratched door glass. • Improper AC compressor engagement. • Loss of power steering in heavy rain or when passing through puddles. • Poor radio reception. • Warning that premium fuel may cause stalling, long cold start times, hesitation, and warm-up sags. • Front suspension popping/creaking noise.

Safety summary/recalls: NHTSA probes: 1995—Steering column fires. • 98 reports of "inappropriate" airbag deployment causing 13 crashes and injuring 28 people. • Sudden steering loss. • Small horn buttons are hard to find in an emergency. Headlight switch is a "hide-and-seek" affair. • Axle shafts may suddenly fail, as the owner of a '95 Neon discovered:

> I was driving in traffic and the car just stopped. I couldn't move forward or backwards but the engine was still going. It turned out that the left front axle of the car had collapsed. I was just lucky that I wasn't driving on the highway when this occurred, because I would have been severely injured or killed. I had the car towed to the dealer, and they repaired the broken axle, but I just don't feel safe in the vehicle....

1995-96—Engine compartment fires. **Recalls: 1995**—Corroded fuel and rear brake tubes may fail. • Steering columns could snap loose from the car's frame during an accident. **1996**—Engine wiring harness may short, causing stalling. **1997**—Airbag module should be replaced to prevent airbags from deploying while vehicle is parked.

Secret Warranties/Service Tips

1995—Tips on how to fix paint fogging and stained white bumpers are offered. • Faulty radios will be replaced for free under a secret warranty. **1995-97**—If water drips into the vehicle from the roof-rail weather strip channel, Chrysler will provide, under warranty, a free anti-drip roof-rail retainer channel.

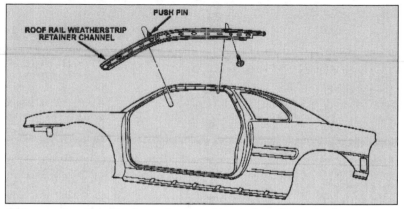

This correction should take one hour and is reimbursable under the warranty.

1996—Water could enter the air cleaner housing, be ingested into the engine, and cause serious engine damage. To prevent this from occurring, the dealer will drill a hole in the housing and seal the hood to cowl weatherstrip. This 30-minute correction is free of charge under Chrysler Customer Satisfaction Notice #660. It's not a safety recall, so you may have a hard time getting Chrysler to acknowledge the problem.

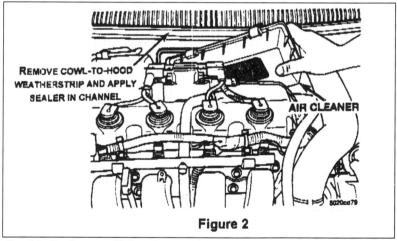

Figure 2

Get this fixed, or you'll face huge engine expenses.

Neon Profile

	1995	1996	1997
Cost Price ($)			
Base	12,195	11,730	12,430
Sport 4d	14,393	14,165	—
Used Values ($)			
Base ↑	8,500	9,700	10,400
Base ↓	7,300	8,400	9,000
Sport 4d ↑	9,400	10,600	—
Sport 4d ↓	8,100	9,300	—
Extended Warranty	Y	Y	Y
Secret Warranty	Y	Y	N
Reliability	❶	❶	❶
Crash Safety	③	④	④

FORD

Aspire

Rating: Average (1994–97). The Aspire's size, engine, and drive-train limitations restrict it to an urban environment. Except for a minor facelift and upgraded side-impact protection, the '97 Aspire is much like its predecessors. **Maintenance/Repair costs**: Higher than average. Repairs are dealer dependent. **Parts**: As with the Festiva, body panels are rare and expensive.

Technical Data

ENGINES	Liters/CID	HP	MPG	Model Years
OHC I-4 FI	1.3L/81	63	28–36	1994–97

Strengths and weaknesses: The Korean-built Aspire comes in three- and five-door versions, and is powered by a fuel-injected, 4-cylinder engine hooked up to either a standard 5-speed manual transmission or an optional 3-speed automatic. With its smooth-shifting 5-speed manual transmission and fuel injection, the Aspire's base powerplant is adequate for short city errands. This car has plenty of front seat room and excellent front and rear visibility. Corrosion protection is enhanced with galvanized steel panels, sealers, and coatings.

The Aspire's engine lacks high-end torque and the widely spaced gear ratios on the manual shifter rob it of much-needed mid-range power. It takes 13 seconds to reach 60 mph and an additional 4 seconds with the automatic gearbox, which is jerky when pushed. Air conditioning slows down the car even more. Steering is heavy and vague at high speeds. Unfortunately, the three-door version doesn't offer power steering. Expect excessive low-speed engine and road/tire noise at higher speeds. Its fuel economy is not all that impressive when compared to entry-level Hondas and Nissans, but their higher cost wipes out any fuel savings.

Dealer service bulletins: **1994**—Rough idle, hesitation, excessive fuel consumption, and poor heater output likely caused by thermostat stuck in open position or opening before it should. **1995**—Automatic transmission fails to upshift in cold weather. • Brake roughness upon application. • Malfunctioning air conditioning and excessive compressor noise. • No-start due to faulty ignition switch. **1996**—Fog/film on windshield/interior glass. • MTX transmission clicks, clunks, and rattles when in Reverse. • Musty and mildewy odors. **1997**—Excessive manual transmission noise. • Delayed automatic transmission engagement. • Door glass won't roll down.

Safety summary/recalls: **NHTSA probes**: This car is unstable in a crosswind. Although fading is minimal, the tiny brakes don't inspire confidence. **1995–96**—Owners have reported ten incidents of steering wheel lockup to NHTSA. **Recalls**: **1994**—Fuel-supply, return, and vapor hoses or lines may leak. Steel fuel lines will be repositioned; get additional corrosion protection, if needed.

Secret Warranties/Service Tips

1994—The upper steering column cover causes the warning flasher to stick. • Fuel leaks from fuel and vapor hoses/lines. 1996–97—Fuel odor in the interior may be caused by a cracked seam weld on the vapor vent valve located in the left quarter panel area.

Aspire Profile

	1994	1995	1996	1997
Cost Price ($)				
Base	9,660	9,860	10,225	10,655
Used Values ($)				
Base ↑	5,500	6,500	7,300	7,800
Base ↓	4,800	5,500	6,500	7,100
Extended Warranty	Y	Y	Y	Y
Secret Warranty	Y	N	N	N
Reliability	③	④	④	④
Air conditioning	③	③	③	③
Body integrity	❷	❷	❷	③
Braking system	❷	❷	③	③
Electrical system	❷	③	③	③
Engines	④	④	④	④
Exhaust/Converter	③	④	⑤	⑤
Fuel system	③	③	⑤	⑤
Ignition system	④	⑤	⑤	⑤

Manual transmission	⑤	⑤	⑤	⑤
- automatic	③	③	③	④
Rust/Paint	④	⑤	⑤	⑤
Steering	④	④	④	⑤
Suspension	⑤	⑤	⑤	⑤
Crash Safety	④	④	④	④

Escort, EXP, Lynx, Tracer

Rating: Recommended (1992–97); Average (1991); Not Recommended (1981–90). The LX became the base Escort during the 1994 model year. Lots of upgraded '97 Escorts will come off lease within the next six months; they represent an exceptionally good buy. For the 1999 model year, the Escort will be replaced by the Focus. **Maintenance/Repair costs**: Higher than average on pre-1991s; below average for later models. Repairs can be done by independents or Ford or Mazda dealers. **Parts**: Expensive, but easily found.

Technical Data

ENGINES	Liters/CID	HP	MPG	Model Years
OHC I-4 2 bbl.	1.6/98	70–80	25–30	1985
OHC I-4 FI	1.6/98	84	26–30	1985
OHC I-4T FI	1.6/98	120	22–26	1985
OHC I-4 2 bbl.	1.9/114	86	26–30	1985–86
OHC I-4 FI	1.9/114	90	25–31	1987–90
OHC I-4 FI	1.9/114	108–115	21–25	1985–90
OHC I-4 FI	2.0/121	110	24–29	1997–98
DOHC I-4 FI	2.0/121	130	23–27	1998
OHC I-4D FI	2.0/121	52–58	27–34	1985–87
OHC I-4 FI	1.9/114	88	24–30	1991–95
DOHC I-4 FI	1.8/109	127	23–27	1991–96

Strengths and weaknesses: These front-drive small cars are usually reasonably priced, are economical to operate, provide a comfortable, though busy, ride, and provide adequate front seating for two adults. However, they have a "Dr. Jekyll and Mr. Hyde" disposition, depending on which model year you buy. From 1982 until 1990, these subcompacts were dull performers with uninspiring interiors. Worse, they had a nasty reputation for being unreliable and expensive to repair.

Be wary of early Escorts (1984–87) that use Mazda's 2.0L diesel 4-cylinder; it's weak, noisy, difficult to service, and prone to expensive cylinder-head and gasket repairs. From 1987 until 1990, model year quality continued to go downhill. The 1.9L engine used from 1985 to 1990 gives respectable highway performance but its failure rate is still much higher than average. The radiator and other cooling components, including the fan switch and motor, are failure prone. Carburetors and fuel-injection systems are temperamental. Ignition modules are often defective. Power steering racks fail prematurely. Front and rear wheel alignment is difficult. Exhaust systems rust rapidly.

The '91 model's changeover to mostly Mazda 323 components greatly enhanced the car's overall reliability and performance. The model adopted a longer wheelbase, making for a more comfortable ride and a bit more roomy interior. The 1.9L engine runs more smoothly, as well. The GT and Tracer LTS are equipped with Mazda's powerful 127-hp, 1.8L, 4-cylinder engine, and their overall highway performance and fuel economy are far superior to what previous models offered. Wagon versions are particularly versatile and spacious. The front seats on the Tracer GS and LS are very comfortable and the cargo area is especially spacious in the wagon. Rear seat room is a bit cramped on all other models.

Owner complaints for later models concern air conditioning and fuel pump failures, minor ignition system glitches, electrical short circuits caused by corroded fuel pump wiring, engine malfunctions, and a difficult-to-access oil filter.

The 1997 models were significantly improved to make them look more attractive and to ride and handle better. They gained 25 percent more horsepower with the 2.0L engine (the 1.8L was axed) and featured improved comfort, a quieter interior, and more standard equipment. The car is four inches longer, mostly taken up by a larger trunk. New standard features included power steering, rear heat ducts, intermittent wipers, a battery-saver system, a 24-watt, four-speaker stereo unit that can be upgraded to an 80-watt system hooked to a trunk-mounted CD player, and solar glass. Three-door, five-door, and GT models were dropped and the ZX2, a revived coupe, made its debut in late '97 as a '98 model.

Dealer service bulletins: 1994—Rough idle, hesitation, excessive fuel consumption, and poor heater output (likely caused by thermostat stuck in open position or opening before it should). • Fuel pump wiring short circuits (see "Service Tips"). • Defective electric rear window defrosters. • Lots of water leaks, rattles, and squeaks. **1995**—Insufficient AC cooling or excessive clutch end gap. • Rear view mirrors that fall off. • Lots of wind noise. • Brake roughness upon application. • Fuel pump buzz/whine heard through radio speaker. • Brake drag or lit brake light when not braking (covered under secret warranty #95B63). • Steering wheel shake at idle. • Faulty temperature gauge. • Wind noise. **1996**—Stalling or hard starts. • Transaxle whine upon deceleration. • Front disc brakes knock when applied. • Fuel pump buzz/whine through radio speaker. • Intermittent horn operation. • Fog/film on windshield/interior glass. • Windshield wipers streak or clean unevenly. • Musty and mildewy odors. **1997**—Hard starts with 2.0L engine. • Automatic transmission clicking noise. • Delayed automatic transmission engagement. • Inoperative AC or heater temperature control. • Blower motor chirping/squeaking. • Loose catalyst/muffler heat shields. • Instrument panel buzzing. • Exhaust noise from behind instrument panel.

Safety summary/recalls: **Escort recalls**: **1983–93**—Ford will replace fire-prone ignition switches on designated Escorts/Tracers. **1985**—Rocker arm oil leakage could cause a fire. • Cars with 1.9L engines may fail to return to idle. **1985–86**—Manual gearshift lever may accidentally slip into Neutral in cold weather. **1985–87**—Driver's seat could come loose in an accident. **1986–88**—Fuel line leakage could cause a fire. **1987**—Stainless-steel lug nuts may fracture, causing the wheel to fall off. **1990**—Windshield could come out in a frontal collision. **1991**—Accelerator pedal could stick wide open. • Steering column could lock up. **1991–92**—Fuel vapor could escape from a full fuel tank, causing a fire. **1993**—Faulty driver's seat could fail in a collision. **1995**—Airbag mounting bolts may be missing or improperly torqued. **Tracer recalls**: **1991**—Fuel vapor could escape from fuel tank, causing a fire. **1992**—Steering column may lock up.

Secret Warranties/Service Tips

Escort: **1983–94**—Hesitation, a rough idle, or poor heater output may all be caused by a faulty thermostat. **1986–89**—Hard starting/stalling may be caused by a defective fuel pump or sender assembly. **1988**—Owner notification M59 says that any fuel pump malfunction that drains the battery, makes for hard starts, or cuts engine performance can be corrected by installing an upgraded fuel pump diode (#E8FZ-14A411-A). **1990**—Owner notification B91 allows for the free modification of faulty dealer AC units with condenser fans that rotate backwards. Now, after eight years, you may be asked to pay for this repair. Ask for a pro rata discount. **1991**—Eliminate knocking heard after a cold start or when returning to idle speed after freeway driving by installing new engine camshafts (after ruling out the possibility of lifter noise). **1991–93**—Metallic ticking heard after initial start-up or when returning to idle speed may be caused by a faulty lifter, low amount of oil in the crankcase, incorrect oil filter, or oil deterioration. **1991–94**—Under Service Program #94B55, Ford will install at no charge a fused jumper harness in the fuel pump electrical circuit. This will prevent short-circuit problems such as stalling, erratic instrument gauge readings, and extensive wiring damage, which are caused by water intrusion (see the following article).

Free Fuel Pump Fix
Overview of Program 94B55

September 1994
TO: All Ford and Lincoln-Mercury Dealers
SUBJECT:
Owner Notification Program 94b55 - Fuel Pump/Sender Electrical Circuit Modification on Certain
1991–1994 Escort and Tracer Cars
OASIS   - Yes
OWNER LIST   - Yes
PARTS RETURN   - No
PROGRAM TIMING - There are NO limitations for this program.
AFFECTED VEHICLES:
1991–1994 Escort and Tracer cars produced from Job # 1, 1991 through June 17, 1994, at the Wayne
Assembly Plant and from Job # 1, 1991, through June 28, 1994, at the Hermosillo Assembly Plant
that were originally sold or are currently registered in the following states:
Connecticut, Illinois, Indiana, Maine, Massachusetts, Michigan, New Hampshire, New York, New
Jersey, Ohio, Pennsylvania, Rhode Island, Vermont and Wisconsin.
REASON FOR THIS PROGRAM:
Salt water intrusion between the fuel pump/sender wiring harness connector and fuel pump/sender flange
may cause electrolytic corrosion resulting in an electrical short circuit. The corrosion is the result of heavy
use of calcium and sodium chloride salts for road dust and ice control in the above noted states. Should a
short circuit occur, the instrument cluster gauges may act erratically, the driver may see or smell smoke
inside the passenger compartment due to the wiring overheating and the fuel pump may stop operating.

• Fix a timing belt that's noisy during cold weather by installing an upgraded, more rigid belt tensioner. • A missing or loose front valance panel will be replaced or secured with longer bolts free of charge. **1992–93**—A high idle rpm after heavy use may be corrected by installing a new idle air control valve. **1994–98**—Tips on eliminating wind noise around doors are given in DSB # 97-15-1 (see below).

Article No.
97-15-1
07/21/97
WINDNOISE - AROUND SIDE DOOR(S) - SERVICE TIPS
FORD:
1994–97 CROWN VICTORIA, TAURUS
1994–98 ESCORT
1995–98 CONTOUR
LINCOLN-MERCURY:
1994–97 GRAND MARQUIS, SABLE
1994–98 CONTINENTAL, MARK VIII, TOWN CAR, TRACER
199–98 MYSTIQUE
LIGHT TRUCK:
199–97 EXPLORER, F-150, F-250, RANGER
199–98 WINDSTAR
1997–EXPEDITION, MOUNTAINEER
1998 NAVIGATOR

ISSUE:
Windnoise from the side doors may be heard on some vehicles. This may be caused by the door weatherstrip seal. This TSB article provides service tips for correcting this concern.

ACTION:
Diagnose and repair any windnoise from door weatherstrip concerns using Windnoise Service Tips.

All models/years—Owners report that Ford has been covering the cost of repairs for premature engine head gasket, ring, and valve wear under its emissions warranty. • Three components that frequently benefit from Ford "goodwill" warranty extensions are catalytic converters, fuel pumps, and computer modules. If Ford balks at refunding your money, apply the emissions warranty for a full or partial refund. • For paint delamination, fading, peeling, hazing, and "microchecking," see page 67–75 for details on claiming a refund.

Escort, EXP, Lynx, Tracer Profile

	1990	1991	1992	1993	1994	1995	1996	1997
Cost Price ($)								
Base/LX	7,948	8,586	9,883	8,831	10,510	11,115	11,615	12,225
GT	10,928	12,593	12,800	12,800	12,675	13,530	14,040	—
Used Values ($)								
Base/LX ↑	3,700	4,600	5,200	5,600	6,500	7,500	8,600	10,200
Base/LX ↓	2,800	3,700	4,200	4,600	5,400	6,400	7,400	9,200
GT ↑	4,300	4,500	5,800	6,700	8,000	9,000	10,200	—
GT ↓	3,300	3,800	4,800	5,800	6,800	8,000	9,200	—
Extended Warranty	Y	N	N	N	N	N	N	N
Secret Warranty	Y	Y	Y	Y	Y	Y	Y	Y
Reliability	2	3	4	4	5	5	5	5
Air conditioning	2	1	2	2	3	3	3	3
Body integrity	2	2	2	2	3	3	3	3
Braking system	1	2	3	3	4	4	4	4
Electrical system	1	1	2	3	4	4	4	4
Engines	2	3	3	3	5	5	5	5
Exhaust/Converter	3	3	4	5	5	5	5	5
Fuel system	2	3	3	3	3	4	5	5
Ignition system	2	3	4	5	5	5	5	5
Manual transmission	5	5	5	5	5	5	5	5
- automatic	3	3	4	5	5	5	5	5
Rust/Paint	2	3	4	5	5	5	5	5
Steering	2	3	5	5	5	5	5	5
Suspension	2	3	5	5	5	5	5	5
Crash Safety								
*Escort 2d	2	5	5	1	1	4	4	4
Lynx	2	—	—	—	—	—	—	—
Tracer	2	5	5	1	1	—	—	—
Side Impact	—	—	—	—	—	—	—	3

*The low crash scores represent severe leg trauma rated for the first time.

GENERAL MOTORS

Cavalier, Sunbird, Sunfire

Rating: Average (1996–97); Not Recommended (1984–95). Early models are particularly unforgiving if maintenance schedules aren't followed to the letter. An incredibly slow depreciation rate means that recent models are no bargains. Still, I'd buy a Cavalier or Sunbird/Sunfire over a Saturn any day. The base Sunbird became the LE in 1989 and then changed its name to the Sunfire in 1995. The Z24 convertible was replaced by the LS in 1995. **Maintenance/Repair costs**: Average; repairs aren't dealer dependent, however, ABS troubleshooting is a real head-scratcher. **Parts**: Reasonably priced; often bought for much less from independent suppliers.

Technical Data

ENGINES	Liters/CID	HP	MPG	Model Years
		Cavalier		
OHV I-4 FI	2.0/121	85–90	21–25	1985–89
OHV I-4 FI	2.2/133	95–120	21–25	1990–94
OHV I-4 FI	2.2/132	120	25–31	1995–98
DOHC I-4 FI	2.3/138	150	21–30	1995
DOHC I-4 FI	2.4/146	150	21–31	1996–98
OHV V6 FI	2.8/173	120–130	19–23	1985–89
OHV V6 FI	3.1/173	135–140	19–23	1990–94
		Sunbird/Sunfire		
OHC I-4 FI	1.8/109	82–84	24–27	1985–86
OHC I-4T FI	1.8/109	150	20–24	1985–86
OHV I-4 FI	2.0/122	88	21–26	1985
OHC I-4 FI	2.0/121	96–111	22–26	1987–94
OHC I-4T FI	2.0/121	165	19–24	1987–90
OHV I-4 FI	2.2/132	120	25–31	1995–98
DOHC I-4 FI	2.4/146	150	21–31	1996–98
OHV V6 FI	3.1/191	140	18–22	1991–94

Strengths and weaknesses: Snappy road performance (with the right engine and transmission hookup) has been marred by abysmally poor reliability. The basic versions are lackluster performers. The 2.0L 4-cylinder engine gets overwhelmed by the demands of passing and merging. On top of that, major reliability weaknesses afflict all J-body mechanical and body components. Engine, transmission, electronic module, and brake failures are common for all model years. 2.0L engine blocks crack, cylinder heads leak, and the turbocharged version frequently needs expensive repairs. Oil leakage from the rear crankshaft seal is common. Oil filters on all model years tend to wear out quickly.

1986–89 model year improvements simply changed the nature, not the frequency, of breakdowns. Power-steering rack and front suspension components aren't durable. Consider replacing the original components with front gas struts and rear cargo coil springs to improve handling and durability. Owners also report that a change to high-octane fuel can help improve engine performance and reduce knocking and engine run-on. The cooling, exhaust, ignition, and fuel systems have had more than the average number of problems. The manifold heat shield tends to be noisy. Front brakes wear out quickly, and rear brakes tend to lock the rear wheels in emergency stops (one cause being the seizure of the rear brake adjusters). The optional 2.8L V6 with 3-speed automatic transmission is the best highway performer, but intake manifold gasket failures, premature head gasket wear, and transmission malfunctions compromise driving pleasure.

For 1990–94 versions, a base 2.2L 4-cylinder and optional 3.1L replaced the failure-prone 2.0L and 2.8L powerplants. Unfortunately, the newer engines already have a checkered reputation, highlighted by reports of head gasket failures causing coolant leakage, overheating, engine seizure, hard starting, stalling, and surging—problems covered by a secret warranty. Air conditioning and hood latch failures, seatbelt defects, and a plethora of body deficiencies are also commonplace. Door bottoms and wheel housings are particularly vulnerable to rust perforation. Premature paint peeling and cracking, discoloration, and surface rust have been regular problems since these cars were introduced.

The 1995–97 versions benefited from some engine tweaks, standard dual airbags and ABS, a longer wheelbase (but shorter body), a stiffer structure, and an improved suspension. Unfortunately, though, the engine head gasket failures have apparently been carried over to the '95s, as well.

Dealer service bulletins: **1993**—3.1L engines hesitate or stall. • No Reverse or slipping while in Reverse with 3T40 automatic transmissions. • Rear brake squawk. **1994**—Body fit deficiencies. • Premature front brake wear. • Faulty ignition switches. • Electrical short circuits. **1995**—Engine failing to crank and no-start. • Brake vibration and/or pedal pulsation. • Longer-life front brake linings. • Low voltage reading and dim lights at idle. • Grinding/growling when in Park on an incline. • Knocking noise when traversing rough roads. • Rear window panel squeaking. • Rear quarter-panel road noise. • Loose door trim panel. • Poor paint application and rust spots. **1996**—Excessive engine roll. • Low speed knocking noise when passing over rough roads. • Air conditioning odors. • Radio frequency interference diagnosis tips. • Water leak diagnostic guide. • Loose door trim panel. • Tips on silencing rear quarter-panel road noise. • Exterior light condensation. • Rear edge of hood rubs windshield when opening. • Twisted seatbelt webbing.

1997—Axle seal leakage. • Scuffed interior quarter trim panels on convertibles. • Coolant odor or leakage. • Deck lid hard to open or close. • Automatic transmission failure. • Low-engine-coolant light flashes. • Popping noise originating from the engine compartment. • Rear seatback rattles/squeaks. • Rear shock noise coming from trunk area. • Engine cranks, but won't run.

Safety summary/recalls: NHTSA probes: 1995—Steering that fails/locks up. • Faulty cruise control. • Windshield wipers that fail in cold weather. • **1995–96—ABS** brakes that fail. • Airbags that fail to deploy or deploy accidentally. • Inoperative horn. • Transmission that slips out of Park. • Sudden acceleration, stalling. • Passenger side seatbacks won't stay upright. **1996**—Injuries suffered from airbags. • Engine gaskets that leak oil. • Mufflers fail frequently. **1996–97**—The NHTSA has received 96 complaints of inadvertent airbag deployment causing 10 crashes and injuries to 53 people. Since GM modified the airbag sensing and diagnostic module in May 1997, no further incidents have been reported. **Recalls: 1983–84**—The floor pan anchor on cars with a manually adjusted driver's seat could break, causing the driver's seat to tip backwards suddenly and causing a potential loss of vehicle control. • Models with 2.0L engines may suddenly accelerate due to a kinked accelerator control cable. **1985**—Air cleaner plastic trim could catch fire. **1986**—A defective headlight switch can cause headlights to flicker or fail. **1987**—It is possible that the fuel feed/return lines will crack, leaking fuel. • The parking brake lever may fail, allowing the vehicle to roll away unexpectedly. • Cars with 2.0L engines may have a frozen accelerator cable that could cause sudden acceleration. **1989**—The fuel tank, which could leak fuel, will be inspected and replaced, if necessary, for free. **1991**—Cracked front-door shoulder-belt guide loops could pull loose in an accident. • Front door frames that anchor the seatbelt housing could collapse in an accident, resulting in seatbelt failure. **1992**—The hood could open suddenly, blocking the driver's view. **1992–93**—Dealer will install a redesigned intake manifold gasket on vehicles with rough-running 2.2L engines. **1993**—Faulty rear brake hoses could cause brake failure. **1994**—Loose drive-axle spindle nuts may cause steering knuckle tire-wheel assembly to separate from the axle. **1995**—Front suspension lower control-arm assemblies may be defective. **1995–96**—Front or rear hazard warning lights could be faulty. **1996**—Accelerator cable may be kinked, requiring excessive pedal effort. **1997**—Driver's wiper blades may be 5 inches too short. **1988 Sunbird**—Backup lights may be inoperative. **1992–93**—Vehicles equipped with 2.0L engines may have defective throttle-cable assemblies that could stick open in cold weather.

Secret Warranties/Service Tips

1985–88—Premature brake lining wear may be caused by a maladjusted cruise-control cutoff or brake light switch. **1985–89**—No first gear and/or slips in first may mean that you need new forward clutch piston seals. **1985–90**—Exhaust boom or moan can be corrected by installing a mass dampener (#10137382). • Noise from rear springs requires the installation of upgraded rear spring insulators (#22555689). **1986–87**—Erratic idle and 2.0L engine surging require the replacement of the PROM or TCC solenoid; another possible cause is a defective mass air flow sensor. **1987–88**—Difficult cold starts with 2.0L engines may require a new drop-in manifold deflector plate (#10112342). • A sagging headliner needs service package #22541347. **1987–90**—A rattle or buzz from the instrument panel may require a new upgraded brake booster check valve (#18012017). **1988–89**—2.0L engine valve train noise can be reduced by adjusting or replacing the rocker arms. **1988–94**—Water leaks at the front upper door frame are treated in depth in a DSB issued in October 1994. **1989**—Product Campaign 89C16 provides for the free replacement of the 5-speed manual transmission. **1990**—Heater and AC blower noise can be reduced by replacing the blower assembly. **1990–91**—Poor starting may be caused by the spring in early starter drives compressing too easily; install an upgraded starter motor drive assembly (#10473700). **1991–94**—A crunching noise coming from the right side of the dash when turning the steering wheel can be silenced by installing a new steering grommet on the right side. **1992–93**—Engine head gasket failures may cause coolant leakage, overheating, and serious engine failure. GM will repair the defect at no charge under a secret warranty (see following page).**1992–97**—Paint delamination, peeling, or fading: GM lets dealers repaint the entire car at no charge to the owner (up to $650), regardless of whether it was bought new or used. Head office permission isn't needed before work commences (see page 96). **1993–94**—Excessive engine vibrations at idle or a clunk upon acceleration are most likely due to a defective engine mount. **1994**—A squeaking noise heard when going over bumps, accelerating, or shifting can be stopped by replacing the exhaust manifold pipe seal. • Water leaks into the front footwell are treated in depth in a December 1993 DSB. **1986–92 Cavalier**—Vehicles equipped with the 3T40 automatic transmission may experience slippage in manual Low or Reverse; install service package #8628222, which includes a Low/Reverse clutch release spring (#8664961) and clutch retainer and snap ring (#656/657). **1987–88**—Engine stalling in Reverse or Drive with the THM 125C automatic transmission may mean that you need an upgraded auxiliary valve body filter (#8664921). • Poor AC cooling may be caused by a faulty pressure switch O-ring seal. **1992**—Engine hesitation or roughness, particularly at idle, may be corrected by installing a new lower intake manifold gasket (#10103647). **1995–97**—Axle seal leakage may be caused by a pinched transaxle vent hose. • Delayed automatic transmission engagement after a cold soak signals the need to install a revised forward clutch housing assembly. • Repair tips are offered for scuffed interior quarter trim panels on convertibles. • A sticking deck lid may need an upgraded lid release cable. • A dome light that won't shut off probably has a corroded door jamb switch. • The left-hand mirror may not adjust if the lever has become disengaged. • A popping noise originating from the engine compartment may mean that the torque strut-mount attaching bolts are loose.

1908 Colonel Sam Drive
Oshawa, Ontario L1H 8P7

Dear General Motors Customer:

As the owner of a 1992 or 1993 Chevrolet Cavalier equipped with a 2.2L engine, your satisfaction with our product is of the utmost concern to us. Your vehicle was provided with a new vehicle warranty, which covers certain parts of your vehicle for a specified period. These warranties are of considerable value to you if you should experience problems with your vehicle.

This letter is intended to make you aware that some 1992 and 1993 Chevrolet Cavalier models with 2.2L engines may develop a failure of the cylinder head gasket that allows coolant to leak from the cylinder head gasket to engine block joint. Early evidence of this would be a loss of coolant in the coolant reservoir and an odor of coolant from the engine compartment, or a low coolant light. There may also be visible coolant deposits at the cylinder head to engine block joint.

General Motors of Canada Limited is therefore taking the following action:

We are providing owners with special coverage. If the above-mentioned condition occurs within seven (7) years of the date your vehicle was originally placed in service or 160,000 km, whichever occurs first, your vehicle will be repaired for you at no charge.

This special policy applies only to repairs requiring cylinder head gasket replacement as a result of cylinder head gasket failure that results in an engine coolant leak. It does not cover engine damage from continuing to operate the engine in an overheated condition after loss of coolant.

This is not a recall campaign. Do not take your vehicle to your GM dealer as a result of this letter unless you believe that your vehicle has the condition as described above. Keep this letter with your other important glove box literature for future reference.

If you have already paid for some or all of the cost to have the cylinder head gasket replaced and in-service time was less than seven (7) years and 160,000 km, you should contact your GM dealer. You may be eligible for partial or complete reimbursement of costs if genuine GM parts were used in the repair. If the work was done by someone other than a GM dealership the amount of reimbursement may be limited to the amount the repair would have cost GM to have it completed by a GM dealership. Please provide your dealer with your original paid receipts or invoices verifying the repair, the amount charged, proof of payment, and the date of payment of those charges by March 1, 1997.

Repairs and adjustments qualifying under this Special Policy coverage must be performed by your GM dealer.

The same head gasket problem has been reported by owners of 1994–95 models; GM hasn't formally included them in this program yet, probably because most vehicles may still be covered by the base warranty. Whatever the reason, remember this: GM IS 100% RESPONSIBLE FOR REPAIRING THIS DEFECT.

• Troubleshooting tips on silencing rear shock noise and rear seatback rattles and squeaks are available. **1996–97**—Coolant odor or leakage may occur at the joint where the radiator outlet pipe is connected to the coolant pump cover or at the joint between the cooling system air bleed pipe and the coolant outlet. **1997**—A low-engine-coolant light may come on to signal that the cooling system surge tank is defective. **All models/years**—Squeaking front brakes can be silenced by replacing the semi-metallic front brake linings with quieter linings (#12321424). The new linings will be 20 percent less durable (DSB 86-5-20). • A rotten-egg odor coming from the exhaust is probably caused by a malfunctioning catalytic converter; this repair is covered by GM's emissions warranty.

Cavalier, Sunbird, Sunfire Profile

	1990	1991	1992	1993	1994	1995	1996	1997
Cost Price ($)								
Cavalier	9,994	10,252	11,046	10,667	11082	12,030	12,872	13,357
Conv.	—	16,929	17,720	17,110	17,470	17,695	17,995	18,265
Z24	13,115	13,700	14,710	14,215	14,965	14,295	15,490	15,760
Sunfire	—	—	—	—	—	12,989	13,514	14,079
Used Values ($)								
Cavalier ↑	3,000	4,000	4,500	5,500	6,500	8,500	9,500	11,000
Cavalier ↓	2,500	3,000	4,000	4,500	5,500	7,500	8,500	10,000
Conv. ↑	—	6,500	7,000	8,000	9,000	11,500	13,000	14,500
Conv. ↓	—	5,500	6,000	6,500	8,000	10,000	11,000	13,000
Z24 ↑	5,000	5,500	6,500	7,500	8,500	9,500	10,500	12,000
Z24 ↓	4,000	4,500	5,500	6,500	7,500	8,000	9,500	11,000
Sunfire ↑	—	—	—	—	—	9,000	10,000	11,500
Sunfire ↓	—	—	—	—	—	8,000	9,000	10,000
Extended Warranty	Y	Y	Y	Y	Y	Y	Y	Y
Secret Warranty	Y	Y	Y	Y	Y	Y	Y	Y
Reliability	①	①	②	②	②	③	③	③
Air conditioning	③	③	③	③	③	③	④	④
Body integrity	①	①	①	②	②	②	②	②
Braking system	①	①	①	②	②	②	②	②
Electrical system	①	①	①	②	②	②	②	②
Engines	②	②	②	②	②	②	③	④
Exhaust/Converter	②	②	③	③	③	④	④	⑤
Fuel system	①	①	①	③	③	③	④	④
Manual transmission	③	③	③	③	③	④	④	④
- automatic	①	①	①	②	②	②	③	③
Rust/Paint	①	①	①	②	②	②	②	②
Steering	②	②	②	②	②	③	③	④
Suspension	①	①	①	②	②	③	③	④
Crash Safety								
Cavalier 4d	②	⑤	⑤	②	②	—	③	④
Side Impact								
Cavalier 4d	—	—	—	—	—	—	—	①

Note: NHTSA says Sunbird/Sunfire safety ratings should be identical to the Cavalier's score.

GENERAL MOTORS/SUZUKI

Metro and Swift

Rating: Above Average (1995–97); Average (1990–94); Below Average (1987–89). Look at the redesigned '95 version for a new body style, standard dual airbags, and a peppier 4-cylinder engine. The convertible version packs plenty of fun and performance into a reasonably priced subcompact body. **Maintenance/Repair costs**: Higher than average. Repairs are dealer dependent. **Parts**: Expensive; sometimes drivetrain and body components are back-ordered several weeks.

Technical Data

ENGINES	Liters/CID	HP	MPG	Model Years
OHC I-3 2 bbl.	1.0/61	46–48	42–55	1985–88
OHC I-3T FI	1.0/61	70	35–39	1987–88
OHC I-3 FI	1.0/61	49–55	44–49	1989–98
OHC I-4 FI	1.3/79	70–79	30–42	1995–98

Strengths and weaknesses: Unlike Ford's discontinued Festiva and Aspire imports, GM's Suzuki-based mini-cars are still being churned out in their Alliston, Ontario, manufacturing plant. These tiny, economical, 3- and 4-cylinder, front-wheel drive, hatchback econoboxes, equipped with either a manual or an automatic transmission, offer impressive all-round performance and economy, particularly for urban dwellers. In fact, these little squirts should be considered primarily city vehicles due to their small size, small tires, low ground clearance, and high-speed average handling. Interior garnishing is decent but plain and there's plenty of room for two passengers, with four fitting in without too much discomfort. The turbocharged convertible model is an excellent choice for high-performance thrills in an easy-to-handle ragtop.

Mechanically speaking, the GM-Suzuki partnership hasn't hurt quality control. These cars have a better-than-average repair history and body components are well assembled and very durable. The only trouble spots indicated so far concern: excessive oil consumption after the fourth year of service; automatic transmission and differential failures around 80,000 km; electrical system shorts; faulty cooling system; premature brake, clutch, and exhaust-system wear out; and minor fuel supply malfunctions. Fogging of the side windows and windshield due to inadequate heat distribution is a common complaint.

Owners of 1990–94 models report that hatches vibrate when windows are open and the rear hatch seems to want to open on its own; push buttons for the lights and wipers tend to fly off the dashboard; fuel economy is often exaggerated by dealers; front metallic brake pads are noisy and the front discs warp easily; and the fuel injection system performs poorly. Owners also point out that the tiny radiator can't stand up to the rigors of northern climates. If it's not checked, the cooling system will eventually fail, causing great damage to the aluminum engine. For '95 and later versions, the chief complaints concern premature clutch and brake wear, paint peeling, early rusting, and sloppy body assembly.

Safety summary/recalls: Side window defogging is slow and sometimes inadequate. **Recalls: 1986**—The push-pull headlight switch will be replaced at no charge. **1989–1991 Geo Metro and Sprint**—Takata seatbelt will be replaced. **1989–93**—Hood may fly up when car is in motion. **1995**—Faulty rear brake drums may lead to sudden wheel separation. **1995 Metro hatchbacks without ABS**—Faulty rear brake drums could cause wheel separation.

Secret Warranties/Service Tips

1989–92—Stalling or loss of power shortly after starting may be due to high pressure in the hydraulic lifter assemblies. **1991–92**—Excessive vehicle vibration when the vehicle is in Reverse is most likely due to poor insulation between the engine/transaxle assembly and the vehicle's chassis. Install upgraded engine mounts. **All models/years**—Paint delamination, fading, peeling, hazing, and "microchecking": See page 95.

Metro, Swift Profile

	1990	1991	1992	1993	1994	1995	1996	1997
Cost Price ($)								
Metro	6,551	7,361	7,585	7,296	7,791	9,481	9,988	10,185
Swift	6,659	6,669	7,184	7,599	7,864	9,029	9,359	9,359
Used Values ($)								
Metro ↑	2,800	3,300	3,800	4,300	5,000	6,500	7,400	7,900
Metro ↓	2,000	2,800	2,800	3,300	4,000	5,500	6,400	7,200
Swift ↑	3,000	3,500	4,000	4,600	5,200	6,700	7,700	8,200
Swift ↓	2,200	2,700	3,100	3,600	4,200	5,700	6,700	7,400
Extended Warranty	Y	Y	N	N	N	N	N	N
Secret Warranty	Y	Y	Y	Y	Y	Y	Y	N
Reliability	③	④	④	⑤	⑤	⑤	⑤	⑤
Air conditioning	②	②	②	②	③	③	③	③
Body integrity	①	①	②	②	③	③	④	④
Braking system	①	②	②	③	③	③	④	④
Electrical system	②	②	②	②	②	③	③	④
Engines	②	②	②	②	②	②	④	⑤
Exhaust/Converter	①	②	②	③	④	⑤	⑤	⑤
Fuel system	②	③	③	③	③	④	④	⑤
Ignition system	③	③	④	④	③	④	④	④
Manual transmission	④	④	⑤	⑤	④	⑤	⑤	⑤
- automatic	③	③	④	⑤	④	④	④	⑤
Rust/Paint	③	③	④	④	⑤	⑤	⑤	⑤
Steering	④	④	④	⑤	⑤	⑤	⑤	⑤
Suspension	④	④	④	⑤	⑤	⑤	⑤	⑤
Crash Safety	①	⑤	⑤	⑤	⑤	④	④	④

HONDA

Rating: Recommended (1993–97); Above Average (1992); Average (1989–91); Below Average (1984–88). The Si was dropped in '95. Depreciation is so minimal that, if you want to get a good buy at a fair price, the '93 is your best bet. **Maintenance/Repair costs**: Average. Repairs can be carried out by independent garages, but the 16-valve engine's complexity means that dealer servicing is a must. To avoid costly engine repairs, owners must check the engine timing belt every 2 years/40,000 miles and replace it every 80,000 miles ($300). **Parts**: Parts are a bit more expensive than most other cars in this class, but they aren't hard to find.

Technical Data

ENGINES	Liters/CID	HP	MPG	Model Years
		Civic		
OHC I-4 3 bbl.	1.3/81	60	33–37	1985–87
OHC I-4 3 bbl.	1.5/91	76	27–31	1985–87
OHC I-4 FI	1.5/91	91	28–32	1986–87
OHC I-4 FI	1.5/91	70	32–36	1988–91
OHC I-4 FI	1.5/91	92	28–33	1988–91
OHC I-4 FI	1.6/91	105–108	25–31	1988–91
OHC I-4 FI	1.5/91	70	34–38	1992–95
OHC I-4 FI	1.5/91	92	39–45	1992–95
OHC I-4 FI	1.5/91	102	29–35	1992–95
OHC I-4 FI	1.6/97	125	26–33	1992–95
OHC I-4 FI	1.6/97	106	27–34	1996–98
OHC I-4 FI	1.6/97	115	30–37	1996–98
OHC I-4 FI	1.6/97	127	26–34	1996–98
		CRX		
OHC I-4 3 bbl.	1.5/91	58	33–37	1985–87
OHC I-4 3 bbl.	1.5/91	76	27–32	1985–87
OHC I-4 FI	1.5/91	91	36–31	1985–87
OHC I-4 FI	1.5/91	62	37–45	1988–91
OHC I-4 FI	1.5/91	92	29–35	1988–91
OHC I-4 FI	1.6/97	105–108	25–31	1988–91
		del Sol		
OHC I-4 FI	1.5/91	102	28–34	1993–95
OHC I-4 FI	1.6/97	125	26–31	1993–95
DOHC VTEC	1.6/97	160	23–27	1994–96

Strengths and weaknesses: The quintessential econobox, Civics have distinguished themselves by providing sports car acceleration and handling with excellent fuel economy and quality control that's better than what American automakers can deliver. Other advantages: a roomy, practical trunk and simple, inexpensive maintenance.

CRXs are a sportier version of the Civic, equipped with a more refined 1.5L and 1.6L engine and stiffer suspension. They give improved handling at the expense of fuel economy, interior space, and a comfortable ride. They also require valve adjustments every 20,000 miles.

Some other Civic disadvantages: power steering isn't offered with the manual 5-speed transmission; there's no ABS available; you won't find much backseat headroom; engine noise may seem excessive when under load; and the Civic's high resale value means bargains are rare.

1984–92 Civics suffer from failing camshafts/crankshafts and prematurely worn piston rings. The 12-valve engine is prone to valve problems and is costly to repair. Early fuel-injection units were also problematic until the system was redesigned in 1988. Manual transmission shifter bushings need frequent replacement and the automatic version needs careful attention once the 5-year/100,000 mile point has been reached.

The 1988 redesign improved handling and increased interior room. There isn't a great deal of torque with the 1.6L engine below 3,500 rpm, however, and serious generic problems present since the car's debut continue to plague the later models. First, the front brakes continue to wear out quickly and are often noisy when applied, causing excessive steering wheel vibration. Premature constant-velocity-joint and boot wear on all cars is another problem area that needs careful inspection before purchasing. The rack-and-pinion steering assembly often needs replacement around the five-year mark. There have also been reports of premature clutch wear with 4X4 Civics.

A large number of 1988–91 Honda Civics and CRXs have faulty distributor igniters. When the igniter fails, the car stalls, and it may be impossible to restart. The only remedy is to call a tow truck and replace the distributor.

1993–97 Civics continue to be both rugged and reliable. The few problems that are reported concern front brake noise and premature wear, AC malfunctions, and minor body faults.

What are minor body faults with recent models turn into major rust problems with older Civics, where simple surface rust rapidly turns into perforations. The underbody is also prone to corrosion, which leads to the severe structural damage that compromises safety. The fuel tank, front suspension, and steering components, along with body attachment points, should be examined carefully in any Civic more than a decade old. Since 1988, Hondas have been much more resistant to rusting and overall body construction has been vastly improved. All hatchbacks let in too much wind/road noise due to poor sound insulation. Owners complain of water leaking into the trunk area through the rear taillights on the 1990 DX four-door sedan. The two-piece tailgate rattles and is complicated, for no good reason.

Safety summary/recalls: A Michigan jury awarded $1.25 million for a death caused by a lack of automatic door locks in a 1989 CRX Si. **Recalls: 1986–1991 Civic**—Takata seatbelts will be replaced. **1989–1991 CRX**—Takata seatbelts will be replaced. **1990**—Front windshield will be replaced. **1992–94**—The automatic transmission's shift lever position may not match the actual gear that's engaged. **1994**—Passenger-side airbag module may carry a defective inflator. **1993 Civic del Sol**—The automatic transmission's shift lever position may not match the actual gear that's engaged.

Secret Warranties/Service Tips

Civic/CRX/del Sol: 1988–90—Excessive valve noise will be corrected with a cam holder kit (#04101-PM3-308). • The dashboard cracks at the center bolt hole. **1988–91**—Distributor igniters are faulty (see "Strengths and weaknesses"). • New front brake pads that minimize front brake squeal are available for all Civic and CRX models. • A clicking noise heard while making a left or right turn may be caused by a worn outboard drive shaft joint. **1988–93**—A creaking noise coming from the window regulator can be corrected by installing an upgraded regulator spiral spring. **1989–91**—An oil leak around the spark plug well will be corrected with a cam holder kit (#04101-PM3-308). **1990**—The horn sounds by itself when the temperature drops. **1992**—A growling noise coming from the wheel area may mean that water has entered the wheel bearing through the hubcap and has damaged the bearing. • A steering wheel shake or body vibration when braking may indicate that the rear brake drum hub is crowned, causing excessive runout when the wheel nuts are torqued. Other factors could be a bent rear wheel, over-torqued wheel nuts, or excessive rust buildup on the brake rotors. **1992–97**—Water leaking into the footwell from under the corner of the dash can be stopped by applying sealer to the seam where the side panel joins the bulkhead.

```
Bulletin No.
92-050
Issue Date
FEB 3, 1997
Mode [NEW]
1992 and
LATER
CIVIC
Applicable To [NEW]
ALL
File Under
BODY
Water Leak From Seam Under Corner of Dash
(Supersedes 92-050, dated May 15, 1995)


SYMPTOM
A water leak into the footwell from under the left or right corner of the dash.

PROBABLE CAUSE
Not enough sealer on the cowl side of the panel-to-bulkhead seam.

CORRECTIVE ACTION
[NEW]
Apply sealer to the seams where the side panel joins the bulkhead. Refer to section 20 of the appropriate Service Manual for
removal and reinstallation of body components.
[NEW]
1. Look for a leak from the lower corners of the dashboard while an assistant runs water over the windshield and cowl. Confirm
   which side is leaking.
[NEW]
2. Remove the windshield wiper arms and the cowl cover.
[NEW]
3. Remove the side sill, the inner fender, and the front fender from the side that is leaking.

4. Insert a scraping tool through the access holes and remove all loose sealer. For better visibility, shine a flashlight through the holes.
```

Honda says this leak can be repaired within 90 minutes and is eligible for "goodwill" warranty consideration.

• An abnormally long crank time before the car starts may be caused by a leaking check valve inside the fuel pump. **1993**—Poor AM reception or a popping sound coming from the speakers is likely due to a poor ground connection between the antenna collar and car body. **1995–97**—In a settlement with the Environmental Protection Agency, Honda paid fines totaling $17.1 million and extended its emissions warranty on 1.6 million 1995–97 vehicles to 14 years or 150,000 miles. This means that costly engine components and exhaust system parts like catalytic converters will be replaced free of charge, as long as the 14-year/150,000-mile limit hasn't been exceeded. Additionally, the automaker will provide a full engine check and emissions-related repairs at 50,000 to 75,000 miles and will give free tune-ups at 75,000 to 150,000 miles. It is estimated the free check-ups, repairs, and tune-ups will cost Honda over $250 million. The story of the settlement was first reported on page 6 of the June 15, 1998, edition of *Automotive News*. **1996**—A clunking noise in the front suspension can be fixed by installing upgraded upper arm flange bolts.

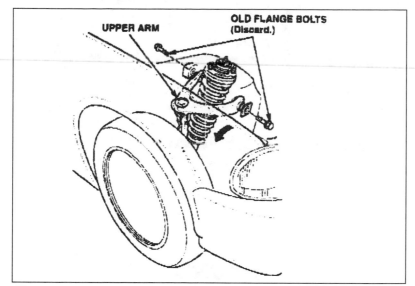

Honda's service bulletin specifically singles out this repair as also eligible for "goodwill" consideration. Refer to "Defect Code 042" and ask Honda to pay the tab.

All models/years—Most Honda DSBs allow for special warranty consideration on a "goodwill" basis even after the warranty has expired or the car has changed hands. Referring to this euphemism will increase your chances of getting some kind of refund for repairs that are obviously related to a factory defect.

Civic, CRX, del Sol Profile								
	1990	**1991**	**1992**	**1993**	**1994**	**1995**	**1996**	**1997**
Cost Price ($)								
Civic	6,880	7,155	8,190	8,730	9,750	10,130	10,360	10,945
Si/EX	10,490	10,555	11,990	12,530	13,520	13,920	15,330	15,645
CRX/del Sol	9,390	9,405	—	13,530	14,450	15,160	15,475	15,475
Used Values ($)								
Civic ↑	5,000	5,500	6,000	7,000	7,500	8,500	9,000	9,500
Civic ↓	4,500	5,000	5,500	6,000	7,000	7,500	8,500	9,000
Si/EX ↑	7,500	8,500	9,000	10,000	11,000	12,000	13,000	14,000
Si/EX ↓	6,500	7,500	8,500	9,000	10,000	11,000	12,000	13,000
CRX/del Sol ↑	7,000	7,500	—	9,500	11,000	12,000	13,000	14,000
CRX/del Sol ↓	5,500	7,000	—	8,500	9,500	11,000	12,000	13,000
Extended Warranty	Y	Y	N	N	N	N	N	N
Secret Warranty	Y	Y	Y	Y	Y	Y	Y	Y
Reliability	③	③	③	④	⑤	⑤	⑤	⑤
Air conditioning	❷	❷	③	③	④	④	⑤	⑤
Body integrity	❶	❷	❷	③	③	③	③	④
Braking system	❷	❷	③	③	③	④	⑤	⑤

Electrical system	②	③	③	③	④	④	④	⑤
Engines	③	③	③	③	③	⑤	⑤	⑤
Exhaust/Converter	②	②	③	③	④	⑤	⑤	⑤
Fuel system	②	③	④	④	④	④	⑤	⑤
Ignition system	②	③	③	④	④	④	④	⑤
Manual transmission	③	③	③	③	④	④	⑤	⑤
- automatic	③	③	③	③	④	⑤	⑤	⑤
Rust/Paint	②	③	③	③	⑤	⑤	⑤	⑤
Steering	③	③	③	④	④	④	④	⑤
Suspension	③	③	③	④	④	④	④	⑤
Crash Safety								
Civic 2d	⑤	⑤	⑤	⑤	⑤	④	④	④
Civic 4d	❶	❷	❷	❷	❷	③	⑤	④
CRX	⑤	⑤	⑤	—	—	—	—	—
Side impact								
Civic 4d	—	—	—	—	—	—	—	③

HYUNDAI

Accent

Rating: Above Average (1995–97). Lots of standard features. **Maintenance/Repair costs**: Higher than average. Repairs are dealer dependent. **Parts**: Expensive and not easily found. Dealer servicing has been substandard in the past. Hyundai says that the timing chain should be replaced every 60,000 miles.

Technical Data

ENGINES	Liters/CID	HP	MPG	Model Years
OHC I-4 FI	1.5L/91	92	28–38	1995–98
DOHC I-4 FI	1.5L/91	105	26–35	1996–97

Strengths and weaknesses: An upgraded Excel masquerading as an Accent, this front-drive, 4-cylinder sedan retains most of the Excel's underpinnings, while dropping the Mitsubishi powerplant in favor of a new home-grown 1.5L 4-cylinder. It's built better than the old Excel, though: upgraded, smoother-shifting automatic transmission; stiffer, better-performing suspension; stronger and quieter-running engine; optional dual airbags; and ABS.

Excels have always had a checkered reliability history, so the Accent has a lot of bad karma to overcome, such as mediocre body assembly and poorly applied paint. Past problem areas include the engine cooling system and cylinder head gaskets, transmission, wheel bearings, fuel system, and electrical components, as well as premature front brake wear and excessive noise when braking.

Dealer service bulletins: **1995**—The exhaust system has a tendency to release a rotten-egg odor. • Troubleshooting tips for locating and plugging interior water leaks. **1996**—Exhaust rattling. • Shift quality improvements. • Sticking headlight flasher switch.

Safety summary/recalls: Horn controls may be hard to find in an emergency, rear head restraints appear to be too low to protect occupants, and rear seatbelt configuration complicates the installation of a child safety seat. **Recalls**: **1995**—The ECM wiring harness may short on vehicles equipped with a manual transaxle. **1996–97**—Faulty wiper motor.

Secret Warranties/Service Tips

1995–96—Harsh shifting may be fixed by installing an upgraded Transaxle Control Module (TCM). • Clutch drag may be caused by a restriction in the hydraulic line from grease used during the assembly of the clutch master assembly. **All models/years**—Apparent slow acceleration upon cold starts is dismissed as normal.

Accent Profile

	1995	1996	1997
Cost Price ($)			
L	9,674	8,690	9,014
Sedan	10,834	11,270	11,819
Used Values ($)			
L ↑	6,000	7,000	7,500
L ↓	5,000	6,500	7,000
Sedan ↑	7,000	8,000	8,500
Sedan ↓	6,000	7,000	7,500
Extended Warranty	Y	Y	Y
Secret Warranty	N	N	N
Reliability	④	④	⑤
Crash Safety	—	③	③

Excel

Rating: Below Average (1992–94); Not Recommended (1986–91). **Maintenance/Repair costs**: Higher than average. Repairs are dealer dependent. To avoid costly engine repairs, check the engine timing belt every 2 years/40,000 miles. **Parts**: Expensive and not easily found.

Technical Data

ENGINES	Liters/CID	HP	MPG	Model Years
OHC I-4 2 bbl.	1.5/90	68	26–31	1986–89
OHC I-4 FI	1.5/90	81	28–33	1990–94

Strengths and weaknesses: Replaced by the 1995 Accent, the Excel is a low-tech and low-quality economy car that was orphaned in 1995. Resale prices are low, but these cars are no bargain in the long run. Although overall comfort and handling are passable, the engine is distinctly short on power and the carburetor provides uneven throttle response, especially when the car is cold, resulting in difficult starts. Poor interior ventilation, with chronic window fogging and poor defrosting, is particularly irritating.

On early models, likely problem areas are defective constant velocity joints, water pumps, oil pan gaskets, oil pressure switches, front struts, and heat exchange under dash, as well as a leaking head gasket. Excels made after 1989 are noted for their noisy automatic transmissions and engines that fail to start when the weather turns cold or wet. Other problem areas are faulty radiator hoses, alternators, Hyundai radios, and wiper motors. Owners also complain of premature brake wear and temperamental carburetors, electrical problems, poor engine performance, and premature rusting due to poor-quality body parts and paint. Body construction is sloppy, giving rise to wind/water leaks, rattles, and breakage. Mufflers last a little over two years.

Dealer service bulletins: **1993**—Harsh shifting with the automatic transmission when accelerating or coming to a stop. • Excessive disc brake noise. • Engine has difficulty reaching recommended operating temperature (MPI fault code #21). • Low fuel pressure. **1994**—Tips for troubleshooting water leaks into the interior.

Safety summary/recalls: **Recalls**: **1986**—A defective brake pedal cotter pin will be changed. **1986–87**—Excessive brake fade can be improved by installing upgraded metallic pads. **1986–89**—Cruise control operation is erratic. • A malfunctioning emission control system could cause an engine compartment fire. • Insufficient gear lubrication could cause drive wheels to lock. **1988–89**—A defective heater stem assembly could allow hot coolant leakage. **1990**—Front wheel hub nut lockwasher could crack, causing a loss of vehicle control. **1990–94**—In frontal crashes, excessive fuel spillage could pose a fire hazard. **1994**—A short circuit in the crank-angle sensor could cause sudden stalling.

Secret Warranties/Service Tips

1990—A fifth-gear noise can be eliminated by replacing the third- and fourth-shift forks and synchronizer hub and sleeve. • Cranking with no spark may be due to a defective noise filter located between the ignition coil and tachometer. **1990–94**—Difficult-to-engage Reverse gear needs an upgraded part. **1991**—Stalling when shifting into gear immediately after starting a cold engine may be corrected by installing Hyundai's Cold Start Enrichment Kit (#39901-24Q00D). **1994**—A harsh downshift usually means that the accelerator switch is out of adjustment. • A rear suspension groaning noise heralds the need to install upgraded shock absorbers. • A rear suspension squeaking noise can be silenced by re-torquing the rear suspension attachment nuts.

Excel Profile

	1988	1989	1990	1991	1992	1993	1994
Cost Price ($)							
Base	5,520	5,774	7,244	7,965	8,390	8,634	9,140
Used Values ($)							
Base ↑	1,300	1,700	1,900	2,300	3,000	4,000	5,000
Base ↓	1,000	1,300	1,700	1,900	2,500	3,000	4,000
Extended Warranty	Y	Y	Y	Y	Y	Y	Y
Secret Warranty	N	N	N	N	N	N	N
Reliability	②	②	②	②	②	②	②
Air conditioning	②	②	②	③	③	③	④
Body integrity	②	②	②	②	②	②	②
Braking system	②	②	②	②	②	②	②
Electrical system	②	②	②	②	②	②	②
Engines	①	①	②	③	③	③	③
Exhaust/Converter	①	②	③	③	③	③	③
Fuel system	②	②	②	③	③	③	③
Ignition system	②	②	②	③	③	③	③
Manual transmission	②	②	②	②	②	②	②
- automatic	②	③	③	③	④	④	④
Rust/Paint	②	②	②	②	②	③	③
Steering	③	③	③	④	③	④	④
Suspension	③	③	③	③	③	③	③
Crash Safety	②	②	②	①	⑤	⑤	⑤

Elantra

Rating: Above Average (1996–97); Average (1991–95). Way overpriced: between 1991 and 1996, the base MSRP rose a whopping $5,000. There's also a $1,000–$3,500 difference between the high-end and entry-level models. **Maintenance/Repair costs**: Higher than average; repairs are dealer dependent. **Parts**: Higher-than-average cost, but not hard to find.

Technical Data

ENGINES	Liters/CID	HP	MPG	Model Years
DOHC I-4 FI	1.6/97	113	22–29	1992–95
DOHC I-4 FI	1.8/110	124	21–27	1993–96
DOHC I-4 FI	1.8/110	130	22–27	1996–98

Strengths and weaknesses: This conservatively styled "high-end" sedan is only marginally larger than the Excel, but its overall reliability is much better. It's a credible alternative to the Toyota Corolla,

Nissan Sentra, and Saturn, and the redesigned 1996–97 versions
actually narrow the handling and performance gap with the Honda
Civic. The 16-valve 1.6L 4-cylinder is smooth, efficient, and adequate when mated to the 5-speed manual transmission. It's not very
quiet, however. The smooth ride causes excessive body lean when
cornering, but overall handling is fairly good, due mainly to the
Elantra's longer wheelbase and more sophisticated suspension.

The 4-speed automatic transmission robs the base engine of at
least 10 horses. Brakes are adequate though sometimes difficult to
modulate. Conservative styling makes the Elantra look a bit like an
underfed Accord, but there's plenty of room for four average-sized
occupants. Tall drivers might find rearward seat travel insufficient,
making head room a bit tight.

1996–97 Elantras are the better buy due to their additional interior room, improved performance and handling, and quieter-
running engine. Moreover, the Elantra was first offered in a wagon
in 1996–97. Still, passing power with the automatic gearbox is per-
petually unimpressive and the trunk's narrow opening makes for
difficult loading.

Surprisingly for a Hyundai, owners report few serious defects.
Nevertheless, be on the lookout for body deficiencies (fit, finish,
and assembly), harsh shifting with the automatic transmission, oil
leaks, and brake defects.

Dealer service bulletins: **1993**—Harsh shifting with the automatic
transmission when accelerating or coming to a stop. • Excessive disc
brake noise. • Engine has difficulty reaching recommended operating temperature (MPI fault code #21). • Low fuel pressure. • Oil
leaks between the oil filter and mounting bracket. • Wheel cover
discoloration. **1994**—Excessive front brake noise and premature
wear. • Rear speaker whine. • Harsh automatic transmission engagement. • Slow windshield defrosting and defogging. **1995**—The
exhaust system releases a rotten-egg odor. • Rear suspension
squeaking noises. • An inaccurate fuel gauge. • Trunk water leaks
and troubleshooting tips for locating and plugging other interior
water leaks. **1996–1997**—Automatic transmission won't engage
Overdrive. • Clutch pedal squeaking. • Tapping noise coming from
the passenger-side dash panel/engine compartment area. •
Exhaust system buzz. • Improved shifting into all gears. • Improved
shifting into Reverse. • Clutch drag.

Safety summary/recalls: **NHTSA probes**: **1996**—Windshield wipers
fail. **Recalls**: **1994–95**—Driver's-side airbag could be defective or the
warning light could illuminate unnecessarily. **1996–97**—A faulty
wiper motor will be replaced.

Secret Warranties/Service Tips

1991–92—A harsh shift when coming to a stop or upon acceleration could be due to a misadjusted accelerator switch TCU. **1992**—Oil leaking from between the oil filter and mounting bracket could be caused by an overly wide mounting surface on the bracket. Correct this by replacing the bracket. **1992–94**—Hyundai has a field fix for manual transaxle gear clash/grind (DSB 9440-004). **1992–94**—The difficult-to-engage Reverse gear needs an upgraded part. **1994**—Rear speaker whine can be stopped by installing an improved noise reduction filter. **1996**—A cold exhaust system buzz can be silenced by installing a sub-muffler resonator. • Improved shifting into all gears can be accomplished by installing an upgraded transaxle control module (TCM). **1996–97**—A tip on eliminating clutch pedal squeaking is offered. • Tips on eliminating clutch drag are offered. **All models/years**—Hyundai has a new brake pad kit (#58101-28A00) that the company says will eliminate squeaks and squeals during light brake application. Hyundai also suggests that you replace the oil pump assembly if the engine rpm increases as the automatic transmission engages abruptly during a cold start.

Elantra Profile

	1992	1993	1994	1995	1996	1997
Cost Price ($)						
Base	11,155	11,749	12,674	13,149	13,434	13,659
Used Values ($)						
Base ↑	4,000	5,500	6,500	7,500	8,500	9,500
Base ↓	3,000	4,500	5,500	6,500	7,500	8,500
Extended Warranty	Y	Y	Y	N	N	N
Secret Warranty	N	N	N	N	Y	N
Reliability	③	③	③	④	④	④
Air conditioning	③	③	④	④	④	⑤
Automatic transmission	❷	❷	❷	❷	③	③
Body integrity	❷	❷	❷	③	③	③
Braking system	❷	③	③	③	③	③
Electrical system	❷	❷	❷	③	③	③
Engines	④	⑤	⑤	⑤	⑤	⑤
Exhaust/Converter	③	④	⑤	⑤	⑤	⑤
Fuel system	③	③	③	④	④	⑤
Ignition system	④	③	③	④	④	⑤
Rust/Paint	④	④	④	④	⑤	⑤
Steering	④	④	⑤	⑤	⑤	⑤
Suspension	④	④	④	④	④	⑤
Crash Safety	❶	❶	❶	❶	③	③

MAZDA

323, GLC, Protegé

Rating: Recommended (1996–97); Above Average (1991–95); Average (1985–90). If you can't find a reasonably priced 323 or Protegé, look for a Ford Escort or Tracer instead—they're basically Mazdas disguised as Fords. The redesigned 1995–96 Protegé offers fresh styling, a larger wheelbase, standard dual airbags, and a new 4-banger. Along with the 1997 versions, which were mostly carried over unchanged with a slightly restyled grille and headlights and interior refinements, they are excellent used-car buys. Plus, they should be plentiful at bargain prices as they come off their two- and three-year leases within the next six months. **Maintenance/Repair costs**: Higher than average. Repairs are dealer dependent. To avoid costly engine repairs, check the engine timing belt every 2 years/40,000 miles ($200). **Parts**: Expensive and not easily found outside the dealer network.

Technical Data

ENGINES	Liters/CID	HP	MPG	Model Years
OHC I-4 FI	1.6/97	82	24–33	1986–94
DOHC I-4 FI	1.5/91	92	25–38	1995–98
DOHC I-4T FI	1.6/97	132	19–23	1988–89
OHC I-4 FI	1.8/112	103	24–31	1990–94
DOHC I-4 FI	1.8/112	125	25–28	1990–94
DOHC I-4 FI	1.8/110	122	23–31	1995–98

Strengths and weaknesses: The GLC was replaced by the 323 in 1986. Both Mazdas are peppy performers with a manual transmission hooked to the base engine. The automatic gearbox, however, produces lethargic acceleration that makes highway passing a bit chancy. Handling and fuel economy are fairly good for a car design this old. However, overall durability is not as good as that of more recent Mazda designs, beginning with the 1991 323/Protegé, which was also sold as the Ford Escort. Catalytic converters plug up easily and other pollution-control components have been troublesome. Automatic transmission defects, air conditioner breakdowns, and engine oil leaks are also commonplace. Oil leaks in the power steering pump may also be a problem. GLCs rust quickly, especially the rocker panels, door bottoms, hood, and rear hatch. A careful corrosion inspection is a must.

The fuel-injected 1.6L engine is a better performer than the 1.5L, but you also get excessive engine and exhaust noise. Stay away from the 3-speed automatic transmission. The car's small engine can't handle the extra burden without cutting fuel economy and performance. Both models are surprisingly roomy, but the Protegé's trunk is small for a sedan.

The 1985–90 models offer mediocre reliability. Owners report hard starting in cold weather, in addition to automatic transmission problems and electrical-system failures. The engine camshaft assembly and belt pulley often need replacing around 80,000 miles. Clutch failure and exhaust-system rust-out are also common. Other areas of concern are constant velocity joint failures, rack-and-pinion steering wear out, and front brake wear. The front brakes wear quickly due to poor-quality brake pads and seizure of the calipers in their housings. Check for disc scoring on the front brakes. Stay away from models equipped with a turbocharger—few mechanics want to bother repairing it or hunting for parts. Many owners report premature paint peeling.

The 1991–95 models are quite reliable and reasonably-priced; however, the '96 and '97 versions are *la crème de la crème*. When the 323 was dropped at the end of 1994, the Protegé became Mazda's least-costly model and underwent a major redesign the next year. It shares platforms with the Escort and Tracer, but keeps its own sheet metal, engine, and interior styling. Powered by a standard, fuel-efficient, 1.5L engine mated to a manual 5-speed transmission, the Protegé is one of the most responsive and roomiest small cars around.

Nevertheless, these cars aren't perfect and owners report problems with weak rear defrosting, rough second gear engagement, engine stalling, noisy suspension, AC failures, and numerous body defects, including wind and water leaks into the interior, paint defects, and power mirror failures.

Dealer service bulletins: **1995**—A tapping, cracking noise that comes from the B- and C-pillars. • Excessive blower motor and brush noise. • Heater and AC unit noise after long storage. • No sound from audio. • A bump sound when opening the sunroof. • Detached sunroof tilt switch knob. • Power outside mirror glass vibration. • Fuse block cover and glove box hinge breakage. • A slightly off-center steering wheel.

Safety summary/recalls: **Recalls**: **1992–93**—Protegé may not meet regulations relative to child restraint tether anchorages. **1995 Protegé with 1.5L engine**—The engine valve springs are defective.

Secret Warranties/Service Tips

1990—Cold weather stalling usually requires the replacement of the ECU, which is under the emissions warranty. **1990–91**—Rough idle or vibration in drive may require changing the No. 1 and No. 4 engine mounts and the radiator lower mounts. **1990–92**—Noise coming from the front of the car when turning may be due to dirt accumulation in the top strut mount bushing. **1990–94**—Clutch squealing is fixed by installing an upgraded clutch cushioning plate. **1995–96**—A horn noise heard from the exhaust will be silenced with a special tail pipe tip furnished by Mazda under its warranty (see below).

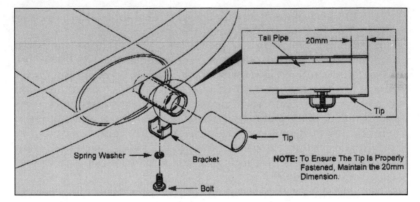

323, GLC, Protegé Profile

	1990	1991	1992	1993	1994	1995	1996	1997
Cost Price ($)								
323	7,913	8,243	8,439	9,219	10,220	—	—	—
Protegé	11,103	11,063	11,769	12,374	10,570	14,010	13,720	14,170
Used Values ($)								
323 ↑	4,000	4,500	5,000	6,000	6,500	—	—	—
323 ↓	3,000	4,000	4,500	5,000	5,500	—	—	—
Protegé ↑	5,000	5,700	6,500	7,000	7,300	9,000	10,000	11,000
Protegé ↓	4,000	4,700	5,500	6,500	6,300	8,000	9,000	10,000
Extended Warranty	Y	N	N	N	N	N	N	N
Secret Warranty	N	N	N	N	N	N	N	N
Reliability	②	③	④	④	④	④	④	⑤
Air conditioning	②	②	③	③	④	⑤	⑤	⑤
Body integrity	③	③	③	③	③	③	③	③
Braking system	①	②	②	②	③	③	③	③
Electrical system	①	②	③	③	③	④	④	④
Engines	③	③	③	④	④	④	④	④
Exhaust/Converter	②	②	②	③	③	⑤	⑤	⑤
Fuel system	②	③	③	④	④	⑤	⑤	⑤
Ignition system	③	④	④	④	④	④	⑤	⑤
Manual transmission	④	④	④	④	④	④	⑤	⑤
- automatic	②	②	③	③	④	⑤	⑤	⑤
Rust/Paint	②	②	②	③	③	③	③	④
Steering	③	③	③	④	④	④	④	④
Suspension	③	③	③	③	③	③	③	④
Crash Safety								
323	②	②	②	②	②	—	—	—
Protegé	—	⑤	⑤	⑤	⑤	—	②	②

NISSAN/DATSUN

Classic, Sentra

Rating: Recommended (1995–97); Above Average (1991–94); Average (1988–90); Not Recommended (1983–87). The redesigned '95 version offers fresh styling, a longer wheelbase, a peppier powerplant, standard dual airbags, and side-door beams. Many of these models should just be coming off their three-year leases and should be reasonably priced. **Maintenance/Repair costs**: Higher than average on early models, but anybody can repair these cars. **Parts**: Reasonably priced and easily obtainable.

Technical Data

ENGINES	Liters/CID	HP	MPG	Model Years
DOHC I-4D FI	1.7/103	55	32–37	1985
OHC I-4 2 bbl.	1.6/97	69	27–31	1985–86
OHC I-4 2 bbl.	1.6/97	70	26–31	1987
OHC I-4 FI	1.6/97	69	26–32	1987–88
OHC I-4 FI	1.6/97	90	26–31	1989–90
DOHC I-4 FI	1.6/97	110	27–32	1991–94
DOHC I-4 FI	1.6/97	115	27–38	1995–98
DOHC I-4 FI	2.0/122	140	23–27	1991–94
DOHC I-4 FI	2.0/121	140	22–26	1998

Strengths and weaknesses: Sentras aren't expensive to buy, they're relatively easy and inexpensive to repair, and they give good fuel economy. On the other hand, ride and handling are mediocre and build quality is spotty at best. Until 1991, mechanical and body components suffered from poor quality control, making these cars quite unreliable and sometimes expensive to repair. Clutches and exhaust systems were particularly problematic. The 1.6L engine is much more reliable, but even there the oil pressure switch may develop a leak that can lead to sudden oil loss and serious engine damage. Quality improved considerably with the '91 version, yet the vehicle's base price rose only marginally, making these later model years bargain buys for consumers looking for a reliable "beater."

1991–94 Sentras are a bit peppier and handle better, although they have their deficiencies, too, such as the motorized two-point front seatbelts on the sedans. Other owner-reported problems: faulty fuel tanks, leaking manual and automatic transmissions, a persistent rotten-egg smell, and noisy engine timing chains and front brakes. With the exception of the carburetor and electronic component failures, repairs are relatively simple to perform.

Redesigned for the 1995 model year, the Sentra sedan is a much improved, larger, and better-performing vehicle. The seatbelts are more comfortable and dual airbags are a standard feature. Most owner complaints concern minor problems like poor body fits, accessories that malfunction, and some stalling and hard starting.

Dealer service bulletins: 1995—AC compressor leaks or noise. •
Excessive brake noise. • C-pillar finisher lifting. • Faulty fuel gauge.
• Self-activating horn. • Poor driveability—Code 45. • Power door
locks that self-activate during periods of high heat or humidity. •
Power windows that won't roll up unless ignition key is cycled. •
Front window misalignment. • Front window won't go completely
down. • DSB NTB 95-052 addresses all the possible causes and reme-
dies for wind noise intruding into the passenger compartment.

Safety summary/recalls: Recalls: 1987–88—These model years have
been recalled because of cracked fuel tanks. 1987–91—Takata seatbelts will be replaced. 1990–91—Frayed front shoulder belts may
lead to improper retraction and inadequate protection. 1991–92—
Valve vacuum hose may loosen. 1995—ABS may be defective.
1995–98—Dealer will install a water diversion seal to prevent water
from entering the windshield wiper linkage.

Secret Warranties/Service Tips

1987–90—Manual transmission fluid leaks can be plugged with upgraded case
bolts. 1989—Install an AIV case assembly if the exhaust smells like rotten eggs.
• If the trunk lid is hard to close or latch, install an upgraded latch and a soft-
er weatherstrip. 1991–92—Noisy front brakes can be silenced by installing
upgraded, non-asbestos front disc brake pads (#41060-63Y90). • Timing chain
rattle may be caused by insufficient oil in the chain tensioner. You can correct
this by replacing the tensioner with a countermeasure part (#13070-53J03).
1991–93—The manual transmission has no Reverse gear—install a Nissan
upgrade kit. 1991–94—Stiffer trunk torsion bars will help keep the trunk lid
from falling. 1993–94—Brake and steering wheel vibrations are most likely
caused by excessive rotor thickness. 1994—Door hinges may have received
inadequate rust protection; Nissan will apply a sealer at no charge. 1995–96—
DSB #NTB96-001 gives lots of troubleshooting tips on finding and correcting
various squeaks and rattles. • Nissan has a special kit to improve brake pedal
feel, according to DSB #NTB96-041 (see below).

Classification:
BR96-004
Reference:
NTB96-041
Date:
May 22, 1996
1995–96 SENTRA/200SX BRAKE PEDAL FEEL IMPROVEMENT
APPLIED VEHICLE.
1995–96 Sentra/200SX (B14) equipped with NT, GA16DE engine, non-ABS

APPLIED VIN:
Smyrna Sentras built before 1N4AB41D1TC720407
Nismex Sentras but before 3N1AB41D9TL009605
Smyrna 200SX built before 1N4AB42D7TC506164

APPLIED DATE:
Smyrna Sentras built before October 16, 1995
Nismex Sentras built before December 13, 1995

SERVICE INFORMATION
Some 1995–96 non-ABS Sentras and/or 200SXs equipped with A/T, GA16DE engines, may experience a hard or low brake
pedal feel. Perform the following procedure to resolve this incident.

DESCRIPTION	PART #/PFP	QUANTITY
Tandem brake booster	47210-1M200	1
Front brake pad kit	41060-1N790	1
Tube assy – Front right	46240-4B010	1
Tube assy – Front left	46242-69Y00	1
Tube assy – Rear right	46282-4B010	1
Tube assy – Rear left	46283-4B010	1
Brake tube clip	46289-81L00	1

SERVICE PROCEDURE
Verify the incident then replace all of the components listed in the Parts Information table.

PARTS INFORMATION

OPERATION	OP CODE	FRT	SYMPTOM	DIAGNOSIS	PFP
RPL brake booster assy.	PF10AA	1.1 hrs.	DA	69	47210-1M200
RPL brake pipe(s)	PH10AA	1.3 hrs.			
RPL pad set – both sides	PB19AA	0.6 hrs.			

CLAIMS INFORMATION
Submit a Primary Part claim using the coding as shown.

Nissan's original warranty covers this correction.

Classic, Sentra Profile

	1990	1991	1992	1993	1994	1995	1996	1997
Cost Price ($)								
Base	8,383	9,099	9,645	10,310	11,924	11,389	11,904	11,919
Used Values ($)								
Base ↑	4,000	5,000	6,000	6,500	7,500	8,500	9,500	10,000
Base ↓	3,000	4,000	5,000	6,000	6,500	7,500	8,500	9,500
Extended Warranty	N	N	N	N	N	N	N	N
Secret Warranty	N	N	N	N	N	Y	Y	N

Reliability	③	③	④	④	④	⑤	⑤	⑤
Air conditioning	③	③	④	⑤	⑤	⑤	⑤	⑤
Body integrity	❷	❷	③	③	③	③	④	④
Braking system	❶	❷	❷	❷	❷	❷	❷	③
Electrical system	❷	❷	③	③	③	③	④	④
Engines	❷	③	④	④	④	⑤	⑤	⑤
Exhaust/Converter	❷	❷	❷	③	④	⑤	⑤	⑤
Fuel system	❷	③	③	❷	❷	③	③	④
Ignition system	❷	③	③	③	③	③	④	④
Manual transmission	⑤	⑤	⑤	⑤	⑤	⑤	⑤	⑤
- automatic	③	④	④	④	④	⑤	⑤	⑤
Rust/Paint	❶	❷	③	③	③	③	④	④
Steering	③	③	③	③	④	④	⑤	⑤
Suspension	③	③	③	③	④	④	⑤	⑤
Crash Safety	❷	⑤	⑤	③	③	—	④	④

Pulsar/NX

Rating: Above Average (1991–93); Average (1987–90). Stay away from failure-prone and expensive-to-repair turbo models. The Pulsar was replaced by the 1991 NX, a similar small car that also shares Sentra components. **Maintenance/Repair costs**: Lower than average and anybody can repair these cars. **Parts**: Reasonably priced and easily obtainable, except for turbocharger components, which are both costly and hard to find.

Technical Data

ENGINES	Liters/CID	HP	MPG	Model Years
OHC I-4 2 bbl.	1.6/97	69	27–31	1985–86
OHC I-4 FI	1.6/97	69	25–30	1987–88
OHC I-4 FI	1.6/97	90–110	24–28	1989–93
DOHC I-4 FI	1.6/97	113	22–26	1987
DOHC I-4 FI	1.8/110	125	21–25	1988–89

Strengths and weaknesses: Early Pulsars weren't very sporty cars. In fact, considering their bland styling, they weren't even all show and no go, like the unlamented Pontiac Fiero. As a Sentra clone, even the turbo models aren't appreciably quicker. The rear seat is such a pain that these coupes should be considered two-seaters only. For 1983–86 models, overall reliability is poor to very poor for the turbos. As with other discontinued Nissans, the 1987–92 models have shown remarkable performance improvement and are all the more attractive due to their depreciated prices.

Pulsars suffer from premature turbocharger failure, premature engine wear, and difficult-to-diagnose electrical problems. The engine oil pressure switch often leaks. 1983–86 models also have a host of clutch problems and fuel system glitches caused by faulty electronic modules. Manual and automatic transmissions on 1985–86 models are failure prone. The base 1.6L engine is inadequate for the heavier post-1986 model years. All Pulsars built before 1991 are prone to premature wear on the front brake pads and discs and faulty air conditioners. From 1991 on, the only problems reported concern minor AC malfunctions, premature wear out of front brakes and suspension components, and exhaust systems that don't last very long (two years, tops). Complaints of premature rusting and paint peeling are legion for the 1983–90 models.

Safety summary/recalls: Recalls: 1987–88—Cracked fuel tank inlet pipe.

Secret Warranties/Service Tips

1987–88—Insufficient alternator output causing repeated dead batteries can be fixed by installing a 70 amp alternator (#2310-70A00R). • Abrupt automatic transmission shifting may be caused by a poorly adjusted throttle wire. • To improve defrosting, install an upgraded center defroster duct (#2780084M00). **1987–90**—Manual transmission fluid leaks are likely due to insufficient case bolt torque. **1991–93**—If there is no Reverse gear with the manual transmission, install an upgrade kit. **1993**—Brake and steering wheel vibrations are likely caused by excessive rotor thickness.

Pulsar, NX Profile

	1986	1987	1988	1989	1990	1991	1992	1993
Cost Price ($)								
Pulsar	8,349	11,274	11,899	12,009	13,334	—	—	—
NX	—	—	—	—	—	12,240	12,900	13,285
Used Values ($)								
Pulsar ↑	2,500	3,500	4,000	4,500	5,000	—	—	—
Pulsar ↓	2,000	3,000	3,500	4,000	4,500	—	—	—
NX ↑	—	—	—	—	—	6,000	6,500	7,500
NX ↓	—	—	—	—	—	5,000	6,000	6,500
Extended Warranty	Y	Y	Y	Y	Y	Y	Y	Y
Secret Warranty	N	N	N	N	N	N	N	N
Reliability	①	①	③	③	③	③	④	④
Air conditioning	—	③	③	③	③	④	④	⑤
Body integrity	①	①	②	②	②	③	③	③
Braking system	①	①	②	③	③	③	③	④
Electrical system	①	①	②	③	③	③	③	④
Engines	②	②	②	④	④	④	④	⑤
Exhaust/Converter	①	①	①	①	②	③	④	④
Fuel system	①	①	②	②	②	③	④	⑤
Ignition system	②	②	③	③	③	③	④	④
Manual transmission	②	②	②	④	④	④	④	⑤
- automatic	②	②	②	④	④	④	④	⑤
Rust/Paint	①	①	②	②	③	③	④	⑤
Steering	③	③	③	③	③	③	④	⑤
Suspension	③	③	③	③	③	③	④	④
Crash Safety	①	①	①	①	①	①	①	①

SATURN

SL, SL1, SL2, SC

Rating: Average (1997); Below average (1992–96). As bizarre as it may appear, the Saturn division has a better reputation than the car it sells. The Geo Storm, Honda Civic LX, and Toyota Corolla perform well and offer better quality for about $1,500–$2,500 more. **Maintenance/Repair costs**: Average; repairs aren't dealer dependent. **Parts**: Higher-than-average cost, but not hard to find through independent suppliers.

Technical Data

ENGINES	Liters/CID	HP	MPG	Model Years
OHC I-4 FI	1.9/116	85	27–33	1991–94
OHC I-4 FI	1.9/116	100	27–35	1995–98
DOHC I-4 FI	1.9/116	123	23–29	1991–98

Strengths and weaknesses: Conceived as an all-American effort to beat the Japanese in the small car market, the Saturn compact isn't any better built than the other GM home-grown compacts we've learned to be wary of over the past 20 years. The car is far from high-tech; it's remained virtually unchanged, except for a minor face-lift and a bit more leg room, since it was launched in 1991. Saturns have exhibited a surprising number of serious body and mechanical problems which GM has covered up by generously applying its base warranty. Second owners aren't treated as well and risk paying for GM's powertrain and body mistakes. With Saturn first-quarter 1998 sales down 20 percent, GM is seriously considering merging Saturn with one of its other divisions. If this occurs, it will make warranty claim servicing even more problematic and routine dealer servicing will likely deteriorate, as well.

Overall, these are competitively priced, roomy, and comfortable small cars. Both two-door coupes and four-door sedans handle nimbly in good weather. Powered by a 4-cylinder aluminum engine, and a multi-valve variation of the same powerplant in the coupe, these cars are remarkably fuel efficient with the base engine hooked to a manual transmission.

The double-cam multi-valve 1.9L powerplant is no neck-snapper, but it does a decent job in most situations when coupled with a manual transmission that's precise and easily shifted. The rack-and-pinion steering is fairly precise and predictable, while the suspension gives a firm, but not harsh, ride. On the other hand, these lightweight vehicles are tricky to handle in snow or ice.

The loud, coarse, standard single-cam engine gives barely adequate acceleration times (12.2 seconds to reach 60 mph) with the manual transmission. This time is increased to a glacial 13.7 seconds with the 4-speed automatic gearbox that robs the engine of what little power it produces. Other generic problems affecting all model years are stalling and hard starting. One Canadian owner of a '94 Saturn plagued with chronic stalling problems had this to say:

> ...After stalling in rush hour traffic, car was towed as hazard lights failed after ten minutes; unable to restart. Car was then towed. Cause indicated: bad fuel tank, pump, battery, ECM and ignition module. Replaced probe, module, pump, tank, valve, module, and battery.
>
> Work order indicated that they performed various diagnostic checks, including: updated computer program, checked fuel pressure, checked ignition module circuit for proper operation, checked circuit from ignition switch to PCM for poor connection, and tried good ignition switch. Monitored voltage at back of ignition switch circuit for Fuse #1 PCM, replaced fuel tank-concaved and fuel pump as per tac, and replaced ECM. Car returned Feb. 27, 1998, but that evening car stalled again.
>
> Car stalled Feb. 28, March 1, 2, and 3 and finally, after stalling a dozen or so times on my way to work and almost getting into an accident with a bus, I told the Customer Service in Toronto that they could come get the car from my work as I was not driving it home...

The 5-speed manual transmission sometimes has trouble going into Reverse. With the automatic, there's lots of gearbox shudder when the kickdown is engaged while passing.

Dealer service bulletins indicate that three major quality problems are likely to crop up: malfunctioning automatic transmissions, electrical short circuits, and numerous wind and water leaks. On early models, the doors were poorly fitted, rear seats had to be lowered half an inch to give much-needed head room, engine mounts were changed to reduce vibrations, the shifter mechanism on the manual transmission was unreliable, and the reclining front seats were recalled because they could suddenly slip backward. Rear head room is still a bit tight, and owners report that the headliner in the rear tends to sag. Despite the dent-resistant plastic body panels, Saturn owners complain that the fascia chips and discolors.

GM's minor refinements to the '97 Saturns don't appear to justify the higher price. The sedans and wagons got upgraded engine mounts to lessen noise and vibration and the coupe was given the sedan's 102-inch wheelbase, providing additional leg room, particularly in the rear. More effective silencing materials were added forward of the dash and the air inlet was redirected away from the passenger compartment. Upgraded seatbelts on all '97s are less prone to tripping passengers trying to access the rear seat.

Dealer service bulletins: 1993—AC may emit foul odors. • The trunk lock assembly may be defective. **1994**—Malfunctioning cruise control assemblies. • Engine knocking, rough running, hard starting, and stalling. • Malfunctioning window cranks. • Paint spotting (white paint only). • Suspension/body noises. • Floor board rattles. •

Inoperative electrically controlled door locks. • Radio static when the power windows are operated. **1995**—Engine flares, loss of power, harsh shifts into Reverse. • Engine knock and/or rattle at normal temperature. • Engine stalls when cold, difficult to restart. • Excessive engine vibration at idle. • ATF leak at automatic transaxle oil pressure filter. • Possible causes of brake pulsation. • More recent info on brake vibration and/or pedal pulsation. • Steering pull, torque steer and wander. • Squealing sound from front of engine during cold starts. • Buzzing noise at rear of vehicle. • Possible other causes of buzzing, rattling, and fluttering noises. • Hoot noise upon light deceleration. • Clicking, ticking noise from instrument cluster odometer. • Ignition noise heard through radio speakers. • Popping noise from front seatback frame. • Rattle or chatter coming from passenger side. • Rattle, pop, or click from front end whenever passing over rough roads. Squeak/squawk noise from rear of vehicle. • Whistling produced by antenna mast. • Troubleshooting tips to silence wind noise at highway speeds. • Low voltage reading or dim lights at idle. • Instrument panel center air outlet closes. • Hard-to-operate sunroof sunshade. • Water drips onto seat/carpet with door open. •.Water leaks into right front footwell from front of dash. • Water leak at front upper door frame. **1996**—Excessive engine vibration at idle. • Radio frequency interference diagnosis. **1997**—Automatic transmission malfunctions. • Failure-prone cylinder head. • Cruise control drops out intermittently or won't reset after drop out. • Faulty switch for front-door jamb causes the dome light to stay on and prevents the alarm from arming. • Ignition key can be removed when vehicle is in gear. • Defective ignition lock cylinders create havoc with accessories (radio, power windows, AC, etc.). • Ignition key may bind in the ignition's Run position. • Excessive front brake noise or pulsation. • Knocking/rattling from front of floor to front of dash area. • Loose rear exterior door panels. • Runs out of fuel while fuel gauge reads one-quarter full. • Automatic transmission whine.

Safety summary/recalls: The optional ABS, while effective, may take what seems to be a long time to grip the discs. **Recalls: 1991**—Seatback recliners will be strengthened at no charge. **1991–92**—The seatbelt retractor may not fully retract the belt. **1991–93**—Faulty trunk lock assemblies will be replaced. • GM dealers will install at no charge a fusible link wiring harness to prevent an engine fire. **1992**—Automatic shift lever may show the wrong gear. **1993**—Sudden brake loss may be caused by faulty brake-booster housing. • The windshield wiper and brake-booster assemblies will be inspected and replaced, if necessary, at no charge under two separate safety recalls. • Battery cable terminal may be defective. **1995 automatic**—Possible to shift from Park with key removed or to remove key when lever is in gear. **1996 wagon**—Some welds between roof and reinforcement panels may not meet specifications. **1997**—Belted front passenger's seat not secure during a frontal impact.

Secret Warranties/Service Tips

1991—Engine misses, surges, or backfires may be caused by a poor ground at the electronic distributorless ignition (DIS). Install another DIS module. • Headlights that stay on when the switch is turned off can be fixed by installing an upgraded switch. • Wind noise from the front and rear doors may be caused by insufficient sealing under the mirror patch gasket, missing sealer at certain locations (for example, the door frame to door assembly at the beltline), insufficient contact of the secondary seals to door openings, or the glass run channels not sealing to the glass at the upper corners. **1991–92**—Owners have reported excessive noise and vibration levels coming from the steering wheel, seat, and floor pan. Saturn officials say that the noise and vibration could be caused by the following: pre-loaded powertrain mounts (1991); a pre-loaded engine strut cradle bracket (1992); improperly positioned or worn exhaust system isolators and muffler band clamp/block (1991–92); lower cooling module grommets and improper positioning of wiring harnesses and upper cooling system module grommets (1991–92); improper routing of AC hoses or hood release cable and air inlet snorkel (1991–92); debris in accessory drive belt pulleys (1991); improper adjustment of hood stop(s) (1991–92); PCV or brake booster check valve noise (1991); DOHC (LLO) automatic transaxle mount assembly replacement (1991); or a malfunctioning engine, electrical, or fuel system (1991–92). **1991–94**—Rough running or surging after a cold start may signal the need to clean carbon or fuel deposits from the engine's intake valves. • The many causes of hard-to-crank windows are covered in DSB 94-T-19. • Inoperative electric door locks may have been shorted by water contamination. Since the design and positioning of the relay for the power door lock allows this to develop, Saturn is accepting claims on a case-by-case basis. • Water leaks into the front footwell and at the front upper door frame are treated in depth in two DSBs published in August and November 1994. • Whistling noises are also treated in two different bulletins published in June and October 1994. **1991–95**—Erratic cruise control operation can be corrected by replacing the cruise control module assembly. • If the engine stalls within five minutes of starting, or when coming to a stop, or is difficult to restart, the oil viscosity or engine's hydraulic lifters may be at fault. • Engine squealing after a cold start can be corrected by installing an upgraded belt idler pulley assembly. **1991–97**—Excessive front brake noise or pulsation requires the installation of upgraded brake pads, according to DSB #96-T-40A. • Engines that run hot or have coolant mixed in the engine oil probably have a defective engine cylinder—a factory-related goof, according to GM's service bulletin (see below).

BULLETIN NO.: 96-T-65A
ISSUE DATE: February 1997
GROUP/SEQ. NO. Engine-15
CORPORATION NO.: 686204R
SUBJECT:
Engine Runs Hot and Engine Oil Mixed with Engine Coolant in Engine Coolant Recovery Reservoir (Replace Cylinder Head Assembly)
This bulletin is revised to replace an incorrect part number for the one gallon container of DEX-COOL(TM) and supersedes bulletin 96-T-65, which should be discarded.
MODELS AFFECTED:
1991–1997 Saturns equipped with SOHC (LKO-1991-1994, L24-1995-1997) engines
CONDITION:
Engine may run hot and/or have engine oil mixed with engine coolant. This condition may be noticeable when checking coolant recovery reservoir level.
CAUSE:
Some 1991–1997 SOHC engines may develop a crack on or near the camshaft journals and surrounding casting areas allowing engine oil to mix with engine coolant. These cracks may be caused by "folds" in the aluminum that occur during the head casting process.
CLAIM INFORMATION

Case Type	Description	Labor Operation Code	Time
VW	Replace Cylinder Head Assembly	T9715	11.2 hrs
Add:	with A/C		0.8 hrs
	with power steering		0.3 hrs

To receive credit for this repair during the warranty coverage period, submit a claim through the Saturn Dealer System as shown.

Don't kid yourself. This is a major engine defect that'll take 11-plus hours to correct. GM will pay, if you refuse to go away.

• If your Saturn runs out of fuel while the fuel gauge reads one-quarter full, it's likely you have a plugged EVAP canister vent which should be repaired free of charge under the emissions warranty. • A whistle or groaning noise heard at highway speeds may be caused by the radio antenna mast. **1992—** An engine that stalls, hesitates, or surges during light acceleration may require new PCM calibrations. • Harsh Reverse engagement can also be corrected with new PCM calibrations. • Engine rattling can be fixed by changing the motor mounts. **1993–94—**A popping noise coming from the base of the left-hand A-pillar, hinge pillar, and engine compartment is caused by a slight flexing in the area where the three are joined together. **1993–97—**Troubleshooting tips are available on diagnosing delayed or harsh automatic transmission shifting into Reverse. **1994—**White Saturns may have yellow stains or spotting along the fenders, fender extension, or quarter panel. If so, the company will change the affected part and repaint the area at no charge to the owner. • A Saturn equipped with manual transmission may have the transaxle stuck in gear due to a defective shift control housing. **1994–95—**Excessive engine knocking can be corrected by changing the clearance between the piston pin and connecting rod bushing. **1995–97—**Electrical accessories may lose power after the car is started or while it's on the road. GM blames the problem on a defective ignition lock cylinder. **1996–97—**If your security alarm won't work properly or your dome light won't go out, GM suggests you change the door jamb switches.

All models/years—A rotten-egg odor coming from the exhaust is likely the result of a malfunctioning catalytic converter, which you can have replaced free of charge under GM's emissions warranty. Paint delamination, peeling, or fading: See page 95.

Saturn Profile							
	1991	1992	1993	1994	1995	1996	1997
Cost Price ($)							
SL	9,045	9,265	10,330	11,210	11,260	11,805	11,925
SL2	11,345	11,465	12,625	13,010	13,260	13,605	13,825
SW1	—	—	12,025	12,910	12,960	13,305	13,525
SC/SC1	12,825	12,945	12,125	12,910	13,130	13,505	13,825
Used Values ($)							
SL ↑	4,500	5,000	6,500	7,500	8,500	9,500	10,000
SL ↓	3,500	4,000	5,500	6,500	7,500	8,500	9,500
SL2 ↑	6,000	7,000	8,000	9,000	10,500	11,500	12,000
SL2 ↓	5,000	5,500	7,000	8,000	9,000	10,000	11,500
SW1 ↑	—	—	8,000	9,000	10,500	11,500	12,200
SW1 ↓	—	—	7,000	8,000	9,200	10,300	11,200
SC/SC1 ↑	6,500	7,000	7,500	8,500	9,500	10,500	11,000
SC/SC1 ↓	5,500	6,000	6,500	7,500	8,500	9,500	10,500
Extended Warranty	Y	Y	Y	Y	Y	Y	Y
Secret Warranty	Y	Y	Y	Y	Y	Y	Y
Reliability	②	②	②	②	②	③	③
Air conditioning	②	②	②	②	③	④	④
Automatic transmission	②	②	②	②	②	③	③
Body integrity	②	②	②	②	②	②	②
Braking system	②	②	②	②	②	②	③
Electrical system	②	②	②	②	②	②	③
Engines	②	②	②	②	②	③	③
Exhaust/Converter	②	③	③	③	③	③	③
Fuel system	②	②	②	②	②	②	②
Ignition system	②	②	②	②	③	③	③
Rust/Paint	③	③	③	③	③	③	④
Steering	③	③	③	④	④	④	⑤
Suspension	③	③	③	④	④	④	④
Crash Safety							
SL2	②	②	①	①	④	④	④

SUBARU

Justy

Rating: Average (1991–95); Not Recommended (1988–90). Only buy a Subaru if the 4X4 capability is essential to your driving needs. Otherwise, choose a less dealer-dependent model from Honda, Mazda, or Toyota. **Maintenance/Repair costs**: Higher than average. CVT transmission and 4X4 repairs must be carried out by a dealer. Make sure you can get dependable service from your local Subaru dealer before your purchase. **Parts**: Expensive and rare.

Technical Data

ENGINE	Liters/CID	HP	MPG	Model Years
OHC I-3 FI	1.2/72	66–73	35–41	1988–95

Strengths and weaknesses: The Justy does everything reasonably well for an entry-level Subaru. Both the front-wheel drive and 4X4 models offer an optional continuously variable transmission (CVT). The design does away with conventional clutches, torque converters, and gears. Instead, the engine's power is transmitted to the drive shaft via a set of pulleys and belts that adjust the engine's power to the messages sent by the gas pedal. CVT increases fuel economy considerably (almost as much as a manual transmission), while making for a simpler and lighter transmission.

Pairing smooth and nimble handling with precise and predictable steering, the 4X4 system is a boon for people who often need easy-to-engage extra traction and an automatic transmission. Dashboard gauges are simple and front seats are firm and supportive.

The Justy's engine is anemic, harsh, and noisy. There are annoying steering wheel vibrations caused by the rough-running engine. The non-power-assisted steering requires maximum effort when parking. The ride is uncomfortable when carrying a full load. You lose some steering stability with hard braking, and cornering at high speeds feels tippy on the 4X4. Larger tires would improve handling. Transmission problems aren't easily diagnosed or repaired due to the transmission's complicated construction. Front shoulder belts are uncomfortable and rear seatbelts are hard to buckle up. The rear seat is for children only. The heater is insufficient and air distribution is inadequate. Trunk space is less than you would expect.

The Justy's reliability record has been about average from the 1991 model on. Some owners complain concerning poor engine idling and frequent cold weather stalling, manual and automatic transmission malfunctions, premature exhaust system rust-out, catalytic converter failures, and paint peeling. With the exception of the CVT, servicing and repairs are made easy due to a very straightforward design.

Safety summary/recalls: **Recalls: 1987–91**—Takata seatbelts will be replaced. **1988**—The 4X4 solenoid hose/alternator wiring stay bracket may present a fire hazard.

Secret Warranties/Service Tips

1988—If the "check engine" light comes on for no reason, install a new diode harness. **1988–89**—A grinding second gear is fixed with an upgraded transmission assembly. **1989**—ECVT clutch rattle can be fixed by installing an upgraded clutch control unit (#30522KA091).

Justy Profile

	1987	1988	1989	1990	1991	1992	1993	1994
Cost Price ($)								
Base	5,596	5,831	6,261	6,261	6,390	7,090	7,783	8,194
Used Values								
Base ↑	1,500	2,000	2,300	2,500	3,000	3,500	4,000	4,700
Base ↓	1,000	1,500	1,800	2,100	2,500	3,000	3,500	4,000
Extended Warranty	Y	Y	Y	Y	Y	Y	Y	Y
Secret Warranty	N	N	N	N	N	N	N	N
Reliability	②	②	②	③	③	③	④	④
Body integrity	②	②	②	③	③	③	④	④
Braking system	②	②	②	③	③	③	④	④
Electrical system	③	③	③	③	④	④	④	④
Engines	②	②	②	④	⑤	⑤	⑤	⑤
Exhaust/Converter	②	②	③	④	⑤	⑤	⑤	⑤
Fuel system	③	③	③	③	④	④	⑤	⑤
Ignition system	③	③	③	③	④	④	④	④
Manual transmission	③	③	③	④	④	④	⑤	⑤
- automatic	②	②	③	④	③	③	④	⑤
Rust/Paint	②	②	②	③	③	④	④	④
Steering	③	③	③	③	④	④	④	④
Suspension	②	②	③	③	④	④	③	④
Crash Safety	②	②	②	②	②	②	②	—

Chaser, DL, GL, Loyale, Impreza, XT

Rating: Recommended (1996–97); Average (1993–95); Below Average (1987–92). The earlier models aren't recommended because of poor-quality emissions components and the premature wear out of major mechanical systems (CV joints, steering, etc.). **Maintenance/Repair costs**: Higher than average and 4X4 repairs must be carried out by a dealer. Only buy a Subaru if you must have AWD and you're confident you can get dependable service from your local Subaru dealer. **Parts**: Expensive and hard to find, especially for the discontinued Chaser. Emission components are often back-ordered for months, but cheap aftermarket components can be found outside the dealer network.

Technical Data

ENGINES	Liters/CID	HP	MPG	Model Years
OHV F-4 2 bbl.	1.6/97	69	23–30	1985–88
OHV F-4 2 bbl.	1.8/109	73	21–29	1985–89
OHC F-4 2 bbl.	1.8/109	82–84	23–28	1985–87
OHC F-4 FI	1.8/109	90–97	23–28	1984–94
OHC F-4T FI	1.8/109	111–115	20–24	1985–90
OHC F-6 FI	2.7/163	145	17–23	1988–91
		Loyale		
OHC flat-4 FI	1.8/109	90–97	23–28	1985–94
OHC flat-4T FI	1.8/109	111–115	19–24	1985–90
OHC flat-6 FI	2.7/163	145	17–23	1988–91
		Impreza		
OHC flat-4 FI	1.8/109	110	23–28	1993–96
OHC flat-4T FI	2.2/135	135	19–26	1995–98
OHC flat-4T FI	2.5/150	165	22–26	1998

Strengths and weaknesses: 1987–92 are the years to avoid. Performance, handling, and ride are mediocre. Engine breakdowns and premature clutch and exhaust system wearout are commonplace. Early hatchbacks came with a weak and growly 1.6L flat 4-cylinder motor; later models have a 1.8L version of the same anemic engine. Expensive catalytic converters are often replaced at the owner's cost before the 5-year emissions warranty has expired. Subaru will reimburse the cost if you raise a fuss.

On 1988 and later models, steering assemblies, CV joints, and front brakes are the main problem areas. These parts generally need replacing after three to five years and Subaru dealers charge the full rate for replacement.

In the early spring of 1993, the Impreza replaced the unpopular and aging Loyale. The Impreza, too, offered sluggish engine performance, jerky full-throttle downshifts, and mediocre fuel economy. Overall reliability was improved, however.

By 1996, when these small cars went AWD, overall quality control improved as well. Powertrain components are more durable and function more smoothly and electronic components have fewer glitches. Rusting is less of a problem than with the earlier models that are particularly susceptible to rapid rusting of the bumpers, door bottoms, rear hatch, and hood.

Safety summary/recalls: **NHTSA probes**: **1994–95 Impreza** and **1995–96 Legacy**—Inadvertent airbag deployment is a problem. Airbags could deploy after the underside of the car scrapes the road or if the car drives over a dip in the road, hits a pothole, or is stuck in a ditch in the snow. **Recalls**: **1985 XT**—Improperly installed bumpers will be fixed. **1985–87**—Corrosion of the rear suspension inner arms could affect the control of the vehicle. **1985–87**

DL/GL/GT—The rear suspension's inner arms could fail. **1987 DL/GL**—Faulty carburetor components could pose a fire hazard. **1988–91 XT6 and 1989–91 XT**—Faulty power steering will be repaired. **1989–90**—Automatic transmission may engage abruptly, causing a sudden lurch into Reverse. **1991 XT 4X4**—5-speed manual gearbox may leak, causing transmission to suddenly seize. **Recalls: 1988–1990 Loyale**—Takata seatbelts will be replaced. **1989–90 Loyale**—Automatic transmission may engage abruptly, causing a sudden lurch into Reverse. **1990 Loyale with 3AT transmission**—Vehicle may jump into gear from Park. **1990–93 Loyale**—5-speed manual transmission may suddenly seize.

Secret Warranties/Service Tips

1985–90—Correct rear gate door rattle with a plastic sheet buffer. **1987**—An overly rich choke condition during cold starts can be corrected by installing a modified auxiliary choke pull-off spring. **1990–91**—A knocking noise from the exhaust flex joint may require the replacement of an exhaust flange gasket with an upgraded gasket (#44022-GA 191). **1990–91 Loyale**—A knocking noise from the exhaust flex joint may require the replacement of the exhaust flange gasket with an upgraded gasket (#44022-GA 191). **1991**—Weak, noisy, AM reception can be corrected by installing a modified antenna feeder cable (#86324AA040). • Banging over bumps is likely caused by the struts, strut mounts, and brake cable clamps on trailing arms or by the rear defogger condenser hitting the quarter panel. • A popping noise heard when going over small bumps may be caused by the front stabilizer bar bushing clamps. **1991–92**—Ignition relay failure is the likely cause of no-starts. **1992–94**—The heater mode door actuator may be the culprit of an annoying clicking in the heater area.

Impreza, Loyale Profile

	1990	1991	1992	1993	1994	1995	1996	1997
Cost Price ($)								
Impreza	—	—	—	11,444	11,645	13,420	—	—
Impreza 4X4	—	—	—	—	—	16,425	13,990	15,290
Loyale	9,694	9,894	10,244	10,923	—	—	—	—
4X4	11,419	—	—	—	13,998	—	—	—
Used Values ($)								
Impreza ↑	—	—	—	7,000	8,000	9,000	• —	—
Impreza ↓	—	—	—	5,500	7,000	8,000	—	—
Impreza 4X4 ↑	—	—	—	—	—	12,000	12,000	13,000
Impreza 4X4 ↓	—	—	—	—	—	10,000	11,000	12,000
Loyale ↑	4,500	5,000	6,000	7,000	—	—	—	—
Loyale ↓	4,000	4,500	5,000	6,000	—	—	—	—
4X4 ↑	6,000	—	—	—	10,000	—	—	—
4X4 ↓	5,000	—	—	—	9,000	—	—	—
Extended Warranty	Y	Y	Y	Y	Y	Y	Y	Y
Secret Warranty	N	N	N	N	N	N	N	N
Reliability	❷	❷	❷	❷	❷	③	④	④

Air conditioning	❷	❷	③	④	④	⑤	⑤	⑤
Body integrity	❷	❷	❷	③	③	③	③	③
Braking system	❷	❷	❷	❷	❷	③	③	④
Electrical system	❷	❷	③	③	③	③	④	④
Engines	❷	❷	❷	③	③	④	⑤	⑤
Exhaust/Converter	③	③	④	④	④	④	⑤	⑤
Fuel system	④	④	④	❷	❷	❷	④	④
Ignition system	❷	❷	❷	❷	❷	④	④	④
Manual transmission	④	④	④	④	④	⑤	⑤	⑤
- automatic	③	③	③	③	③	③	④	⑤
Rust/Paint	❷	❷	③	③	③	④	④	⑤
Steering	③	③	③	③	③	④	④	④
Suspension	③	③	④	④	④	④	④	④
Crash Safety								
Impreza	—	—	—	—	—	—	④	④

SUZUKI

Esteem

Rating: Recommended (1996–97). An incredibly slow rate of depreciation means that bargains will be rare. Nevertheless, both the base GL and upscale GLX come loaded with standard features that cost extra on other models. The GL, for example, comes with power steering, rear-window defroster, remote-trunk and fuel-filler door releases, tinted glass, and a fold-down rear seat (great for getting extra cargo space). GLX shoppers can look forward to standard ABS, power windows and power door locks, and a host of other interior refinements. Shop around for a better-made, second-series (made after March 1996) '96 Esteem rather than a '97 inasmuch as they're practically identical and a late-model '96 should be much cheaper. **Maintenance/Repair costs**: Higher than average; repairs must be carried out by a Geo/Chevrolet or Suzuki dealer. **Parts**: Average cost, but some long waits reported.

Technical Data

ENGINES	Liters/CID	HP	MPG	Model Years
OHC I-4 FI	1.6/92	98	42–45	1996–98

Strengths and weaknesses: The Esteem, Suzuki's largest car, is a small four-door sedan that is a step up from the Swift. Smaller than the Honda Civic and Dodge Neon, it has a fairly spacious interior, offering rear accommodation (for two full-sized adults) that is comparable to òr better than most cars in its class. Suzuki's top-of-the-line econobox stands out with its European-styled body and large array of such standard features as air conditioning, a fold-down back seat, and remote trunk and fuel-door releases.

The Esteem has only been on the market for three years, but early reports indicate a high level of quality and dependability. In this respect, it competes well with rivals like the Chevy Cavalier, Ford Escort, and Honda Civic. However, some owners complain of premature front brake wear, noisy front brakes, and occasional electrical short circuits.

Safety summary/recalls: N/A.

Secret Warranties/Service Tips

1995-97-Uneven wear of the front disc brake pads can be corrected by modifying the upper bushing tolerance, says DSB # TS 5-03-04126.

Esteem Profile

	1995	1996	1997
Cost Price ($)			
GL	11,789	11,989	13,319
GLX	14,789	13,289	14,419
Used Values ($)			
GL ↑	9,000	10,500	11,000
GL ↓	8,000	9,000	10,000
GLX ↑	9,500	11,000	11,500
GLX ↓	8,500	9,500	10,500
Extended Warranty	N	N	N
Secret Warranty	N	N	N
Reliability	⑤	⑤	⑤

TOYOTA

Paseo

Rating: Recommended (1994–97); Above Average (1992–93). Expect resale prices to remain high now that Toyota has announced that 1998 will be the Paseo's last model year. **Maintenance/Repair costs**: Lower than average; repairs can be done anywhere. **Parts**: Reasonably priced and easily found.

Technical Data

ENGINES	Liters/CID	HP	MPG	Model Years
DOHC I-4 FI	1.5/90	100	25–32	1992–95
DOHC I-4 FI	1.5/90	93	26–33	1995–97

Strengths and weaknesses: This baby Tercel's main advantages are a peppy 1.5L 4-cylinder engine, a smooth 5-speed manual transmission, good handling, a supple ride, great fuel economy, and above average reliability. On the other hand, this light little sportster is quite vulnerable to side winds, there's lots of body lean in turns, plenty of engine, exhaust, and road noise, limited front head room and leg room, and very little rear seat space.

Dealer service bulletins show that the 1993s may have defective Panasonic tape and CD players and a radio hum at low volume caused by fuel pump interference. Later models have fewer reliability problems, except for some brake and drivetrain vibrations.

Safety summary/recalls: Thick rear pillars reduce rear visibility. **Recalls**: N/A.

Secret Warranties/Service Tips

1992—Low-volume radio hum can be corrected by installing spacers (insulators) between the radio chassis and the printed circuit board. **1992–93**—Toyota will improve the shift "feel" on its automatic gearboxes by increasing the C1 accumulator control pressure. **1996**—Toyota has developed an upgraded thermostat to improve heater performance. **1997**—Fujitsu radios may not eject/accept CDs. **All models/years**—DSB #B0003-97 recommends the use of a new wind noise repair kit. • DSB #AC002-97 gives lots of troubleshooting tips on eliminating AC odors. • AM radio static is likely caused by a damaged power antenna or by poor grounding due to corrosion.

Paseo Profile

	1992	1993	1994	1995	1996	1997
Cost Price ($)						
Base	14,433	12,663	13,753	14,725	14,383	14,553
Used Values ($)						
Base ↑	7,000	8,500	9,500	10,500	12,000	13,000
Base ↓	6,000	7,000	8,500	9,500	10,500	11,500
Extended Warranty	N	N	N	N	N	N
Secret Warranty	N	N	N	N	N	N
Reliability	④	④	⑤	⑤	⑤	⑤
Crash Safety	❷	—	—	—	—	④

Tercel

Rating: Recommended (1993–97); Above Average (1991–92); Average (1987–90). **Maintenance/Repair costs**: Inexpensive; repairs can be done anywhere. **Parts**: Reasonably priced and easily obtainable.

Technical Data

ENGINES	Liters/CID	HP	MPG	Model Years
OHC I-4 1 bbl.	1.5/89	76–78	27–32	1987–90
OHC I-4 2 bbl.	1.5/89	62	28–33	1987–88
OHC I-4 FI	1.5/89	82	25–31	1991–94
DOHC I-4 FI	1.5/89	93	29–37	1995–97

Strengths and weaknesses: Don't buy a Toyota on reputation alone, because many early models (1985–90) can have serious braking, electrical, and rusting problems and be overpriced, to boot. Stay away from the troublesome 4X4 versions made from 1984–87, as well.

All Tercels should be checked for door panel and underbody rust damage. 1987–90 Tercels are rust-prone around the rear wheels and side mirror mounts, and along the bottoms of doors, hatches, and rear quarter-panels. Early models suffer from extensive corrosion of rear suspension components.

1987–88 Tercels give you more for your money with a restyled aero look, a better-performing multivalve, an overhead-cam engine, the impressive performance of a 5-speed manual gearbox, and additional sound insulation. Their main shortcomings are insufficient power when merging into traffic or hill climbing (particularly when shifting from second to third gear with the automatic transmission), cruise control glitches, fuel system malfunctions, excessive carbon buildup on the engine intake valve, occasional air conditioner breakdowns, cracked front exhaust pipes, and exhaust system/catalytic converter rust-out. Tercels are also plagued by pulsating brakes that wear out much too quickly. Owners of the four-wheel drive wagon complain of manual transmission failures and the occasional bug in the transfer case (these repairs are *very* expensive).

The redesigned 1989–90 versions are roomier, better performing, and above average in quality and reliability (except for some paint peeling and surface rusting). The sunroof is a frill that cuts head room drastically and causes irritating water leaks and wind noise. Tercels have a great reputation for exemplary durability, but overall performance is not outstanding and the interior is cramped.

1991–94 Tercels are pretty reliable, but they're not perfect. They were the first to be fuel-injected, which makes for livelier and smoother acceleration, and the interior space feels much larger than it is. Owners report faulty clutch-sleeve cylinders, hard shifting with the automatic transmission, premature brake and suspension-component wear out, brake pulsation, defective CD players, leaking radiators, windshield whistling, and myriad squeaks and rattles.

Redesigned 1995–97 Tercels offer a bit more horsepower, standard dual airbags, side door beams, aero styling, and a redesigned interior. They continue, however, to have some brake, electrical system, and suspension problems.

Safety summary/recalls: Recalls: 1987–90—Headlights may fail.

Secret Warranties/Service Tips

1989–90—Fix harsh shifting from second to third on automatics by installing a new rubber check ball (#35495-22020). **1994**—A whistling noise coming from the windshield requires a urethane sealant applied at key points. • A steering column that's noisy or has excessive free play may need an upgraded steering main-shaft bushing. **1995**—Windshield molding wind noise troubleshooting is covered in DSB# BO95-005 (see below).

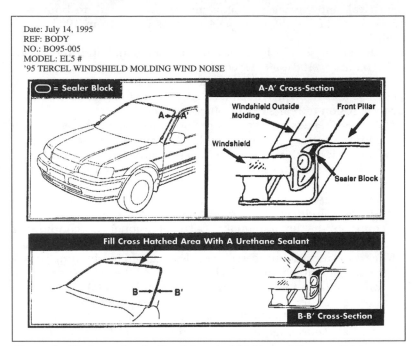

Date: July 14, 1995
REF: BODY
NO.: BO95-005
MODEL: EL5 #
'95 TERCEL WINDSHIELD MOLDING WIND NOISE

Put sealer blocks under the lip of the windshield moulding to silence an annoying whistling noise.

1995–96—Toyota has developed an upgraded thermostat to improve heater performance. • The company will also make available a longer passenger-side seatbelt. **1997**—Fujitsu radios may not eject/accept CDs. **All models/years**—DSB #B0003-97 recommends the use of a new wind noise repair kit. • Interior squeaks and rattles can be fixed with Toyota's kit (#08231-00801). • DSB #AC002-97 gives lots of troubleshooting tips on eliminating AC odors. • Older Toyotas with stalling problems should have the engine checked for excessive carbon buildup on the valves before any other repairs are done. • Improved disc brake pad kits are described in DSB BR94-004. Brake pulsation/vibration, another generic Toyota problem, is fully addressed in DSB BR94-002, "Cause and Repair of Vibration and Pulsation." • A damaged power antenna or poor grounding due to corrosion are the most likely causes of AM radio static.

Tercel Profile								
	1990	1991	1992	1993	1994	1995	1996	1997
Cost Price ($)								
Base	7,698	7,728	8,303	9,223	10,223	11,535	11,981	12,508
Used Values ($)								
Base ↑	4,000	5,000	5,500	6,500	7,000	8,500	9,500	11,000
Base ↓	3,000	4,000	4,500	5,500	6,000	7,500	8,500	10,000

Extended Warranty	Y	N	N	N	N	N	N	N
Secret Warranty	N	N	N	N	N	N	N	N
Reliability	③	③	③	④	⑤	⑤	⑤	⑤
Air conditioning	❷	❷	③	③	⑤	⑤	⑤	⑤
Body integrity	③	③	③	④	④	⑤	⑤	⑤
Braking system	❶	❷	❷	❷	❷	❷	③	④
Electrical system	③	③	③	④	⑤	⑤	⑤	⑤
Engines	④	④	④	④	⑤	⑤	⑤	⑤
Exhaust/Converter	❷	❷	❷	❷	❷	④	⑤	⑤
Fuel system	③	③	③	④	⑤	⑤	⑤	⑤
Ignition system	❷	③	③	④	④	④	④	④
Manual transmission	③	④	④	④	⑤	⑤	⑤	⑤
- automatic	④	④	④	④	⑤	⑤	⑤	⑤
Rust/Paint	③	③	③	③	④	⑤	⑤	⑤
Steering	④	④	④	③	④	④	⑤	⑤
Suspension	③	③	③	③	③	③	④	⑤
Crash Safety	❶	❷	❷	⑤	⑤	③	③	④

Corolla, Prizm

Rating: Recommended (1993–97); Above Average (1991–92); Average (1988–90). Although the '97 model was "decontented," (less soundproofing, fewer standard features, etc.), there has been no reduction in quality or performance. **Maintenance/Repair costs**: Lower than average and repairs can be done anywhere. **Parts**: Reasonably priced and easily found.

Technical Data

ENGINES	Liters/CID	HP	MPG	Model Years
OHV I-4 2 bbl.	1.6/97	70–74	24–30	1985–88
DOHV I-4 FI	1.6/97	108–110	22–27	1987–88
OHC I-4D FI	1.8/112	56	27–33	1985
DOHC I-4 2 bbl.	1.6/97	90	25–30	1988–89
DOHC I-4 FI	1.6/97	100–102	22–26	1989–92
DOHC I-4 FI	1.6/97	115–130	23–27	1988–91
DOHC I-4 FI	1.6/97	105	24–29	1993–97
DOHC I-4 FI	1.8/110	105–115	23–28	1993–97

Strengths and weaknesses: These two small cars are practically identical, except for small differences in body styling, interior trim, and the placement of some controls. They are both economical, high-quality, dependable little cars, but age can take its toll, especially in the Rust Belt, where rust snacks on these cars. 1985–87 versions may appear to be bargains at first glance, but they're likely to have serious rusting problems and need costly brake, steering, and suspension work. Stay away from the 1.8L diesel version; it lacks performance capability and parts aren't easy to find. 4X4 versions

172 — Lemon-Aid

are also risky. Wiper pivot assemblies may seize due to corrosion. Front shocks on rear-wheel-drive models wear out more quickly than average. Exhaust parts aren't very durable.

Post-1987 models are much improved. The two-door models provide sporty performance and good fuel economy, especially when equipped with the 16-valve engine. The engines and drivetrains are exceptionally reliable. Front-drive sedans and five-door hatchbacks offer more room than their rear-drive counterparts. The base engine, however, lacks power and is especially deficient in low-end torque, making for agonizingly slow merging and passing on the highway. Owners report problems with premature front suspension strut and brake wear, brake vibration, faulty defrosting that allows the windows to fog up in winter, and rusting of body seams, especially door bottoms, side mirror mounts, trunk and hatchback lids, and wheel openings.

The 1990–97 Corollas' and Prizm's problems are limited to harsh automatic shifting, early front brake pad and strut/shock wear out, and some interior squeaks and rattles. They do, however, still require regular valve adjustments to prevent serious engine problems. Less of a problem with later models, rusting is usually confined to the undercarriage and other areas where the moldings attach to sheet metal.

Safety summary/recalls: **NHTSA probes**: Some owners find the driver's foot room inadequate to safely operate the accelerator, brake, and clutch pedals. **1993–96**—Researchers are looking into 20 similar incidents where the turn signal failed after the hazard warning light activated. **Recalls**: **1993–94**—An unused harness connector for vehicle accessories located under the carpet may cause an electrical short circuit or fire. **1993–95**—Liquid spilled onto the console could make the airbags deploy. **1994**—Seatbelt anchor straps may be faulty. **1995**—Defective terminal could drain the battery or make it explode. Dealer will replace the battery.

Secret Warranties/Service Tips

1987–88—Engines that run on, surge, or have flat power spots may need an upgraded carburetor assembly, cold-mixture heater temperature switch, or engine sub-wire harness. **1993–96**—Toyota has upgraded the hazard switch to improve turn signal performance in cold climates. **1993–97**—Inoperative front-passenger power side window switch may be caused by lubricant from the wire harness contaminating the window switch contacts. **1994**—A loose rear-seat bolster cover is a common problem, according to DSB B094-005. • Windshield A-pillar wind noise can be stopped by modifying the molding lip. **1995–96**—To enhance the performance of the rear door glass, Toyota has upgraded the mounting channel rubber insert and offers it as a service part. **All models/years**—Improved disc brake pad kits are described in DSB BR94-004. • Brake pulsation/vibration, another generic Toyota problem, is fully addressed in DSB BR94-002, "Cause and

Repair of Vibration and Pulsation." • Complaints of steering column noise may require the replacement of the steering column assembly, a repair covered under Toyota's base warranty. • Insiders tell me Toyota will pay for the repair under a "goodwill" secret warranty if the warranty has expired and the customer won't take "no" for an answer.

Corolla, Prizm Profile

	1990	1991	1992	1993	1994	1995	1996	1997
Cost Price ($)								
Base Corolla	10,368	10,508	11,123	12,983	13,308	13,782	14,538	15,028
Prizm	11,849	11,555	11,995	11,662	12,480	13,435	14,300	14,375
Used Values ($)								
Base Corolla ↑	5,000	5,500	6,500	8,000	9,000	10,000	11,500	12,000
Base Corolla ↓	4,000	5,000	5,500	7,000	8,000	9,000	10,000	11,000
Prizm ↑	4,500	5,000	6,000	7,000	8,000	9,000	10,000	11,000
Prizm ↓	3,500	4,000	5,000	6,000	7,000	8,000	9,000	10,000
Extended Warranty	Y	N	N	N	N	N	N	N
Secret Warranty	N	N	N	Y	Y	Y	Y	Y
Reliability	③	③	④	④	⑤	⑤	⑤	⑤
Air conditioning	④	⑤	⑤	⑤	⑤	⑤	⑤	⑤
Body integrity	③	③	③	④	④	④	④	④
Braking system	❷	❷	❷	❷	❷	③	③	④
Electrical system	❷	❷	③	③	③	④	④	⑤
Engines	③	④	④	④	④	⑤	⑤	⑤
Exhaust/Converter	❷	❷	③	③	④	④	⑤	⑤
Fuel system	❷	❷	③	③	③	⑤	⑤	⑤
Ignition system	❷	③	③	③	④	④	⑤	⑤
Manual transmission	④	④	④	④	④	⑤	⑤	⑤
- automatic	④	③	③	④	④	⑤	⑤	⑤
Rust/Paint	③	③	③	④	④	④	④	⑤
Steering	③	③	④	④	④	④	⑤	⑤
Suspension	③	③	③	③	④	④	⑤	⑤
Crash Safety	❷	❷	❷	⑤	⑤	④	④	④
Side Impact	—	—	—	—	—	—	—	③

VOLKSWAGEN

Fox

Rating: Below Average (1990–93); Not Recommended (1987–89).
Maintenance/Repair costs: Higher than average; repairs are dealer dependent. **Parts**: Expensive and sometimes hard to find.

Technical Data

ENGINE	Liters/CID	HP	MPG	Model Years
OHC I-4 FI	1.8/109	81	24–28	1987–93

Strengths and weaknesses: Smooth acceleration with good passing ability. The car handles very well and takes a surprisingly large load. The Fox's old design can't offer the mechanical or interior efficiency that newer cars provide, though. Other failings are the absence of power steering and an automatic transmission. It's true that these cars are fun to drive and provide lots of extra equipment for the money, but they have a checkered reputation as far as reliability and durability are concerned. Furthermore, as time goes on, these cars become more troublesome and difficult to repair.

Owners report common failures with engine timing belts, starter motors, and brake cylinders. Other problem areas include electrical, engine cooling, and fuel systems and there are body hardware glitches. The manual transmission shift linkage needs frequent adjustment, and the front brakes, as on most VWs, need more frequent servicing than those of comparable makes. Assembly and paint application quality vary considerably and interior trim and dashboard controls are easily broken. Towing is not recommended.

Safety summary/recalls: **Recalls**: **1987–89**—Steering wheel shaft nut may be too loose. **1987–93**—Hot coolant could spill onto the front passenger's feet and legs or steam up the vehicle interior. **1988–91**—Hood may fly open. **1991**—Metal fuel lines may rub against exhaust manifold, posing a fire hazard.

Secret Warranties/Service Tips

1988–93—Poor driveability may be caused by a deteriorated oxygen sensor wire shield or ground connection. **1991–1993**—If the vehicle loses power and bucks and jerks after several hours of driving, the likely cause is a faulty mass airflow sensor that creates a vibration resonance, sending an intermittent signal to the ECM. This repair may be covered by the emissions warranty. **1993**—Wind noise from the top of the door may be fixed by installing a new auxiliary door seal. **All models/years**—If the engine fails to crank or the battery is constantly discharged, you may have a loose fastening nut on terminal 30 of the starter motor. • Water leaking between the sunroof's glass panel and seal can be stopped with VW's Water Management System kit (I swear to God, they call it that) #302877005. • Install a self-adhesive shim kit (#171698993) to quiet noisy disc brakes.

Fox Profile

	1987	1988	1989	1990	1991	1992	1993
Cost Price ($)							
Base	6,015	6,310	7,210	8,260	8,405	8,770	9,065
Used Values ($)							
Base ↑	2,000	2,300	2,500	3,000	3,500	4,000	4,500
Base ↓	1,700	1,800	2,000	2,500	3,000	3,500	4,000
Extended Warranty	N	N	N	N	N	N	N
Secret Warranty	N	N	N	N	N	N	N
Reliability	②	②	②	③	③	③	③
Air conditioning	②	②	③	③	③	③	③
Body integrity	②	②	②	②	③	③	③
Braking system	②	②	②	②	②	③	③
Electrical system	②	②	②	②	②	③	③
Engines	②	②	②	③	③	③	③
Exhaust/Converter	②	②	②	③	③	③	⑤
Fuel system	②	②	②	③	③	③	③
Ignition system	②	③	③	③	④	④	④
Manual transmission	④	④	④	⑤	⑤	⑤	⑤
- automatic	③	③	③	③	④	④	⑤
Rust/Paint	②	②	②	③	③	③	③
Steering	③	③	③	④	④	④	④
Suspension	②	③	③	④	④	④	④
Crash Safety	②	①	②	②	②	②	②

Cabrio, Golf, and Jetta

Rating: Above Average (1993–97); Not Recommended (1988–92). There was no '94 model Cabrio. Expect the '96 Cabrio (convertible) version to cost almost double what you would pay for a base Golf. **Maintenance/Repair costs**: Higher than average; repairs are dealer dependent. **Parts**: Expensive, but generally available from independent suppliers.

Technical Data

ENGINES	Liters/CID	HP	MPG	Model Years
OHC I-4 FI	1.8/109	85–105	23–27	1985–93
DOHC I-4 FI	1.8/109	123	21–25	1987–89
OHC I-4D FI	1.6/97	52	35–42	1985–91
OHC I-4TD FI	1.6/97	68	35–40	1985–86
OHC I-4TD FI	1.6/97	59	35–40	1992
OHC I-4TD FI	1.9/116	90	39–46	1997–98
DOHC I-4 FI	2.0/121	134	20–25	1990–92
OHC I-4 FI	2.0/121	115	22–26	1994–98
OHC V6 FI	2.8/170	172	18–23	1994–98

Strengths and weaknesses: The Golf was much better executed than the failure-prone Rabbit, the model it replaced. The Golf has proven to be much more reliable and it performs as well or better than its American and Japanese counterparts. The 1.8L gasoline engine is very peppy and the diesel engines (not offered in '88 and '89) are very reliable and economical. Both engines are easily started in cold weather.

Reliability is impressive—for the first five years. Then the brake components, fuel, and electrical systems start to self-destruct as your wallet gets lighter. Exhaust-system components aren't very durable, body hardware and dashboard controls are fragile, and many owners have reported that the paint often discolors and is easily chipped.

Although the 1990–93 models are improved a bit, Volkswagen still has lots of quality problems. Owners report electrical short circuits, heater/defroster resistor and motor failures, leaking transmission and stub axle seals, defective valve-pan gaskets, head gaskets, timing belts, steering assemblies, suspension components, alternator pulleys, catalytic converters, and trim items. Diesel versions are a bit slow to accelerate, and fourth gear can't handle highway speeds above 50 mph.

The redesigned 1994–97 models are much more reliable and safer. Nevertheless, service-bulletin-disclosed problems for these model years include poor driveability, water leaks, trim defects, and premature rear tire wear. Owners report the following: electric door locks that take a long time to lock; paint that is easily nicked, chipped and marked; a variety of trim defects; premature rear tire wear; and poor-quality seat cushions. One owner of a 1996 Golf relates this "goodwill" experience with Volkswagen:

> ...Enclosed is a copy of a work order...to replace both front seat cushions—the second replacement for the driver's side since we purchased the vehicle in January 1996.
>
> The work order states "Goodwill Repair," as we are out of warranty. We feel this statement is rather misleading. Goodwill repair would have been if, when we brought the problem to the dealership's attention, they had offered to have the problem rectified with no hassle and without our having to resort to pressure from an outside source.
>
> The seat cushions have been replaced, but we feel they will only go again. Whether this is a flaw in the design of them or what, we can't say. The store manager seemed to think it was the way we "entered the vehicle" that caused the problem. As someone commented, entry was gained via the door!

For 1997, Golfs and Jettas equipped with the 115-hp 4-cylinder engine got a redesigned cylinder head that cuts engine noise. The Golf GTI VR6 rides lower, thanks to new shocks, springs, and anti-roll bars. The Cabrio Highline got standard AC, 14-inch alloy wheels, halogen driving lights, and leather upholstery. The base convertible lost its standard ABS and a few other goodies in order to keep a lid on price.

Jetta

Jettas provide slightly more comfort and better road performance than their Golf hatchback counterparts. The 1.6L 4-cylinder found on early Jettas was surprisingly peppy, and the diesel engine is very economical, although quite slow to accelerate. Diesels have a better overall reliability record than gasoline models and are popular as taxis. Jettas are far more reliable than Rabbits, but they, too, suffer from rapid body deterioration and some mechanical problems after their fourth year in service. For example, on post-'88 Jettas, starters often burn out because they are vulnerable to engine heat; as well, sunroofs leak, door locks jam, window cranks break, and windows bind. Owners also report engine head gasket leaks and water pump and heater core breakdowns. It's axiomatic that all diesels are slow to accelerate, but VW's fourth gear can't handle highway speeds above 50 mph. Engine noise is deafening when shifting down from fourth gear.

Problems on 1990–93 versions include electrical short circuits, vacuum hose misrouting, and defective steering assemblies, suspension components, catalytic converters, and trim items.

1994–97 models are much more reliable, but, nevertheless, owners report problems with leaky sunroofs, malfunctioning speedometers, broken trunk latches, and defective security systems.

Dealer service bulletins: 1995—CD changer skipping or grounding. • Slow or inoperative central locking. • Clutch pedal noise and vibration. • Front end knock. • Wind noise at A-pillar door glass seal. • Exterior door locks freezing. • Release handle won't open hood. • Faulty instrument cluster control light. • Poor fuel system performance. • Pulsating or clicking noise from engine. • Shifting difficulties. • Rotten-egg odor from exhaust. • Sunroof noise and vibration. • Water leaks from sunroof area. • Noise from 5-speed transmission when cornering. • Vehicle drifts or pulls to one side. • Suggestions for correcting wheel/tire vibrations. • Skipping wiper blades. **1996**—Front-end knock. • Noise in rear center console. • Vehicle drifts to one side. • Skipping wiper blades. **1997**—Anti-theft alarm sounds for no apparent reason and car won't start. • Automatic transmission fluid seeps from final drive breather vent. • Battery cable clamp won't tighten. • Frequent causes for inoperative window regulator motor. • Tips on eliminating front and rear door air leaks. • Excessive vibration or knocking of the shifter lever. • Transmission may not shift in or out of Reverse. • Troubleshooting windshield wiper failures.

Safety summary/recalls Recalls: 1985—The brake master cylinder is faulty. • Front seatbelt retractors on two-door models may not lock properly. **1985–90 Jetta** —The heat exchanger—located underneath the instrument panel—could rupture, spraying hot engine coolant throughout the passenger compartment.**1985–86**—Excessive fuel spillage could occur during a collision. **1985–87**—The engine may suddenly stall due to a seized fuel pump. **1987**—Loose lug nuts on alloy wheels could cause wheel separation. **1988**—The seatbelt retractor pawl is weak. • The brake booster is faulty. **1988–91**—The engine preheating tube may interfere with braking. **1988–92**—VW will replace the fuel hose and install new spring-type hose clamps. **1993**—The windshield wiper motor may fail. **1985–90 Golf/Jetta**—Hot coolant could escape into the passenger compartment. **1990**—Omitting air ducts could cause brake fluid to overheat. **1993–95**—The jack could collapse during use. **1985 Jetta**—The plastic clip that holds the brake line may be a fire hazard. **1987–89**—An incorrectly contoured brake line could result in brake failure. **1990**—The power steering pump bracket is faulty. **1991**—Too-short front brake hoses may rupture. **1985 Cabriolet**—The fuel supply hose is faulty. **1987–90**—The fuel tank may leak. **1990**—The airbag harness wire is poorly located. **1990–91**—A bent water separator panel could cause sudden acceleration. **1990–92**—A faulty fuel hose retaining clamp could be a fire hazard. **1991**—Defective track control arms used to support front wheels cause wheel misalignment and steering pull to one side.

Secret Warranties/Service Tips

1988–94—Poor driveability may be caused by a deteriorated oxygen sensor wire shield or poor ground connection. **1990**—Hard winter starting may require the installation of a new high-energy ignition coil, high-tension wires, and spark plugs. **1992–94**—Poor 2.8L engine performance or a rough idle may be due to a misrouted EVAP vacuum hose. **1993–94**—DSB 95-04 gives simple service tips for frozen door locks. **1994**—Water leaks into the engine bulkhead. **1996–97**—Tape player may have distorted sound or may snack on tapes. • A shifter that's hard to move side-to-side or won't go into Reverse may signal that the selector shaft is binding in the selector shaft housing bearing. **1997**—Erratic electrical functions may be caused by a loose ground at one of two grounding studs located under the battery tray. • If the transmission pops out of gear, check for a hairline crack on the selector shaft shift detent sleeve. • Buzzing noise from right side air outlet may be caused by loose outlet mounting screws.

Golf, Jetta, Cabrio Profile

	1990	1991	1992	1993	1994	1995	1996	1997
Cost Price ($)								
Golf	10,095	10,330	11,135	12,830	13,565	11,915	14,435	14,830
Jetta	11,120	11,355	12,580	14,030	14,365	12,915	15,535	15,930
Cabrio	16,630	17,740	18,585	19,665	—	21,215	21,260	20,785

Used Values ($)

Golf ↑	5,000	5,500	6,500	8,500	9,500	10,000	12,000	13,000
Golf ↓	4,000	4,500	5,500	7,500	8,500	9,500	11,000	12,000
Jetta ↑	5,000	5,500	6,500	8,000	9,500	10,000	12,500	13,000
Jetta ↓	4,500	5,000	5,500	7,000	8,500	9,500	11,500	12,000
Cabrio ↑	6,500	7,500	8,500	10,000	—	16,000	17,000	18,000
Cabrio ↓	6,000	6,500	7,500	8,500	—	14,500	16,000	17,000
Extended Warranty	Y	Y	Y	Y	Y	N	N	N
Secret Warranty	N	N	N	N	N	N	N	N
Reliability	①	②	②	③	④	④	④	④
Air conditioning	②	②	④	④	⑤	⑤	⑤	⑤
Body integrity	①	①	①	①	①	②	②	③
Braking system	②	②	②	③	③	③	③	③
Electrical system	①	①	①	①	①	②	②	③
Engines	②	②	②	③	④	④	⑤	⑤
Exhaust/Converter	②	②	②	③	③	④	④	⑤
Fuel system	②	②	②	③	③	③	③	④
Ignition system	③	③	③	③	④	④	④	④
Manual transmission	④	④	④	⑤	⑤	⑤	⑤	⑤
- automatic	③	③	③	③	④	⑤	⑤	⑤
Rust/Paint	②	③	③	④	④	⑤	⑤	⑤
Steering	③	③	③	③	④	⑤	⑤	⑤
Suspension	②	③	③	③	③	④	④	⑤
Crash Safety								
Golf	—	—	—	—	—	—	—	③
Jetta	—	—	—	—	—	③	③	③

MEDIUM CARS

A medium-sized car is a trade-off between size and fuel economy, offering more room and comfort but a bit less fuel economy (25–30 mpg) than a small car. These cars are popular because they combine the advantages of a smaller cars with those of larger vehicles. Because of their versatility and upsizing and downsizing throughout the years, these vehicles shade into both the small and large car niches. The trunk is usually large enough to meet average baggage requirements and the interior is spacious enough to meet the needs of the average family (seating four persons in comfort and five in a pinch). It's the best car for combined city and highway driving.

Recommended

Ford Taurus SHO
Honda Accord (1992–97)
Honda Prelude (1992–97)
Mitsubishi Diamante

Mitsubishi Galant (1994–97)
Subaru Legacy (AWD)
Toyota Camry (1990–97)
Mitsubishi Galant (1994–97)

Above Average

Acura Integra (1990–97)
Acura Vigor (1992–94)
Chrysler Avenger, Breeze, Sebring
Ford Taurus, Sable (1997)
Honda Accord (1990–91)
Honda Prelude (1988–91)

Mazda 626, MX–6 (1993–97)
Mitsubishi Galant (1990–93)
Nissan Stanza (1990–92)
Subaru Legacy AWD (1995–97)
Toyota Camry (1988–89)

Average

Acura Integra (1988–89)
Acclaim, LeBaron, Spirit (1991–95)
Ford Contour, Mystique (1996–97)
Ford Taurus, Sable (1996)
GM Achieva, Calais, Grand Am,
  Skylark (1995–97)
GM Corsica, Beretta (1993–96)
Honda Accord (1988–89)

Hyundai Sonata (1995–97)
Mazda 626, MX–6 (1991–92)
Nissan Altima (1993–97)
Nissan Stanza (1988–89)
Subaru Legacy AWD (1990–94)
Toyota Camry (1985–86)
Volvo 240 (1989–93)

Below Average

Chrysler Breeze, Cirrus, Stratus
Chrysler Duster, Shadow,
  Sundance (1993–94)
Ford Contour, Mystique (1995)
GM Achieva, Calais, Grand Am,
  Skylark (1988–94)
GM 6000, Celebrity, Century,
  Ciera (1997)

GM Bonneville, Cutlass Supreme,
  Delta 88, Grand Prix,
GM LeSabre, Lumina, Malibu,
  Monte Carlo, Regal (1988–97)
Volvo 240 (1985–88)
VW Corrado (1992–94)
VW Passat (1995–97)

Not Recommended

Acura 2.2 CL, 3.0 CL

Chrysler Acclaim, LeBaron, Spirit (1989–90)

Chrysler Aries, Reliant (1983–89)

Chrysler Duster, Shadow, Sundance (1987–92)

Chrysler Lancer, LeBaron GTS (1985–89)

Ford Contour, Mystique

Ford Tempo, Topaz (1985–94)

Ford Taurus, Sable (1986–95)

GM 6000, Celebrity, Century, Ciera (1982–96)

GM Corsica, Beretta (1988–92)

Hyundai Sonata (1989–93)

Mazda 626, MX-6 (1988–90)

Nissan Stanza (1985–88)

VW Corrado (1990–91)

VW Passat (1991–94)

1993 Ford Tempo: Along with its Topaz twin, these are Ford's quintessential lemons. Both cars were replaced none too soon in 1995 by the Contour and Mystique.

ACURA

Integra

Rating: Above Average, compromised by a stiff price (1990–97); Average (1988–89). **Maintenance/Repair costs**: Higher than average; repairs are dealer dependent. **Parts**: Expensive, but can be bought from cheaper independent Honda suppliers.

Technical Data

ENGINES	Liters/CID	HP	MPG	Model Years
DOHC I-4 FI	1.6/97	113–118	24–28	1986–89
DOHC I-4 FI	1.7/102	160	22–26	1992–93
DOHC I-4 FI	1.8/112	130–160	23–27	1990–93
DOHC I-4 FI	1.8/112	142	23–29	1994–98
DOHC I-4 FI	1.8/109	170	22–28	1994–98

Strengths and weaknesses: A Honda spin-off, early Integras (1986–89) came with lots of standard equipment and are a pleasure to drive, especially when equipped with a manual transmission. The high-revving 1.7L powerplant growls when pushed and lacks guts (read, torque) in the lower gears. The 4-speed automatic saps the base engine's power considerably. Engine and tire noise are intrusive at highway speeds. The car corners well and is more agile than later 1990–93 models. Its hard ride can be reduced a bit by changing the shocks and adding wide tires. The front seats are very comfortable, but they're set a bit low, and the side wheel wells leave little room for your feet. Rear seat room is very limited, especially on the three-door version.

A large number of 1989–90 Integras have faulty distributor igniters. When the igniter fails, the car stalls and it may be impossible to restart. The only remedy is to call a tow truck and have a garage replace the distributor.

Overall, assembly and component quality are good but not exceptional, as you can see from the "Service Tips" list. To avoid costly engine repairs, check the engine timing belt every 2 years/40,000 miles.

For model years 1990–93, the 1.8L engine is smoother running but delivers the same maximum horsepower as the 1.7L it replaced. Surprisingly, overall performance has been toned down and is seriously compromised by the 4-speed automatic gearbox. Interior design is more user friendly, with the front seating roomier than in previous years, but reduced rear seating is still best left to small children.

Mechanical reliability is impressive, but that's the case with most Hondas that sell for far less, and many mechanical components are so complex that self-service can pretty well be ruled out. The Integra's front brakes may require more attention than those of other Hondas. Surprisingly, what Integras give you in mechanical reliability they take away in poor quality control of body components and accessories. Water leaks, excessive wind noise, low-quality trim items, and plastic panels that deform easily are all commonplace. Owners also report severe steering shimmy, excessive brake noise, premature front brake pad wear-out, and radio malfunctions.

In the 1994 model year, the Integra was dramatically restyled with a more aerodynamic profile and a few more horses were wrung out of the venerable 1.8L 4-banger through variable valve timing. The 1994–97 models also offer a smoother ride than previous versions. But, overall, there are too few improvements to justify the high prices that late-model Integras command.

Owners report that steering wheel shimmy, fit and finish deficiencies, and malfunctioning accessories continue to be problematic on later models. Premature front brake wear is also an ongoing concern. Squeaks and rattles frequently crop up in the door panels and hatches and the sedan's frameless windows often have sealing problems.

Safety summary/recalls: **Recalls**: **1986–87**—An upgraded contact unit retainer needs to be attached to the front windshield wiper assembly. **1986–1991**—Takata seatbelts will be replaced. **1987–88**—Acura will repair or replace defective heaters for free. **1990–91**—Takata seatbelts will be replaced. **1994**—Automatic transmission retaining clip may show wrong gear.

Secret Warranties/Service Tips

1986–89—A faulty fuel pump check valve or fuel pressure regulator may be the cause of hard starts. Correct this problem by installing an improved fuel pressure regulator (#16740-PG7-663) or fuel pump (#16700-PG7-663). **1990–91**—DSB 91-015 is an excellent troubleshooting guide to the myriad squeaks and rattles in the dash, front doors, hatch, steering shaft, and sunroof. **1990–93**—Poor AM radio reception is likely caused by a poor ground connection between the antenna collar and the car body. **1992–97**—A defective seatbelt tongue stopper will be replaced free of charge with no ownership, time, or mileage limitations. **1994**—Rear hatch rattles are usually caused by a poorly adjusted striker. • Lots of troubleshooting bulletins are offered dealing with in-dash cellular phone problems. • Power door locks that cycle from locked to unlocked require a new power door lock control unit. **1994–95**—A partially open window that rattles may be caused by excess clearance between the window guide pin and the center sash guide or by the glass run channel having come out of the center channel. These are also likely causes of moon roof chattering or shuddering. **1996–97**—In a settlement with the Environmental Protection Agency, Honda paid fines totaling $17.1 million and extended its emissions warranty on 1.6 million 1995–97 models to 14 years or 150,000 miles. This means that costly engine components and exhaust system parts like catalytic converters will be replaced free of charge, as long as the 14-year/150,000-mile limit hasn't been exceeded. Additionally, the automaker will provide a full engine check and emissions-related repairs at 50,000 to 75,000 miles and will give free tune-ups at 75,000 to 150,000 miles. It is estimated the free check-ups, repairs, and tuneups will cost Honda over $250 million. The story of the settlement was first reported on page 6 of the June 15, 1998, edition of *Automotive News*. **All models/years**—Severe and persistent steering wheel shimmy is likely due to an imbalanced wheel/tire/hub/rotor assembly.

Integra Profile

	1990	1991	1992	1993	1994	1995	1996	1997
Cost Price ($)								
RS	13,145	13,870	14,335	14,045	16,695	17,390	18,080	17,335
Used Values ($)								
RS ↑	7,500	8,500	9,500	10,500	11,500	13,000	14,500	15,500
RS ↓	6,500	7,500	8,500	9,500	10,500	12,000	13,500	14,500
Extended Warranty	N	N	N	N	N	N	N	N
Secret Warranty	N	N	Y	Y	Y	Y	Y	Y
Reliability	④	④	⑤	⑤	⑤	⑤	⑤	⑤
Air conditioning	❷	③	④	④	⑤	⑤	⑤	⑤
Body integrity	③	③	③	③	③	③	③	④

Braking system	③	③	③	③	③	③	④	④
Electrical system	③	③	③	③	③	④	④	④
Engines	④	④	④	④	④	⑤	⑤	⑤
Exhaust/Converter	③	④	④	⑤	⑤	⑤	⑤	⑤
Fuel system	③	③	③	④	④	⑤	⑤	⑤
Ignition system	④	④	④	④	④	⑤	⑤	⑤
Manual transmission	⑤	⑤	⑤	⑤	⑤	⑤	⑤	⑤
- automatic	④	④	④	④	⑤	⑤	⑤	⑤
Rust/Paint	③	③	④	④	⑤	⑤	⑤	⑤
Steering	③	③	④	④	④	④	④	⑤
Suspension	③	③	④	④	④	④	④	⑤
Crash Safety	❶	⑤	⑤	❶	—	④	④	—

2.2 CL, 3.0 CL

Rating: Not recommended (1997); their first year on the market has brought out a surprising number of serious deficiencies that will hopefully be corrected during the second year's production. Overpriced and hard to find. **Maintenance/Repair costs**: Predicted to be higher than average; repairs are dealer dependent. **Parts**: Predicted to be expensive once the warranty expires.

Technical Data

ENGINES	Liters/CID	HP	MPG	Model Years
OHC I-4 FI	2.2/132	145	21–27	1996–97
OHC I-4 FI	2.3/138	150	20–25	1998
OHC V6 FI	3.0/183	200	23–28	1997–98

Strengths and weaknesses: The only difference between these two coupes is the 3.0 CL's larger engine, different wheels, and larger exhaust tip. Other vehicles worth considering, but with fewer standard features: the BMW 318, Honda Accord, Lexus SC300, Nissan Maxima, and Toyota Camry.

The most distinctive features of the 2.2L CL and its 3.0L CL twin are the engine and wheels. These cars are both stylish, front-drive, five-passenger, American built and designed luxury coupes. They have a flowing, slanted back end and no apparent trunk lock (a standard remote keyless entry system opens the trunk from the outside and a lever opens it from the inside). And while other Japanese automakers are taking content out of their vehicles, Acura has put content into the CL, making it one of the most feature-laden cars in its class.

Sure, we all know that the coupe's mechanicals and platform aren't that different from the Accord's, but when you add up all of its standard bells and whistles, you get a fully loaded small car that costs thousands of dollars less than such competing luxury coupes as the BMW 318 and the Lexus SC300. Consider this array of standard features: power windows, power mirrors, power moon roof, six-way power driver seat, remote keyless entry system, ABS, leather-wrapped steering wheel, simulated wood trim, automatic climate control, dual airbags, tilt steering wheel, cruise control, CD player, and AM/FM stereo with six speakers.

Although no one would consider the CL a high performance car, it gets plenty of power from its all-new 3.0L 24-valve SOHC Variable Valve Timing and Lift Electronic Control (VTEC) V6, in addition to the Accord's 2.2L, single overhead cam 4-cylinder VTEC engine. That engine's 145 horses (same as the Accord's) take the CL from 0 to 60 mph in a respectable nine seconds. Handling is better than average, thanks to the Accord's upgraded suspension, variable-assisted steering, and 16-inch wheels, which are one inch larger than the Accord's (I told you there was a lot of Accord in the CL).

Now that I've whetted your appetite with all that's right about these little Acuras, let's look at some of the problems reported with the '97 models. This is not a car for seating passengers in the rear. Back-seat room is insufficient, unless the front seats are pushed all the way forward, and the rear windows don't roll down. Furthermore, owners have become so incensed at what they perceive as Acura's arrogant stonewalling of customer complaints that one owner set up his own Acura Lemon website to air Acura gripes and put pressure on the company. He got his money back and shows how others can do the same in Part 2. Some of the common defects reported on this web site: faulty transmission control unit; transmission downshift problems; chronic brake rotor pulsation and other brake problems leading to resurfacing of brake rotors and replacement of brake pads, rotors, calipers, and springs; repeated front end realignments; door and wind noise leading to replacement of door; and sunroof won't stop at closed position, requiring replacement of sunroof switch and controller. Honda's 14-year free repair secret warranty applies to all 1996–97 Acuras, except for the type R models.

It's obvious to me that these first-year cars are a risky buy.

CL Profile

	1997
Cost Price ($)	
2.2 CL	24,395
3.0L	26,895
Used Values ($)	
2.2 CL ↑	21,000
2.2 CL ↓	20,000
3.0 CL ↑	22,000
3.0 CL ↓	21,000
Extended Warranty	N
Secret Warranty	N
Reliability	④
Crash Safety	—

Vigor

Rating: Above Average (1992–94). **Maintenance/Repair costs**: Higher than average; repairs are dealer dependent. **Parts**: Expensive, but most mechanical components can be bought cheaper from independent suppliers. Accord parts can be used for most maintenance chores. Body panels and engine components, however, are more difficult to find.

Technical Data

ENGINE	Liters/CID	HP	MPG	Model Years
OHC I-5 FI	2.5/152	176	19–23	1992–94

Strengths and weaknesses: A spin-off of the Honda Accord sedan, the 5-cylinder Vigor went through only three model years (1992–94). Due to its high cost and the absence of a more economical, smoother, and easier-to-repair 6-cylinder powerplant, most buyers chose the cheaper Accord, instead. This compact has power to spare, handles well, and has an impressive reliability/durability record. On the other hand, owners report the following problems: lots of engine, tire, and road noise intrude into the passenger compartment at highway speeds; the engine and transmission lack smoothness; and the brakes aren't easy to modulate. The suspension is firm but not unpleasant, rear leg room is limited, and there have been some complaints of fit and finish deficiencies. Vigors are also notoriously thirsty for premium fuel.

Safety summary/recalls: **Recalls**: 1992—Inadequate venting could allow moisture to build up in the distributor cap and prevent the engine from starting.

Secret Warranties/Service Tips

1992—DSB 92-034 goes into great detail on ways to silence the Vigor's many squeaks and rattles. **All models/years**—Excessive steering wheel shimmy is likely due to an imbalance of the wheel/tire/hub/rotor assembly in the front end.

Vigor Profile

	1992	1993	1994
Cost Price ($)			
LS	24,340	25,380	27,485
Used Values ($)			
LS ↑	12,000	13,500	15,000
LS ↓	10,500	12,000	14,000
Extended Warranty	Y	Y	Y
Secret Warranty	N	N	N
Reliability	④	④	④
Crash Safety	❷	—	—

CHRYSLER/EAGLE

Aries, Reliant

Rating: Not Recommended (1983–89). Don't buy an Aries or Reliant if you can find a similarly equipped Chrysler Spirit or Acclaim. **Maintenance/Repair costs**: Inexpensive repairs can be done by any garage. **Parts**: Not hard to find and cheap when bought from independent suppliers.

Technical Data

ENGINES	Liters/CID	HP	MPG	Model Years
OHC I-4 2 bbl.	2.2/135	96	23–27	1985
OHC I-4 2 bbl.	2.6/156	101	20–25	1985
OHC I-4 2 FI	2.2/135	93–97	22–27	1986–89
OHC I-4 2 FI	2.5/153	96–100	21–26	1986–89

Strengths and weaknesses: A low selling price, uncomplicated mechanical components, and a roomy interior made these cars attractive buys when new, but once in service, they quickly deteriorate. Both cars use dirt-cheap, low-tech components that tend to break down frequently.

Manual transmission shifters are imprecise and balky. All cars have a problem with idle shake caused by the transverse-mounted 4-cylinder engine, as well as driveability problems, especially in cold or damp weather. The "gutless" 2.2L Chrysler-built 4-cylinder motor is a bit more reliable than the 2.6L Mitsubishi engine, which has a tendency to self-destruct. It also suffers from premature wear of the timing belt guide and piston ring and leaky camshaft oil plugs. The 2.2L powerplant has multiple problems, the main ones being a weak cylinder head gasket and timing belt failures. The turbocharged version often requires expensive repairs. The MAP sensor fails frequently and is costly to replace.

The best powertrain choices are either the fuel-injected 2.2L or 2.5L engine. Some transaxle and front suspension components wear out quickly, and power-steering rack seals develop leaks. Front brake rotors warp and rust, and hand brake cables seize. Carbureted engines are renowned for stalling and poor driveability. Exhaust systems, wheel bearings, and air conditioning components aren't durable. Water infiltration around the windshield and into the trunk are common. Surface rust due to chipped paint occurs frequently. More serious corrosion generally starts along the trunk line and along the edges of the rear wheel wells. Perforations tend to develop along the bottom door edges, around the windshield, and on the floor. Front doors stick when opened wide and make loud creaking and cracking noises when they're closed.

Safety summary/recalls: **Recalls**: 1989—Faulty engine valve cover gasket could leak oil.

Secret Warranties/Service Tips

1987–88—Harsh or abrupt shifting into Drive may mean that the rear clutch discs need changing. • If the manual transmission fails to engage second or third gear, consider replacing the second and third thrust washer snap ring (#6033348). **1987–89**—2.2L and 2.5L engines with an erratic low idle and/or no fast idle with fault code 25 may require that the throttle body wiring harness be tie-wrapped and positioned away from the valve cover edge. **1988**—An engine that stalls in cold weather may require a new SMEC module (#4557522). **1988–89**—A power-steering gear hissing noise may mean that the lower steering column coupling is defective. **1988–90**—2.2L and 2.5L engines running roughly at idle may need a new EGR valve. **1989–90**—2.2L engine knock may require a new engine controller module (#4557518). • Surging or bucking at 35–55 mph with an A413 or A670 automatic transmission can be fixed with driveability kit (#4419447). **All models/years**—A rotten-egg odor coming from the exhaust is probably the result of a malfunctioning catalytic converter. • The 2.6L Mitsubishi engine balancer chains frequently wear out prematurely and often cause serious damage (up to $2,000) to the engine's internal components. The problem can be prevented by adjusting the chain every 20,000 miles, changing the oil every three months or 3,000 miles, and by using SAE 5W-30 motor oil rated for both gas and diesel.

Aries, Reliant Profile

	1983	1984	1985	1986	1987	1988	1989
Cost Price ($)							
Aries, Reliant	8,551	8,855	8,957	9,085	9,840	9,018	9,600
Used Values ($)							
Base ↑	1,500	1,800	2,000	2,200	2,500	2,700	3,000
Base ↓	1,000	1,300	1,500	1,700	1,900	2,100	2,400
Extended Warranty	Y	Y	Y	Y	Y	Y	Y
Secret Warranty	N	N	N	N	N	N	N
Reliability	②	②	②	②	③	③	③
Crash Safety	②	②	②	②	②	②	②

Acclaim, LeBaron, Spirit

Rating: Average only with an extended warranty (1991–95); Not Recommended (1989–90). These front-drives are a better choice than the Aries/Reliant due to their more recent vintage and more refined engines and suspension. 1995 was their last model year. Some early LeBaron GTC convertibles cost only about $2,000 to $3,000 more than the standard LeBaron sedan. **Maintenance/Repair costs**: Lower than average; repairs can be easily done by independent garages. The ease with which the Spirit and Acclaim can be repaired and the low cost of most replacement parts add to their attractiveness as relatively inexpensive five-passenger, fuel-efficient used cars. **Parts**: Reasonably priced, with good availability through independent suppliers.

ENGINES	Liters/CID	HP	MPG	Model Years
Technical Data				
DOHC I-4T FI	2.2/135	224	17–23	1991–92
OHC I-4 FI	2.5/153	100	22–28	1989–95
OHC I-4 FI	2.5/153	150–152	19–23	1989–92
OHC V6 FI	3.0/181	141–142	18–24	1989–95

Strengths and weaknesses: Although these cars have an outdated design, Chrysler improved their assembly quality and backed these cars with a strong base warranty that's transferable to second owners. The 100-hp 2.5L 4-cylinder engine and 3-speed automatic are models of ruggedness. Acceleration is adequate with the standard 4-cylinder engine and quite fast and smooth with the 150-hp Chrysler-bred 2.5L turbo.

The following are all prone to rapid wear: the cylinder head gaskets on the 2.5L engine, the front suspension, brakes, fuel system, and air conditioning. The Mitsubishi-built V6 has generated complaints about premature oil leaks and fuel system problems. The Ultradrive A604 4-speed automatic transmissions (renamed the 41TE in 1992) were found early in production to have poor shifting, internal fluid leakage leading to clutch burn-out, and sudden second gear lockup. The problem first becomes apparent when the transmission tries to engage third and fourth gears simultaneously, causing either clutch failure or sticking in second gear. Between 1989 and July 1991, Chrysler tried 28 different changes to resolve the Ultradrive's clutch failures, second gear lockup, and excessive shifting on hills. The 41TE automatic transmissions on 1992–96 models are also failure-prone.

The air conditioner switches on and off continuously. The following parts often need replacing: windshield wiper and interior fan motors, speedometer-sending unit and MAP sensor, and steering rack, bushings, and front stabilizer bar. Owners report that the steering wheel's vinyl coating rubs off on hands and clothing and the plastics used in the seats and dash area give off vapors that collect as a film on inside window surfaces.

All model years have fragile body hardware and sloppy body assembly. Many owners report water infiltration, especially around the windshield and into the trunk. Surface rust is common, especially around the windshield, door bottoms, and rear lip of the trunk lid.

LeBarons are a bit more high-tech, but overall road performance and reliability are just as disappointing. The ride is rough and vibrations and rattles are constant. Automatic transmission torque converters frequently malfunction. The front suspension is particularly trouble prone, and electrical bugs and major computer module failures are common. Wheel bearings, fuel pumps, and rear window motors tend to wear out prematurely.

Owners of 1991–95 models report that oil leaks and oil pump failures are common, rear brakes are noisy, the heating, air conditioning, and ventilation systems often malfunction, and electrical components (notably electronic modules) aren't very durable. Paint and assembly quality are also below par, characterized by body hardware and trim that rust out, break, or fall off.

Safety summary/recalls: In all three cars, the front wheels tend to lock prematurely when braking heavily. • According to the Washington-based Center for Auto Safety (CFAS), engine fires due to fuel and oil leaks from 1978–90 front-drive Chryslers have generated hundreds of complaints. • Rear brake lockup and master cylinder failures on 1978–92 models are also common, according to the CFAS. **Recalls: 1989–90**—Engine oil leakage means a new engine valve cover gasket is needed. **1991**—Pin bolts on the front-disc brake caliper guide might be too loose. • Both airbag front-impact sensors might be improperly mounted. • Outboard front seatbelts might not latch properly. **1992**—The coupling bolts on the steering column shaft could be faulty. **1994**—Seatbelt assembly could fail in an accident. **1990 LeBaron**—Airbag inflator module could be defective.

Secret Warranties/Service Tips

1989—Leaking fuel injectors are a common problem. • If the AC heater check valve freezes, install a new vacuum-control check valve (#5264270). • Models with 3.0L engines that lose power may need a new throttle body base gasket. • 3.0L engines that burn oil, stall, or lack power may have excessive sludge accumulation in the left bank (front) rocker cover baffle oil drain hole. • 2.5L turbo engines that lose power may need the Chrysler driveability kit (#4419460), or, during hot weather, a new vacuum connector (#5277577). **1989–90**—A604 automatic transmissions with excessive upshifting/downshifting require a new A604 controller (#4557585). • Rough idling might require the replacement of the EGR valve. **1989–91**—A604 automatic transmissions with 1–2 upshift shudder may need the 2–4 clutch replaced. **1989–93**—3.0L engines that burn oil or produce a smoky exhaust at idle can be fixed by installing snap rings on the exhaust valve guides and replacing all of the valve guide stems or the cylinder head. **1989–95**—Intake valve deposits are the likely cause of stalling, loss of power, hesitation, or hard starting. • Failure to go into Reverse is likely caused by faulty low/reverse piston. • Various tips are offered on correcting third gear shuddering. **1990**—A604 automatic transmissions that limp or fail to shift require the replacement of the PRNDL and Neutral safety switch. **1990–91**—Surging or bucking at 35–55 mph with A413 or A670 automatic transmission can be fixed with driveability kit (#4419447). **1990–92**—Erratic idle speeds that occur after deceleration from a steady cruising speed can be corrected by replacing the idle air-control motor with a revised motor. **1990–94**—Harsh automatic shifts can be tamed by installing the following revised parts: kickdown, accumulator, reverse servo cushion springs, and accumulator piston. **1991**—Customer Satisfaction Notifications #499 and #521 set out Chrysler's commitment to correct, free of charge, engine oil pump failure. **1991–92**—Engines with a rough idle and stalling following a cold start may require a new Single Board Engine Controller (SBEC). **1991–93**—The serpentine belt may come off the pulley after driving the vehicle through snow. Install an upgraded shield, screw, and retainers. **1991–94**—Engines that stall following a cold start may need an upgraded Park/Neutral/start switch. **1991–95**—Poor AC performance while the AC blower continues to operate is likely due to the evaporator freezing. **1992**—If the heater and ventilation system changes to defrost mode during acceleration, trailer towing, or hill climbing, the installation of a revised vacuum check valve should cure the problem. • Long crank times, a rough idle, and hesitation may be corrected by replacing the intake manifold assembly. • A low-frequency moan or groan coming from the rear brakes can be reduced by installing an upgraded rear disc pad set (#4423667). **1992–93**—Rough idling after a cold start with 2.2L and 2.5L engines can be corrected by installing an upgraded powertrain control module (PCM). • Some 41TE transaxles may produce a buzzing noise when shifted into Reverse; this problem can be corrected by replacing the valve body assembly or valve body separator plate. • Deceleration shudder can be eliminated by replacing the powertrain control module with an upgraded version. **1992–95**—Tips are offered on eliminating AC odors and tracing likely causes of a rotten-egg exhaust smell. **1993**—Failure of the fuel pump check valve can cause start-up die-out, reduced power, or erratic shifting. **1993–94**—Acceleration shudder may be caused by automatic transmission front pump leakage. • Improve automatic shifting by installing an upgraded transmission control module. **1993–95**—Troubleshooting tips are offered concerning excessive brake noise. **1994–95**—Poor AC performance is likely due to defective compressor suction or discharge lines. **1995**—Transmission limp-in may be caused by an intermittent transaxle input speed-sensor signal. **All models/years**—Excessive effort required to disengage Park may mean a new Park rod assembly is required (#4431530). • Headlight condensation requires installing vents in the headlight assemblies. • A rotten-egg odor coming from the exhaust is likely the result of a defective catalytic converter, which should be replaced free under the emissions warranty.

Acclaim, LeBaron, Spirit Profile

	1989	1990	1991	1992	1993	1994	1995
Cost Price ($)							
Acclaim, Spirit	11,489	12,418	12,852	13,343	13,455	14,154	14,828
LeBaron Sedan	13,256	14,561	16,915	15,253	15,594	17,226	—
Convertible	18,956	18,816	19,160	18,631	19,569	18,239	18,709
Used Values ($)							
Acclaim, Spirit ↑	3,500	4,000	4,500	5,500	6,500	7,500	8,500
Acclaim, Spirit ↓	3,000	3,500	4,000	4,500	5,500	6,500	7,500
LeBaron Sedan ↑	4,000	4,500	6,500	6,500	7,000	9,000	—
LeBaron Sedan ↓	3,000	4,000	5,500	6,000	6,000	8,000	—
Convertible ↑	4,500	6,000	6,500	7,500	8,500	10,000	11,000
Convertible ↓	4,000	5,000	6,000	6,500	7,500	8,500	10,000

| Extended Warranty | Y | Y | Y | Y | Y | Y | Y |
| Secret Warranty | Y | Y | Y | Y | Y | Y | Y |

Reliability	②	③	③	③	③	④	④
Air conditioning	①	①	②	②	②	③	③
Body integrity	①	①	③	③	③	③	③
Braking system	②	②	②	②	②	③	③
Electrical system	②	②	②	②	③	③	④
Engines	②	②	③	③	④	④	④
Exhaust/Converter	③	②	②	④	⑤	⑤	⑤
Fuel system	③	③	③	③	③	④	⑤
Ignition system	②	③	③	④	④	④	④
Manual transmission	—	—	—	—	—	—	—
- automatic	②	②	②	②	②	②	③
Rust/Paint	②	②	②	②	②	③	③
Steering	②	③	③	⑤	⑤	⑤	⑤
Suspension	②	②	③	③	③	④	⑤
Crash Safety							
Acclaim, Spirit	①	①	⑤	⑤	①	②	④

Lancer, LeBaron GTS

Rating: Not Recommended (1985–89). **Maintenance/Repair costs**: Higher than average; repairs aren't dealer dependent. **Parts**: Higher-than-average cost (independent suppliers sell for much less), but not hard to find.

Technical Data

ENGINES	Liters/CID	HP	MPG	Model Years
OHC I-4 FI	2.2/135	93–99	20–23	1985–89
OHC I-4T FI	2.2/135	146	18–23	1985–88
OHC I-4T FI	2.2/135	174	17–22	1987–89
OHC I-4 FI	2.5/153	96–100	18–23	1986–89
OHC I-4T FI	2.5/153	150	18–23	1989

Strengths and weaknesses: These cars suffer from many of the same problems as the Aries and Reliant K cars and their 1989 replacements, the Spirit and Acclaim. Road performance is sedate with the standard engines and suspension, and snappy with turbocharging. The interior will seat five comfortably and offers all the advantages of the hatchback design. The manual transmission is balky and its clutch has a poor durability record. Turbo models are risky buys at all times.

Head gaskets are prone to leaks on all engines. Shock absorbers, MacPherson struts, and brakes wear out quickly. Front brake rotors are prone to rusting and warping. The electrical system is troublesome: the distributor pickup and computer modules malfunction constantly, causing stalling and hard starting. Air-conditioning components have a short life span and body hardware is fragile.

Safety summary/recalls: **Recalls**: **1985**—Seatbelts might be missing. Driver's seat frame could be weakened by fatigue cracks. **1985-86**—Seatback could have excessive rearward movement. **1985-87 Turbo**—Fuel leaking from the supply hose could create a fire hazard. **1987 Shelby**—Parking brake could malfunction. **1989**—Original brake pads fail due to excessive corrosion. • Engine valve cover gasket could leak oil, creating a fire hazard.

Lancer, LeBaron GTS Profile

	1985	1986	1987	1988	1989
Cost Price ($)					
Lancer	10,390	11,113	11,589	12,275	12,956
LeBaron GTS	10,700	11,440	11,890	12,591	17,370
Used Values ($)					
Lancer ↑	1,500	2,000	2,500	3,000	3,500
Lancer ↓	1,200	1,500	2,000	2,500	3,000
LeBaron GTS ↑	1,800	2,300	2,800	3,300	4,700
LeBaron GTS ↓	1,400	1,800	2,200	2,800	4,000
Extended Warranty	Y	Y	Y	Y	Y
Secret Warranty	N	N	N	N	N
Reliability	❶	❶	❶	❶	❷
Crash Safety	❷	—	—	—	—

Duster, Shadow, Sundance

Rating: Below Average (1993–94); Not Recommended (1987–92). 1994 was the last model year, then these cars were replaced by the Neon. **Maintenance/Repair costs**: Average; repairs aren't dealer dependent. **Parts**: Average cost, but can be bought for less through independent suppliers.

Technical Data

ENGINES	Liters/CID	HP	MPG	Model Years
OHC I-4 FI	2.2/135	93–96	22–25	1987–94
OHC I-4 FI	2.2/135	146	18–22	1987–88
OHC I-4 FI	2.2/135	174	18–22	1990
OHC I-4 FI	2.5/153	96–100	19–24	1988–94
OHC I-4T FI	2.5/153	150–152	18–22	1989–91
OHC V6 FI	3.0/181	142	18–24	1992–94

Strengths and weaknesses: Fairly rapid depreciation makes these cars relatively inexpensive to buy. They're better built than other Chryslers in their class, but they still have many of the same mechanical and body weaknesses that Chrysler owners have suffered with throughout the years.

On early models, the turbocharged engine isn't very reliable and can be quite expensive to repair. The fuel-injection system can be temperamental and the MacPherson struts leak or wear out prematurely. Front brakes are particularly prone to rapid wear and parking brake cables need frequent service. Convertible tops on the 1991 Shadow tend to leak profusely and non-metallic paint chips easily.

Owners of 1989–92 models report cylinder head, oil pan gasket, and rear crankshaft seal leakage; the air conditioning compressor rarely lasts more than two years; windshield wiper fluid often freezes in hoses; and the power-steering assembly seldom lasts longer than five years. Fortunately, the assembly isn't that expensive to replace. The upgraded '92 41TE automatic transmission is problematic, engine head gaskets often need replacing, oil leaks and oil pump failures are common, rear brakes are noisy, the heating, air conditioning, and ventilation systems often malfunction, electrical components (notably electronic modules) aren't very durable, and excessive suspension vibrations are common. Body assembly is sloppy, paint discolors or peels prematurely, door moldings fall off, and doors freeze shut.

Safety summary/recalls: According to the Center for Auto Safety (CFAS), hundreds of owners have complained about engine fires caused by fuel and oil leaks in 1978–90 front-drive Chryslers. • Rear brake lockup and master cylinder failures on 1978–92 models are also common, according to the CFAS. **Recalls: 1987 Turbo**—Fuel can leak at supply hose/pressure regulator/fuel rail connections. **1987 Shelby**—The parking brake may be faulty. **1988**—The front passenger seatbelt retractor may be faulty, compromising child safety seat protection. **1988–89**—The automatic shoulder restraint system could malfunction in a collision. **1989–91**—The possibility of engine oil leakage means that owners can get a new engine valve cover gasket. **1991**—Guide pin bolts on front disc brake calipers may be too loose. **1991–92**—Steering wheel cracks may cause the wheel to loosen. **1991 Shadow**—Both airbag front-impact sensors may be improperly mounted. • Outboard front seatbelts may not latch properly. **1991–92**—The driver's seatback attaching bolt may fail. **1992**—Coupling bolts are faulty in the steering column shaft.

Secret Warranties/Service Tips

1987–88—If the manual transmission fails to shift into Reverse, install a pull-up ring service kit (#4443404). **1987–89**—Heat from exhaust system may scorch or melt carpet; install a heat shield kit (#4549356). **1989**—Leaking fuel injectors are a common problem. • 2.5L turbo engines that lose power may need Chrysler driveability kit (#4419460) or, during hot weather, a new vacuum connector (#5277577). **1989–90**—Rough idling may require the replacement of the EGR valve. • Squeaking from the exhaust flex joint requires a revised exhaust manifold-to-exhaust-pipe sealing ring. **1990**—Clearcoat paint delamination cause and cure are outlined in a special bulletin. **1990–91**—Surging or bucking at 35–55 mph with A413 or A670 automatic transmission can be fixed with driveability kit

(#4419447). • 2.2L and 2.5L engines with oil leaks at the valve cover need a new cover. **1990–92**—Erratic idle speeds occurring after deceleration from a steady cruising speed can be corrected by replacing the idle air control motor. **1991–93**—The serpentine belt may come off the pulley after driving through snow; install an upgraded shield, screw, and retainers. **1991–94**—Engines that stall following a cold start may need an upgraded Park/Neutral/start switch. • Poor AC performance while the AC blower continues to operate is likely due to the evaporator freezing. **1992**—If the heater and ventilation systems change to the defrost mode during acceleration, trailer towing, or hill climbing, the installation of a revised vacuum check valve should cure the problem. • Long crank times, a rough idle, and hesitation could be corrected by replacing the intake manifold assembly. **1992–93**—A buzzing heard when the 41TE automatic transmission shifts into Reverse can be fixed by replacing the valve body assembly or the valve body separator plate. • A deceleration shudder can be eliminated by replacing the powertrain control module with an upgraded version. • 3.0L engines that burn oil or produce a smoky exhaust at idle can be fixed by installing snap rings on the exhaust valve guides and replacing all of the valve guide stems or the cylinder head. • Engines that stall following a cold start may need an upgraded Park/Neutral/start switch. **1992–94**—Rough idling after a cold start with 2.2L and 2.5L engines can be corrected by installing an upgraded powertrain control module (PCM). • Harsh automatic shifts can be tamed by installing the following revised parts: kickdown, accumulator, reverse servo cushion springs, and accumulator piston. **1993**—Failure of the fuel pump check valve can cause start-up die-out, reduced power, or erratic shifting. **1993–94**—Acceleration shudder may be caused by automatic transmission front pump leakage. • Improved automatic shifting can be achieved by installing an upgraded transmission control module. **1994**—Poor AC performance is likely due to defective compressor suction or discharge lines. **All models/years**—A rotten-egg odor coming from the exhaust is likely the result of a malfunctioning catalytic converter, possibly covered under the emissions warranty.

Duster, Shadow, Sundance Profile

	1987	1988	1989	1990	1991	1992	1993	1994
Cost Price ($)								
Shadow/ Sundance	9,204	9,652	10,050	10,585	10,086	10,610	10,623	11,052
Duster V6	—	—	—	—	—	11,924	12,440	13,008
Used Values ($)								
Shadow/Sundance ↑	2,500	3,000	3,500	4,000	4,500	5,000	5,500	6,500
Shadow/Sundance ↓	2,000	2,500	3,000	3,500	4,000	4,500	5,000	6,000
Duster V6 ↑	—	—	—	—	—	5,500	6,500	7,500
Duster V6 ↓	—	—	—	—	—	4,500	5,500	6,500
Extended Warranty	Y	Y	Y	Y	Y	Y	Y	Y
Secret Warranty	Y	Y	Y	Y	Y	Y	Y	Y
Reliability	❶	❷	❷	❷	❷	❷	❷	③
Air conditioning	❶	❷	❷	❷	❷	❷	❷	❷
Body integrity	❶	❶	❶	❶	❶	❶	❷	③
Braking system	❶	❶	❷	❷	③	③	③	④

Electrical system	①	①	②	②	②	②	③	③
Engines	①	②	③	③	③	③	③	④
Exhaust/Converter	②	②	②	②	②	③	③	③
Fuel system	①	②	③	③	②	③	③	③
Ignition system	①	②	③	③	②	③	④	⑤
Manual transmission	③	③	③	④	④	⑤	⑤	⑤
- automatic	②	②	②	②	②	②	②	③
Rust/Paint	①	①	①	①	①	①	②	③
Steering	②	②	②	③	③	③	④	④
Suspension	②	②	③	③	③	③	④	⑤
Crash Safety	①	—	—	—	⑤	⑤	②	—

Breeze, Cirrus, Stratus

Rating: Below Average (1995–97). Stay away from any model carrying the anemic and failure-prone four-cylinder engine. **Maintenance/Repair costs**: Higher than average, but repairs aren't dealer dependent. **Parts**: Higher-than-average cost (independent suppliers sell for much less), but not hard to find. Nevertheless, don't even think about buying any one of these cars without a three- to five-year supplementary warranty.

Technical Data

ENGINES	Liters/CID	HP	MPG	Model Years
OHC I-4 FI	2.0L/122	132	23–29	1995–98
DOHC I-4 FI	2.4L/148	150	21–28	1995–98
OHC V6 FI	2.5L/152	164–168	20–27	1995–98

Strengths and weaknesses: Roomy and stylish, well appointed, comfortable, and smooth, the Chrysler Cirrus and Dodge Stratus are mid-sized sedan replacements for the LeBaron. The Breeze, launched as a '96 model, is essentially a decontented version of the more expensive Cirrus and Stratus.

Most components have been used for some time on other Chrysler models, particularly the Neon subcompact and Avenger/Sebring sports coupes. Power is supplied by three engines: a 2.0L 4-cylinder engine, shared with the Neon; a 2.4L 4-banger; and the recommended optional 2.5L V6. Carrying Chrysler's "cab forward" design a step further up the evolutionary ladder, these cars have short rear decks, low noses, and massive sloping grilles. A wheelbase that's two inches longer than the Ford Taurus makes these cars comfortable for five occupants, with wide door openings and plenty of trunk space.

These cars aren't all that impressive, either from a performance or a quality control standpoint. Furthermore, owners have serious misgivings as to whether these vehicles can withstand a harsh climate. One radio producer relates the following "adventure" with his '95 Cirrus:

...as I left a shopping mall parking lot, I heard a slight 'pop.' I instantly lost power steering. I had it towed to Triple Seven. They diagnosed the same problem that the university professor had: it appears Chrysler engineers made the sender hose from the power steering pump too long. In our severe climate, the line freezes, contracts, starves the power steering pump, and sends it into coronary arrest. And the professor and I weren't alone. Two other Cirruses with the same problem were seen Saturday at this dealer alone. Probably, this model was collapsing in large numbers across the West this last week in our record-breaking low temperatures.

Other problems reported by owners include the following: excessive road noise and vibrations, chronic automatic transmission failures, erratic engine operation, ABS malfunctions and sudden brake loss, paint delamination, electrical short circuits, weak headlights, AC glitches, water leaks into the trunk area and interior, easy-to-break trim items, and lots of squeaks and rattles.

Dealer service bulletins: 1995—Inoperative AC system. • Misaligned windshield washer nozzles. • Faulty deck-lid and door latches. • Rattling exhaust-system crossover pipes. • Faulty radios. **1996**—Won't start due to faulty neutral safety switch. • Single cylinder misfire. • Cold engine sag or rough idle. • A number of transmission problems and upgrades, including: intermittent control module failures; reduced transmission limp-in default sensitivity; changes to lock-up control system; and an upgraded Overdrive clutch hub. • Difficulty going into second gear or Reverse after a cold start. • Shuddering during upshifts or when torque converter is engaged. • Steering noise on right turns. • Vehicle drifts or leads at high speeds. • Cowl plenum water leaks. • Inoperable door glass. • Erratic windshield-wiper delay intervals. • Exhaust cover pipe rattle, buzz, and moan. • Ratcheting sound when coming to a stop. • Headlight pattern improvement. • Interior window film buildup. **1997**—Troubleshooting tips are available for poor AC performance. • The powertrain "bumps" when AC engages. • The CD changer rattles. • A low frequency rumbling sound can come from the front of the car while highway cruising. • Transmission shudders.

Safety summary/recalls: NHTSA probes: 1995—The lower control-arm ball joint fails. **1995 Sebring**—The ignition key gets stuck when shift lever is in Park; sometimes the key can be removed when the lever isn't in Park. • Night driving can get scary due to the poor performance of the front headlights, which aren't bright enough and so have an unsafe range. You shouldn't buy any one of these used cars without an evening test drive on a rural secondary road. This problem with weak headlights also affects the 1993–95 Concorde, Intrepid, Vision, LHS, and New Yorker. **Recalls: Cirrus, Stratus,**

Breeze 1995–96—Rusting in the ABS unit could cause the car to jerk to one side when stopping. **1995 Cirrus and Stratus**—Following an NHTSA lawsuit, Chrysler has been ordered to replace the rear seat-belt anchor belts. **1995–97 Cirrus, Stratus, and Breeze**—Dealers may replace, free of charge, prematurely corroded ball-joint components. **1996–97**—The hood could fly up. **1996–97 Breeze**—Dealers may replace, free of charge, prematurely corroded ball-joint components. **1997 Sebring**—The support bracket for the front-passenger head restraint could break; dealers must replace the entire seatback assembly. **1996–97 vehicles equipped with a 2.4L engine**—An engine oil leak could pose a fire hazard.

Secret Warranties/Service Tips

1995–96—Water leaks into the passenger compartment from behind the door trim panel. Correct the leakage by installing new door panel clips, door watershields, and additional tape to seal the watershield. • Front brake lining wears prematurely.

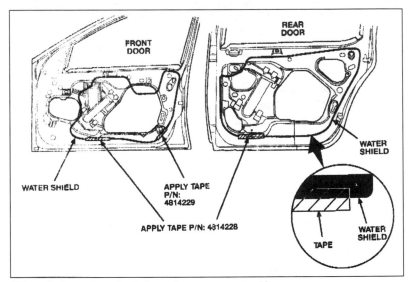

Water leakage from both doors is a common problem.

```
NO: 05-01-96
GROUP: Brakes
DATE: Jan. 26, 1996
SUBJECT: Premature Front Brake Lining Wear
MODELS: 1995-1996 (JA) Breeze/Cirrus/Stratus
SYMPTOM/CONDITION:
Grinding or squeaking noise from front brakes. This condition can result from premature front pad wear in
city commuter type driving or commercial use where the brakes are operated at elevated temperatures for
extended periods of time.
DIAGNOSIS:
Inspect the front disc brake lining, as described on page 5-234 of the 1996 Cirrus/Strauts Service Manual
(Publication No. 8`-270-6121). If one or more of the front brake linings are excessively worn, perform the
Repair Procedure.
PARTS REQUIRED:
1      4874548         Shoe Lining Set, Front Heavy Duty
REPAIR PROCEDURE:
This bulletin involves replacing the front disc brake linings with a heavy duty lining set.
NOTE:
This heavy duty front lining could generate customer vehicle brake applied noise and is not recommended
for replacement on vehicles with front brake noise complaints that do not exhibit premature wear. Use PIN
4798885 brake lining for normal replacement.
1. Replace the front brake disc brake lining, P/N 4874548, as outlined in the Service Manual, page 5-24.
POLICY: Reimbursable within the provisions of the warranty.
TIME ALLOWANCE:
Labor Operation No:    05-70-24-90    0.5 hrs.
FAILURE CODE:         P8 - New Part
```

Upgraded linings will reduce wear, but might increase noise.

1995–97—Troubleshooting tips are available to correct poor AC performance. • A powertrain "bump" when the AC engages is normal, according to Chrysler. • Transmission shudder could be caused by using the wrong transmission fluid. **1997**—Send a rattling CD changer back to the factory. • A low-frequency rumble heard while at highway cruising speed can be silenced by replacing the front hub bearing assemblies.

Breeze, Cirrus, Stratus Profile

	1995	1996	1997
Cost Price ($)			
Breeze	—	15,650	16,380
Cirrus	17,970	18,895	18,570
Stratus	15,230	15,820	16,545
Used Values ($)			
Breeze ↑	—	11,000	12,500
Breeze ↓	—	9,500	11,000
Cirrus ↑	11,500	13,000	14,500
Cirrus ↓	10,000	11,500	13,500
Stratus ↑	9,500	11,000	12,700
Stratus ↓	8,000	9,500	11,200
Extended Warranty	Y	Y	Y
Secret Warranty	Y	Y	Y
Reliability	❷	❷	③
Crash Safety	③	③	③
Side Impact	—	—	③

FORD

Tempo, Topaz

Rating: Not Recommended (1985–94). Be wary of the all-wheel drive's low price; it's no bargain at any price. The V6 is the powerplant of choice, but found only on '92 and later versions. In 1994, these cars were replaced by the '95 Contour and Mystique. **Maintenance/Repair costs**: Higher than average; repairs aren't dealer dependent, but troubleshooting usually costs an arm and a leg. **Parts**: Higher-than-average cost, but can be bought for much less from independent suppliers.

Technical Data

ENGINES	Liters/CID	HP	MPG	Model Years
OHV I-4 FI	2.3/141	86–100	22–26	1985–94
OHC I-4D FI	2.0/121	52	33–37	1985–86
OHV V6 FI	3.0/182	130–135	21–24	1992–94

Strengths and weaknesses: This front-drive compact's strong points are its attractive, rounded styling, and smooth, quiet V6, which works well with the automatic gearbox, and a roomy interior. On the downside, these cars are under-powered with the base 2.3L 4-cylinder engine, fuel thirsty when coupled with an automatic transmission, and failure prone. They are riddled with design and manufacturing bugs. The engine, transmission, electrical systems, electronic modules, fuel pump, power steering, suspension components, and cruise control all tend to fail prematurely. The 2.0L Mazda diesel engine is unreliable and doesn't deliver traditional diesel durability.

The 2.3L gas engine isn't much better. Cylinder head gaskets tend to leak and the engine's cooling, fuel, and ignition systems are plagued by a multitude of breakdowns. Stalling and hard starting are often caused by a malfunctioning catalytic converter. If the car still won't start, mechanics advise owners to tap the solenoid switch behind the battery. The starter motor is weak and the oil pan gasket tends to leak. There are many complaints of prematurely worn front axles and leaking seals. The air conditioning fails frequently and is expensive to repair. Heater noise often signals the need to change the heater motor. Power-steering rack seals deteriorate quickly. Suspension components such as tie-rod ends and strut bearings need replacement almost annually. Shocks, for example, last barely 20,000 km. Front brakes wear out almost as quickly and rotors are easily damaged. Even though these cars have been dropped, parts are plentiful, but they cost more than the North American average.

Body components are substandard and poorly assembled on all models and all years, with peeling paint and premature rusting being the main offenders. The front door seal tears every time the seatbelt doesn't retract properly, the car's air dam often works loose, and the hood cable-release mechanism tends to jam. Radio reception is mediocre. The 4X4 models are particularly unreliable, with most of the complaints centering on driveline deficiencies.

Safety summary/recalls: NHTSA probes: 1991 and 1995—Engine cooling-fan motor may overheat and cause a fire. Owners report that their cars' chronic stalling places them constantly at risk. One owner of a '91 Tempo says:

> The car will stall in all weather conditions and in all driving conditions. The engine failure is most apparent when decelerating or stopping after exiting from highways. The car frequently, and dangerously, stalls in the midst of left-hand turns. There is absolutely no warning. The car engine dies and there is occasionally some difficulty re-igniting the engine.

Other owners report the opposite problem with their '93 Topaz—the car may suddenly accelerate. **Recalls: 1985**—Rear-suspension control-arm bolts may fail. • 2.3L engine stalling, hesitation, and hard starting is due to a faulty ignition module. **1985–86**—Manual shift lever may accidentally slip into Neutral gear. **1986**—Sudden acceleration on cars with 2.3L engines may be due to a defective electronic control module. **1987**—Again, a faulty 2.3L engine electronic control module may cause high idling, loss of power, and stalling. **1987 Tempo**—Stainless-steel lug nuts may cause stud failure/wheel separation. **1988**—Faulty throttle sensor could cause unintended acceleration. **1988–93**—The ignition switch could experience an internal short circuit, creating the potential for overheating, smoke, and possibly fire in the steering column area of the vehicle. **1989–1994**—Cars with 2.3L engines may suffer a frozen PCV system when operated in extremely cold weather for extended periods at sustained highway speeds. Oil forced out through the dipstick tube or past some other gasket or seal area of the engine could pose a fire hazard. **1990**—Fan motor could overheat and cause engine damage. **1992–94**—Engine cooling-fan motor may overheat and cause a fire.

Secret Warranties/Service Tips

1983–90—Buzzing or humming coming from the fuel pump when the engine is shut off, a low battery, and hard or no-starts signal the need to install an upgraded fuel pump relay (#F19Z-9345-A). **1984–86**—Surging and bucking during acceleration is likely due to a loose intake manifold damaging the gasket. **1984–88**—2.3L engines with Duraspark II ignition may have starting problems; correct with a new module (#D9UZ-12A199-A). • Hard starting/stalling is caused by defective TFI modules that link the vehicle's distributor to its microprocessor and signal the plugs. • Coolant and oil leaks that plague 2.3L and 2.5L HSC engines can be stopped by installing an improved cylinder head gasket (#E83Z-6051-A). • Inoperative power door locks require an upgraded retainer clip assembly (#E8AZ-5421952-A). **1985–92**—An exhaust buzz or rattle can be fixed by installing new clamps to secure the heat shield attachments. **1985–94**—The in-tank fuel pump is the likely cause of all that radio static you hear; squelch the noise by installing an electronic noise RFI filter (#F1PZ-18B925-A). • Install worm clamps to silence heat shield/muffler buzzing (falls under the emissions warranty). **1986–94**—Ford offers an upgraded wiper-motor service kit for wiper motor malfunctions. **1987**—Rough idle or stall at idle may be caused by a shorted 12A581 wire harness. • No power on accelera-tion, stalling, or high engine idle may require the replacement of the EEC IV processor. **1987–94**—Loss of Reverse gear in cold weather may be due to defec-tive inner and outer Reverse clutch piston seals. • A rusty catalytic converter inlet pipe flange may be replaced free of charge with a stainless-steel flange under the emissions warranty. **1988**—Loss of AC when switching between AC and Max-AC can be fixed by installing an upgraded fan controller (#E83Z-8B658-A). **1988–89**—Loose or missing air deflector may cause engine over-heating; install new deflector. Engine bucks, jerks, hesitates, and stumbles; install upgraded engine fan controller (#E932-88658-A). **1988–92**—Cold hesi-tation when accelerating, rough idle, long crank times, and stalling may all sig-nal the need to clean out excessive intake valve deposits. **1989–90**—Owner Notification #B90: cooling fans on AC may loosen; replace with upgraded fan (#F03Z-8600-B). **1990**—Loss of AC cooling may be due to a cracked spring lock connector. Put in a new discharge manifold and discharge hose. **1990–93**—Noise heard from the power-steering pump may be caused by air in the system. **1992–93**—An inoperative air conditioner may be due to a faulty cooling fan relay (#E93Z-8Z658-A). **1992–94**—If the idle speed fluctuates excessively in cold weather, you may need to change the powertrain control module (PCM). **All models/years**—If the transmission seems erratic in shifting from sec-ond gear to third or downshifting from third to second, a newly designed governor spring will have to be installed. • A rotten egg odor coming from the exhaust is the result of a malfunctioning catalytic converter. • Three components that frequently benefit from Ford "goodwill" warranty exten-sions are catalytic converters, fuel pumps, and computer modules. If Ford balks at refunding your money, apply the emissions warranty for a full or partial refund. Regarding paint delamination, fading, peeling, hazing, and "microchecking": see pages 67–74 for details on claiming a refund.

Tempo, Topaz Profile

	1987	1988	1989	1990	1991	1992	1993	1994
Cost Price ($)								
GL	9,813	10,311	10,785	11,293	11,376	11,808	11,599	12,065
LX	10,974	11,390	11,884	12,415	12,498	12,936	13,605	13,350
Used Values ($)								
GL ↑	2,500	2,700	3,200	3,700	4,300	4,800	5,500	6,500
GL ↓	1,800	2,200	2,500	3,000	3,500	4,000	4,500	5,500
LX ↑	2,700	3,000	3,500	4,000	4,500	5,000	6,000	7,000
LX ↓	2,000	2,300	2,700	3,200	3,500	4,200	5,000	6,000
Extended Warranty	Y	Y	Y	Y	Y	Y	Y	Y
Secret Warranty	Y	Y	Y	Y	Y	Y	Y	Y
Reliability	❶	❶	❶	❶	❷	❷	❷	❷

Air conditioning	1	2	2	2	2	2	2	2
Body integrity	2	2	2	2	2	2	3	3
Braking system	1	1	2	2	2	2	2	2
Electrical system	2	2	1	1	2	2	2	2
Engines	1	1	1	1	2	2	3	3
Exhaust/Converter	1	1	1	1	3	3	3	3
Fuel system	1	1	1	1	2	2	2	2
Ignition system	1	1	1	2	2	2	3	3
Manual transmission	4	4	4	4	4	4	5	5
- automatic	2	2	2	2	2	3	3	3
Rust/Paint	1	2	2	3	3	3	3	4
Steering	1	1	2	2	3	3	3	3
Suspension	1	1	1	1	2	2	2	3
Crash Safety	—	—	—	1	5	5	5	1

Contour, Mystique

Rating: Average (1996–97); Below Average (1995). Mazda's 626 is a worthwhile alternative to the Contour and Mystique. It's a more stylish, highway-proven sedan with a better-than-average warranty and excellent parts supply and has been powered by a 2.0L and 2.5L V6 for the past several years. If you absolutely must have a Contour/Mystique, choose the much-improved (better seating, upgraded mechanicals) '96 or a later version. **Maintenance/Repair costs**: Higher than average, and most repairs are dealer dependent. **Parts**: Higher-than-average cost and sometimes hard to find.

Technical Data

ENGINES	Liters/CID	HP	MPG	Model Years
DOHC I-4 FI	2.0L/121	125	24–34	1995–98
DOHC V6 FI	2.5L/155	170	21–29	1995–98

Strengths and weaknesses: These front-drive, mid-sized twin sedans (Contour has a more angular nose and different dashboard) are based on the European-designed Mondeo, which has met with respectable sales after many years on the market. The four-door, five-passenger Contour sells for a bit less than its practically identical Mercury counterpart.

The main advantages of the Contour and Mystique are exceptional handling and a powerful, limited-maintenance V6 engine. Their drawbacks are an unacceptably high base price, cramped rear seating, a wimpy, noisy 4-banger, and spotty quality control. Both vehicles are set on a wheelbase slightly larger than that of the Taurus and come with two engines and transmissions: a base 16-valve 125-hp 2.0L 4-cylinder and an optional 24-valve 170-hp 2.5L V6. Either engine may be hooked to a standard 5-speed transaxle or an optional 4-speed automatic. A smooth but firm ride and crisp handling are guaranteed by the standard MacPherson strut front suspension, an anti-roll bar, and fully independent rear suspension. Other interesting standard features include dual airbags, adjustable head restraints, 60/40 split-fold rear seats, rear heater ducts, and a sophisticated air filtration system for the passenger compartment. Four-wheel disc brakes, a sport-tuned suspension, and high performance tires are standard features on the V6.

These cars have had lots of first-year problems. Owners report frequent computer module failures and a long wait for parts. One CompuServe member had this to say:

> My '95 Mystique ran fine for six months, but has been in the dealer repair shop—still not fixed—for three weeks now. First the 'overlock' froze, so you couldn't shift out of Park—even with a foot on the brake. The dealer said an 'electrical short circuit kept making a module fail.' They told me the part was part of a recall that had not yet been announced. No sooner had they fixed that when the Overdrive on-off button on the automatic gearshift stopped working. That's still not fixed after 11 working days. First the dealer claimed they couldn't 'locate the cause.' They sent the car out to a transmission expert who found another 'failed module.' The current problem is that the replacement part is 'much in demand,' and they're 'trying to locate one.'

Dealer service bulletins: **1995**—Fluid leaking from the transaxle pump seal. • Reduced power due to throttle plate icing. • Reduced steering assist during wet weather. • Insufficient AC cooling or excessive clutch end gap. • Delayed transmission engagement and shift errors, or no forward engagement or third gear. • Brake roughness upon application. • PCV tube wear-through. • Excessive vibration upon acceleration. • Noise upon hard acceleration or when turning. • Faulty speedometer. • Stuck fuel filler door. • Water dripping on floor. **1996**—Stalling or hard starts. • Grinding or clashing noise when shifting into third gear. • CD4E transaxle vent right-hand differential leak. • Fluid seeping from CD4E transaxle vent. • CD4E transaxle makes a whistle noise when in Park. • Harsh ride or rubbing noise from rear of vehicle. • Inoperative fuel filler door. • Fog/film on windshield/interior glass. • Musty and mildew-type odors. • Water dripping on floor from AC condensate leak. • **2.5L engine**—Squealing noise from water pump. • Stall or hooting noise from engine compartment. **1997**—Air blows out the defroster ducts only. • AC has a musty odor. • Transaxle fluid seepage. • Harsh transmission shifting. • Chirping or squeaking blower motor. • Fog/film on windshield/interior glass. • Front-end accessory drive-belt slippage. • Parking brakes stick or bind. • Poor carpet fit. • Tips on preventing brake vibration. • Wind noise around doors. • Stall, hooting, or moosing noise from engine compartment. • Stall and/or exhaust sulfur smell.

Safety summary/recalls: There are reports of gas tank leaks. **Recalls**: **1995**—The rear door window will be replaced. • The addition of a ground strap prevents an electrostatic charge from building up and igniting fuel vapors when refueling. • The hardware that attaches the outboard ends of the front seatbelts to the front seat frames may be cracked or fractured. • The passenger airbag may not inflate properly. • The fuel filler pipe opening reinforcement may leak fuel. Tank replacement includes a new fuel filter and a FREE FILL UP! The last item in the recall procedure involves filling up the tank (at Ford's expense) in order to confirm that there are no leaks at the tank-to-filler-neck seal. **1995–96**—Faulty traction control throttle cables may prevent the engine from returning to idle.

Secret Warranties/Service Tips

1995–97—Stall and/or exhaust sulfur smell requires a revised power control module. • Stall, hooting, or moosing noise from engine compartment can be fixed by replacing the air intake duct, idle air resonator, and idle air hose with a revised duct and resonator assembly (#F6RZ-9B659-CA). **1995–98**—Air that blows out the defroster ducts only may signal that the defrost actuator door linkage has become disconnected from the crank. • Transaxle fluid seepage can be corrected by servicing with a remote vent kit or by replacing the main control cover. • Parking brakes that stick or bind need a parking brake cable service kit. • Front-end accessory drive-belt slippage can be corrected by installing an upgraded FEAD belt, steel idler pulley, and splash shield kit.

Contour, Mystique Profile

	1995	1996	1997
Cost Price ($)			
Contour GL	15,470	15,980	16,020
SE V6	18,355	18,865	19,350
Used Values ($)			
Contour GL ↑	8,500	9,500	11,000
Contour GL ↓	7,500	8,500	9,500
SE V6 ↑	9,500	11,500	12,500
SE V6 ↓	8,500	10,000	11,500
Extended Warranty	Y	Y	Y
Secret Warranty	Y	Y	Y
Reliability	❷	③	③
Crash Safety	⑤	⑤	⑤
Side Impact	—	—	③

Sable, SHO, Taurus

Rating: The SHO is a Recommended buy. Other versions: Above Average (1997); Average (1996) if you can stomach the 1996's ugly redesign, which restricts side/rear views via arching rear pillars and windows like portholes; Not Recommended (1986–95). Serious 3.8L engine headgasket failures, automatic transmission glitches (especially the 1–2 shift), and chronic paint/rust problems are the main reasons these cars' rating has been downgraded this year. An extended warranty is a prerequisite for any 1986–95 Sable or Taurus. Frankly, I'm ticked off at Ford's poor quality control on its Sable and Taurus models over the past decade. If you look at most car guide magazines, they'll tell you that quality control has improved over the past several years. I disagree. That's not what Ford's service bulletins show. I've tolerated Ford's deteriorating quality control because Chrysler and GM's defects were more serious and more frequent. Plus, Ford set up a number of effective "goodwill" programs to compensate owners. Unfortunately, all that "goodwill" has dried up during the past several years. And, my ratings of the Taurus, Sable, and Windstar are lower, as a consequence. **Maintenance/Repair costs**: Higher than average, but repairs aren't dealer dependent. **Parts**: Average cost (independent suppliers sell for much less) and very easy to find, except for the SHO's Yamaha engine, which is practically indestructible, anyhow.

Technical Data

ENGINES	Liters/CID	HP	MPG	Model Years
OHV I-4 FI	2.5/153	88–90	21–25	1986–90
OHV I-4 FI	2.5/153	105	21–25	1991
OHV V6 FI	3.0/181	140–145	20–24	1986–98
DOHC V6 FI	3.0/181	200	18–24	1989–98
DOHC V6 FI	3.2/192	200–225	17–23	1993–95
OHV V6 FI	3.8/232	140	20–24	1992–95
DOHC V8 FI	3.4/207	235	16–22	1996–98

Strengths and weaknesses: Although they lack pickup with the standard 4-cylinder engine, these mid-size sedans are excellent family cars, offering lots of interior room, nice handling, and plenty of safety and convenience features. The best combination of high performance engine and transmission for all driving conditions: the 3.0L or 3.8L V6 hooked to a 4-speed for the family sedan and the Yamaha powerplant harnessed to a manual gearbox on the high performance SHO. Two caveats, however: the automatic transmission is failure-prone (1991–95 models, in particular) and is slow to shift—an annoying drawback if you need to rock the car out of a snowbank and fairly dangerous if you need to pull onto a busy roadway. The transmission is also a bit sluggish when downshifting from Overdrive while climbing steep hills. The other problem concerns the 3.0L engine's less-than-sparkling acceleration. The 3.8L V6 that equips most of the late-model cars offers much better highway performance with above-average fuel economy, and better reliability than its weaker 3.0L cousin, although there have been many cases of head gasket failures around the three-year mark. (These engine repairs are covered by Ford's 98M01 secret engine warranty covering engine failures.)

The problem-plagued 1986–95 models are the object of multiple safety-related recalls, secret warranties, and service adjustments. The 4-cylinder engine is a dog that no amount of servicing can change. It's slow, noisy, prone to stalling and surging, and actually consumes more gas than the V6.

The 3.0L engine is noted for cylinder head bolt failures and piston scuffing and is characterized by hard starting, stalling, excessive engine noise, and poor fuel economy. Changing the oil filter and spark plugs is particularly difficult and messy. Transmission cooler lines leak, heater hoses blow, and fuel gauge sending units often malfunction. Brakes need constant attention; in front, they're noisy, pulsate excessively, tend to wear out prematurely, require a great deal of pedal effort, and are hard to modulate. Master cylinders need replacing around 60,000 miles.

Although these sedans and wagons were redesigned in 1992, quality wasn't improved that much. In fact, only the latest 1996 redesign seems to have tackled some of the cars' quality shortcomings. Owners are keeping their fingers crossed, though, because the reduction in quality complaints may simply be caused by the vehicle's relative low mileage.

1988–95 models continue to have defective ignition modules, oxygen sensors, and fuel pumps, causing rough running, chronic stalling, hard starting, and electrical system short circuits. Other problem areas include the following: defective engine mounts; an automatic transmission that's slow to downshift, hunts for Overdrive, and gives jerky performance; air conditioners that are failure prone and can cost up to $1,000 to fix; malfunctioning heaters that are slow to warm up and don't direct enough heat to the floor (particularly on the passenger side); a defective heater core that costs big bills to replace (buy from an independent supplier); and noisy, prematurely worn rack-and-pinion steering assemblies. Front suspension components also wear out quickly and body/trim items are fragile on all cars (did somebody mention door handles?). Other electrical components like windshield wipers, fuel pumps, and the rear defroster interfere with radio reception. The automatic antenna often sticks, electric windows short-circuit, power door locks fail, and the electronic dash gives inaccurate readings. Owners report that electrical short circuits— which illuminate the "Check Engine" light and cause flickering lights and engine surging—are frequently misdiagnosed. Customers end up paying for the unnecessary replacement of the alternator, voltage regulator, or battery, in addition to unnecessary tune-ups. The speedometer is noisy and often inaccurate in cold weather.

1996–97 models were radically redesigned with a totally new, more rounded styling that turned off as many buyers as it turned on. Other '96 model changes included an upgraded Duratec 3.0L V6, new electronic controls for the LX, and a revamped, oval dash panel. Other improvements: better handling and ride quality, more effective soundproofing, and some transmission refinements (beginning with the '97 models). Despite these changes, however, owners still report that the non-Duratec 3.0 V6 is noisy and slow, the automatic transmission shifts roughly, and the suspension gives a stiff ride.

SHO

The Taurus SHO (Super High Output) sedan, debuting in 1989, carries a Yamaha 24-valve 3.0L V6 with 220 horsepower, a stiff, performance-oriented suspension and 5-speed manual transmission. As of 1993, a 4-speed automatic transmission became available. In mid-'96, a redesigned SHO debuted with a standard Yamaha 32-valve V8. Unfortunately, the manual transmission was dropped at that time, a move that has turned off most die-hard performance enthusiasts.

The SHO is an impressive high performance car that is apparently better built than regular-production Taurus and Sable versions. In fact, early SHOs escaped Ford's powertrain problems due to its reliance upon Yamaha for its engines and the wide use of a manual gearbox.

Is the SHO a good buy? The answer is yes, but only if you're willing to spend big bucks for your performance thrills. SHOs hold their value well and give impressive performance. On the other hand, they're hard to find (only 10,000 units a year are sold and only 3 percent of Taurus buyers opt for a SHO), they're expensive, and engine repairs may become a problem now that Ford has announced that 1998 may be the SHO's last model year. If the SHO is dropped next year, its price is likely to remain stable inasmuch as most buyers feel it's already overpriced.

Paint delamination

Over the past seven years, there have been frequent complaints of paint delamination, peeling, and premature rusting. One owner of a 1990 Sable found pinpoint rust spots during the first year of ownership and had the entire car repainted at Ford's expense. Unfortunately, the problem didn't go away. According to the owner, "...I have recently noticed continued paint defects causing the car to rust prematurely, specifically under the front edge of the hood....I maintain that the sealer and paint were improperly applied when the car was manufactured and that this is a defect that the Ford Motor Company should correct."

That *Lemon-Aid* reader is right and that's why this year's guide includes a comprehensive list of web sites, DSBs, and other secret-warranty documents that will help other Ford owners get their cars, minivans, trucks, and 4X4s repainted for free by Ford.

Article No. 93-8-4	
April 14, 1993	
PAINT - EXTERIOR CLEARCOAT "MICROCHECKING," HAZING OR PEELING	
FORD:	LINCOLN-MERCURY:
1983–93 THUNDERBIRD	1983–93 COUGAR
1984–93 TEMPO	1984–92 MARK VII
1985–93 ESCORT	1984–89 TOPAZ
1986 LTD	1985–89 TRACER
1986–93 TAURUS	1986 MARQUIS
1989–93 CROWN VICTORIA, MUSTANG, PROBE	1986–93 SABLE
	1988–93 CONTINENTAL, TOWN CAR
LIGHT TRUCK:	1989–93 GRAND MARQUIS
1983–93 RANGER	1991–93 TRACER
1986–93 AEROSTAR	1993 MARK VIII
1987–90 BRONCO II	
1988–93 F SUPER DUTY, F-47	
1991–93 ECONOLINE, EXPLORER	
1992–93 F-150-350 SERIES	
1993 VILLAGER	

ISSUE: The clearcoat layer of the basecoat/clearcoat paint system may "microcheck" (crack and erode), turn white, flake or peel off vehicle. This condition is noticeable on the horizontal surfaces only.
ACTION: Inspect the vehicle and if repair is necessary, refer to the following procedure for service details. This is a wet on wet procedure. Sanding is not required after the seal coat is applied.

Paint delamination is a problem that goes back to the 1983 model year, according to Ford's DSB 93-8-4.

Paint adherence is particularly poor on plastic components, weld joints, and the underside, even with mud guards. Owners also report that water leaks into the trunk through the taillight assembly and that 1986–95 versions produce an annoying sound of fuel sloshing when accelerating or stopping.

Dealer service bulletins: **1993**—Poorly performing air conditioning systems caused by a slipping clutch at high ambient temperatures. • Growling AC FX-15 compressor. • Fuel odors in the passenger compartment. • Noisy power-steering units. • Inoperative power door locks. • Under-hood squeaks, chirps, and knocks; wind noise coming from front door windows. • Intermittent long cranks or no-starts. • A service engine light that has a mind of its own and may go on for no apparent reason. **1994**—A faulty 3.8L engine rocker arm assembly may be the cause of squeaking, chirping, and knocking noises. • A rough idle, hesitation, and excessive fuel consumption. • Defective fuel pumps often produce extraneous noise in radio speakers. • Faulty electric rear window defrosters. • Inadequate AC operation caused by a faulty cold engine lockout switch and hose assembly. **1995**—Hesitation, no-start, reduced power, stalling, no-crank due to solenoid corrosion (see bulletin on following page).

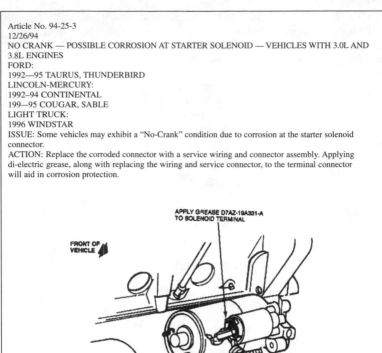

Article No. 94-25-3
12/26/94
NO CRANK — POSSIBLE CORROSION AT STARTER SOLENOID — VEHICLES WITH 3.0L AND 3.8L ENGINES
FORD:
1992—95 TAURUS, THUNDERBIRD
LINCOLN-MERCURY:
1992–94 CONTINENTAL
199—95 COUGAR, SABLE
LIGHT TRUCK:
1996 WINDSTAR
ISSUE: Some vehicles may exhibit a "No-Crank" condition due to corrosion at the starter solenoid connector.
ACTION: Replace the corroded connector with a service wiring and connector assembly. Applying di-electric grease, along with replacing the wiring and service connector, to the terminal connector will aid in corrosion protection.

This electrical problem affects 1992–96 model cars and minivans.

• Delayed transmission engagement and shift errors, harsh shifts, no 3–4 shift, erratic shifts, Forward/Reverse gear malfunctions and transaxle click when in Reverse. • Insufficient AC cooling or excessive clutch end gap; AC compressor has moans, chirps, or squeaks coming from the blower motor at low speeds. • Fuel pump buzz/whine heard through the radio speaker. • Faulty temperature gauge. • No-crank caused by a corroded starter solenoid (carried over several model years). • Brake roughness upon application and a clacking/thumping noise when braking. • Premature inner edge wear on the rear tires. • A fuel tank sloshing noise. **1996**—No-start or stall. • Stall or hard start after 1–4 hour soak. • Cold engine hesitation/stumble. • Harsh automatic transmission shifting. • Click from transmission when going into Reverse. • Transaxle driveline noises. • Case breakage at rear planet support. • Grunt or groan noise during steering wheel return. • Reduction in power-steering assist. • Door hinge correction. • Fog/film on windshield/interior glass. • Musty and mildewy odors. • Dead battery diagnosis. • Blower motor noise. • Acceleration or deceleration clunk noise. • Wind noise at A-pillar at highway speeds. • A-pillar creaking noise. • Front suspension creak/groan. • Hard starting, long crank, stalling. • Rear headliner sag. • Door handle malfunctions. • High idle, surge, stall, harsh transmission engagement. • Loose catalyst or muffler heat shields. • Click noise when going into Reverse. • AM static. • Warm weather stalling. • Thump, clunk, or chuckle noise from front end. • Troubleshooting driveline noises. • Water leaking onto passenger compartment floor. • Excessive wind noise. **1997**— Harsh automatic shifting. • Chronic dead battery. • Excessive blower motor noise. • Acceleration or deceleration clunk. • Front suspension clunk. • A-pillar creaking noise. • Front end accessory drive belt (FEAD) may slip during wet conditions causing a reduction in steering power assist. • Steering wheel grunt or honk noise. • Loose catalyst or heat shields. • AM band static. • Stall or surging with automatic transmission engagement. • Water leaks onto passenger floor area.

Safety summary/recalls: NHTSA probes: 1993—Front coil springs may fracture causing the suspension to collapse. **1995**—Sudden windshield shattering. • AC failures. • Headlight failures. **1995–96**—Fuel pump failures. • ABS failures. • Airbag fails to deploy or is accidentally deployed. • Transmission slips out of Park. • Sudden acceleration. • Stalling. • Engine compartment fires. • Defective door locks. **1996**—Cruise control won't slow vehicle on slopes. • Defective power steering. • Transmission shifts erratically. • Left front wheel may separate from car. **Recalls: 1986**—Ignition key can be removed when the ignition switch isn't locked. • Faulty cooling fan motor resistor may cause the air conditioner to malfunction. • Misrouted battery wire may lead to premature radiator leakage. **1986 wagon**—The right-quarter tinted window was improperly tempered. **1986–87 wagons**—Rear windows may break suddenly. **1986–87**—A faulty spring-lock fuel line coupling is a fire hazard. **1986–91**—The front brake rotors may snap as a result of corrosion. **1986–92 wagons**—The rear storage compartment is a hazard to children because it can't be opened from the inside. Owners should deactivate the slam-down latching mechanism with a screwdriver then get a dealer to install a replacement mechanism. **1986–93**— Vehicles may have detached body mounts at the rear corners of the car's subframe. This defect could allow the subframe to drop and make steering difficult. The mounts will be inspected and a reinforcement plate installed with new attaching bolts. **1987**—Lower steering shaft may separate. • A defective rear spindle assembly could separate and cause loss of vehicle control. **1988 3.0L**—The air conditioner compressor shaft seal is faulty. **1988 3.8L**—The power-steering pump pulley may fail causing loss of power steering and other accessories. **1988–89**—A misrouted power seat switch could cause an electrical fire. **1988–90**—Engine mount failure could lead to engine surges, a stuck throttle, or power-steering hose failures. **1989–90**—End release seatbelt buckles may not latch properly. **1991–95**—Cruise control units and throttle control cable are faulty. **1992**—The inner tie-rod may collapse suddenly. The son of a West Coast '92 Taurus owner relates this incident:

> ...The right inner tie-rod, a piece of the suspension critical to the steering and thus safety of my 1992 Taurus, broke while my father was attempting to make a right turn from a stop sign. The car lost all steering control and the front wheels were seized. Fortunately, the car was barely moving, and no collision occurred...I can tolerate a radio or AC failure on a "medium aged" car but critical safety components should have a longer service life designed into them. I hope you can inform all Taurus/Sable owners of the inherent dangers lurking in their steering system. And for those cars still under warranty, specify that the part be thoroughly inspected by first removing the rubber protecting boot...

1992 wagon—Children could lock themselves in the foot well area or storage area. • The liftgate could open while the vehicle is in motion. **1992–95**—The engine cooling fan may freeze and cause the cooling fan motor to overheat, in turn causing wiring damage and sparking a fire (3.0L and 3.8L engines only). • The throttle can stick and not return to idle if water enters the throttle cable area and freezes (3.8L engines only). **1993 ABS**—Rear-drive controllers were installed in error. **1995**—Brake master cylinder may be defective. **1996**—The brake fluid indicator may malfunction. **1996 Taurus**—Fuel may leak from a faulty fuel pressure regulator. **1996–97 Taurus and Sable**—The transmission may not engage; PRNDL may give a false reading. • Defective fuel rail may deliver fuel to the injectors at more than 43 psi; it may cause chronic stalling under low-speed deceleration or acceleration. • Transmission fluid leakage could cause a fire. **1996 SHO**—Faulty fuel pressure regulator could cause a fire.

Secret Warranties/Service Tips

1986–89—A great deal of door handle and tailgate rusting occurs around the bottom horizontal window sill, usually after the third year. Ford will assume part of the repair cost on a case-by-case basis. • A glove compartment rattle may require rerouting the AC vacuum hoses. • If the accessories frequently cut out, install a new ignition switch wire harness. **1986–90**—Extended or no 3–4 shift may require a reassembled direct clutch piston and spring retainer. • No shifts, harsh shifts, or extended shifts may be due to faulty oil pump body and valve body check balls. • AC evaporator water leaks onto the carpet require a new core and seal assembly (#E9DZ-19860-A). • Poor AM radio reception may be caused by interference from the heated windshield system. **1986–91**—Poor forward shifting may require a new clutch piston. • Engine knocking at idle may require the installation of a new, thicker thrust plate to reduce camshaft end play.

1986–92—A buzz or rattle from the exhaust system may be caused by a loose heat shield catalyst. **1986–94**—A squeak or chirp coming from the blower motor can be stopped by installing an upgraded blower motor with improved brush-to-commutator friction. • A rear suspension clunk or rattle when a wagon goes over a bump may be caused by a loose rear tension strut. • A speaker whine or buzz caused by the fuel pump can be stopped by installing an electronic noise RFI filter. **1986–95**—A cracked forward clutch piston may cause Forward/Reverse problems. Install the improved clutch piston as indicated below and ask Ford to cover the cost inasmuch as their bulletin admits that it's a design defect.

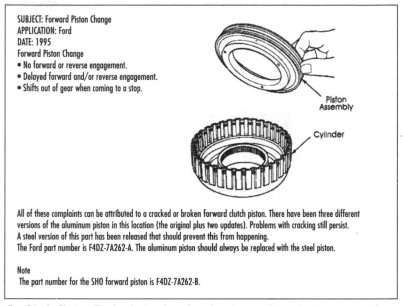

SUBJECT: Forward Piston Change
APPLICATION: Ford
DATE: 1995
Forward Piston Change
• No forward or reverse engagement.
• Delayed forward and/or reverse engagement.
• Shifts out of gear when coming to a stop.

Piston
Assembly

Cylinder

All of these complaints can be attributed to a cracked or broken forward clutch piston. There have been three different versions of the aluminum piston in this location (the original plus two updates). Problems with cracking still persist. A steel version of this part has been released that should prevent this from happening. The Ford part number is F4DZ-7A262-A. The aluminum piston should always be replaced with the steel piston.

Note
The part number for the SHO forward piston is F4DZ-7A262-B.

In this bulletin, Ford admits that the aluminum piston is prone to cracking; the automaker changed the design on its 1996 models, yet, subsequent bulletins show 1996–98 models may have the same affliction.

• Premature wear on the inner edges of the rear tires calls for the installation of Ford's rear suspension adjustable camber kit. **1988–89**—Harsh downshifts may require a new 1990 level pump and main control assembly. **1988–91**—The fist-sized hydraulic engine mounts on cars equipped with a 3.8L V6 engine may deteriorate, causing a vibrating noise. The problem is covered by Ford for 6 years/100,000 km (60,000 miles). **1988–92**—Cold hesitation when accelerating, rough idle, long crank times, and stalling may all signal the need to clean out excessive intake valve deposits. **1989–93**—A persistent fuel odor in the interior when the AC is running signals the need to install a new auxiliary vapor-tube service kit and relocate the vapor tube near the rear bumper. **1990–93**—Noise coming from the power-steering pump may be caused by air in the system; purge the system. **1991**—When Ford modified the automatic transmission for easier shifting, it also made it less reliable. In fact, *Consumer Reports*' annual member survey shows that

almost 20 percent of owners of 1991 Tauruses, Sables, and Continentals said
that they had experienced a serious transmission failure in the preceding 12
months—four times the average for '91 vehicles, says *Consumer Reports*. Ford
extended the warranty on these transmissions for up to six years (see bulletin below). Although it's too late for a full refund under this program, you
should strive for a satisfactory pro rata adjustment and, if not successful,
challenge Ford's refusal before the small claims court.

Ford's No-Charge Transmission Repair

Owner Letter

Serial Number:12345678901234567   94M84   Date, Here
Mr. John Sample
123 Main Street
Anywhere, USA 12345

Ford Motor Company is providing a no-charge Service Program, Number 94M84, to owners of
1991 Model Year Taurus/Sable and Continental cars equipped with Automatic Transmissions.

REASON FOR THIS PROGRAM
Your vehicle may experience erratic transmission operation.

WHAT WE WILL DO
If you should experience erratic transmission operation, at no charge to you, your dealer will
repair, or if necessary, replace your automatic transmission. This no-charge service is available for
6 years or 60,000 miles, whichever occurs first, from original warranty start date, or for 6 months
from the date of this letter, whichever provides greater coverage.

WHAT YOU SHOULD DO
PLEASE KEEP THIS LETTER. If your car should exhibit the condition described above within
the indicated time/mileage limitations, contact your dealer. Show the dealer this letter. If you mis-
place this letter, your dealer will still do the work free of charge.

COURTESY CARS
While your transmission is being repaired or replaced, your dealer will provide you with a free
(except for fuel) courtesy vehicle.

REFUNDS
If you paid to have this service done before the date of the letter, Ford is offering a full refund. For
the refund, please give your original paid work order to your dealer.

Ask for a partial refund if your transmission shifts erratically.

1991–93—Growling from the FX-15 AC compressor can be eliminated by
installing a new compressor rubber damped disc and hub assembly.
1991–95—A sloshing noise from the fuel tank when accelerating or stopping requires the installation of an upgraded tank. Cost may be covered
under the emissions warranty. **1992**—A 3.0L engine that stalls or idles
roughly after a cold start may require a new EEC IV processor. **1992–95**—
A corroded solenoid may be the cause of starter failures. **1993–94**—An
inoperative AC blower probably needs an improved cold engine lockout
switch and hose assembly. • Stalling or hard starts in high ambient temperatures or high altitudes may be due to fuel tank contamination, which causes damage to the fuel pump. Ford paid for a fuel tank flush and a new fuel
pump/sender and in-line fuel filter until May 31, 1997, under Service
Program 94B48. **1993–97**—If the front end accessory drive belt (FEAD)
slips during wet conditions, it can cause a reduction in steering power
assist; Ford suggests the belt be replaced. **1994–95**—A thumping or clank-
ing noise heard from the front brakes signals the need to machine the
front disc brake rotors. **1996–98**—Water leaking onto the passenger floor
area is likely caused by insufficient sealing of the cabin air filter to the cowl
inlet. **1996–97**—An acceleration or deceleration clunk is likely caused by

the rear lower subframe isolators allowing movement between the mounts and the subframe. • A front suspension clunk may signal premature sway bar wear. • Harsh automatic shifting 1–2 may be caused by a malfunctioning electronic pressure control or the main control valves sticking in the valve body (see below).

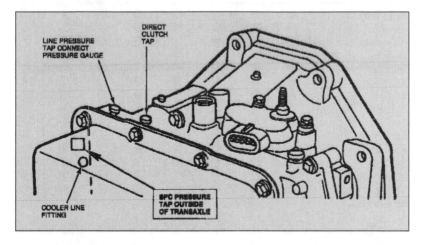

1997—Stalling or surging of 3.0L engines when shifting may signal the need to reprogram the power control module (PCM). **All models/years**— A rotten-egg odor coming from the exhaust probably means that you have a faulty catalytic converter. • Vehicles equipped with 3.0L engines where piston scuffing is evident (hard starting, stalling, excessive engine noise, poor fuel economy) may be eligible for free engine repairs or replacement on a case-by-case basis. • On other engines, Ford has been repairing premature engine head gasket, ring, and valve wear for free when the emissions warranty applies. • Three other components that frequently benefit from Ford "goodwill" warranty extensions are catalytic converters, fuel pumps, and computer modules. If Ford balks at refunding your money, apply the emissions warranty for a full or partial refund. Paint delamination, fading, peeling, hazing, and "microchecking" are also candidates for secret warranty compensation: See pages 94–95 for details on claiming a refund.

Sable, SHO, Taurus Profile

	1990	1991	1992	1993	1994	1995	1996	1997
Cost Price ($)								
Taurus L/G	15,510	16,075	17,164	—	—	—	18,545	19,000
Taurus GL	16,050	16,595	17,619	18,840	18,280	18,295	19,390	19,780
L Wagon	16,420	16,986	18,195	—	—	—	—	—
SHO	22,088	22,551	24,262	25,960	25,240	26,465	27,800	28,220
Used Values ($)								
Taurus L/G ↑	5,000	5,500	6,500	—	—	—	11,500	13,000
Taurus L/G ↓	4,000	4,500	5,500	—	—	—	10,000	11,500
Taurus GL ↑	5,500	6,000	7,000	9,000	9,500	10,500	12,000	14,000
Taurus GL ↓	4,500	5,000	6,000	7,500	8,500	9,500	11,000	13,000
L Wagon ↑	6,000	6,500	7,500	—	—	—	—	—
L Wagon ↓	5,000	5,500	6,500	—	—	—	—	—

216 Lemon-Aid

SHO ↑	6,500	7,200	8,000	10,000	12,500	13,500	15,000	18,000
SHO ↓	5,500	6,500	7,000	8,500	11,000	12,500	13,500	17,000
Extended Warranty	Y	Y	Y	Y	Y	Y	N	N
Secret Warranty	Y	Y	Y	Y	Y	Y	Y	Y
Reliability	①	①	②	②	②	③	④	④
Air conditioning	①	①	①	②	②	③	③	③
Automatic transmission	①	①	②	②	②	②	②	③
Body integrity	②	②	②	②	②	③	③	③
Braking system	②	②	②	②	②	②	③	③
Electrical system	①	①	①	①	①	②	③	④
Engines	①	①	①	②	②	②	④	⑤
Exhaust/Converter	②	②	③	③	③	⑤	⑤	⑤
Fuel system	②	②	②	③	③	③	④	④
Ignition system	③	③	③	③	③	③	④	④
Rust/Paint	②	②	②	②	②	③	③	③
Steering	②	②	②	②	③	③	③	④
Suspension	②	②	②	③	④	⑤	⑤	⑤
Crash Safety	①	⑤	⑤	①	①	④	④	④
Side Impact	—	—	—	—	—	—	—	③

Note: The low frontal crash ratings represent the inclusion of leg trauma in the overall score. The low engine ratings reflect the 3.8L engine's chronic head gasket failures.

GENERAL MOTORS

6000, Celebrity, Century, Ciera

Rating: Below Average (1997); Not Recommended (1982–96). The same failure-prone components have been used year after year. The '96 Century isn't in the same league as the more expensive, revised '97 version. You'll probably find a cheaper '96 Ciera but you won't have the important mechanical and body upgrades offered by its '97 replacement, the Cutlass, a new mid-size sedan similar to the new Malibu. The '97 Century moved over to the W platform that also serves the Chevrolet Lumina, Pontiac Grand Prix, and 1998 Oldsmobile Intrigue. The Ciera was replaced by the Olds Cutlass. Be careful not to confuse the new Cutlass with the Cutlass Supreme, a ten-year-old model that was replaced by the Intrigue, which is equipped like the Century. **Maintenance/Repair costs**: Higher than average, but repairs aren't dealer dependent. **Parts**: Higher-than-average cost (independent suppliers sell for much less), but not hard to find. Nevertheless, don't even think about buying one of these front-drives without a three- to five-year supplementary warranty.

Technical Data

ENGINES	Liters/CID	HP	MPG	Model Years
OHV I-4 FI	2.2/133	110–120	21–25	1993–96
OHV I-4 FI	2.5/151	92–110	19–24	1985–92
OHV V6 2 bbl.	2.8/173	112	18–24	1985–86
OHV V6 FI	2.8/173	125	18–24	1987–88
OHV V6 2 bbl.	3.0/181	110	17–24	1985
OHV V6 FI	3.1/191	160	18–25	1994–98
OHV V6 FI	3.3/204	160	18–24	1989–93
OHV V6 FI	3.8/231	125	16–21	1985
OHV V6 FI	3.8/231	150	17–22	1986–88
OHV V6D FI	4.3/262	85	23–28	1985

Strengths and weaknesses: The A-body line, long a mainstay in GM's family sedan market, has disappeared. This is good news, because these cars are outclassed by the competition and are in desperate need of high-quality components and fresher styling. Overall quality has improved somewhat since the introduction of these cars in 1982, but with the arrival of the Ford Taurus 11 years ago and better-quality Japanese imports, these derivatives of the X-bodies aren't really in the running.

Nevertheless, these cars were consistently popular with fleet buyers and car rental agencies because they were useful as comfortable family sedans and wagons. Handling and other aspects of road performance varied considerably depending on the suspension and powertrain chosen.

1988–96 models are particularly unreliable. The 2.5L 4-cylinder engine suffers from engine-block cracking and a host of other serious defects. The 2.8L V6 engine hasn't been durable either; it suffers from premature camshaft wear and leaky gaskets and seals, especially the intake manifold gasket. The 3-speed automatic transmission is weak and the 4-speed automatic frequently malfunctions. Temperamental and expensive-to-replace fuel systems (including the in-tank fuel pump) afflict all models/years, causing chronic stalling, hard starting, and poor fuel economy (use the emissions warranty to get compensation). Fuel-system diagnosis and repair for the 3.0L V6 (Buick and Oldsmobile) are difficult and the electronic controls are often defective. Air conditioners frequently malfunction and the cooling system is prone to leaks.

Prematurely worn power-steering assemblies are particularly commonplace. Brakes are weak and need frequent attention due to premature wear and dangerously rapid corrosion, front-brake rotors warp easily, excessive pulsation is common, and rear drums often lock up. Shock absorbers and springs wear out quickly. Rear wheel alignment should be checked often. Electric door locks frequently malfunction. Premature and extensive surface rust—due to poor paint application, delamination, and defective materials—is common for all years.

The 1997 Century got a complete make-over that includes the following: gobs of room and trunk space (rivaling that of the Taurus, Concorde, Accord, and Camry); sleeker styling; a much quieter interior; and an upgraded, standard ABS system that produces minimal pedal pulsation. Engine noise was also reduced. Other new features include a starter that has an anti-grind feature in case you turn the key with the engine running, upgraded door seals, steering-wheel mounted radio controls, and additional heating ducts for rear passengers. On the downside, you can get only the 160-hp 3.1L V6 engine; the new Century's speed-dependent power steering is too light and vague; and its suspension and handling are more tuned to comfort than performance.

Dealer service bulletins: **1993 vehicles equipped with 3.3L V6 engines**—Converter seal leaks on 4T60E automatic transmissions. • Loss of power. • Unexpected downshifts. • Defective cruise control. • Stalling when decelerating. • Extended cranking. • Faulty Reverse gear on 3T40 automatic transmissions. • Additionally, the Buick Century may experience brake drag and loss of power. **1994**—Fuel pumps may fail prematurely. • A front-end squeak may require the replacement of the exhaust manifold pipe springs with dampers. • Excessive noise or vibrations can be caused by defective rear transmission mounts. • Engine wiring harnesses could melt. • Exhaust moan. • Temperature gauges could give false readings. **1995**—The cruise control fails to engage. • Oil leaks at the rocker cover. • Grinding/growling when in Park on an incline. • Popping, banging, and rattling upon hard acceleration. • Engine tick/rattle upon cold start-up. • Cold start stall, hesitation, and sag; cold rough idle. • Cold start rattle with the 4T60E automatic transmission. • Brake vibration and/or pedal pulsation. • Low voltage reading or dim lights at idle. • Exhaust manifold seal squeaks and exhaust boom/moan at idle. • Loose windshield garnish molding. • Wind rush at top of doors. • Poor paint application and rust spots. **1996**—Second gear starts; poor 1–3 shifting. • Vibration at high speeds. • Steering column noise. • Air conditioning odors. • Radio frequency interference diagnosis. **1997 Century**—Air temperature from HVAC outlets doesn't change. • Rear brake clicking or squealing. • Door glass creaking noise. • Insufficient heater performance on passenger side floor area. • Intermittent Neutral/loss of Drive at highway speeds. • Loose airbag housing door on passenger side dash. • Low voltage reading/dim lights at idle. • Pop, groan, or moan from rear of vehicle. • Remote keyless entry range is shorter than expected. • Slow window operation. • Front brake squealing, grinding noise. • Wiper arms/blades park at incorrect positions.

Safety summary/recalls: Drivers report that the head restraints don't stay up. **Recalls**: **1983–87**—The fuel system on the 2.5L engine may leak fuel, creating a fire hazard. • Some wagons were recalled due to poor braking performance. **1985**—Throttle on V6 engines may stick open, causing sudden acceleration. • Misrouted clutch cable could cause fluid leakage from the brake master cylinder. **1986**—Defective headlight switch can cause headlights to flicker or fail. **1988**—GM will repair a leaking fuel feed hose on vehicles with 2.8L engines. • Dealer will inspect and repair the front suspension. • The lower arm bracket could develop cracks and cause the disengagement of the lower control arm, resulting in steering loss. **1989–90 Celebrity, 1989–91 6000, 1989–96 Ciera**—Rear seat anchor bolts don't meet federal load standards. **1990–91**—A short circuit in the six-way power seat or power recliner could set the seat on fire. **1992**—Automatic 4-speed transmissions were recalled because they performed poorly or remained in Reverse while the indicator showed Neutral. • Wagons may have erratically operating interior lights and suffer a sudden tailgate opening. **1992–93**—Dealers will install a redesigned intake manifold gasket at no charge on vehicles with rough-running 2.2L engines. **1993**—Right front brake hoses are defective. **1986 Century**—Cars with 2.8L engines could suffer an under-hood fire due to misrouted wiring. **1989–96**—Rear seat anchor bolts don't meet federal load standards. **1994 Century**—Sudden acceleration may occur when the 3.1L primary accelerator spring binds. • Water leakage into the power door lock may cause a short-circuit fire.

Secret Warranties/Service Tips

1984–90—Frequent loss of Drive with 440-T4 transmissions is likely caused by a misadjusted 1–2 band stop unit. **1986–90**—Vehicles equipped with the 3T40 automatic transmission may experience slippage in manual Low or Reverse gears. Install service package #8628222, which includes a Low/Reverse clutch release spring (#8664961) and a clutch retainer and snap ring (#656/657). **1987–88**—Poor engine performance troubleshooting shortcuts are detailed in DSB No. 88-T-47B. **1987–90**—A rattle or buzz from the instrument panel may require a new, upgraded brake booster check valve (#18012017). **1989–93**—Vehicles equipped with a 3300 or 3800 engine that experience stalling upon deceleration or hard starts may need a new air control motor (IAC). **1990**—Door lock rods that fall off need an upgraded inside handle to lock the rod. **1994**—Loss of Drive or erratic shifts may be caused by an intermittent short to ground on the A or B shift solenoid or an electrical short circuit in the transaxle. • A front-end clunking noise when driving over rough roads may require the repositioning of the diagonal radiator support braces. **1994–95**—DSB 43-81-29 troubleshoots cruise controls that fail to engage. **1995–97**—Intermittent Neutral/loss of Drive at highway speeds can be fixed by replacing the control valve body assembly. **1997**—Rear brake clicking or squealing may be caused by a maladjusted park brake cable. • Insufficient heater performance on the passenger-side floor area can be fixed by installing a new I/P insulator panel and bracket. **1991–92 Ciera**—Uncomfortable front seat shoulder belts will be replaced at no charge. **1994**—Loss of Drive or erratic shifts may be caused by an intermittent short to ground on the A or B shift solenoid or an electrical short circuit in the transaxle. **All models/years**—A rotten-egg odor coming from the exhaust is probably the result of a malfunctioning catalytic converter. **3.8L V6 engines**—Low oil pressure is likely caused by a failure-prone oil pump. A temporary remedy is to avoid low-viscosity oils and use 10W-40 in the winter and 20W-50 for summer driving. • A spark knock on the 2.5L engine can be fixed with the installation of a new PROM module (#12269198; DSB 804-5812) under the emissions warranty. • THM 44C-T4 automatic transaxles with V6 engines are particularly failure prone, due to pinched or kinked vacuum lines that cause oil starvation. Paint delamination, peeling, or fading: See page 95.

6000, Celebrity, Century, Ciera Profile

	1990	1991	1992	1993	1994	1995	1996	1997
Cost Price ($)								
6000	15,114	15,628	—	—	—	—	—	—
Celebrity	15,764	—	—	—	—	—	—	—
Century	16,076	15,798	16,337	16,627	17,325	19,171	18,235	18,590
Ciera S/SL	16,135	15,945	15,855	16,234	17,725	16,595	15,305	—
Used Values ($)								
6000 ↑	5,000	6,000	—	—	—	—	—	—
6000 ↓	4,000	5,000	—	—	—	—	—	—
Celebrity ↑	4,500	—	—	—	—	—	—	—
Celebrity ↓	4,000	—	—	—	—	—	—	—
Century ↑	5,500	6,200	6,700	7,700	8,700	10,000	11,500	16,500
Century ↓	4,500	5,200	5,600	6,500	7,500	9,000	10,000	14,500
Ciera S/SL ↑	5,000	5,500	6,000	7,000	8,000	9,500	11,000	—
Ciera S/SL ↓	3,500	4,000	5,000	5,500	7,000	8,000	9,500	— —
Extended Warranty	Y	Y	Y	Y	Y	Y	Y	Y
Secret Warranty	Y	Y	Y	Y	Y	Y	Y	Y
Reliability	②	②	②	②	②	②	③	③
Air conditioning	②	②	②	②	③	③	③	③
Automatic transmission	②	②	②	②	②	②	②	②
Body integrity	①	①	①	①	①	②	②	②
Braking system	②	②	②	②	②	②	②	②
Electrical system	②	②	②	②	②	②	②	②
Engines	②	②	②	②	③	③	③	③
Exhaust/Converter	②	②	③	③	④	⑤	⑤	⑤
Fuel system	②	②	②	②	②	③	③	②
Ignition system	②	②	②	②	②	③	④	④
Rust/Paint	①	①	①	①	①	②	②	②
Steering	②	②	②	②	③	③	③	④
Suspension	②	②	②	②	②	②	③	④
Crash Safety								
Century 4d	—	②	②	①	②	④	④	—
Ciera	—	—	—	①	—	—	—	—

Bonneville, Cutlass Supreme, Delta 88, Grand Prix, LeSabre, Lumina, Monte Carlo, Regal

Rating: Front-drives are Not Recommended (1988–97); rear-drives, if you can find them, are Above Average (1984–87). Although generally classed as medium-sized cars, some of these GM models move in and out of the large car class, as well. **Maintenance/Repair costs**: Higher than average, but repairs aren't dealer dependent. **Parts**: Higher-than-average cost (independent suppliers sell for much less), but not hard to find. Nevertheless, don't even think about buying one of the front-drives without a three- to five-year supplementary warranty.

Technical Data

ENGINES	Liters/CID	HP	MPG	Model Years
OHC I-4 FI	2.2/133	110	21–24	1993
OHC I-4 FI	2.5/151	110	20–23	1990–92
OHV V6 2 bbl.	3.8/231	110	18–21	1985–87
OHV V6 FI	3.0/181	125	18–22	1986
OHV V6 FI	3.8/231	150–165	16–21	1986–91
OHV V6 FI	3.8/231	170	17–22	1992–95
OHV V6 FI	3.8/231	205–240	16–20	1992–98
OHV V6 FI	4.3/262	140	17–22	1987
OHV V8 4 bbl.	5.0/305	150–165	16–18	1985–87
DOHC I-4 FI	2.3/138	160	21–24	1990–91
OHV V6 FI	2.8/173	130	18–23	1988–89
OHV V6 FI	3.1/191	140–160	17–22	1989–95
OHV V6 FI	3.1/191	160	19–28	1995–98
OHV V6T FI	3.1/191	205	15–19	1989–90
DOHC V6 FI	3.4/207	200–210	16–21	1991–95
DOHC V6 FI	3.4/207	210–215	16–21	1995–97

Strengths and weaknesses: **Rear-drives**: The rear-drives are competent and comfortable cars, but they definitely point to a time when handling wasn't a priority and fuel economy was unimportant. Their overall reliability isn't impressive, but at least repairs are easy, defects are obvious, and any independent garage can service them. Models equipped with diesel engines or with the turbocharged gas V6 should be approached with extreme caution. These cars have a higher-than-average incidence of repairs, but parts are inexpensive and all mechanical work is very easy to perform.

Original-equipment shock absorbers and springs aren't durable and electrical malfunctions increase proportionally with extra equipment. The AC module and condenser and wheel bearings (incredibly expensive) also have short life spans. The 4-speed automatic transmission available in later models isn't reliable. Surface rust caused by poor paint quality and application is common. The rear edge of trunk lids, roof areas above doors, and the windshield and windshield posts rust through easily.

Front-drives: The front-drives are a different breed of car: less reliable and more expensive to repair, with a considerable number of mechanical and electrical deficiencies directly related to their front-wheel drive configuration. Nevertheless, acceleration is adequate, fuel economy is good, and they're better at handling than their rear-drive cousins—except in emergencies, when their non-ABS brakes lock up and directional stability is the first to go. The front-drive's many design and manufacturing weaknesses make for unimpressive high-speed performance, mediocre interior comfort, a poor reliability record, and expensive maintenance costs. That's why most fleets and police agencies use rear-drives when they can get them. They've seen the rear-drive's safety and operating cost advantages.

These aren't driver-friendly cars. Many models have a dash that's replete with confusing push-buttons and gauges. The digital display panel showing speed, oil pressure, temperature, and other information may freeze and not light up when the temperature reaches 0°F. Drivers must wait at least ten minutes for their cars to warm up sufficiently before this vital information is displayed. The keyless entry system often fails, the radio's memory is frequently forgetful, and the fuel light comes on when the tank is below the "1/2" fuel-level mark. The electronic climate control frequently malfunctions and owners report that warm air doesn't reach the driver-side heating vents. Servicing, especially for the electronic engine controls, is complicated and expensive.

Other major problem areas: the engine, automatic transmission, leaking and malfunctioning AC systems—due mainly to defective AC modules—faulty electronic modules, rack-and-pinion steering failure, bursting steering hoses on 1991 models, weak shocks, excessive front brake pad wear and seizure of the rear brake calipers, rear brake/wheel lockup, myriad electrical failures requiring replacement of the computer module (a $500–$750 repair job if the emissions warranty has expired), leaking oil pan, and suspension struts.

Owners report that 3.8L engines won't continue running after a cold start, the exhaust system booms, 3T40 automatic transmissions may have faulty Reverse gears, and the instrument panel may pop or creak.

The Lumina's engine is buzzy and anemic, giving out only 140 hp with the V6; the instruments and steering column shake when the car is traveling over uneven road surfaces; and lots of road and wind noise comes through the side windows thanks to the inadequately soundproofed chassis. Seating isn't very comfortable due to the lack of support caused by low-density foam, knees-in-your-face low seating, and the ramrod-straight rear backrest. The ride is acceptable with a light load, but when fully loaded, the car's back end sags and the ride deteriorates.

Body assembly is notoriously poor and is no doubt one of the main reasons why GM has lost so much market share over the past decade. Premature paint peeling and rusting, water and dust leaks into the trunk, squeaks and rattles, and wind and road noise are all too common. Accessories are also problem plagued, with defective radios, power antennas, door locks, cruise control, and alarm systems leading the pack.

Dealer service bulletins: **1993–94**—3.8L engine stalls after a cold start. • Converter seal leaks on 4T60E automatic transmissions. • AC hisses from the instrument panel and it becomes too warm on extended idle. • Poor heat distribution. • Door speakers buzz. **1993–94 LeSabre**—Remedies for stalling and hard starts. • Whistling when the AC is in recirculate mode. • Rattling when car passes over bumps. **1994 Olds 88 and Bonneville**—3T40 automatic transmissions have faulty Reverse gears. **All 1995 models**—A knocking noise from the accessory drive belt tensioner. • Continuous spark knock. • Excessive oil consumption and oil leaks at the rocker cover. • Coolant leak near the throttle body. • Grinding/growling when in Park on an incline and a cold start rattle with the 4T60E automatic transmission. • Harsh 1–2 upshifts. • Brake vibration and/or pedal pulsation. • Low voltage reading or dim lights at idle. • Headlights/parking lights remain on. • An upgraded wire protector shield is needed to correct a noisy steering column. • Squeak/creak from rear of vehicle, whistle noise coming from the heater/AC unit, and excessive radio static. • Door window rattle, popping noise during moderate braking or acceleration, front suspension pop noise, and rear-strut-related squeaking/thumping noise. ˜ Left rear door binds. • Poor paint application and rust spots. • Frequent reports of wind noise affecting the 1990–95 Cutlass, Grand Prix, and Regal and the 1988–94 Lumina have led to the publication of DSB 53-15-16, which outlines the causes of and remedies for persistent wind noise complaints. **Supreme**—Snapping noise from door window and exhaust manifold seal squeak. • Door lock/power-window switches binding. **Regal**—Left rear door binds when opening. **Olds 88**—Inadvertent low fuel chime. **Bonneville**—Headrest cover splits, loosens, or separates. **All 1996 models**—Second gear starts, poor 1–3 shifting. • Steering column noise. • Air conditioning odors and diagnosis of AC noises. • Whistle noise from HVAC. • Diagnosis and correction of fluttering, popping, ticking, and clunking noises. • Popping noise from the front of vehicle when turning. • Radio frequency interference diagnosis. • Rear door rattle when closing. • Excessive wrinkles in seat cushion trim. • Exterior light condensation. **1997**—AC flutter or moan. • Cold start rattle. Engine cranks but will not run. • Engine oil leak at oil pan sealing flange and rear of engine near flywheel cover. • Engine oil level indicates over-full. • Excessive vibration of electrochromic mirror. • High beams are intermittent. • Inoperative power door locks. • Intermittent AC noise. • Intermittent Neutral/loss of Drive at highway speeds. • Instrument panel buzz and rattle when the brakes are applied. • Popping or thump noise from the left rear of vehicle is normal, according to GM. • Transmission gear whine at 25–40 mph. **1996 Supreme**— Stalls at low rpm and high loads, extended crank time. • Front suspension popping. • HVAC blower motor noise/vibration. • Loose left side instrument panel access cover. • Inoperative antenna, power mirrors, and door locks.

Safety summary/recalls: NHTSA probes: 1988–93 Lumina, Regal, Cutlass, and Grand Prix—Corroded brake calipers may cause brake failures. **1986–88**—Brakes either fail or the pedal goes to the floor when depressed. **1994 Grand Prix**—Windshield wiper failures. **1991–92 Olds 88**—Damaged fuel lines. **1992 Olds 88**—A poorly aligned PRNDL indicator may allow shifts from Park to Reverse while the engine is running. There are reports of the driver's seat breaking from its moorings. **1990 Cutlass Supreme**—ABS is tough to modulate; it doesn't always engage quickly enough or it's sometimes too sensitive. **1990–91 Lumina**—Wheels may crack and fracture, leading to wheel failure and loss of control. **Recalls: 1986**—Faulty headlight switch may cause erratic operation of lights. **1987**—200-4R transmissions may engage the wrong gear or start in gear. **1988**—Three separate recalls will correct faulty tie-rod nuts or lower control arms that could cause steering loss, a faulty transmission cable that indicates the wrong gear, and a leaking left-front-brake hose. • Parking brake cable may separate from the left rear brake caliper. **1988–91**—Faulty front shoulder belt guide loop. **1989–90**—Faulty brake lights. **1992**—4-speed automatic transmissions that slip in Reverse, lock in Reverse when the indicator shows Neutral, or generally perform poorly. **1993**—The seatback may suddenly recline. **1996–97**—Backfire can break upper intake manifold, making car hard to start and possibly starting a fire. **1997**—Seatbelt may not latch properly. **1990 Lumina**—Cracks can develop in the Kelsey Hayes steel wheels. **1996 Chevy Lumina and Buick Regal**— Brake line could rub against the transaxle mounting bracket. **Monte Carlo**—Improperly installed brake booster. **1991 Regal**— The fuel-feed hose on vehicles with 3.8L V6 engines may leak fuel; dealer will install a new fuel-feed hose. **1994–95 Regal**—Improperly installed brake hoses could leak fluid and cause partial brake loss. **1995 Regal**—Steering could fail if the bolts on the steering-column support bracket aren't tightened. **1990 models with 2.3L Quad 4 engine**—Faulty ignition coils that may cause engine misfiring will be replaced under an emissions recall campaign. **1991 Olds 88 and 1992 LeSabre and Bonneville**—Parking brakes may not hold well enough, allowing the car to roll when the brake is on. **1994 Cutlass Supreme**—Improperly installed brake hoses could leak fluid and cause partial brake loss. **1994–95**—Washer wiper may malfunction. **1995**—Seatbelt anchor could fracture in a crash. **1994–95 Olds 98**—Headlight switch may not work. **1988–90 Regal, Cutlass, and**

Grand Prix—Cracks can develop in the Kelsey Hayes steel wheels. **1992–93 LeSabre, Park Avenue, 88, 98, and Bonneville with 4T60-E automatic transmission**—Oil cooler line can leak transmission fluid, posing a fire hazard.

Secret Warranties/Service Tips

1980–89 Front-drives—First gear malfunctions with the THM 125C transmission may require new forward clutch piston seals (#8631986). **1984–89**—No third gear with the automatic 440-T4 transmission means that a new thrust bearing assembly should be installed. **1985–89**—Wind noise around the doors can be cured by using several kits mentioned in DSB 89-286-10. **1986–87**—Serious stalling problems can usually be traced to a defective PROM module or a malfunctioning TCC solenoid. **1986–88**—Models with anti-lock brakes may have defective hoses. • 3.8L V6 engines have a history of low oil pressure caused by a failure-prone oil pump. A temporary remedy is to avoid low viscosity oils and use 10W-40 in the winter and 20W-50 in the summer. **1987**—Frequent engine stalling may require that a different PROM be put in the ECM (DSB 87-6-17A). **1987–89**—If the engine constantly stalls and won't restart, consider replacing the fuel pump and installing a fuel-sender kit. **1988**—Poor engine performance diagnostic shortcuts are detailed in DSB No. 88-T-47B. **1988–89**—Poor FM reception can be improved by installing an RFI suppresser harness (#25027405). • If your door hinge breaks, GM will replace it for free for up to ten years under a special policy. • Rear suspension thud noise may be reduced by replacing the strut assemblies. **1988–93**—A vehicle equipped with a 3,300 or 3,800 engine that stalls when decelerating or is hard to start may need a new air-control motor (IAC). **1989**—Constant stalling with the 2.8L engine may be fixed by installing a new service MEMCAL. **1989–90**—Hard cold starts may require a new MEMCAL. **1990**—Sunroof failures may be due to static electricity blowing the sunroof's electric module; install a plastic button switch. **1990–92**—A vehicle equipped with a 3.1L or 3.4L engine that is hard to start when cold or that chronically stalls may need an engine calibration or an upgraded MEMCAL module. **1991–94**—Loss of Drive or erratic shifts may be caused by an intermittent short to ground on the A or B shift solenoid or an electrical short circuit in the transaxle. • Harsh automatic transmission upshifts can be corrected by installing an upgraded accumulator valve in the control valve body. **1992–94**—A front-end engine knock troubleshooting chart is found in DSB 306001. • Water leaking from the doors into the passenger compartment has a number of causes and remedies, according to DSB 431003. **1993–94**—Knocking from the accessory drive belt tensioner requires an upgraded replacement. • Owners who complain of automatic transmission low-speed miss, hesitation, chuggle, or skip may find relief with an improved MEMCAL module. **1995–96**—Wind noise around front and rear doors; diagnosis and repair. **1995–97**—Intermittent Neutral/loss of Drive at highway speeds can be fixed by replacing the control valve body assembly. **1991–92 LeSabre**—Premature bore corrosion of the front-brake caliper bolt can be fixed by changing the rubber bushings and honing out the bores. **1991–94**—A scraping noise or increased effort required to open the front doors can be fixed by bending the door's lower check ear. • Water leaking from the doors into the passenger compartment has a number of causes and remedies (DSB 431003). **1992–94**—Loss of Drive or erratic shifts may be caused by an intermittent short to ground on the A or B shift solenoid or an electrical short circuit in the transaxle. **1995–97**—Intermittent Neutral/loss of Drive at highway speeds can be fixed by replacing the control valve body assembly (see below).

File In Section: 7 - Transmission
Bulletin No.: 67-71-64
Date: February 1997
Subject:
Intermittent Neutral or Loss of Drive at Highway Speeds or from Fourth Gear
(Replace Control Valve Body Assembly)
Models:
1995–96 Buick Skylark, Regal Century, Park Avenue, Riviera, LeSabre
1997 Buick Skylark, Regal, Century, LeSabre
1995 Cadillac DeVille
1995–96 Chevrolet Beretta, Corsica, Lumina APV, Lumina, Monte Carlo 1997 Chevrolet Lumina, Monte Carlo, Venture
1995–96 Oldsmobile Cutlass Ciera, Cutlass Cruiser, LSS, Ninety Eight, Ninety Eight Regency, Eighty Eight, Achieva, Silhouette, Cutlass Supreme
1997 Oldsmobile Eighty Eight, Achieva, Cutlass Supreme, LSS, Silhouette
1995–97 Pontiac Bonneville, Grand Am, Trans Sport, Grand Prix with HYDRA-MATIC 4T60-E Transaxle (RPO M13)
Condition
Some owners may comment about an intermittent, neutral condition while driving at highway speeds or intermittent neutral from fourth gear.
Cause
The 3–2 Manual Downshift valve may be sticking intermittently. When the 3–2 downshift valve sticks, this allows the 2–3 shift valve to float in its bore either exhausting 2ND, 3RD and 4TH clutch oil or sending D-4 oil into the AUX input clutch feed. Exhausting the 3RD and 4TH clutch oil could cause an intermittent loss of drive. Sending D-4 oil into the input circuit could cause a potential tie up condition by engaging the input clutch and 4TH clutch.
Correction
Inspect the transmission fluid and pan for signs of distressed clutches or any abnormal amounts of debris. Remove and disassemble the 1–2 and 2–3 accumulator housing assembly. Inspect the accumulator housing and cover for any signs of scoring, sediment, or abnormalities that could generate debris. If any of the above conditions are found, make the necessary repairs to those items. Then inspect the 2–3 (357) and 3–2 (356) valve line up. If the valves are scored, replace the control valve body assembly.
Parts Information
Refer to the latest service parts catalog for the proper control valve body assembly part numbers. Anodized valves are being installed into the 2–3 (357), and 3–2 (356) valve line up, and the machining operation for the valve body has been refined to produce a clean valve bore.
Warranty Information
For vehicles repaired under warranty use:

Labor		
Operation	Labor Time	
K5570	Use published labor operation time and appropriate add time for accumulator housing inspection	

This major transmission repair should be covered by GM's base warranty or a "goodwill" warranty since the bulletin clearly shows it's a factory-related defect.

• Transmission gear whine at 25–45 mph means the final drive assembly may have to be replaced. **1990 Lumina**—Vehicles equipped with a 3.1L engine may exhibit piston scuffing, which produces cold engine knock at low ambient temperatures. GM recommends a partial engine replacement rather than changing the pistons. **1990–91**—Late transaxle upshifts may be fixed by resetting the TV cable. **1994**—Excessive brake-pedal effort when cold can be fixed by installing upgraded brake pads. **1994–95**—A steering-wheel clicking or scrubbing noise when turning can be fixed by installing an upgraded wire protector shield. **1990–91 Lumina and Regal with 3.1L V6 engine**—If the starter makes a grinding noise or won't engage the engine, the fault may be a weak starter spring. Replace the starter-motor drive assembly with #10473700. • A defective sending unit will cause a display of high oil pressure or erratic readings. Replace the old pressure sender with #25605389. • Excessive brake-pedal effort can be corrected by replacing the original pads with modified parts. **1990–92**—Vehicles equipped with the 3T40 automatic transmission may experience slippage in manual Low or Reverse. Install service package #8628222, which includes a Low/Reverse clutch release spring (#8664961) and clutch retainer and nap ring (#656/657). **1991–92 Lumina**—A delayed shift between Drive and Reverse is likely caused by a rolled or cut input-clutch-piston outer seal. **1991–94**—Loss of Drive or erratic shifts may be caused by an intermittent short to ground on the A or B shift solenoid or an electrical short circuit in the transaxle. **1992–93**—No Reverse or slipping in Reverse can be corrected by installing an upgraded Low/Reverse clutch return spring and spiral retaining ring. **1991–94 Regal**—Loss of Drive or erratic shifts may be caused by an intermittent short to ground on the A or B shift solenoid or an electrical short circuit in the transaxle. **1992**—Front-door wind noise and water leaks can be fixed by replacing the run channel retainer and adding sealer between the retainer and the door frame. **1995–97**—Intermittent Neutral/loss of Drive at highway speeds can be fixed by replacing the control-valve body assembly. **1997 Regal and Grand Prix**—Insufficient heater performance on passenger-side floor area can be fixed by installing a new I/P insulator panel and bracket. **1990–91 2.3L Quad 4 engine**—Head-gasket leaks are a problem that was once covered by a secret warranty extension. The first sign of trouble is a loss of power caused by combustion gases mixing with coolant. This is followed by a cloud of steam and coolant loss through the exhaust system. If these warnings are ignored, cylinder-bore scoring, a warped cylinder head, and piston seizure will likely result as the engine continues to overheat. Up to 6 years/60,000 miles, GM has replaced at no charge the head gasket with an improved version. **All models/years**—A rotten-egg odor coming from the exhaust is probably caused by a malfunctioning catalytic converter, covered by the emissions warranty. • Paint delamination, peeling, or fading: See page 95.

Bonneville, Cutlass Supreme, Delta 88, Grand Prix, LeSabre, Lumina, Malibu, Monte Carlo, Regal Profile

	1990	1991	1992	1993	1994	1995	1996	1997
Cost Price ($)								
Bonneville	17,473	18,550	19,677	20,522	21,627	21,584	22,374	22,914
Delta 88	17,999	18,969	20,502	21,251	22,480	20,995	21,370	23,100
Grand Prix	16,064	15,869	16,575	16,245	17,094	17,589	18,049	19,250
LeSabre	17,919	19,019	19,615	19,554	22,541	23,481	22,345	23,040
Lumina	15,225	15,200	15,850	15,550	16,650	16,840	17,860	18,480
Malibu	—	—	—	—	—	—	—	15,995
Monte Carlo	—	—	—	—	—	17,510	18,012	18,220
Regal	16,405	17,295	18,370	18,190	19,670	20,650	20,280	23,495
Supreme	16,862	16,812	17,450	17,170	18,830	18,995	17,995	19,500

Used Values ($)

Bonneville ↑	5,500	6,500	8,000	9,500	11,500	13,500	15,500	17,500
Bonneville ↓	4,500	5,500	7,000	8,500	10,000	12,000	14,500	16,000
Delta 88 ↑	6,000	7,000	8,000	9,500	11,000	13,000	15,500	17,000
Delta 88 ↓	5,000	5,500	6,500	8,000	9,500	12,000	14,000	15,500
Grand Prix ↑	5,000	6,000	6,500	7,500	9,500	11,000	12,500	15,000
Grand Prix ↓	4,000	5,000	6,000	6,500	8,500	10,000	11,500	14,500
LeSabre ↑	5,500	6,000	8,000	9,500	11,500	13,500	15,500	17,000
LeSabre ↓	4,500	5,500	7,000	8,500	10,000	12,000	14,000	16,500
Lumina ↑	4,500	5,500	6,000	7,000	8,000	10,500	11,500	13,500
Lumina ↓	4,000	4,500	5,500	6,000	7,000	9,500	10,500	12,500
Malibu ↑	—	—	—	—	—	—	—	13,500
Malibu ↓	—	—	—	—	—	—	—	12,500
Monte Carlo ↑	—	—	—	—	—	11,000	12,500	14,500
Monte Carlo ↓	—	—	—	—	—	9,500	11,500	13,000
Regal ↑	5,500	6,500	7,500	9,000	10,500	12,000	14,000	17,000
Regal ↓	4,500	5,500	6,500	7,500	9,000	10,500	13,000	15,500
Supreme ↑	5,500	6,000	8,000	9,500	11,500	13,500	15,500	17,000
Supreme ↓	5,500	6,000	8,000	9,500	11,500	13,500	15,500	17,000
Extended Warranty	Y	Y	Y	Y	Y	Y	Y	Y
Secret Warranty	Y	Y	Y	Y	Y	Y	Y	Y

Reliability	❷	❷	❷	❷	❷	❷	❷	③
Air conditioning	❷	❷	❷	❷	❷	❷	❷	③
Automatic transmission	❶	❶	❶	❶	❶	❷	❷	❷
Body integrity	❶	❶	❶	❶	❶	❷	❷	③
Braking system	❶	❶	❶	❶	❶	❷	❷	③
Electrical system	❶	❶	❶	❶	❶	❶	❶	③
Engines	❷	❷	❷	❷	❷	③	③	④
Exhaust/Converter	❷	❷	❷	❷	③	④	④	④
Fuel system	❷	❷	❷	❷	❷	③	③	④
Ignition system	❷	❷	③	③	③	③	③	④
Rust/Paint	❶	❶	❶	❶	❶	❶	❷	③
Steering	❷	❷	❷	❷	❷	③	③	③
Suspension	❷	❷	❷	❷	❷	❷	③	③
Crash Safety								
Bonneville 4d	⑤	⑤	⑤	❶	❶	⑤	—	⑤
Delta 88 2d	⑤	⑤	⑤	⑤	—	—	—	—
Delta 88 4d	❷	❷	❷	❶	❶	—	—	④
Grand Prix 2d	❷	❷	❷	❷	❶	④	④	④
Grand Prix 4d	—	❶	❶	❶	❶	—	—	—
LeSabre 2d	—	❷	❷	❷	❷	—	—	④
Lumina 4d	—	⑤	⑤	❷	❷	—	⑤	⑤
Monte Carlo	❷	—	—	—	—	④	—	—
Monte Carlo 2d	—	—	—	—	—	—	④	—
Regal 2d	—	⑤	⑤	—	—	—	—	—
Regal 4d	❷	—	—	⑤	❶	—	—	—
Supreme 2d	❷	❷	❷	❷	❷	—	—	—
Supreme 4d	❷	❶	❶	❶	❶	—	—	—
Side Impact								
Cutlass	—	—	—	—	—	—	—	❶
Lumina	—	—	—	—	—	—	—	④

Beretta, Corsica

Rating: Average buy (1993–96) if you can adjust to the brakes' poor performance; Not Recommended (1988–92). The Corsica was the entry-level model, followed in price by the Beretta. Best bet is an ABS-equipped and V6-powered version available from 1992–96. **Maintenance/Repair costs**: Higher than average; repairs aren't dealer dependent. **Parts**: Higher-than-average cost, but can be bought for much less from independent suppliers.

Technical Data

ENGINES	Liters/CID	HP	MPG	Model Years
OHV I-4 FI	2.0/121	90	22–27	1987–89
OHV I-4 FI	2.2/133	95–120	21–25	1990–96
DOHC I-4 FI	2.3/138	170–180	19–25	1990–94
OHV V6 FI	2.8/173	130	19–25	1987–89
OHV V6 FI	3.1/191	135–160	18–24	1990–96

Strengths and weaknesses: These reasonably priced, roomy compacts came with standard anti-lock brakes as of the 1992 model year. Overall road performance is unimpressive, however, and emergency handling is below par. From a quality standpoint, these compact coupes, sedans, and hatchbacks are almost as unreliable as the Skyhawk, Firenza, J2000, and 2000 they replaced. The anemic, failure-prone, and expensive-to-repair 2.0L 4-cylinder engine with its faulty computer modules is a major disappointment. You need to shift into low gear on modest inclines. Owners report frequent no-starts and stalling with all engine variations, mainly due to temperamental electronic modules, particularly in conjunction with multi-port fuel-injection systems. Fuel system and ignition glitches are legion and the cruise control operation is erratic. Servicing is difficult because of the tight engine compartment. The V6 engine is seriously weakened by air conditioning and the automatic transmission's poor quality control. The lockup on the automatic engages and disengages constantly. The 5-speed manual performs better, but it too is unreliable, being handicapped by long clutch-pedal travel and a tendency to stall at light throttle. Owners report some instances where the clutch has shifted into Reverse rather than first gear. Steering is vague and components are unreliable. Braking is terrible and the front brakes rust and wear out quickly. The standard suspension offers poor ride control on bumpy roads, produces excessive body roll in turns, and is characterized by imprecise handling, especially at highway speeds. The sport suspension option (standard on some models) offers better handling and a firmer but more comfortable ride. Shock absorbers often begin leaking before 50,000 km and the replacement of the suspension struts is sometimes an annual affair. Electrical components often short circuit. Owners report that the windshield wiper motor fails frequently.

1990–96 models also have more than their share of performance problems and factory-related defects. Braking is still scary, even with ABS, and cornering is a white-knuckle affair. The 2.2L engines have a "piston scuffing" problem and the Quad 4 engine's head gaskets fail prematurely. Hard starting, stalling, and engine surging are common and AC operation is erratic.

Body panels are poorly assembled, paint delaminates and peels away, and rattles are a constant companion. GM announced in the January 18, 1993, edition of *Automotive News* that Corsica and Beretta paint peeling would be covered for six years under a special extended warranty. This change in GM's policy was first communicated to American dealers on October 16, 1992, in a series of letters and bulletins sent to each division's dealers.

Amazingly, GM weasels out of paying many claims for paint repairs by ignoring the *Automotive News* article or by pretending that the extended warranty never existed. Owners who won't take no for an answer and turn to small claims court usually get their cars repainted for free (see "Service Tips").

Safety summary/recalls: There have been many reports of rear-wheel lockup and sudden brake loss on non-ABS equipped models, and ABS brake performance hasn't been impressive. **Recalls**: **1987–88**—The hood could fly up. • Replace broken front-door hinges with upgraded hinges (#10092242-3). **1988–89**—Front shoulder belt retractors could fail in a collision. **1989**—Dealers will install a front seatbelt latch plate and buckle for free. • The fuel tank could leak. • Dealers will replace both front seat frames if found defective. • The port fuel injector on 2.8L engines will be replaced for free based on the emissions warranty. **1994–95**—The reinforcement panel is missing from the right-side rocker assembly. **1989 Corsica**—A steel wheel fracture could cause wheel separation. **1991**—A loose steering wheel nut may cause steering wheel separation. **1992**—The brakelight switch is faulty. **1992–93**—Dealers will install a redesigned intake manifold gasket on vehicles with rough-running 2.2L engines. **Models with 2.3L Quad 4 engines**: **1988–89**—Vehicles may have a cracked fuel-hose feed, causing a fuel leak. **1990**—Faulty ignition coils that cause engine misfiring may be replaced under an emissions recall campaign.

Secret Warranties/Service Tips

1987–88—Brake pulsations may be caused by unevenly worn brake rotors. Install upgraded, reduced-diameter caliper slide pins (#18016164). • Difficult cold starts with 2.0L engines may require a new drop-in manifold deflector plate (#10112342). • High accelerator pedal effort or inoperative cruise control may require a new throttle body actuating linkage. • Rear speaker ignition noise calls for the installation of a separate jumper cable harness. **1987–89**—Excessive 2.0L engine knock may indicate a need for tighter fitting pistons. • AC refrigerant loss can be corrected by installing a new valve and cap seal. • No first gear and/or slips in first may mean that you need new forward clutch piston seals. **1987–91**—Vehicles equipped with the 3T40 automatic transmission may experience slippage in manual Low or Reverse. Install Service Package #8628222; it includes a Low/Reverse clutch release spring (#8664961) and a clutch retainer and snap ring (#656/657). **1988**—Erratic performance of the window motor may call for a replacement brush package (#22094719). • 2.0L engine valve-train noise can be reduced by adjusting or replacing the rocker arms. • Lack of heat in the rear may require upgraded floor heater outlets. **1988–95**—A binding or popping noise coming from the front door glass when the glass is rolled down means that the regulator arm stabilizer plate is misadjusted. **1988–89**—Product Campaign #89C06 provides for the rewiring of a faulty 2.0L engine coolant switch. • 2.0L engines that fail to run or stall in cold weather probably need a new PROM. **1989**—Product Campaign #89C16 provides for the replacement of the 5-speed manual transmission. **1989–91**—A power-steering shudder, moan, or vibration signals the need for a "tuned" power-steering return hose and/or high-expansion pressure hose between the steering pump and gear. **1990**—Engine piston scuffing may cause cold engine knock. GM DSB 90-433-6A recommends a partial engine replacement. **1990–91**—No-starts, stalling, and rough running may be caused by a DIS ignition wiring short circuit. • Poor starting may be caused by the spring in early starter drives compressing too easily. Install an upgraded starter motor drive assembly (#10473700). • Engine overheating or poor AC performance may be due to an inoperative engine cooling fan. **1990–92**—Poor braking may be due to excessive corrosion of the front-disc brake-caliper bolt bore. **1991–94**—A crunching noise coming from the right side of the dash when turning the steering wheel can be silenced by installing a new steering grommet on the right side. • Water leaking onto the right front carpet from a gap between the air inlet screen and windshield can be stopped by applying a urethane sealing strip. **1992**—Chafing of the engine harness wires can cause hard starting, engine surging, stalling in gear, the display of the "Service Engine Soon" warning, and an inoperative temperature gauge. • Engine hesitation or roughness, particularly at idle, may be corrected by installing a new lower intake manifold gasket (#10103647). **1992–93**—No Reverse or slipping in Reverse can be corrected by installing an upgraded Low/Reverse clutch return spring and spiral retaining ring. **1992–94**—Front brake linings can be made to last longer by replacing the front brake pads with new 8100 lining compound (#18022600). **1993–96**—A front suspension squawk noise heard when passing over small bumps can be silenced by using a special GM service kit (see following bulletin).

File In Section: 3 Steering/Suspension
Bulletin No.: 73-33-01
Date: April 1997

Subject:
Squawk Noise Coming From Front Suspension or Engine Compartment Area
(Install Ultra High Molecular Tape)

Models:
1993–97 Buick Skylark
1993–94 Chevrolet Cavalier
1993–96 Chevrolet Beretta, Corsica
1993–97 Oldsmobile Achieva
1993–94 Pontiac Sunbird
1993–97 Pontiac Grand Am

Condition
Some owners may comment on a "squawk" noise coming from the front suspension or engine compartment area. This noise may be more noticeable over small bumps, entering parking lots, and including any irregular road surfaces. This condition may also be more noticeable in cold weather conditions.

Cause
The squawk noise may be caused by the rubber stabilizer bushing material bleeding through the Teflon/Polyester sock (on later models) and coming into contact with the stabilizer shaft. On earlier models, the squawk may be caused from friction when the stabilizer bushing is grabbing and releasing the stabilizer shaft.

Correction
If the above conditions exist, perform the following repair:
1. Remove front stabilizer bushing clamps and bushings. Refer to Section 3C of the Service Manual.
2. Inspect stabilizer bushings for excessive wear, replace if necessary.
3. Use crocus cloth (or equivalent) to sand the stabilizer shaft where the stabilizer bushings contact the stabilizer shaft. Sand all rough corrosion thoroughly.
4. Install UHM (Ultra High Molecular) tape (provided in kit, P/N 22602686) into stabilizer bushing; adhesive side of tape should be installed onto the bushing. Install UHM tape to the opening of the bushing (the slit) as well as the circumference (this will secure the tape in place). Kit provides enough tape for two bushings (one vehicle).

1994—Insufficient AC cooling may be due to a leak at the low-charge primary port seal. • Automatic transaxle gear whine may be eliminated by installing a redesigned transaxle final drive assembly. • A squeaking noise heard when going over bumps, accelerating, or shifting can be stopped by replacing the exhaust manifold pipe seal. • Harsh automatic transmission upshifts can be corrected by installing an upgraded accumulator valve in the control valve body. • Loss of Drive or erratic shifts may be caused by an intermittent short to ground on the A or B shift solenoid or an electrical short circuit in the transaxle. **1994–96**—If the accelerator pedal is difficult to depress or if the accelerator cable separates, install an upgraded accelerator cable and clip. • Chronic engine miss or a loss of power can be caused by a micro-arcing corroded spark plug wire or ignition coil. **1990–91 2.3L Quad 4 engine**—Head gasket leaks are covered by a secret warranty extension. The first sign of trouble is a loss of power caused by combustion gases mixing with coolant. This is followed by a cloud of steam and coolant loss through the exhaust system. If these warnings are ignored, cylinder bore scoring, a warped cylinder head, and piston seizure will likely result as the engine continues to overheat. Up to 6 years/60,000 miles, GM will replace the head gasket with an improved version and carry out a new multi-step head-bolt tightening procedure at no cost to the owner. The deductible will be also refunded. Others who bought their cars used or had repairs done at an independent garage are eligible for this free repair and a refund if the engine has already been fixed. Althought this program has expired, one should still ask for a pro rata refund of the repair cost. **1995–96 Chevrolet Beretta Corsica**—Intermittent Neutral/loss of Drive at highway speeds can be fixed by replacing the control valve body assembly. **All models/years**—A rotten-egg odor coming from the exhaust is probably caused by a malfunctioning catalytic converter, which is covered by GM's emissions warranty. Paint delamination, peeling, or fading: See page 95.

Beretta, Corsica Profile

	1989	1990	1991	1992	1993	1994	1995	1996
Cost Price ($)								
Corsica LT	11,650	11,240	11,845	12,834	13,230	13,630	14,385	14,885
Beretta GT/Z	13,600	13,465	14,145	16,620	17,025	15,795	16,790	17,190
Used Values ($)								
Corsica LT ↑	3,500	4,000	4,500	5,000	6,000	7,000	8,000	9,500
Corsica LT ↓	2,500	3,500	4,000	4,500	5,000	6,000	7,000	8,500
Beretta GT/Z ↑	4,500	5,000	5,500	6,500	7,500	8,500	9,500	11,000
Beretta GT/Z ↓	3,500	4,500	4,500	5,500	6,500	7,500	8,500	10,000
Extended Warranty	Y	Y	Y	Y	Y	Y	Y	Y
Secret Warranty	Y	Y	Y	Y	Y	Y	Y	Y
Reliability	①	②	②	②	②	②	②	②
Air conditioning	②	②	②	②	②	②	②	③
Body integrity	①	①	①	①	①	②	②	②
Braking system	①	①	①	①	①	②	②	②
Electrical system	①	①	②	②	②	②	③	③
Engines	①	①	②	②	②	②	③	③
Exhaust/Converter	②	②	②	②	③	③	③	④
Fuel system	①	①	②	②	③	③	③	④
Ignition system	①	②	②	②	③	③	③	④
Manual transmission	②	②	③	③	③	④	④	⑤
- automatic	②	②	②	②	②	②	②	②
Rust/Paint	①	②	②	②	②	②	②	③
Steering	①	②	②	③	③	④	④	⑤
Suspension	①	②	②	③	③	④	④	⑤
Crash Safety								
Corsica 4d	—	②	⑤	⑤	①	①	③	③
Beretta 2d	—	①	⑤	⑤	⑤	—	—	—

Achieva, Calais, Grand Am, Skylark

Rating: Average (1995–97); Below Average (1988–94). The '92 Achieva replaced the Calais; except for styling, this Achieva is practically identical to the others. There is little to recommend in these cars. More reliable, reasonably priced family haulers and sporty sedans are available from other domestic automakers, principally Ford. **Maintenance/Repair costs**: Higher than average; repairs aren't dealer dependent. **Parts**: Higher-than-average cost, but can be bought for much less from independent suppliers.

Technical Data				
ENGINES	**Liters/CID**	**HP**	**MPG**	**Model Years**
		Achieva		
OHC I-4 FI	2.3/138	115–120	21–25	1992–94
DOHC I-4 FI	2.3/138	150–160	20–24	1992–95
DOHC I-4 FI	2.3/138	170–190	20–24	1992–94
DOHC I-4 FI	2.4/146	150	21–26	1996–97
OHC V6 FI	3.1/191	155	20–25	1994–97
OHC V6 FI	3.3L/204	160	19–23	1992–93
	Calais, Grand Am, Skylark			
OHC I-4T FI	2.0/121	165	18–22	1987–89
DOHC I-4 FI	2.3/138	150–160	22–26	1988–91
DOHC I-4 FI	2.3/138	180	21–25	1990–91
OHC I-4 FI	2.3/138	115–120	21–25	1992–94
OHC I-4 FI	2.3/138	150	22–26	1995
DOHC I-4 FI	2.4/146	150	21–26	1996–98
OHV I-4T FI	2.5/151	92–98	22–25	1985–88
OHV I-4T FI	2.5/151	110	21–25	1989–91
OHV V6 FI	3.0/181	125	18–21	1985–87
OHC V6 FI	3.1/191	155	20–25	1994–98
OHV V6 FI	3.3/204	125	19–24	1989–91
OHC V6 FI	3.3/204	160	19–23	1992–93

Strengths and weaknesses: The Achieva uses the Grand Am and Skylark platform, Quad 4 powerplant, and suspension. The base car carries a 150-hp Quad SOHC engine, a 5-speed transaxle, and ABS. The basic front-wheel drive platform continues to be a refined version of the Sunbird and Cavalier J-body. These cars are too cramped to be family sedans (rear entry/exit can be difficult), too sedate for sporty coupe status, and too ordinary for inclusion in luxury car ranks.

In their basic form, these cars are unreliable, unspectacular, and provide barely adequate performance. An upgraded and more reliable 3.1L V6 powerplant gives you only five more horses than the Pontiac's four. There's been a lot of hype about the new Quad 4 16-valve engine, available with all models, but little of this translates into benefits for the average driver. A multi-valve motor produces more power than a standard engine, but always at higher rpms and with a fuel penalty and excess engine noise. The Quad 4 is rougher than most multi-valve engines when revved to cruising speed and so does little to encourage drivers to get the maximum power from it.

These cars ride and handle fairly well but share chassis components with the failure-prone J-bodies. This explains why engine, transmission, brake, and electronic problems are similar. Water leaks and body squeaks and rattles are so abundant that GM has published a six-page troubleshooting DSB that pinpoints the noises and lists fixes (see "Service Tips").

The 2.5L 4-cylinder engine doesn't provide much power and has a poor reliability record. Avoid the Quad 4 and 3.0L V6 engine with SFI (sequential fuel injection) because of their frequent breakdowns and difficult servicing. If you have a blown head gasket or other problems with the Quad 4 engine, keep in mind that GM once had a secret warranty covering its defects; ask for a pro rata refund for the repair, even though the warranty coverage has expired (again, see "Service Tips"). Poor engine cooling and fuel-system malfunctions are common; diagnosis and repair are more complicated than average, however. The engine computer on V6 models has a high failure rate and the oil pressure switch often malfunctions. The electrical system is gremlin plagued. Seals in the power-steering rack deteriorate rapidly. Front brake discs need more frequent replacement than average. Paint defects are common; consequently, surface rust may occur sooner than expected.

Dealer service bulletins: 1993 Achievas and other cars equipped with 2.3L and 3.1L V6 engines—They won't continue running after a cold start. • The converter seal leaks on 4T60E automatic transmissions. • Front door windows may be hard to roll up and seal poorly. • Intermittent electrical problems. • Stalling when decelerating. • Hard starting. • Faulty Reverse gear on 3T40 automatic transmissions. • Rear brake squawk. **1994**—V6-equipped models may experience excessive second-gear vibration caused by a defective hub shaft bearing and sleeve assembly. • Loss of engine coolant likely caused by faulty surge tank caps. • Power steering may lead or pull. • A faulty automatic transmission fluid-level indicator could give false readings. • A poorly running 2.3L Quad 4 engine can often be traced to a moisture-contaminated or corroded ECM connector; correction requires the re-sealing of the engine harness pass-through. **1995**—Oil leaks at the rocker cover. • Engine tick/rattle upon cold start-up. • Cold start stall or tip-in hesitation. • Grinding/growling when in Park on an incline. • AC cut off after an extended idle. • A cold start rattle with the 4T60E automatic transmission. • Longer-life front brake linings. • Brake vibration and/or pedal pulsation. • Rear wheel brake drag. • Inoperative washer pump. • A low voltage reading or dim lights at idle. • A flickering check oil/check gauges light. • Water entering into spoiler (Grand AM). • Poor paint application and rust spots. • Right rear-quarter window wind noise and water leaks. • By the way, DSB 43-1007A gives an exhaustive review of all the possible causes and remedies for body squeaks and rattles afflicting 1992–95 models. **1996**—Second gear starts, poor 1–3 shifting. • Driveability problems, whistling noise, or reduced fuel economy. • Engine overheating/faulty cooling fan. • Excessive engine roll. • Air conditioning odors. • Front seatbelt webbing twists and won't retract. • Fuel filler door won't open. • Radio frequency interference diagnosis. • Wind noise at front-door outer-belt sealing strip.

• Water entering rear compartment at tail light area. • Water leaking into tail light harness. **1997**—Cold start rattle noise is normal, according to GM and no fix is planned (see following page). • "Premature" separation of the accelerator cable and the pedal may require a lot of effort to depress. • Inoperative power door locks. • Noisy instrument panel. • Intermittent loss of drive at highway speeds. • No-starts. • Engine popping noises. • Power window malfunctions. • Front suspension squawk noise.

Safety summary/recalls: **Recalls**: **1985**—A faulty throttle return spring on 2.5L engines could lead to sudden acceleration. **1985–86**—The door pillar could crack. **1986–1990**—Headlights could operate erratically. **1987**—The fuel feed or return hose could leak. **1991**—Power windows could short circuit and remain in the down position or start an electrical fire. **1994**—Weak fuel tank welds could create a fire hazard in a rear-end collision. **1987–90 2.3L Quad 4 engine**—Faulty ignition coils that cause engine misfiring will be replaced under an emissions recall campaign. **1988–89**—It's possible that a cracked fuel-hose feed could leak. **1996**—Front or rear hazard warning lights could be faulty. • The airbag could deploy behind the instrument panel. • A loose steering column bolt could cause loss of steering.

File In Section: 7 - Transmission
Bulletin No.: 57-71-06A
Date: December 1996
Subject:
Cold Start Rattle Noise
(Diagnosis/Service Procedure)
Models:
1991 Buick Reatta
1991–96 Buick Riviera
1991–96 Buick Park Avenue, Ultra
1991–97 Buick Regal
1992–97 Buick LeSabre
1994–96 Buick Century
1994–97 Buick Skylark
1991–93 Cadillac Eldorado, Seville, Sixty Special and Fleetwood (FWD)
1991–95 Cadillac DeVille
1991–97 Chevrolet Lumina
1992–96 Chevrolet Lumina APV
1997 Chevrolet Venture
1994–95 Chevrolet Beretta, Corsica
1995–97 Chevrolet Monte Carlo
1991–92 Oldsmobile Toronado, Trofeo
1991–95 Oldsmobile Ninety Eight
1991–97 Oldsmobile Cutlass Supreme
1992–97 Oldsmobile Eighty Eight, Silhouette
1994–96 Oldsmobile Cutlass Ciera
1994–97 Oldsmobile Achieva
1991–97 Pontiac Grand Prix
1992–97 Pontiac Bonneville, Trans Sport
1994–97 Pontiac Grand Am
with HYDRA-MATIC 4T60-E (RPO M13)
This bulletin is being revised to add models and 1996-97 model years. Please discard Corporate Bulletin Number 57-71-06 (Section 7 - Transmission).
Condition
Some owners may notice a rattle noise from the engine compartment after a cold start that lasts for less than one minute. This condition will usually only occur once per day after the vehicle is started after sitting overnight or an extended period of time.
Cause
This rattle noise may be assumed to be an engine related noise (piston slap, bearing knock, lifter rattle, etc.) but may actually be a 4T60-E transaxle noise caused by a combination of oil pump starvation/cavitation and pressure regulator valve instability. This transaxle noise condition DOES NOT DAMAGE THE TRANSAXLE AND DOES NOT CAUSE A DURABILITY CONCERN. This transaxle noise condition is more noticeable with engines that exhibit a "fast" start (short crank times and immediate engine RPM increase after start). The 3.1L engine (VIN M - RPO L82) is a good example of a "fast" starting engine, though other 4T60-E/engine combinations may exhibit this noise also.
Correction
If the diagnostic steps listed under SERVICE PROCEDURE lead to the 4T60-E transaxle as the cause of the cold start rattle noise, NO REPAIRS SHOULD BE ATTEMPTED. There is no repair for this noise condition at this time. This bulletin will be updated when a repair becomes available.

Let's see if I got this right: GM says its rattling engine is a transmission problem, but it's really not a problem; however, another bulletin will be issued when a repair for the problem becomes available, although said repair has eluded GM's engineers since 1991. Is it any wonder GM's market share over the past several decades has plummeted from 50 percent to 30 percent?

Secret Warranties/Service Tips

1991–95—Front brake linings can be made to last longer by replacing the front brake pads with new 8100 lining compound (#18022600); see below.

More Durable Front Brakes

FILE IN SECTION: 5 - Brakes
BULLETIN NO.: 43-50-06A
DATE: May 1995
SUBJECT:
Longer Life Front Brake Lining (Install New Brake Pads)
MODELS:

1991–95	Buick Skylark
1992–95	Chevrolet Cavalier: Corsica, Beretta
1991	Oldsmobile Cutlass Calais
1992–95	Oldsmobile Achieva
1991–95	Pontiac Grand Am
1992–94	Pontiac Sunbird
1995	Pontiac Sunfire

This bulletin is being revised to include the 1995 model year and revise part number information. Please discard Corporate Bulletin Number 43-50-6 (Section 5 - Brakes).
CONDITION: Some owners may comment on the life of the front brake linings.
CORRECTION: This condition can be addressed by replacing front brake pads with the new 8100 lining compound, P/N 12510050, (Canadian P/N 18022395). The new brake pads incorporate wear sensors on each brake pad.
Important:
DO NOT resurface rotors unless there is a pulsation concern or deep scoring in excess of .060 (up to the head on a dime) is measured. U.S. Dealers — Pontiac vehicles should replace rotors; not resurface if the above conditions are met. Canadian dealers — use current policy.

1992–93—A front-end engine knock troubleshooting chart is found in DSB 306001. **1992–94**—Corrosion of the ECM connectors can lead to a host of driveability problems (DSB 338109A). • DSB 431007 is an excellent troubleshooting guide to finding and correcting squeaks and rattles; it contains six charts that show noise sources and remedies. **1994**—Gear whine with the 4T60E automatic transaxle can be stopped by replacing the final drive and updating the PCM calibration. • Insufficient AC cooling may be due to a leak at the low-charge primary-port seal. • Loss of Drive or erratic shifts may be caused by an intermittent short to ground on the A or B shift solenoid or an electrical short circuit in the transaxle. • A front-end clunking noise when driving over rough roads may require the repositioning of the diagonal radiator support braces. **1987–91 2.3L Quad 4 engine**—Head gasket leaks are covered by a secret warranty extension that's now expired. Try for a pro rata partial refund. The first sign of trouble is a loss of power caused by combustion gases mixing with coolant. This is followed by a cloud of steam and coolant loss through the exhaust system. If these symptoms are ignored, cylinder bore scoring, a warped cylinder head, and piston seizure will likely result as the engine continues to overheat. **1988–89**—Power loss in cold weather can be corrected by installing ventilation kit (#12339306). • A whistle or whine coming from the engine is likely caused by a noisy oil pump; replace it with an improved oil pump (#22538689). • The engine wiring harness may have been cut by constant rubbing on the alternator. This will cause a rough-running engine, inoperative air conditioner/alternator, the illumination of the check engine light, failure of the ECM module, and excessive white smoke (DSB 88-8-11). **1992–97**—Inoperative power door locks may need an upgraded external bumper on the actuator arm. **1995–97**—Intermittent loss of drive at highway speeds may require the replacement of the control valve body assembly. • Engine popping noises can be silenced by tightening the torque strut mount bolts. **1997**—No starts may be due to an improperly routed and pinched wire from the generator to the wiring harness. **2.5L engine**—Excessive oil consumption may be caused by one or more damaged intake valve guides. • Hard starting and engine pinging can be fixed by the installation of a new PROM module (#16121217) TSB 88-6E-11. • Frequent engine overheating is caused by a defective thermostat; replace it with an upgraded part (#3059793). **1995–97 Skylark**—Intermittent Neutral/loss of Drive at highway speeds can be fixed by replacing the control valve body assembly. **All models/years**—A rotten-egg odor coming from the exhaust may be the result of a malfunctioning catalytic converter—covered by the emissions warranty. Stand your ground if GM or the dealer claims that you must pay. • Paint delamination, peeling, or fading: See page 95.

Achieva, Calais, Grand Am, Skylark Profile

	1990	1991	1992	1993	1994	1995	1996	1997
Cost Price ($)								
Achieva S	—	—	14,675	15,009	16,045	14,750	15,790	15,750
Calais S	11,680	12,793	—	—	—	—	—	—
Grand Am	12,439	12,089	13,859	14,484	14,484	15,084	15,624	15,969
Skylark	11,811	12,036	15,180	14,260	14,914	16,070	15,995	16,495
Used Values ($)								
Achieva S ↑	—	—	5,500	6,000	7,000	8,000	9,000	10,500
Achieva S ↓	—	—	4,500	5,000	6,000	7,000	8,000	9,500
Calais S ↑	4,000	5,000	—	—	—	—	—	—
Calais S ↓	3,000	4,000	—	—	—	—	—	—
Grand Am ↑	4,500	5,000	6,000	7,000	8,000	9,500	10,500	11,500
Grand Am ↓	3,500	4,000	5,000	6,000	7,000	8,000	9,500	11,000
Skylark ↑	4,500	5,000	5,500	6,000	7,000	8,000	9,500	11,000
Skylark ↓	3,500	4,000	4,500	5,000	6,000	7,000	8,000	9,500
Extended Warranty	Y	Y	Y	Y	Y	Y	Y	Y
Secret Warranty	Y	Y	Y	Y	Y	Y	Y	Y
Reliability	②	②	②	②	②	②	③	④
Air conditioning	②	②	②	③	③	④	④	④
Body integrity	①	②	②	②	②	②	②	②
Braking system	①	①	①	②	②	②	③	③
Electrical system	①	①	②	②	②	②	②	②
Engines	②	②	②	②	②	③	③	③
Exhaust/Converter	①	①	②	③	③	③	④	⑤
Fuel system	①	②	②	②	②	②	③	③
Ignition system	②	②	②	③	③	③	③	③
Manual transmission	③	③	③	③	④	⑤	⑤	⑤

- automatic	②	②	②	②	②	②	②	②
Rust/Paint	①	①	①	②	②	②	③	③
Steering	②	②	②	②	③	④	⑤	⑤
Suspension	②	③	③	③	⑤	⑤	⑤	⑤
Crash Safety								
Calais 4d	—	⑤	—	—	—	—	—	—
Grand Am 4d	—	—	—	①	—	—	④	—
Grand Am 2d	—	⑤	—	—	—	—	—	—
Skylark 4d	—	—	—	①	—	—	—	—
Achieva 2d	—	—	②	②	—	④	—	⑤
Achieva 4d	—	—	—	①	—	④	—	⑤
Side Impact								
Achieva 2d	—	—	—	—	—	—	—	①

HONDA

Accord

Rating: Recommended (1992–97); Above Average (1990–91); Average (1988–89). Fast and nimble without a V6, this is the car of choice in the compact sedan class for drivers who want maximum fuel economy and comfort along with lots of space for grocery hauling and occasional highway cruising. **Maintenance/Repair costs**: Lower than average; repairs aren't dealer dependent. **Parts**: Higher-than-average cost, but can be bought for much less from independent suppliers. Owners report that Honda frequently charges for parts that should be replaced for free under the emissions warranty and that those charges are far in excess of what other automakers ask.

Technical Data

ENGINES	Liters/CID	HP	MPG	Model Years
OHC I-4 2 bbl.	2.0/119	98	24–28	1986–89
OHC I-4 FI	2.0/119	110–122	23–28	1986–89
OHC I-4 FI	2.2/132	125–130	23–27	1990–97
OHC I-4 FI	2.2/132	140–145	23–27	1991–97
OHC V6 FI	2.7/163	170	20–24	1995–97

Strengths and weaknesses: The Accord doesn't really excel in any particular area; it's just very, very good at everything. It's smooth, quiet, mannerly, and competent, with outstanding fit and finish, inside and out. Every time Honda redesigned the line it not only caught up with the latest advances but went slightly ahead. Strong points are comfort, fit and finish, ergonomics, impressive assembly quality, reliability, and driveability. With the optional 16-valve 4-cylinder engine or V6, the Accord is one of the most versatile compacts you can find. It offers something for everyone, and its high resale value means there's no way you can lose money buying one.

Despite all the foregoing praise, this hasn't always been a great car. During the '80s, Accords were beset with severe premature rusting, frequent engine camshaft and crankshaft failures, and severe front brake problems. Engines leaked or burned oil and blew their cylinder head gaskets easily and carbureted models suffered from driveability problems through 1986.

Between 1986 and 1989, the brakes, automatic transmission (particularly the 2–4 clutch assembly), rack-and-pinion steering, suspension (coils are practically biodegradable), and electrical system became the major problem areas. Also, water pumps and alternators need replacing about every three years. Rapid front brake wear and frequent brake rotor replacements are common. The automatic transmission shifts a bit harshly upon hard acceleration. Shock absorbers go soft quickly, and replacement prices are often beaten by independent suppliers. To avoid costly engine repairs, check the engine timing belt every 2 years/40,000 miles.

Early Accords were surprisingly vulnerable to paint chipping, flaking, and premature surface rust. If left untreated, sheet metal perforations develop unusually quickly. Especially vulnerable spots are front fender seams, door bottoms, and areas surrounding side view mirrors and door handles, rocker panels, wheel openings, windshield posts, front cowls, and trunk and hatchback lids.

1990–93 models got more room (stepping up to the mid-size car niche) and additional power through a new quieter 2.2L 4-cylinder engine. Nevertheless, rear seating is still inadequate, the added weight saps the car's performance, and the automatic transmission shifts harshly at times. Owners report prematurely worn automatic transmissions, constant velocity joints, and power-steering assemblies. Poor quality control in the choice of body trim and assembly leads to numerous air and water leaks.

Redesigned again for the 1994 model year, the Accord continues to add interior room and other refinements. However, the addition of the V6 powerplant in the 1995 model year gives the Accord plenty of power in reserve without the high rpms. The automatic transmission still works poorly with the 4-banger, producing acceleration times that are far from impressive, and owners still complain of excessive road noise and tire whine. Nevertheless, no significant reliability problems have been reported with the latest redesign.

Confidential dealer service bulletins show that the 1994s may have faulty door weather stripping that bunches up and slides in the channel and excessive wind noise emanating from the outside mirror. Usually, these problems are simple to repair and Honda customer relations staff are helpful; however, Honda staffers may be getting a bit too arrogant in their dealings with the public. One *Lemon-Aid* reader wrote:

We returned the car to the dealer several times (at least six) to have the doors adjusted to reduce wind noise affecting my 1994 Accord

LX sedan. They were finally able to reduce the noise a small amount. A letter written to Honda explaining our dissatisfaction with the car resulted in a response letter with very definite 'screw you' overtones.

Dealer service bulletins: **1994**—Buzzing when the turn signals are activated. • A clunking noise from the door glass and instrument panel creaking. • Damaged door handle seals. • Faulty fuel filler doors. • Rattling moon roof deflectors. • Outside mirror wind noise. • Power door locks that unlock themselves. • Difficulty in closing the trunk lid. • Lots of water leaks and wind noise. **1995**—Noise from the front passenger's footwell, exhaust system, and shoulder belt anchors; rear shelf will buzz. • The dash panel and clutch pedal may creak. • A screeching noise occurs when the driver's window is lowered. • A wind whistle emanates from the top of the windshield. • Heater control indicators may not light. DSB 95-017 shows which rear brake pads produce less noise and which ones last the longest. **1996**—Instrument panel creaking. • Poor fit of wheel center cap. • Screeching noise when lowering the driver's window. • Seatbelt is slow to retract. **1997**— Seatbelt malfunctions.

Safety summary/recalls: **NHTSA probes**: **1995**—Rear seatbelt buckle has insufficient slack, preventing buckle from latching. • Airbag warning light stays on. Excessive windshield glare. • AC failure. • Headlight failure. • Cruise control malfunctions. • Premature front/rear brake wear. **1995–96**—Faulty power windows. • Brake failures/lockup. • Airbag failed to deploy or accidentally deployed. • Injury from airbag. • Sudden acceleration, stalling. • Passenger side seatbacks won't stay upright. **1996**—Front passenger seatbelt locks up. • The door lock design gives a boost to thieves. • The check-engine light is always on. • The defroster could be faulty. • Faulty power door locks. • The steering column separates from the shaft. **Recalls**: **1985**—A defective electric control unit could cause the airbags to deploy outside of a crash situation. **1986–1991**— Takata seatbelts will be replaced. **1990–91**—Defective crank pulleys connected to the drive generator and power-steering pump could fail, preventing the battery from recharging. **1991**—The power window malfunctions. • The module may overheat and cause a fire. **1991–93**—Faulty rear seatbelts won't pull out if the car is parked on a steep incline. **1994**—Faulty tire stems may lead to sudden air loss.

Secret Warranties/Service Tips

1988–93—A creaking sound coming from the window regulator can be corrected by installing an upgraded regulator spiral spring. **1990**—Delay after shifting into Drive is corrected by adjusting the cable (87-040). • A right rear suspension clunking noise can be fixed with a new spring silencer tube. • An interior roaring noise can be silenced by installing blind body plugs (#95550-15000) in the door rocker panels. • If the front inside door handle doesn't work, check for a loose or broken actuator rod clip. • A moaning sound heard when the steering wheel is turned may mean that the steering-pump outlet-hose orifice has slipped out of position or that the outlet hose is faulty. • Water leaks behind the dashboard require sealing near the windshield locating blocks and frame panel seams in the cowl. • Whistling from the front of the car is likely caused by poor hood sealing. **1990–91**—A faulty automatic transmission countershaft nut will be replaced free under a product update program. • A new distributor body and kit will help cars that have a starting problem. **1990–93**—Poor AM reception or a popping noise from the speakers is likely due to poor ground connection between the antenna collar and car body. **1992**—A faulty oil pressure switch will be replaced free under a product update program. **1994**—Damaged door handle seals will be replaced for free under a "goodwill" warranty. **1995**—A whistling or howling noise coming from the top of the windshield can be silenced by applying sealant under the upper windshield molding (see illustration below). • Honda will supply an exhaust buzz silencing kit for free on a case-by-case basis. • The Accord's noise problems will be fixed for free only if the dealer makes the request to Honda. **1995–96**—A creaking noise coming from the instrument panel can be silenced through a variety of measures. **1996–97**—In a settlement with the Environmental Protection Agency, Honda paid fines totaling $17.1 million and extended its emissions warranty on 1.6 million 1995–97 models to 14 years or 150,000 miles. This means that costly engine components and exhaust system parts like catalytic converters will be replaced free of charge, as long as the 14-year/150,000-mile limit hasn't been exceeded. Additionally, the automaker will provide a full engine check and emissions-related repairs at 50,000 to 75,000 miles and will give free tune-ups at 75,000 to 150,000 miles. It is estimated the free check-ups, repairs, and tune-ups will cost Honda over $250 million. The story of the settlement was first reported on page 6 of the June 15, 1998, edition of *Automotive News*. **All models/years**—Steering wheel shimmy is a frequent problem taken care of in DSB 94-025.

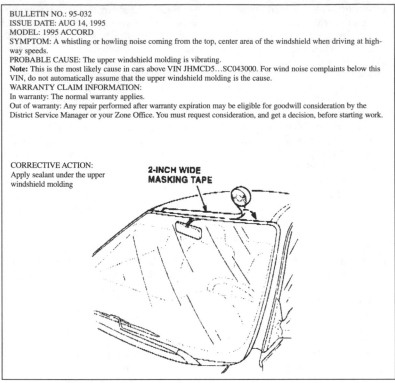

BULLETIN NO.: 95-032
ISSUE DATE: AUG 14, 1995
MODEL: 1995 ACCORD
SYMPTOM: A whistling or howling noise coming from the top, center area of the windshield when driving at high-way speeds.
PROBABLE CAUSE: The upper windshield molding is vibrating.
Note: This is the most likely cause in cars above VIN JHMCD5…SC043000. For wind noise complaints below this VIN, do not automatically assume that the upper windshield molding is the cause.
WARRANTY CLAIM INFORMATION:
In warranty: The normal warranty applies.
Out of warranty: Any repair performed after warranty expiration may be eligible for goodwill consideration by the District Service Manager or your Zone Office. You must request consideration, and get a decision, before starting work.

CORRECTIVE ACTION:
Apply sealant under the upper windshield molding

2-INCH WIDE MASKING TAPE

The Accord's noise problem will be fixed for free, but only *if the dealer makes the request to Honda.*

Accord Profile

	1990	1991	1992	1993	1994	1995	1996	1997
Cost Price ($)								
DX	13,340	13,555	14,265	15,030	12,100	15,930	16,280	16,295
EX	17,590	17,805	19,285	20,050	16,090	21,440	21,780	21,895
Used Values ($)								
DX ↑	8,000	9,000	10,000	10,700	11,500	12,500	13,500	15,000
DX ↓	6,500	8,000	8,500	9,500	10,000	11,000	12,500	14,000
EX ↑	9,500	10,500	11,500	13,000	14,000	15,500	17,000	18,500
EX ↓	8,500	9,000	10,000	11,500	12,500	14,000	15,500	17,000
Extended Warranty	Y	N	N	N	N	N	N	N
Secret Warranty	Y	Y	Y	N	Y	Y	Y	Y
Reliability	③	④	⑤	⑤	⑤	⑤	⑤	⑤
Air conditioning	③	③	③	③	③	④	④	④
Body integrity	❷	❷	❷	❷	③	③	③	④
Braking system	❷	❷	❷	❷	③	③	③	④
Electrical system	③	③	③	③	④	⑤	⑤	⑤
Engines	④	④	④	⑤	⑤	⑤	⑤	⑤

Exhaust/Converter	②	③	②	④	④	⑤	⑤	⑤
Fuel system	④	④	④	⑤	⑤	⑤	⑤	⑤
Ignition system	③	④	④	⑤	⑤	⑤	⑤	⑤
Manual transmission	⑤	⑤	⑤	⑥	⑥	⑥	⑥	⑤
- automatic	④	④	④	④	⑤	⑤	⑤	⑤
Rust/Paint	③	④	④	④	④	④	⑤	⑤
Steering	②	②	③	③	③	④	⑤	⑤
Suspension	③	③	③	④	⑤	⑤	⑤	⑤
Crash Safety								
4d	—	⑤	⑤	⑤	②	④	④	④
LX wagon	—	⑤	—	②	—	—	—	—
SE	—	—	—	❶	—	—	—	—
Side Impact								
4d	—	—	—	—	—	—	—	②

HYUNDAI

Sonata

Rating: Average (1995–97); Not Recommended (1989–93). The 1994 model year was skipped and the 1995s were launched in April 1994. These cars aren't rated very high because of their poor quality control and crash rating, inadequate parts supply, and the uncertain future of the parent company in Canada. If you must have a Sonata, I suggest you buy a 1996–97 version, plan to keep it at least five years to shake off the depreciation, and put some of the savings on the purchase price into a comprehensive supplementary warranty to protect you during that period. **Maintenance/Repair costs**: Higher than average; repairs aren't dealer dependent. **Parts**: Higher-than-average cost and often back-ordered.

Technical Data

ENGINES	Liters/CID	HP	MPG	Model Years
OHC I-4 FI	2.0/122	128	19–24	1992–94
DOHC I-4 FI	2.0/122	137	21–27	1995–98
OHC I-4 FI	2.4/143	110–116	20–25	1989–91
OHC V6 FI	3.0/181	142	18–22	1990–98

Strengths and weaknesses: This mid-size front-drive sedan was built under Mitsubishi licensing, but its overall reliability isn't anywhere near as good as what you'll find with Mitsubishi's cars and trucks. Acceleration is impressive with the manual gearbox and only passable with the automatic. Handling and performance are also fairly good, although emergency handling isn't confidence-inspiring, particularly due to the imprecise steering and excessive lean when cornering. As with other Hyundai models, the automatic transmission performs erratically, the engine is noisy, and reliability is a problem: it's way below average for the 1989–93 models; the

1995–97 models are moderately improved.

Redesigned for the 1995 model year, the car got additional interior room, more horsepower, and an upgraded automatic transmission. Nevertheless, acceleration with an automatic is still below average with the 4-banger and the automatic gearbox still downshifts slowly. 1995–97 Sonatas came with more standard features, like air conditioning, power steering, and a 2.0L 16-valve 4-cylinder engine.

Consumer Reports magazine reports that owners of 1990–92 Sonatas had 120 percent more complaints than the average car owner. Sonatas have had body assembly and preparation deficiencies that show that Hyundai doesn't yet have a firm grip on quality control. For example, the sloppily applied paint pits like an orange peel and the sun visors and headliner look cheap and fragile. If the experience of Stellar and Pony owners is any guide, Sonata owners will notice serious deficiencies by the third and fourth year.

Hyundai dealer service bulletins indicate that the Sonata's automatic transmission could exhibit what Hyundai describes as "shift shock" as well as delayed shifting. Problems reported by owners in the past: poor engine performance (hard starting, poor idling, stalling); the engine runs hot, and when you're stopped at a traffic light, it shakes like a boiling kettle; #3 spark plug often needs replacing or cleaning; rough engine rattle; high oil consumption (one liter every two–three months); excessive front brake pulsation and premature wear; steering defects (when the steering wheel is turned to either extreme, it makes a sound like metal cracking); cruise control malfunctions and electrical short circuits; battery life of only 18 months; malfunctioning lights; radio failures; falling interior roof liner; faulty hood locks; rotten-egg smell coming from the catalytic converter; broken muffler; faulty resonator; defective exhaust pipe; poor door and window sealing (water leaking into the interior when the car is washed); premature paint peeling; and rusting.

Safety summary/recalls: There are reports of electrical fires for the 1989–90 models. • Emergency handling leaves lots to be desired. The owner of a '93 Sonata reports:

> I almost lost control once when I had to cut the wheel sharply to avoid a collision. I wasn't traveling especially fast at the time and weather and highway conditions were ideal. The car rocked and swerved violently and would not respond to any corrective measures I tried. It was just pure luck that I managed to keep it on the road or avoid colliding with other vehicles.

Recalls: **1986–91**—Part of the wiring harness connecting the alternator to the battery could detach, create a short circuit, and result in the loss of electrical power or an engine fire. **1989–90**—Fuel leaks into engine compartment. • Hood could fly up. **1989–94**—The motorized shoulder belt could malfunction. **1995**—There is the potential of loss of rear spring support. **1996–97**—The wiper motor is faulty.

Secret Warranties/Service Tips

1989–90—Vibrations caused by excessive hub and brake disc run-out require a new hub, machining of the disc, or new brake discs. • Cold-start stalling with the 2.4L engine can be fixed by installing start enrichment kit #39901-326000D. • Engine oil drain-plug leaks are likely caused by a faulty gasket or incorrect gasket installation. **1990**—Difficult shifts into fourth gear require a new transmission restrict ball assembly. **1992**—Oil leaking between the oil filter and mounting bracket could be due to an overly wide mounting surface on the bracket; correct this leakage by replacing the bracket. **1992–93**—Hyundai has a field fix for manual transaxle gear clash/grind (DSB 9440-004). **1992–95**—Difficult-to-engage Reverse gear needs an upgraded part. **1995–96**—Harsh shifting might be fixed by installing an upgraded Transaxle Control Module (TCM). **1995–97**—Lots more tips are offered on getting the automatic transmission to shift properly. **All models/years**—Harsh shifting when coming to a stop or upon initial acceleration is likely caused by a misadjusted accelerator pedal switch TCU. • A faulty air exhaust plug could cause harsh shifting into second and fourth gear on vehicles with automatic transmission. • Brake pedal pulsation can be corrected by installing upgraded front discs and pads (see following bulletin).

Number: 96-50-004
Date: AUGUST, 1996
Model: SONATA (ALL)
Subject: BRAKE PEDAL PULSATION: DIAGNOSIS AND REPAIR
DESCRIPTION: Some Sonata vehicles may experience brake pedal pulsation during light brake application if brake disc thickness variation exceeds specifications. A pulsating brake pedal condition does not affect the stopping distance of the vehicle. If a road test has confirmed that the vehicle has this condition, the front brake discs and pads should be replaced.
SERVICE PROCEDURE:
1. Remove front brake discs and pads, following the procedure outlined in the shop manual.
2. Discard brake discs, pads, and return springs.

Part Name	Part Number	
	Previous	Current
Disc-FR Brake	51712-33001	51712-33001
Pad Kit-FR Disc Brake	58101-35A10	58101-34A10

Insist that this repair should be covered under warranty up to 2 years/ 25,000 miles.

Sonata Profile

	1989	1990	1991	1992	1993	1995	1996	1997
Cost Price ($)								
Base	11,325	12,104	12,540	13,130	13,554	14,614	15,204	15,964
Used Values ($)								
Base ↑	2,500	3,000	3,500	4,500	5,500	8,000	9,500	11,000
Base ↓	2,000	2,500	3,000	3,500	4,500	7,000	8,500	10,000

| Extended Warranty | Y | Y | Y | Y | Y | N | N | N |
Secret Warranty	N	N	N	N	N	Y	Y	Y
Reliability	②	②	②	②	③	③	③	③
Air conditioning	③	③	③	③	④	④	④	—
Body integrity	②	②	②	②	②	③	③	③
Braking system	③	③	③	③	③	③	③	③
Electrical system	②	②	②	②	②	④	④	④
Engines	⑤	⑤	⑤	⑤	⑤	⑤	⑤	⑤
Exhaust/Converter	③	③	④	④	⑤	⑤	⑤	⑤
Fuel system	④	③	⑤	⑤	④	⑤	⑤	⑤
Ignition system	④	④	④	⑤	⑤	⑤	⑤	⑤
Manual transmission	④	④	④	③	③	④	⑤	④
- automatic	②	②	②	②	②	③	④	④
Rust/Paint	②	②	③	③	③	④	④	④
Steering	③	③	④	④	④	⑤	⑤	⑤
Suspension	②	②	③	④	④	⑤	⑤	⑤
Crash Safety	①	—	—	—	—	③	③	③
Side Impact	—	—	—	—	—	—	—	①

MAZDA

626, Cronos and MX-6, Mystère

Rating: Above Average (1993–97); Average (1991–92); Not Recommended (1988–90). 1997 was the last model year for the MX-6 and Probe, its Ford twin. **Maintenance/Repair costs**: Higher than average; repairs aren't dealer dependent. Mazda suggests changing the engine timing chain after 60,000 miles. **Parts**: High repair and parts costs. Try independent suppliers to keep costs down.

Technical Data

ENGINES	Liters/CID	HP	MPG	Model Years
OHC I-4 2 bbl.	2.0/122	84	22–27	1985
OHC I-4 FI	2.0/122	93	22–26	1986–87
OHC I-4T FI	2.0/122	120	19–24	1986–87
OHC I-4D FI	2.0/122	61	30–35	1985
OHC I-4 FI	2.2/133	110	22–26	1988–92
OHC I-4T FI	2.2/133	145	18–23	1988–92
DOHC I-4 FI	2.0/122	118	22–27	1993–97
DOHC V6 FI	2.5/153	164	19–24	1993–97

Strengths and weaknesses: Although far from being high performance vehicles, these cars ride and handle fairly well and still manage to accommodate four people in comfort. The 1988–92 versions incorporated a third-generation redesign that added a bit more horsepower to the 4-banger. Apart from that improvement, these cars are still easy riding, fairly responsive, and not hard on gas. On the downside, the automatic transmission downshifts roughly, the power steering is imprecise, and the car leans a lot in turns.

The earlier models had a bit more interior room than post-1987 models. Electronically adjustable shock absorbers on the 1983–85 coupes and touring sedans became optional in 1986. The five-door hatchback touring sedan offers lots of sports and luxury extras as well.

4-wheel steering was part of the sedan's equipment in 1988, but it was added exclusively to the MX-6 a year later. Wise buyers should pass over this option and look instead for anti-lock brakes and airbags on 1992 LG and GT versions. The manual transmission is a better choice because the automatic robs the engine of much-needed horsepower, as is the case with most cars this size.

Mid-sport, mid-compact hybrids, the MX-6 and Mystère are coupe versions of the 626. They have more sophisticated suspensions, more horsepower, and better steering response than their sedan alter ego. The 1993 models gained a base 2.5L 165-hp V6 powerplant. Overall reliability and durability are on par with the 626.

Mazda 626 and MX-6 reliability was mediocre until 1984, improved in the car's middle years, and is now on the upswing again. Additionally, the newer models have a strong, comprehensive factory warranty that protects subsequent purchasers. The original rear-drive is a good compact sedan marred by steady deterioration of mechanical and body components as it ages. Newer front-wheel drive models are doing better, which is unusual, since front-drives are generally less durable than rear-drive vehicles. Air conditioning malfunctions, poor body assembly (leaks and paint problems), automatic transmission glitches, and premature exhaust system rust-out are commonplace, particularly on 1987–88 versions. The steering rack is failure-prone on pre-1988s.

1988–92 626s still generate complaints concerning automatic transmission failures and jerky downshifts when the 4-cylinder is at full throttle (corrected on the 1994s). The automatic transmission on turbo-equipped models is particularly troublesome. Shocks and struts are expensive to replace. MacPherson strut defects are common, especially when the model is equipped with the electronic adjustment feature. The electronically controlled shock absorbers haven't been durable and they cost a lot to replace. Front and rear brakes are troublesome and often need replacing within 2 years/40,000 miles. The exhaust system will rarely last more than two years, and wheel bearings fail repeatedly within the same period.

You want to buy a 1993–97 626 for the improved acceleration; however, the manual gearbox doesn't shift quickly and the automatic transmission still handles downshifts badly. Still, you get good performance and handling, reasonable fuel economy (premium grade, though), and less body lean when cornering. Reliability was also improved.

All model years have door and hatch locks that often freeze up, headliner rattles, and the metal surrounding the rear wheel wells is prone to rust perforation, as are hood, trunk, and door seams. Interestingly, the paint seems particularly prone to chipping. The underbody and suspension components on cars older than five years should be examined carefully for corrosion damage.

Safety summary/recalls: NHTSA probes: 1995–96—Inadvertent airbag deployments. **1997 626 ES**—Head restraints are too low. One West Coast neurologist says the 626's head restraints are set too low and cannot extend to a safe level. He says there is an additional two inches required for a six-foot-tall occupant. When informed of his assessment, the dealer replied that Mazda "cannot help you with your problem." The doctor maintains his Mazda 626 cannot be safely operated by a driver over five-foot ten-inches in height. He concludes: "As a result of my occupation, I see many motor vehicle accident neck injuries and have a keen interest in making my new vehicle, and those of others, safe." **Recalls: 1979–82**—The free replacement of suspension components, including the idler arm, is authorized under recall #17510. **1986**—The throttle could stick open due to a defective nylon rotor. **1986–87**—An ignition switch failure will result in faulty wipers, washer, engine fan, heater blower, and air conditioner compressor. **1988**—Automatic shoulder belt could break. • The floor mat could interfere with the gas pedal. • Frost could accumulate in the throttle body. • A rear brake shoe could separate from a wheel cylinder piston. • Band flexing could cause the fuel tank to leak. **1988–91**—Mazda will replace original door handles with new handles that are more durable so that door won't fly open. **1988–1989 MX-6**—Takata seatbelts will be replaced. **1995**—Airbags malfunction.

Secret Warranties/Service Tips

1993–94—Freezing door and hatch lock cylinders are addressed in DSB 021/94. • Headliner rattles can be fixed by using Mazda's fastener kit. • The driver's-side power seat might not work if the wiring harness touches the seat frame. • A clunking noise coming from the steering gear is caused by excessive backlash in the steering gear assembly. **1995–96**—A 3–4 shift hunt is probably caused by failure in the 3–4 shift solenoid hydraulic circuit. • Front strut squeaks on turns could be caused by interference between the spring upper seat and the strut dust cover or between the dust cover and the rubber bump stopper. **All models/years**—Non-turbo models that idle roughly after a warm restart could have fuel vaporizing in the distribution pipe due to high under-hood temperatures; to eliminate this problem, the emission control unit has been redesigned to allow higher fuel pressure at lower temperatures (DSB 023/87R). • Excessive rear brake squealing can be reduced with improved brake pads (DSB 015/89-11). • Excessive vibrations felt in the brake pedal, steering wheel, floor, or seat when applying the brakes can be fixed by installing a redesigned brake assembly.

626, Cronos and MX-6, Mystère Profile

	1990	1991	1992	1993	1994	1995	1996	1997
Cost Price ($)								
626, Cronos	14,488	14,448	15,685	17,495	15,450	17,630	17,960	18,160
MX-6, Mystère	14,298	14,384	15,475	18,300	19,540	20,713	21,745	22,345
Used Values ($)								
626, Cronos ↑	6,000	7,000	8,000	9,000	10,000	11,000	12,000	13,500
626, Cronos ↓	5,000	6,000	7,000	8,000	9,000	10,000	11,000	12,500
MX-6, Mystère ↑	6,100	7,100	8,000	9,200	10,500	11,500	12,500	14,500
MX-6, Mystère ↓	5,100	6,200	7,000	8,200	9,500	10,500	11,500	13,500
Extended Warranty	Y	Y	Y	N	N	N	N	N
Secret Warranty	N	N	N	N	N	Y	Y	N
Reliability	②	②	③	③	③	③	④	⑤
Air conditioning	③	③	②	②	③	③	④	④
Body integrity	③	③	②	③	③	③	③	③
Braking system	③	④	④	③	③	③	③	④
Electrical system	③	③	③	③	④	⑤	⑤	⑤
Engines	④	④	④	⑤	⑤	③	③	④
Exhaust/Converter	⑤	⑤	⑤	③	④	⑤	⑤	⑤
Fuel system	④	④	③	④	④	④	⑤	⑤
Ignition system	④	④	④	④	⑤	⑤	⑤	⑤
Manual transmission	④	④	④	④	⑤	⑤	⑤	⑤
- automatic	③	③	③	③	③	③	③	④
Rust/Paint	③	③	③	③	③	④	④	④
Steering	③	③	③	④	④	⑤	⑤	⑤
Suspension	③	③	④	④	④	④	④	④
Crash Safety								
626 4d	—	—	—	❶	❶	④	④	④
Side Impact								
626 4d	—	—	—	—	—	—	—	❷

MITSUBISHI

Galant

Rating: Recommended (1994–97); Above Average (1990–93).
Maintenance/Repair costs: Higher than average, but repairs aren't dealer dependent. **Parts**: Parts are relatively inexpensive when compared with other cars in this class. Parts availability is about average.

Technical Data

ENGINES	Liters/CID	HP	MPG	Model Years
OHC I-4 FI	2.0/122	102	19–24	1989–92
OHC I-4 FI	2.0/122	121	19–24	1993
DOHC I-4 FI	2.0/122	135–144	18–22	1989–92
DOHC I-4 FI	2.0/122	195	17–21	1991–92

| OHC I-4 FI | 2.4/144 | 141 | 19–25 | 1994–98 |
| DOHC I-4 FI | 2.4/144 | 160 | 17–23 | 1994 |

Strengths and weaknesses: The Galant is a recommended family-car buy because of its reasonable price, spacious, comfortable interior, good fuel economy, and better than average reliability and durability.

1987–93 models have few problems, except for premature brake wear, and excessive noise and vibrations. Add to this poor body assembly, and you can see the Galant is far from perfect.

Totally redesigned, the 1994–97, Galant got larger—now rivaling the Mazda 626, Nissan Altima, and the Toyota Camry. It's powered by a potent base 2.4L 141-hp 4-cylinder engine and an optional twin-cam variant that unleashes 160 horses. Either engine will be mated to a 5-speed manual or an electronically controlled 4-speed automatic. The latest redesign has improved the car's overall reliability, however, brakes and body deficiencies continue to be its Achilles heel.

Safety summary/recalls: **NHTSA probes**: **Recalls**: **1989**—Front seatbelt release button may fail. **NHTSA probes**: **1994–97**—After the ignition key is turned off, the sunroof immediately stops when opening the driver's door. This meets the requirements of FMVSS No. 118, "Power-operated Window Systems." However, the sunroof does not stop when the passenger's door is opened and the government has issued a recall order which Mitsubishi is fighting. **1994**—Brake lights may fail and cruise control not disengage due to faulty stop light switch. **1995**—Vehicle suddenly caught fire; believed to be caused by an electrical short. • Sticking accelerator pedal. • Mat slips under accelerator pedal. • Sudden stalling. • Airbag failed to deploy. • Airbag deployed for no reason. • Sudden brake failure. • Brakes suddenly lock up when driving. • Parking brake fails to hold, vehicle rolled downhill. • Doors lock when brakes are applied. • Premature brake wear. • Driver-side seatbelt failure. • Seatbelt wouldn't loosen, had to be cut off. • Transmission frequently downshifts. • Transmission slippage, locks up and premature failure. • Gear shift lever fails to go from Park to Reverse or Drive. • Control arm failure. • Window fogging. Instrument light failure. • Excessive vibration when AC is engaged. • AC emits a foul odor. • Fuel odors in the interior. **1996**—ABS brake failure. • Airbag failed to deploy. • Hard to secure child safety seat due to excessive length of seatbelts. • Front axle collapsed when passing over a bump, causing loss of steering. • Transmission gasket failure. • Defective electric door locks. • Excessive windshield fogging. • Faulty rear door rubber seals.

Secret Warranties/Service Tips

1994–96—If the ABS warning light comes on for no apparent reason, it's likely the ABS ECU needs replacing under warranty. • Door trim panel gaps

or peeling can be fixed by following the tips given in DSB #96-52A-001.
1995–96—Sunroof water leaks are tackled in DSB #964-42A-008. **1996**—
Rough automatic transmission shifting can be corrected by installing an
upgraded transmission control module under warranty. **All models/years**—
Troubleshooting tips to correct spark plug fouling and window fogging.

Galant Profile

	1990	1991	1992	1993	1994	1995	1996	1997
Cost Price ($)								
Base	14,041	22,145	15,487	16,024	16,204	17,017	18,535	17,964
Used Values ($)								
Base Coupe ↑	6,000	8,500	7,500	9,000	10,000	11,000	12,500	14,000
Base Coupe ↓	5,000	7,500	6,500	7,500	8,500	9,500	11,000	13,000
Extended Warranty	N	N	N	N	N	N	N	N
Secret Warranty	N	N	N	N	N	N	N	N
Reliability	⑤	⑤	⑤	⑤	⑤	⑤	⑤	⑤
Air conditioning	④	④	④	⑤	⑤	⑤	⑤	⑤
Body integrity	❷	❷	❷	❷	③	③	③	④
Braking system	❷	❷	❷	❷	③	③	③	④
Electrical system	③	③	④	④	④	⑤	⑤	⑤
Engines	③	④	④	④	⑤	⑤	⑤	⑤
Exhaust/Converter	❷	❷	④	④	④	⑤	⑤	⑤
Fuel system	③	③	③	④	④	③	④	⑤
Ignition system	③	③	③	④	④	④	⑤	⑤
Manual transmission	④	④	④	⑤	⑤	⑤	⑤	⑤
- automatic	③	③	③	⑤	⑤	④	④	⑤
Rust/Paint	❷	❷	❷	❷	③	③	③	④
Steering	③	③	③	③	③	⑤	⑤	⑤
Suspension	③	③	④	④	④	⑤	⑤	⑤
Crash Safety	❶	❶	❶	❶	❶	④	④	④
Side Impact	—	—	—	—	—	—	—	③

NISSAN

Altima

Rating: Average (1993–97). The V6 provides the necessary versatility needed to match the competition: the Toyota Camry, Mazda 626
Cronos, updated Ford Probe, or larger Ford Taurus and Sable.
Don't buy a 1997 Altima if a cheaper '96 model is available. The '97
version was carried over relatively unchanged, except for upgraded
side-impact protection. Although the SE gives the sportiest performance, the less-expensive GXE is the better deal from a price/qual-
ity standpoint. **Maintenance/Repair costs**: Higher than average.
Dealer dependent. **Parts**: Owners complain of parts shortages; parts
are more expensive than those for most other cars in this class.

Technical Data

ENGINE	Liters/CID	HP	MPG	Model Years
DOHC I-4 FI	2.4/146	150	21–26	1993–96

Strengths and weaknesses: The Altima's wheelbase is a couple of inches longer than the Stanza's and the car is touted by Nissan as a mid-size, even though its interior dimensions put it in the compact league. The small cabin only seats four and rear seat access is difficult to master due to the slanted roof pillars, inward-curving door frames, and narrow clearance.

The base engine gives average acceleration and fuel economy. Good maneuverability around town. No reliability problems reported with the 16-valve powerplant or transmission. Uncluttered under-hood layout makes servicing easy. Good body assembly.

With its noisy and rough engine performance, this car cries out for a V6 like the one used in the Maxima. The 4-banger has insufficient top-end torque and gets buzzier the more it's pushed. In order to get the automatic to downshift for passing, for example, you have to practically stomp on the accelerator. The 5-speed manual transmission is sloppy. The Altima's sporty handling is way overrated; there's excessive body roll and front-end plow in hard cornering, tires squeal at moderate speeds, and steering isn't as precise or responsive as befits a car with performance pretensions. In spite of the car's independent suspension, it gives a busy, uncomfortable ride that's punishing over bumps. Lots of engine, road, and tire noise.

Dealer service bulletins: **1993**—A creaking, squeaking, or tapping noise coming from the window and door areas. • Water leaks. • Electrical system, heater, air conditioning, and defrosting malfunctions. • Body/trim deficiencies. **1994**—No Reverse (automatic). • Excessive brake and steering wheel vibration. • Inaccurate fuel gauges. • Rear suspension noise. **1995**—Front cover oil leakage. • No or low line pressure rise (control valve). • Poor driveability—Code 45. • AC compressor leaks or is noisy. • Troubleshooting excessive front and rear brake noise. • Some windshield cracks are covered under warranty.

Safety summary/recalls: **Recalls**: **1993–94**—Throttle cable may not return to idle. **1995**—Automatic shift lever plate can break, causing unintended vehicle movement. • Brake hose may leak. **1996**—AC refrigerant leaks. • Leaking AC evaporator drain hose causes ECM damage.

Secret Warranties/Service Tips

1993—Center caps on alloy wheels may not fit properly. Order upgraded caps (#40315-D9000). • An exhaust rattle during acceleration can be resolved by installing an upgraded muffler assembly-exhaust (#203000-IE860). • Inadequate defrosting on vehicles made before February '93 can be resolved by following Nissan's suggestions in its NTB93-059 bulletin. • NTB93-086, a lengthy Nissan bulletin sent out May 25, 1993, troubleshoots the Altima's most common water leaks into the interior. • Poor AC performance can be corrected by installing a thermal control unit (TCU). • An inoperative AC and heater may have a kinked heater/water valve cable that has damaged the air mix door actuator. **1993–94**—No Reverse gear with the manual transmission: install a Nissan upgrade kit. • Fuel gauge is inaccurate or it may be difficult to fill a fuel tank fixed with upgraded parts. **1993–96**—DSB #NTB96-046 gives lots of useful tips for troubleshooting squeaks and rattles

Altima Profile

	1993	1994	1995	1996	1997
Cost Price ($)					
XE	16,229	16,904	17,848	18,783	18,798
Used Values ($)					
XE ↑	9,000	10,000	11,500	12,500	14,000
XE ↓	8,500	9,000	10,000	11,500	13,000
Extended Warranty	N	N	N	N	N
Secret Warranty	Y	Y	N	N	N
Reliability	③	④	④	④	⑤
Air conditioning	❷	③	④	④	④
Manual transmission	⑤	⑤	⑤	⑤	⑤
Automatic transmission	⑤	⑤	⑤	⑤	⑤
Body integrity	❷	③	③	③	③
Braking system	❷	③	③	③	③
Electrical system	❷	③	③	③	③
Engines	④	⑤	④	⑤	⑤
Exhaust/Converter	③	④	④	⑤	⑤
Fuel system	③	③	④	⑤	⑤
Ignition system	④	⑤	⑤	⑤	⑤
Rust/Paint	③	④	⑤	⑤	⑤
Steering	③	③	③	④	⑤
Suspension	③	③	③	④	④
Crash Safety	⑤	⑤	—	④	④

Stanza

Rating: Above Average (1990–92); Average (1988–89); Not Recommended (1985–88). **Maintenance/Repair costs**: Lower than average; repairs aren't dealer dependent. The Stanza was replaced by the Altima in 1993. **Parts**: Average cost, but can be bought for much less from independent suppliers.

Technical Data

ENGINES	Liters/CID	HP	MPG	Model Years
OHC I-4 FI	2.0/120	97	23–27	1985–89
OHC I-4 FI	2.4/146	138	20–25	1990–92

Strengths and weaknesses: 1988–89 Stanzas were mini Maximas in that they were redesigned along luxury Maxima lines. Unfortunately, they were under-powered, the automatic transmission was reluctant to downshift, the engine was noisy, and the base suspension allowed the car to bounce about. This is not the car for a full passenger or cargo load.

1990–92 Stanzas are roomy, reasonably priced, four-passenger compacts that offer peppy performance, more responsive steering, nimble handling, and good fuel economy. Overall reliability has been fairly good during the past six years. Except for some road noise, suspension thumps, starting difficulties, transmission malfunctions, and a biodegradable exhaust system, no major problems have been reported on 1988–92 Stanzas.

Owners complain that the automatic transmission vibrates annoyingly when the car is idling in gear, clutches are noisy, and steering wheel vibrations are frequent. Power antenna malfunctions, premature front brake wear, and surface rust complaints are common for all years; wheel openings, the front edge of the hood, rear hatch, and door bottoms are especially prone to rust perforation.

Safety summary/recalls: Recalls: 1986 Wagon 2X4—Cover for the fuel filler pipe for increased accident protection.

Secret Warranties/Service Tips

1982–88—Improved brake pad material will cut brake noise and add to pad durability. Upgraded semi-metallic pads carry the Hitachi HP12 FE designation. **1987–89**—Trunk lid torsion bars won't fall off if you install a torsion bar spacer (#84449-D4060). **1989–92**—Clutch shudder and steering wheel vibration can be eliminated by checking brake rotor thickness or installing an upgraded pressure plate release lever. **1990**—Starting in D4 or delayed downshifting requires a new valve body separator plate. **1990–91**—Starting difficulties can often be traced to an ECU connector not fully seated in the ECU. **1990–92**—Clutch whine or screech in cold temperatures requires the installation of an upgraded clutch disc. **All models/years**—A rotten-egg smell could be caused by a defective catalytic converter; have it replaced free of charge if the emissions warranty still applies.

Stanza Profile

	1987	1988	1989	1990	1991	1992
Cost Price ($)						
Base	12,144	12,869	13,654	13,335	13,900	14,000
Used Values ($)						
Base ↑	3,500	4,000	4,500	5,000	6,000	7,000
Base ↓	3,000	3,000	4,000	4,500	5,000	6,000

Extended Warranty	Y	Y	Y	Y	N	N
Secret Warranty	N	N	N	N	N	N
Reliability	②	③	③	③	④	④
Air conditioning	③	④	④	④	⑤	⑤
Body integrity	②	②	③	③	③	③
Braking system	②	②	③	③	③	③
Electrical system	②	②	②	③	③	③
Engines	②	③	④	④	④	④
Exhaust/Converter	②	②	②	②	③	③
Fuel system	②	③	③	③	③	③
Ignition system	③	③	③	③	③	③
Manual transmission	③	④	④	④	④	④
- automatic	②	③	③	③	③	③
Rust/Paint	②	②	③	③	③	③
Steering	②	③	③	④	④	④
Suspension	②	③	③	③	③	④
Crash Safety						
Stanza 4d	—	—	—	❶	⑤	⑤

SUBARU

Legacy

Rating: Only the AWD models are Above Average (1995–97); Average (1990–94). The 1995–97 models are way overpriced, considering they don't offer much more than AWD. Before buying a front-drive Subaru, first consider what Honda, Mazda, or Toyota have to offer. The only reason to buy a Subaru is for its 4X4 capability and on most used models you'll have to pay a $1,500–$2,000 premium to get it. If it's not what you need for your basic driving requirements, pick a car with a conventional drivetrain. **Maintenance/Repair costs**: Higher than average; repairs are dealer dependent. **Parts**: Higher-than-average cost can't be attenuated through purchasing from independent suppliers.

Technical Data

ENGINES	Liters/CID	HP	MPG	Model Years
OHC flat-4 FI	2.2/135	130	19–25	1990–94
OHC flat-4 FI	2.2/135	135	19–25	1995–98
OHC flat-4T FI	2.2/135	160	17–22	1991–94
OHC flat-4 FI	2.5/150	155	18–22	1996–98

Strengths and weaknesses: First launched in 1989 as front-drives, these compacts are a bit slow off the mark. The 5-speed is a bit notchy and the automatic gearbox is slow to downshift and has difficulty staying in overdrive. Early Legacys are noisy, fuel-thirsty cars

with bland styling that masks their solid, dependable AWD performance. Actually, the availability of a proven 4-wheel drive powertrain in a compact family sedan and wagon makes these cars
appealing for special use. In spite of their reputation for dependability, though, Subarus are not trouble-free—engine, clutch,
turbo, and driveline defects are common on the early models
through to the '94 models.

The redesigned 1995–97 models have sleeker styling, additional
interior room, a bit more horsepower with the base engine, and a
new 2.5L 4-cylinder driving the 1996 AWD GT and LSi. The
Outback was transformed into a sport-utility wagon with a taller
roof. Even with the improvements noted above, acceleration is still
only passable (if you don't mind the loud engine), but handling
and ride are remarkably good. Overall, it's a competent small car
with few faults and only one outstanding feature—AWD. If you
don't need that feature, there are better-performing, less-expensive
vehicles available. Another word of warning: *Consumer Reports* says
that the Outback upgrade isn't worth the extra $3,000. They point
out that Subaru's ads are misleading when they show Paul Hogan
zipping around off-road. The publication also reports that the
Subaru's handling isn't as competent as that of the regular Legacy
(something to do with the higher center of gravity, no doubt).

Subaru's overall product lineup for 1997 marked a return to the
company's four-wheel drive roots with the repackaging of its Legacy
and Impreza 4X4 lineup as Outbacks. (Half of all Legacys sold are
Outbacks.) A Legacy 2.5L GT all-wheel drive sporting sedan, or
wagon variant, also joined the group that year. In addition to these
re-designated models—and the squeezing out of a bit more horsepower from its limited range of engines—Subaru continued to tap
the sport-utility craze through lower prices for its AWD and ABS
options and by offering a greater variety of AWD vehicles.

Are Subarus good buys? Devotees will insist that there's no other
car as versatile and the manufacturer is justifiably proud of the high
J.D. Power owner satisfaction rating earned in the U.S. On the other
hand, I have found that a Subaru can be a good used-car choice only
if its AWD feature is essential for your driving needs, it's been maintained carefully, the body hasn't begun to rust, and dealer servicing
is easily available. This last point is crucial because these cars are very
dependent on the dealer network for parts and servicing.

Through 1996, premature exhaust-system rust-out and automatic transmission (front seals, especially) and clutch breakdowns are
the more common complaints. Brakes require frequent attention.
Shock absorbers, constant velocity joints, and catalytic converters
often wear out prematurely. Other problems that appear over many
model years include starter and ignition relay failures and front-end
suspension noises. Subarus are rust-prone. Fenders, door bottoms,
rocker panels, wheel openings, bumpers and supports, rear quarter-
panels, tailgates, trunk lids, and hoods are particularly vulnerable.

Additionally, the underbody and chassis components should be examined very carefully for corrosion damage.

Safety summary/recalls: NHTSA probes: 1995—Inadvertent airbag deployment: airbags deployed after the underside of the car scraped the road or the car drove over a dip in the road, hit a pothole, or was stuck in a ditch in the snow. **Recalls: 1989–93**—Frost could build up in the manual transmission dipstick vent, causing transmission oil leakage and eventual wheel lockup. **1990–91**—The defroster is faulty. • Help! Door might not open from the inside. • Automatic transmission could engage abruptly, causing a sudden lurch into Reverse. **1990–93 4X4**—Cold weather or high humidity could cause the manual transmission to seize. **1993**—The top of the fuel tank could leak.

Secret Warranties/Service Tips

1990–91—The defroster is faulty. • Front door malfunction could make it impossible to open the door from the inside. • The 4EAT automatic transmission Park gear might not engage properly. **1990–93 AWD**—The manual gearbox could leak, causing the transmission to seize. **1993**—Legacys could have a headliner droop which is addressed in a March 1994 DSB. **1994**—Torque converter squeaking is addressed in a June 1993 DSB. **1995**—Tips are provided on silencing excessive front strut noise and engine oil pump leaks. **1995–96**—If the antenna won't fully retract, Subaru suggests cleaning the antenna mast and replacing the dress nut. **1995–97**—Troubleshooting tips on a sticking anti-lock brake relay are offered. **1997**—Troubleshooting tips are offered on transfer clutch binding and/or bucking on turns. **All models/years**—A rotten-egg smell could be caused by a defective catalytic converter. It will be replaced, after a bit of arguing, free of charge under the emissions warranty.

Legacy Profile

	1990	1991	1992	1993	1994	1995	1996	1997
Cost Price ($)								
Legacy	12,444	12,444	15,259	16,220	17,495	17,395	16,517	—
4X4	17,204	17,204	19,294	21,030	22,100	22,300	17,643	18,490
Used Values ($)								
Legacy ↑	5,500	6,500	7,500	8,500	9,500	11,500	12,500	—
Legacy ↓	4,500	5,500	6,500	7,500	8,500	10,500	11,000	—
Legacy 4X4 ↑	7,500	8,500	9,500	11,000	12,500	13,500	14,500	16,000
Legacy 4X4 ↓	6,500	7,500	8,000	10,000	11,000	12,000	13,500	14,500
Extended Warranty	Y	Y	Y	Y	Y	Y	Y	Y
Secret Warranty	N	N	N	N	N	N	N	N
Reliability	❷	③	❷	❷	③	④	④	④
Air conditioning	❷	❷	③	③	④	⑤	⑤	⑤
Body integrity	❷	❷	❷	❷	③	③	③	④
Braking system	❷	❷	❷	❷	③	③	③	④

Electrical system	②	②	②	②	③	③	③	④
Engines	③	④	④	⑤	⑤	⑤	⑤	⑤
Exhaust/Converter	①	①	②	②	③	④	⑤	⑤
Fuel system	③	③	④	④	④	④	⑤	⑤
Ignition system	②	②	③	③	④	⑤	⑤	⑤
Manual transmission	③	③	③	④	⑤	⑤	⑤	⑤
- automatic	②	②	③	③	③	③	⑤	⑤
Rust/Paint	②	③	③	③	④	④	⑤	⑤
Steering	③	③	④	④	⑤	⑤	⑤	⑤
Suspension	③	③	③	③	⑤	⑤	⑤	⑤
Crash Safety								
Legacy 4d 2X4, 4X4	①	①	①	①	①	④	④	④

TOYOTA

Camry

Rating: Recommended (1990–97); Above Average (1988–89); Average (1985–86). 1996 was the wagon's last model year. **Maintenance/Repair costs:** Higher than average, but repairs aren't dealer dependent. **Parts:** Parts are more expensive (alternator and ignition module, for example) than for most other cars in this class. Parts availability is excellent.

Technical Data

ENGINES	Liters/CID	HP	MPG	Model Years
OHC I-4 FI	2.0/122	92–95	25–29	1985–86
OHC I-4TD FI	1.8/112	73	27–33	1985
OHC I-4TD FI	2.0/121	79	27–33	1986
DOHC I-4 FI	2.0/122	115	24–29	1987–91
DOHC V6 FI	2.5/153	156	16–22	1988–91
DOHC I-4 FI	2.2/132	125–135	22–27	1992–96
DOHC I-4 FI	2.2/132	133	23–28	1996–97
DOHC V6 FI	3.0/180	185–188	17–23	1992–96
DOHC V6 FI	3.0/183	194	18–24	1997

Strengths and weaknesses: The Camry is an excellent family-car buy because of its spacious, comfortable interior, good fuel economy, and impressive reliability and durability.

1987–93 models have few problems, although they're far from perfect. Main areas of concern are failure-prone cylinder head gaskets, suspension and electrical system failures, defective starter drive and ring gear, premature brake wear, and some paint peeling and rusting. Mufflers last only two years on earlier models and sunroofs are rattle prone.

Persistent problems with all Toyota vehicles are premature brake wear, excessive noise, and vibrations. Stung by consumer criticism that these problems haven't been fixed for over a decade and that owners are charged for useless repairs, Toyota published a "Brake Repair" service bulletin (POL94-18) in October 1994. This bulletin finally defines those repairs that will be done under warranty. Toyota has promised that premature brake wear and noise will be fixed under warranty for the first 12 months/12,500 miles and that vibrations will be attended to, under warranty, for up to 3 years/36,000 miles.

Front suspension bushings wear out quickly, leading to clunking and squeaking noises when going over bumps or when stopping quickly. There's also the so-called "Camry chop" (exceptionally rough rides when passing over uneven roadways) reported by owners of 1992–94 models. Cruise-control fails frequently on all years. Owners of the 1992 Camry have reported that a chronic drone noise, along with a vibration felt from the floor and gas pedal, occurs mostly when the automatic transmission changes from second to third gear at 1,800–2,000 rpm.

1992–94 model body problems include excessive wind noise coming from the front windshield, back doors, and sunroof. Older Camrys have trim items that rust and fall off, door handles that pull away, and mufflers with a short life span. No reports of rust perforation problems, but weak spots are door bottoms, rear wheel openings, and trunk and hatchback edges. There are complaints concerning premature rusting on cars painted white. Toyota generally corrects these rust/paint deficiencies for free.

1995–97 Camrys are almost perfect, except for an annoying surging and shuddering when decelerating, which appears to be more common with the 1995–96 models. It seems as though it's a sticking throttle position sensor, but mechanics say that the problem is intrinsic to the way the engine/transmission computer module is calibrated. Other deficiencies reported by owners: brake vibrations, premature brake pad wear, AC malfunctions, and occasional harsh automatic-transmission shifting.

Totally redesigned, the '97 Camry is taller, longer, wider, quieter, more powerful, and cheaper, both in a literal and figurative sense. Gone are the coupe and station wagon variants. The wheelbase was extended by two inches, giving backseat passengers more room. Other changes: It's powered by a base 2.2L 133-hp 16-valve 4-cylinder engine (taken from the Celica) and an optional 3.0L 24-valve V6 that unleashes 194 horses. Either engine will be mated to a 5-speed manual or an electronically controlled 4-speed automatic. ABS is standard on all but the base 4-cylinder version, traction control is standard on all V6-equipped Camrys, rear seats have shoulder belts for the middle passenger, brighter low beam lights, optional heated mirrors, more cup holders, a sunglasses holder, and an additional power port in the center console.

Decontenting hit Toyota's '97 lineup hard, resulting in many changes that cheapened the Camry in subtle ways the average driver may not notice (note: reliability doesn't appear to have been affected, but there has been an increase in noise complaints). The changes include: less expensive S-rated tires on models with 4-cylinder engines, less expensive heating/ventilation system components, no more assist handles for front occupants, no more chrome trim around the windshield, one door seal instead of three (greater chance for wind and water leaks), fewer airbag sensors, an LCD odometer, a distributorless ignition with the 4-cylinder, and a windshield-embedded antenna. Owners report the '97 models have limited rear visibility (due to the side pillars and high trunk lid), less steering "feel," and more squeaks and rattles than previous versions.

Dealer service bulletins: 1997—CD player won't accept/eject CDs. • Charcoal canister humming noise. • Difficulties with moon roof operation. • Front shoulder belt anchor buzzes. • Front suspension groans. • Headliner buzzes or rattles. • Moon roof rattles. • Radio volume control too sensitive. • Rattle, popping suspension noise. • Rubbing noise from door trim. • Seat cover loose at lower rear corners. • Seat movement. • Tailpipe contact with heat shield. • Wind noise repair kit.

Safety summary/recalls: NHTSA probes: 1987–91—Leaking fuel tanks. **1995**—Injury from airbag. Premature front/rear brake wear. Defective, poor performance (wet) Goodyear Invicta tires. Windshield reflects dashboard image. **1995–96**—Brake failure. • Noisy, vibrating brakes. • Premature front and rear brake wear. • Excessive engine noise. • Transmission lever can slip from Drive to Neutral. • Airbag fails to deploy or is accidentally deployed. • Sudden acceleration, stalling. • Passenger side seatbacks won't stay upright. • Passenger seatbelts over-retract. • Defective radio antenna. • Taillight and turn signal bulbs frequently burn out. • **1996**—Vehicle wanders over road. • Door bottom/undercarriage rusting. • Airbag warning light and check engine light always on. • Windshield film buildup. • Window water leaks. **Recalls: 1987**—Liquid spilled on console could short out the automatic seatbelt motor. **1987–89**—Front seatbelt guides that stay retracted will be changed. **1987–90**—Malfunctioning power door locks. **1988 station wagon**—Original equipment jack may collapse. **1991**—Dealer will replace faulty electrical components in Fujitsu Ten radios to eliminate the chance of fire. **1994**—Steering wheel may disengage from the steering column or shaft assembly. One owner of a '92 Camry reports that her car suddenly went out of control. She found that the left rear tire was turned to a 45 degree angle: the front control arm that holds the tire in alignment had completely broken off at the tire end of the arm. **1996**—Taillight assembly lacks sufficient heat resistance. **1997**—Ignition key can be removed when vehicle not in Park.

Secret Warranties/Service Tips

1987–90—Engine ping, surging, or jerk can be fixed with an upgraded ECU. **1987–91**—A front-inner shoulder belt guide is available to keep the belt away from the neck and face. This free accessory is covered under the seatbelt warranty. **1988**—Harsh 2–3 shifts may require the replacement of worn valve body rubber check balls. **1988–89**—Hard starting may require a new cold start time switch. **1989–90**—A rattling sunroof will be silenced with an upgraded sliding mechanism and new cables and shoes. • Wind noise coming from the upper windshield molding requires that sealant be injected underneath the molding. **1992**—Noisy rear brakes can be silenced by installing upgraded brake pads identified by the letter "N" stamped on the part number label. **1992–93**—Upgraded brake rods will reduce front brake groan/grind. **1993**—Under a special program, Toyota has paid for the repair of AC units that fail to cool due to a faulty expansion valve. **1993–96**—Suspension squeaks and groans are addressed in DSB SU95-003. **1994**—A steering column clicking noise calls for the replacement of the steering main shaft assembly and steering column tube assembly. • Rear window wind noise can be stopped by replacing the front centering-type bolt with a non-centering-type bolt and a washer. **1995–96**—Use upgraded brake pad material to eliminate brake groaning, says DSB BR002-96 shown below.

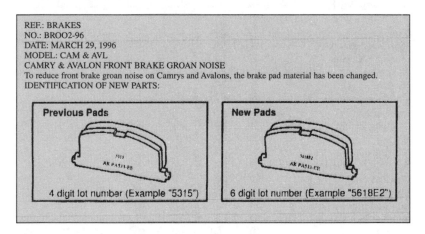

REF.: BRAKES
NO.: BR002-96
DATE: MARCH 29, 1996
MODEL: CAM & AVL
CAMRY & AVALON FRONT BRAKE GROAN NOISE
To reduce front brake groan noise on Camrys and Avalons, the brake pad material has been changed.
IDENTIFICATION OF NEW PARTS:

Previous Pads — 4 digit lot number (Example "5315")

New Pads — 6 digit lot number (Example "5618E2")

1996–97—A charcoal canister humming noise can be silenced by installing an upgraded vacuum hose. **1997**—A front suspension groan can be fixed by replacing the front spring bumper under Toyota's three-year warranty. • If the driver's seat "rocks," Toyota has an upgraded assembly that will secure the seat. **All models/years**—A decade-old brake pulsation/vibration problem is fully described and corrective measures are detailed in DSB BR94-002, issued February 7, 1994. Sometimes only the parts are covered; the owner has to pay for labor. • To reduce front brake squeaks on ABS-equipped vehicles, ask the dealer to install new, upgraded rotors (#43517-32020). • Owner feedback over the last decade plus dealer service managers who wish to remain anonymous tell me that Toyota has a secret warranty that will pay for replacing front disc brake components that wear out before 2 years/40,000 miles. If you're denied this coverage, threaten small claims court action. • A wind-noise repair kit is now available.

Camry Profile

	1990	1991	1992	1993	1994	1995	1996	1997
Cost Price ($)								
Base Coupe	—	—	—	—	18,963	19,430	19,458	—
Base Sedan	14,143	14,513	16,713	17,578	19,293	19,815	19,850	19,918
LE	11,338	16,242	17,293	18,235	19,613	19,955	20,588	20,288
4X4	16,722	17,010	—	—	—	—	—	—
Wagon	15,432	15,837	19,095	19,553	20,703	21,370	22,030	—
LE Wagon V6	18,133	18,483	—	—	—	—	—	—
Used Values ($)								
Base Coupe ↑	—	—	—	—	13,000	14,500	16,000	—
Base Coupe ↓	—	—	—	—	11,500	13,000	14,500	—
Base Sedan ↑	7,000	7,700	9,500	11,500	13,000	15,000	16,500	17,500
Base Sedan ↓	5,500	7,000	9,000	10,000	12,000	13,500	15,000	16,000
LE ↑	7,300	7,900	9,700	11,800	13,300	15,400	16,700	17,800
LE ↓	5,800	7,300	9,300	10,300	12,400	13,800	15,500	16,500
4X4 ↑	7,500	8,500	—	—	—	—	—	—
4X4 ↓	6,500	7,500	—	—	—	—	—	—
Wagon ↑	7,500	8,500	11,000	12,500	14,000	15,500	17,000	—
Wagon ↓	6,000	7,000	9,500	11,000	13,000	14,500	16,000	—
LE Wagon V6 ↑	8,500	9,500	—	—	—	—	—	—
LE Wagon V6 ↓	7,000	8,000	—	—	—	—	—	—
Extended Warranty	N	N	N	N	N	N	N	N
Secret Warranty	Y	Y	Y	Y	Y	Y	Y	N
Reliability	⑤	⑤	⑤	⑤	⑤	⑤	⑤	⑤
Air conditioning	④	④	④	⑤	⑤	⑤	⑤	⑤
Body integrity	③	③	④	④	④	④	④	④
Braking system	❷	❷	❷	❷	③	③	③	④
Electrical system	③	③	④	④	④	⑤	⑤	⑤
Engines	③	④	④	④	⑤	⑤	⑤	⑤
Exhaust/Converter	❷	❷	④	④	④	⑤	⑤	⑤
Fuel system	③	③	③	④	④	③	④	⑤
Ignition system	③	③	③	④	④	④	⑤	⑤
Manual transmission	④	④	④	⑤	⑤	⑤	⑤	⑤
- automatic	③	③	③	⑤	⑤	④	④	⑤
Rust/Paint	④	④	④	④	④	④	④	⑤
Steering	③	③	③	③	③	⑤	⑤	⑤
Suspension	③	③	④	④	④	⑤	⑤	⑤
Crash Safety	—	—	⑤	⑤	⑤	④	④	④
Side Impact	—	—	—	—	—	—	—	③

VOLKSWAGEN

Corrado

Rating: Below Average (1992–94); Not Recommended (1990–91).
Maintenance/Repair costs: Way higher than average and only a VW
dealer can repair these cars. **Parts**: Frequently back-ordered; outrageously high parts cost. Owners complain that the alloy wheels are
easily damaged and can cost over $350 to replace. Improved wheels
cost over $600 each.

Technical Data

ENGINES	Liters/CID	HP	MPG	Model Years
OHC I-4 FI	1.8/109	158	23–28	1990–92
OHC V6 FI	2.8/170	178	18–25	1992–94

Strengths and weaknesses: The Corrado is an attractive mid-size
two-door coupe with a comfortable interior for the driver and front
passenger. It gives good all-round performance, with the accent on
smooth acceleration, a firm but not harsh ride, and excellent handling with little body roll.

The manual transmission's long shift throw is annoying and rear
passenger room is quite limited. The following systems can be troublesome: heating, defrosting, brake, electrical, and fuel. Although
the V6 engine runs quietly, there's lots of road/wind noise intrusion into the passenger compartment.

Safety summary/recalls: **NHTSA probes**: Rear visibility is seriously
compromised by the high tail and spoiler. One owner of a '93
Corrado reports that his car suddenly fishtailed out of control while
rounding a curve at a moderate speed. **1992**—NHTSA is looking
into reports of heater cores that rupture and spew hot coolant into
the passenger compartment. **Recalls: 1989–90**—Hot water could
leak onto driver's feet and steam up the vehicle's interior.

Secret Warranties/Service Tips

1990–91—Abnormal engine noise that occurs when the engine is warm can
be corrected by installing an upgraded crankshaft (#026-105-101E). • If the
radiator fan stays on high speed when the ignition is off, thus discharging
the battery, replace the radiator fan high-speed relay with part number
#321-919-505A. **1991–93**—AC expansion valve noises require the installa-
tion of an upgraded expansion valve. **1990–95**—On Corrados equipped
with an automatic transmission, an engine that won't start could have a
loose contact in the ECM power supply relay; if so, replace the power supply relay. **1992–94**—Poor 2.8L engine performance or a rough idle could
be due to a misrouted EVAP vacuum hose or an improperly routed positive
crankcase ventilation hose that causes a vacuum leak. **1993**—If the ABS
warning light won't go out, a faulty start switch/lock is the likely culprit.

1993–94—AC expansion valve noise can be silenced with an upgraded expansion valve. Troubleshooting tips are offered for insufficient AC cooling. • If the ABS light won't go off, you might have a faulty ignition switch/lock. **All models/years**—Poor driveability (hard starts, surging, stalling, low fuel economy) could be due to a deteriorated oxygen sensor (02S) wire shield or an improper oxygen sensor wire shield ground; ask that it be replaced under the emissions warranty. • Manual transmissions that are difficult to shift in or out of gear could require the installation of a clutch disc with a nickel-plated hub.

Corrado Profile

	1990	1991	1992	1993	1994
Cost Price ($)					
Base	18,220	19,440	20,230	23,260	25,540
Used Values ($)					
Base ↑	6,500	7,500	9,000	12,000	14,500
Base ↓	5,500	6,500	7,500	10,500	13,500
Extended Warranty	Y	Y	Y	Y	Y
Secret Warranty	N	N	N	N	N
Reliability	②	②	③	③	③
Air conditioning	③	③	④	④	④
Body integrity	③	③	③	④	④
Braking system	②	②	②	②	③
Electrical system	②	②	③	③	③
Engines	②	②	③	③	⑤
Exhaust/Converter	⑤	⑤	⑤	⑤	⑤
Fuel system	②	②	②	②	③
Ignition system	③	③	③	④	④
Manual transmission	⑤	⑤	⑤	⑤	⑤
- automatic	②	②	②	②	②
Rust/Paint	④	⑤	⑤	⑤	⑤
Steering	⑤	⑤	⑤	⑤	⑤
Suspension	③	③	③	④	④

Note: No crash tests have been carried out on the Corrado.

Passat

Rating: Below Average (1995–97); Not Recommended (1991–94). Be wary of any Passat sold as a 1994; all '94s were carried over from the 1993 model year. Don't buy any Passat without a comprehensive extended warranty. If you must have a Passat, wait until the Audi spin-off '98 Passats come off their two-year leases. **Maintenance/Repair costs**: Much higher than average; most major repairs are dealer dependent. **Parts**: Parts and service are more expensive than average and dealers complain that VW support is spotty. The '98 Passat is much improved over previous models.

Technical Data

ENGINES	Liters/CID	HP	MPG	Model Years
OHC I-4D FI	1.9/116	90	35-42	1996–97
DOHC I-4 FI	2.0/121	134	19–24	1990–94
DOHC I-4 FI	2.0/121	115	19–24	1995–96
OHC V6 FI	2.8/170	172	17–22	1993–97

Strengths and weaknesses: This front-drive compact sedan and wagon uses a standard 2.0L engine and other mechanical parts borrowed from the Golf, Jetta, and Corrado. Its long wheelbase and squat appearance give the Passat a massive, solid feeling, while its styling makes it look sleek and clean. As with most European imports, it comes fairly well appointed.

As far as overall performance goes, the Passat is no slouch. The multi-valve 4-cylinder engine is adequate and its handling is superior to that of most of the competition. The 2.8L V6 provides lots of power when revved and is the engine that works best with automatic transmission.

The redesigned '95 version came with standard dual airbags, a restyled interior, rear headrests, a softened suspension, and a much-improved crashworthiness rating. The '98 Passat, however, is practically an entirely different car, based upon the Audi A4 and A6, and offers much better performance and reliability.

Passats are infamous for transmission malfunctions that are costly to repair. Even when they're operating as they should, Passat's manual and automatic gearboxes leave a lot to be desired. For example, the 5-speed manual transmission gear ranges are too far apart: there's an enormous gap between third and fourth gear and the 4-speed automatic shifts poorly with the 4-banger. Also, owners report problems with the front brakes, MacPherson struts, and fuel and electrical systems as the car ages. Interior trim and controls are fragile.

Competent servicing and parts aren't easy to find away from the larger cities and many of the above-mentioned deficiencies can cost you an arm *and* a leg to repair.

Dealer service bulletins: **1993**—AC expansion valve noise. • Faulty ABS warning lights. • Excessive diagonal tire wear. • Frequent windshield wiper failures. **1995**—Skipping CD changer. • Instrument cluster loss of memory. • Poor fuel system performance. • Excessive rear tire wear. • Drifting, pulling to one side. • Skipping wiper blades. • Engine won't start. **1996–97**—Transmission fluid seepage. • Malfunctioning CD player. • Shifter is hard to move or won't go into Reverse. • Knocking/vibrating shift lever. • Transmission pops out of gear. • Vehicle will not move into any forward gear.

Safety summary/recalls: Recalls: **1989–90**—Hot water could leak onto driver's feet and steam up the vehicle's interior. **1993**—Axle could separate from struts, causing loss of vehicle control. **1993–95**

VR6 engine—Faulty radiator fan motor could cause engine to overheat and stall.

Secret Warranties/Service Tips

1990–91—If the radiator fan stays on high speed with the ignition off, running down the battery, replace the fan's high-speed relay with part number
#321-919-505A. **1990–95**—On Passats equipped with an automatic trans-
mission, an engine that won't start could have a loose contact in the ECM
power supply relay; fix this by replacing the power supply relay. **1991–93**—
AC expansion valve noises require the installation of an upgraded expansion valve. • Poor driveability could be caused by magnetic interference
due to a deteriorated oxygen sensor wire shield or improper oxygen sensor
wire shield ground connection. **1992–94**—Poor 2.8L engine performance
or a rough idle could be due to a misrouted EVAP vacuum hose or an
improperly routed positive crankcase ventilation hose, which will cause a
vacuum leak. **1993**—If the ABS warning light won't go out, a faulty start
switch/lock is the likely culprit. **1995–96**—Troubleshooting tips are offered
on automatic transmission fluid seepage. **1996–97**—If the transmission
pops out of gear, check for a hairline crack on the selector shaft shift detent
sleeve. **All models/years**—Vehicles that won't move into any forward gear
could have broken retaining lugs for selector plugs of B2/K1, which causes the selector valve to partially protrude or fall out of the valve body.

Passat Profile

	1991	1992	1993	1995	1996	1997
Cost Price ($)						
Base	17,085	17,355	16,955	19,215	19,715	19,930
Used Values ($)						
Base ↑	6,000	8,000	8,700	12,000	13,500	16,000
Base ↓	5,000	7,000	7,700	10,500	12,500	14,500
Extended Warranty	Y	Y	Y	Y	Y	Y
Secret Warranty	N	N	N	N	N	N
Reliability	③	③	③	③	④	④
Air conditioning	②	②	③	④	④	④
Automatic transmission	①	①	①	②	②	③
Body integrity	③	③	③	③	④	④
Braking system	②	②	②	②	②	③
Electrical system	②	②	②	②	③	③
Engines	⑤	⑤	⑤	⑤	⑤	⑤
Exhaust/Converter	⑤	⑤	⑤	⑤	⑤	⑤
Fuel system	②	②	②	③	④	⑤
Ignition system	②	②	②	③	④	⑤
Rust/Paint	③	③	⑤	⑤	⑤	⑤
Steering	③	③	③	③	④	④
Suspension	③	③	③	③	④	④
Crash Safety	②	②	①	④	④	④

VOLVO

240

Rating: Average (1989–93); Below Average (1985–88).
Maintenance/Repair costs: Higher than average; repairs are dealer dependent. **Parts**: Higher-than-average cost and hard to find.

Technical Data

ENGINES	Liters/CID	HP	MPG	Model Years
OHC I-4T FI	2.1/130	162	17–21	1985
OHC I-4 FI	2.3/141	111–114	19–23	1985–93
OHC I-6D FI	2.4/145	80	25–29	1985

Strengths and weaknesses: Problems with entry-level Volvos like the 240 mirror the quality-control problems manifested by Saab, the other Swedish automaker, except for the fact that Volvo styling is more bland than bizarre. The 240 is a solid and spacious car. Unfortunately, it doesn't live up to Volvo's advertising as an automotive longevity wonder. Volvo reliability is, in fact, a bit below average, if you consider the Japanese competition.

The V6 is an honest, though imperfect, engine. Avoid the turbocharged 4-cylinder engine and failure-prone air conditioning systems. Diesels suffer from cooling system breakdowns and leaky cylinder head gaskets. The brakes on all model years need frequent and expensive service and exhaust systems are notorious for their short life span. The GL and GLE suffer from occasional electrical bugs. Volvos are fairly rust-prone and the front and rear wheel openings are especially susceptible to perforation. The lower edges of the side cargo windows on station wagons rust prematurely, as do the lower tailgate lips.

Confidential dealer service bulletins address the following deficiencies affecting models over the past few years: hard cold starting, electronic module defects, excessive brake and cruise control noise, knocking sway bar bushings, and leaking sunroofs.

Safety summary/recalls: NHTSA probes: 1986–91—Interestingly, the only Volvo 240 ever crash tested was the '79 model; researchers concluded both the driver and passenger would have sustained severe head trauma. Nevertheless, the 240 had the lowest rate of driver deaths among popular passenger vehicles on U.S. roads during 1989–93, says an IIHS study. Furthermore, the 240 didn't record a single driver death during the five years of the study. The NHTSA is looking into front seat/center console fires. **Recalls: 1985–86**—A low-speed frontal collision could cause unintended sudden acceleration. **1986–87**—Erratic cruise control operation is caused by a voltage drop. **1992**—The ball joint and strut could separate, leading to loss of vehicle control.

Secret Warranties/Service Tips

1988–90—Brake pulsation, a common problem, is addressed in DSB 51/111. • If you're having problems starting your Volvo on cold mornings, see DSBs 23/135 and 23/21A. **1989–93**—To improve cold starting, Volvo will install an improved fuel injection control module for free if the emissions warranty still applies. Under another program, Volvo will replace the MFI EPROM to improve cold starting and idle quality. **1990–93**—Noise coming from the cruise control vacuum pump can be stopped by modifying the pump bracket mounting. **1991–93**—Under Service Campaign 62, Volvo will replace the sway bar bushing. The bushing can pull away from the retainers and create a knocking noise; Volvo says the problem isn't safety related. Cost is to be borne by the owner, but Volvo sometimes makes pro rata "goodwill" adjustments. **All models/years**—An April 1993 DSB lists front and rear brake pad kits that have been specially developed to eliminate brake noise.

240 Profile

	1986	1987	1988	1989	1990	1991	1992	1993
Cost Price ($)								
240 DL	14,370	16,025	16,920	17,600	17,735	19,680	21,220	22,215
Used Values ($)								
240 DL ↑	4,000	5,000	6,000	7,500	9,000	11,000	13,000	15,000
240 DL ↓	3,000	4,000	5,000	6,500	8,000	10,000	11,500	13,500
Extended Warranty	Y	Y	Y	Y	Y	Y	Y	Y
Secret Warranty	N	N	N	N	N	N	N	N
Reliability	③	③	③	③	③	③	③	④
Air conditioning	❷	❷	❷	③	③	③	③	③
Body integrity	❶	❶	❶	❶	❷	③	③	④
Braking system	❶	❶	❶	❷	❷	③	③	③
Electrical system	❶	❶	❶	❶	❶	③	❷	③
Engines	③	③	③	③	③	③	③	④
Exhaust/Converter	❷	❷	❷	❷	③	③	③	④
Fuel system	❶	❶	❶	❷	❷	❷	③	③
Ignition system	④	④	④	④	③	③	④	⑤
Manual transmission	③	③	③	③	③	③	③	④
- automatic	④	④	④	④	③	③	③	④
Rust/Paint	❷	❷	③	③	③	④	④	⑤
Steering	❶	❶	④	④	④	⑤	③	④
Suspension	④	④	④	④	④	❷	③	③
Crash Safety	❶	—	—	—	—	—	⑤	⑤

LARGE CARS/WAGONS

These are excellent cars for extensive highway driving by motorists who are able to write off relatively high gasoline consumption, maintenance costs, and insurance premiums. Gas consumption is particularly high in city driving, unless you have a 6-cylinder engine, but then you're likely to have insufficient power to run all the bells and whistles that add to comfort and convenience. A smaller powerplant also compromises highway performance and reduces resale value.

The term "large car" is relative. Now that the automakers have shortened most of the wheelbases of their large cars, reduced their weight, and switched to front-wheel drive, existing definitions may no longer be accurate indicators of a car's size. Some large cars, like GM's Caprice and Roadmaster, bucked this trend, however, and remained long and heavy.

Owners have to pay a considerable amount of money for these vehicles, but large cars offer plenty of comfort and stability at high speeds. They also can seat six adults comfortably, and make excellent cars for families that take motoring vacations. Their high-speed performance isn't spectacular, but they're effortless to drive.

Recommended

Chrysler Caravelle, Diplomat, New Yorker (1988–89)

Ford Crown Victoria, Grand Marquis (1995–97)
Ford Thunderbird, Cougar

Above Average

Ford Crown Victoria, Grand Marquis (1992–94)
Ford Thunderbird, Cougar (1989–97)

1996 Crown Victoria: Along with the Grand Marquis, a recommended buy. The perfect car for highway cruising with all the comforts of home.

Average

Chrysler Caravelle, Diplomat,
 New Yorker (1986–87)
Ford Crown Victoria, Grand
 Marquis (1986–91)
Ford Thunderbird, Cougar
 (1986–88)

GM Caprice, Custom Cruiser,
 Impala SS, Roadmaster,
 Wagon (1991–96)
GM Olds 98/Regency, Park
 Avenue (1994–97)

Below Average

Chrysler Concorde, Intrepid, LHS,
 New Yorker, Vision (1995–97)

Olds 98/Regency, Park
 Avenue (1991–93)

Not Recommended

Chrysler Caravelle, Diplomat,
 New Yorker (1984–85)
Chrysler Concorde, Intrepid, LHS,
 New Yorker, Vision (1993–94)
Chrysler Dynasty, Fifth Avenue,
 Imperial, New Yorker (1988–93)

GM Caprice, Custom Cruiser,
 Impala SS, Roadmaster,
 Wagon (1991–96)
GM Olds 98/Regency, Park
 Avenue (1988–90)

*1994 Chrysler Concord (Vision, Intrepid, and LHS): Not recommended.
All style and little substance. Imagine inadequate night driving lights,
leaky trunks, transmissions made by Mattel, and paint delamination,
which Chrysler once blamed on bird droppings.*

Station wagons (full-size)

If passenger and cargo space and car-like handling are what you
want, a large station wagon may not be the answer—a used minivan,
van, light truck, or compact wagon can fill the same need for less
cost and will probably still be around a decade from now. Popular
(though troublesome) wagons—like the Caprice and Roadmaster,
both axed in '96—into which you could cram a Little League team,
are an endangered species, losing out to the van and minivan craze.

Some disadvantages of large station wagons: difficulty in keeping the interior heated in winter, atrocious gas consumption, sloppy handling, and poor rear visibility. Exterior road noise is also a frequent problem, since the vehicle's interior has a tendency to amplify normal road noise. Rear hatches tend to be rust prone. Crash safety is variable.

No full-sized station wagons are recommended.

1991 Buick Roadmaster: An average buy. Look out for the below average crash rating, poor quality electronics, sloppy body assembly, and mediocre powertrain performance.

CHRYSLER

Caravelle Salon, Diplomat, N.Y. Fifth Avenue (RWD)

Rating: Recommended (1988–89); Average (1986–87); Not Recommended (1984–85). Reasonably reliable and simple-to-repair throwbacks to a time when land yachts ruled the highways. **Maintenance/Repair costs**: Lower than average, and repairs aren't dealer dependent. **Parts**: Average cost (independent suppliers sell for much less) and not hard to find.

Technical Data

ENGINES	Liters/CID	HP	MPG	Model Years
OHV V8 2 bbl.	5.2/318	140	15–19	1985–89

Strengths and weaknesses: Both the 6- and 8-cylinder engines will practically run forever with a minimum of care. Repairs and maintenance are simple. The fuel-efficient "slant 6" powerplant was too small for this type of car and was changed to a gas-guzzling, though smooth and reliable, V8 after 1983. Handling is vague and sloppy and emergency braking is often accompanied by rear-wheel lockup.

Overall reliability is average, but inexpensive parts are available anywhere. Carburetor, ignition, electrical system, brake, and suspension

274   *Lemon-Aid*

(premature idler-arm wear) problems predominate. It's a good idea to adjust the torsion bars frequently for better suspension performance. Front door locks and exterior chrome trim pieces fall off, chip paint, and promote premature rusting. Surface rust is very common. Doors, windshield pillars, the bottoms of both front and rear fenders, and the trunk lid rust through more quickly than average.

Safety summary/recalls: **Recalls**: **1985**—Driver's seat frame may be weakened by fatigue cracks. **1985–86**—Seat backs on power bucket or 50/50 seats may have a sudden backwards movement. **1985–87 turbo**—Supply-hose fuel leakage may cause a fire. **1986 600**—Electronic instrument panel resistor could overload and result in a fire. **1988 with cruise control**—Incorrectly routed fusible link wires may cause an under-hood fire. **1988–89 Diplomat**—the steering wheel could separate.

Secret Warranties/Service Tips

1985–90—Excessive 3.9L, 5.2L, or 5.9L engine tappet noise requires upgraded tappets (#4636794). • 5.2L engine vapor locking diagnosis and repair (18-09-88). **1986–87**—The erratic operation of the right-rear-door lock requires a revised lock motor (#4467252). **1988**—Engine die-out during cold start or rough running during warm-up requires an upgraded ESA/EFC module and EGR valve. • Diplomats require a filter jumper harness (#4414708) to correct low-speed engine bucking and surging. **1988–89**—To prevent auxiliary oil cooler freeze-up, install an oil cooler bypass connector (#4401013).

Caravelle Salon, Diplomat, N.Y. Fifth Avenue Profile

	1984	1985	1986	1987	1988	1989
Cost Price ($)						
Caravelle Salon	—	10,042	10,424	11,121	11,906	—
Diplomat	10,447	10,748	11,385	11,922	12,622	13,355
N.Y. 5th Avenue	15,269	15,496	16,241	17,831	18,820	20,040
Used Values ($)						
Caravelle Salon ↑	—	2,300	2,700	2,900	3,200	—
Caravelle Salon ↓	—	1,800	2,100	2,300	3,000	—
Diplomat ↑	1,500	1,800	2,100	2,300	2,500	3,200
Diplomat ↓	1,000	1,300	1,800	2,000	2,300	2,400
N.Y. 5th Avenue ↑	2,400	2,700	3,100	3,500	4,000	4,500
N.Y. 5th Avenue ↓	2,000	2,400	2,500	3,000	3,500	3,700
Extended Warranty	N	N	N	N	N	N
Secret Warranty	N	N	N	N	N	N
Reliability	③	③	③	③	④	④

Dynasty, Fifth Avenue, Imperial, New Yorker

Rating: Not Recommended (1988–93). The 1994 LHS New Yorker is a completely different car from previous New Yorkers. Even though the top-of-the-line Imperial has a rapid depreciation rate, it's no bargain at any price. **Maintenance/Repair costs**: Higher than average; repairs aren't dealer dependent. **Parts**: Higher-than-average cost, but can be bought for much less from independent suppliers. Body parts are often back-ordered. Imperial body parts are rare and costly.

Technical Data

ENGINES	Liters/CID	HP	MPG	Model Years
OHC I-4 FI	2.5/153	96–100	20–24	1986–93
OHC I-4 2 bbl.	2.6/156	101	19–24	1985
OHC I-4T FI	2.2/135	146	18–23	1985–88
OHC V6 FI	3.0/181	136–141	17–22	1988–93
OHV V6 FI	3.3/201	164	17–22	1990–93

Strengths and weaknesses: These relatively fuel-efficient four-door sedans handle and ride like the average mid-size car popular two decades ago. Compared to large rear-drives equipped with V6 or V8 engines, they can't tow as much weight, their unit-body construction makes for a noisier ride, and long-term reliability is way below average.

The base 2.5L engines are a major source of mechanical woes and, when turbocharged, can cost you a small fortune to repair. Owners complain of substandard piston rings, faulty oil seals, and a failure-prone timing-chain mechanism that can lead to severe engine damage unless it's checked and adjusted frequently.

The Mitsubishi 3.0L V6 engine, offered since 1988, has generated complaints concerning oil leaks, electronic malfunctions, and fuel-system problems. Chrysler's 3.3L V6, available since 1989, is more reliable. The electronic 4-speed automatic has elicited a number of complaints about erratic and noisy shifting. The A604 automatic transmission is a nightmare and Chrysler is replacing it by the ton, paying the warranty deductible and compensating consumers for consequential damages.

Front suspension components and brakes wear out quickly. The electrical system is bug-plagued; avoid the electronic dashboard. Air conditioning malfunctions occur all the time, accompanied by the evaporator freezing up. Windshield-wiper motors short-circuit and often the motor is unnecessarily replaced. Owners report erratic horn operation and leaky radiators. Knobs and levers break very easily. Front seats lack lower-back support and the middle passenger is punished by the hard edges of the split seat and folded armrest. Mediocre heating—when the Dynasty accelerates, there isn't enough engine vacuum to operate the actuators that maintain a consistent heat range. There aren't any ducts to distribute warm air to the rear. When going over bumps, these cars shake and rattle like old taxicabs. Many owners report water infiltration, especially around the windshield and into the trunk. Surface rust is common, especially around windshields, door bottoms, and the rear lip on trunk lids.

Safety summary/recalls: Recalls: 1989–90 Dynasty/all 1990s—The dealer will install a free bypass valve to prevent automatic transmission damage in cold weather. **1990–91 ABS**—The high-pressure hose could leak. **1991**—The front outboard seatbelt latch is faulty. **1992**—The coupling bolts for the steering column shaft are faulty. **1990 Fifth Avenue**—The airbag could be defective on cars with gray interior. **1991 Fifth Avenue**—Pin bolts for the front disc brake caliper guide could be too loose. • A short circuit in the heater blower motor could cause a fire in the cowl area.

Secret Warranties/Service Tips

1988–93—3.0L engines that burn oil or produce a smoky exhaust at idle can be fixed by installing snap rings on the exhaust valve guides and replacing all of the valve guide stems or the cylinder head. **1990–93**—Harsh automatic shifts can be tamed by installing the following revised parts: kickdown, accumulator, reverse servo cushion springs, and accumulator piston. **1991–92**—Engines with a rough idle and stalling following a cold start could require a new single board engine controller (SBEC). **1991–93**—Poor AC performance while the AC blower continues to operate is likely due to the evaporator freezing; the evaporator freezes when the powertrain control module (PCM) isn't properly disengaging the AC clutch via the relay. • An engine that stalls following a cold start might need an upgraded Park/Neutral/Start switch. • The serpentine belt could come off the pulley after driving through snow; install an upgraded shield, screw, and retainers to overcome this problem. **1992**—Long crank times, a rough idle, and hesitation can be corrected by replacing the intake manifold assembly or ECT/sensor connector. **1992–93**—Eliminate a deceleration shudder by replacing the powertrain control module with an upgraded version. • Rough idling after a cold start with 2.2L and 2.5L engines can be corrected by installing an upgraded powertrain control module (PCM). **1993**—Acceleration shudder could be caused by a leaking automatic-transmission front pump. • For improved automatic shifting, install an upgraded transmission control module. • Fuel-pump check-valve failure can cause startup die-out, reduced power, or erratic shifting. **All models/years**—Defective valve springs on the 3.3L V6 engine will be replaced free of charge (DSB R#466). • There is excessive air conditioner noise with 3.3L engine (DSB 24-8-89). • Most model years with A-604 automatic transmission suffer clutch slippage (DSB 21-09-90). • A rotten-egg odor coming from the exhaust is probably caused by a malfunctioning catalytic converter and might be covered under the emissions warranty.

Dynasty, Fifth Avenue, Imperial, New Yorker Profile

	1988	1989	1990	1991	1992	1993
Cost Price ($)						
Dynasty	13,598	13,580	15,945	16,740	17,000	17,540
Fifth Avenue	—	—	23,990	23,405	23,906	22,725
Imperial	—	—	25,550	27,515	29,063	30,000
New Yorker	19,949	20,015	20,986	18,990	20,134	20,000
Used Values ($)						
Dynasty ↑	3,500	4,000	5,000	6,000	7,000	8,000
Dynasty ↓	3,000	3,500	4,500	5,000	6,000	7,000
Fifth Avenue ↑	—	—	7,500	8,500	9,500	10,500
Fifth Avenue ↓	—	—	6,000	7,500	8,500	9,500
Imperial ↑	—	—	8,000	9,000	10,000	11,000
Imperial ↓	—	—	7,000	8,000	9,000	10,000
New Yorker ↑	4,500	5,500	6,500	7,000	7,500	9,000
New Yorker ↓	3,500	4,500	6,000	6,500	6,000	7,500
Extended Warranty	Y	Y	Y	Y	Y	Y
Secret Warranty	N	N	N	Y	Y	Y
Reliability	❶	❶	❶	❶	❶	❶
Air conditioning	❶	❶	❶	❶	❷	❷
Automatic transmission	❷	❷	❶	❶	❶	❶
Body integrity	❷	❷	❷	❷	❷	❷
Braking system	❶	❶	❶	❷	❷	③
Electrical system	❷	❷	❷	❷	③	③
Engines	❶	❶	❶	❷	❷	❷
Exhaust/Converter	❷	❷	❷	⑤	⑤	⑤
Fuel system	❶	❶	③	③	③	③
Ignition system	❶	❶	❷	❷	❷	③
Rust/Paint	❷	③	③	③	③	③
Steering	❶	❶	❶	❷	❷	③
Suspension	❶	❶	❶	❷	③	③
Crash Safety						
Dynasty	❶	—	—	—	—	❷
Imperial	—	—	❷	❷	—	—
New Yorker	❶	—	—	—	—	❶

Concorde, Intrepid, LHS, New Yorker, Vision

Rating: Below Average (1995–97); Not Recommended (1993–94). If you want maximum passenger room, choose the 1995–96 LHS or New Yorker. They're about five inches longer and use the larger engine. Whichever vehicle you're considering buying, before paying a cent, make sure you get an extended warranty and take a test drive at night to assess the efficacy of the headlights. **Maintenance/Repair costs**: Higher than average, but most repairs aren't dealer dependent. **Parts**: Higher-than-average cost (independent suppliers sell for much less), but not hard to find. Only vehicles that still carry Chrysler's seven-year powertrain and body warranty are worthy of any consideration.

Technical Data

ENGINES	Liters/CID	HP	MPG	Model Years
OHV V6 FI	3.3/201	153–161	18–23	1993–97
OHC V6 FI	3.5/215	214	17–21	1993–97

Strengths and weaknesses: These sleek-styled front-wheel drives are Chrysler's mid-size flag bearers. They're roomy, fuel efficient, and highly maneuverable. The base engine is a 3.3L 153-hp 6-banger, but 70 percent of buyers chose the 3.5L for its 61 extra horses. Both engines provide plenty of low-end torque and acceleration; they blow the Camry and Accord away with a 0–60 time of 8.9 seconds. This advantage is lost somewhat when traversing hilly terrain: the smaller V6 powerplant strains to keep up. You'll find good or better handling and steering response than in the Taurus and Sable and the independent suspension maximizes control, reduces body roll, and provides lots of suspension travel so that you don't get bumped around too much on rough roads.

With all these positives, why aren't these cars recommended? Simple: they're unreliable. One '94 Intrepid owner's comments posted on the Internet sums it up: "...The lack of overall quality and dangerous headlights made me dump the car after only 15 months' use."

A perusal of dealer service bulletins and comments from car rental agencies and other owners tell me that these cars continue to have many serious safety- and performance-related shortcomings that can no longer be explained away as "first series" teething problems that all new cars experience.

Owners report lots of interior noise, uneven fit and finish, poor-quality trim items that break or easily fall off, exposed screw heads, faulty door hinges that make the doors rattle and hard to open, windows that come off their tracks or are misaligned and poorly sealed, power window motor failures, and steering wheel noise when the car is turning. The automatic climate control system operates erratically, blowing cold air when it's set for warm and warm air when it's set for cool. The instrument panel must be removed before servicing the ventilation system because the AC ducts are molded into the plastic panel.

The shift console needs lighting, the radio and climate controls are too small, the trunk release is hidden in the glove compartment, the hood release is on the floor, the rear view mirror is too narrow, and the fuel filler door needs a lock. The trunk has a high deck lid, making for difficult loading and unloading, and there's no inside access by folding down the rear seat, as in the Camry.

Owner reports confirm that there are chronic problems with leaking 3.3L engine head gaskets and noisy lifters that wear out prematurely around 20,000 miles. Water pumps often self-destruct and take the engine timing chain along with them (a $1,000 repair). Other common complaints: a poor fit between the exhaust manifold and engine block often results in oil leaks and noisy engine operation; if you wash your car during extremely cold weather, the resulting ice buildup and leaking deck lid seals can easily damage the heater fan motor (the drain hole has to be enlarged).

The 4-speed LE42 automatic transmission is a spin-off of Chrysler's failure-prone A604 version—and owner reports show it to be troublesome as well. Owners tell of chronic glitches in the computerized transmission's shift timing and computer malfunctions, which result in driveability problems (stalling, hard starts, and surging).

Body problems abound, with lots of interior noise, uneven fit and finish, poor-quality trim items that break or fall off easily, exposed screw heads, faulty door hinges that make the doors rattle and hard to open, windows that come off their tracks or are misaligned and poorly sealed, power-window motor failures, and steering wheel noise when turning. Other body defects specifically addressed in dealer service bulletins include: noisy front suspension; glue oozing out at the backlight and windshield molding; water collecting in the park/turn lights; noisy rear upper strut mounts; water draining into the trunk when the deck lid is raised; and water entering into the AC-heater housing.

Dealer service bulletins: **1993**—AC operates erratically. • ATC (automatic temperature control) works poorly in warm weather. • An ominous clicking noise comes from the passenger compartment and the 3.3L engine emits a ticking sound when cold. • Hard starting and long crank times when the engine is hot. • Ignition noise on the AM band. • Malfunctioning AC ducts that blow different temperatures of air. **1993–95**—Upgraded spark plugs will improve cold starting; ask for part number 56027275. **1994**—Acceleration shudder. • Faulty engine timing belts. • The transmission wiring harness bracket could break, transmission wires could short-circuit, and the floor shifter knob could stick. • The radio often "locks up." **1995**— Glitches in the computerized transmission's shift timing cause driveability problems (stalling, hard starts, and surging). Amazingly, the 4-speed LE42 automatic transmission—a spin-off of Chrysler's failure-prone A604—appears to be just as problem-plagued as its predecessor. • AC refrigerant leaks. • Heater/AC housing leaks water and there's moisture in headlights. • Excessive engine noise is likely caused by carbon buildup on the top of the pistons. • Engine mount rattles. • Transmission clicks and clunks. • Fuel line rattles caused by faulty fuel rail assembly. • Squeaking front or rear brakes require upgraded brake linings. • A-pillar wind noise. • Rattling C-post appliqué or poor fit of the appliqué to the back glass. • Front hub clicks and clunks. • B-pillar and rear spring rattles. • Upper strut mount squeaks. • Excessive road noise from the front wheels and rear seat require reduced tire pressure and the addition of foam/sealer insulation to the front upper load beam or the C-pillar.

1996—3.3L/3.8L lower engine oil leaks. • Reduced transmission limp-in default sensitivity. • Shuddering on upshift or whenever the torque converter is engaged. • Upgraded Overdrive clutch hub. • Front suspension clunking or rattling. • Metallic knocking from front of vehicle when passing over bumps. • High-speed windshield washer spray knockdown. • Trunk water leaks (see "Service Tips"). • Polycast wheel center falls off. • Cup holder improvements. **1997**— Tips on troubleshooting noisy brakes. • AC evaporator leaks. • AC suction line failure. • Warped or poor-fitting passenger airbag door. • A metallic popping noise might be heard coming from the front of the vehicle. • Sticking sunroof or sunshade. • Rear drum brake ticking. • Water ingestion into heater/AC housing.

Upscale LHS and New Yorker versions haven't escaped Chrysler's notorious poor-quality body components and sloppy assembly. In addition to the above-mentioned owner and bulletin-related problems, other service bulletins for these cars indicate that they're likely to have their own persistent problems, such as faulty fuel pumps causing stalling, reduced power, or erratic transmission shifting, radio lockups, water leaks coming from the heater/AC housing, and moisture in the headlights. Bulletins also address how to silence a noisy AC compressor, a squeaking or creaking noise coming from the rear window when traveling at slow speeds over rough roads, and a high-pitched whistling noise caused by a defective idle air control motor.

Safety summary/recalls: NHTSA probes: 1993–95 LH and LHS with 3.5L engines—Faulty fuel injector components could cause an engine compartment fire. • Headlights are too dim for safe motoring, and some owners report that the headlights sometimes cut out completely. This problem also affects 1994 versions. • Defrosting is inadequate on some '93s, allowing ice and moisture to collect at the base of the windshield. Chrysler has a fix for these two problems that requires the installation of a new headlight lens and small foam pads into the defroster outlet ducts. • Non-ABS brakes perform poorly, resulting in excessively long stopping distances—more so than for other cars in this class. • The overhead digital panel is distracting and forces you to take your eyes from the road. • The emergency brake pedal catches pant cuffs and shoelaces as you enter or exit the vehicle. • A high rear window sill obstructs rear visibility. • These cars have safety-related peculiarities that you wouldn't believe. The owner of a '93 Intrepid recounts his unforgettable experience in these words:

> I started having trouble getting the key out of the ignition after I shut the car off. This happened on a Saturday afternoon. I called the dealer and was told I was pretty much out of luck until a mechanic was available on Monday. If I had been smart, I would have left the keys in the ignition and prayed some stupid thief would steal the car.

I finally had to call a friend who works at Transport Canada's Road Safety department here in Ottawa. He had the answer—you have to smack the gearshift lever from right to left so the internals under the button on the gearshift lever pop out. Lo and behold, this worked. Nifty feature on a $27,000-plus car. I still have to do this to this day, especially during colder weather....The power remote locks would not work and the driver's side door could not even be unlocked with the key (some rod was broken). The only way I could get into the car was to unlock the passenger door with the key and crawl across the front seat! Who is the brainiac who decided the location of the horn button? The horn is impossible to locate in an emergency.

Recalls: **1993**—Dealers will re-route the wiring harness to prevent shorting. • Replace fuel injector rail seals that may leak. **1994**— Faulty transmission wiring might cause the car to start when not in the Park position. **1993 Intrepid and Vision**—Defective lower control arm washers could cause loss of steering.

Secret Warranties/Service Tips

1993—Failure of the fuel pump check valve could cause start-up die-out, reduced power, or erratic shifting. • Doors that are hard to open or close or that make a snapping sound likely need four-check door straps, which Chrysler will provide free of charge. **1993–94**—Acceleration shudder could be caused by automatic-transmission front pump leakage. • A-pillar wind noise requires sealing the upper load beam and A-pillar or sealing the roof rail body seam. • AC belt rollover requires the installation of a revised AC belt and idler pulley. • Exchange the base body control module (BCM) for an upgraded version if dash instruments and gauges suddenly quit working. • Upgraded disc brake linings will help reduce front or rear squeaking noises. • AM radio static (poor reception of distant stations) can be corrected by installing a supplemental engine-suppression strap to the left side of the engine. • Engine mount rattles signal the need to replace the engine mounts (always replace in pairs). • Cold start-up piston knocking noise can be eliminated by replacing the piston and connecting rod assembly. • No-starts, poor engine performance, and loud noises when attempting to start can be corrected by installing a snubber over the timing-belt tensioner plunger. (This applies to the 3.5L engine only.) • Dealers will exchange small head restraints for larger ones free of charge. • A heater AC housing that leaks water into the passenger compartment can be plugged by enlarging the right plenum drain hole. • Rear disc brake noise can be stopped by installing upgraded rear disc brake adapters. • Rear glass rattling is likely caused by a loose backlight. • Excessive rear road noise can be reduced by indexing the spring to the upper strut mount; in cases where indexing doesn't work, you may have to replace the rear upper strut mounts with revised mounts. • A transmission buzz or rattle can be stopped by replacing the transfer chain snubber and attaching screws. • If water leaks or dust accumulates inside the trunk, try sealing the quarter panel to the outer wheel house panel seam. **1993–97**—The blower motor could seize or freeze from water seeping into the heater/AC housing. • AC evaporator leaks caused by premature corrosion can be prevented by installing a cowl plenum screen; Chrysler says this is a warranty repair.

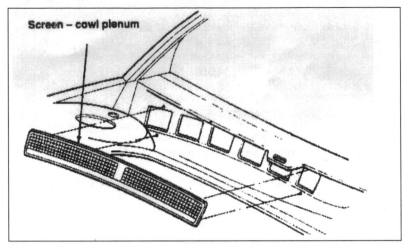

Both the screen and its installation are covered by Chrysler's warranty.

1994—Harsh, erratic, or delayed transmission shifts can be corrected by replacing the throttle position sensor (TPS) with a revised part. **1994–95**—The intermittent or total loss of air conditioning can be corrected by installing a revised AC pressure transducer. **1995–96**—More troubleshooting tips are offered on diagnosing and fixing trunk water leaks.

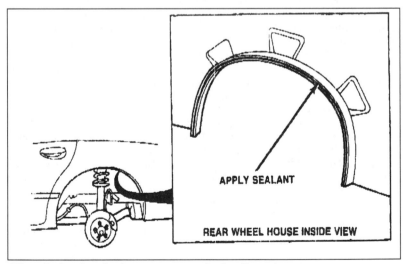

Water leaks often lead to premature wheel well rusting.

1995–97—If the AC suction line fails, replace it and install a revised right-side engine ground strap; the original ground strap probably caused the failure. **1996–97**—If you hear a metallic popping noise coming from the front of the vehicle when you accelerate from a stop, install two new upper and two new lower cradle mounting isolators. • Rear drum brake ticking can be silenced by burnishing the rear brakes. **All models/years—** A rotten-egg odor coming from the exhaust is probably caused by a malfunctioning catalytic converter; this is covered by Chrysler's original warranty *and* the emissions warranty. Don't take no for an answer. The same advice goes for all the squeaks and rattles and the water and wind leaks that afflict these vehicles. Don't let Chrysler or the dealer pawn these problems off as maintenance items. They're all factory related and should be covered for at least five years.

Concorde, Intrepid, LHS, New Yorker, Vision Profile

	1993	1994	1995	1996	1997
Cost Price ($)					
Concorde	19,720	21,020	21,090	19,990	20,980
Intrepid	18,000	19,100	19,230	18,990	19,950
LHS	—	30,870	30,190	30,850	30,850
New Yorker	—	26,125	26,190	27,890	—
Vision	18,725	20,272	20,232	19,795	20,860
Used Values ($)					
Concorde ↑	9,500	11,000	12,500	14,500	16,500
Concorde ↓	8,000	9,500	11,500	13,000	15,500
Intrepid ↑	8,500	10,000	11,500	13,000	15,000
Intrepid ↓	7,000	8,500	10,000	11,500	13,500
LHS ↑	—	14,000	16,000	17,500	21,000
LHS ↓	—	12,500	14,500	16,000	18,000
New Yorker ↑	—	12,500	14,000	17,000	—
New Yorker ↓	—	11,000	13,000	15,000	—
Vision ↑	8,500	9,500	11,500	13,000	15,000
Vision ↓	7,000	8,500	10,000	12,000	13,500
Extended Warranty	Y	Y	Y	Y	Y
Secret Warranty	Y	Y	Y	Y	Y
Reliability	②	②	②	②	③
Air conditioning	①	①	①	②	②
Automatic transmission	①	①	①	②	③
Body integrity	①	①	①	②	②
Braking system	②	②	③	③	③
Electrical system	①	①	②	②	③
Engines	③	③	③	④	④
Exhaust/Converter	④	④	④	④	④
Fuel system	③	③	③	④	④
Ignition system	②	②	③	④	④
Rust/Paint	④	④	④	④	④
Steering	④	⑤	⑤	⑤	⑤
Suspension	②	②	②	③	④
Crash Safety					
Concorde	②	②	—	—	④
Intrepid	②	②	④	④	④
LHS	—	②	—	④	④
New Yorker	—	②	④	④	—
Vision	②	②	—	—	④

Side Impact

Concorde	❶	—	—	—	④
Intrepid	❶	❶	④	④	④
LHS	—	❷	—	—	④
New Yorker	❷	❶	④	④	—
Vision	❶	—	—	—	④

Note: All these vehicles are practically identical and should have similar crashworthiness scores, even though not every model was tested each year.

FORD

Crown Victoria, Grand Marquis

Rating: Recommended (1995–97); Above Average (1992–94); Average (1986–91). Overall, these cars aren't as reliable as Japanese luxury vehicles, but they're the best of the domestic crop. Don't waste your money buying a '97 model. A used '96 version will cost much less and give you the same features. The Marquis is a slightly more luxurious version that costs more but gives little of consequence for the extra expense. **Maintenance/Repair costs**: Average, but some AC and electronic repairs can be carried out only by Ford dealers. **Parts**: Higher-than-average cost (independent suppliers sell for much less), but not hard to find.

Technical Data

ENGINES	Liters/CID	HP	MPG	Model Years
OHC I-4 1 bbl.	2.3/140	88	17–22	1985
OHV V6 FI	3.8/232	120	16–21	1985–86
OHV V8 FI	5.0/302	140–165	15–18	1985–91
OHC V8 FI	4.6/281	190–210	17–22	1992–98

Strengths and weaknesses: Built in Canada, these cars are especially suited to people who need lots of room or who prefer the safety blanket provided by road-hugging, gas-guzzling weight. Handling is mediocre, but it's about average for cars this size. Both the 4.6L and 5.0L V8s provide adequate though sometimes sluggish power, with most of their torque found in the lower gear ranges. The fuel pump, sender, fuel filter, and fuel-hose assemblies are failure-prone. There are many complaints of EEC IV ignition module malfunctions that cause hard starting and frequent stalling. Brakes, shock absorbers, and springs wear out more quickly than they should.

Some owners complain of rust perforations around the windshield, trunk, and lower body areas, but these problems concern cars that have a lot of years and mileage.

Dealer service bulletins: **1993**—Poorly performing AC systems caused by a slipping clutch at high ambient temperatures. • Ticking, pinging, or popping when the AC clutch cycles and a noisy FX-15 AC compressor. • Premature front brake rotor wear and vibrations when braking. • Noisy power-steering units. • Inoperative or malfunctioning cellular phones. • Power door locks that may not work. **1994**—Transmission shudder under light to moderate acceleration. • Radio speaker noise caused by a faulty fuel pump. • Defective electric rear window defrosters. **1995**—Delayed transmission engagement and shift errors, loose transmission connector, intermittent loss of torque at 3–4 upshift, irregular or no-torque converter operation, and shifts to Neutral at heavy throttle. • Insufficient AC cooling or excessive clutch end gap. • Water intrusion of the MLP/TR sensor. • A clacking/thumping noise when braking and brake roughness upon application. • A fuel pump buzz/whine continues to be heard through the radio speaker. **1996**—Stalling or hard starts. • Delayed 1–2 shift. • Transmission valve body cross leaks. • Chatter during turns. • Fog/film on windshield/interior glass. • Musty and mildew-type odors. • Right-front-door window requires much effort to roll up. **1997**—ABS brakes may activate on their own or produce a grinding, pulsing, fluttering effect on the brake pedal. • AC musty odor. • Air rush and/or flutter noise from center register. • Erratic or prolonged 1–2 shift. • Spark knock during acceleration. • Door latch sticks open. • Driver's-side seat cushion is uncomfortable, sags. • Fog/film on windshield/interior glass. • Front door panel crack on rear edge. • Loose catalyst or muffler heat shields. • Wind noise around doors. • Shudder or vibration while in third or fourth gear. • Steering wheel noise or vibration. • Suspension leans to right side. • Axle whine at 60 mph.

Safety summary/recalls: One Marquis owner writes:

> "Fuel is delivered from the gas tank to the engine via a pressurized fuel line. There is a gas return line that brings fuel back from the engine to the gas tank. At the location of the wheel well, the return line is installed slightly higher than the fuel line. Because of this, the return line is exposed to intermittent rubbing from the chassis. Since the fuel line is metal, it will not wear right away. In my car, it took six years, but now the line is leaking gasoline. I don't know whether all Marquis cars have this problem; however, the Alberta Motor Association mechanic, the Canadian Tire mechanic and the City Ford dealer mechanic all indicated that the car came from the factory this way. There's a serious risk of both fire and explosion while driving the car."

• One police agency reports that four 1992–93 vehicles have had incidents of unintended sudden acceleration and on two occasions the brakes failed. • Ford has received 19 complaints of reduced power-steering assist during high-speed maneuvers with 1992–93 Crown Victoria police cars. Lawsuits have been filed and the NHTSA is also involved. • There are reports of hoods suddenly flying up and shattering the windshield while 1992–93 vehicles are in motion. • There are also complaints of poor traction on ice, a hard-to-see shift indicator, and the instrument panel washing out in sunlight. **Recalls**: **1984**—Seatbelt anchors may not meet federal regulations. **1987**—Faulty fuel-injection tube assembly may cause fuel leakage and create a fire hazard. **1987–88 station wagons with dual-facing rear seats**—Automatic seatbelt retractors are faulty. **1988–89**—A faulty ignition module may cause a fire. **1991**—The car may roll away even though the automatic transmission lever says that it's in Park. **1992–93**—A short circuit could cause a front seat fire. • On non-ABS-equipped vehicles, an abraded rear brake line can cause loss of brake fluid and loss of braking power. **1992–97**—Hoods may fly open on taxis and police cars. **1995**—Fuel could leak from the tank and pose a fire hazard; dealer will replace the fuel-filler pipe seat. • Faulty headlight and power-window circuit breakers may unexpectedly turn the headlights off. • Rear seatbelt attachments may be faulty. • Airbag may not inflate properly and the end cap could separate. **1996**—Driver's door may not sustain the specified load when in the secondary latch position. **1995–96 fleet cars**—Pittman arm corrosion can cause abnormal wear. **1994 Grand Marquis**—The metal cylinder that holds the airbag can be projected into the passenger area as the airbag deploys.

Secret Warranties/Service Tips

1985–92—An exhaust buzz or rattle can be fixed by installing new clamps to secure heat shield attachments. **1986–94**—A speaker whine or buzz caused by the fuel pump can be stopped by installing an electronic noise RFI filter. **1987–90**—Excessive oil consumption is likely caused by leaking gaskets, poor sealing of the lower intake manifold, defective intake and exhaust valve stem seals, or worn piston rings. Install new guide-mounted valve stem seals for a more positive fit and install new piston rings with improved oil control. **1988–91**—The intermittent loss of the AC may be due to a defective suction accumulator (#E6VY-19C836-A). Change the accumulator and install a larger AC liquid line and a new 1992 condenser (#F2AZ-19712-A). **1989–90**—Program B89 provides for the inspection and replacement of the Overdrive gear and installation of a repair kit (#E9AZ-7L22B-A). • No Overdrive or an extended 3–4 shift may require a new Overdrive band, transmission separator plate kit, overhaul kit, and reverse drum. • Harsh or rough shifting may be caused by sticking control valves. • Poor AM radio reception due to ignition static can be improved by securing the antenna ground connection. **1990**—Excessive transmission noise, delayed shifts, or no engagements may be due to metal particles from the thrust washer that have plugged the filter or burnt clutch plates. • Install a new "service only" EEC IV processor to correct driveline clunk when the throttle is closed. • If the AC blower won't change speed, consider installing a new switch assembly. If the blower sometimes cuts out, look for a loose connection at the variable-blower speed control. • If the front seats move in their tracks or make noise, Ford will install new seat tracks and a memory track on the driver's side free of charge. • A sluggish speed-control response can be remedied by installing a new EEC IV processor. • A loose or wobbly steering wheel requires putting in a new bearing tolerance ring service kit (#F0DZ-3L539-D). **1990–91**—Fuel pump whining can be reduced by adding tank insulation material. **1990–93**—Brake pedal and steering vibration when braking can be reduced by installing improved brake rotors (#F1VY-1125-A) and linings (#F3AZ-2001-A). **1992**— Premature brake wear and seizure due to overheating can be corrected by installing air scoops to cool the brakes. **1992–94**—A moaning or loud noise coming from the engine compartment of cars equipped with the 4.6L engine can be corrected by installing a new air-idle bypass tube and resonator assembly. • Automatic transmissions with delayed or no forward engagement, or a higher-than-expected engine rpm when coming to a stop, are covered in DSB 94-26-9. **1992–97**—An erratic or prolonged 1–2 shift can be cured by replacing the cast aluminum piston with a one-piece stamped steel piston that has bonded lip seals and by replacing the top accumulator spring. These upgraded parts will increase the transmission's durability, according to Ford. **1995–97**—ABS brakes that activate on their own or produce a grinding, pulsing, fluttering effect on the brake pedal probably need upgraded wiring connectors at the ABS sensors.

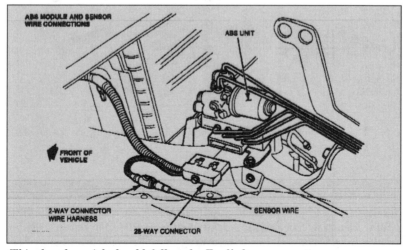

This three-hour job should fall under Ford's base warranty.

1996–97—Spark knock during acceleration can be silenced by replacing the MAF sensor and reprogramming the power control module. **All models/years**—Three components that frequently benefit from Ford "goodwill" warranty extensions are catalytic converters, fuel pumps, and computer modules. If Ford balks at refunding your money, apply the emissions warranty for a full or partial refund. • Paint delamination, fading, peeling, hazing, and "microchecking": See page 94-95 for details on claiming a refund.

Crown Victoria, Grand Marquis Profile

	1990	1991	1992	1993	1994	1995	1996	1997
Cost Price ($)								
Crown S/LTD	17,760	18,776	21,051	21,250	19,350	21,320	21,780	21,430
Marquis GS	18,915	19,920	21,455	23,425	21,125	22,130	22,600	23,145
Used Values ($)								
Crown S/LTD ↑	5,500	6,000	8,000	10,000	11,500	13,500	15,000	17,500
Crown S/LTD ↓	4,500	5,000	7,000	8,500	10,000	12,000	14,000	16,000
Marquis GS ↑	5,500	6,200	8,500	10,500	12,000	14,000	15,500	18,500
Marquis GS ↓	4,500	5,500	7,500	9,000	10,500	12,500	14,500	17,000
Extended Warranty	Y	N	N	N	N	N	N	N
Secret Warranty	Y	Y	Y	Y	Y	Y	Y	N
Reliability	③	③	④	④	④	⑤	⑤	⑤
Air conditioning	②	②	②	②	③	③	③	④
Automatic transmission	③	③	③	③	③	④	④	⑤
Body integrity	②	②	③	③	③	④	④	④
Braking system	②	②	②	②	②	②	②	③
Electrical system	②	②	②	②	③	③	③	④
Engines	④	④	④	④	④	④	⑤	⑤
Exhaust/Converter	④	④	④	③	③	③	⑤	⑤
Fuel system	②	②	③	③	③	③	③	④
Ignition system	②	③	③	③	③	③	③	④
Rust/Paint	②	②	②	②	③	③	③	④
Steering	③	③	③	③	③	③	③	④
Suspension	②	②	③	③	③	④	⑤	⑤
Crash Safety	—	—	⑤	②	②	④	⑤	⑤
Side Impact	—	—	—	—	—	—	—	④

Note: The 1993–94 models' low crash scores represent severe leg trauma rated for the first time.

Cougar, Thunderbird

Rating: Above Average (1989–97); Average (1986–88). **Maintenance/Repair costs**: About average and repairs aren't dealer dependent. **Parts**: Higher-than-average cost (independent suppliers sell for much less) and not hard to find. Despite the fact that 1997 is the last model year for both models, parts should remain plentiful.

Technical Data

ENGINES	Liters/CID	HP	MPG	Model Years
OHC I-4 FI	2.3/140	45–155	21–25	1985–86
OHC I-4 FI	2.3/140	190	18–24	1987–88
OHV V6 FI	3.8/232	120–140	16–21	1985–88
OHV V8 FI	5.0/302	140–150	15–18	1985–88
OHV V6 FI	3.8/232	140	17–22	1989–97

OHV V6 FI	3.8/232	210–230	15–21	1989–95
OHC V8 FI	4.6/281	205	17–22	1994–97
OHV V8 FI	5.0/302	200	17–22	1991–93

Strengths and weaknesses: These are no-surprise, average-performing, two-door luxury cars that have changed little over the years. Nevertheless, they offer more performance and greater reliability than GM rear-drives and most of the Big-Three-produced front-drives. Handling and ride are far from perfect, though, with considerable body lean and rear-end instability when taking curves at moderate speed.

The reliability of 1989–97 models has been average to better than average, as long as you stay away from the turbocharged 4-cylinder engine. True, it offers lots of power, but excessive noise and expensive repairs are the price you pay. Front suspension components wear out quickly, as do power-steering rack seals. Owners of recent models have complained of EEC IV ignition module defects, electrical system bugs, parking brake cables that seize, steering-pump hoses that burst repeatedly (one owner of a '94 Cougar wrote that he replaced the hose twice in the same year), transmission shudder in Overdrive during cold weather, numerous squeaks and rattles, faulty heater fans, and failure-prone power window regulators.

Safety summary/recalls: Recalls: 1988–93—The ignition switch could experience an internal short circuit, creating the potential for overheating, smoke, and possibly fire in the steering column. **1989**—Rear suspension wheel knuckles could fracture. • There is excessive brake pedal travel. **1990–91**—Wiper motor nuts may loosen or fall off. **1996**—The automatic transmission may disengage or fail to engage when shift lever is moved to Park. • Driver's door may not sustain the specified load when it's in the secondary latch position. • The semi-automatic temperature control blower may malfunction.

Secret Warranties/Service Tips

1985–92—A buzz or rattle from the exhaust system may be caused by a loose heat shield catalyst. **1989–94**—Water dripping from the floor ducts when the AC is working requires a relocated evaporator core. **1990–93**—Noise from the power-steering pump may be caused by air in the system. **1992–95**—A corroded solenoid may be the cause of starter failures. **1994**—Automatic transmissions with delayed or no forward engagement or a higher engine rpm than expected when coming to a stop are covered in DSB 94-26-9. • A no-crank condition in cold weather may be due to water freezing in the starter solenoid. • Hesitation or stumble in vehicles equipped with a 3.8L engine may be fixed by installing an upgraded PCM (powertrain control module) that allows for low-grade fuel. **1994–95**—A thumping or clacking noise heard from the front brakes signals the need to machine the front disc brake rotors; Ford will pay for this repair under its base warranty. **1994–97**—An erratic or prolonged 1-2 shift can be cured by replacing the cast aluminum piston with a one-piece stamped steel piston that has bonded lip seals and by replacing the top accumulator spring. These upgraded parts will increase the transmission's durability, according to Ford. **All models/years**—Ford's "goodwill" warranty extensions cover fuel pumps and computer modules that govern engine, fuel injection, and transmission functions. If Ford balks at refunding your money for a faulty computer module, say that you wish to have the 5-year/50,000-mile emissions warranty applied either by the company or by the courts. There's nothing like a small claims court action to focus Ford's attention. The same advice applies if you notice a rotten-egg odor coming from the exhaust. It's likely the result of a malfunctioning catalytic converter—not last night's sumptuous helpings of franks 'n' beans. • Paint delamination, fading, peeling, hazing, and "microchecking": See page 94-95 for details on claiming a refund.

Cougar, Thunderbird Profile

	1990	1991	1992	1993	1994	1995	1996	1997
Cost Price ($)								
Cougar	16,670	16,890	17,790	17,830	18,360	18,960	18,450	19,690
T-bird	16,473	16,550	17,675	15,830	17,325	17,890	17,990	18,390
Used Values ($)								
Cougar ↑	5,500	6,600	7,700	8,700	9,200	11,300	13,000	14,000
Cougar ↓	4,500	5,700	6,800	7,700	8,200	9,800	12,000	13,000
T-bird ↑	5,500	6,500	7,500	8,500	9,000	11,000	12,500	13,500
T-bird ↓	4,500	5,500	6,500	7,500	8,000	9,500	11,000	12,500
Extended Warranty	Y	Y	Y	Y	N	N	N	N
Secret Warranty	Y	Y	Y	Y	Y	Y	Y	Y
Reliability	③	③	③	③	③	④	④	⑤
Air conditioning	②	②	②	②	②	③	③	④
Body integrity	②	②	②	②	②	③	③	③
Braking system	②	②	②	②	②	②	②	③
Electrical system	②	②	②	②	②	②	③	③
Engines	④	④	④	⑤	⑤	⑤	⑤	⑤
Exhaust/Converter	②	③	③	③	④	⑤	⑤	⑤
Fuel system	③	③	③	③	③	③	③	④
Ignition system	③	③	③	④	④	⑤	⑤	⑤
Manual transmission	—	—	—	—	—	—	—	—
- automatic	②	②	③	③	③	③	⑤	⑤
Rust/Paint	①	①	②	②	②	②	②	③
Steering	②	②	②	③	③	③	③	⑤
Suspension	②	②	③	③	④	④	④	⑤
Crash Safety	—	⑤	⑤	①	②	⑤	⑤	⑤

Note: The 1993–94 models' low crash scores represent severe leg trauma rated for the first time.

GENERAL MOTORS

Olds 98/Regency, Park Avenue

Rating: Average (1994–97); Below Average (1991–93); Not Recommended (1988–90). **Maintenance/Repair costs**: Higher than average, but repairs aren't dealer dependent. **Parts**: Higher-than-average cost (independent suppliers sell for much less), but not hard to find. Nevertheless, don't even think about buying one of these front-drives without a three- to five-year extended warranty backed by GM.

Technical Data

ENGINES	Liters/CID	HP	MPG	Model Years
Park Avenue				
OHV V6 2 bbl.	3.0/181	110	15–20	1985
OHV V6 FI	3.8/231	125–150	17–20	1985–87
OHV V6 FI	3.8/231	165	17–20	1988–90
OHV V6D FI	4.3/262	85	20–23	1985
Olds 98/Regency				
OHV V6 FI	3.8/231	140–170	18–22	1986–94
OHV V6 FI	3.8/231	205	18–21	1995–98
OHV V6 FI*	3.8/231	205–225	17–21	1992–96
OHV V6 FI*	3.8/231	240	16–20	1997–98

*supercharged

Strengths and weaknesses: These attractive, luxurious cars are billed as six-seaters, but only four passengers can ride in comfort. Although the 1991–96 Park Avenue and Olds 98/Regency were improved over the years, they've compiled the worst repair history among large cars. Main problem areas are the engine, automatic transmission, fuel system, brakes, electrical system (including defective PROM and MEMCAL modules), starter and alternator, and badly assembled, poor-quality body hardware. The 3.0L V6 engine is inadequate for cars this heavy and the 3.8L has been a big quality disappointment. Stay away from the failure-prone diesel engine. Under-hood servicing is complicated. Automatic transmission and engine computer malfunctions are common. The fuel-injection system is temperamental. Window mechanisms are poorly designed. The power-steering assembly is failure-prone. There are frequent electrical failures. Front brake pads and rotors require frequent replacement. Shock absorbers leak or go soft very quickly. Extensive surface corrosion has been a problem because of poor and often incomplete paint application at the factory.

The revised '97 models have had fewer complaints, perhaps because of the short time they've been out and the fact that GM's warranty is still in effect. Nevertheless, the main problem areas continue to be the following: powertrain malfunctions; engine and transmission leaks; a concerto of squeaks, rattles, moans, and whines; AC not performing properly; and numerous body and trims defects.

1997 models
Like the LeSabre, the '97 Park Avenue and Ultra were redesigned to include a reworked powertrain, a stiffer body, improved interior amenities, upgraded four-wheel disc brakes, and an upgraded ventilation system.

Aficionados of full-size luxury sedans love the flush glass, wraparound windshield and bumpers, and clean body lines that lend the latest makeover an aerodynamic, pleasing appearance. But these cars are more than just pretty packages; they provide lots of room, luxury, style, and, dare I say, performance. Plenty of power is available with the Park Avenue's 205-hp 3.8L V6 engine and the Aurora's 240-hp supercharged version of the same powerplant. It does 0–60 mph in under 9 seconds (impressive, considering the heft of these vehicles), and improves low and mid-range throttle response. Power is transmitted to the front wheels through an electronically controlled transmission that features "free-wheeling" clutches designed to eliminate abrupt gear changes. Both the Park Avenue and Ultra use a stretched version of the more rigid Buick Riviera and Olds Aurora platform.

Safety summary/recalls: Recalls: 1986—Faulty headlight switches. • Power-steering hose leaks could cause an under-hood fire. • ABS may suddenly fail due to fluid leaking from system. **1987**—A faulty fusible link could cause an under-hood fire. • Some throttle cables may not return to idle position. **1991 Park Avenue and Olds 98/Regency**—Parking brakes might not hold. • Console shift lever could disengage. **1992–93**—Transmission-cooler line could separate at low temperatures. **1994–95 Olds 98/Regency**—Headlight switch may not work. **1995 models with Twilight Sentinel**—Current leakage can cause loss of headlights and parking lights or the lights may suddenly come on while the car is parked. **1996**—Damaged capacitor could cause confusing electronic warnings to be displayed. • Backfire upon start-up can damage the intake manifold and cause hard starting or a fire. **1997 Park Avenue**—Center seatbelt anchor bolts were improperly installed. • Brake/Traction Control Module could cause ABS to lose its effectiveness and make for longer stopping distances.

Secret Warranties/Service Tips

1988–93—Vehicles equipped with a 3800 engine that stalls upon deceleration or is hard to start may need a new air-control motor (IAC). **1991–94**—Harsh automatic transmission upshifts can be corrected by installing an upgraded accumulator valve in the control valve body. **1991–94 Park Avenue and Olds 98/Regency**—Loss of Drive or erratic shifts may be caused by an intermittent short to ground on the Λ or B shift solenoid or an electrical short circuit in the transaxle. • Water leaking from the doors into the passenger compartment has a number of causes and remedies (DSB 431003). **1993–94**—Owners who complain of automatic-transmission low-speed miss, hesitation, chuggle, or skip may find relief with the improved MEMCAL module that GM developed to remedy the problem. **1994**—Inadequate heating, ventilation, and AC operation is addressed in DSB 431219. **1995–96**—Wind noise around front and rear doors; diagnosis and repair. **1995–97**—Transmission gear whine at 40–70 km/h means the final drive assembly may have to be replaced. **All models/years**—A rotten-egg odor coming from the exhaust is probably caused by a malfunctioning catalytic converter and may be covered under GM's emissions warranty. • The THM 44C-T4 automatic transaxles on front-drive models equipped with V6 engines are particularly failure-prone: their pinched or kinked vacuum lines result in low oil pressure. • Paint delamination, peeling, or fading: see page 95.

Olds 98, Park Avenue, Regency Profile

	1990	1991	1992	1993	1994	1995	1996	1997
Cost Price ($)								
Olds 98/Regency	22,615	25,129	25,943	25,839	25,695	26,695	28,800	—
Park Avenue	—	25,595	26,570	26,650	27,625	28,880	28,850	30,650
Used Values ($)								
Olds 98/Regency ↑	6,000	9,000	9,500	11,000	13,000	16,000	18,000	—
Olds 98/Regency ↓	5,000	7,500	8,000	9,500	12,000	14,500	17,000	—
Park Avenue ↑	—	9,500	11,500	13,000	14,500	18,000	20,000	22,500
Park Avenue ↓	—	8,000	10,000	12,000	13,000	16,500	18,000	20,500
Extended Warranty	Y	Y	Y	Y	Y	Y	Y	Y
Secret Warranty	N	Y	Y	Y	Y	Y	Y	Y
Reliability	②	②	②	②	③	③	③	③
Air conditioning	②	②	②	②	②	③	③	③
Automatic transmission	②	②	②	②	②	③	③	③
Body integrity	①	①	①	①	①	①	①	③
Braking system	②	②	②	②	②	③	③	③
Electrical system	②	②	②	②	②	②	②	②
Engines	②	②	②	③	③	③	③	③
Fuel system	②	②	②	②	②	②	③	③
Ignition system	②	②	②	②	③	③	③	③
Rust/Paint	①	①	①	①	①	①	②	③
Steering	①	①	①	①	②	②	②	③
Suspension	②	②	②	②	②	③	③	③
Crash Safety								
Park Avenue	①	—	—	—	—	—	—	—

Caprice, Custom Cruiser, Impala SS, Roadmaster, Wagon

Rating: Average (1991–96); Not Recommended (1988–90). The '95 and '96 versions carry the best crash ratings. This group of cars ceased production in 1995. A good alternate choice would be any rear-drive Buick LeSabre or a Ford Crown Victoria or Grand Marquis. **Maintenance/Repair costs**: Higher than average, but repairs can be done practically anywhere. **Parts**: Higher-than-average cost (independent suppliers sell for much less), but not hard to find. Don't buy one of these rear-drives without a three- to five-year supplementary warranty backed by GM.

Technical Data

ENGINES	Liters/CID	HP	MPG	Model Years
OHV V6 FI	4.3/262	130–140	18–21	1985–88
OHV V8 4 bbl.	5.0/305	150–170	14–17	1985–88
OHV V8 FI	5.0/305	170	15–16	1989–90
OHV V8 4 bbl.	5.0/307	140	14–17	1987–90
OHV V8D FI	5.7/350	105	22–25	1985
OHV V8 FI	4.3/265	200	18–22	1994–96
OHV V8 FI	5.0/305	170	16–20	1991–93
OHV V8 FI	5.7/350	180	16–23	1992–93
OHV V8 FI	5.7/350	260	17–23	1994–96

Strengths and weaknesses: These cars are large, comfortable, and easy to maintain. The trunk is spacious. Overall handling is acceptable, but expect a queasy ride from the too-soft suspension. Gas mileage is particularly poor. Despite the many generic deficiencies inherent in these rear-drives, the LeSabre has scored highest in this group for overall reliability and durability, even after passing over to front-wheel drive. The Impala SS is basically a Caprice with a 260-hp Corvette engine and high-performance suspension.

On all cars, engine problems include crankshaft and head-gasket failures, cracked cylinder heads, injection-pump malfunctions, and oil leaks. Engine knocking is a common V8 problem that's hard to correct inexpensively due to the various possible causes that have to be eliminated. Cars equipped with the 5.7L diesel V8 should be approached with caution. All V8s suffer from premature camshaft wear and the 350-cubic-inch V8s often fall prey to premature valve-guide wear caused by a faulty EGR valve. The 4-speed automatic transmission was troublesome until 1987. Burnt-out clutches and malfunctioning torque converters are quite common.

The 1991–96 models have shown the following deficiencies: powertrain failures; chronic AC glitches; prematurely worn suspension components, especially shock absorbers and rear springs; serious electrical problems; poor-quality body and trim items; sloppy body assembly; poor paint quality and application; excessive surface rusting (door bottoms, windshield posts, and roof panels are especially vulnerable); wagons have a rust problem around cargo-area side windows; and hubcaps on later models tend to fly off.

Dealer service bulletins: **1993**—Buzzing at idle coming from the 4L60E automatic transmission, along with a maladjusted shift linkage, causing loss of Reverse or lack of power in second gear. • Improperly adjusted automatic-transmission shift linkage leading to a burnt-out Low/Reverse clutch and increased rpms with downshifts. • Noisy power-steering units. • Intermittent cruise-control operation. • Extreme temperature difference when the AC is put in a bi-level mode and inoperative AC compressors. **1994**—Excessive oil consumption. • Faulty door-mounted radio speakers. • Poor AC performance. • Inadequate interior air flow. **1995**—1–2 and 2–3 shifting malfunctions (Caprice). • Front brake pulsation. • An exhaust-system moan or boom; inadvertent horn honking; a low voltage reading or dim lights at idle. • Automatic door lock may not work (Roadmaster). • A steering system crunch or popping noise. • Wiper-blade chatter. • Poor paint application and rust spots. **1996**—Engine noise (install new valve-stem oil seal). • 3–2 part throttle downshift flare and delayed transmission engagement. • Transmission chuggle/surge. • Transmission fluid leak from pump body (replace bushing). • Steering column noise. • Radio frequency interference diagnosis. • AC odorous.

Safety summary/recalls: **NHTSA probes**: **1994–95 Chevy Caprice police series**—Steering wheel may break at the crossbar. **Recalls**: **1985**—Leaking fuel feed and return pipe may cause a fire. • Cars equipped with a 4.3L engine could have a battery-cable short that creates a fire hazard. **1985–88**—Faulty cruise control could lead to sudden acceleration. **1987**—Cars equipped with 200-4R automatic transmission could start in gear or engage the wrong gear. **1989**—GM will inspect and replace the AC condenser inlet pipe. **1991**—Seatbelts malfunction because of defective shoulder-belt guide loop. **1991–92**—Rear seatbelts that are uncomfortable will be changed for free by GM. • Corrosion could prevent the hood from latching properly, making it hard to open or causing it to fly open. **1992**—A rattling front-door lock rod can be silenced by installing a corrective kit (#10222731). • The 4.3L engine fuel-feed and return pipes may leak. **1994**—A leaking oil cooler inlet hose is a fire hazard. • Fractured wheel studs may allow the wheel to separate from the car. • Faulty fuel tank strap fasteners. **1994–95**—Accelerator pedal may stick. **1995–96 Roadmaster, Fleetwood, and Caprice**—Loose wheel lug nuts could cause the wheel to fall off.

Secret Warranties/Service Tips

1982–91—Hydramatic 4L60/700R4 automatic transmission may have no upshift or appear to be stuck in first gear. The probable cause is a worn governor gear. It would be wise to replace the retaining ring as well. **1982–93**— Vehicles equipped with a Hydramatic 4L60 transmission that buzzes when the car is in Reverse or at idle may need a new oil-pressure regulator valve. **1985–88**—The 307-cid V8 is the most reliable and durable engine in this lineup. In 1985–86, it was plagued with camshaft/lifter problems due to the small offset from lifter bore to cam lobe. The problem was rectified in 1987 when GM adopted roller-lifters. The engine's aluminum intake manifold and gasket can be eaten away by extensive corrosion in each of the four corners where they contact a coolant port; serious coolant leaks result. Flush the radiator yearly and use a good-quality antifreeze in order to extend the life of these components. **1987–91**—This bulletin lists the different types of tailpipe smoke signals that alert you to the need for different repairs: cars with V8 engines that emit blue or bluish-white smoke may require a valve seal kit (#12511890); models with port fuel injection that emit black smoke after long starter cranks may have fuel leaking into the engine from the injectors; models with throttle body injection and port fuel injection that emit white or bluish smoke and have normal oil consumption likely have poor sealing between the intake manifold joint and the cylinder head. **1989–91**—If the transmission won't go into Reverse or is slow to shift into Reverse, GM suggests that the Reverse input clutch housing be changed. **1991**—A poor-running 5.0L or 5.7L engine may require an EGR valve kit and PCV valve in addition to a new PROM. **1994**—Excessive oil consumption is likely due to delaminated intake manifold gaskets. Install an upgraded intake manifold gasket kit. • GM campaign 94C15 will adjust at no charge a maladjusted automatic-transmission shift linkage that could, if left alone, burn out the Low/Reverse clutch. **1994–96**—Excessive engine noise can be silenced by installing an upgraded valve stem oil seal (see the following bulletin).

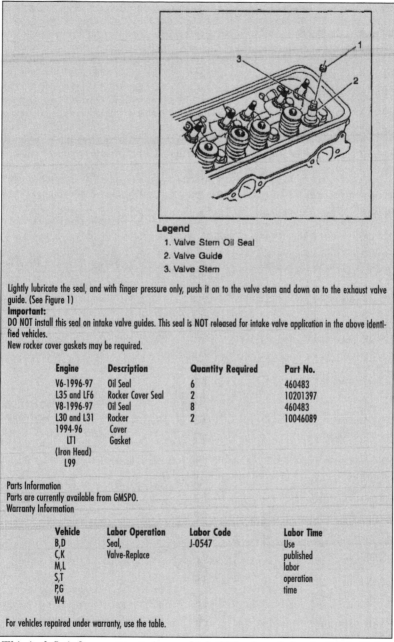

Legend

1. Valve Stem Oil Seal
2. Valve Guide
3. Valve Stem

Lightly lubricate the seal, and with finger pressure only, push it on to the valve stem and down on to the exhaust valve guide. (See Figure 1)

Important:

DO NOT install this seal on intake valve guides. This seal is NOT released for intake valve application in the above identified vehicles.

New rocker cover gaskets may be required.

Engine	Description	Quantity Required	Part No.
V6-1996-97	Oil Seal	6	460483
L35 and LF6	Rocker Cover Seal	2	10201397
V8-1996-97	Oil Seal	8	460483
L30 and L31	Rocker	2	10046089
1994-96	Cover		
LT1	Gasket		
(Iron Head)			
L99			

Parts Information

Parts are currently available from GMSPO.

Warranty Information

Vehicle	Labor Operation	Labor Code	Labor Time
B,D	Seal,	J-0547	Use
C,K	Valve-Replace		published
M,L			labor
S,T			operation
P,G			time
W4			

For vehicles repaired under warranty, use the table.

This is definitely a warranty item, which GM acknowledges in this bulletin.

1994–96 with 5.7L engine—A chuggle or surge condition will require a reflash calibration. **1991 Roadmaster**—If the starter makes a grinding noise or won't engage the engine, the fault could be a weak starter spring. • Front doors that won't stay open on an incline or are hard to open need an improved hold-open door spring. **1992**—Water leaks into the trunk from the fixed mast antenna: install an upgraded antenna base (#25610633) and bezel (#25609129). • If the front seat doesn't have enough upward travel, GM will provide a special kit (#12520796) to raise it. • A chuggle or shudder at 44mph on vehicles equipped with a 5.7L engine may be corrected by installing a new torque converter assembly. **1994**—Excessive oil consumption is likely due to delaminated intake manifold gaskets. Install an upgraded intake manifold gasket kit. • Poor AC performance can be improved by replacing the temperature control cable. • Delayed automatic-transmission shift engagement is a common problem addressed in DSB 47-71-20A. **1995–96**—Delayed automatic-transmission shift engagement may require the replacement of the pump cover assembly. **All models/years**—A rotten-egg odor coming from the exhaust is usually the result of a malfunctioning catalytic converter covered by the emissions warranty. • Paint delamination, peeling, or fading: See page 95.

Caprice, Custom Cruiser, Impala SS, Roadmaster, Wagon Profile

	1990	1991	1992	1993	1994	1995	1996
Cost Price ($)							
Caprice	15,990	18,040	19,020	19,225	20,698	21,798	21,495
Caprice wagon	17,786	19,590	20,433	21,318	22,703	24,375	22,995
Roadmaster	—	—	24,255	25,895	27,224	28,425	28,595
Wagon	—	24,642	25,110	27,895	29,078	30,370	30,250
Impala SS	—	—	—	—	23,360	24,390	24,995
Used Values ($)							
Caprice ↑	5,000	7,000	8,000	9,500	11,500	12,500	15,500
Caprice ↓	4,000	6,000	7,000	8,000	10,000	11,500	14,000
Caprice wagon ↑	6,000	9,000	10,500	12,000	14,000	16,000	18,500
Caprice wagon ↓	5,000	7,500	9,000	10,500	12,500	14,500	17,000
Roadmaster ↑	—	—	11,000	12,500	14,000	15,000	17,500
Roadmaster ↓	—	—	9,500	11,000	13,000	14,000	16,000
Wagon ↑	—	10,500	12,500	14,000	17,500	19,000	22,000
Wagon ↓	—	9,000	11,000	12,500	16,000	17,500	20,000
Impala SS ↑	—	—	—	—	18,000	20,500	22,000
Impala SS ↓	—	—	—	—	16,500	19,000	21,000
Extended Warranty	Y	Y	Y	Y	Y	Y	Y
Secret Warranty	Y	Y	Y	Y	Y	Y	Y
Reliability	②	②	②	②	③	③	③
Air conditioning	②	②	②	②	②	②	②
Automatic transmission	①	①	①	①	①	②	②
Body integrity	②	②	②	②	②	③	③
Braking system	③	③	③	③	③	③	③
Electrical system	②	②	②	②	②	②	③
Engines	③	③	③	③	③	③	③
Exhaust/Converter	②	②	②	②	③	④	④
Fuel system	③	③	③	③	③	③	③
Ignition system	③	③	③	③	③	④	④

Rust/Paint	2	2	2	2	2	2	2
Steering	2	2	2	2	3	4	4
Suspension	2	2	2	2	2	3	3
Crash Safety							
Caprice	—	2	2	1	1	4	4

Note: The 1995–96 Caprice models scored four stars for driver protection but only two for front passenger protection in government-run crash tests.

LUXURY CARS

Used luxury cars are attractive buys because they project a flashy image that can be bought for 50 percent of the new price after three years or so. They can be bargains if the selling price is reasonable, independent servicing is available, and used parts can be found. But on the downside, they're complicated to service and the cost of new parts can be horrendous.

Traditionally, the luxury-car niche has been dominated by American and German automakers. During the past decade, however, buyers have gravitated towards Japanese models. This shift in buyer preference has forced GM, Ford, and Chrysler to downsize and adopt front-drive. It has also forced GM to drop its rear-drive Caprice, Roadmaster, and Fleetwood. Despite these moves to better respond to buyers' preferences, American luxury cars are still seen by most consumers as overweight and unreliable land yachts.

You don't always have to spend big bucks to get true luxury and iron-clad reliability. Smart buyers can target fully equipped Toyota's Camrys and Cressidas, Honda's Accord, Nissan's Maxima, and Mazda's 929, all of which offer the same equipment, reliability, and performance as Lexus, Infiniti, and Acura models but for much, much less.

There are few used American luxury cars that can stand up to a six-year-old Japanese or German luxury vehicle. And this fact is reflected in the head-spinning, high depreciation rates seen with most luxury cars put out by the Big Three. Chrysler's rear-drive New Yorker and Ford's Crown Victoria/Mercury Grand Marquis and Lincoln Town Car come closest to meeting the imports in overall reliability and durability. On the other hand, the discontinued Chrysler Imperial was more show than go and the front-drive New Yorker and its LHS variant are unremarkable and were plagued by serious powertrain reliability problems, as can be seen by the numerous dealer service bulletins I've intercepted. GM's Cadillacs aren't even in the running; in fact, *AutoWeek* magazine has dubbed the Catera a "lame duck."

Recommended

BMW 5 Series (1992–97)
Lexus ES 250, ES 300,
  LS 400, SC 400
Mercedes 300, 400, 500 Series,
  E-Class (1993–97)

Mitsubishi Diamante
Nissan Maxima (1996–97)
Volvo 850 Series
Volvo 900 Series

Above Average

Acura Legend (1989–95)
Audi A4, A6, S6 (1993–97)
BMW 3 Series (1992–97)
BMW 5 Series (1991)
Cadillac (RWD) DeVille,
  Fleetwood (1995–96)
Infiniti G20, I30, J30, Q45
Lincoln Mark VII/VIII
  (1993–97)
Lincoln Town Car (1990–97)

Mazda 929 (1992–95)
Mazda Millenia (1995–97)
Mercedes 190 Series, C-Class
  (1994–97)
Mercedes 300, 400, 500 Series
  (1988–92)
Nissan Maxima (1989–95)
Toyota Avalon (1995–97)
Toyota Cressida (1985–92)
Volvo 700 Series (1992)

Average

BMW 3 Series (1986–91)
BMW 5 Series (1988–90)
Cadillac Concours, DeVille,
  Fleetwood (1994–97)
Cadillac (RWD) DeVille,
  Fleetwood (1988–94)
GM Aurora, Riveria, Toronado,
  Trofeo (1995–97)

Lincoln Continental (1995–97)
Lincoln Mark VII/VIII (1992)
Lincoln Town Car (1990–97)
Mazda 929 (1988–91)
Mercedes 190 Series, C-Class
  (1988–93)
Nissan Maxima (1986–88)
Volvo 700 Series (1991)

Below Average

Cadillac Allanté, Catera,
  Eldorado, Seville (1992–97)
Cadillac Concours, DeVille,
  Fleetwood (1988–93)
Lincoln Continental (1988–94)
Lincoln Mark VII/VIII
  (1986–91)

Mercedes 190 Series, C-Class
  (1984–87)
Mercedes 300, 400, 500 Series
  (1985–87)
Saab 900, 9000 (1994–97)

Not Recommended

Acura Legend (1988)
Audi (1984–92)
Cadillac Allanté, Catera,
  Eldorado, Seville (1988–91)

GM Aurora, Riveria, Toronado,
  Trofeo (1986–93)
Saab 900, 9000 (1986–93)
Volvo 700 Series (1986–90)

1996 Nissan Maxima GXE: The Maxima GXE is a recommended buy for 1995–97. This is a more affordable alternative to the high-priced Infiniti and Lexus offerings.

1988 Merkur XR4Ti: Not recommended. This European luxury import turned into a luxury lemon and then was dropped by Ford.

ACURA

Legend

Rating: Above Average (1989–95); Not Recommended (1988). Resale value is high on all Legend models, but especially so with the coupe. Shop instead for a cheaper 1989 or later base Legend with the coupe's upgraded features. In fact, the '90 Legend combines the lowest price with the best crash rating score. **Maintenance/Repair costs**: Higher than average, and most repairs are dealer dependent. To avoid costly engine repairs, check the engine timing belt every two years. **Parts**: Higher-than-average cost (some independent suppliers sell for much less under the Honda name), but not hard to find.

Technical Data

ENGINES	Liters/CID	HP	MPG	Model Years
OHC V6 FI	2.5/152	151	19–25	1986–87
OHC V6 FI	2.7/163	161	18–24	1987–90
OHC V6 FI	3.2/196	200	18–24	1991–95
OHC V6 FI	3.2/196	230	17–24	1994–95

Strengths and weaknesses: **1986–90**—Early Legends were upscale, enlarged Accords that were unimpressive performers with both 6-cylinder powerplants. Dependability, acceptable road handling, and a spacious interior are the car's main advantages. In spite of occasional clutch malfunctions, the 5-speed manual gearbox is the transmission of choice. The automatic shifts harshly and its lockup torque converter is constantly cutting in and out, reducing both performance and fuel economy. An overly soft suspension gives the car a bouncy ride and it easily bottoms out when the vehicle is loaded or traversing rough roads. Front-end components get noisier as time passes. Long-term durability is better than average, with the only problems centered around body hardware and accessory equipment malfunctions, notably poor radio performance.

1991–95—The 3.2L V6 is by far a better performer than the 2.5L and 2.7L engines of earlier models. Ride quality improved, power steering is more responsive, and rear seating is more spacious. Automatic shifting is still rough (especially during acceleration), fuel economy is disappointing, and the coupe's rear seat room is a joke. Owners report that suspension struts soften quickly, minor electrical problems occasionally occur, radio reception is poor, and brake servicing is too frequent. The windshield-washer pump frequently malfunctions on the '91 and '92 versions.

Safety summary/recalls: **NHTSA probes**: **1986–87**—Fuel tank over-pressurization may result in fuel spewing out when the cap is removed. **1986–88**—These Legends have one of the highest rates of accidental sudden acceleration reported by owners. **1992–93**—Inadvertent airbag deployment. **Recalls**: **1986–1990**—Takata seatbelt replacement. **1991**—A faulty automatic transmission shift cable should be replaced. **1992**—Vehicles may not have an igniter for the passenger-side airbag.

Secret Warranties/Service Tips

1986–95—A clicking noise heard while turning means you need to replace the constant-velocity joint. **1990**—Water collects in the spare tire well; diagnosis and repair DSB 89-021. • Malfunctioning security-system control unit; diagnosis and repair DSB 90-002. **1991**—Poor AM radio reception or interference from the car's electrical equipment may be due to a poor ground connection between the antenna collar and car body. **1991–92**—Static on the AM radio band may also be caused by a faulty Bose amplifier as well as poor antenna grounding due to loose mounting nuts. • If the remote audio volume controls cause static or operate erratically, change the volume control motor inside the audio unit. • Poor AC performance is often caused by a mal-adjusted heater valve cable. **1991–93**—Engine knocking after a cold start-up is likely due to carbon buildup in the piston ring land. **1991–94**—To prevent the lower bumper face from pulling loose, Acura will reinforce the mounting points and reverse the overlap of the lower bumper face and the splash shield. • Power-steering speed sensor failures. **1995**—You can correct the gap in the front-door-sill molding at the B-pillar by trimming back the nylon carpet retainer. Honda has a 14-year/150,000-mile free engine repair and tuning secret warranty (see Integra "Service Tips"). **All models/years**—Like Hondas, most Acura DSBs allow for special warranty consideration on a "goodwill" basis even after the warranty has expired or the car has changed hands. Referring to this euphemism will increase your chances of getting some kind of refund for repairs that are obviously factory defects. Acura will repair or replace defective steering assemblies, constant velocity joints, and catalytic converters free of charge for up to 5 years/100,000 miles on a case-by-case basis. There's no labor charge or deductible. Used vehicles and repairs carried out by independent garages aren't covered by this special program. But, since the converter is an emissions component, it's almost always automatically covered under the emissions warranty. • Steering wheel shimmy can be reduced by re-balancing the wheel/tire/hub/rotor assembly in the front end. • Poor radio reception or interference is addressed in DSB 94-011, issued August 30, 1994. • The automaker will install air intake screens to keep debris away from the blower motor. • Vertical scratches on the door window result from the window making contact with the molding's metal clips. • Seatbelts that fail to function properly during normal use will be replaced for free under the company's lifetime seatbelt warranty.

Legend Profile

	1988	1989	1990	1991	1992	1993	1994	1995
Cost Price ($)								
Base	23,735	24,580	24,580	27,910	28,580	30,370	36,490	38,220
Used Values ($)								
Base ↑	7,500	8,500	9,500	13,500	15,000	17,000	21,000	23,500
Base ↓	6,000	7,000	8,000	12,000	13,500	15,500	19,000	22,000
Extended Warranty	N	N	N	N	N	N	N	N
Secret Warranty	N	N	N	N	N	Y	Y	Y
Reliability	③	③	③	④	④	④	⑤	⑤
Air conditioning	④	④	④	⑤	⑤	⑤	⑤	⑤
Body integrity	③	③	③	③	③	③	③	③
Braking system	③	③	③	④	④	④	④	⑤
Electrical system	③	③	③	③	③	③	③	④
Engines	④	④	④	⑤	⑤	⑤	⑤	⑤
Exhaust/Converter	④	④	⑤	⑤	⑤	⑤	⑤	⑤
Fuel system	④	④	④	④	④	⑤	⑤	⑤
Ignition system	③	③	④	④	④	⑤	⑤	⑤
Manual transmission	③	**❷**	④	⑤	⑤	⑤	⑤	⑤
- automatic	③	③	③	③	③	④	④	⑤
Rust/Paint	**❷**	③	③	③	④	④	⑤	⑤
Steering	④	④	④	④	⑤	⑤	⑤	⑤
Suspension	③	③	④	④	⑤	⑤	⑤	⑤
Crash Safety	⑤	—	⑤	—	—	**❷**	**❷**	③

AUDI

80, 90, 100, 200, 5000, Coupe, Quattro, V8 Series, A4, A6, S6

Rating: Above average (1993–97); Not Recommended (1984–92). **Maintenance/Repair costs**: Higher than average, and almost all repairs have to be done by an Audi dealer. **Parts**: Way-higher-than-average cost, and independent suppliers have a hard time finding parts. Don't even think about buying one of these front-drives without a three- to five-year supplementary warranty backed by Audi.

Technical Data

ENGINES	Liters/CID	HP	MPG	Model Years
OHC I-5 FI	1.8/109	102	22–25	1985–87
OHC I-5T FI	2.1/131	140	17–23	1985
OHC I-5 FI	2.2/136	115	20–24	1985–87
OHC I-5T FI	2.2/136	158–162	17–23	1986–91
DOHC I-5T FI	2.2/136	217	17–23	1991
DOHC I-5T FI	2.2/136	227	17–23	1992–95
OHC I-5 FI	2.3/141	130	18–23	1987–91
OHC V6 FI	2.8/169	172	20–25	1993–98

Strengths and weaknesses: These cars are attractively styled, handle well, are comfortable to drive, and provide a spacious interior. Yet the pre-'93 models have a worse-than-average reliability record and are plagued by mechanical and electrical components that don't stand up to the rigors of driving in Canada. Furthermore, it seems that VW has written off these failure-prone cars in favour of the better-built and more recent A4 and A6 models. The dealer body isn't strong enough to adequately service all of these vehicles when things go wrong, so owners of older models are generally left to independent garages to serve their needs. Premium fuel is required for vehicles equipped with the 6-cylinder engine.

A4, A6, S4, S6, and Sport 90

This is the pick of the Audi litter starting with the 1995 model year. Although Audi continued its alphabet name game by grouping its 100 series under a new A6 heading, these cars were substantially improved. Packed with standard features, the A6 is a comfortable, spacious, front-drive or all-wheel-drive luxury sedan that comes with dual airbags and ABS. It uses the same V6 powerplant as the A4, its smaller sibling. The S4 is a limited-production, high performance spin-off that carries a 227-horsepower turbocharged rendition of the old 5-cylinder powerplant. Restyled for '95, they were rebadged as the A6 and S6. The S6 wasn't sold in 1996–97, however.

These cars are conservatively styled, slow off the mark (in spite of the V6 addition when hooked to an automatic), and plagued by electrical glitches. The 4-speed automatic shifts erratically and the

2.8L V6 engine needs full throttle for adequate performance. Handling is acceptable, but the ride is a bit firm and the car still exhibits considerable body roll, brake dive, and acceleration squat when pushed. Handling is on a par with the BMW 300 series and acceleration times beat out those of the Mercedes. Quattro's AWD is extended to entry-level models at a time when most automakers are dropping the option on passenger cars.

Overall quality control has really improved over the past several years, with fewer body, brake, and electrical glitches than exhibited by previous models. A perusal of this year's internal service bulletins shows a dramatic improvement in quality control over earlier versions.

Dealer service bulletins: 1995—Oil leakage from the rear and upper engine. • Coolant circulation pump leakage. • Delayed first- and second-gear shift. • A malfunctioning climate control. • Inaccurate fuel gauge and temperature gauges. • Door lock key binding. • Skipping wiper blades. **1996**—ABS light comes on inadvertently. • Front speaker buzzing. • Cruise control won't maintain set speed. • Delayed 1–2 shift on cold start warm-up. • Inaccurate Delta Bose radio display. • Friction noise from front and rear door seals. • Fuel gauge doesn't register full. • Carbon buildup in the intake valve and combustion chamber. • Exhaust popping and rasping noise. • Radio volume goes to maximum when adjusted. • Binding rear ashtray lid. • Rear differential noise and vibration while driving. • Loose rear reading light. • Tachometer sticking and erratic AC display. **1997**—False ABS light warning. • Delayed 1–2 shift on cold start warm-up. • Friction noise from front and rear door seals. • Rasping noise from exhaust.

80, 90, and 100 series

Launched in 1988, these entry-level Audis share the same wheelbase, front-drive, and 4X4 components. Equipped with an efficient but wimpy 2.0L 4-cylinder (dropped in 1991) or the more powerful 2.3L 5-cylinder engine, 4-wheel disc brakes, and galvanized body panels, these small sedans are leagues ahead of Audi's mid-1980s vehicles. The 1991 models are clearly a better choice; they use an improved 4-speed automatic transmission hooked up to a more powerful engine. 1992 was basically a carry-over year in which unsold '91 models were recycled. Some of their more common problems include AC, electrical system, and brake malfunctions.

Dealer service bulletins: 1993 Audi 100s—Misaligned deck lids that are hard to close. • Noisy steering column and squeaking and rattling coming from the front seats and inside the B-pillar. • Excessive wind noise because of poor window sealing. • Smearing, chattering wiper blades. • The 1992–94 models have quirky AC systems that often malfunction and have to be constantly readjusted. The fresh air fan for the same model years will also misbehave, suddenly going into high-speed operation for no reason.

5000

Renamed the 100 and 200 in 1989, these sedans have had a terrible repair record. The diesel engine is a nightmare, as are the turbocharged gasoline engines coupled to automatic transmissions. Front-drive mechanicals are unreliable and very complex to troubleshoot. Steering racks aren't durable and the engine cooling and electrical systems require frequent repair. Front brake rotors and calipers wear out very quickly and exhaust-system components have a short life span. Other common problems include electrical short circuits in the taillights, AC failures, hot starting difficulties, and leaking transmission seals. The top of the front fenders and the front edge of the hood and rear-wheel housings are susceptible to rust perforations. Furthermore, the persistently poor alignment of lower side moldings is a common body problem. Resale value is much lower than average and owners who've been sucked into buying them because of their bargain-basement price face frequent and outrageously expensive "routine" servicing that's anything but routine.

4000

Gasoline engines require constant and expensive adjustments, the cooling and electrical systems are weak, front brakes require frequent and expensive servicing, and the front MacPherson struts don't last long. Additionally, exhaust-system parts rust through quickly and the fuel-injection system needs constant adjusting. Door panel trim peels away from the body on 1988–89 models. Later models have fewer complaints, probably due to their comprehensive base warranty.

Safety summary/recalls: NHTSA probes: 1993 90, 100—Underhood fires. **Recalls: 1984–90 80, 90, 4000**—Dealers will fix leaky or cracked brake hoses. **1985–86**—Defective idle stabilizer valve on the 5-cylinder version with automatic transmission may cause the vehicle to surge and buck. **1985–91**—Evaporation of the differential oil could result in bearing and gear failure, which saps power from the front wheels or locks them up. **1986**—Rear or right-front seatbelt locks may malfunction. **1990**—Faulty steering lock bolts may block steering wheel movement. A faulty idle control module may cause erratic or increased idle speed. **1990 Quattro**—Faulty front seat back hinges. **1984–85 100, 200, 5000 Quattro, V8**—A faulty idle control module may cause erratic or increased idle speed. **1984–86**—Audi will install a transmission/brake interlock. **1984–88**—Audi will install a vent line valve or modify the fuel filler neck to prevent fuel vapor ignition on Turbo models. **1984–89 Turbo and Quattro**—Hardened fuel injector seals allow fuel to leak onto the engine. **1985–86**—A maladjusted fuel distributor may cause fuel vapors to collect in the air filter and ignite if the engine backfires. • Defective idle stabilizer valve on the 5-cylinder version with automatic transmission may cause the vehicle to surge and buck. **1985–91**—An extension of the previous recall to prevent bearing and gear failure from sapping power from the front wheels or locking them up. **1986**—Malfunctioning rear or right-front seat-belt locks. **1990–91 V8 with cruise control**—Cruise control may not return to idle. **1992 100 series**—Audi will modify the brake vacuum booster system to improve brake pedal assist. **1994–96 90, 100, A6, Cabriolet, S4, and S6**—Defective ignition switches will cause mal-functioning turn signals, windshield wipers, lights, power windows, and air conditioners. **1995–96 90, A4, A6, and Cabrio**—If the cruise control won't maintain speed, add additional vacuum or change the vacuum servo unit. **1996 A4**—A fuel gauge that won't register full signals a short circuit. • Inoperative horn is due to insufficient electrical ground contact.

Secret Warranties/Service Tips

100, 200, 5000 Quattro, V8: 1991–92—A clacking noise occurring whenever the vehicle passes over a bump is caused by plastic-to-plastic contact between the door lock latch and the door wedge. **1992–94**—DSB 94-09 troubleshoots common AC problems. • DSB 94-05 recommends replacing the fresh air fan with an upgraded part. **1995–97**—Delayed 1–2 shift on cold start warm-ups is a normal condition resulting from the emissions control settings, according to Audi. **All models/years**—Defective catalytic converters that cause a rotten-egg smell may be replaced free of charge under the emissions warranty.

80, 90, A4, A6, S6 Profile

	1990	1991	1992	1993	1994	1995	1996	1997
Cost Price ($)								
80	19,235	21,400	23,055	—	—	—	—	—
90	24,910	26,045	—	26,295	28,265	26,115	—	—
A4	—	—	—	—	—	—	26,975	28,905
A6	—	—	—	—	—	31,045	32,775	33,100
S6	—	—	—	—	—	45,720	—	—
Used Values ($)								
80 ↑	6,000	7,500	9,000	—	—	—	—	—
80 ↓	5,000	6,500	7,500	—	—	—	—	—
90 ↑	7,500	8,500	—	12,500	14,500	16,500	—	—
90 ↓	6,000	7,000	—	11,000	13,000	15,000	—	—
A4 ↑	—	—	—	—	—	—	16,500	16,500
A4 ↓	—	—	—	—	—	—	16,500	16,500
A6 ↑	—	—	—	—	—	21,000	24,000	27,000
A6 ↓	—	—	—	—	—	19,000	22,500	25,000
S6 ↑	—	—	—	—	—	34,000	—	—
S6 ↓	—	—	—	—	—	31,000	—	—
Extended Warranty	Y	Y	Y	Y	Y	Y	Y	Y
Secret Warranty	N	N	N	N	N	N	N	N
Reliability	①	①	②	②	③	④	④	④
Air conditioning	①	①	①	①	②	②	②	③
Body integrity	④	④	④	④	④	④	④	④

Braking system	2	2	2	1	2	2	2	3
Electrical system	1	1	1	1	1	2	2	3
Engines	1	1	1	2	3	3	3	4
Exhaust/Converter	2	2	2	1	4	5	5	5
Fuel system	1	2	2	5	4	4	4	4
Ignition system	2	2	2	1	3	3	3	3
Manual transmission	3	3	3	3	3	4	5	5
- automatic	2	2	4	4	4	5	5	5
Rust/Paint	2	1	4	4	4	4	4	4
Steering	2	2	3	3	3	3	3	4
Suspension	2	3	3	3	3	3	3	3
Crash Safety								
A4	—	—	—	—	—	—	4	4
A6	—	—	—	—	—	5	5	5

100, 200, 5000, V8 Profile

	1988	1989	1990	1991	1992	1993	1994
Cost Price ($)							
100	—	25,315	27,235	28,505	28,105	30,845	35,565
100Q	—	31,140	29,805	30,865	36,805	41,395	43,465
200	—	33,340	33,740	34,935	—	—	—
200TQ	—	36,690	36,140	42,755	—	—	—
5000	23,535	—	—	—	—	—	—
5000Q	27,320	—	—	—	—	—	—
V8	—	—	47,785	50,555	53,505	58,945	59,145
Used Values ($)							
100 ↑	—	6,000	7,500	8,500	12,000	13,500	16,500
100 ↓	—	4,500	6,000	7,000	10,500	12,000	14,500
100Q ↑	—	9,000	10,000	11,000	15,500	18,000	20,000
100Q ↓	—	7,000	8,500	9,500	14,000	16,000	18,500
200 ↑	—	8,000	9,000	10,000	—	—	—
200 ↓	—	6,500	8,000	8,500	—	—	—
200TQ ↑	—	10,000	11,500	12,500	—	—	—
200TQ ↓	—	8,500	10,000	11,000	—	—	—
5000 ↑	4,000	—	—	—	—	—	—
5000 ↓	3,500	—	—	—	—	—	—
5000Q ↑	4,500	—	—	—	—	—	—
5000Q ↓	3,000	—	—	—	—	—	—
V8 ↑	—	—	15,000	14,500	22,000	26,000	30,000
V8 ↓	—	—	13,000	16,000	20,000	24,000	28,000

	1988	1989	1990	1991	1992	1993	1994
Extended Warranty	Y	Y	Y	Y	Y	Y	Y
Secret Warranty	N	N	N	N	N	N	N
Reliability	1	1	1	2	2	2	3
Air conditioning	2	2	3	3	3	3	3
Body integrity	4	4	4	4	4	4	5
Braking system	2	2	2	2	2	2	3
Electrical system	1	1	1	1	2	2	2
Engines	1	1	1	2	2	4	5
Exhaust/Converter	2	2	2	3	3	5	5
Fuel system	1	2	2	2	2	3	3

Ignition system	②	②	②	②	②	③	③
Manual transmission	④	④	④	—	—	⑤	⑤
- automatic	②	②	④	④	④	⑤	⑤
Rust/Paint	②	③	④	④	④	④	⑤
Steering	②	②	②	②	③	④	④
Suspension	②	②	②	③	③	⑤	⑤
Crash Safety							
100	—	⑤	—	⑤	—	—	—

BMW

3 Series, 5 Series

Rating: **3 series**: Above Average (1992–97); Average (1986–91). **5 series**: Recommended (1992–97); Above Average (1991); Average (1988–90). These cars come with a reputation that far exceeds what they actually deliver. **Maintenance/Repair costs**: Higher than average, but many repairs can be done by independents who specialize in BMW repairs. Unfortunately, they're concentrated around large urban areas. **Parts**: Higher-than-average cost and often back ordered.

Technical Data

ENGINES	Liters/CID	HP	MPG	Model Years
		3 Series		
OHC I-4 FI	1.8/108	101	23–28	1985
DOHC I-4 FI	1.8/110	134	23–27	1991–93
DOHC I-4 FI	1.8/110	138	23–27	1991–95
DOHC I-4 FI	1.9/116	138	22–27	1996–98
OHC I-6FI	2.5/152	168	18–24	1988–93
DOHC I-6FI	2.5/152	189	18–24	1992–95
DOHC I-6FI	2.8/170	190	19–23	1996–98
		5 Series		
OHC I-6TD FI	2.4/149	114	19–25	1986–87
OHC I-6FI	2.5/152	168	18–24	1989–90
DOHC I-6FI	2.5/152	189	18–24	1991–96
OHC I-6 FI	2.7/164	121–127	19–23	1986–88
DOHC I-6 FI	2.8/170	190	18–22	1997–98
DOHC V8 FI	3.0/183	215	16–21	1994–96
OHC I-6 FI	3.4/209	208	15–20	1989–93
DOHC V8 FI	4.0/243	282	14–18	1994–96
DOHC V8 FI	4.4/268	282	14–18	1997–98

Strengths and weaknesses: **1984–91**—Great 6-cylinder performance with the manual gearbox and ride and handling are commendable. The 318's small engine is seriously compromised by an automatic transmission; the 325e is more pleasant to drive and delivers lots of low-end torque. The 4-cylinder engines that first appeared on the '91 models aren't well-suited to the demands of the automatic gearbox. These cars are fun to drive as long as you keep in mind that the rear end is unstable on slippery pavement. Rear passenger and cargo room is limited and overall reliability is average. Whenever a problem arises, however, repair costs are particularly high, due to the small number of dealers, the relative scarcity of parts, and the acquiescence of affluent owners.

The electrical system is the source of most complaints. The automatic transmission isn't durable and front brakes require frequent attention. Owners also report chronic surging at idle and a rotten-egg smell from the exhaust (all models/years).

Door seams, rocker panels, rear-wheel openings, and fender seams are particularly rust prone. Early BMWs were poorly rust-proofed and deteriorated very quickly, especially along the door bottoms and within the front- and rear-wheel wells. Check the muffler bracket for premature wear and weather seals and door adjustments for leaks.

1992–97—Peppy 4-cylinder acceleration, but only with high revs and a manual transmission. Keep in mind that city driving requires lots of manual gear shifting characterized by an abrupt clutch. If you must have an automatic, look for a used model with the 6-cylinder engine or see if you can get by with the larger 1.9L 4-cylinder that went into the mid-'96 models. 1997 models came with traction control.

Confidential dealer service bulletins confirm that the 1993 3 series has noisy, poorly performing AC, the cellular phone interferes with FM radio reception, doors don't close easily, accelerator pedals buzz and vibrate, there are excessive engine-compartment noises, the odometer display flickers, the radiator expansion tank seals leak, there is a rough idle caused by a loose or broken carbon canister, a rotten-egg odor comes from the exhaust, excessive brake vibrations are caused by Jurid brake pads, the reverse switch pins are defective, and the power windows malfunction.

Dealer service bulletins: 1994—Coolant leakage from the timing case profile gasket. • A binding/sticking ignition leading to starter failures. • Sagging convertible headliners. • Water leaking into the driver's side footwell and into the E-box area, flooding the DME control module. • Self-activating emergency flashers and flickering instrument lighting. • A rotten-egg smell caused by faulty catalytic converters. **1995**—Excessive brake squealing. • Insufficient interior air distribution. • Leaking door contact switches, binding air-distribution knobs, and noisy, ineffective wipers. **1996–97**—AC evaporator ices up. • ABS warning light glows for no reason. • CD skips when road surface is rough. • Delayed gear engagement or adapter case leak. • Electrical troubleshooting tips. • Electronic mobilizer malfunctions. • False alarms caused by glass breakage sensor. • General module malfunctions. • Noise from AC expansion valve on 318ti. • Noise from AC compressor area. • Sun visor pops out of clip. • Sunroof fails to close. • Transmission shudders. • Whistle noise when cooling fan runs on high speed. • Wind noise troubleshooting tips.

5 series
No problem with rear seat or cargo room with this Bimmer. Handling and ride are superb, although these weighty upscale models do strain when going over hilly terrain if they have the automatic gearbox. There was no 1996 version.

5-series owners report numerous electrical and fuel glitches, faulty turn signal indicators, starter failures, self-activating emergency flashers, rotten-egg odors from the exhaust, and excessive steering wheel/brake vibration. In 1993–94, BMW used a V-8 aluminum 4.0L engine designated as the M60 in its 540, 740, and 840 models. The engine was advertised as having a galnikal cylinder lining, which was to be wear resistant. Unfortunately, around 20,000 miles, many will experience chronic rough idling.

BMW knows that they have a problem and are working to fix it by raising the temperature of the engine from 185°F to 200°F. According to BMW, the idea is to burn off the sulfur. This applies to all M60 V8s, both the 4.0 and 3.0 liter, in the 5, 7, and 8 series cars. They've stopped selling these engines and are back to steel-lined cylinder sleeves, according to the November '95 edition of *BMW Magazine*. In addition, BMW has increased the warranty from 4 years/50,000 to 6 years/100,000 on all 1993–95 V8 engines. BMW has notified its owners that if they have a model made before April '95 they should come into a dealer to have the engine control system updated at no charge.

Dealer service bulletins: **1995**—AC belt tensioner noise. • Leaking door contact switches. • Faulty trunk lock actuator. • Noisy, ineffective wipers. **1996**—N/A. **1997 528 and 540**—Brakes momentarily won't release. • CD skips when road surface is rough. • Electronic mobilizer malfunctions. • Glove-box lock broken. • Radio with DSP switches off intermittently. • Right front door won't lock. • Wind noise troubleshooting tips.

Safety summary/recalls: **Recalls**: **1984**—Sudden acceleration on 318i models may be caused by a faulty engine idle control valve. • A binding heater control valve can cause the solenoid to malfunction, resulting in an instrument panel fire. **1984–91**—Leaks caused by a cooling-system malfunction will be corrected at no charge. **1985–86**—Supporting plates will be installed to reinforce the steering column. **1985–90**—Fuel-pump relay failures that cause no-starts require a new relay. **1986–87**—Faulty center-mounted brake light switch needs to be replaced. **1988 325iX**—A bent oil dipstick tube could prevent the throttle from returning to idle when the accelerator is released. **1991–92 318**—Ice buildup in the throttle housing can lead to increased idle speed or impaired deceleration. **1991 318 and 325**—Erratic wiper operation caused by an electrical short circuit. **1991 318i and 325iS**—The knee booster will be relocated so that it won't interfere with the steering column's absorption of crash forces. **1991 325i**—Faulty windshield-wiper-switch ground screw. **1991 325iX**—The transfer case leaking at the weep hole signals the need to revise the depth of the inner seal. **1992**—On 318 versions, a faulty cooling system may spray hot water into the interior. • **318i, 318iS, 325i, and 325iS**—Airbag may not deploy. **1992–93**—Fuel lines can harden and "set" over time. **1992–94 325i and 325iS and 1994 325C**—Brake light switch may fail. **1993–94 325i/is**—Defective front transmission crossmember support.

Secret Warranties/Service Tips

3 series: **1986–89**—A cracked intake manifold purge valve is a common problem. **1990–91 vehicles with E34 and M50 engines**—Cylinder head cover leaks require a new, upgraded cover (11-12-1-722-385 or 11-12-738-171 for later models). **1990–93**—Vehicles equipped with Jurid 506 brake pads may exhibit a steering vibration. **1992**—If the heater blower performs erratically, chances are the blower resistor unit needs replacing. **1994**—A starter motor failure may be caused by a faulty steering lock and electrical switch. • A sagging convertible headliner requires reinforced plastic clips that hold the headliner bracket to the bow. • Water intrusion into the driver's footwell area and the subsequent corrosion of the X13 and X14 connectors can be prevented by sealing off the hood's mounting flange just inboard of the left gas strut. • Water leaks into the E-box can be prevented by installing an improved capacity air intake drain hose in the right side drain, in addition to installing another drain hose. **1996**—Transmission shuddering requires the installation of a modified transmission control module. **1996–97**—Delayed gear engagement or adapter case leak requires the installation of new transmission seal kit (#21-41-422-762). **5 series**: **1989**—A fusible link could fail, shorting out all electrical power. **1990–93**—Change the Jurid 506 brake pads. **1990–94 525i, 1992–94 525iT, and 1994 530i and 530iT**—Brake light switch may fail. **1991**—Inoperative power accessories may require the installation of a Reinshagen general module (version 5.2 or later). **1991–92 525i and 535i**—Airbag may not deploy. **1993–94**—Emergency flashers may self-activate. • Tips on fixing starter motor failures. **7 series**: **1990–92 735i and 735iL, 1993–94 740i and 740iL, and 1990–92 750i**—Brake-light switch may fail. **1991–92 735i, 735iL, and 750iL**—Airbag may not deploy. **All models/years**—According to BMW, a rotten-egg smell coming from the exhaust is due to fuel impurities and can't be resolved by changing the catalytic converter. • BMW insiders tell me 3 Series engine head gasket failures are covered by a "goodwill" policy.

3 Series Profile

	1990	1991	1992	1993	1994	1995	1996	1997
Cost Price ($)								
318ti	—	—	—	—	—	25,295	26,180	26,535
318i 4d	—	20,275	23,275	25,420	26,720	27,645	30,120	30,745
Convertible	—	28,875	29,245	—	31,945	33,965	35,745	36,145
325i/328	25,695	26,700	30,265	32,055	33,350	34,120	36,410	36,845
Convertible	34,895	35,650	37,495	36,725	40,150	40,970	42,875	42,935
Used Values ($)								
318ti ↑	—	—	—	—	—	17,500	20,000	22,000
318ti ↓	—	—	—	—	—	16,000	18,000	21,000
318i 4d ↑	—	10,000	14,500	16,000	18,000	20,000	22,000	25,000
318i 4d ↓	—	8,500	13,000	14,500	16,500	18,500	20,500	23,000
Convertible ↑	—	13,000	15,500	—	23,000	25,000	28,000	31,000
Convertible ↓	—	12,000	14,000	—	21,000	23,500	26,000	29,000
325i/328 ↑	10,500	12,000	17,500	20,000	22,500	25,000	28,000	31,000
325i/328 ↓	9,000	11,000	15,500	18,000	20,500	23,000	26,000	29,000
Convertible ↑	14,500	16,000	21,000	23,000	29,000	32,000	35,000	37,000
Convertible ↓	13,000	14,000	18,500	21,500	27,500	30,000	33,000	36,000
Extended Warranty	Y	Y	N	N	N	N	N	N
Secret Warranty	N	N	N	N	N	N	N	N
Reliability	②	②	③	④	④	④	④	④
Air conditioning	②	②	②	②	②	③	④	④
Body integrity	②	②	③	③	③	③	④	④
Braking system	②	②	③	③	③	③	③	③
Electrical system	②	②	②	②	②	③	④	④
Engines	③	④	④	④	⑤	⑤	⑤	⑤
Exhaust/Converter	②	②	②	③	③	③	③	④
Fuel system	②	②	③	③	③	③	④	④
Ignition system	③	③	③	③	④	④	④	④
Manual transmission	③	③	③	④	⑤	⑤	⑤	⑤
- automatic	③	③	③	③	④	⑤	⑤	⑤
Rust/Paint	②	②	③	④	④	⑤	⑤	⑤
Suspension	④	④	④	④	④	⑤	⑤	⑤
Crash Safety								
325i	②	②	⑤	②	—	④	—	—
325i Convertible	—	—	—	—	⑤	—	—	—
328i	—	—	—	—	—	—	④	④

5 Series Profile

	1989	1990	1991	1992	1993	1994	1995
Cost Price ($)							
525i	37,325	34,245	35,600	37,975	38,355	39,775	40,125
535i	44,775	44,775	43,625	45,725	45,755	—	—
Used Values ($)							
525i ↑	15,000	16,500	18,500	20,500	22,000	25,000	28,000
525i ↓	13,000	15,000	16,500	18,500	20,000	22,000	26,000
535i ↑	17,000	18,500	20,500	22,500	25,000	—	—
535i ↓	14,500	17,500	18,500	21,000	22,500	—	—

Extended Warranty	Y	Y	Y	Y	Y	Y	Y
Secret Warranty	N	N	N	N	Y	Y	N
Reliability	❷	③	④	⑤	⑤	⑤	⑤
Air conditioning	❷	④	⑤	⑤	⑤	⑤	④
Body integrity	❷	③	③	③	③	③	④
Braking system	❷	❷	❷	③	③	③	④
Electrical system	❷	❷	③	③	③	③	④
Engines	④	④	④	⑤	⑤	⑤	⑤
Exhaust/Converter	③	③	③	③	③	③	④
Fuel system	③	③	③	③	④	④	⑤
Ignition system	③	③	③	④	④	④	⑤
Manual transmission	③	③	④	⑤	⑤	⑤	⑤
- automatic	③	③	③	④	⑤	⑤	⑤
Rust/Paint	❷	③	④	④	④	④	⑤
Suspension	④	④	④	④	⑤	⑤	⑤

GENERAL MOTORS

Aurora, Riviera, Toronado, Trofeo

Rating: Average (1995–97); Not Recommended (1986–94). GM skipped the '94 model year and introduced an all-new '95 version. **Aurora**: Above Average (1995). **Maintenance/Repair costs**: Higher than average, but repairs aren't dealer dependent. **Parts**: Higher-than-average cost (independent suppliers sell for much less), but not hard to find. Nevertheless, don't even think about buying one of the earlier front-drives without a three- to five-year supplementary warranty.

Technical Data

ENGINES	Liters/CID	HP	MPG	Model Years
OHV V6 FI	3.8/231	140–170	17–23	1986–93
OHV V6 FI	3.8/231	205	19–28	1995–97
OHV V6 FI*	3.8/231	225–240	17–26	1995–98
Aurora				
DOHC V8 FI	4.0/244	250	17–23	1995–96

*supercharged

Strengths and weaknesses: Although the redesigned 1988–93 cars got more horsepower and handling and ride upgrades, they kept the same low level of quality control with multiple design and manufacturing defects, including serious fuel injection, engine computer, and electrical-system problems. One particularly poor design was the complex Graphic Control Center, which used an oversensitive video screen and small push buttons. It's both distracting and expensive to repair. The automatic transmission is notoriously failure-prone, and brakes wear out prematurely and perform poorly. Surface rust and poor paint quality are the most common body complaints on all years. The dashboard control screen (Riviera) is awkward to use and dangerously distracting. Shock absorbers wear out quickly and the diesel engine seldom runs properly. Mechanical parts are easy to find, but body panels have to be ordered from GM at a premium.

The 1995–97 models offer lots more luxury features but continue their checkered repair history. GM improved the quality over the years, but generic deficiencies affecting the automatic transmission, engine, computer modules, suspension, and fit and finish make these cars less than luxury from a quality-control standpoint.

Dealer service bulletins: **1995**—Engine misfires, rough idle, white exhaust smoke, and a continuous spark knock. • Excessive oil consumption. • A cold-start rattle with the 4T60E automatic transmission. • A starter motor that runs continuously. • Reduced heater performance on the driver's side. • Brake vibration and/or pedal pulsation. • Instrument-panel trim may separate from the upper-trim pad. • Low voltage reading or dim lights at idle. • A scraping noise and increased effort to open the doors. • Inoperative fuel filler door. • ABS/traction light stays on. • Poor paint application and rust spots. **1996**—Second gear starts and erratic 1–3 shifts. • AC odor in humid climates. • Steering column noise. • Cold-start rattle noise. • Engine cranks but won't start. • Engine oil leaks. • Excessive vibration of electrochromic mirror. • Exterior light condensation. • Troubleshooting tips for fluttering, popping, ticking, and clunking noises. Gap between door opening weather strip and roof line. • Inoperative power door locks. • Intermittent Neutral/loss of Drive at highway speeds. • Instrument panel buzz or rattle when the brakes are applied. • Popping noise, growl or vibration when making a right turn. • Reduced heater performance on the driver's side. • Reduced retention of door trim lace. • Roof panel running front to back has a wavy/dimpled appearance and transmits excessive rain noise. • Underbody noise from rear of vehicle. • Wet or smelly carpet from water leaks. **1997**—Front brake noise. • Engine cranks but won't start. • Engine oil leaks. • Engine oil level indicates over-full. • Excessive vibration of electrochromic mirror. • Harsh shift from Reverse to Drive. • Inoperative power door locks. • Instrument panel buzz or rattle when the brakes are applied. • Popping noise, growl or vibration when making a right turn. • Steering vibration, shudder, or moan when parking. • Roof panel running front to back has a wavy/dimpled appearance and transmits excessive rain noise.

Aurora

This front-drive luxury sedan is aimed at the Acura, Infiniti, and Lexus crowd. It uses the same basic design as the Riviera but, fortunately, doesn't share the same major mechanical features or styling. The Aurora's main advantages are its sporty handling and unusual aero styling. In contrast to the Riviera and Toronado, the Aurora only seats five and uses the Cadillac 4.6L V8 Northstar engine. Acceleration is underwhelming (this is a heavy car) but adequate for highway touring. Road and wind noise is omnipresent and the rear trunk's small opening compromises the large trunk's ability to handle odd-sized objects.

Dealer service bulletins: 1995—White exhaust smoke, engine oil leak at the rear main seal or T joint, and loss of oil pressure or lack of power. • A popping noise is heard during cranking, or the starter motor continues to run or crank after shutoff. • Reduced heater performance on the driver's side. • Brake vibration and/or pedal pulsation. • A clicking noise emanating from the dash or hood, creak noise at the right side of vehicle, and a thumping from the rear of the vehicle. • Loose, rattling headliner and clicking emanating from the sunroof. • Excessive radio static. • Instrument-panel trim that may separate from the upper-trim pad. • Wet, smelly carpet from water leaks. • Wind noise at the front door A-pillar. 1996—Engine oil leaks from upper to lower crankcase joint. • Oil leakage from the oil pan to lower crankcase attaching bolts. • Loss of oil pressure and/or lack of power. • Steering column noise. • Popping noise from front of vehicle when turning. • Underbody noise from rear of vehicle. • Reduced heater performance. • Rear-compartment lid-assist rod separating from lid. • Gap between door opening weather strip and roof line. • Reduced retention of door trim lace. • Exterior light condensation. • Wet or smelly carpet from water leaks.

Safety summary/recalls: **Recalls**: 1986–87—The power-steering pump hose may leak, creating the possibility of an engine fire. 1989—ABS brakes may fail due to a faulty brake line. 1990—Faulty transmission cable may indicate that the wrong gear is engaged. 1990–93—Front shoulder seatbelt may stick in retractor. • Poorly aligned rear shoulder seatbelt retractor assemblies. 1992—Possible steering loss due to the disengagement of the steering shaft. 1996—Driver warning alarms and displays may malfunction. • Backfire can break the intake manifold and cause a fire.

Secret Warranties/Service Tips

1989–90—Stalling from a cold start and a chuggle at 44 mph require a new MEMCAL. 1990–91—A revised headrest guide loop will be installed on Rivieras if the shoulder seatbelt rests uncomfortably on the neck. 1990–93—An engine ticking at idle can be traced to rattling piston pins, which must be replaced with upgraded parts. 1991–93—Loss of Drive or erratic shifts may be caused by an intermittent short circuit to ground on the A or B shift solenoid, or an electrical short circuit in the transaxle. 1992–93—Harsh automatic transmission upshifts can be corrected by installing an upgraded accumulator valve in the control valve body. • A front-end engine knock troubleshooting chart and extensive diagnostic tips are found in DSB 306001. **1990–92 Toronado and Trofeo**—A body-mount creak that occurs whenever the vehicle passes over a bump may be due to one or more of the body mounts being poorly positioned in the frame; correct by installing a new lower insulator. • Chronic wind noise coming from the front-door window can be corrected by reinstalling the run channel retainer. • A shake or vibration in the front end when going over smooth roads may be caused by an internal leak in the engine mount. **1990–93**—An engine ticking at idle can be traced to rattling piston pins. **1991–92**—Harsh automatic transmission upshifts can be corrected by installing an upgraded accumulator valve in the control valve body. **1995–96**—Intermittent Neutral/loss of Drive at highway speeds can be fixed by replacing the control valve body assembly. **All models/years**—A rotten-egg odor coming from the exhaust is likely the result of a malfunctioning catalytic converter covered by GM's emissions warranty. • Paint delamination, peeling, or fading: See page 95.

Riviera, Toronado, Trofeo Profile

	1990	1991	1992	1993	1995	1996	1997
Cost Price ($)							
Riviera	25,985	26,250	27,080	28,120	28,857	30,715	31,375
Toronado	24,609	25,579	26,539	—	—	—	—
Trofeo	25,545	27,075	27,895	—	—	—	—
Used Values ($)							
Riviera ↑	7,500	9,000	10,500	12,500	16,500	20,000	24,000
Riviera ↓	7,000	8,000	9,500	11,000	15,000	18,000	22,000
Toronado ↑	7,000	8,500	9,500	—	—	—	—
Toronado ↓	5,500	7,000	8,000	—	—	—	—
Trofeo ↑	7,500	8,800	9,900	—	—	—	—
Trofeo ↓	6,000	7,500	9,500	—	—	—	—
Extended Warranty	Y	Y	Y	Y	Y	Y	Y
Secret Warranty	Y	Y	Y	Y	Y	Y	Y
Reliability	②	③	③	③	③	④	④
Air conditioning	③	③	④	④	④	④	④
Automatic transmission	②	②	③	③	③	③	③
Body integrity	②	②	②	②	③	③	③
Braking system	②	②	②	②	②	③	③
Electrical system	②	②	②	②	②	②	③
Engines	③	③	③	④	④	④	④
Exhaust/Converter	④	④	④	⑤	⑤	⑤	⑤
Fuel system	②	③	③	③	③	③	④
Ignition system	③	③	③	③	③	③	④
Rust/Paint	②	②	②	②	②	②	③
Steering	③	③	③	④	④	④	④
Suspension	②	③	③	③	③	④	④

Aurora Profile

	1995	1996	1997
Cost Price ($)			
Aurora	43,020	43,695	46,045
Used Values ($)			
Aurora ↑	24,500	29,000	34,000
Aurora ↓	22,000	26,500	31,000
Extended Warranty	Y	Y	Y
Secret Warranty	Y	Y	Y
Reliability	④	④	④
Crash Safety	—	③	—

Allanté, Catera, Eldorado, Seville

Rating: Below Average (1992–97); Not Recommended (1988–91). **Maintenance/Repair costs**: Higher than average, but repairs aren't dealer dependent. **Parts**: Higher-than-average cost (independent suppliers sell for much less), but not hard to find. Don't buy one of the front-drives without a three- to five-year supplementary warranty.

Technical Data

ENGINES	Liters/CID	HP	MPG	Model Years
OHV V8 FI	4.1/249	130	16–21	1986–87
OHV V8 FI	4.5/273	155	16–21	1988–89
OHV V8 FI	4.5/273	180	16–20	1990
DOHC V8 FI	4.6/279	270–300	16–20	1993–98
OHV V8 FI	4.9/300	200	16–20	1991–93

Strengths and weaknesses: The early Cadillacs are luxury embarrassments and later models barely pass muster. Even though most use the same mechanical components with the same deficiencies as the Riviera and Toronado models, they're far more failure-prone due to the complexity of their different luxury features.

Eldorado and Seville
From 1992 on, the Eldorado's styling became more distinctive, even though it shares most powertrain and chassis components with the Seville. Although the base 4.9L V8 provides brisk acceleration, the 32-valve Northstar V8, first found on the '93 Touring Coupe, gives you almost 100 more horses with great handling and a comfortable ride. Overall, the Touring Coupe or Sport Coupe will give you the best powertrain, handling, and braking features. Of course, you'll have to contend with poor fuel economy, limited rear visibility that's obstructed by the huge side pillars (a Seville problem, as well), confusing and inconvenient climate controls, and a particularly complex engine compartment.

Sitting on the same platform as the Eldorado, the Seville has European-style allure, with a more rounded body than the Eldorado. Apart from that, since its latest redesign in 1992, its engine, handling, and braking upgrades have followed in lockstep fashion the Eldorado's improvements.

Whether you buy a used Eldorado or Seville, keep in mind that the most improved versions came out with the '95 models. They carried on unchanged until their redesign for 1998. So, if you must buy one of these two models, remember that the only distinguishing difference between the two is styling not performance. Then you'll have to decide whether the Seville's styling is worth the extra $2,000–$3,000 it will cost you over the Eldorado.

The 4.1L V8 is best avoided. It may be simpler to work on but it, too, is fuel thirsty and easily overpowered by the Eldorado's weight. These cars have generic deficiencies that fall into the same categories: poorly calibrated and failure-prone engines, transmissions, and fuel and ignition systems; a multiplicity of electrical short circuits; and sloppy body assembly using poor-quality components.

Specifically, engines and fuel systems often produce intermittent stalling, rough idling, hesitation, and no-starts; the Overdrive automatic is prone to premature failure; oil pumps fail frequently; front brakes and shock absorbers wear out quickly; paint is often poorly applied, fades, or peels away prematurely; fragile body hardware breaks easily; and there are large gaps between sheet-metal panels and doors that are poorly hung and not entirely square. Other body problems include cracking of front outside door handles, door rattles (Eldorado), poor bumper fit, loose sun visor mounting, rear taillight condensation, fading and discoloring appliqué moldings (Seville), interior window fogging, "creaking" body mounts, water leaking into the trunk from the licence-plate holder (Eldorado), noisy roof panels and seat back lumbar motors, and a creaking noise at the upper-front-door hinge area.

Allanté
Introduced in 1987, the Allanté was essentially a "kit car" Cadillac 2-seat roadster with body components flown in from Italy and mechanicals assembled in Detroit. This car got the more powerful Northstar V8 in 1993—the same year it was discontinued. Originally selling for $77,475, an '87 model would fetch no more than $8,000 today. Does it have any value as a collector's item? Not a chance.

Owners report many reliability problems, especially with brake, electronic control, and powertrain glitches, and woefully poor-quality body assembly. Also, the convertible top is a chore to put up or down.

Catera
Assembled in Germany and based on the Opel Omega, the rear-drive, mid-size Catera comes with a 200-hp V6 engine, four-speed automatic transmission, 16-inch alloy wheels, 4-wheel disc brakes, a

limited-slip differential, traction control, and standard dual front airbags. Designed to compete with the BMW 328i, Lexus ES 300, and Mercedes Benz C280, GM hoped that its conservatively-styled '97 Catera—the uninspired styling has Lumina written all over it— won't drive away its more traditional "empty-nesters" (I guess that's a polite term for "old folks") while luring more baby boomers to its higher-performance variations.

The last time Cadillac introduced an entry-level model was in 1981 when the automaker launched the Cimarron, a fully-loaded, Chevrolet Cavalier-derived Cadillac that carried a $4,000 premium over the comparably equipped Cavalier. Back then, most auto critics and consumer advocates considered the Cavalier to be at the rear of the pack as far as performance and quality control were concerned. The Catera, on the other hand, has received good reviews from the European press for its quiet, spacious, and comfortable interior, responsive handling, precise steering, fine-tuned suspension, and almost nonexistent lean or body roll when cornering. Without a doubt, this is one Cadillac that's meant to be driven. On the downside, though, the controls aren't easy to figure out, some gauges are hard to read, and the driver's rear view is hindered by the large rear head restraints and narrow-back windshield. Furthermore, owners report chronic stalling and hard starts, possibly due to a malfunctioning idle control valve, constant warning-light illuminations, poor AM radio reception (requiring an additional amplifier), and loose interior panels. Two other performance problems reported by owners: when you pass over a large expansion joint the floorpan vibrates annoyingly; drive over a bump when turning and the steering wheel kicks back in your hands.

A few other points you may wish to consider: GM dealers are notoriously bad when it comes to understanding and repairing European-transplanted cars (just ask any Saab owner). As well, first-year cars don't generally have an adequate supply of replacement parts in the pipeline until their second or third year on the market. So get ready for long service waits and high parts costs for those repairs not covered under warranty. Finally, the fact that they're European-built doesn't necessarily mean that these Cadillacs will be reliable or durable. GM first learned that lesson with the British-built Vauxhall Firenza it unleashed on an unsuspecting public in the '70s. A few years later, it settled out of court several class actions that were piloted by this author, and paid a $20,000 fine to the federal government for misleading advertising. (On a nationally advertised road trip, GM said the cars excelled. Truth is, they required a team of engineers just to get started.)

Dealer service bulletins: 1993 models equipped with 3.8L or 4.9L engines—May be hard to start, frequently stall, lose power, and may not maintain the cruise control set speed. • Condensation in the taillights. • Radio static. • Excessive front-end vibrations when passing

over bumps. • Faulty engine oil pumps (Allanté only). •
Transmission gear whine and rear suspension noise. • **Eldorado**—
Squeaks and squealing after a cold start. • Warped windshield and
rear-window molding. **1994**—Faulty engine oil pumps and noisy
fuel pumps. • Engine oil leaks. • 4.6L engines may run roughly,
miss, surge, or hesitate. • Engine accessory belt noise. • An inoperative cruise control or brake/transmission interlock. • Erratic shifting. • AC hissing noise and rear suspension noise. • Condensation
dripping from the heater duct and poor heat distribution (driver's
feet get cold). • Doors won't stay open on slight grades and parking
brake binds. **1995**—Engine cranks but won't start; no fuel pressure;
loss of oil pressure, or lack of power. • Engine oil leak at the rear
main seal or T joint. • Starter motor runs continuously. • Lack of
power; loss of oil pressure. • Metallic knocking sound from the
engine. • A grinding or scraping noise in Park or Neutral. • Front
brake vibration and/or pedal pulsation. • Annoying AC odor. • A
low-voltage reading or dim lights at idle. • Remote keyless entry
malfunctions. • Rattle noise from front of vehicle, front-seat clicking noise, clicking noise from under the hood or dash, and rubbing noise when the front wheels are turned all the way. • Door
window slaps or rattles when closing door. • Excessive radio static. •
Wet or smelly carpet from water leaks. • Poor paint application and
rust spots. **1996**—Engine oil leaks from upper to lower crankcase
joint. • Loss of oil pressure and/or lack of power. • Oil leakage from
the oil pan to lower crankcase attaching bolts. • Second-gear starts,
poor 1–3 shifting. • Steering column noise. • Poor AC cooling in
traffic and high ambient temperatures. • Insufficient heat distribution or lack of air flow. • Coolant temperature gauge reads hot. •
Erratic or inaccurate instrument panel displays and gauges. •
Insufficient remote keyless entry operating range. • Positive battery
cable won't tighten properly. • Radio clock stuck on 12:00. • Radio
frequency interference diagnosis. • Whistle noise from HVAC. •
Exhaust rattles. • Rattling heard when vehicle goes over bumps. •
Clicking noise from front seats. • Squawk noise from rear of vehicle
in cold temperature. • Slow parking brake release or slow HVAC
mode changes. • Water leak from rear-door side-window area. • Wet
or smelly carpet from water leaks. • Abnormal condensation in taillights and other lights. • Faulty cup holders. **1997**—Front brake
noise. • Remote won't open doors or trunk. • Excessive vibration of
electrochromic mirror. • Fuel tank won't fill to capacity/always
reads full. • Horn hard to operate when cold. • Inoperative power
door locks. • Metallic buzz or rattle at the instrument panel when
the brakes are applied. • No warning light or driver-information-
center message. • Power window inoperative after express down feature is used. • Torque converter clutch buzz or moan.

Dealer service bulletins: **1997 Catera**—Brake squealing. • Clunk
noise from engine compartment on vehicles with cruise control. •

Ignition key binds, drags, or sticks in ignition. • Loose fuel cap. • Low voltage reading or dim lights at idle. • Noise in AM band of radio with rear defogger on. • Oil leak from engine timing cover. • Inoperative power door locks. • Inoperative rear defogger. • Windshield wiper slap/flop noise.

Safety summary/recalls: NHTSA probes: 1994 Seville—Owners report that the throttle may stick in the open or closed position. Dealers will modify the throttle control cable to secure it in place. Drivers also complain that the shoulder belt chafes at the neck and that the Eldorado's wide rear pillars obstruct their view to the right rear. • NHTSA is looking into dash-trim panels that fly apart when the airbag is deployed. • Excessive moisture in 1995–96 Eldorados and Sevilles—for example, due to a window left open when it rains—may cause the airbag to deploy when the ignition is switched on. There have been 70 reported incidents, 39 of them with injuries to drivers, passengers or both. GM has sent notices to car owners advising them to take precautions if their vehicle interiors become wet. (No, I haven't read the letter and I can't imagine what kind of precautions you can take.) **Recalls:** See comments on Riviera and Toronado. **1986–87**—Faulty headlight circuit. **1989**—ABS may be defective. **1990**—Gear indicator may be poorly aligned. • Faulty rear seatbelt shoulder retractors. **1990–91**—Front outer shoulder belt web may stick in retractor. **1992**—Possible loss of steering control. **1993 with 4.6L engine**—Fuel leakage in engine compartment. **1993–94 with 4.6L engine**—Leaking engine oil cooler hose may cause a fire. **1994**—Faulty throttle cable. **1995**—A short circuit caused by wet carpets could cause the airbags to deploy suddenly.

Secret Warranties/Service Tips

1990–94—A rear suspension squawk can be eliminated by installing upgraded stabilizer shaft insulators. **1991–95 Cadillacs with 4.9L engines**— GM will install a new computer chip that also reduces stalling, pursuant to an agreement with the U.S. Justice Department and the EPA. **1993**—DSB 476506 gives lots of tips on fixing 4.6L engines that run roughly, miss, surge, or hesitate. **1993–94**—DSB 476003 goes into great detail about troubleshooting the various engine oil leaks afflicting 1993–94 models. • Noisy fuel pumps can be silenced only by installing an upgraded fuel pump under warranty. • Poor heat distribution (driver's feet get cold) can be fixed by replacing the floor outlet assembly. **1994**—Condensation dripping from the heater duct requires the installation of a watertight dam in the HVAC case. • An inoperative cruise control or brake/transmission interlock may signal a maladjusted stop-light switch assembly. • A binding parking brake may need a new park-brake vacuum-release switch. **1996–97**—A torque converter clutch buzz or moan requires the installation of an upgraded case-cover-assembly spacer plate and the upper-control-valve body. **1997**—Excessive front-brake noise can be cured by installing upgraded front brake pads. **1997 Catera**—Brake squealing can be silenced by installing redesigned calipers. • Oil leakage from the engine timing cover can be corrected by installing a new oil pump gasket.

324   *Lemon-Aid*

Allanté, Catera, Eldorado, Seville Profile

	1990	1991	1992	1993	1994	1995	1996	1997
Cost Price ($)								
Allanté	51,550	55,250	58,470	61,675	—	—	—	—
Catera	—	—	—	—	—	—	—	33,635
Eldorado	30,875	32,380	33,720	35,240	38,565	39,505	41,020	39,883
Seville	33,780	34,975	36,225	38,240	42,265	43,220	44,420	41,883
Used Values ($)								
Allanté ↑	16,000	18,00	21,000	30,000	—	—	—	—
Allanté ↓	14,000	16,000	19,000	26,000	—	—	—	—
Catera↑	—	—	—	—	—	—	—	27,000
Catera ↓	—	—	—	—	—	—	—	24,000
Eldorado ↑	9,000	10,500	14,000	16,500	20,000	23,000	27,000	28,000
Eldorado ↓	7,500	9,000	12,500	15,000	17,500	21,000	25,000	26,000
Seville ↑	10,000	11,500	14,500	18,000	22,000	25,000	29,000	34,000
Seville ↓	8,500	10,000	13,000	16,500	20,000	23,000	27,000	31,000
Extended Warranty	Y	Y	Y	Y	Y	Y	Y	Y
Secret Warranty	N	Y	Y	Y	Y	Y	N	N
Reliability	②	②	②	②	②	②	③	③
Air conditioning	②	③	③	③	③	④	④	④
Automatic transmission	②	②	②	②	②	②	②	②
Body integrity	②	②	②	②	②	③	③	③
Braking system	②	②	②	②	②	②	③	③
Electrical system	②	②	②	②	②	②	③	③
Engines	③	③	③	③	③	③	②	③
Exhaust/Converter	②	②	②	③	③	④	④	⑤
Fuel system	②	②	③	③	③	③	③	③
Ignition system	②	②	②	②	②	③	③	③
Rust/Paint	②	②	②	②	②	②	③	③
Steering	②	②	②	②	④	④	④	④
Suspension	②	②	②	②	②	③	③	④

Note: Reliability figures only apply to the Eldorado and Seville; Allanté and Catera reliability information is given in the text. None of the above vehicles has been recently crash tested.

Concours, DeVille, Fleetwood (FWD)

Rating: Average (1994–97); Below Average (1988–93). **Maintenance/Repair costs**: Higher than average, and most repairs must be done by a dealer. After the 1992 model year, only the rear-drive Fleetwood remained (see following rating). **Parts**: Higher-than-average cost (independent suppliers sell for much less), but not hard to find. All of these front-drives require a three- to five-year supplementary warranty.

Technical Data

ENGINES	Liters/CID	HP	MPG	Model Years
OHV V8 FI	4.1/249	130	16–20	1985–87
OHV V6D FI	4.3/262	85	21–25	1985
OHV V8 FI	4.5/273	155	15–19	1988–89
OHV V8 FI	4.5/273	180	15–19	1990
OHV V8 FI	4.6/279	270–300	16–20	1994–98
OHV V8 FI	4.9/300	200	16–20	1991–98

Strengths and weaknesses: Although they have better handling and are almost as comfortable as the old series, these early model luxury coupes and sedans aren't worth considering because of their dismal reliability and overly complex servicing. Redesigned 1994–97 versions have posted fewer complaints; however, they are still far below the industry norm for quality and reliability. As with the Eldorado and Seville, you get the best array of handling, braking, and performance features with the '96 and later versions. They do ride more quietly and comfortably, but fuel economy is still poor, the dash controls and gauges are confusing and not easily accessible, and the rear view is obstructed by the high trunk lid and large side pillars.

The 4.1L, 4.3L, and 4.5L V8 engines and 4-speed automatic transmission suffer from a variety of terminal maladies including oil leaks, premature wear, poor fuel economy, and excessive noise. The electrical system and related components are temperamental. The suspensions go soft quickly and the front brakes often wear out after only 18 months/12,000 miles. The digital fuel-injection and engine-control systems are very difficult to diagnose and repair. Poor body assembly is characterized by premature paint peeling and rusting, excessive wind noise in the interior, and fragile trim items.

Dealer service bulletins: 1993 DeVille—Buzzing or whining 4L60 automatic transmissions. • Fuel tank popping during start-up. • Noisy fuel pumps and faulty engine oil pumps. • A noisy cooling fan, power-steering moaning, and rattles from the rear strut area. • Rear quarter-panel gaps. • Squeaks and squealing after a cold start and whistling when the AC is in re-circulate mode. **1994 (except Fleetwood)**—4.6L engines may run roughly, miss, surge, or hesitate. • Engine oil leaks. • Engine accessory belt noise and AC hissing. • Erratic shifting. • Inoperative cruise control or brake/transmission interlock. • Parking brake binding. • Condensation dripping from the heater duct and poor heat distribution (driver's feet get cold). • Doors won't stay open on slight grades. • Rear compartment water leaks. **1995–96**—Engine oil leaks from upper to lower crankcase joint. • Loss of oil pressure and/or lack of power. • Oil leakage from the oil pan to lower crankcase attaching bolts. • Poor AC cooling in traffic and high ambient temperatures. • AC defrost creaking noise.

• AC odors. • Steering column noise. • Insufficient heat distribution or lack of air flow. • Erratic or inaccurate instrument panel displays and gauges. • Insufficient remote keyless entry operating range. • Positive battery cable won't tighten properly. • Radio clock stuck on 12:00. • Radio frequency interference diagnosis. • Inaccurate fuel gauge. • Exhaust rattles. • Rattling heard when vehicle goes over bumps. • Clicking noise from front seats. • Squawk noise from rear of vehicle in cold temperature. • Slow parking brake release or slow HVAC mode changes. • Vertical seat height adjustment tips. • Abnormal condensation in taillights and other lights. • Wet or smelly carpet from water leaks. **1997**—Fuel tank won't fill to capacity/always reads   full. • Front brake noise. • Remote won't open doors or trunk. • Excessive vibration of electrochromic mirror. • Front-door front auxiliary weather strip loose. • Uncomfortable front seat back. • Horn hard to operate when cold. • Inoperative power door locks. • Metallic buzz or rattle at the instrument panel when the brakes are applied. • No warning light or driver-information-center message. • Power window inoperative after express down feature is used. • Torque converter clutch buzz or moan. **Concours**—Harsh suspension performance.

Safety summary/recalls: **NHTSA probes**: **1994–97 Cadillac DeVille**—Rear turn signal lights may not flash. **1995–96 DeVille and Concours**—A short circuit caused by wet carpets could cause the airbags to suddenly deploy. Excessive moisture in the vehicles—for example, due to a window left open when it rains—may cause the airbag to deploy when the ignition is switched on. **Recalls**: **1986**—Faulty headlight switch. **1986–87**—Anti-lock brake fluid may leak onto the pump motor and cause partial or complete loss of front or rear braking. **1991–93 DeVille with 4.9L engines**—Upper transaxle oil cooler hose could come loose and create a fire hazard. **1991–95 Cadillacs with 4.9L engines**—GM will install a new computer chip that also reduces stalling, pursuant to an agreement with the U.S. Justice Department and the EPA. **1994**—Engine oil cooler inlet hoses may be too close to the steering gear, causing it to leak and creating a fire hazard. **1994–95**—Accelerator pedal may stick. **1996**—Hood may fly up. **1997**—Faulty Brake Traction Control module could increase stopping distance.

Secret Warranties/Service Tips

1991–94—Loss of Drive or erratic shifts may be caused by an intermittent short to ground on the A or B shift solenoid, or an electrical short circuit in the transaxle. **1994**—Condensation dripping from the heater duct requires the installation of a watertight dam in the HVAC case. • An inoperative cruise control or brake/transmission interlock may signal a maladjusted stoplight switch assembly. • DSB 476003 goes into great detail about how to troubleshoot the various engine oil leaks afflicting '94 models. • Doors that won't stay open on slight grades require upgraded door springs.

• Noisy fuel pumps can be silenced only by installing an upgraded fuel pump under warranty. • DSB 476506 gives lots of tips on fixing 4.6L engines that run roughly, miss, surge, or hesitate. • Poor heat distribution (driver's feet get cold) can be fixed by replacing the floor outlet assembly. • Rear compartment water leaks are addressed in DSB 311510. **1994–96 with 5.7L engine**—A chuggle or surge condition will require a reflash calibration. **1994–96**—Excessive engine noise can be silenced by installing an upgraded valve-stem oil seal. **1995**—Intermittent Neutral/loss of Drive at highway speeds can be fixed by replacing the control valve body assembly. **1996–97**—A torque converter clutch buzz or moan requires the installation of an upgraded case-cover-assembly spacer plate and the upper-control-valve body. **All models/years**—Defective catalytic converters that cause a rotten-egg smell in the interior will be replaced free of charge under the emissions warranty. • Paint delamination, peeling, or fading: See page 95.

Concours, DeVille, Fleetwood Profile

	1990	1991	1992	1993	1994	1995	1996	1997
Cost Price ($)								
DeVille	29,931	31,925	32,910	34,160	34,440	36,320	37,420	38,445
Concours	—	—	—	—	37,215	40,935	41,135	42,660
Fleetwood	34,090	36,095	37,530	—	—	—	—	—
Used Values ($)								
DeVille ↑		9,000	10,500	12,000	14,000	18,000	22,000	25,000	28,000
DeVille ↓		7,500	9,000	10,500	12,500	16,500	20,000	23,000	26,000
Concours ↑	—	—	—	—	19,500	24,000	27,000	30,000
Concours ↓	—	—	—	—	18,000	22,000	25,000	28,000
Fleetwood ↑	9,500	11,500	13,000	—	—	—	—	—
Fleetwood ↓	8,000	9,500	11,500	—	—	—	—	—
Extended Warranty	Y	Y	Y	Y	Y	Y	Y	Y
Secret Warranty	N	N	N	Y	Y	Y	Y	Y
Reliability	❷	❷	❷	❷	❷	③	③	③
Air conditioning	❷	❷	❷	❷	❷	❷	❷	③
Automatic transmission	❷	❷	③	③	③	③	③	④
Body integrity	❷	❷	❷	❷	❷	❷	③	③
Braking system	❷	❷	❷	❷	❷	❷	③	③
Electrical system	❷	❷	❷	❷	❷	❷	③	③
Engines	❷	❷	③	③	③	③	④	④
Exhaust/Converter	③	③	③	③	③	④	④	④
Fuel system	❷	❷	❷	❷	③	③	③	③
Ignition system	❷	❷	❷	❷	③	③	③	③
Rust/Paint	❷	❷	❷	❷	❷	③	④	④
Steering	❷	❷	❷	❷	③	④	④	④
Suspension	❷	❷	❷	❷	③	③	④	④
Crash Safety								
DeVille	❶	⑤	⑤	❶	❶	—	③	④
Side Impact								
DeVille	—	—	—	—	—	—	—	④

Note: The DeVille's low scores represent severe leg trauma measured in 1990, 1993, and 1994.

Brougham, Fleetwood (RWD)

Rating: Above Average (1995–96); Average (1988–94). **Maintenance/Repair costs**: Average, and repairs aren't dealer dependent. **Parts**: Reasonably priced (independent suppliers sell for much less) and not hard to find.

Technical Data

ENGINES	Liters/CID	HP	MPG	Model Years
OHV V8 FI	4.1/249	135	13–16	1985
OHV V8 FI	5.0/305	170	15–19	1991–92
OHV V8 4 bbl.	5.0/307	140	15–18	1986–90
OHV V8 FI	5.7/350	175–185	13–17	1990–93
OHV V8 FI	5.7/350	260	14–17	1994–96
OHV V8D FI	5.7/350	105	20–23	1985

Strengths and weaknesses: The quintessential land yacht, these cars emphasize comfort over handling with their powerful engines and large chassis. The most serious problem areas are the fuel-injection system, which frequently malfunctions and costs an arm and a leg to repair; automatic transmissions that shift erratically; a weak suspension; computer module glitches; poor body assembly; and paint defects. From a reliability/durability standpoint, the rear-drives are slightly better made than their front-drive counterparts.

GM dealer service bulletins show that these vehicles also have noisy power-steering units and cooling fans, the AC bi-level mode produces extreme temperature differences, the instrument panel squeaks and rattles, there are rear-quarter-panel gaps and rusting at the rear-side-door window molding, and water leaks into the passenger side of the front compartment.

Safety summary/recalls: **Recalls**: **1984–88**—A sticking throttle could lead to sudden acceleration. **1986**—Vehicles with a 5.0L engine could also have a sticking throttle. **1987**—Cars equipped with an automatic transmission could start in gear or engage the wrong gear. **1993**—Passenger-side airbag may have a defective igniter. **1994**—Oil-cooler inlet hose leaks. • Lug nuts may loosen. • Fuel-tank strap fasteners can detach. **1994–95**—Throttle control spring may stick in low temperatures.

Secret Warranties/Service Tips

1993 Fleetwood—Noisy transmissions, power-steering units, and cooling fans. • AC bi-level mode produces extreme temperature differences. • Instrument panel squeaks and rattles. • Rusting at the rear-side-door-window molding. • Water leaks into the passenger side of the front compartment. **1994 Fleetwood and Brougham**—Instrument panel displays that are too dim. GM installed an upgraded cluster in mid-1994. • Intermittent loss of power door locks, seats, and mirrors due to a short circuit in the door lock circuit. **1995**—A popping noise during cranking, the engine cranks but won't start, no fuel pressure, or extended crank time after cold soak. • Lack of power. • Engine oil leak at the rear main seal or T joint. • Low oil pressure, loss of oil pressure, or lack of power. • AC odor. • Grinding or scraping noise in Park or Neutral (Concours). • A cold-start rattle with the 4T60E automatic transmission. • Front-brake vibration and/or pedal pulsation. • A rubbing noise when the front wheels are turned all the way. • Door window scraping noise or sticking, rattle noise from front of vehicle, and excessive radio static. • A clicking noise from under the dash or hood (Concours). • A front-seat clicking noise. • Erroneous fuel gauge readings, a low voltage reading or dim lights at idle, and frequent blown fuse or battery drain. • Malfunctioning remote keyless entry. • Wet or smelly carpet from water leaks. • Poor paint application and rust spots. **1996 Fleetwood Brougham**—3–2 part throttle downshift flare. • Engine noise (install new valve stem oil seal). • Transmission chuggle/surge. • Transmission fluid leak from pump body (replace bushing). • Crunch/pop noise in steering system. • AC odors. • Radio frequency interference diagnosis. **All models/years**—Defective catalytic converters that cause a rotten-egg smell in the interior will be replaced free of charge under the emissions warranty. • Paint delamination, peeling, or fading: See page 95.

Brougham, Fleetwood (RWD) Profile

	1990	1991	1992	1993	1994	1995	1996
Cost Price ($)							
Brougham/Fleet	30,128	31,375	32,910	35,160	35,185	37,015	38,420
Used Values ($)							
Brougham/Fleet ↑	8,500	10,000	11,500	14,000	17,500	21,000	25,000
Brougham/Fleet ↓	7,000	8,500	10,000	13,500	16,000	19,000	22,000
Extended Warranty	Y	Y	Y	Y	Y	Y	Y
Secret Warranty	N	N	N	Y	Y	Y	Y
Reliability	③	③	③	③	③	③	④
Air conditioning	③	③	③	③	③	③	④
Automatic transmission	②	②	②	②	②	③	③
Body integrity	②	②	②	③	③	③	③
Braking system	②	②	②	③	③	③	③
Electrical system	②	②	②	②	②	②	②
Engines	③	③	③	③	③	③	③
Exhaust/Converter	②	②	②	②	③	③	④
Fuel system	②	②	②	③	③	③	③
Ignition system	②	②	②	③	③	③	③
Rust/Paint	②	②	②	③	③	③	③
Steering	②	②	②	③	④	④	④
Suspension	②	②	②	③	③	③	③

Note: Neither the Brougham nor the Fleetwood have been crash tested.

INFINITI

G20, I30, J30, Q45

Rating: Above Average. The fully equipped Maxima, Accord, Camry, Avalon, Millenia, and 929 are better buys from a price/quality standpoint, but they don't have the same luxury cachet. **Maintenance/Repair costs**: Higher than average, and they must be done by either an Infiniti or a Nissan dealer. **Parts**: Higher-than-average cost, but not hard to find (except for body panels).

Technical Data

ENGINES	Liters/CID	HP	MPG	Model Years
ES 250, 300				
DOHC V6 FI	2.5/153	156	17–23	1990–91
DOHC V6 FI	3.0/181	185–88	17–22	1992–96
DOHC V6 FI	3.0/181	200	17–22	1997–98
GS 300				
DOHC V6 FI	3.0/183	220	15–19	1993–97

Strengths and weaknesses: With its emphasis on sporty handling, the Infiniti series takes the opposite tack from the Lexus, which puts the accent on comfort and luxury. Still, the Infiniti comes fully equipped and offers owners the prestige of driving a comfortable, reliable, and nicely styled luxury car. One serious weakness, however, is the 1993 airbag-equipped J30's poor crash rating—all the more surprising when one considers that the 1992 Nissan Maxima passed the NHTSA 35-mph crash tests with flying colours.

G20

The least expensive Infiniti, the G20 is a front-drive luxury sports sedan that uses a base 2.0L 140-hp 16-valve, twin-cam, 4-cylinder powerplant to accelerate smoothly, albeit noisily, through all gear ranges. It does this while delivering 24 miles to a gallon of gasoline. Dual airbags came on line midway through the 1993 model year and ABS is standard. Towing capacity is 1,000 lbs. Cruise control is a bit erratic, particularly when traversing hilly terrain. The automatic transmission is silent and engine power is reduced automatically when shifting. Steering is precise and responsive under all conditions. However, the rear end tends to swing out sharply following abrupt steering changes. Early Infinitis rode a bit too firmly, leading to a softening of the suspension on the '94 model. Now drivers say that the suspension tends to bounce and jiggle occupants whenever the car goes over uneven pavement or the load is increased.

Overall, however, the Infiniti models aren't as refined as the Lexus in interior space, drivetrain, or convenience features. Owners have complained that the engine's lack of low-speed torque means that it has to work hard above 4,000 rpm—while protesting noisily—to produce brisk engine response in the higher gear ranges. The automatic transmission shifts roughly, particularly when passing (a problem corrected in the '94 models); the power steering needs more assist during parking maneuvers; and the dealer-installed fog lights cost an exorbitant $500 to replace. Poorly thought-out control layout is best exemplified by the hard-to-reach heat/vent controls, an armrest-mounted trunk and filler release that's inconvenient to operate, and center-console-mounted power window switches that are hard to find while driving. Tall drivers will find the leg room insufficient. The trunk is spacious, but its small opening is limited by the angle of the rear window.

There are three helpful bulletins containing troubleshooting tips for AC compressor leaks and noise, Code 45 driveability alerts, and brake shudder and steering wheel shimmy.

J30

Resembling the 929 Serenia, the rear-drive, four-door J30, and its high-performance variant, the I30, are sized and priced midway between the G20 and the top-of-the-line Q45. It uses a modified version of the Nissan 300ZX's 3.0L 210-hp V6 engine. Although the J30 is replete with important safety features and accelerates and handles well, its engine is noisy, passenger and cargo room have been sacrificed to styling, and fuel economy hovers around 16 mph in the city.

The J30 comes with a standard airbag, ABS, and traction control. It's changed very little over the years, meaning that there's no reason to choose a more recent model over a much cheaper older version. Consider buying an Acura Legend, Lexus ES 300, or a fully equipped Accord, Maxima, 929, Cressida, or Camry.

Dealer service bulletins list the following two defects affecting the '95s: a front seat rattling noise and a loose B-pillar lower finisher. For all J30 model years, there are a number of other helpful bulletins containing troubleshooting tips for AC compressor leaks and noise, brake clunking noises and pedal pulsation, hard starts, rough idle, water leaks, Code 45 driveability alerts, and brake shudder and steering wheel shimmy.

Q45

This luxury sedan provides performance while its chief rival, the Lexus ES 400, provides luxury and quiet. Faster and glitzier than other cars in its category, the Q45 uses a 32-valve 278-hp 4.5L V8 tire burner not frequently found on a Japanese luxury compact. It accelerates faster than the Lexus, going 0–60 mph in 7.1 seconds without a hint of noise or abrupt shifting. Unlike the base G20, though, the Q45's engine supplies plenty of upper-range torque as well. The suspension was softened in '94, but the car still rides much more firmly than its Lexus counterpart. The 4-wheel steering is precise, but the standard limited-slip differential is no help in preventing the car's rear end from sliding out on slippery roads, due mainly to the original equipment "sport" tires designed mainly for 130-mph Autobahn cruising. There's not much foot room for passengers and cargo room is disappointing. Fuel economy is nonexistent. ABS is standard, but a passenger-side airbag wasn't available before 1994. A redesigned '94 version got a restyled front end, chrome grill, and an updated instrument panel. Three years later, the car was again made over with the addition of a downsized 4.1L V8 set on a smaller platform.

Owners report excessive wind noise around the A-pillars, sunroof wind leaks, tire thumping noise, cellular telephone echoing, faulty CD players, and a popping sound coming from the radio.

Dealer service bulletins list the following defects affecting the '95s: AC not blowing cold, front brake pad noise, low or rough idle, and inside-edge tire wear. You may also be interested in reviewing other helpful bulletins containing troubleshooting tips for AC compressor leaks and noise, brake clunking noises and pedal pulsation, hard starts, rough idle, suspension noise, Code 45 driveability alerts, and brake shudder and steering wheel shimmy.

Safety summary/recalls: **NHTSA probes**: **1991 Q45**—NHTSA is looking into reports of fires that may ignite in or around rear stereo speakers. **Recalls**: **1991–92 G20**—Rear seatbelt buckle may only partially engage. **1991–96**—Possible fuel leakage from a corroded fuel filler tube. **1993–95**—Harness connector protector near seatbelt pre-tensioner can ignite. **1993–95 G20 and 1993 and 1994 J30**—Cabin may catch fire in a collision.

Secret Warranties/Service Tips

1991 G20—An intermittent slip of the sunroof motor requires the installation of an improved motor assembly. • Noisy 2–3 shifting requires the installation of a countermeasure input shaft and an improved high clutch assembly with less free play. • Reverse gear blocking can be corrected by installing an improved Reverse idle gear set. **1991–92**—If the engine's timing chain rattles, install an upgraded chain tensioner (#13070-53J03). • If the air conditioner emits a stale odor or blows out small white flakes, Infiniti will install an improved evaporator core that should correct the problem. **1991–94**—Condensation may prevent the CD player from reading the CD. The only recourse is to wait until the optic sensor dries (10–20 minutes; longer for trunk-mounted players). **All models/years**—Troubleshooting tips to correct hard starts. • Vehicles with sunroofs may have wind noise coming from the sunroof area because of a small pinhole in the body sealer at the rear C-pillar. • Windshield cracking. **1990 Q45**—An idle vibration felt through the steering, floor, and seat can be corrected by idle adjustments. • Air and wind noise coming from the windshield, dash, or A-pillar may be corrected by resealing the problem areas. • The following noises require the following repairs according to DSB ITB90-039: valve ticking—replace valves/guides; front engine block knocking—

replace tensioners; tapping from valves during warm-up—replace pivot/rocker; tapping from valves at all times—check cam bearings. **1990–91**—Front-suspension clicking may require that the shock-absorber upper bushing be re-greased. • A driveline vibration or drone at moderate speeds can be eliminated by installing a new balance propshaft assembly. • Takata seatbelt replacement. **1991**—Reports of transmission overheating and failures have forced Infiniti to extend the warranty to 7 years in order to compensate owners whose transmissions have insufficient cooling and filtration. Furthermore, the company will install an external cooler and filter at no charge. **All models/years**—Erratic operation of the power antenna requires that the antenna rod be replaced.

G20, I30, J30, Q45 Profile

	1991	1992	1993	1994	1995	1996	1997
Cost Price ($)							
G20	18,650	19,585	22,750	25,625	26,625	27,630	—
I30	—	—	—	—	—	32,000	30,395
J30	—	—	34,450	37,400	39,000	40,400	36,245
Q45	40,385	42,385	45,850	50,900	52,850	54,000	48,395
Used Values ($)							
G20 ↑	9,000	10,000	11,500	12,500	14,500	16,500	—
G20 ↓	8,000	9,000	10,500	11,500	13,000	15,000	—
I30 ↑	—	—	—	—	—	22,000	24,000
I30 ↓	—	—	—	—	—	20,000	22,000
J30 ↑	—	—	16,000	18,000	21,000	23,000	26,000
J30 ↓	—	—	14,500	16,500	19,000	21,000	24,000
Q45 ↑	15,000	16,500	18,500	25,000	27,000	31,000	38,000
Q45 ↓	13,000	15,000	17,000	22,000	25,000	29,000	35,000
Extended Warranty	N	N	N	N	N	N	N
Secret Warranty	N	N	N	N	N	N	N
Reliability	②	③	③	④	④	⑤	⑤
Air conditioning	②	③	③	③	⑤	⑤	⑤
Automatic transmission	②	②	③	③	④	⑤	⑤
Body integrity	②	②	③	③	③	③	④
Braking system	②	②	②	②	③	③	③
Electrical system	②	②	③	③	③	③	③
Engines	⑤	⑤	⑤	⑤	⑤	⑤	⑤
Exhaust/Converter	③	③	③	⑤	⑤	⑤	⑤
Fuel system	③	③	④	④	④	④	④
Rust/Paint	③	③	⑤	⑤	⑤	⑤	⑤
Steering	②	③	④	④	⑤	⑤	⑤
Suspension	③	③	③	⑤	⑤	⑤	⑤
Crash Safety							
J30	—	—	—	②	④	④	④
Side Impact							
J30	—	—	—	—	—	—	④

LEXUS

ES 250, ES 300, LS 400, SC 400

Rating: Recommended (1991–97). A bit more reliable and better built than the Infiniti, but more costly too. A fully equipped Legend, Accord, Maxima, Camry, Taurus, or Sable will provide airbags, comparable highway performance, and reliability at far less initial cost. But if you do pay top dollar for a used Lexus, its slow rate of depreciation virtually guarantees that you'll get much of your money back. **Maintenance/Repair costs**: Higher than average, and repairs must be done by either a Lexus or Toyota dealer. **Parts**: Higher-than-average cost, but not hard to find (except for body panels).

Technical Data

ENGINES	Liters/CID	HP	MPG	Model Years
		G20		
DOHC I-4 FI	2.0/122	140	21–27	1991–96
		J30		
DOHC V6 FI	3.0/181	210	17–22	1993–97

Strengths and weaknesses: Like the Acuras and Infinitis, Lexus models all suffer from some electrical, body, trim, and accessory deficiencies that are confirmed by confidential dealer service bulletins.

ES 250

The ES 250's 32-valve V8 engine gives exceptional, smooth acceleration and gets 19 mpg. The 4-speed Overdrive transmission makes subtle changes by reducing the engine power just before shifting. Trailers of up to 2,000 lbs. can be towed by cutting out Overdrive. One of the best-riding front-drive cars money can buy, the ES 250's seating offers plenty of support and a comfortable driving position that can be automatically adjusted for two drivers. Braking and handling aren't very impressive, however.

ES 300

Resembling an LS 400 dressed in sporty attire, the ES 300 was launched in 1992 to fill the gap between the ES 250 and the LS 400. In fact, the ES 300 has many of the attributes of the LS 400 sedan for much less money. A five-passenger sedan based on the Camry, it comes equipped with a standard 3.0L 24-valve engine that produces 181 horsepower coupled to either a 5-speed manual or a 4-speed electronically controlled transmission. Unlike the Infinitis, the ES 300 accelerates smoothly and quietly, while averaging about 20 mpg in mixed driving. The suspension is soft and steady. Passenger and cargo room is plentiful, with lots of leg and head room (except on sunroof-equipped versions). ABS is standard, but a second airbag is available only on the '94 model. Moon-roof wind noise is a common problem addressed in dealer service bulletins.

Dealer service bulletins: 1995–96 ES 300—Ambient temperature displays –220⁰ C. • CD changer won't eject magazine. • Direct clutch improvements. • Front brake groan. • Moon-roof-panel wind noise. • Static noise on weak AM stations.

LS 400

The Lexus flagship, the LS 400 rear-drive outclasses all other luxury sedans in reliability, styling, and function. The base engine is a 242-hp 4.0L V8 that provides smooth, impressive acceleration and superior highway passing ability at all speeds. Its transmission is smooth and efficient. The suspension gives an easy ride without body roll or front-end plow during emergency stops, thereby delivering a major comfort advantage over other luxury compacts. There's an absence of engine and wind noise. ABS and dual airbags are standard.

Owners have complained that the brakes don't inspire confidence, owing to their mushy feel and average performance. Furthermore, there's limited rear foot room under the front seats, and the rear-middle passenger has to sit on the transmission hump. This car is a gas guzzler that thirsts for premium fuel.

GS 300

This four-door luxury sedan fits right in between the top-of-the-line LS 400 and the entry-level ES 300. It has all the bells and whistles seen with most of the other Lexus offerings, plus, a new 5-speed automatic transmission that went into the 1996 models. Although the GS 300 handles very well and is more reasonably priced than the LS 400, its six-cylinder powerplant is a bit sluggish in accelerating, fuel economy isn't very good, and the driveline hump limits comfortable rear seating to two adults. Furthermore, the short trunk's utility is compromised and rear visibility is restricted by the large side rear pillars and narrow rear windshield. May make you wonder whether the price savings were worth it. It might be a better idea to consider the following vehicles that compete well with the GS 300: BMW's 3 Series, the Ford Taurus SHO, Crown Victoria, or Mercury Grand Marquis, the Infiniti J30, Volvo 850, or Mercedes' C Class and E Class models.

SC 300, 400

These two coupes are pratically identical, except for their engines and luxury features. The cheaper SC 300 gives you the same high-performance six-cylinder engine used by the GS 300 and Toyota Supra, while the SC 400 uses the same 4.0L V8 engine found in the LS 400. You're likely to find fewer luxury features with the SC 300 because they were sold as options. Nevertheless, look for an SC with traction control for additional safety during poor driving conditions. On the downside, V8 fuel consumption is horrendous, rear seating is cramped, and trunk space is unimpressive. Also, invest in a good anti-theft device, or your Lexus relationship will be over almost before it begins.

Dealer service bulletins: **1995 LS 400**—Engine knocking, front seat cushion noise, front stabilizer bushing noise, strut bar cushion noise, and sun visor rattling. **1995 SC300 and SC400**—Rear suspension rattling or clacking, probably caused by a faulty rear spring bumper (replace with an upgraded spring bumper). **1996**—Ambient temperature displays –220⁰ C. • Front brake groan. • Static noise on weak AM stations.

Safety summary/recalls: **Recalls**: **NHTSA probes**: **1990–91 ES 250**—Fuel tank leak. **1990 400**—Cruise control may not return to its former position. • Prolonged illumination of the center-mounted brake light. **1993–94 GS 300**—Premature ball joint wear could affect steering and handling. An upgraded ball joint socket will be installed. **1995–97 LS 400 and 1996–97 SC 400**—A faulty starter-motor magnetic switch may cause a fire or render the starter inoperative.

Secret Warranties/Service Tips

1990 ES 250—To reduce front brake squeaks, Lexus has changed the rotors (#43517-32020). **1990–91**—Front brake squeaking can also be reduced by using revised brake pads (#04491-32390). **1991**—Cellular-telephone-antenna wind noise can be eliminated by installing a newly designed antenna. • A cruise control that cancels after setting needs a filter circuit added to the cruise control ECU. **1992 ES 300**—Inaccurate fuel gauges require an improved indicator needle. **1992–93**—Sun visor rattles can be fixed by using the Lexus Squeak and Rattle Repair Kit. • Rear brake squeaks can be reduced by using upgraded rear brake pads. • Rear stabilizer bar bushing noise can be eliminated by installing upgraded bushings. **1993**—Problems with hot start or poor engine performance when going downhill require the installation of an upgraded ECM. • Front seat headrest rattles can be corrected by installing an improved headrest support. **1992 SC 300/SC 400**—Popping from the Nakamichi radio has been eliminated with an upgraded model containing improved volume control resistors. **1990 LS 400**—Front brake popping can be corrected by installing a modified pad support plate and applying new adhesive. • Moon-roof wind noise may be corrected by realigning the roof panel. • Faulty cruise control assemblies will be replaced with an improved assembly (SSC 901). • Warped center high-mounted brake-light housings will be replaced free under a goodwill program (SSC 902). **1990–91**—A difficult-to-open rear door may be reduced by modifying the rear door check arm. • To prevent transmission clicking when shifting from Neutral to Drive or Reverse, reduce the depth of the flange yoke assembly. • Windshield upper molding noise requires that the molding be changed and a thicker adhesive tape applied. • AC groaning can be eliminated by reducing the expansion valve flow rate and adding an O-ring to the EPR piston.

ES 250, ES 300, LS 400, SC 400 Profile

	1991	1992	1993	1994	1995	1996	1997
Cost Price ($)							
ES 250	24,500	—	—	—	—	—	—
ES 300	—	28,650	31,030	31,070	34,180	34,895	33,045
GS 300	—	—	40,130	40,370	45,380	48,445	48,595
LS 400	41,650	43,600	48,030	50,370	52,680	54,445	54,495
SC 400	—	39,100	42,730	45,570	49,780	53,845	52,295
Used Values ($)							
ES 250 ↑	10,000	—	—	—	—	—	—
ES 250 ↓	8,500	—	—	—	—	—	—
ES 300 ↑	—	16,000	19,000	21,000	24,000	27,000	30,000
ES 300 ↓	—	15,000	17,000	19,000	22,000	25,000	28,000
GS 300 ↑	—	—	22,000	25,000	28,000	32,000	35,000
GS 300 ↓	—	—	20,000	23,000	26,000	30,000	33,000
LS 400 ↑	20,000	23,000	26,000	28,000	37,000	41,000	46,000
LS 400 ↓	18,000	21,000	24,000	26,500	35,000	38,000	44,000
SC 400 ↑	—	23,000	25,500	28,000	33,000	37,000	42,000
SC 400 ↓	—	21,000	23,500	26,000	29,000	35,000	40,000
Extended Warranty	N	N	N	N	N	N	N
Secret Warranty	N	N	N	N	N	N	N
Reliability	④	④	④	⑤	⑤	⑤	⑤
Air conditioning	③	④	⑤	⑤	⑤	⑤	⑤
Automatic transmission	③	④	⑤	⑤	⑤	⑤	⑤
Body integrity	❷	③	④	⑤	⑤	⑤	⑤
Braking system	❷	❷	❷	❷	❷	③	④
Electrical system	③	③	③	④	④	④	④
Engines	④	④	④	⑤	⑤	⑤	⑤
Exhaust/Converter	⑤	⑤	⑤	⑤	⑤	⑤	⑤
Fuel system	④	④	⑤	⑤	⑤	⑤	⑤
Ignition system	④	⑤	⑤	⑤	⑤	⑤	⑤
Rust/Paint	⑤	⑤	⑤	⑤	⑤	⑤	⑤
Steering	④	⑤	⑤	⑤	⑤	⑤	⑤
Suspension	❷	❷	③	⑤	⑤	⑤	⑤
Crash Safety							
ES 250	⑤	—	—	—	—	—	—
ES 300	—	—	—	—	—	⑤	—
GS 300	—	—	—	⑤	③	—	③

LINCOLN

Continental, Mark VII, Mark VIII, Town Car

Rating: **Continental**—Average (1995–97); Below Average (1988–94).
Mark VII/VIII—Above Average (1993–97); Average (1992); Below
Average (1986–91). **Town Car**—Above Average (1990–97); Average
(1988–89). Redesigned for 1998. **Maintenance/Repair costs**: Higher
than average, and they must be done by a Lincoln dealer. **Parts**:
Higher-than-average cost, but not hard to find (except for electronic components and body panels).

Technical Data

ENGINES	Liters/CID	HP	MPG	Model Years
		Continental		
OHC 1-6TD FI	2.4/149	115	22–27	1985
OHV V6 FI	3.8/232	140	17–22	1988–90
OHV V6 FI	3.8/232	155–160	16–20	1991–94
OHV V8 FI	5.0/302	140–200	14–19	1985–95
OHV V8 FI	5.0/302	225	14–20	1988–92
DOHC V8 FI	4.6/281	260	14–21	1995–98
		Mark VII		
OHV V8 FI	5.0/302	225	13–17	1988–92
		Mark VIII		
DOHC V8 FI	4.6/281	280–290	14–18	1993–98
		Town Car		
OHV V8 FI	5.0/302	150	14–16	1986–90
OHC V8 FI	4.6/281	190–210	14–18	1991–97

Strengths and weaknesses: These large luxury cruisers are proof
that quality isn't proportional to the money you spend. Several
designer series offer all the luxury options anyone could wish for,
but the two ingredients most owners would expect to find—high
quality and consistent reliability—are sadly lacking, especially when
it comes to the automatic transmission, electrical system, brakes,
body hardware, and fit and finish.

These cars aren't lemons (at least the later models aren't), but
they don't offer the kind of trouble-free driving one would normally expect in a new vehicle selling for over $40,000. The automatic
leveling air-spring suspension system makes for a stiff ride (especially on early models), while still allowing the Continental to "por-
poise" due to its heavy front end. The anemic V6 powertrain is
poorly suited to a car of this heft. The engine hesitates in cold
weather and the automatic transmission shifts roughly due to malfunctioning computer modules.

Major mechanical defects affect the engine (frequent flywheel replacements), transmission, ABS, electrical, suspension, and steering systems, and electronic modules. The mass of electrical gadgets increases the likelihood of problems as the cars age. For example, automatic headlight doors fail frequently, and the electronic antenna seldom rises to the occasion. The computerized dashboard is particularly failure prone.

Other reliability complaints concern transmission fluid leakage due to misplaced bolts, rough upshifting caused by a defective valve body, and air conditioning and heating that sometimes work in reverse order (you often get heat when opening the AC and air conditioning frequently comes on when the heater is engaged).

Continental (front-drive)

When the Continental went front-drive in 1988, it made a bad situation worse. The frequency and cost of repairs increased considerably, and parts became more difficult to find. The automatic transmission continued to malfunction, particularly on 1988–91 models; electrical components became even less reliable; stopping performance was compromised by premature brake wear and rear wheel lockup; and body hardware continued to be second class. The redesigned '95 Continental featured a new V8 powerplant, more aerodynamic styling, and fiberglass panels. However, powertrain, electrical system, and brake problems remained.

Dealer service bulletins: 1993 Continental—Poorly performing AC systems caused by a slipping clutch at high ambient temperatures, and AC FX-15 compressor growling. • Service engine light may go on for no apparent reason. • A-pillars may make cracking noises in cold weather. • Power steering units may be noisy and power door locks may not work. • Frequent under-hood squeaks, chirps, and knocks. • Premature wear on the inner edge of the rear tires, corrected by a new camber kit. **1994**—Faulty 3.8L engine rocker arm assemblies could cause squeaking, chirping, and knocking. • Inadequate AC operation caused by a faulty cold engine lockout switch and hose assembly. • Faulty electric rear window defrosters. **1995**—Engine misfires, no-start, hard start, and spark plug fouling. • Faulty in-tank fuel delivery modules causing the engine to stall and not restart will be replaced for free under Ford Program #95B71. • The Virtual Image Cluster will also be replaced at no charge under Program #95B71. (Ford will pay for a loaner car at $30 per day whenever carrying out these Program repairs.) • Harsh shifts, no 3–4 shift, erratic shifts, delayed transmission engagement and shift errors, low transaxle fluid level improperly setting the DTC and causing serious transmission malfunctions, and clicking noise when shifting into Reverse. • Insufficient AC cooling or excessive clutch end gap. • Brake roughness upon application or a thumping, clacking noise when braking. • Power steering grunt or groan. • Rocker arm noise. • A ticking noise from the cooling fan or AX4N transaxle. **1996**—Stall or hard start after 1–4 hour soak. • Vehicle drifts or pulls while driving. • Transaxle click noise during Reverse engagement. • Transaxle driveline noises. • Case breaks at rear planet support. • Air suspension leaks down overnight. • Fog/film on windshield/interior windows. • Musty and mildew-type odors. **1997**—Harsh automatic shifting. • Chronic dead battery. • Excessive blower motor noise. • Acceleration or deceleration clunk. • Front suspension clunk. • A-pillar creaking noise. • Front end accessory drive belt (FEAD) may slip during wet conditions, causing a reduction in steering power assist. • Steering wheel grunt or honk noise. • Loose catalyst or heat shields. • Stall or surging with automatic transmission engagement.

Safety summary/recalls: NHTSA probes: 1988–90—Power-steering fluid leakage and 3.8L engine fires. **1991 and 1995**—Reports of ice causing the cooling fan to freeze to the shroud, possibly leading to an engine fire. • Side windows on 1988 and 1989 models tend to fog up when carrying a few passengers. **Recalls: 1986**—Throttle may fail to return to idle. • Defective brake master cylinder warning sensor. **1986–87**—Fuel-line coupling may leak. **1987–88**—Body mounts will be inspected and a reinforcement plate installed. • Faulty transmission shift cable. • Power steering pump pulley could separate from engine. **1988–93**—Advanced front subframe fastener corrosion. **1989**—Faulty left rear seatbelt retractor. **1992–94**—Engine cooling fan motor may overheat and cause a fire. **1994**—Missing or improperly installed brake pedal push rod retainer. **1995–96**—"Autolamp" control module may fail. **1996–97**—Transmission may not engage; PRNDL may give a false reading.

Town Car
The rear-drive Town Car is the pick of the Lincoln litter. Nevertheless, it's still afflicted by the Lincoln's generic problems: transmission, AC, and electrical glitches and body hardware deficiencies. Nevertheless, thanks to its rear-drive configuration it's relatively inexpensive to repair and parts aren't hard to find. Try to find a '91 or better version with the 4.6L engine to optimize performance and economy.

Dealer service bulletins: 1994 Town Car—A rough idle, hesitation, excessive fuel consumption, and a poor heater output that's likely caused by a thermostat sticking in an open position or opening before it should. • Transmission shudder under light-to-moderate acceleration. • Radio speaker noise caused by fuel pump malfunctions. • Faulty electric rear window defrosters. **1995**—Problems with the '95 Town Car are identical to those listed for the Crown Victoria, except for one bulletin addressing a rough idle after a cold soak start-up. **1996**—Stall or hard start after 1–4 hour soak. •

Squealing noise from the engine compartment. • Transmission valve body cross leaks. • Chatter during turns. • Creaking from A-pillar area. • Rough idle or stalling at high altitudes. • Inoperative power-assisted deck lid. • Fog/film on windshield/interior windows. • Musty and mildew-type odors. **1997**—Erratic transmission shifting, especially the 1–2 shift. • Spark knock upon acceleration. • Door latch stuck open. • Fog/film on windshield/interior windows. • Loose catalysts or muffler heat shields. • Diagnosing and correcting wind noise around doors. • Shudder or vibration while in third or fourth gear. • Steering wheel noise and vibration. • Suspension leans to right side. • Whining noise from rear axle at highway speeds. **1994–97 Mark VIII**—An erratic or prolonged 1–2 shift can be cured by replacing the cast aluminum piston with a one-piece stamped steel piston with bonded lip seals and by replacing the top accumulator spring. These upgraded parts will increase the transmission's durability, says Ford. **1995**—Intermittent loss of torque at 3–4 upshift, shifts to Neutral at heavy throttle, delayed transmission engagement and shift errors, and irregular or no torque converter operation. • Brake roughness upon application. • Insufficient AC cooling or excessive clutch end gap. • Faulty fuel gauge. • Hard start in low temperatures. **1996**—Stall or hard start after 1–4 hour soak. • Transmission valve body cross leaks and shudder/downshift bump. • Growling noise from steering column when turning. • Squealing noise from the engine compartment. • Fog/film on windshield/interior windows. • Musty and mildew-type odors. **1997**—Erratic transmission shifting, especially the 1–2 shift. • Chirping and squeaking from blower motor. • No start or crank; anti-theft system not responding. • Radio AM band static while driving. • Troubleshooting wind noise around doors.

Safety summary/recalls: **NHTSA probes**: **1992–95 Mark VIII**—Headlight failures. **Recalls**: **1988–89**—Faulty ignition switches may be a fire hazard. **1990**—Ford will install new seat tracks and a memory track on the driver's side. **1990–91**—Hood can pop open during highway driving. **1991–92**—Secondary hood latch may not engage. **1991–94**—Faulty cruise control units and speed control cable. **1992–94**—Overheated engine cooling fan may start a fire. **1994**—Rear brake adapter to axle housing flange could loosen or separate. • Missing or improperly installed brake pedal push rod retainer. **1995**—Fuel could leak from tank. • Passenger airbag may not deploy properly. **1996**—Driver's door may not sustain specified load. • Seatbelts with switchable retractors for child restraints may not have the right components. **1997**—Driver's airbag may malfunction.

Secret Warranties/Service Tips

1984–94 Continental—A hum from the air suspension system can be corrected by replacing the compressor isolators with upgraded parts. **1988–90**—Hard cold start, hesitation, and stalling during idle or when decelerating may be corrected by removing excessive sludge deposits or an oil film from the throttle body bore and plate, or the idler air bypass valve. • High effort during wide turns at highway speeds signals the need to install a new power-steering short rack. • The intermittent loss of the AC may be due to a defective suction accumulator (#E6VY-19C836-A). **1988–94**— A squeak or chirp coming from the blower motor can be stopped by installing an upgraded blower motor with improved brush-to-commutator friction. • A cracked forward clutch piston may cause forward/reverse problems. Install an improved clutch piston. • A speaker whine or buzz caused by the fuel pump can be stopped by installing an electronic noise RFI filter. **1989**—A rough idle or lean fuel flow may require the installation of deposit-resistant injectors. **1989–93**—A persistent fuel odor in the interior when the AC is running signals the need to install a new auxiliary vapor tube kit and relocate the tube near the rear bumper. **1991**—When Ford modified the automatic transmission for easier shifting it also made it less reliable. In fact, *Consumer Reports'* annual member survey shows that almost 20 percent of the owners of the 1991 Taurus, Sable, and Continental said that they had experienced a serious transmission failure in the preceding 12 months— four times the average for '91 vehicles, according to *CR.* Ford has extended the warranty on these transmissions to up to six years. • Delayed transaxle 3–2 downshifts may require a new, more durable spring retainer clip (#F1DZ-7F194-A). **1991–94**—A sloshing noise from the fuel tank when accelerating or stopping requires the installation of an upgraded tank. Cost is covered under the emissions warranty. **1992–94**—A corroded solenoid may be the cause of starter failures. **1993–94**—An inoperative AC blower probably needs an improved cold engine lockout switch and hose assembly. • Stalling or hard starts in high ambient temperatures or high altitudes may be due to fuel tank contamination damaging the fuel pump. Ford paid for a fuel tank flush and a new fuel pump/sender and in-line fuel filter until May 31, 1997, under Service Program 94B48. **1994–95**—A thumping or clacking heard from the front brakes signals the need to machine the front disc brake rotors. Ford will pay for this repair under its base warranty. **1995–97**—An acceleration or deceleration clunk is likely caused by the rear lower subframe isolators allowing movement between the mounts and the subframe. • A front suspension clunk may signal premature sway bar wear. **1985–92 Mark VII and Mark VIII**—An exhaust buzz or rattle may be caused by a loose heat shield catalyst. **1986–94**—The in-tank fuel pump is the likely cause of radio static. Install an electronic noise RFI filter (#F1PZ-18B925-A). **1993–94**—A squeak or chirp coming from the blower motor can be stopped by installing an upgraded blower motor with improved brush-to-commutator friction. • Automatic transmissions with delayed or no forward engagement, or a higher engine RPM than expected when coming to a stop, are covered in DSB 94-26-9. **1983–90 Town Car**—A buzzing or humming from the fuel pump when the engine is shut off, a low battery, and hard or no-starts signal the need to install an upgraded pump relay (#F19Z-9345-A). **1987–90**—Excessive oil consumption is likely caused by leaking gaskets, poor sealing of the lower intake manifold, defective intake and exhaust valve stem seals, or worn piston rings. Install new guide-mounted valve stem seals for a more positive fit and new piston rings with improved oil control. **1989–90**—No Overdrive or an extended 3–4 shift may require the installation of a new Overdrive band, transmission separator plate kit, overhaul kit, and reverse drum. **1990**—A no-start condition may be caused by a defective Neutral start switch. • A pull to the right when braking can be corrected by installing a new brake pad and lining kit (#F1VY-20001-A). **1990–92**—Brake pedal and steering vibration when braking can be reduced by installing improved rotors (#F1VY-1125-A) and linings (#F3AZ-2001-A). **1991–92**—Secondary hood latch may not engage. **1992–94**—Automatic transmissions with delayed or no forward engagement, or a higher engine rpm than expected when coming to a stop, are covered in DSB 94-26-9. **1993–94**—A speaker whine or buzz caused by the fuel pump can be stopped by installing an electronic noise RFI filter. **1997**—Driver-side airbag may lack two mounting bolts. **All models/years**—Stalling at idle, poor fuel economy, and inadequate heating can all be traced to the thermostat being stuck in a partially open position (DSB 86-17-12). • Three components that frequently benefit from Ford "goodwill" warranty extensions are catalytic converters, fuel pumps, and computer modules. If Ford balks at refunding your money, apply the emissions warranty for a full or partial refund. • Paint delamination, fading, peeling, hazing, and "microchecking": See pages 94–95 for details on claiming a refund.

Continental Profile

	1990	1991	1992	1993	1994	1995	1996	1997
Cost Price ($)								
Continental	31,352	32,175	34,237	33,918	34,375	41,370	42,440	37,850
Used Values ($)								
Continental ↑	7,500	9,000	10,000	12,000	14,500	20,000	24,000	27,000
Continental ↓	6,000	7,500	9,000	11,000	13,000	18,000	22,000	25,000
Extended Warranty	Y	Y	Y	Y	Y	Y	Y	Y
Secret Warranty	N	Y	Y	Y	Y	Y	Y	N
Reliability	2	1	2	2	2	2	3	3
Air conditioning	1	1	1	1	1	2	3	3
Automatic transmission	2	1	1	1	2	2	3	4
Body integrity	2	2	2	2	2	2	3	3
Braking system	1	1	1	1	2	3	3	4
Electrical system	2	2	2	2	2	2	2	2
Engines	2	2	2	3	3	4	4	4
Exhaust/Converter	3	3	4	4	5	5	5	5
Fuel system	3	3	3	3	3	3	3	3
Ignition system	1	1	2	3	3	3	3	4
Rust/Paint	4	4	4	4	4	4	4	4
Steering	2	2	3	3	4	4	4	4
Suspension	2	2	2	2	3	4	4	4
Crash Safety	—	5	5	1	1	—	—	4

Mark VII, VIII Profile

	1990	1991	1992	1993	1994	1995	1996	1997
Cost Price ($)								
Mark VII/VIII	29,801	30,942	32,746	37,230	38,675	39,425	40,290	36,950
Used Values ($)								
Mark VII/VIII ↑	8,000	9,500	11,000	13,000	16,000	19,000	22,000	26,000
Mark VII/VIII ↓	7,000	8,000	9,500	12,000	14,000	17,000	20,000	24,000

Extended Warranty	Y	Y	Y	Y	Y	Y	Y	Y
Secret Warranty	N	Y	Y	Y	Y	Y	Y	N
Reliability	②	②	②	②	②	③	③	③
Air conditioning	②	②	②	③	③	③	③	③
Automatic transmission	②	②	②	②	②	③	④	⑤
Body integrity	②	②	②	②	②	②	②	③
Braking system	②	②	②	②	②	③	④	④
Electrical system	②	②	②	②	②	②	②	②
Engines	④	④	③	③	④	④	④	④
Exhaust/Converter	②	②	③	④	④	④	⑤	⑤
Fuel system	③	③	③	③	③	③	④	④
Ignition system	③	③	③	③	③	③	④	③
Rust/Paint	②	②	②	②	③	③	③	④
Steering	②	②	③	④	④	④	⑤	⑤
Suspension	②	②	②	③	③	③	③	④

Town Car Profile

	1990	1991	1992	1993	1994	1995	1996	1997
Cost Price ($)								
Town Car	31,218	31,909	33,585	35,350	35,930	37,595	38,120	38,720
Used Values ($)								
Town Car ↑	8,500	10,000	12,000	14,000	17,000	20,000	24,000	27,000
Town Car ↓	7,000	8,500	10,500	12,000	15,500	18,000	22,000	25,000
Extended Warranty	N	N	N	N	N	N	N	N
Secret Warranty	Y	Y	Y	Y	Y	Y	Y	Y
Reliability	②	②	②	③	④	④	④	④
Air conditioning	②	②	②	③	③	③	③	④
Automatic transmission	②	②	②	②	②	③	④	④
Body integrity	①	①	①	②	②	③	③	③
Braking system	①	①	①	①	②	③	④	⑤
Electrical system	①	①	①	②	③	③	③	③
Engines	④	④	④	④	④	④	④	④
Exhaust/Converter	②	②	③	③	④	④	⑤	⑤
Fuel system	②	③	③	③	③	③	③	④
Ignition system	②	②	③	③	③	③	③	④
Rust/Paint	②	②	②	③	③	③	④	⑤
Steering	③	③	③	④	④	③	③	④
Suspension	②	②	③	③	③	④	④	④
Crash Safety	②	⑤	⑤	②	②	⑤	④	④

Note: The Continental and Town Car registered low scores for the 1993 and '94 model years because leg trauma was included in the ratings.

MAZDA

929

Rating: Above Average (1992–95); Average (1988–91). **Maintenance/Repair costs**: Higher than average, and they must be done by a Mazda dealer. **Parts**: Higher-than-average cost, but not hard to find through cheaper independent suppliers.

Technical Data

ENGINES	Liters/CID	HP	MPG	Model Years
OHC V6 FI	3.0/180	158	17–21	1988–91
DOHC V6 FI	3.0/180	190–195	17–22	1990–95

Strengths and weaknesses: The key word for the 929 is understatement: the engine is unobtrusive, the exterior is anonymous, and the interior is far from flashy. In spite of its lack of pizzazz and imprecise power steering, the 929 will accelerate and handle curves as well as the best large European sedans. The 929 has proven to be fairly reliable.

The car's main drawbacks are its limited interior room and trunk space. The driver's seat doesn't have enough rear travel for tall drivers and head room is tight. Owners report some problems with premature disc brake wear, electrical glitches, exhaust system rust-out, electronic shock absorber durability (particularly with the 1989–91 models), and fit and finish deficiencies.

Redesigned as a '92 model, the 929 got a more rounded body, and a longer wheelbase that added to interior room while sacrificing trunk space. Despite these improvements, tall occupants will still feel cramped.

Shocks are very expensive to replace. Manual transmission isn't offered, and the automatic's many settings can be confusing. Furthermore, the transmission's lockup feature frequently cuts in and out. The rear end sometimes wants to slide out a bit on slippery surfaces, and the front end bounces around on bumpy roads. The optional automatic adjusting suspension does little to improve the car's ride or handling.

Dealer service bulletins: 1995—Heater and AC unit noise after long storage. • Rattling sunroof and outer door handles. • A slightly off-center steering wheel. • Brake pulsation repair. • Inoperative rear door window. • Brake shudder repair. • Scratched or peeling B-pillar trim. • Troubleshooting various causes of engine noise.

Safety summary/recalls: Recalls: 1988–91—Mazda will replace door handles with handles that won't break as easily. • Takata seatbelt replacement.

Secret Warranties/Service Tips

1988–91—Cold engine piston slapping requires replacement pistons to fix the problem. • Constant brake pulsation or shudder is likely caused by an uneven rotor surface or excessive rotor run-out. • Hard shifting after cold weather starts can be corrected by installing upgraded synchronizer rings and clutch hub assemblies. **1988–92**—Valve train noise occurring just after start-up may be caused by air trapped in the hydraulic lash adjuster. Correct by installing redesigned rocker arm shafts that promote better oil flow. **1989**—Mazda has modified the bushing assembly to reduce shudder and make for a more comfortable ride. The new assembly part is #H260-34-230C. **1990**—A power seat that won't adjust up or down smoothly likely has a broken gear in the seat motor. **1990–91**—Difficult starts in hot weather can be corrected by installing an upgraded cold start thermo-switch (#JE27-18-870). **1992–94**—Freezing door and hatch lock cylinders are addressed in DSB 021/94. **All models/years**—DSB 006/94 covers all the possible causes and remedies for excessive vibrations when braking. • Water intrusion into the lock actuator connectors may cause the unintended operation of the rear defroster.

929 Profile

	1988	1989	1990	1991	1992	1993	1994	1995
Cost Price ($)								
Sedan	19,534	22,189	23,579	23,799	28,150	29,550	31,895	36,235
Used Values ($)								
Sedan ↑	6,000	6,500	7,500	8,500	11,000	12,500	14,500	16,500
Sedan ↓	5,000	6,000	6,500	7,000	10,000	11,500	13,000	15,000
Extended Warranty	Y	Y	Y	Y	N	N	N	N
Secret Warranty	N	N	N	N	N	N	N	N
Reliability	②	②	③	③	③	④	⑤	⑤
Air conditioning	②	②	③	③	③	④	⑤	⑤
Automatic transmission	②	②	②	③	④	④	⑤	⑤
Body integrity	②	②	②	②	②	②	③	③
Braking system	②	②	②	②	②	②	②	③
Electrical system	②	②	②	②	④	④	④	④
Engines	②	③	③	④	⑤	④	④	⑤
Exhaust/Converter	②	②	②	②	③	③	④	⑤
Fuel system	③	③	③	④	③	④	④	④
Ignition system	②	③	④	⑤	⑤	⑤	⑤	⑤
Rust/Paint	④	④	④	④	⑤	⑤	⑤	⑤
Steering	③	③	③	③	④	⑤	⑤	⑤
Suspension	②	②	②	③	④	⑤	⑤	⑤
Crash Safety	②	②	②	②	②	②	②	—

Millenia

Rating: Above Average (1995–97). Lots of power and sophisticated mechanicals makes this luxury tourer a winner. From a performance standpoint, the Camry V6 with its less complicated powertrain outruns the Millenia. **Maintenance/Repair costs**: Higher than average, and repairs must be done by a Mazda dealer. **Parts**: Higher-than-average cost and limited availability.

Technical Data

ENGINES	Liters/CID	HP	MPG	Model Years
DOHC V6 FI	2.5L/152	170	20–26	1995–96
DOHC V6 FI	2.3L/138	210	20–28	1995–96

Strengths and weaknesses: Smaller than the Mazda 929, the front-drive Millenia carries the same 2.5L 170-hp V6 used by the 626. An optional 2.3L Miller-Cycle "S" 6-cylinder engine, although smaller than the base powerplant, still manages to pump out 210 horsepower. Both engines use a standard 4-speed automatic transmission that shifts a bit harshly when pushed. As with all luxury cars, the Millenia comes with a wide array of standard features that would normally cost thousands of dollars more. Although billed as a five-passenger car, the middle occupant in the rear seat is cramped and has to sit on a hump—a problem that 929 owners are familiar with.

Assembly and component quality are high, despite the few problems mentioned in the Mazda DSBs.

Dealer service bulletins: **1995**—Cruise control surging. • Transmission position indicator light failure. • AC evaporator freeze-up. • Battery discharge due to the trunk light staying on. • Snap noise around the A-pillar. • Steering wheel may be off-center. • Roof insulator peeling off. **1996**—Brake pulsation repair. • Cracked center sun-visor holder. • Creaking or knocking noise from rear of vehicle. • Rattle noise from rear package tray. **1997**—Brake pulsation repair.

Safety summary/recalls: It's easy to hit your head on the low trunk lid and latch. **Recalls**: N/A.

Secret Warranties/Service Tips

1995–96—A creaking or knocking noise from the rear of the vehicle is likely caused by loose diagonal braces behind the rear seat.

Millenia Profile			
	1995	1996	1997
Cost Price ($)			
Base		29,335	28,445 29,446
Used Values ($)			
Base ↑		18,500	19,500 21,000
Base ↓		17,000	18,500 19,500
Extended Warranty		N	N N
Secret Warranty		N	N N
Reliability		④	⑤ ⑤
Crash Safety		④	④ ④

MERCEDES-BENZ

190 Series, C-Class

Rating: Above Average (1994–97); Average (1988–93); Below Average (1984–87). Although these cars are above average in reliability and comfort, every model—other than the 300 series—is overpriced and overrated. The 190 version is not recommended. Consider buying a '97 C-class only if you feel you need the 2.3L engine's 12 additional horses and improved automatic gearbox. Keep in mind, though, that you'll have to keep the car much longer to amortize its higher cost. **Maintenance/Repair costs**: Higher than average, and most repairs must be done by a Mercedes dealer if you don't live in an area where independent shops have sprung up. **Parts**: Higher-than-average cost. Parts supply and servicing have become problematic now that the 190 series has been off the market for almost three years.

Strengths and weaknesses: Mercedes introduced the 190 "baby" Benz in 1984 in an effort to downsize its entry-level compact and make it more affordable. It never caught on due to its serious drivetrain deficiencies, cramped interior, and rounded styling (a real departure from Mercedes' traditional squared-off look). The best choice from a quality/price standpoint is any post '89 version equipped with the in-line 6-cylinder powerplant.

C-class (1994–97)
The '94 models were renamed the C-class and gained interior room and more powerful engines. The standard 2.6L 6-cylinder motor is a real powerhouse in this small car, and its power is used effectively when coupled to the 5-speed manual transmission. The 4-speed automatic is a big disappointment—it requires a lot of throttle

effort to downshift and prefers to start out in second gear. The '94 versions add much-needed horsepower, but lacks the manual 5-speed transmission that would set those extra horses free. Rear seat room is limited and there's lots of road noise intrusion into the passenger compartment.

Three entry-level versions based on the 190 platform were offered for 1997: a $36,950 148-hp 2.3L-equipped Special Edition C230; a $42,950 standard 2.3L-equipped C230; and an upscale $50,995 C280 offered with a 194-hp 2.8L V6 engine. An awesome 276-hp 3.6L in-line 6-cylinder powered the top-of-the-line $72,365 C36.

The base 2.3L engine is acceptable around town, but highway cruising requires more grunt to handle the car's heft and accessories. And speaking of grunt, the 2.8L powerplant is a real powerhouse in this small car. Although its power is used most effectively when coupled to the new 5-speed manual transmission, its performance with the new 5-speed automatic is quite acceptable. On '96 models, some owners have complained that the 4-speed automatic requires a lot of throttle effort to downshift.

Keep in mind that owner surveys give the entry-level cars a "just" better than average rating, while the 300 and higher series have always scored way above average in owner satisfaction. The 190's reliability is a notch below that of other Mercedes; the '94 model C-class is the better buy from a quality and reliability standpoint. Owners report frequent problems with drivetrain noise and vibration, and slipping or soft shifts. Brakes, AC, electrical system, and fit and finish are also failure prone.

Dealer service bulletins: 1993 190 and 1994 C220—Drivetrain noise and vibration. • Harsh shifts or erratic shift quality. • High coolant temperature. • Rough reverse release. • Handling of fuel system complaints. **1995**—Drivetrain noise and vibration. • High coolant temperature. • Slipping or soft shifts.

Safety summary/recalls: Recalls: 1994–95 C-class—Secondary hood latch may not work properly.

Secret Warranties/Service Tips

1989–92—Excessive oil consumption may be corrected by replacing the valve stem seals with upgraded Viton seals. **1990–91**—A jerking that occurs when driving downhill with the cruise control engaged can be corrected by installing a relay to disable the deceleration fuel shut-off switch. **All models/years**—Excessive engine valve train noise may be caused by a stretched timing chain. After 30,000 miles the camshaft and timing chain drive should be checked carefully, especially if excessive noise is heard.

190 Series, C-Class Profile

	1990	1991	1992	1993	1994	1995	1996	1997
Cost Price ($)								
190E 2.3	—	31,260	30,200	33,930	—	—	—	—
190E 2.6	32,750	34,050	35,250	36,865	—	—	—	—
C220	—	—	—	—	31,085	32,000	33,055	—
C230	—	—	—	—	—	—	—	33,235
C280	—	—	—	—	37,105	38,400	37,815	37,985
Used Values ($)								
190E 2.3 ↑	—	13,500	15,000	16,500	—	—	—	—
190E 2.3 ↓	—	12,000	14,000	15,000	—	—	—	—
190E 2.6 ↑	14,500	16,500	18,500	20,000	—	—	—	—
190E 2.6 ↓	13,000	14,500	16,000	18,500	—	—	—	—
C220 ↑	—	—	—	—	22,500	25,000	28,000	—
C220 ↓	—	—	—	—	21,000	23,000	26,000	—
C230 ↑	—	—	—	—	—	—	—	30,000
C230 ↓	—	—	—	—	—	—	—	28,000
C280 ↑	—	—	—	—	26,000	28,000	32,000	35,000
C280 ↓	—	—	—	—	25,000	27,000	31,000	33,000

	1990	1991	1992	1993	1994	1995	1996	1997
Extended Warranty	Y	Y	Y	Y	Y	Y	Y	Y
Secret Warranty	N	N	N	N	N	N	N	N
Reliability	②	②	③	③	④	④	⑤	⑤
Air conditioning	②	②	②	③	③	④	④	④
Automatic transmission	②	③	③	③	④	④	⑤	⑤
Body integrity	②	③	③	③	③	③	④	④
Braking system	②	②	②	②	②	③	④	④
Electrical system	②	②	②	②	③	③	④	④
Engines	②	③	③	③	③	③	⑤	⑤
Exhaust/Converter	③	③	③	④	④	④	⑤	⑤
Fuel system	②	②	②	③	③	④	⑤	⑤
Ignition system	②	③	③	③	④	⑤	⑤	⑤
Rust/Paint	④	④	③	③	④	④	⑤	⑤
Steering	②	②	③	④	④	⑤	⑤	⑤
Suspension	②	②	②	②	③	④	⑤	⑤
Crash Safety								
190	②	⑤	—	—	—	—	—	—
C220	—	—	—	—	❶	④	④	④

300, 400, 500 Series

Rating: Recommended (1993–97); Above Average (1988–92); Below Average (1985–87). The '94 and later models are referred to as E-class, with the entry-level model a 300 diesel. **Maintenance/Repair costs**: Higher than average, and repairs must be done by a Mercedes dealer. **Parts**: Higher-than-average cost and limited availability.

Strengths and weaknesses: These cars are ideal mid-size family sedans. They're reliable, depreciate slowly, and provide all the interior space that the pre-'94 190 series and C-class leaves out. Their only shortcomings are a high resale value that murders bargain hunters and a weak dealer network that limits parts distribution. The 300 series offers a traction-control system that prevents wheel spin upon acceleration—somewhat like ABS in reverse.

Another interesting feature is a 24-valve 220-hp high performance version of the in-line 6-cylinder engine that powers the 300 series. All this has its price, though. If, ironically, you'd like to drive one of these cars but are of an economical frame of mind, choose the 260E—it offers everything the 300 does but for much less. The 300CE is a coupe version, appealing to a sportier crowd, while the 300TE is the station wagon variant.

Dealer service bulletins: Bulletins show that the '95 300 series may have transmission gasket leaks, in addition to drivetrain noise and vibration, and slipping or soft shifts. 1996–97 models have no bulletins listing factory-related problems or troubleshooting tips.

Safety summary/recalls: Recalls: 1992–95 300-series and E-class— Front passenger's footrest could abrade the wiring harness underneath. The ensuing short circuit could stall the engine or deploy the airbag.

Secret Warranties/Service Tips

1987–90—A cruise control that surges or maintains a speed that's 3–4 miles above the set speed may have a faulty amplifier or reference resistor gasket. **1987–92**—Excessive brake vibrations can be reduced by installing upgraded Jurid 226 front brake pads. **1988–90**—A gurgling heater core noise can be silenced by Mercedes' "gurgling kit." **1990–91**—Excessive exhaust noise between the exhaust manifold flange and rear muffler may be caused by a leak at the O_2 sensor or the clamped joints. If this isn't the cause, change the catalytic converter.

300, 400, 500 Series Profile

	1990	1991	1992	1993	1994	1995	1996	1997
Cost Price ($)								
300E	40,200	41,350	43,300	46,115	—	—	—	—
300CE	56,450	57,700	60,750	61,400	—	—	—	—
300D	39,950	41,350	43,300	46,115	—	—	—	—
E300D	—	—	—	—	—	43,100	42,465	42,475
E420	—	—	—	—	51,475	52,975	—	51,585
E500/S500	—	—	—	—	82,975	89,675	88,095	89,795
Used Values ($)								
300E ↑	18,000	21,000	23,000	25,000	—	—	—	—
300E ↓	16,000	17,500	20,000	23,500	—	—	—	—
300CE ↑	24,000	25,500	29,000	34,000	—	—	—	—
300CE ↓	20,000	23,000	26,000	31,000	—	—	—	—

300D ↑	19,000	21,000	23,500	26,000	—	—	—	—
300D ↓	17,000	19,000	21,000	24,000	—	—	—	—
E300D ↑	—	—	—	—	—	32,000	36,000	38,000
E300D ↓	—	—	—	—	—	29,000	35,000	36,000
E420 ↓	—	—	—	—	32,000	38,000	—	48,000
E420 ↑	—	—	—	—	30,000	35,000	—	46,000
E500/S500 ↑	—	—	—	—	57,000	60,000	66,000	74,000
E500/S500 ↓	—	—	—	—	53,000	57,000	61,000	79,000

Extended Warranty	N	N	N	N	N	N	N	N
Secret Warranty	N	N	N	N	N	N	N	N

Reliability	③	③	③	③	③	④	④	⑤
Air conditioning	❷	❷	③	③	④	⑤	⑤	⑤
Automatic transmission	③	③	③	③	④	⑤	⑤	⑤
Body integrity	③	③	③	③	④	④	④	⑤
Braking system	❷	❷	③	③	③	③	④	④
Electrical system	❷	❷	❷	③	③	⑤	⑤	⑤
Engines	③	③	③	③	③	⑤	⑤	⑤
Exhaust/Converter	③	③	③	③	③	⑤	⑤	⑤
Fuel system	③	③	③	③	③	③	⑤	⑤
Ignition system	③	③	③	⑤	⑤	⑤	⑤	⑤
Rust/Paint	④	④	④	④	④	④	④	⑤
Steering	③	③	③	③	③	④	④	④
Suspension	❷	❷	❷	③	③	⑤	⑤	⑤

Note: These Mercedes models haven't been recently crash tested by the NHTSA.

MITSUBISHI

Diamante

Rating: Recommended. Think of the Diamante as an upscale Camry with lots of electronic gadgets. **Maintenance/Repair costs**: About average, best of all, repairs aren't dealer dependent. **Parts**: Parts are easily found and relatively inexpensive.

Technical Data

ENGINES	Liters/CID	HP	MPG	Model Years
DOHC V6 FI	3.0	175–202	19–24	1992–96

Strengths and weaknesses: The Diamante is an excellent family-car buy because of its spacious, comfortable interior, fair fuel economy, and impressive reliability. Virtually unchanged, the 1992–95 wagons and sedans targeted the sports sedan buyer, while the revamped 1996–97 models moved up into the luxury sedan niche where it now competes against BMW, Lexus, and Nissan's Maxima.

1992–95 models have few problems, although they're far from perfect. Main areas of concern are a failure-prone automatic transmission on the '93 models, and electrical shorts and brake problems plaguing all model years. Early models also may have excessive wind noise coming from the side windows, fragile trim items that break or fall off, premature paint peeling, and sound system glitches.

1996–97 model Diamante deficiencies reported by owners include brake vibrations, premature brake pad wear and electrical system malfunctions.

Safety summary/recalls: NHTSA complaints: 1995—Automatic transmission suddenly shifted into Neutral. • Airbag deployment caused severe injuries to occupants. **1996**—Sudden ABS failure. • Transmission failure. • Electronic control unit failure causes excessive hesitation when shifting gears. • Premature wear of the front brake rotors. • Windows leaking, mirror falling off, door locks freeze too easily. **Recalls: 1992–95**—Right front wheel-side brake hose can crack, resulting in leakage. A revised brake hose will be installed. **1993**—The rear outboard lower safety belt attachment bolt may have been inadequately torqued.

Secret Warranties/Service Tips

1994–95—Horn buttons tend to pop out due to their holding claws being too short. Mitsubishi will replace the horn buttons and switch under its "goodwill" warranty on a case-by-case basis. **All models/years**—Troubleshooting tips to correct excessive valve noise at startup are included in DSB #95-11-001.

Diamante Profile

	1992	1993	1994	1995	1996	1997
Cost Price ($)						
Base/ES	21,375	22,842	25,995	28,370	27,550	26,370
Used Values ($)						
Base/ES ↑	9,500	11,000	13,000	14,500	17,000	21,000
Base/ES ↓	8,000	9,500	11,000	13,000	15,000	19,000
Extended Warranty	N	N	N	N	N	N
Secret Warranty	N	N	N	N	N	N
Reliability	③	③	③	④	④	⑤
Air conditioning	④	⑤	⑤	⑤	⑤	⑤
Automatic trans.	⑤	❷	③	④	⑤	⑤
Body integrity	③	③	③	③	④	④
Braking system	❷	❷	③	③	③	④
Electrical system	❷	❷	❷	❷	④	⑤
Engines	④	④	⑤	⑤	⑤	⑤
Exhaust/Converter	④	④	④	⑤	⑤	⑤
Fuel system	③	④	④	③	④	⑤
Ignition system	③	④	④	④	⑤	⑤
Rust/Paint	❷	③	③	④	⑤	⑤
Steering	③	③	③	⑤	⑤	⑤
Suspension	④	④	④	⑤	⑤	⑤
Crash Safety	⑤	❷	—	—	—	—

NISSAN

Maxima

Rating: Recommended (1996–97); Above Average (1989–95); Average (1986–88). The redesigned 1995–98 version offers a peppier engine, more rounded styling, and a bit longer wheelbase. **Maintenance/Repair costs**: Higher than average, but repairs can be done practically anywhere. **Parts**: Higher-than-average cost, but easy to find.

Technical Data

ENGINES	Liters/CID	HP	MPG	Model Years
OHC V6 FI	3.0/181	152	17–23	1985–88
OHC V6 FI	3.0/181	160	18–24	1989–94
DOHC V6 FI	3.0/181	190	18–22	1995–98

Strengths and weaknesses: These front-wheel drive sedans are very well equipped and nicely finished, but cramped for their size. Although the trunk is spacious, only five passengers can travel in a pinch (pinch, in the literal sense). The 6-cylinder engine, borrowed from the 300ZX, offers sparkling performance; the fuel injectors, however, are problematic. Early Maximas are less expensive to buy, but more costly to maintain—for example, replacing the exhaust manifold, a common component failure, will set you back $300–$500. Owners report that the '95 Maxima's suspension was cheapened to the detriment of both the ride and handling.

Minor electrical and front suspension problems afflict early Maximas. Brakes and engine timing belts need frequent attention in all years. Newer models have a weak automatic transmission and the ignition system can malfunction. There have also been reports of "cooked" transmissions. This is due to a poorly designed transmission cooler. Mechanics say that this breakdown can be avoided by installing an externally mounted transmission cooler with a filter and replacing the transmission filter cooler at every oil change.

Owners report that the V6-equipped Maxima is sometimes hard to start in cold weather due to the engine's tendency to flood easily. The cruise-control unit is another problematic component. When it's engaged at moderate speeds it hesitates or "drifts" to a lower speed, acting as if the fuel line were clogged. It operates correctly only at much higher speeds than needed. Incidentally, owners say that a new fuel filter will *not* correct the problem. Additionally, though warped manifolds were once routinely replaced under a "goodwill" warranty, Nissan now makes the customer pay. The warpage causes a manifold bolt to break off, thereby causing a huge exhaust leak. Most fuel injector malfunctions are caused by carbon clogging up the injectors; there are additives you can try that might reduce this buildup. There have also been internal problems with the coil windings on the fuel injectors. Your best bet is to replace the entire set.

Nissan has had problems with weak window regulators for some time. If the window is frozen, *don't open it.* The rubber weather stripping around the window is also a problem. It cuts easily and causes the window to go off track, which in turn causes stress on the weak regulators. Driver's side window breakage is common and can cost up to $300 to repair. Costly aluminum wheels corrode quickly and are easily damaged by road hazards. There have been a few reports of surface rust and paint problems. Pre-'90s Maximas suffer from rust perforation on the sunroof, door bottoms, rear wheel wells, front edge of the hood, and bumper supports. The underbody should also be checked carefully for corrosion damage. Premature wear-out of the muffler is a frequent problem. It's often covered by Nissan's "goodwill" warranty, wherein the company and dealer contribute 50 percent of the replacement cost.

1995–97 models
These redesigned Maximas have a longer wheelbase (adding to interior room), a new 3.0L engine and more rounded styling. They compete well with fully equipped Camrys and entry-level Infinitis and Lexus models. Nevertheless, tall passengers will find the interior a bit cramped, the automatic transmission is often slow to downshift and isn't always smooth. Quality control and overall reliability is apparently much better with these more recent iterations.

Dealer service bulletins: 1995—Hard cranking, no or low line pressure rise (control valve), and poor driveability (Code 45). • Clutch slippage. • AC compressor leaks or is noisy. • Troubleshooting excessive front and rear brake noise. • Rear brake, spare tire cover, and exhaust heat shield rattling. • Faulty center console lid latch. • Wind noise around the front door. • Certain windshield cracks are covered under warranty. **1996**—Brake squeak or squeal. • Center console lid latch replacement. • Hard starts or no-starts. • Timing chain noise.

Safety summary/recalls: NHTSA probes: There have been 548 complaints of leaks in the fuel-injection system and 300 reports of engine fires caused by leaks on models built in the late 1980s. Nissan says that owners should inspect injector hoses and connecting hoses every few years. **Recalls: 1986**—Windshield may detach in a collision. **1992–93**—Dealers will install a new airbag sensor so that the airbags won't inadvertently deploy whenever the car passes over a speed bump. **1993–94**—Loose wheel nuts on aluminum wheels could allow wheels to fall away.

Secret Warranties/Service Tips

1985–91—Excessive brake noise can be corrected with upgraded front and rear pads, caliper pins, and baffle plates. **1989**—Insufficient heating may be caused by air bubbles trapped in the heater core. • Ice-induced heater motor failure requires a new blower (#27200-85E02). **1989–91**—Starting difficulties can often be traced to a connector not fully seated in the ECU. **1989–92**—Nissan has developed a variety of brake pads to respond to a number of customer complaints regarding excessive noise when braking. • Clutch shudder can be eliminated by installing an upgraded pressure plate release lever. **1995–96**—Timing chain rattling noise can be silenced by replacing the timing chain tensioner and slack guide. Covered by the warranty under the "Primary Failed Part" claim category. • Brake squeak or squeal can be corrected by installing front and rear brake kits. This repair is also covered by Nissan's base warranty (see below).

Front Brake Pad Replacement⁵

OPERATION	OP CODE	PNC¹	SYMPTOM	DIAGNOSIS	FRT
RPL Front Pad Sets— Both Sides²	PB19AA	41061	DD	69	0.7 hrs

NOTE: 1. New Claims System dealers: Submit a Primary Part claim using P/N 41060-40U92 as the PFP.
2. Brake rotor turning in combination with pad replacement is NOT required for this countermeasure.

Rear Brake Pad Replacement⁵

OPERATION	OP CODE	PNC³	SYMPTOM	DIAGNOSIS	FRT
RPL Rear Pad Sets— Both Sides⁴	PD19AA	44061	DD	69	0.7 hrs

NOTE: 3. New Claims System dealers: Submit a Primary Part claim using P/N 41060-31U92 as the PFP.
4. Brake rotor turning in combination with pad replacement is NOT required for this countermeasure.
5. If both front and rear brake pads are replaced, "old" claims system dealers should put both Op Codes on the same claim using PNC 41060. New Claims System dealers should submit a separate line for each OP.

Nissan can't pretend the above brake repairs are the owner's responsibility when it suggests in the above bulletin that dealers submit a "Primary Part claim."

All models/years—Defective catalytic converters that cause a rotten-egg smell may be replaced free of charge under Nissan's emissions warranty. Bulletin P195-006 looks at the many causes and remedies for excessive brake noise.

Maxima Profile

	1990	1991	1992	1993	1994	1995	1996	1997
Cost Price ($)								
Base	17,959	18,975	19,997	23,525	22,579	21,989	23,084	23,665
Used Values ($)								
Base ↑	8,000	9,000	10,500	11,500	13,000	14,500	16,500	18,000
Base ↓	7,000	8,000	9,500	10,000	11,500	13,000	15,000	17,000

Extended Warranty	Y	N	N	N	N	N	N	N
Secret Warranty	N	N	N	N	N	Y	Y	N

Reliability	③	④	④	④	④	④	⑤	⑤
Air conditioning	③	④	④	⑤	⑤	⑤	⑤	⑤
Body integrity	❷	❷	❷	③	④	④	④	④
Braking system	❷	❷	❷	❷	③	③	④	④
Electrical system	❷	❷	❷	❷	③	③	④	④
Engines	④	④	④	④	⑤	⑤	⑤	⑤
Exhaust/Converter	❷	③	③	③	③	⑤	⑤	⑤
Fuel system	③	③	③	④	④	④	④	④
Ignition system	③	③	③	④	③	④	④	④
Manual transmission	❷	❷	③	③	③	⑤	⑤	⑤
- automatic	③	③	③	④	④	⑤	⑤	⑤
Rust/Paint	③	③	③	④	④	⑤	⑤	⑤
Steering	③	③	④	④	④	⑤	⑤	⑤
Suspension	③	③	④	④	④	⑤	⑤	⑤
Crash Safety	—	⑤	⑤	❷	❷	④	④	④

Note: The low frontal crash ratings represent the inclusion of leg trauma in the overall score.

SAAB

900, 9000

Rating: Below Average (1994–97); Not Recommended (1986–93). Interestingly, the upscale 9000 series isn't as crashworthy as the cheaper 900 versions. **Maintenance/Repair costs**: Higher than average, and repairs must be done by a GM/Saab dealer. **Parts**: Higher-than-average cost and limited availability.

Technical Data

ENGINES	Liters/CID	HP	MPG	Model Years
900				
OHC I-4 FI	2.0/121	110	21–24	1985–88
DOHC I-4T FI	2.0/121	160–175	20–25	1985–94
DOHC I-4 FI	2.0/121	128	21–26	1986–90
DOHC I-4 FI	2.1/129	140	20–25	1991–94
DOHC I-4 FI	2.3/140	150	19–24	1994–98
DOHC I-4T FI	2.3/140	185	20–25	1995–98
DOHC V6 FI	2.5/152	170	18–23	1994–96
9000				
DOHC I-4 FI	2.0/121	125–130	20–23	1987–90
DOHC I-4T FI	2.0/121	160–165	19–22	1986–90
DOHC I-4 FI	2.3/140	150	19–22	1990–94

DOHC I-4 FI	2.3/140	170	19–23	1995–96
DOHC I-4T FI	2.3/140	200–225	17–20	1991–98
DOHC V6 FI	3.0/180	210	17–20	1995–97

Strengths and weaknesses: These Swedish-built luxury cars don't offer the refinement and ride comfort of most other cars in their class; the redesigned '99 models will, however. They do combine excellent handling and great interior ergonomics (one of the few imports with the EPA's "large car" label) without all the bells and whistles found in domestic luxury breeds. Convenience items like a fuse box in the glove box, a toolbox in the hatchback, and easy-to-replace bulbs add to your comfort.

Unfortunately, Saabs don't live up to the Swedish reputation for exceptional reliability and are quirky in design. Servicing is inadequate and will probably get much worse in the future. Parts are already costly and hard to find outside major urban areas. Take the tires, for example. Those for the 1992 9000 aren't a common size (205/50ZR16), and therefore command a not-so-common price—about $200–$400 per tire, depending on the manufacturer.

Generally, the 900 and 9000 series have similar deficiencies affecting the engine cooling—biodegradable water pumps and electrical systems, brakes, automatic transmission (clutch O-rings), and body hardware. The 9000 is assembled with greater care, but owner reports show only a marginal improvement in overall reliability and durability.

Short circuits are legion and run the gamut from minor annoyances to fire hazards (see "Recalls," following). Electrical glitches in the Traction Control System's relay module give a false reading that the tires are spinning, which shuts the engine down.

Turbos produce much stronger acceleration and better handling than other 9000s without compromising their overall reliability. Nevertheless they should be approached with caution, because owner abuse or poor maintenance can quickly lead to turbocharger deterioration. Air conditioners and exhaust-system parts have a short life span, and leaky seals and gaskets are common. Rust perforations tend to develop along door bottoms and the rocker panels. The underbody, especially the floor, should be inspected for corrosion damage on older models.

Dealer service bulletins: **1995 900**—Battery drain due to climate control system. • Excessive exhaust vibration. • Loose center cover on rear belt member. • Rear floor duct noise. • Creaking noise in right hand A-pillar. • Evaporative loss system leaks. • Excessive clutch pedal freeplay. • Hard brake pedal when starting a cold engine. • Binding ignition switch contacts. • Inoperative blower motor. • Leaking sunroof or wet headliner. • Loosening seat upholstery. • Noise from rear speaker, secondary air injection pump, vacuum pump, dash, or front seat. • Pedal raising kit. • AM band radio interference. • Airbag warning light comes on. • Sulfur smell from exhaust. • Vibration caused by tires or rims. **1995 9000**—Poor EDU illumination. • Loose dome light. • Evaporative loss system leaks. • Excessive fuel line pressure. • Failing fan control. • Secondary air injection pump noise. • Noise when shifting from second to third gear (automatic). • Rain or washer fluid running over rear window. • Dashboard squeaks and rattles. • Smell from climate control system. • Inoperative speedometer. • Airbag warning light comes on. • Sulfur smell from exhaust. • Tire or rims causing excessive vibration. • Whistling noise from windshield. **1996 900**—Rear floor duct noise. • Excessive clutch pedal freeplay. • Inoperative blower motor. • Leaking sunroof or wet headliner. • Loosening seat upholstery. • Front seat or dash noise. • Pedal raising kit. • AM band radio interference. • Clutch plate rattling. • Sulfur smell from exhaust. **1996 9000**—Failing fan control. • Interior lights won't go out. • Noise when shifting from second to third gear (automatic). • Rattling noise from clutch plate. • Climate system smells. • Whistling noise from windshield. • Inoperative speedometer.

Safety summary/recalls: NHTSA probes: 1990 900—Leaking fuel pumps. **1990–91**—Damage to the fuel tank by the in-tank fuel gauge, resulting in the release of vapor or fuel. **1986–91 9000**—Reports of passenger compartment fires. The American government is investigating reports that Saab officials destroyed key documents that described the problem. A class action suit has been filed in Los Angeles, and a second suit has been filed in Atlanta, Georgia. **Recalls: 1989 900**—Recall #274 provides for the free replacement of the fuel filter. **1994**—Front seats may not lock into position properly. **1994 hatchback**—Fatigue cracks could allow seat to suddenly fold backwards. **1985 Turbo 900**—Flexible fuel hose may leak. **1986 Turbo 900**—Steering shaft could pull out of joint. **1986–87 Turbo 900**—Fuel hose may rupture. **1987–88 Turbo 900**—Wiring harness may chafe, creating a fire hazard. **1988 Turbo 900**—Front lower control arm may fail. **1989 Turbo 900**—Leaking fuel filter may create a fire hazard. • Heater fan resistor may overheat. **1993 Turbo 900**—Front brakes are very vulnerable to salt and slush, which compromises braking. **1994–95**—Transmission may be in Neutral when shifter is in Reverse. • Car could roll away if it's parked with the parking brake disengaged. **1996**—Seatbelt anchorage may not hold. **1994–95 5d and Coupe with manual transmissions**—A shift linkage defect may cause an unexpected movement if transmission is in gear. **1995 with 2.3L engines**—Faulty electronic system. **1995 Saab 900 convertibles**—Possible loss of steering control due to a misaligned steering shaft. **1986 9000**—Wiring harness may short-circuit, creating a fire hazard. **1986–91**—Fire may be caused by a short circuit in the driver console. **1988**—Faulty cruise control may lead to unintended acceleration. • Recall No. 272 provides for the free replacement of the lower control arm attachment bolts. **1988–89**—Fluid leakage may compromise braking effectiveness. **1988–90**—Fire may erupt in the backup light circuit. **1989**—Leaking fuel filter may create a fire hazard. **1991**—Car may be started in gear. **1992–93**—Dealers will install a new fuel filler and fuel filler vent hose to prevent fuel leakage. • Vehicles equipped with an engine oil cooler may catch fire in a collision. **1992–94**—ABS corrosion can lead to loss of full braking power. **1993–94**—Brake lights may operate erratically.

Secret Warranties/Service Tips

1988–91 900—Cold weather starting problems may be fixed with service kit #8819070. **1990–91**—A new valve and new O-rings will correct starting problems caused by a sticking fuel pump check valve. **1993–94**—Binding ignition switch contacts can lead to electrical failures. **1994**—A-pillar wind noise is addressed in DSB 08194-0486. • DSB 88/94-0480 lists the causes and remedies of AC malfunctions. **1992–94 9000**—A noisy climate control unit may have excess pressure building up at the fresh air intake. **1993–94**—A stuck shift lever may be caused by a blown #3 fuse. A faulty sun visor/vanity mirror causes the short circuit.

900, 9000 Profile

	1990	1991	1992	1993	1994	1995	1996	1997
Cost Price ($)								
900	18,478	19,812	20,435	21,400	22,750	24,545	24,490	25,520
9000	26,378	24,077	26,175	28,570	30,670	32,695	32,695	35,360
Used Values ($)								
900 ↑	5,000	7,000	8,500	12,000	15,000	17,500	20,000	22,000
900 ↓	4,000	6,000	7,500	11,000	13,500	16,000	18,500	21,000
9000 ↑	7,000	10,000	11,500	15,000	19,000	22,000	26,000	28,000
9000 ↓	6,000	8,500	10,000	13,000	17,500	19,000	25,000	26,000
Extended Warranty	Y	Y	Y	Y	Y	Y	Y	Y
Secret Warranty	N	N	N	N	N	N	N	N
Reliability	②	②	②	②	②	②	③	③
Air conditioning	②	②	③	③	③	③	③	③
Body integrity	②	②	②	②	③	②	③	③
Braking system	②	②	②	②	②	②	②	③
Electrical system	①	①	①	②	②	②	②	②
Engines	②	②	②	②	②	③	④	④
Exhaust/Converter	②	②	②	②	③	③	④	④
Fuel system	③	③	②	②	②	③	③	③
Ignition system	②	②	③	③	③	③	③	③
Manual transmission	③	③	③	③	③	⑤	⑤	④
- automatic	②	②	②	②	②	③	③	④
Rust/Paint	②	②	③	③	③	③	④	⑤
Steering	③	③	④	⑤	⑤	⑤	⑤	⑤
Suspension	③	③	③	③	④	④	④	④
Crash Safety								
900	—	—	—	—	—	④	④	④
9000	—	—	—	②	—	—	—	—

TOYOTA

Avalon

Rating: Above Average (1995–97). A Camry knock-off; if you want a more driver-involved experience in a Toyota, consider a Lexus ES 300 or GS 300. **Maintenance/Repair costs**: Higher than average, and repairs must be done by a Toyota dealer. **Parts**: Higher-than-average cost and limited availability.

Technical Data

ENGINES	Liters/CID	HP	MPG	Model Years
DOHC V6 FI	3.0L/180	192	20–27	1995–98

Strengths and weaknesses: This near-luxury four-door offers more value, interior space, and reliability than do other cars in its class that cost thousands of dollars more. A front-engine, front-drive mid-size sedan, based on a stretched Camry platform, the Avalon is similar in size to the Ford Taurus and bigger than the rear-drive Cressida it replaced. Sure, there's a fair amount of Camry in the Avalon, but it's quicker on its feet than the Camry, better attuned to abrupt maneuvers, and two inches longer. In fact, there's more rear-seat leg room than you'll find in either the Taurus or the new Chevrolet Lumina. It's close to the Dodge Intrepid in this respect.

Quality control is above reproach. Body construction and assembly are solid, with few gaps. Owners have some performance gripes, however—power steering that's a bit too light, excessive body lean, and understeering when cornering.

Dealer service bulletins: 1995–96—Air conditioning odors. • AM band radio static on vehicles with an automatic antenna. • Front brake groan and rear brake moan. • Rear seat popping noise. • Wind noise from front door A-pillar area.

Safety summary/recalls: **NHTSA probes**: 1995—Researchers are looking into 20 incidents of turn signal failures after the hazard warning lights have been activated.

Secret Warranties/Service Tips

1995–96—Use an upgraded rear brake pad material to eliminate rear brake moan. • To reduce wind noise from the front door A-pillar area, consult DSB #B0010-97. **1996**—Use an upgraded brake pad material to eliminate brake groan noise.

Avalon Profile

	1995	1996	1997
Cost Price ($)			
XL	23,155	23,838	23,958
XLS	27,085	27,868	27,468
Used Values ($)			
XL ↑	17,000	19,000	20,000
XL ↓	15,500	17,500	19,000
XLS ↑	19,000	21,000	23,000
XLS ↓	17,500	19,500	21,500
Extended Warranty	N	N	N
Secret Warranty	N	N	N
Reliability	⑤	⑤	⑤
Crash Safety	—	④	④

Cressida

Rating: Above Average (1985–92). The Cressida was dropped in 1992 and then replaced with the Avalon for the 1995 model year. **Maintenance/Repair costs**: Higher than average, but repairs can be done by an independent garage. **Parts**: Higher-than-average cost and limited availability.

Technical Data

ENGINES	Liters/CID	HP	MPG	Model Years
DOHC I-6 FI	2.8/168	156	17–23	1985–88
DOHC I-6 FI	3.0/180	190	16–23	1989–92

Strengths and weaknesses: The Cressida offers an excellent combination of dependable, no-surprise, rear-drive performance, comfort, and luxury. There is little to find at fault when it comes to overall reliability, and the engine is a model of smooth power. Its only shortcomings: a bit less interior and trunk space than one would find with the Nissan Maxima or Acura Legend, inconvenient, confusing dash controls, and poor fuel economy.

Surprisingly, the newer models aren't as reliable and trouble-free as earlier versions, owing primarily to quality cutbacks in body and electronic components. Two complaints, however, have been frequent throughout the decade: premature front brake wear and excessive pulsation/vibration. AC glitches and electrical short circuits are commonplace. Exhaust-system parts rust quickly.

Safety summary/recalls: **Recalls**: N/A.

Secret Warranties/Service Tips

1989—Speaker static when the power mirror is activated requires a noise filter in the power-mirror circuit. **All models/years**—Older Toyotas with stalling problems should have the engine checked for excessive carbon buildup on the valves before any more extensive repairs are authorized. • The brake pulsation/vibration problem is fully outlined and corrective measures are detailed in DSB BR94-002, issued February 7, 1994.

Cressida Profile

	1985	1986	1987	1988	1989	1990	1991	1992
Cost Price ($)								
Base	15,690	16,130	20,475	21,238	21,753	21,763	22,473	23,783
Used Values ($)								
Base ↑	4,500	5,500	6,500	7,000	8,500	9,500	10,500	11,500
Base ↓	4,000	4,500	5,500	6,500	7,000	8,000	9,500	10,500
Extended Warranty	N	N	N	N	N	N	N	N
Secret Warranty	N	N	N	N	N	N	N	N
Reliability	2	2	2	2	3	3	3	3
Air conditioning	1	1	1	2	2	2	3	3
Body integrity	4	4	4	4	4	4	4	4
Braking system	2	2	2	2	2	3	3	3
Electrical system	2	2	3	3	3	3	3	4
Engines	4	4	4	4	4	4	4	4
Exhaust/Converter	2	2	2	2	2	2	2	3
Fuel system	4	4	4	4	4	4	4	4
Ignition system	3	3	3	3	3	3	3	4
Manual transmission	3	3	3	3	—	—	—	—
- automatic	4	4	4	4	4	4	4	4
Rust/Paint	4	4	4	4	4	4	4	4
Steering	3	3	3	3	3	4	4	4
Suspension	1	1	1	2	3	3	3	4
Crash Safety	1	—	—	—	1	—	5	5

VOLVO

700 Series

Rating: Above Average (1992); Average (1991); Not Recommended (1985–90). **Maintenance/Repair costs**: Higher than average, and repairs must be done by a Volvo dealer. **Parts**: Higher-than-average cost and limited availability.

Technical Data

ENGINES	Liters/CID	HP	MPG	Model Years
OHC I-4 FI	2.3/141	114	20–24	1985–92
DOHC I-4 FI	2.3/141	153	20–24	1989–91

OHC I-4T FI	2.3/141	157–162	19–24	1985–92
OHC V6 FI	2.8/174	134–145	17–22	1985–90
OHC 1-6TD FI	2.4/145	108	24–29	1985–86
DOHC 1-6 FI	2.9/178	181–201	18–22	1992

Strengths and weaknesses: The 700 series is more spacious, luxurious, and crashworthy than the entry-level 240. Its standard engine and transmission perform well, but aren't as refined as the 850. Furthermore, the 700 series suffers from the same generic brake, electrical, engine cooling, air conditioning, and body problems as does its cheaper cousin. Brakes tend to squeak or grind, wear rapidly, and require expensive service. Exhaust systems usually need replacing after a few years.

Owners complain of hard cold starts on 1987–89 models. Power windows fail to operate, as a result of either dirt getting into the mechanism or the wiring short-circuiting. Air conditioning units that emit a musty odor or fail to work properly when the car is idling are a common problem. Body and interior trim pieces are fragile—dashboard cracks often appear after the third year. The windshield wiper motor malfunctions after two years. There have been some complaints of sunroof rattles, premature surface rust (the paint chips easily), and rusted-out exhaust systems.

Safety summary/recalls: **NHTSA probes**: **1986–91**—Front seat/center console fires. **Recalls**: **1985**—Water pump pulley may be defective. **1985–87**—Possible engine wiring harness short circuit. **1985–88**—On vehicles with B230F engines, the driveshaft could separate from the transmission. **1986 wagons**—Locked tailgate can be opened from inside the vehicle. **1988**—Headlight switch may short-circuit. **1989–90**—Fuel may seep from fuel tank. Cars are eligible for new fuel tanks. **1992**—Faulty front seatbelts could detach from anchors. • The seatbelt webbing guide may break.

Secret Warranties/Service Tips

1988–90—Brake pulsation, a common problem, is addressed in DSB 51/111. • If you're having problems starting your Volvo on cold mornings, see DSB 23/135 and 23/21A. **1989–90**—Service Campaign No. 54 calls for the free installation of a cable harness. **1989–92**—To improve cold starting, Volvo will install an improved fuel injection control module gratis if the emissions warranty applies. Under another program, Volvo will replace the MFI E PROM to improve cold starting. **1990–91**—AM band radio interference will be stopped with kit #3533250-1. **1992**—Volvo Special Service Campaign No. 59 provides for the free replacement of AC pressure switches and harness, the Regina fuel control units, and Rex ignition control units. These repairs are to be carried out regardless of vehicle mileage or number of previous owners. • A decrease in idling speed when the AC engages can be corrected by installing a capacitor kit. **All models/years**—Check the valve cover nuts at every servicing interval to prevent oil leakage.

700 Series Profile

	1985	1986	1987	1988	1989	1990	1991	1992
Cost Price ($)								
740 GLE/GL	17,240	18,240	21,485	22,330	20,335	22,050	23,135	24,680
Used Values ($)								
740 GLE/GL ↑	4,500	5,500	6,500	7,000	8,000	9,500	11,000	12,500
740 GLE/GL ↓	4,000	5,000	5,500	6,500	7,000	8,000	9,500	11,000
Extended Warranty	Y	Y	Y	Y	Y	Y	Y	Y
Secret Warranty	N	N	N	N	N	N	N	N
Reliability	②	③	③	③	③	③	③	④
Air conditioning	①	①	①	①	②	②	③	④
Body integrity	②	②	②	②	②	②	②	③
Braking system	①	①	①	①	①	①	①	②
Electrical system	①	①	①	①	①	①	①	②
Exhaust/Converter	①	①	①	①	②	③	④	④
Fuel system	③	③	③	③	③	③	③	④
Ignition system	③	③	③	④	③	③	③	③
Manual transmission	③	③	③	③	③	③	③	④
- automatic	②	②	②	④	③	③	③	④
Rust/Paint	③	③	③	③	③	③	③	④
Steering	③	③	③	③	③	③	③	③
Suspension	③	③	③	③	③	③	③	④
Crash Safety	—	—	—	①	—	—	⑤	⑤

850 Series

Rating: Recommended (1993–97). Don't waste your money on a '97 850: the 1996 models are virtually identical to the more expensive '97 versions and are a real bargain if the selling price has been reduced sufficiently. **Maintenance/Repair costs**: Higher than average, and repairs must be done by a Volvo dealer. The '98 model 850s were redesignated the S70/V70. **Parts**: Parts are less expensive than other cars in this class, according to CAA. Limited availability.

Technical Data

ENGINES	Liters/CID	HP	MPG	Model Years
DOHC I-5 FI	2.4/149	168	20–27	1993–98
DOHC I-5 FI	2.4/149	190	19–26	1997–98
DOHC I-5T FI	2.3/192	222–240	19–25	1994–98

Strengths and weaknesses: Bland, but practical to the extreme with plenty of power, good handling, and plenty of capacity. For 1997, the 850 GLT got a bit more lower-end torque, while the turbo version was upgraded with electrically adjusted front-passenger seats and an in-dash CD player. The base 850 sedan uses a 2.4L 24-valve 168-hp 5-cylinder engine hooked to a front-drive powertrain. An all-wheel drive version is available only in Canada and Europe. Wagons use the same base powerplant, hooked to a 5-speed manual or optional 4-speed electronic automatic. GLTs have a torquier, turbo variant of the same powerplant that boosts horsepower to 190.

The "sports" sedan T5 is a rounder, sportier-looking Volvo that delivers honest, predictable performance but comes up a bit short on the "sport" side. Volvo's base turbo boosts horsepower to 222, but its new T-5R variant uses an upgraded turbocharger that boosts power to 240 horses—for up to seven seconds.

Passenger space, seating comfort, and trunk and cargo space are unmatched by the competition. Braking on dry and wet pavement is also exemplary. The rides of both the sedan and wagon deterio- rate progressively as the road gets rougher and passengers are added. Turbo versions are particularly stiff and passengers are con- stantly bumped and thumped.

So far the 850 has escaped the traditional AC, electrical system, and brake problems that afflict its predecessors. Owners have complained that the early models have uncomfortable seatbelts, insufficient rear travel for the front seats, and some body hardware deficiencies, resulting in excess noise invading the interior.

Dealer service bulletins: **1993–94**—Faulty engine accessory mount- ing brackets. • Electrical short circuits. • Water contamination of the accessory drive belt. • Poor radio reception on the FM band. **1995**—Faulty cruise control. • Climate control system odor. • Steering knock at full lock, rattle from tailgate lock, sunroof rat- tling, doorstop and interior fittings noise, and auxiliary belt noise. • Poor performance of the engine belt tensioner, and prematurely worn crankcase ventilation hoses. **1996**—AM band radio interfer- ence. • Cruise control won't engage. • Damage to tailgate by tailgate handle. • Generator noise in the loudspeakers. • High oil consumption. • Starting difficulties. • Improvements to ventilation and defrosting. • New shims to reduce rear resonance vibrations. • Remedies for noise from evaporative canister hose. • Repair tips for loose door stops in A and B posts. • Repair tips for roof panel unevenness. • Loose windshield upper trim strip.

Safety summary/recalls: **Recalls**: **1993–96**—Block heater could loosen and overheat, seriously damaging the engine. **1994**—Frozen throttle linkage could result in erratic engine operation. **1995**— The threaded insert that attaches the seatbelt catch to the front seat was incorrectly manufactured. • Some jacks may fail. **1996–97**— Throttle may not return to idle when foot is taken off the accelera- tor pedal.

Secret Warranties/Service Tips

1993—A jerking sensation while accelerating may be caused by electrical interference between the rpm sensor wiring and the secondary ignition system. • Accessory drive belt noise due to water infiltrating into the system can be corrected by installing a special right front fender liner extension manufactured by Volvo to fix the problem. • Headlight wiper and washer motors may cause radio interference on the FM band. Eliminate this noise by installing suppressed wiper motors and a suppressor between the washer pump and the existing wiring. • Under Service Campaign 62, Volvo dealers will install at no charge an improved engine accessory mounting bracket. **1993–94**—Steering column spring noise can be silenced by using upgraded bolts to secure the upper bracket to the airbag retaining plate. **1993–96**—Tips on repairing roof panel unevenness. **1995**—If the cruise control won't engage, check the vacuum supply and vacuum supply pipe first. **All models/years**—Check the valve cover nuts at every servicing interval to prevent oil leakage.

850 Series Profile

	1993	1994	1995	1996	1997
Cost Price ($)					
Base	24,495	24,725	25,540	26,620	28,180
Turbo	—	31,900	32,000	33,145	33,525
TLA/AWD	—	—	—	37,380	36,190
Used Values ($)					
Base ↑	15,500	17,500	18,500	21,000	23,000
Base ↓	14,000	16,000	17,500	19,500	22,000
Turbo ↑	—	21,500	24,000	27,000	28,500
Turbo ↓	—	20,000	22,500	25,000	27,000
TLA/AWD ↑	—	—	—	29,000	31,000
TLA/AWD ↓	—	—	—	27,500	29,000
Extended Warranty	Y	Y	Y	Y	Y
Secret Warranty	Y	N	N	N	N
Reliability	⑤	⑤	⑤	⑤	⑤
Air conditioning	③	③	④	⑤	⑤
Automatic transmission	③	④	⑤	⑤	⑤
Body integrity	④	④	④	④	④
Braking system	⑤	⑤	⑤	⑤	⑤
Electrical system	❷	❷	③	③	④
Engines	⑤	⑤	⑤	⑤	⑤
Exhaust/Converter	⑤	⑤	⑤	⑤	⑤
Fuel system	④	④	④	⑤	⑤
Ignition system	③	③	④	⑤	⑤
Rust/Paint	④	④	⑤	⑤	⑤
Steering	⑤	⑤	⑤	⑤	⑤
Suspension	③	④	⑤	⑤	⑤
Crash Safety	—	❶	⑤	⑤	⑤

Note: The low frontal crash ratings represent the inclusion of leg trauma in the overall score.

900 Series

Rating: Recommended (1991–97). The '98 model 900s were redesignated the S90/V90. **Maintenance/Repair costs**: Higher than average, and repairs must be done by a Volvo dealer. **Parts**: Higher-than-average cost and limited availability.

Technical Data

ENGINES	Liters/CID	HP	MPG	Model Years
DOHC I-4T FI	2.3/141	153	18–23	1991
OHC I-4 FI	2.3/141	114	20–24	1992–95
OHC I-4T FI	2.3/141	162	19–24	1991–95
DOHC 1-6 FI	2.9/178	181–201	18–22	1992–98

Strengths and weaknesses: Essentially a repackaged 760, these flagship rear-drive sedans and wagons have a much better reliability record than do the 240 and 700 series, and are on par with the 850 over the past five model years. Both the 940 and 960 offer exceptional roominess and comfort, and are capable of carrying six people with ease. The wagon provides lots of cargo space and manages to do it in great style. Some owner gripes: the base 114-hp 2.3L engine is overpowered by the car's weight, excessive fuel consumption with the turbo option, and excessive road and wind noise at highway speeds.

Dealer service bulletins: **1993–94**—Hard starting and stalling caused by low fuel volatility. • Excessive vibrations when idling on vehicles equipped with an automatic transmission. • Whistling from the bulkhead and wiper-well cover panel. **1995**—Evaporator odor treatment. • Front brake squealing. • Poor AC performance.

Safety summary/recalls: NHTSA probes: **1986–91**—Front seat/center console fires. **1991**—Sudden airbag deployment. These cars come with reinforced sides that Volvo claims exceed federal regulations. **1994–95**—Airbags deploy for no reason. **Recalls**: **1989–90**—Fuel may seep from fuel tank. **1991 Turbo**—Throttle may jam. • Child car seat may not conform to federal safety standards. **1992–93**—Front seatbelts may detach from anchorage. • The seatbelt webbing guide may break. **1993 Turbo 944/945**—Erratic throttle operation. **1995**—Driver-side airbag may not deploy properly. **1996–97**—Throttle may not return to idle when foot is taken off the accelerator pedal.

Secret Warranties/Service Tips

1989–93—To improve cold starting, Volvo will install an improved fuel-injection control module free of charge if the emissions warranty applies. Under another program, Volvo will replace the MFI E PROM to improve cold starting. **1992**—Volvo Special Service Campaign No. 59 provides for

the free replacement of AC pressure switches and harness, the Regina fuel
control units, and Rex ignition control units. These repairs are to be carried out regardless of the vehicle mileage or the number of previous owners. **1992–94**—A decrease in idling speed when the AC engages can be
corrected by installing a capacitor kit. **All models/years**—Check the valve
cover nuts at every servicing interval to prevent oil leakage.

900 Series Profile

	1991	1992	1993	1994	1995	1996	1997
Cost Price ($)							
940 GLE	28,265	25,390	25,390	23,325	24,315	—	—
960	—	34,370	36,070	33,875	30,360	34,455	34,795
Used Values ($)							
940 GLE ↑	11,000	13,000	13,500	15,000	17,500	—	—
940 GLE ↓	10,000	11,500	12,500	14,000	16,000	—	—
960 ↑	—	14,500	16,500	19,000	21,000	24,000	27,000
960 ↓	—	13,500	14,500	17,000	19,000	22,500	25,000
Extended Warranty	Y	Y	Y	Y	Y	N	N
Secret Warranty	Y	Y	Y	N	N	N	N
Reliability	③	③	④	⑤	⑤	⑤	⑤
Air conditioning	③	③	④	⑤	⑤	⑤	⑤
Automatic transmission	③	④	⑤	⑤	③	⑤	⑤
Body integrity	❷	❷	❷	❷	③	③	③
Braking system	❷	❷	❷	❷	③	④	④
Electrical system	❷	❷	❷	❷	❷	③	③
Engines	❷	❷	③	④	⑤	⑤	⑤
Exhaust/Converter	⑤	⑤	⑤	⑤	⑤	⑤	⑤
Fuel system	④	④	⑤	⑤	⑤	⑤	⑤
Ignition system	④	③	⑤	⑤	⑤	⑤	⑤
Rust/Paint	⑤	⑤	⑤	⑤	⑤	⑤	⑤
Steering	⑤	⑤	⑤	⑤	⑤	⑤	⑤
Suspension	③	④	⑤	⑤	⑤	⑤	⑤
Crash Safety	—	—	—	—	—	—	④

SPORTS CARS

The average sports car should be able to go from 0 to 60 mph in under 10 seconds and top 80 mph at the end of a quarter mile. Luxury sports sedans, like the Infiniti Q45 and Lexus LS 400, have produced exceptional acceleration times of 60 mph in less than 8 seconds and have exceeded 90 mph after a quarter mile. Nevertheless most sports cars—or "high-performance vehicles," as they're euphemistically named—sacrifice reliability, fuel economy, interior space, and comfortable suspension for speed, superior road handling, and attractive styling. Those which don't have these handicaps are usually loaded to the gills with high-tech, complex powertrain and suspension systems that make the car overweight, over-priced, difficult to troubleshoot, expensive to repair, and unreliable to boot.

Sports cars come with a whole slew of expensive high performance packages, mainly because they're not very sporty in their basic form. By carefully browsing through classified ads and dealer car lots you should find many fully-loaded offerings at a fraction of their original cost. Remember that models which have been taken off the market, like the Toyota Supra, Nissan 300ZX, and Chevrolet Corvette ZR1, aren't likely to become collectors' cars with soaring resale values. In fact, discontinued Japanese sports cars like the Nissan 1600 haven't done nearly as well as some of the British roadsters taken off the market about the same time.

Recommended

Chrysler Avenger, Sebring
Chrysler Stealth (1993–96)
Eagle Laser, Talon, 4X4
  (1995–97)
Ford Mustang (1994–97)
Ford Probe (1994–97)
GM Camaro/Firebird V6
  (1995–97)
Honda Prelude (1992–97)

Mazda MX-3, Precidia
  (1993–95)
Mazda MX-5, Miata (1993–97)
Mazda RX-7 (1991–95)
Mitsubishi 3000GT (1993–97)
Mitsubishi Eclipse (1995–97)
Nissan 240SX (1995–97)
Toyota Celica (1994–97)
Toyota MR2 (1988–95)

Above Average

Chrysler Stealth (1992)
Eagle Laser, Talon, 4X4
  (1995–97)
Ford Probe (1993–94)
GM Camaro/Firebird V6
  (1993–94)
GM Corvette (1995–97)
Honda Prelude (1988–91)

Mazda MX-5, Miata (1990–92)
Mazda RX-7 (1985–90)
Mitsubishi 3000GT (1992)
Mitsubishi Eclipse (1990–94)
Nissan 200SX
Nissan 240SX (1989–94)
Toyota Celica (1990–93)
Toyota MR2 (1988–90)

Hyundai Tiburon   Toyota Supra (1993–97)
Mazda MX-3, Precidia (1992)

Average

Chrysler Stealth (1991)   Nissan 300ZX (1990–96)
Ford Probe (1989–92)   Toyota Celica (1988–89)
GM Camaro/Firebird V6 (1991–92) Toyota MR2 (1986–87)
GM Corvette (1993–94)   Toyota Supra (1988–92)
Mitsubishi 3000GT (1991)

Below Average

Chrysler Daytona, Laser, Shelby   GM Camaro/Firebird V6 (1990)
  (1990–93)   Hyundai Scoupe (1991–95)
Ford Mustang (1988–93)   Nissan 300ZX (1988–89)

Not Recommended

Chrysler Daytona, Laser, Shelby   GM Corvette (1980–92)
  (1984–89)
GM Camaro/Firebird V6
  (1988–89)

1996 Pontiac Firebird: The Firebird is a recommended buy from 1995 to '97. This rear-drive sports car is both powerful and sleek. Too bad GM is seriously thinking of dropping it and its Camaro brother.

1990 Chrysler Daytona ES: Not recommended. "The Little Car That Couldn't." Another car with sports car styling and commuter car substance.

CHRYSLER

Daytona, Laser, Shelby

Rating: Below Average (1990–93); Not Recommended (1984–89). **Maintenance/Repair costs**: Higher than average, but repairs can be done by any garage. **Parts**: Higher-than-average cost and limited availability.

Technical Data

ENGINES	Liters/CID	HP	MPG	Model Years
OHC I-4 FI	2.2/135	96	19–24	1985–86
OHC I-4T FI	2.2/135	149	18–23	1985–88
OHC I-4T FI	2.2/135	174	17–21	1987–90
DOHC I-4T FI	2.2/135	224	17–21	1992–93
OHC I-4 FI	2.5/153	100	19–24	1986–93
OHC I-4 FI	2.5/153	152	17–21	1989–92
OHC V6 FI	3.0/181	141	17–21	1990–93

Strengths and weaknesses: The high-performance Daytonas—the Turbo Z, Pacifica, and Shelby Z—can run with the best of them for a little while, and then the service bills start piling up. Without the failure-prone turbocharged engine and sport suspension, these coupes provide mediocre handling and acceleration.

All engines are troublesome. If they're not maintained meticulously from the very beginning, the turbocharger is likely to fail around the 50,000-mile mark and cause serious damage to the engine and your wallet. Fuel system problems are common on all versions, requiring the frequent replacement of electronic computer modules. The manual transmission has a sloppy shift linkage and a heavy clutch that doesn't stand up to hard use. Models loaded with electrical accessories have a higher failure rate than stripped-down versions. Electronic instrument panels and other electrical items are temperamental. The body is particularly poorly assembled and water/wind leaks are common.

Safety summary/recalls: Recalls: 1985—Fatigue cracks could allow the seat to suddenly move backwards. **1985–87 Turbo**—Fire hazard caused by fuel supply hose leak. **1987–89**—Exhaust system heat may melt carpet. Install free heat shield kit #4549356. **1989–90**—Leaking cylinder heads and gaskets will be replaced free of charge under Recall No. 467. **1990**—Airbag may be defective on cars with a gray interior. **1991**—Front disc brake caliper guide pin bolts may be too loose. **1992**— Coupling bolts on steering column shaft may be faulty. **1992–93**—Dealers will install additional bolts to better secure the dash panel. • Inadequate spot welds attaching the front rails to the dash panel could cause structural damage, including door-opening interference and sheet metal cracking.

Secret Warranties/Service Tips

1989—Leaking fuel injectors are a common problem. • Corrosion of the oxygen sensor connector is a common problem that's no longer covered by the emissions warranty. **1989–90**—Defective valve stem seals are the likely cause of high oil consumption with 2.2L and 2.5L engines (DSB HL-49-89C). **1990–92**—Erratic idle speeds occurring after deceleration from a steady cruising speed can be corrected by replacing the idle air control motor with a revised motor. **1991–92**—Engines with a rough idle and stalling following a cold start may require a new single board engine controller (SBEC). **1992**—If the heater and ventilation system change to the defrost mode during acceleration, trailer towing, or hill climbing, the installation of a revised vacuum check valve should cure the problem. • Long crank times, a rough idle, and hesitation may be corrected by replacing the intake manifold assembly. • A leak in the oil filter area may be corrected by installing a special oil filter bracket gasket (#MD198554). **1992–93**—Some 41TE transaxles may produce a buzzing noise when shifted into Reverse. Replace the valve body assembly or valve body separator plate. **All models/years**—A rotten-egg odor coming from the exhaust is probably caused by a defective catalytic converter that may be covered by the emissions warranty.

Daytona, Laser, Shelby Profile

	1986	1987	1988	1989	1990	1991	1992	1993
Cost Price ($)								
Daytona	10,070	11,524	11,807	11,045	12,589	12,428	12,918	13,500
IROC	—	—	—	—	—	15,687	15,254	15,980
Laser	11,051	—	—	—	—	—	—	—
Shelby	—	14,474	15,176	14, 634	16,066	15,752	15,254	—
Used Values ($)								
Daytona ↑	2,500	3,000	3,500	4,000	4,700	5,500	6,500	7,000
Daytona ↓	2,000	2,500	3,000	3,200	4,000	4,700	5,500	6,000
IROC ↑	—	—	—	—	—	6,500	7,500	8,500
IROC ↓	—	—	—	—	—	5,500	6,000	7,500

Laser ↑	2,500	—	—	—	—	—	—	—
Laser ↓	2,000	—	—	—	—	—	—	—
Shelby ↑	—	3,500	4,000	4,700	5,500	6,500	7,500	—
Shelby ↓	—	2,500	3,000	3,700	4,500	5,500	6,500	—

Extended Warranty	Y	Y	Y	Y	Y	Y	Y	Y
Secret Warranty	N	N	N	N	N	N	N	N

Reliability	③	③	❷	❷	③	③	③	③
Crash Safety								
Daytona	—	—	—	⑤	—	⑤	⑤	⑤

Avenger, Sebring

Rating: Recommended (1995–97). The Avenger, and its more luxuriously appointed Sebring twin, have had fewer factory-related defects than other new Chrysler designs, probably because they're built at its Illinois plant—by Mitsubishi. **Maintenance/Repair costs**: Higher than average, and repairs must be done by a Chrysler dealer. **Parts**: Higher-than-average cost and limited availability.

Technical Data

ENGINES	Liters/CID	HP	MPG	Model Years
DOHC I-4 FI	2.0L/122	140	22–31	1995–98
OHC V6 FI	2.5L/152	155–163	20–28	1995–98

Strengths and weaknesses: Like the Eagle Talon and Mitsubishi Eclipse, both the Avenger and Sebring are surprisingly agile—which isn't that surprising considering they share many of the same components. This also explains why quality control is above reproach and body construction is solid, with few gaps. Interior space is more than ample for driver and passengers, though the rear seating may be uncomfortable for long trips.

The convertible, made in Mexico, is six inches longer than the Sebring coupe and is powered by a standard 2.0L twin cam, while the upscale JXi gets a performance injection with the 2.5L 6-cylinder powerplant.

Acceleration is fairly good with the base engine, but the optional V6 powerplant is the engine of choice to overcome the power-hungry automatic transmission. Engine, tire, and road noise at higher speeds can be disconcerting. Rear seat access can be literally a pain.

Dealer service bulletins: **1995**—Poor engine performance, hard starts, and stalling caused by a faulty powertrain control module. • Tendency to drift to the left requires upgraded compression lower arm assemblies. • Loss of air conditioning (corrected by installing a revised AC pressure transducer). • Headliner sagging. • Difficulty in closing the sunroof owing to a faulty lever mechanism. **1996**—Troubleshooting excessive brake noise. • Door buzz and rattle. • Hard start, misfire, or rough idle. • Interior window film buildup. • No-start condition. • Poor driveability. • Engine compartment popping or knocking. • Power seat switch can stick. • Ratcheting sound when coming to a stop. • Rear shock noise. • Sag or hesitation on acceleration. • Shudders during upshift. • Sunroof inoperative or opens by itself. • Sunroof ratcheting sound or jerky operation; binding or coming off its track. • Speed control undershoot or overshoot. • Engine compartment ticking noise. • Transaxle shudder. • Vehicle drift or lead.

Safety summary/recalls: NHTSA probes: 1996–97—Sebring convertible top flies off. • Small horn buttons on the steering wheel spokes may be hard to reach in an emergency. **Recalls: 1996–97**—Prematurely corroded ball-joint components will be replaced. **1996**—Faulty power mirror switch. • Power brake booster hose mislocated. **1997**—Front passenger head restraint support bracket may break. Dealers must replace the entire seat back assembly.

Secret Warranties/Service Tips

1995—One of the causes of premature brake wear, shudder, and noise is a misadjusted brake light switch. **1995–96**—Engine compartment ticking can be silenced by replacing the duty cycle purge solenoid with a quieter solenoid assembly. **1995–97**—Engine compartment popping or knocking may require an upgraded EGR valve. • Tips for reducing transaxle shudder are found in DSB #21-05-97.

Avenger, Sebring Profile

	1995	1996	1997
Cost Price ($)			
Avenger	16,309	17,008	—
V6	18,260	19,190	18,857
Sebring	17,636	18,418	18,541
V6	20,548	20,685	21,555
Convertible	—	25,210	—
Used Values ($)			
Avenger ↑	12,000	13,500	—
Avenger ↓	10,500	12,000	—
V6 ↑	13,000	15,000	16,000
V6 ↓	12,000	13,500	15,000
Sebring ↑	12,500	14,000	15,500
Sebring ↓	11,000	13,000	14,500
V6 ↑	14,000	16,000	17,500
V6 ↓	12,500	14,500	16,000
Convertible ↑	—	17,500	—
Convertible ↓	—	16,500	—

Extended Warranty	N	N	N
Secret Warranty	N	N	N
Reliability	⑤	⑤	⑤
Crash Safety			
Avenger	—	⑤	⑤
Sebring	—	—	⑤
Sebring convertible	—	—	④

CHRYSLER/MITSUBISHI

Eclipse, Laser, Talon, 4X4

Rating: Recommended (1995–97); Above Average (1990–94). The '95 version offers fresh styling, dual airbags, and a more powerful engine. The 1996 models are identical to the more expensive, restyled '97 versions, and are the better buy if they're substantially cheaper. **Maintenance/Repair costs**: Higher than average, but repairs can be done practically anywhere. **Parts**: Good parts availability. Dealers have had some trouble adequately servicing these high-tech vehicles, and parts are a bit more expensive than other cars in this class.

Technical Data

ENGINES	Liters/CID	HP	MPG	Model Years
OHC I-4T FI	1.8/107	92	22–26	1990–94
DOHC I-4 FI	2.0/122	135	21–25	1990–94
DOHC I-4T FI	2.0/122	195	17–23	1990–94
DOHC I-4 FI	2.0/122	140	21–25	1995–98
DOHC I-4 FI	2.0/122	205–210	21–25	1995–98

Strengths and weaknesses: These sporty Mitsubishi-made cars combine high performance, low price, and reasonable durability. The base 1.8L engine is adequate and the suspension is comfortable, although a bit soft. The optional 16-valve, turbocharged 2.0L comes with a firmer suspension and gives more horsepower for the dollar than most other front-drive sports coupes, without much turbo lag. The 5-speed manual is the gearbox of choice. Torque steer makes the car appear to try to twist out of your hands when all 195 turbocharged horses are unleashed. The 4-speed automatic transmission cuts into the Laser's highway performance. Overall handling is impressive, with the 4X4 system giving sure-footed foul weather stability. Keep in mind that the all-wheel-drive (AWD) model has a smaller trunk area than the front-drive.

The '97 Talon was dramatically restyled with wide air openings under the front bumper, new body cladding, and a redesigned rear end which includes a spoiler housing the center-mounted stop light. A new, decontented (a fancy word that means it lacks many of the bells and whistles of the ESi, TSi, and TSi AWD) base model was also added. The TSi got 17-inch wheels and better high performance tires.

The ESi comes with a 140-hp 2.0L engine (borrowed from the Neon Sport), while the TSi is powered by a 210-hp 2.0L Mitsubishi-bred engine. Two additional powerplants are available: a 2.0L double overhead cam with 135-hp, and a turbocharged version of the same engine rated at a sizzling 195-hp. A manual 5-speed is standard, and an optional 4-speed automatic is available on all models except the Turbo RS. AWD is offered on both '96 car models, but only the '97 TSi offers AWD.

All high performance models cost thousands of dollars less than their Japanese competitors, without compromising quality or performance. The 16-valve Talon/4X4 is at the top of the trim list and provides five more horses than the turbocharged TSi.

Mitsubishi products have an above-average reliability record, as several decades of Colts have shown. Nevertheless, beginning with the 1990–94 models, owners report glitches with the 1.8L engine and electrical system, driveline vibrations, premature brake wear and excessive noise, and poor fit and finish. Some problems reported with 1995–97 versions were unstable idling, poor idling, and reduced rpm when the AC is running; cold weather hard starts and stalling; cold weather transmission shift delays (2–3 and 3–4) that take up to two minutes; transmission defaults into second gear (limp-in mode); a tendency to drift or lead to the right; speed control undershoot or overshoot; false theft alarm; center exhaust pipe heat shield buzz; door buzz and rattle; misadjusted door glass causing water leaks and wind noise; noisy clutch pedal; interior window film buildup; headliner sagging; power seat switch can stick; stress marks on the quarter trim panel; buzz or rattle from the rear quarter trim; inoperative, noisy, and jerky sunroof operation; faulty lever latch pin; and the sunroof may open by itself.

Dealer service bulletins: 1994—Turbocharger bolts may be poorly torqued (Chrysler will re-torque them for free—DSB JE-41-89). • Excessive engine noise caused by carbon buildup on the top of the pistons. • Excessive driveline vibration. • Rear brake squeak, and standard brakes often lock up or require long stopping distances. **1995**—Poor idling and reduced rpm when the AC engages (requires an upgraded powertrain control module). • Cold weather hard starts and stalling, and cold weather transmission shift delays (2–3 and 3–4) that take up to two minutes. • Vehicle tends to drift or lead to the right, requiring upgraded compression lower arm assemblies. • Center exhaust pipe heat shield buzz and noisy clutch pedal. • Headliner sagging. • Stress marks on the quarter trim panel. • Faulty sunroof lever latch pin. **1996**—No-start due to faulty neutral safety switch. • Hard start, misfire, or rough idle. • Erratic idle. • Single cylinder misfire. • Driveability improvements. • Shuddering during upshifts or when torque converter is engaged. • Reduced limp-in default sensitivity. • Difficulty going into second gear or Reverse after a cold start. • Speed control overshoots or undershoots. • Vehicle drifts or leads at high speeds. • Excessive brake noise. • Intermittent theft alarm activation. • Power seat switch can stick. • Ratcheting sound when coming to a stop. • Sunroof is inoperative or opens by itself. • Sunroof operation produces a ratcheting sound or is jerky. • Sunroof or sunshade binds or comes off its track. • Door buzz and rattle. • Rear quarter trim buzz or rattle. • Engine compartment ticking noise. • Interior window film buildup. **1997**— Excessive brake noise. • Inoperative CD player. • Poor driveability. • Transmission shudder. • Loose side body moldings.

Safety summary/recalls: Standard brakes often lock up or require long stopping distances. Choose the optional ABS. • Three deficiencies that compromise comfort and safety on many of these cars are the absence of airbags and ABS on the Laser, a small, shallow trunk with a high sill, and head restraints that block rear visibility. **Recalls**: **1990**—Sunroof glass may detach from roof. • Poor windshield retention during a collision. **1990 Laser**—Headlight wiring harness may short, causing the lights to fail. **1990 Talon/4X4**—Early production oxygen sensors that can't withstand the turbo engine's high temperatures will be replaced for free under an emissions recall. **1990–91**—Takata seatbelt replacement. **1995–96**— Incorrectly installed fuel gauge/pump gaskets may cause a fire. Requires a new fuel tank. **1997 Talon/4X4 and Eclipse**—Front passenger head restraint support bracket may break. Dealers must replace the entire seat back assembly.

Secret Warranties/Service Tips

1991–92—Tappet/lash adjuster noise is a common problem that's covered by DSB 09-53-91. **1990 Laser**—To correct transmission case gasket leaks, use gasket kit #MD730803. **1990 Talon**—Turbocharger bolts may be poorly torqued. • Warping of the headliner molding can be fixed by installing an improved molding. • If the headlights won't retract when the switch is turned off, replace the passing control relay, heat shrink tube, and tie straps. • Hard shifting/gear clash can be prevented by installing a modified 1–2 synchronizer sleeve, spring, and 3–4 spring. **1990–91**—A loose rear-quarter trim panel may require new clips. **1990–94**—Driveline vibrations on smooth roads can be eliminated by installing upgraded engine and transmission mounting brackets. **1992–94**—Rear brake squeaks can be silenced with a Mitsubishi shim kit. **1997**—Tips available on repairing loose side body moldings. **All models/years**—A rotten-egg odor coming from the exhaust may be the result of a malfunctioning catalytic converter, which may be covered by the emissions warranty.

Eclipse, Laser, Talon, 4X4 Profile

	1990	1991	1992	1993	1994	1995	1996	1997
Cost Price ($)								
Eclipse	12,526	12,655	12,894	13,399	13,686	15,891	15,135	15,821
Laser	12,890	12,958	13,398	13,876	14,042	—	—	—
Turbo RS	16,135	16,150	17,110	17,680	17,887	—	—	—
Talon	14,944	14,906	15,854	13,910	14,080	16,927	15,954	16,701
Talon AWD	18,386	18,429	19,382	20,034	20,270	20,758	21,695	21,666
Used Values ($)								
Eclipse ↑	5,000	6,000	6,500	7,500	9,000	11,500	12,500	13,500
Eclipse ↓	4,000	5,000	6,000	6,500	7,500	10,000	11,500	12,500
Laser ↑	5,000	5,500	6,500	7,500	8,500	—	—	—
Laser ↓	4,000	4,500	5,500	6,500	7,500	—	—	—
Turbo RS ↑	5,500	6,500	7,500	8,500	9,000	—	—	—
Turbo RS ↓	4,500	5,500	6,000	7,500	8,000	—	—	—
Talon ↑	5,500	6,500	7,500	8,500	9,000	12,000	13,000	14,500
Talon ↓	5,000	5,500	6,000	7,500	8,500	10,500	12,000	13,500
Talon AWD ↑	6,500	7,500	8,500	9,500	11,000	14,000	16,000	17,500
Talon AWD ↓	5,500	6,500	7,500	8,500	9,500	12,500	14,500	16,000
Extended Warranty	N	N	N	N	N	N	N	N
Secret Warranty	N	N	N	N	N	N	N	N
Reliability	②	③	③	④	④	④	⑤	⑤
Air conditioning	③	③	④	⑤	⑤	⑤	④	④
Body integrity	②	②	②	②	②	②	③	③
Braking system	②	②	②	②	③	①	④	④
Electrical system	②	②	②	②	②	②	②	③
Engines	①	②	②	③	③	②	③	④
Exhaust/Converter	③	③	③	④	⑤	⑤	⑤	⑤
Fuel system	④	③	③	④	④	④	④	⑤
Ignition system	③	②	②	③	③	④	⑤	⑤
Manual transmission	③	③	③	④	④	④	⑤	⑤
- automatic	②	②	③	③	④	⑤	⑤	⑤
Rust/Paint	②	②	②	③	③	②	③	④
Steering	④	④	④	④	⑤	⑤	⑤	⑤
Suspension	③	④	④	④	④	⑤	⑤	⑤
Crash Safety	①	—	—	—	—	—	—	④

3000GT, Stealth

Rating: Recommended (1993–97); Above Average (1992); Average (1991). The Mitsubishi 3000GT and Dodge Stealth are serious, reasonably priced sports cars that are as much go as show. **Maintenance/Repair costs**: Average, and repairs must be done by a Chrysler or Mitsubishi dealer. **Parts**: Higher-than-average cost and limited availability. The small engine compartment means that some of the simplest jobs will require special tools and take an inordinate amount of time to complete.

Technical Data

ENGINES	Liters/CID	HP	MPG	Model Years
3000GT				
SOHC V6 FI	3.0/181	161	16–20	1997–98
DOHC V6 FI	3.0/181	222	18–28	1991–98
DOHC V6T FI	3.0/181	300–320	16–21	1991–98
Stealth				
SOHC V6 FI	3.0/181	164	18–23	1991–96
DOHC V6 FI	3.0/181	222	18–23	1991–96
DOHC V6T FI	3.0/181	300–320	18–23	1991–96

Strengths and weaknesses: An impressive highway performer with a good reliability record. The base V6 engine accelerates well and provides more than enough power for all driving conditions. The awesome twin turbo power on the R/T Turbo rivals the engine performance of sports cars selling for far more. Power steering is crisp and predictable and provides just the right amount of road feel. Standard disc brakes work very well, but the ABS is particularly impressive in stopping the car in a short distance without any loss of steering stability or fading after repeated application. Where the Stealth disappoints is in its limited driver head room (a Ford Probe problem, too), confusing and hard-to-find interior instrumentation and controls, hard-to-service engine compartment, and mediocre quality control when it comes to body hardware, fit, and finish. The Stealth isn't a car for short drivers, since they may have trouble seeing over the hood or reaching the clutch pedal. When the seat is moved forward, short drivers may be unable to see the overhead lights. Rear seating is very cramped—the norm with most sports cars. The dash control that adjusts the exhaust system sound is more gimmick than innovation. The Turbo's excessive weight taxes fuel economy.

Dealer service bulletins and a small number of owner complaints show that the first-year (1991) Stealth had an unusually large number of factory defects that were corrected in the second year. For example, owners report frequent gearbox and fit problems, including drivetrain noise, grinding noise when shifting, gear clash, hard shifting into all gears, difficulty shifting into Reverse, door glass rattling, excessive wind noise along door glass, water leaks, and sluggish window operation. Other problems reported by owners and confirmed by dealer service bulletins: cruise-control failure due to improper wiring connection, noisy engine lash adjuster, power transfer unit and viscous coupling failure, 1–2 gear clash, faulty exhaust manifold nuts, noisy steering column, rear suspension tapping noise, and faulty turn signals.

Safety summary/recalls: **NHTSA probes**: **1992–93**—Sunroof glass shattering. **Recalls**: **1991**—Takata seatbelt replacement. **1991 R/T Turbo**—Oil leaking from the AWD transfer case may cause bearing damage/failure. **1991–94**—Front-wheel brake hoses may crack.

Secret Warranties/Service Tips

1991–94—Rear cargo cover rattling or failure to stay in the holder requires a new clip. **1992**—Vehicles that won't start may have corroded wiring in the A-67 12-connector. **1994**—Door glass weather stripping may pull out, requiring the installation of upgraded weather stripping. **All models/years**— A rotten-egg odor coming from the exhaust is probably the result of a malfunctioning catalytic converter, which may be covered by the emissions warranty.

3000GT, Stealth Profile

	1991	1992	1993	1994	1995	1996	1997
Cost Price ($)							
Base 3000GT	21,161	21,826	24,102	27,645	28,920	31,110	28,400
Turbo	32,265	34,288	37,693	41,370	43,520	46,878	45,060
Base Stealth	18,484	19,525	20,863	23,659	24,572	25,651	—
RT	24,443	25,868	27,766	26,404	27,756	29,207	—
RT Turbo	30,438	32,096	34,350	38,785	38,785	35,355	—
Used Values ($)							
Base 3000GT ↑	9,500	11,000	13,000	15,000	17,500	20,000	23,000
Base 3000GT ↓	8,000	9,500	11,000	13,500	16,000	18,500	22,000
Turbo ↑	13,500	16,000	18,500	21,000	23,000	27,500	30,000
Turbo ↓	12,500	14,000	16,500	18,500	22,000	25,500	28,000
Base Stealth ↑	8,500	10,000	11,000	13,500	15,500	18,500	—
Base Stealth ↓	7,000	8,500	10,000	12,500	14,500	17,000	—
RT ↑	10,000	12,000	14,000	15,000	17,000	20,000	—
RT ↓	8,500	10,000	12,000	14,000	15,000	17,500	—
RT Turbo ↑	13,500	15,000	18,000	20,000	23,000	26,000	—
RT Turbo ↓	12,000	13,500	16,000	18,000	22,000	24,500	—
Extended Warranty	N	N	N	N	N	N	N
Secret Warranty	Y	Y	Y	Y	Y	Y	Y
Reliability	③	③	④	⑤	⑤	⑤	⑤
Air conditioning	③	⑤	⑤	⑤	⑤	⑤	⑤
Body integrity	❷	❷	❷	❷	④	④	⑤
Braking system	③	③	❷	③	④	④	④
Electrical system	❷	❷	❷	❷	③	③	④
Engines	⑤	⑤	④	④	⑤	⑤	⑤
Exhaust/Converter	⑤	⑤	⑤	⑤	⑤	⑤	⑤
Fuel system	⑤	⑤	⑤	⑤	⑤	⑤	⑤
Ignition system	❷	③	④	⑤	⑤	⑤	⑤
Manual transmission	③	③	③	③	⑤	⑤	⑤
- automatic	③	③	③	③	⑤	⑤	⑤
Rust/Paint	③	③	③	③	③	④	⑤
Steering	⑤	⑤	⑤	⑤	⑤	⑤	⑤
Suspension	③	③	③	④	⑤	⑤	⑤
Crash Safety	—	—	❶	—	—	—	—

FORD

Mustang, Cobra

Rating: Recommended (1994–97); Below Average (1988–93). GM's Camaro and Firebird are the Mustang's traditional competition as far as performance is concerned. All 4-cylinder versions should be shunned. **Maintenance/Repair costs**: Average, particularly because repairs can be done anywhere. **Parts**: Average cost and often sold for much less through independent suppliers.

Technical Data

ENGINES	Liters/CID	HP	MPG	Model Years
OHC I-4 1 bbl.	2.3/140	88	18–21	1985–86
OHC I-4 FI	2.3/140	88	19–23	1987–90
OHC I-4 FI	2.3/140	105	20–24	1991–93
OHC I-4T FI	2.3/140	155–205	17–20	1985–86
OHV V6 FI	3.8/232	120	16–19	1985–86
OHV V6 FI	3.8/232	145–150	19–24	1994–98
OHC V8 FI	4.6/281	215–225	17–22	1996–98
OHC V8 FI	4.6/281	305	17–22	1996–98
OHV V8 4 bbl.	5.0/302	210	13–16	1985
OHV V8 FI	5.0/302	165–225	13–17	1985–95
OHV V8 FI	5.0/302	215–240	16–20	1994–95

Strengths and weaknesses: Rear-wheel drive Mustangs remain popular because they offer sporty styling and high performance thrills, usually for less money than GM's Camaro and Firebird, the Mustang's main domestic competitors. Ford has the price advantage, with a base Mustang costing a bit less than the cheapest Camaro, but it lags from a performance standpoint—10 horses with the V6 and 60 horses with the V8. The GM models offer crisper handling, standard ABS, a 6-speed transmission, and more comfortable rear seats. The 1988–93 Mustangs provide competent highway performance with a minimum of surprises when equipped with the optional 5.0L V8 powerplant. The 4-cylinder engine, used through 1993, isn't just failure prone—it also doesn't carry half the horses as the 5.0L V8 and has no redeeming qualities. A limited-edition Cobra debuted in 1993, sporting a 245-hp V8. Unfortunately, the 1993 Mustang fell behind its GM competition when the Camaro and Firebird were radically restyled that year.

Don't waste your money on a '97 Mustang if a '96 version is available in good condition. The '96 models were substantially improved and can be a real bargain if the price is right.

1994–97 models

Ford fought back with its own redesign of the '94 model which replaced the 4-banger with a V6, added four-wheel disc brakes, made the chassis more rigid (especially the convertible version), and dropped the hatchback. Mustangs now carry a base 3.8L V6 and an optional 4.6L V8. In addition, the high performance, limited-edition Cobra variation delivers 90 more horses than what the stock 4.6L V8 offers. The single and twin cam V8 options make the Mustang a powerful, if a bit unsophisticated, street machine. V6 models are an acceptable compromise, even though the engine fails to deliver the gobs of power most performance enthusiasts expect from a Mustang. Base models come equipped with a host of luxury and convenience items, which can be a real bargain once the base price has sufficiently depreciated—say, after the first three or four years. Off-lease models are particularly good buys these days.

This is definitely not a family car. For example, a light rear end makes the car dangerously unstable on wet roads or when cornering at high speeds. But for those who want a sturdy and stylish second car, or who don't need room in the back or standard ABS, the 1994–97 Mustang is a pretty good sports car buy. And if GM carries out its threat to drop its rear-drive Camaro and Firebird by the year 2000, the Mustang will be the main alternative for rear-drive sports car enthusiasts.

Like Camaros, Mustangs have never been very reliable cars. The first Mustang, launched in 1964 and now worth more than $25,000, had serious rusting, electrical, and suspension problems. And guess what? Thirty-five years later Mustangs still have electrical systems and electronic modules that are constantly breaking down and a base suspension and front brakes that wear out quickly.

The less said about the infamous 2.3L 4-cylinder engine, the better. The V6 and V8 engines are reasonably reliable, but the V8 has a definite performance and reliability edge. Turbocharged models aren't recommended because of their frequent and expensive mechanical breakdowns. If you want high-performance action, you'll have to pay a premium—and be prepared for some monstrous repair bills. Sport trim models feature an upgraded suspension and wheel package that improves handling considerably. The SVO rivals many expensive sports cars in performance but commands a very high resale price.

Common problems with the pre-'94 models are failure-prone 4-cylinder engines, manual transmission malfunctions, worn-out power-steering assemblies, prematurely worn front suspension components, and temperamental carburetors. Troublesome EEC IV ignition modules have provoked many stalling and hard starting complaints. Hood and trunk lid edges are prone to rust perforation.

The redesigned '94 and later versions produced less body complaints (although paint delamination became more severe) and a more durable engine and automatic transmission. This said, keep in mind that the electronic modules that govern engine and transmission performance are often on the fritz, producing chronic hard starts, stalling, and overall poor city and highway performance. Furthermore, the 3.8L 6-cylinder engine has begun to tally up a record number of head gasket failures around the 80,000 mile mark. Other problem areas: the front brakes, fuel pumps and front suspension remain consistent weak spots and MacPherson struts and various steering components are likely to wear out before their time. The parking brake cable also seizes easily. The EEC IV engine computer can be temperamental, and electrical problems are common. Assembly quality is still not on par with Japanese vehicles.

Dealer service bulletins: **1993**—AC odors. • Minor surface damage to bumper covers. • Noisy power steering units. **1994**—Faulty 3.8L engine rocker arm assembly that causes squeaking, chirping, or knocking. • Rough idle, hesitation, and excessive fuel consumption. • Poor heater output is likely caused by a thermostat stuck in an open position or opening before it should. • Transmission shudder under light-to-moderate acceleration. • Noise in radio speakers caused by the fuel pump. **1995**—Misaligned or worn accessory drive belt. • Delayed transmission engagement and shift errors, intermittent loss of torque at 3–4 upshift, and shifts to Neutral during heavy throttle. • Insufficient AC cooling or excessive clutch end gap. • Rear brake squeak, brake roughness upon application, and a thumping/clacking sound when braking. • Water intrusion of the MLP/TR sensor. • Faulty rear view mirror, loose rocker panel moldings, a temperature control knob that doesn't reach full cool position, and a malfunctioning temperature gauge. • Fuel pump buzz/whine heard through the radio speaker in addition to poor radio reception. **1996–97**—Stalling or hard starts. • Noisy 4.6L engine. • Transmission valve body cross leaks. • Erratic or prolonged 1–2 shift. • Squeal or hoot noise from engine compartment. Accessory belt damaged or comes off. • Coolant leaks from upper radiator hose. • Chatter during turns. • Front suspension rattle. • Fuel pump buzz/whine is still heard through the radio speaker. • Musty and mildew-type odors. • Blower motor noisy or inoperative in cold weather. • Convertible top leaks. • Sticking or clicking odometer/trip meter. • Overheating; AC shuts off. • Hard starting, long crank, stalling. • Loose catalyst or muffler heat shields. • Fog/film on windshield/interior glass.

Safety summary/recalls: Regularly equipped Mustangs, like most rear-drive Fords, don't handle sharp curves, wet roads, or sudden acceleration very well. The rear end swings out suddenly, and the car tends to spin. Furthermore, when the car loses traction on wet pavement, braking is barely adequate. **Recalls**: **1984–85**—Front seatbelt buckles may break and separate from the belt webbing. **1985**—Defective ignition module. • Faulty plastic sleeve in front seatbelt tongue assembly. • Power brake booster could come apart. **1986–87**—Fuel line coupling may leak fuel. **1987**—Faulty fuel-injection tube assemblies may cause fuel leakage and create a fire hazard. **1988–93**—Faulty ignition module may pose a fire hazard.

1991—Vehicle could roll away with the shift lever in Park position. **1995**—Defective tie-rod ends could cause an excessive shake or shimmy, resulting in an accident. **1995 GT**—Front seat cushion supports could abrade wiring harness, posing a fire hazard.

Secret Warranties/Service Tips

1980–88—Inoperative power door locks need an upgraded retainer clip assembly (#E8AZ-5421952-A). **1982–86**—Wind noise and water leaks with T-roofs and convertibles are usually caused by misaligned doors. Install door alignment kit #E72Z-6123042-A or -B. **1982–90**—An unusual engine metal-to-metal noise may be caused by the flexing of the torque converter. Install six new flywheel bolts with reduced head height to provide additional clearance. **1985–97**—A buzz or rattle from the exhaust system may be caused by a loose heat shield catalyst. **1986–94**—The in-tank fuel pump is the likely cause of all that radio static you hear. Stop the noise by installing an electronic noise RFI filter (#F1PZ-18B925-A). **1987–90**—Excessive oil consumption is likely caused by leaking gaskets, poor sealing of the lower intake manifold, defective intake and exhaust valve stem seals, or worn piston rings. Install new guide-mounted valve stem seals for a more positive fit and new piston rings with improved oil control. **1988–92**—Cold hesitation when accelerating, rough idle, long crank times, and stalling may all signal the need to clean out excessive intake valve deposits. These problems also may result from the use of fuels that have low volatility, such as high octane, premium blends. **1990**—Excessive transmission noise, delayed shifts, or no engagements may be due to thrust washer metal particles that have plugged the filter or burnt out the clutch plates. **1990–93**—Noise heard from the power-steering pump may be caused by air in the system. **1991**—A rough idle or lean fuel flow may require the installation of deposit-resistant injectors. **1994**—Automatic transmissions with delayed or no forward engagement, or a higher engine rpm than expected when coming to a stop, are covered in DSB 94-26-9. • A cracked cowl top vent grille should be replaced with an upgraded version. • A driveline boom can be silenced by replacing the rear upper control arms. • A noisy fuel pump needs to be replaced by an improved "guided check valve" fuel pump. • Models with laser red paint may have serious paint decay problems requiring a repainting of the entire body. • A ticking or tapping sound coming from the engine at idle can be silenced by installing an improved fuel hose/damper assembly. **1994–95**—A thumping or clacking heard from the front brakes signals the need to machine the front disc brake rotors. Ford may pay for this repair under its base warranty. • Loss of torque during or just after 3–4 shift may be caused by a hydraulic condition in the transmission or an intermittent signal from one of the powertrain system sensors. **1994–97**—An erratic or prolonged 1–2 shift can be cured by replacing the cast aluminum piston with a one-piece stamped steel piston with bonded lip seals and by replacing the top accumulator spring. These upgraded parts will increase the transmission's durability, says Ford. **1996**—Stalling or hard starts may be due to the idle air control valve sticking. **All models/years**—Three components that frequently benefit from Ford "goodwill" warranty extensions are catalytic converters, fuel pumps, and computer modules. If Ford balks at refunding your money, apply the emissions warranty for a full or partial refund. • Paint delamination, fading, peeling, hazing, and "microchecking": See pages 94–95 for details on claiming a refund.

Mustang, Cobra Profile

	1990	1991	1992	1993	1994	1995	1996	1997
Cost Price ($)								
LX/Coupe	11,341	12,321	12,343	12,847	16,455	17,550	18,485	18,810
Convertible	16,926	18,271	18,873	19,706	22,840	23,610	23,935	23,710
Cobra	—	—	—	19,935	22,425	23,060	26,645	27,195
Used Values ($)								
LX/Coupe ↑	5,000	5,500	6,000	7,000	10,000	12,000	13,500	15,000
LX/Coupe ↓	4,000	4,500	5,000	6,000	8,500	10,000	12,000	14,000
Convertible ↑	6,500	7,000	7,500	8,500	12,500	14,500	16,000	18,500
Convertible ↓	5,000	5,500	6,500	7,000	11,000	13,000	15,000	17,000
Cobra ↑	—	—	—	13,000	16,000	18,500	21,000	23,500
Cobra ↓	—	—	—	11,000	14,500	16,500	19,000	21,500
Extended Warranty	Y	Y	Y	N	N	N	N	N
Secret Warranty	Y	Y	Y	Y	Y	Y	Y	Y
Reliability	2	3	3	3	4	4	4	4
Air conditioning	1	1	1	1	1	2	4	5
Body integrity	1	1	2	2	2	2	3	3
Braking system	1	1	2	2	2	2	3	3
Electrical system	1	1	1	1	2	3	4	4
Engines	3	3	3	4	4	4	4	4
Exhaust/Converter	2	3	3	3	3	4	5	5
Fuel system	2	3	3	3	3	4	5	5
Ignition system	3	3	3	3	4	4	4	4
Manual transmission	3	3	3	3	4	5	5	5
- automatic	2	2	2	2	3	3	3	4
Rust/Paint	1	1	1	1	1	1	1	2
Steering	2	3	3	3	3	4	5	5
Suspension	2	3	3	3	3	4	5	5
Crash Safety								
Base	—	—	—	—	1	4	4	4
Convertible	1	5	5	1	—	—	5	5

Probe

Rating: Recommended (1995–97); Above Average (1993–94); Average (1989–92). **Maintenance/Repair costs**: Average, and repairs can be done by independent garages or Mazda dealers. Nevertheless, the under-hood layout is crowded, making for high routine maintenance costs. **Parts**: Despite the fact that 1997 was the Probe's last model year (Mazda's MX-6 bit the dust as well), parts should remain plentiful and reasonably priced.

Technical Data

ENGINES	Liters/CID	HP	MPG	Model Years
OHC I-4 FI	2.2/133	110	20–26	1989–92
OHC I-4T FI	2.2/133	145	19–23	1989–92

OHV V6 FI	3.0/182	140–145	17–23	1990–92
DOHC I-4 FI	2.0/122	115–118	21–27	1993–97
DOHC V6 FI	2.5/153	164	19–23	1993–97

Strengths and weaknesses: The sporty four-seater Probe coupe was launched in May 1988 as the front-wheel drive replacement for the aging Mustang. Don't get the impression that the Mazda MX-6 and Probe are twins because they share most mechanical features. In fact, they differ markedly in handling and appearance. Ford engineers took more control of the chassis tuning and suspension geometry to give the car a smoother and firmer sporty demeanor, and its stylists chopped and pulled the body to give it a more aero-dynamic, aggressive personality.

Available only as a two-door hatchback, there are two models, each with its own powerplant: a 2.0L 4-cylinder and a 2.5L V6 engine. These engines give the car much-needed power and smoothness not found in the anemic and brutish powertrains used in the past.

Mazda's mechanicals are above reproach but, despite gobs of torque, the GT doesn't give the muscle-car performance found in the more brutish and less refined 5.0L Mustang GT. Performance is sapped considerably by the automatic transmission. Early models are beset by severe "torque steer," a tendency for the chassis to twist when the vehicle accelerates. Nevertheless, overall handling is precise and predictable on all models without sacrificing ride quality, which is a bit on the hard side.

Refinements of the 1993 and later versions include two new Mazda-designed engines that give the car a small horsepower boost, more interior room, all-disc brakes on the GT, and eliminate torque steer.

The Probe's overall mechanical reliability is very good, but, like its Mustang cousin, body assembly is a big letdown. Paint quality and rust protection are pretty good, though. The turbocharged engine has been relatively trouble-free, but owners have complained of frequent stalling and stumbling with the base 2.2L powerplant. Many experience excessive ABS noise and vibrations when braking, and the front brakes tend to wear out very quickly. AC components have a short life-span of three to five years and are outrageously expensive to troubleshoot and repair.

The car is essentially a 2+2 with the rear reserved for children or cargo. The interior is short on head room for tall drivers (especially when equipped with a sunroof), but cargo room is increased with the folding rear seat backs. Multiple squeaks and rattles, wind and water leaks, and cheap interior appointments are the most common body complaints. The digital read-outs are distracting and often incorrect.

388   *Lemon-Aid*

Dealer service bulletins: **1993**—Poorly performing 4EAT automatic transmissions produce harsh 3–2 downshifts. • The "service engine" light may go on for no apparent reason. **1994–1995**—Fluid leak from the transaxle pump seal. • Brake roughness upon application. • Inaccurate fuel gauge. • Erratic headlight door operation. • Off-center steering wheel. **1996–97**—Engine misses, stalls, runs rough, or has reduced power. • Excessive engine noise. • Upper engine noise service tip. • Hesitation, low power, rough idle. • 3–4 shift hunt. • CD4E transmission has harsh shifting, fluid seeping from the vent, and produces a buzz or a clicking vibration. It may also make a whistling noise in Park. • Fluid leaks at axle shaft. • Inaccurate fuel gauge reading when the tank is full. • Loose catalyst or muffler heat shields. • Fog/film on windshield/interior glass. • Door glass makes a pop or snap noise when rolled up or down. • Musty and mildew-type odors.

Safety summary/recalls: The driver's motorized shoulder belt is literally a pain in the neck. It rides high on the neck, fails to retract properly, tangles easily, and often hangs too loose. It also requires that the driver attach the lapbelt separately. **Recalls**: **1985**—A defective ignition may make 2.3L engines hard to start. • Defective plastic sleeve in front seatbelt tongue assembly. • Power brake booster could come apart (except in police cars and taxicabs). **1986–87**—Fuel line coupling could leak fuel. **1990–92**—Motorized shoulder belts may not work. **1991**—Vehicle could roll away when in Park. **1991 GL**—There's a free fix of welds that anchor the front shoulder belt retractors. **1993**—A faulty rear hatch strut may cause the hatch to drop without warning. Dealer will replace rivets that have undersized heads on the strut pivot pins. **1994–95**—Passenger side airbag may not inflate properly. **1996**—Incorrect warning regarding rearward-facing child safety seats.

Secret Warranties/Service Tips

1989—2.2L engines with hairline cracks in the cylinder head must have the head replaced. • Hard cold starts or chronic stalling may require a cold stall pressure regulator kit (#900809A). • No-starts/low battery may mean that you need a new alternator pulley and belt kit (#E92Z-10344-D). **1989–92**—An exhaust buzz or rattle may be fixed by installing new clamps to secure the heat shield. **1989–91**—Constant fogging and moisture on the interior windows and windshield signal the need to adjust the re-circulation/fresh control cable. **1989–94**—A no-start condition, or inoperative heater or lights, may be caused by water and corrosion in the wiring connector, or a short-to-ground at splice 102 (circuit 9). **1990 GT**—Service Program No. 96 provides for the rerouting of the wiring harness and hose clamp to prevent transmission failure. **1990–91**—Rear disc brake squeal can be corrected by installing revised brake pads (#E92Z-2200-A). • Taillight condensation can be prevented by installing a new outer lens kit. • Engine knocking at idle may require the installation of a thicker thrust plate. **1990–94**—A speaker whine or buzz caused by the fuel pump can be stopped by installing an electronic noise RFI filter. **1993–94**—A clunk or knock from the steering assembly when turning is likely due to an insufficient yoke plug (pinion) preload. • Wind/water leaks require the readjustment of the front door glass, as outlined in DSB 994-5-4. • Inoperative power door locks may have a corroded wiring harness connection. Frozen door locks, a common problem, are addressed in DSB 94-8-6. • A ticking noise coming from the 2.0L engine's hydraulic lash adjusters can be stopped by a longer oil pump control plunger that prevents air from passing through to the oil pump. **1994**—A rough idle affecting 2.0L engines could be caused by spark leakage from a damaged number 1 or number 2 spark plug wire. **1994–97**—Transaxle fluid seepage can be corrected by servicing with a remote vent kit or by replacing the main control cover. **All models/years**—Three components that frequently benefit from Ford "goodwill" warranty extensions are catalytic converters, fuel pumps, and computer modules. If Ford balks at refunding your money, apply the emissions warranty for a full or partial refund. • Paint delamination, fading, peeling, hazing, and "microchecking": See pages 94-95 for details on claiming a refund.

Probe Profile

	1990	1991	1992	1993	1994	1995	1996	1997
Cost Price ($)								
Base	13,434	13,680	14,140	15,119	15,975	15,890	16,240	16,235
GT	16,570	17,016	16,740	17,687	19,105	19,485	19,545	18,735
Used Values ($)								
Base ↑	5,000	5,500	6,000	8,000	9,000	10,000	12,000	13,000
Base ↓	4,000	4,500	5,000	6,500	7,500	9,000	10,500	12,000
GT ↑	5,500	6,000	7,000	9,000	10,000	12,000	13,500	15,000
GT ↓	4,500	5,000	5,500	7,500	9,000	10,500	12,000	14,000
Extended Warranty	Y	Y	Y	N	N	N	N	N
Secret Warranty	Y	Y	Y	Y	Y	Y	Y	Y
Reliability	③	③	③	③	④	④	⑤	⑤
Air conditioning	②	②	②	②	③	③	③	④
Body integrity	①	①	①	①	①	①	②	②
Braking system	①	①	①	①	①	②	②	②
Electrical system	①	①	②	②	②	②	②	③
Engines	③	③	③	④	⑤	⑤	⑤	⑤
Exhaust/Converter	②	②	②	③	⑤	⑤	⑤	⑤
Fuel system	③	③	③	③	④	⑤	⑤	⑤
Ignition system	②	③	③	⑤	⑤	⑤	⑤	⑤
Manual transmission	④	④	④	④	⑤	⑤	⑤	⑤
- automatic	③	④	⑤	④	⑤	④	⑤	⑤
Rust/Paint	①	①	①	①	①	①	②	②
Steering	③	③	③	③	④	④	④	⑤
Suspension	③	③	③	③	④	④	④	⑤
Crash Safety	—	⑤	⑤	①	①	⑤	⑤	⑤

Note: The low frontal crash ratings represent the inclusion of leg trauma in the overall score. Although the '90 Probe wasn't crash tested, the '89 crash test results showed minimal injury would be sustained by the driver and front-seat passenger.

GENERAL MOTORS

Camaro, Firebird, IROC-Z, Trans Am, Z28

Rating: Recommended (1995–97); Above Average (1993–94); Average (1991–92); Below Average (1990); Not Recommended (1988–89). The 1996 Camaro and Firebird are essentially the same as the more expensive '97 versions. A V8-equipped Camaro or convertible is the best choice for retained value a few years down the road. But you can do quite well with a used base coupe equipped with the performance handling package and 235 tires. GM has announced it may drop the Camaro and Firebird sometime during the 1999 model year. If it does, this move is unlikely to affect the cars' resale value or parts supply. **Maintenance/Repair costs**: Average, and repairs can be done by any independent garage. **Parts**: Reasonably priced and easy to find.

Technical Data

ENGINES	Liters/CID	HP	MPG	Model Years
OHV I-4 F	I2.5/151	88	19–22	1985–86
OHV V6 FI	2.8/173	135	17–22	1985–89
OHV V6 FI	3.1/191	140	17–22	1990–92
OHV V6 FI	3.4/207	160	18–23	1993–96
OHV V6 FI	3.8/231	200	17–22	1995–98
OHV V8 4 bbl.	5.0/305	150–190	14–16	1985–87
OHV V8 FI	5.0/305	195–230	16–19	1985–87
OHV V8 FI	5.0/305	170	16–19	1988–92
OHV V8 FI	5.7/350	225–245	15–18	1987–92
OHV V8 FI	5.7/350	275–285	15–19	1993–98
OHV V8 FI	5.7/350	305–320	14–17	1998

Strengths and weaknesses: When compared with the Mustang, Camaros and Firebirds are safer, better-performing rear-drive muscle cars that produce excellent crash protection scores and high resale values. They also take the lead over the Mustang with their standard ABS and slightly better reliability record. However, brute power is combined with almost-as-brutal repair charges. The Camaro and Firebird's overall performance varies a great deal depending on the engine, transmission, and suspension combination in each particular car. Base models equipped with the V6 powerplant accelerate reasonably well, but high performance enthusiasts will find them slow for sporty cars. Handling is compromised by poor wet road traction, minimal comfort, and a suspension that's too soft for high-speed cornering and too bone-jarring for smooth cruising. The Z28, IROC-Z, and Trans Am provide smart acceleration and handling at the expense of fuel economy.

1984–92—Much like Ford's embarrassing 4-banger, the puny and failure-prone 2.5L 4-cylinder powerplant was the standard engine up to 1987—part of the legacy of an earlier fuel crisis and the subsequent downsizing binge. Trans Ams offered three more reliable engines: the Buick 3.8L V6, the 4.3L Oldsmobile V8, and the Buick 5.0L V8. The turbocharged V8 offered on some Trans Am models should be viewed with caution because of its many durability problems.

Camaro flat seats don't offer as much support as the better-contoured Firebird seats. These cars are also plagued by chronic fuel-system problems, especially on the Cross-Fire and multi-port fuel-injection controls. Automatic transmissions, especially the 4-speed, aren't durable. The standard 5-speed manual gearbox has a stiff shifter and a heavy clutch. Clutches fail frequently and don't stand up to hard use. The 2.8L V6, used through 1989, suffers from leaky gaskets and seals and premature camshaft wear. The larger 3.1L 6-cylinder has fewer problems. Electrical problems and malfunctioning dash gauges are common. Exhaust parts rust quickly. Dual outlet exhaust systems on V8 engines are expensive to replace. Front suspension components and shock absorbers wear out very quickly.

Like its Mustang rival, body hardware is fragile, poor paint quality and application are common and lead to premature rusting, and squeaks and rattles are legion. Body integrity is especially poor on cars equipped with a T-roof. Windshield and rear wheel openings, door bottoms, and rear quarter panels are particularly vulnerable to rusting. The assorted add-on plastic body parts found on sporty versions promote corrosion by trapping moisture along with road salt and grime.

1993–97—These cars are much better overall performers, with a more powerful, reliable base engine, increased body rigidity that hushes some of the squeaks and rattles so prevalent with previous years, a redesigned, easier-to-read dash, a bit more rear head room, and additional standard safety features. A more powerful 3.8L V6 arrived in spring 1995 and became standard for '96.

On 1997 models GM offered a 30th birthday styling package for the Camaro and some interior upgrades, V6 engine dampening for smoother running at high speeds, optional Ram Air induction, and racier-looking ground-effects body trim for the Firebird.

These sporty convertibles and coupes are almost identical in their pricing and in the features they offer (the Firebird has pop-up headlights, a more pointed front end, a narrower middle, and a rear spoiler). As noted above, both cars got a complete make-over in 1995, making them more powerful and aerodynamic with less spine-jarring performance. They were given new plastic skins, dual airbags, standard anti-lock brakes, new suspension and steering systems, a new 5-speed manual transmission, a reworked interior, and minor cosmetic improvements.

As one moves up the scale, overall performance improves considerably. The V8 engine gives these cars lots of sparkle and tire-spinning torque, but there's a fuel penalty to pay. A 4-speed automatic transmission is standard on the 5.7L-equipped Z28; other versions come with a standard 5-speed manual gearbox or an optional 6-speed. Many of these cars are likely to have been ordered with lots of extra performance and luxury options, including a T-roof package guaranteed to include a full assortment of creaks and groans.

Both cars are equipped with an impressively effective pass key theft-deterrent system similar to the one used successfully in the Corvette. A resistor pellet in the ignition disables the starter and fuel system when the key code doesn't match the ignition lock.

Not everything is perfect, however. Owners report that the base engine is noisy, though the 3.8L doesn't have the head gasket failures seen with Ford's 3.8L powerplant (covered by a secret warranty). Fuel economy is practically nonexistent, the air conditioner malfunctions (but not to the same extent as Ford-produced units), front brakes and MacPherson struts wear out quickly, servicing the fuel injection system is an exercise in frustration, and body problems just won't go away. Yes, body defects are still a major problem, in spite of the millions of dollars GM spent redesigning the car in 1993. These cars are still afflicted by door rattles, misaligned doors and hatch, a sticking hatch power release, and poor fit and finish. Owners also complain that the steering wheel is positioned too close to the driver's chest, the low seats create a feeling of claustrophobia, visibility is limited by wide side pillars, and trunk space is sparse with a high liftover.

Dealer service bulletins: **1994**—Poor radio reception. • A rough-running AC compressor on V8-equipped vehicles requires an upgraded compressor pulley. **1995**—Transmission fluid leak from the pump body. • Excessive rear axle noise. • Steering pull, usually to the right. • Front brake vibration and/or pedal pulsation and unevenly worn rear brake pads. • A low voltage reading or dim lights at idle. • Rear compartment lid water leaks. • Door glass rattles. • Poor paint application and rust spots. **1996**—Engine rpm flare during gear shifts. • Engine oil leak at rear of engine near flywheel cover and spark knock at idle. • 3–2 part throttle downshift flare and delayed transmission engagement. • Transmission fluid leak from pump body (replace bushing). • Steering column noise. • Steering lead or pull, usually to the right. • Steering column click or snap noise. • Uneven brake pad wear. • Convertible top leaks water. • Coolant leak at engine coolant heater assembly. • AC odors. • Radio frequency interference diagnosis. • Exterior light condensation. • Water leaks at rear compartment lid when vehicle is parked on an incline. • Water leak diagnostic guide. • Cannot remove ignition key. • Anti-theft alarm may sound if vehicle gets wet. • Inoperative power door locks. • Rattle or buzz from parking brake handle release button. **1997**—Oil leaks between the intake manifold and engine block. • Troubleshooting a malfunctioning convertible top. • Erratic headlight or turn signal operation. • Inoperative power door locks. • Low voltage reading or dim lights at idle. • Premature burnout of rear tail/stop light bulbs. • Rattle or buzz from parking brake handle release button.

Safety summary/recalls: **NHTSA probes**: **1991–92**—Inadvertent airbag deployments. **1994–97**—Vehicles equipped with the 5.7L V8 may pose a fire hazard due to the fuel line touching the exhaust. **Recalls**: **1985**—Shoulder seatbelt may not retract. **1985–86**—For vehicles with rear disc brakes and manual transmissions, the parking brake adjuster may not hold the vehicle when parked on an incline. **1985–90**—Defective seatbelt buckle assemblies may not latch. **1986**—Faulty push-pull headlight switch. **1988**—GM will inspect and repair the power-steering pump support brace and mounting bracket. **1988–89**—Fuel feed hoses may leak on vehicles equipped with a 2.8L V6 engine. **1989 convertible**—Rear seatbelts may be too long. **1990**—Fuel return hoses may leak on vehicles equipped with a V8 engine. **1991**—Poor windshield retention in an accident. • Defective seatbelt latchplates will be fixed for free. • Defective front seats. **1991–92**—Fuel filler neck may leak. **1992**—The automatic transmission shift control cable may separate and hamper shifting. **1994**—Fuel line on V8-equipped cars may leak fuel into the engine compartment. **1995**—Faulty lower steering shaft coupling could lead to loss of steering.

Secret Warranties/Service Tips

1982–93—Vehicles equipped with a Hydramatic 4L60 transmission that buzzes when the car is in Reverse or idle may need a new oil pressure regulator valve. **1984–87**—Left side cowl leaks can be plugged by sealing the wiper transmission mounting area. **1985–87**—Hard starting or reduced acceleration may require an upgraded catalytic converter. **1985–88**—A long crank time with the 5.7L engine may be due to a faulty cold start injector, fuel pump clutch valve, or fuel pressure regulator, or the fuel injector may be leaking pressure and shutting down. **1985–91**—Hydramatic 4L60/700R4 automatic transmission may have no upshift or appear to be stuck in first gear. The probable cause is a worn governor gear. It would be wise to replace the retaining ring as well. **1987–88**—If cold weather makes your THM 200-4R automatic transmission difficult to downshift 2–1, the likely cause is a defective 1–2 throttle valve spring (#8634619) in the valve body (DSB 88-164-7A). • Port fuel injections that emit black smoke after long starter cranks may have fuel leaking into the engine from the injectors. • Throttle body injections and port fuel injections that emit white or bluish-white smoke and have normal oil consumption likely have poor sealing between the intake manifold joint and the cylinder head. **1989**—If the rear brakes moan when they're slightly applied while backing up or turning, a redesigned caliper mounting plate may be needed (DSB 89-162-5). • Knocking from a cold 5.0L engine means that the PROM module has to be replaced (DSB 89-284-6E). • No-start or stalling may be caused by a disconnected fuel pump coupler. **1989–90**—Campaign 90-C-11 provides

for free convertible top latch handles. **1990**—Cold start stalling with the
3.1L engine may be corrected by replacing the MEMCAL. **1993–94**—DSB
431028 covers all aspects of securing loose door outer panels. • A loose, rattling instrument panel or upper trim panel requires new dual lock riveted
fasteners. • Rear brake squeal can be silenced by installing upgraded disc
brake pads. **1993–96**—Uneven rear brake pad wear, or premature wear can
be corrected by replacing the caliper anchor bracket, guide pins, and the
brake pads with upgraded parts. This is a warranty item, as set out in GM's
chart, shown below.

File In Section: 5 - Brakes
Bulletin No: 53-50-20
Date: November 1995

Subject:
Taper Wear and/or Uneven Wear on Rear Disc Brake Pads (Replace Caliper Mounting Brackets)

Models:
1993–96 Chevrolet Camaro
1993–96 Pontiac Firebird

Condition
Some of the above vehicles may exhibit taper wear and/or uneven wear on the rear disc brake pads. (Taper wear is defined
as uneven wear of the pad from end to end or inboard versus outboard uneven wear.) Maximum taper allowed is 0.15 mm
(0.006 inch).

Cause
Wear of the caliper guide pins and the bores on the caliper anchor brackets may result in the caliper not sliding freely.

Correction
Replace the caliper anchor bracket, the guide pins and the brake pads. Refer to Section 5B2 of the Service Manual.

Description	P/N
Rear Caliper Mounting Bracket (2 required)	18020432
Bracket Mount Bolt (4 required)	10229606
Rear Caliper Guide Pin (4 required)	18022147
Boot – Rear Caliper Guide Pin (4 required)	14087552
Caliper Mounting Bolts (2 required)*	14067559
Pads – Rear Brakes (1 required)	18021875

* (4 bolts required, but 2 bolts come with new pads)

1993–97—Oil leaks between the intake manifold and engine block are
most often caused by insufficient RTV bonding between the intake manifold and cylinder block. **1994**—Excessive oil consumption is likely due to
delaminated intake manifold gaskets. Install an upgraded intake manifold
gasket kit. • Delayed automatic transmission shift engagement is a common
problem addressed in DSB 47-71-20A. • Install a new "flash" PROM to cure
erratic increases in engine rpm or start/stall/hesitation upon acceleration
with automatic transmission-equipped cars. **Engines 2.5L**—Spark knock
can be fixed with the free installation of a new PROM module (#12269198)
if the emissions warranty applies. • Frequent stalling may require a new
MAP sensor (DSB 90-142-8A). **3.8L V6**—These engines have a history of
low oil pressure caused by a failure-prone oil pump. A temporary remedy

is to avoid low viscosity oils and use 10W-40 in the winter and 20W-50 for summer driving. **1990–91**—Stalling on deceleration or at stops requires a new MEMCAL that refines idle speed control and throttle follower operation. **1991**—Poor starting may be caused by the spring in early starter drives compressing too easily. Install an upgraded starter motor drive assembly (#10473700). **1992**—Oil leaks from the rear of a 5.0L or 5.7L engine may be caused by insufficient sealing around the camshaft plug. **1995–96**—Delayed automatic transmission shift engagement may require the replacement of the pump cover assembly. **All models/years**—A rotten-egg odor coming from the exhaust is probably the result of a malfunctioning catalytic converter, which is covered by the emissions warranty. • Paint delamination, peeling, or fading: See page 95.

Camaro, Firebird, Iroc-Z, Trans Am, Z28 Profile

	1990	1991	1992	1993	1994	1995	1996	1997
Cost Price ($)								
Base	13,731	14,496	14,132	16,385	16,250	17,536	18,411	18,786
Z28	—	18,276	18,112	20,125	19,900	21,236	21,951	22,721
Convertible	19,474	20,134	23,405	—	25,351	26,388	27,016	28,091
Firebird	16,603	14,624	15,070	16,710	16,735	17,764	19,408	19,209
Trans Am	18,468	19,174	19,840	22,480	21,005	22,344	22,709	23,339
Used Values ($)								
Base ↑	5,500	6,500	7,500	9,000	10,000	11,000	13,000	15,000
Base ↓	4,500	5,500	6,500	7,500	8,000	10,000	11,500	13,500
Z28 ↑	—	7,500	9,000	11,000	12,000	14,000	16,000	18,000
Z28 ↓	—	6,500	7,500	9,000	10,000	12,000	14,000	16,000
Convertible ↑	9,000	10,000	12,000	—	15,000	17,000	19,000	21,000
Convertible ↓	8,000	9,000	9,500	—	13,000	15,000	17,000	19,000
Firebird ↑	6,000	6,500	8,000	9,000	11,500	12,500	13,500	15,000
Firebird ↓	5,000	5,500	7,000	7,500	10,000	11,500	12,500	14,000
Trans Am ↑	6,500	7,500	9,000	11,500	13,000	15,000	17,000	19,500
Trans Am ↓	5,500	6,500	7,500	10,000	11,500	13,000	15,500	18,000
Extended Warranty	Y	Y	Y	N	N	N	N	N
Secret Warranty	Y	Y	Y	Y	Y	Y	Y	Y
Reliability	②	②	③	③	④	④	④	⑤
Air conditioning	②	③	③	③	④	⑤	⑤	⑤
Body integrity	①	①	①	①	②	②	②	③
Braking system	①	①	①	③	③	③	③	③
Electrical system	①	①	①	①	①	①	③	③
Engines	①	①	②	①	②	②	②	③
Exhaust/Converter	①	②	③	③	③	④	④	⑤
Fuel system	①	②	②	③	③	④	④	⑤
Ignition system	②	②	②	③	③	④	④	⑤
Manual transmission	③	③	③	④	④	⑤	⑤	⑤
- automatic	③	③	③	③	④	⑤	⑤	②
Rust/Paint	①	②	③	③	③	④	⑤	⑤
Steering	③	③	③	③	③	③	④	⑤
Suspension	②	②	③	③	③	③	④	⑤
Crash Safety								
Camaro	—	⑤	⑤	—	⑤	⑤	⑤	⑤

Side Impact

Camaro   —   —   —   —   —   —   —   ③

Note: Although the '90 Camaro wasn't crash tested in a frontal collision, the '87 crash test results showed minimal injury would be sustained by the driver and front-seat passenger.

Corvette

Rating: Above Average (1995–97); Average (1993–94); Not Recommended (1980–92). The cheaper 1996 Corvette won't have the cachet or the mechanical and body refinements of the redesigned '97 version. If you choose the '97 model, try to get a second-series car that was made after June 1997. Keep in mind that premium fuel and astronomical insurance rates will further drive up your operating costs. **Maintenance/Repair costs**: Higher than average, although most repairs can be done by any independent garage. **Parts**: Pricey, but easy to find. Surprisingly, parts for older Corvettes are often more easily found through collectors' clubs than are many of the high-tech components used today.

Technical Data

ENGINES	Liters/CID	HP	MPG	Model Years
OHV V8 FI	5.7/350	225–245	17–26	1988–93
OHV V8 FI	5.7/350	300–330	17–26	1992–96
OHV V8 FI	5.7/350	375–405	17–24	1988–95
DOHC V8 FI	5.7/350	375	17–24	1990–93

Strengths and weaknesses: Corvettes made in the late '60s and early '70s are acceptable buys, due mainly to their value as collector cars and their uncomplicated repairs. The Corvette's overall reliability has declined over the years as its price and complexity have increased. This is due in large part to GM's updating its antiquated design with high-tech, complicated add-ons, rather than coming up with something original. Consequently, the car has been gutted and then retuned using failure-prone electronic circuitry. Miles of emissions plumbing have also been added to make it a fuel-efficient, user-friendly, high-performance vehicle. Unfortunately, the Corvette has missed these goals by a large margin.

The electronically controlled suspension systems have been glitch-plagued over the past several years. Servicing the different sophisticated fuel-injection systems isn't easy—even (especially) for GM mechanics. The noisy 5.7L engine frequently hesitates and stalls, there's lots of transmission buzz and whine, the rear tires produce excessive noise, and wind whistles through the A- and C-pillars. These, and the all-too-familiar fiberglass body squeaks, continue to be unwanted standard features throughout all model years.

The electronic dash also never works quite right (speedometer lag, for example).

On the other hand, Corvette ownership of more recent models does have its positive side. For example, the ABS vented disc brakes, available since 1986, are easy to modulate and fade-free. The standard European-made Bilstein FX-3 Selective Ride Control suspension can be preset for touring, sport, or performance. Under speed, an electronic module automatically varies the suspension setting, finally curing these cars of their earlier endemic over-steering, wheel spinning, breakaway rear ends, and other nasty surprises.

If you're planning to buy a used Corvette, be wary of any model made between 1979 and 1993—and make sure that you get a GM-backed supplementary warranty with later models! The frequency of repairs and high repair costs are outrageously expensive on all but the more recent versions. Although older cars are likely to be junked or already restored, here are some of the things that can put a large dent in your wallet if they haven't been fixed already:

1977–83—Major mechanical failings affect the air conditioning, transmission, clutch, shift linkage, camshaft lifters and rear half-shaft soft yokes, carburetor, steering, rear brakes, and starter and electrical system, including the lights. As far as body assembly goes, the major deficiencies are poor panel fits, faulty and fragile interior/exterior parts and trim items, quirky instruments, cheap upholstery, and defective window lifts. Owners also complain of poor workmanship/shoddy assembly causing a cacophony of squeaks and rattles, poor dealer servicing, unavailable and expensive parts, and excessive labor charges.

1984–90—Incredibly difficult to service. One *Lemon-Aid* reader had a faulty engine bearing at 10,000 miles and spent $2,500 to remove the engine. It takes half a day to change the spark plugs on the passenger side. Likely mechanical problem areas are the emission-control systems (injectors, computer-controlled sensors, fuel injection, and engine gaskets), AC, and ignition/distributor. Owners also experience engine and drivetrain failures, Bosch radio malfunctions, and the need to make frequent wheel alignments. Fragile body hardware, poor fit and finish, wind/road noise, and water intrusion into the interior are still major weaknesses. Owners complain of faulty controls and window lifts, defective paint (the base coat comes through the finish), interior/exterior parts and trim, glass and weather-stripping, instruments, lights, door locks, upholstery, and carpeting.

1991–96—Though the restyled '91 Corvette remained the same mechanically, all models got the convex tail and square taillights previously used only on the upscale ZR-1 coupe. A new LTI engine with 55 more horses came on the scene with the '92 'Vette, and the following year the ZR-1 got a 405-hp variant of the same power-plant, shortly before the model was replaced in the spring of 1995 by the Grand Sport. A more substantial redesign was carried out for the 1997 model year.

Owners rave about the redesigned models' improved performance, better handling, and additional safety features, but continue to find fault with the stiff ride, poor fuel economy, and excessive interior noise. From a reliability standpoint, '93 and later models are much improved, with problems affecting mostly the electronic and electrical system, body hardware, fit and finish, suspension, and air conditioning.

Dealer service bulletins: **1995**—A high effort to shift into gear in cold, wet weather and high shift effort into Reverse. • A 3–2 downshift flare and erratic downshifting with the automatic transmission. • Starter clicks but won't start engine. • Front brake pulsation. • A low voltage reading or dim lights at idle. • Right-hand wiper blade chatter • Excessive radio static. • Door glass scratches. • Poor paint application. **1996**—Oil leaks between the intake manifold and engine block. • 3–2 part throttle downshift flare and delayed transmission engagement. • Transmission fluid leak from pump body (replace bushing). • Steering column noise. • Radio frequency interference diagnosis. • Low voltage reading or dim lights at idle. • Door trim armrest lid hard to open. • Water leak diagnostic guide. • Exterior light condensation. **1997**—Air temperature from HVAC outlets doesn't change. • Erratic fuel gauge readings. • Low voltage reading or dim lights at idle. • Hatch won't pop up when activated in cold weather. • Water drips into rear compartment.

Safety summary/recalls: Although frontal crash protection is excellent, the Insurance Institute for Highway Safety found that fatality rates from all kinds of crashes involving Corvettes during 1985–89 were the highest of any car. In fact, the Corvette's relative death rate was more than three times the average for other vehicles. **Recalls**: **1988–89**—The rear wheel tie-rod end could fracture. GM will replace any defective tie-rod assembly free of charge. **1990**—Inoperative parking brakes will get a new brake lever assembly. • The fuel feed and return line connectors may leak fuel. **1992–93**—Power steering hose leakage may cause an engine compartment fire.

Secret Warranties/Service Tips

1982–91—Hydramatic 4L60/700R4 automatic transmission may have no upshift or appear to be stuck in first gear. The probable cause is a worn governor gear. It would be wise to replace the retaining ring as well. **1982–93**—Vehicles equipped with a Hydramatic 4L60 transmission that "buzzes" when the car is in Reverse or idle may need a new oil pressure regulator valve. **1987–89**—Revised cylinder head gaskets provide better sealing (DSB 89-283-6A).**1990–91**—Engine wiring short circuits may be caused by an abraded electrical harness at the mounting clamp just below the oil pressure sensor. **1992**—5.7L engines may develop leaks at the oil filter area. GM Campaign 92COS has covered the repair cost in the past. • 5.7L engines may backfire excessively when shifting from first to second gear with the throttle wide open. Correct by changing the MEMCAL module. • Oil leaks from the rear of a 5.0L or 5.7L engine may be caused by insufficient sealing around the camshaft plug. Replace the plug and reseal. **1992-96**—Oil leaks between the intake manifold and engine block are most often caused by insufficient RTV bonding between the intake manifold and cylinder block. **1994**—Excessive oil consumption is likely due to delaminated intake manifold gaskets. Install an upgraded intake manifold gasket kit. • Delayed automatic transmission shift engagement is a common problem, and is addressed in DSB 47-71-20A. **1995-96**—Delayed automatic transmission shift engagement may require the replacement of the pump cover assembly. **All models/years**—A rotten-egg odor coming from the exhaust is probably caused by a defective catalytic converter, which may be covered by the emissions warranty. • Clearcoat paint degradation, whitening, and chalking, long a problem with GM's other cars, is also a serious problem with the fiberglass-bodied Corvette, says DSB 331708. It too is covered by a secret warranty for up to six years.

Corvette Profile

	1990	1991	1992	1993	1994	1995	1996	1997
Cost Price ($)								
Base	33,444	33,999	35,270	36,230	37,345	37,955	38,400	38,365
Convertible	38,729	40,305	41,780	42,830	44,120	44,835	46,235	—
ZR-1	59,555	64,668	72,378	66,828	67,993	68,603	—	—
Used Values ($)								
Base ↑	14,000	15,000	17,000	19,000	21,000	24,000	27,000	38,000
Base ↓	12,000	13,500	15,000	17,000	19,000	22,000	25,000	35,000
Convertible ↑	16,500	19,500	21,500	22,500	25,000	27,500	30,000	—
Convertible ↓	14,000	17,000	19,000	21,000	22,000	25,000	28,000	—
ZR-1 ↑	25,000	27,000	30,000	33,000	36,000	48,000	—	—
ZR-1 ↓	23,000	24,000	27,000	30,000	33,000	46,000	—	—
Extended Warranty	Y	Y	Y	Y	Y	Y	Y	Y
Secret Warranty	N	N	Y	Y	Y	Y	Y	N
Reliability	2	2	2	3	3	4	4	4
Air conditioning	2	2	2	3	3	3	3	4
Body integrity	2	2	2	2	2	2	2	3
Braking system	2	2	2	2	2	2	3	3
Electrical system	2	2	2	2	2	2	3	4
Engines	2	2	3	3	3	3	3	4
Exhaust/Converter	2	2	2	3	3	4	4	5
Fuel system	2	2	2	2	2	3	3	4
Ignition system	2	2	2	2	2	3	4	5
Manual transmission	2	2	3	3	3	4	4	5
- automatic	2	2	2	2	3	3	3	3
Rust/Paint	2	2	2	2	3	3	3	4
Steering	2	2	2	3	3	4	4	4
Suspension	2	2	2	2	2	3	4	4

HONDA

Prelude

Rating: Recommended (1992–97); Above Average (1988–91). **Maintenance/Repair costs**: Average; repairs aren't dealer dependent. To avoid costly engine repairs, check the engine timing belt every 2 years/40,000 miles. **Parts**: Higher than average cost, but independent suppliers sell for much less.

Technical Data

ENGINES	Liters/CID	HP	MPG	Model Years
OHC I-4 2X1 bbl.	1.8/113	100	20–25	1985–87
OHC I-4 FI	2.0/119	110	20–25	1985–87
OHC I-4 2X1 bbl.	2.0/119	105	19–24	1988–90
DOHC I-4 FI	2.0/119	135	19–24	1988–91
DOHC I-4 FI	2.1/125	140	18–23	1991
OHC I-4 FI	2.2/132	135	21–26	1992–96
DOHC VTEC	2.2/132	190–195	20–24	1993–98
DOHC I-4 FI	2.3/138	160	21–25	1992–96

Strengths and weaknesses: Unimpressive as a high performance sports car, the Prelude instead delivers a stylish exterior, legendary reliability, and excellent resale value.

1985–87 first-generation Preludes were described as luxury sport cars, but didn't offer much of either. They should be inspected carefully for engine problems and severe underbody corrosion, particularly near the fuel tank. Noisy front brakes, premature disc warping, high oil consumption, and worn engine crankshaft or camshaft lobes are the main problem areas with these models. They're also prone to extensive rusting around wheel openings, door bottoms, the trunk lid, fenders, rear taillights, bumper supports, chassis members, suspension components, and the fuel tank.

1988–91 models offer more and smoother engine power, excellent handling, and improved reliability. There are some generic complaints that continue to crop up, including rapid front brake wear, scored and warped front brake rotors, automatic transmission failure, defective constant velocity joints, premature exhaust system rust-out, and a warping hood.

1992–96 models are shorter, wider, and heavier. They're not very fast, except for the VTEC-equipped Si. The 4-wheel steering found on the '92 4WS version is more a gimmick than anything else. It was dropped after '94. The automatic transmission is smoother, although it still saps some of the Prelude's power. Both the rear seating and tiny trunk are inadequate for most people. You can expect fewer yet familiar glitches, including minor electrical problems, body and accessory defects, brake squealing, and prematurely warped front brake rotors. Most independent mechanics are ill-equipped to service these cars because Preludes have become increasingly complicated to repair.

1997 was the year for big Prelude changes. The car was restyled, re-powered, and given handling upgrades that make it a better per-forming, more comfortable-riding sports coupe. The base 2.2L VTEC engine got 5 additional horses, a new Automatic Torque Transfer System (ATTS), an upgraded suspension, standard ABS, air condi-tioning, 16-inch wheels, and a CD player with six speakers. The Sequential SportShift automatic transmission (a variation of the one used in the NSX) equips the base Prelude. Overall, the car is roomier (the extended wheelbase gives added stability and provides more room in the rear seating area), has a more solid body structure, and includes a totally redesigned, user-friendly dash with analogue gauges.

Owners report that air-conditioner condensers frequently fail after a few years and often need cleaning to eliminate disagreeable odors. Other problems include minor electrical glitches, brake squealing, and prematurely warped front brake rotors. A host of new technical features add to the Prelude's complexity and guarantee that you'll never stray far from the dealer's service bay. In fact, most corner mechanics are ill-equipped to service these cars and the Automatic Torque Transfer System (ATTS) won't make their job any easier.

Safety summary/recalls: Recalls: 1978–85—Severe chassis corro-sion around fuel tank and body seams prompted Honda to provide free chassis repairs and to replace suspension/steering components and fuel tanks under a "silent" recall campaign. **1983–87**—Road salt could cause the fuel filler and/or breather pipe to rust through, resulting in leaks. A recall campaign has been organized to fix this defect. **1986–91**—Takata seatbelt replacement. **1988**—Rusty coil spring support could cause loss of control. • Power-steering hose leaks could cause a fire.

Secret Warranties/Service Tips

1988–93—Poor AM reception or popping from the speakers is likely due to a poor ground connection between the antenna collar and car body. Correct the reception by improving the ground connection and tightening the antenna-assembly mounting nuts in the proper sequence. • Creaking from the window regulator can be corrected by installing an upgraded regulator spiral spring. **1990**—Defective AC compressor pickup sensors are a common problem. **1992**—A rattle from the front of the car that occurs when driving over rough surfaces but goes away when brakes are lightly applied can be corrected by installing new front brake pad retainers. **1994–96**—Silence rear headliner rat-tling by applying EPT sealer 5T to the rear headliner where it contacts the wiring harness. **1996–97**—In a settlement with the Environmental Protection Agency, Honda paid fines totaling $17.1 million and extended its emissions warranty on 1.6 million 1995–97 models to 14 years or 150,000 miles. This means that costly engine components and exhaust system parts like catalytic converters will be replaced free of charge as long as the 14-year/150,000 mile limit hasn't been exceeded. Additionally, the automaker will provide a full engine check and emissions-related repairs at 50,000 to 75,000 miles and will give free tune-ups at 75,000 to 150,000 miles. It is estimated that the free check-ups, repairs, and tune-ups will cost Honda over $250 million. The story of the settlement was first reported on page 6 of the June 15, 1998, edition of *Automotive News*. **All models/years**—Steering wheel shimmy can be reduced by rebalancing the wheel/tire/hub/rotor assembly in the front end. • Seatbelts that fail to function properly during normal use will be replaced for free under Honda's lifetime seatbelt warranty. Honda will also repair or replace defective steering assemblies, constant velocity joints, and catalytic converters free of charge for up to 5 years/80,000 miles on a case-by-case basis. There's no labor charge or deductible. Used vehicles and repairs carried out by independent garages aren't covered by this special program. • The converter is almost always covered under the emissions warranty.

Most Honda DSBs allow for special warranty consideration on a "good-will" basis for most problems even after the warranty has expired or the car has changed hands.

Prelude Profile

	1990	1991	1992	1993	1994	1995	1996	1997
Cost Price ($)								
Base/S	14,955	15,955	16,540	17,330	18,450	19,930	20,340	23,595
Used Values ($)								
Base/S ↑	8,000	9,500	10,500	11,500	13,500	15,000	17,000	20,500
Base/S ↓	7,000	8,000	9,000	10,000	12,000	13,500	15,000	19,000
Extended Warranty	N	N	N	N	N	N	N	N
Secret Warranty	N	N	N	N	N	N	Y	Y
Reliability	⑤	⑤	⑤	⑤	⑤	⑤	⑤	⑤
Air conditioning	②	③	③	④	⑤	⑤	⑤	⑤
Body integrity	③	③	③	③	③	③	③	④
Braking system	①	①	③	③	③	③	④	④
Electrical system	②	②	③	③	④	④	④	⑤
Engines	④	⑤	⑤	⑤	⑤	⑤	⑤	⑤
Exhaust/Converter	②	③	⑤	⑤	⑤	⑤	⑤	⑤
Fuel system	④	④	④	④	⑤	⑤	⑤	⑤
Ignition system	④	④	④	④	⑤	⑤	⑤	⑤
Manual transmission	⑤	⑤	⑤	⑤	⑤	⑤	⑤	⑤
- automatic	③	③	④	⑤	⑤	⑤	⑤	⑤
Rust/Paint	②	④	⑤	⑤	⑤	⑤	⑤	⑤
Steering	②	②	③	③	③	③	④	④
Suspension	③	③	④	⑤	⑤	⑤	⑤	⑤
Crash Safety	②	②	⑤	⑤	—	—	—	—

HYUNDAI

Scoupe

Rating: Below Average (1991–95). An Excel cross-dressing as a sports car. **Maintenance/Repair costs**: Higher than average, although most repairs can be done by any independent garage. **Parts**: Higher-than-average cost with limited availability.

Technical Data

ENGINES	Liters/CID	HP	MPG	Model Years
OHC I-4 FI	1.5/90	81	25–31	1991–92
OHC I-4 FI	1.5/91	92	25–32	1993–95
OHC I-4T FI	1.5/91	115	23–29	1993–95

Strengths and weaknesses: This is essentially a cute coupe with an engine more suited to high gas mileage than hard driving. Except for its lighter weight, less luggage space, and shorter overall length, the Scoupe is really an Excel clone, and there are better performing and more reliable sports coupes available. Plenty of interior room up front, but the roof is too angular; if you're short and have to pull the seat up, your head almost touches the roof. The rear interior room is inadequate. The Scoupe is fuel efficient and has a good heating and ventilation system.

This is far from a performance car, mainly due to the Excel's underpinnings and drivetrain. The 4-speed automatic transmission robs the base engine of much-needed horsepower, making for poor acceleration on inclines and constant shifting between 2,500 and 3,500 rpms when pushed. Suspension may be too firm for some. There's plenty of body roll in turns, and mediocre steering. Brakes are hard to modulate.

Customer service has improved, if only because dealers have more factory support. Body construction is sloppy, giving rise to wind/water leaks, rattles, and breakage. Lots of engine and road noise intrudes into the interior. Owners also report frequent brake and wheel-bearing problems.

Dealer service bulletins: **1993**—Engine has difficulty reaching recommended operating temperature (MPI fault code #21), low fuel pressure, and possible fuel leak at fuel gauge connection valve. • Harsh shifting with the automatic transmission when accelerating or coming to a stop. • Excessive disc brake noise. **1994**—Starting difficulties. • Transmission glitches. • AC failures. • Noisy shock absorbers and radio malfunctions. **1995**—Automatic transmission won't engage Overdrive. • Exhaust system releases a rotten egg odor. • Rear suspension squeaks. • Trunk water leaks. • Troubleshooting tips for locating and plugging other interior water leaks.

Safety summary/recalls: **Recalls**: N/A.

Secret Warranties/Service Tips

1991—Stalling when shifting into gear immediately after starting a cold engine may be corrected by installing a Cold Start Enrichment Kit (#39901-24Q00D). **1991–92**—A difficult-to-engage Reverse gear needs an upgraded part. • A harsh shift when coming to a stop or upon acceleration may be due to a misadjusted accelerator switch TCU. **1992–94**—Hyundai has a field fix for manual transaxle gear clash/grind (DSB 9440-004). **1993–94**—Hyundai has also developed an improved spark plug (painted yellow on the tip) for better cold weather starting. **1994**—Hyundai may replace the AC discharge hose for free under a special service campaign (DSB 94-01-010). **All models/years**—An automatic transmission that won't engage Overdrive may need the oil temperature sensor replaced, could have faulty wiring, or a defective Transmission Control Module.

Scoupe Profile

	1991	1992	1993	1994	1995
Cost Price ($)					
Base	10,030	10,569	10,879	11,409	11,905
LS/GLS	10,815	11,174	11,414	11,889	12,735
Used Values ($)					
Base ↑	3,000	3,700	5,500	6,500	7,500
Base ↓	2,500	3,000	4,500	5,500	6,500
LS/GLS ↑	3,500	4,200	6,000	7,000	8,000
LS/GLS ↓	3,000	3,500	5,000	6,000	7,000
Extended Warranty	Y	Y	Y	Y	Y
Secret Warranty	N	N	Y	Y	N
Reliability	②	②	②	②	③
Air conditioning	②	③	④	④	④
Automatic transmission	②	②	②	②	③
Body integrity	②	②	②	②	②
Braking system	②	②	②	②	②
Electrical system	②	②	②	②	②
Engines	④	④	④	④	⑤
Exhaust/Converter	⑤	⑤	⑤	⑤	⑤
Fuel system	③	③	③	③	④
Ignition system	②	②	②	③	④
Rust/Paint	②	②	②	③	③
Steering	③	③	③	③	④
Suspension	③	③	③	④	④
Crash Safety	⑤	⑤	❶	❶	④

Tiburon

Rating: Above Average buy. A high performance Elantra. Keep in mind that for about $1,000 more you can get the better performing FX model. **Maintenance/Repair costs**: Higher than average, although most repairs can be done by any independent garage. **Parts**: Higher-than-average cost with limited availability.

Technical Data

ENGINES	Liters/CID	HP	MPG	Model Years
DOHC I-4 FI	1.8/110	130	20–26	1997–98
DOHC I-4 FI	2.0/122	140	19–25	1997–98

Strengths and weaknesses: This is a fun-to-drive, reasonably sporty car that's based on the Elantra sedan. Although it's too early to have a definitive opinion, overall reliability looks promising. The Tiburon is a credible alternative to the Ford Probe, Nissan 200SX, Mitsubishi Eclipse, or Toyota Celica. The base 16-valve 1.8L 4-cylinder is smooth, efficient, and adequate when mated to the 5-speed manual transmission. Put in an automatic transmission and performance heads south, and engine noise increases proportionally. Overall handling is crisp and predictable, due mainly to the Tiburon's long wheelbase and sophisticated suspension.

The FX gets the more sprightly 2.0L engine along with optional ABS. Standard brakes are adequate though sometimes difficult to modulate. As with most sporty cars, interior room is cramped for average-sized occupants. Tall drivers, especially, might find rearward seat travel insufficient, making head room a bit tight.

Although no serious defects have been reported, be on the lookout for body deficiencies (fit, finish, and assembly), harsh shifting with the automatic transmission, oil leaks, and minor brake glitches.

Dealer service bulletins: **1997**—Automatic transmission won't engage Overdrive. • Clutch pedal squeaking. • Tapping noise coming from the passenger-side dash panel/engine compartment area. • Exhaust system buzz. • Improved shifting into all gears. • Improved shifting into Reverse. • Clutch drag.

Safety summary/recalls: **NHTSA probes**: **Recalls**: **1997**—A faulty wiper motor will be replaced.

Secret Warranties/Service Tips

1997—A tip on eliminating clutch pedal squeaking is offered. • Tips on eliminating clutch drag are offered. **All models/years**—Hyundai has a new brake pad kit (#58101-28A00) that the company says will eliminate squeaks and squeals during light brake application. Hyundai also suggests that you replace the oil pump assembly if the engine rpm increases as the automatic transmission engages abruptly during a cold start.

Tiburon Profile

	1997
Cost Price ($)	
Base	15,609
FX	17,539
Used Values ($)	
Base ↑	12,500
Base ↓	11,000
FX ↑	13,500
FX ↓	12,000

Extended Warranty	Y
Secret Warranty	N

Reliability	④
Air conditioning	⑤
Automatic transmission	③
Body integrity	③
Braking system	③
Electrical system	③
Engines	⑤
Exhaust/Converter	⑤
Ignition system	⑤
Rust/Paint	⑤
Steering	⑤
Suspension	⑤
Crash Safety	—

MAZDA

MX-3, Precidia

Rating: Recommended (1993–95); Above Average (1992).
Maintenance/Repair costs: Higher than average, and most repairs have to be done by a Mazda dealer. **Parts**: Higher-than-average cost, with limited availability.

Technical Data

ENGINES	Liters/CID	HP	MPG	Model Years
OHC I-4 FI	1.6/98	88	24–33	1992–93
DOHC I-4 FI	1.6/98	105	23–31	1994–95
DOHC V6 FI	1.8/113	130	20–26	1992–94

Strengths and weaknesses: The base 1.6L engine supplies plenty of power for most driving situations. When equipped with the optional 1.8L V6 powerplant (Mazda's smallest V6) and high performance options, the MX-3 and Precidia transform themselves into 130-horsepower pocket rockets. In fact, the MX-3 and Precidia GS sports coupes easily outperform the 4-cylinder Honda del Sol, Toyota Paseo, and Geo Storm for comfort and high performance thrills. They do fall a bit short of the Saturn SC due to their limited low-end torque, fuel economy that is disappointing, and reverse gear that is sometimes hard to engage.

Brake and wheel-bearing problems are commonplace. Most of the MX-3 and Precidia's parts are used on other Mazda cars, so their overall reliability should be outstanding.

Body assembly is average and rattles/squeaks are common. Owners have complained of paint defects and sheet metal that's too thin above the door handles—dents in the metal appear where you would ordinarily place your thumb when closing the door. Some owners report wind and water leaks around the doors and windows. Moderate engine noise increases dramatically above 60 mph.

Small door openings are a hardship for tall occupants upon entry and exit. Steering wheel rubs against thighs even when the seat is pushed as far back as it will go. Rear head room and leg room are limited. A high beltline and cowl add to a claustrophobic feeling. The trunk has a high liftover.

Dealer service bulletins: 1995—Shift feel complaints. • Brake pulsation troubleshooting tips. • Heater and AC unit noise after long storage. • Luggage compartment hinge holder breakage. • A slightly off-center steering wheel.

Safety summary/recalls: The NHTSA is looking into reports that an alternator short circuit may cause an engine fire on 1992–94 models. The car's tendency to under-steer can be unnerving when taking corners at moderate speed. **Recalls: 1990–91**—Malfunctioning automatic shoulder belts will be replaced, gratis.

Secret Warranties/Service Tips

1992—A front-end snapping noise during tight turns at walking speed is probably caused by excessive clearance between the wheel bearing and steering knuckle. Install modified wheel bearings. • Idle fluctuation when applying an electrical load during idle, or after deceleration from a high rpm, can be corrected by installing a new Electronic Control Unit. • Poor AC performance may be due to insufficient airflow across the AC condenser. • A noisy rear hatch can be silenced by changing the rear hatch glass, hinge, or molding. • Squeaking noise from the rear pillars is due to interference between the rear inner pillar and its reinforcement. • A sulfurous odor coming from the exhaust can be eliminated by installing an upgraded catalytic converter. **1992–94**—Freezing door and hatch lock cylinders are addressed in DSB 021/94. • Clutch squealing can be silenced by installing an upgraded part with a thicker clutch cushioning plate. **1994**—Timing belt noise can be silenced by replacing the tensioner pulley with an upgraded part. **All models/years**—DSB 006/94 gives all of the possible causes and remedies for brake vibrations.

MX-3, Precidia Profile

	1992	1993	1994	1995
Cost Price ($)				
Base	12,630	13,055	14,840	15,780
GS	15,430	15,825	17,340	—
Used Values ($)				
Base ↑	6,500	7,500	8,500	10,000
Base ↓	5,500	6,000	7,500	8,500
GS ↑	8,000	9,000	10,000	—
GS ↓	7,000	8,000	9,000	—
Extended Warranty	N	N	N	N
Secret Warranty	N	N	N	N
Reliability	③	⑤	⑤	⑤
Air conditioning	❷	③	③	④
Automatic transmission	③	④	⑤	⑤
Body integrity	❷	③	④	④
Braking system	❷	③	③	③
Electrical system	❷	③	③	④
Engines	⑤	⑤	⑤	⑤
Exhaust/Converter	③	④	④	⑤
Fuel system	⑤	⑤	⑤	⑤
Ignition system	⑤	⑤	⑤	⑤
Rust/Paint	③	③	④	⑤
Steering	⑤	⑤	⑤	⑤
Suspension	③	③	⑤	⑤
Crash Safety	⑤	❷	—	—

Note: The low frontal crash ratings represent the inclusion of leg trauma in the over-all score.

MX-5, Miata

Rating: Recommended (1993–97); Above Average (1990–92). **Maintenance/Repair costs**: Higher than average, and dealer dependent. **Parts**: Higher-than-average cost with limited availability (save money with an after-market gel battery).

Technical Data

ENGINES	Liters/CID	HP	MPG	Model Years
DOHC I-4 FI	1.6/98	116	23–31	1990–93
DOHC I-4 FI	1.8/112	133	22–26	1994–97

Strengths and weaknesses: The base 1.6L engine delivers adequate power and accelerates smoothly with a top speed of 115 mph. Acceleration from 0 to 60 mph is in the high 8-second range. The 5-speed manual transmission shifts easily and has well-spaced gears. Their lightness and 50/50 weight distribution make these easy cars to toss around corners, but they're quite jittery on uneven roads.

Top owner performance gripes target the same characteristics that make sports car enthusiasts swoon: inadequate cargo space, cramped interior for large adults, excessive interior noise, and limited low-end torque, which makes for frequent shifting.

Owners also say it's important to change the engine timing chain every 80,000 miles. Other reported problems: 1990–91 model crankshaft failures, leaky rear end seals and valve cover gaskets, torn drive boots, electrical system glitches, brake pulsation, valvetrain clatter on start-up (changing the oil may help), early worn-out shock absorbers and catalytic converter, a leaking or squeaky clutch, and minor body and trim deficiencies.

Dealer service bulletins: **1995**—Brake pulsation troubleshooting tips. • Clutch release bearing squeal. • Steering wheel may be off-center. • Clogged side sill drain holes. • Heater unit noise after long storage. **1996**—Brake pulsation repair. • Side sill paint damage from scuff plate. **1997**—Brake pulsation repair.

Safety summary/recalls: **Recalls**: **1990–93**—80 percent of Miatas are estimated to have some collision damage. • The optional hard-top's hoist accessory kit may have plastic buckles that break and allow the hardtop to suddenly fall. **1991**—Faulty ABS.

Secret Warranties/Service Tips

1990—A hard-to-close trunk lid requires an upgraded rubber cushion (#B48156786). • Poor AC performance is likely caused by the misalignment of the AC harness. • A rattling noise coming from the exhaust manifold may require the replacement of the insulator bracket. • Water may damage door speakers unless a speaker cover assembly (#B4Y5 7696X) is installed. • A musty odor coming from the AC system can be cured by installing an upgraded resin-coated evaporator core (#NA0J 61II0A). **1990–91**—Hard shifting into second gear before the vehicle has warmed up can be corrected by installing an upgraded second gear synchronizer ring and clutch hub sleeve (#JM1NA351-M-232720). **1990–95**—Dirt and debris can clog up side sill drain holes, allowing water to collect and corrosion to occur. Drill larger drain holes. **1992–94**—If the window won't open fully, install a new cable fastener. **1994**—Timing belt noise can be silenced by replacing the tensioner pulley with an upgraded part. **All models/years**—DSB 006/94 gives all of the possible causes and remedies for brake vibration.

MX-5, Miata Profile

	1990	1991	1992	1993	1994	1995	1996	1997
Cost Price ($)								
Base	14,069	14,499	15,150	15,650	17,045	17,940	18,900	20,775
Used Values ($)								
Base ↑	7,500	8,500	9,500	10,500	12,000	13,500	15,000	17,000
Base ↓	6,000	7,000	8,000	9,500	10,500	12,000	14,000	15,500

| Extended Warranty | N | N | N | N | N | N | N | N |
Secret Warranty	N	N	N	N	N	N	N	N
Reliability	④	④	④	⑤	⑤	⑤	⑤	⑤
Air conditioning	④	④	④	⑤	⑤	⑤	⑤	⑤
Body integrity	②	②	③	③	③	④	④	④
Braking system	②	③	③	④	④	⑤	⑤	⑤
Electrical system	②	②	②	③	③	④	④	④
Engines	②	②	③	④	④	⑤	⑤	⑤
Exhaust/Converter	④	④	④	④	④	④	⑤	⑤
Fuel system	③	④	④	⑤	⑤	⑤	⑤	⑤
Ignition system	②	③	③	③	④	④	④	⑤
Manual transmission	⑤	⑤	⑤	⑤	⑤	⑤	⑤	⑤
- automatic	—	—	—	—	—	—	—	—
Rust/Paint	②	②	③	③	③	④	④	⑤
Steering	⑤	⑤	⑤	⑤	⑤	⑤	⑤	⑤
Suspension	⑤	⑤	⑤	⑤	⑤	⑤	⑤	⑤
Crash Safety	②	⑤	⑤	②	—	—	④	④

RX-7

Rating: Recommended (1991–95); Above Average (1985–90). 1995 was the RX-7's last model year. **Maintenance/Repair costs**: Higher than average, and most repairs have to be done by a Mazda dealer. **Parts**: Higher-than-average cost with limited availability. Parts shortage may become chronic now that the RX-7 has been discontinued.

Technical Data

ENGINES	Liters/CID	HP	MPG	Model Years
Wankel FI	1.3/80	160	15–18	1986–91
Wankel FI	1.3/80	200	14–17	1986–91
Wankel FI	1.3/81	255	13–17	1991–95

Strengths and weaknesses: The RX-7 is an impressive performer that goes from 0 to 60 mph in 8 seconds and covers the same distance in 6.2 seconds when equipped with a turbocharger. The ride can be painful on bad roads, though, due primarily to the car's stiff suspension. The GSL and Turbo models are very well equipped and luxuriously finished. Except for some oil-burning problems, apex seal failures, and leaking engine O-rings, the RX-7 has served to dispel any doubts concerning the durability of rotary engines.

Nevertheless, careful maintenance is in order, since contaminated oil or overheating will easily damage the rotary engine. Clutches wear quickly if used hard. Disc brakes need frequent attention paid to the calipers and rotors. The MacPherson struts get soft more quickly than average. AC malfunctions and fuel, exhaust system, and electrical glitches are also common. Be wary of leaky sunroofs. Radiators have a short life span. Rocker panels and body seams are prone to more serious rusting. The underbody on older cars should be inspected carefully for corrosion damage. Fuel economy has never been this car's strong suit.

Age has improved the RX-7's reliability. In fact, dealer service bulletins list only two possible problems with the '95 RX-7: AC unit noise after long storage and a slightly off-center steering wheel.

Safety summary/recalls: Safety investigators believe that 1993 RX-7s could experience engine overheating and engine failure caused by a faulty turbocharger. **Recalls: 1979–83**—Idler arms may corrode, freeze, or break after prolonged exposure to road salt. **1986–87**—Road salt may also cause excessive front brake disc pad liner corrosion. **1989–91**—Shoulder belts may fail. **1993–94**—Engine heat could make fuel hoses deteriorate and leak prematurely, posing a fire hazard. **1991–95**—Fuel hoses may crack and leak fuel. • Poor braking after an overnight park is caused by engine oil mist clogging the brake vacuum check valve.

Secret Warranties/Service Tips

1979–91—Hard shifting into second gear before the vehicle has warmed up can be corrected by installing an upgraded second gear synchronizer ring and clutch hub sleeve (#JM1NA351-M-232720). **1986–88**—A hard-to-start cold engine can be fixed by switching to air gap spark plugs and disconnecting the sub-zero starting assist device. • Misfire and hesitation over 6,000 rpm can be corrected by installing an upgraded air flow meter. • A rough idle may be caused by a short circuit in the water temperature switch wiring. • Erratic power window operation may require a new regulator guide assembly, motor bracket, and sprocket. **1987–88**—Turbo models with a rough idle or cold starting problems may need a new air control valve (#N332 13990). **1993–94**—To eliminate slipping clutch problems, Mazda may install, at no charge, an improved clutch disc. **All models/years**—DSB 006/94 gives all of the possible causes and remedies for brake vibration.

RX-7 Profile

	1988	1989	1990	1991	1992	1993	1994	1995
Cost Price ($)								
RX-7	17,938	19,178	19,768	20,799	—	—	—	—
Convertible	22,668	27,478	28,418	29,199	—	—	—	—
Turbo	23,509	26,219	26,809	28,149	—	32,850	36,395	37,950
Used Values ($)								
RX-7 ↑	5,000	6,200	7,000	8,000	—	—	—	—
RX-7 ↓	4,000	5,000	5,800	6,500	—	—	—	—
Convertible ↑	8,000	9,000	10,500	11,500	—	—	—	—
Convertible ↓	7,500	8,000	9,000	10,000	—	—	—	—
Turbo ↑	6,000	7,000	8,000	9,000	—	17,000	20,000	23,000
Turbo ↓	5,000	5,500	6,500	7,500	—	15,000	18,000	21,000
Extended Warranty	Y	Y	Y	Y	Y	Y	Y	Y
Secret Warranty	N	N	N	N	N	Y	Y	N
Reliability	③	③	④	⑤	⑤	⑤	⑤	⑤

Air conditioning	②	②	③	③	③	③	③	③
Body integrity	③	③	③	③	③	③	④	⑤
Braking system	②	②	③	③	③	③	③	③
Electrical system	②	②	②	②	③	③	③	③
Engines	⑤	⑤	⑤	⑤	⑤	⑤	⑤	⑤
Exhaust/Converter	③	③	③	④	⑤	⑤	⑤	⑤
Fuel system	③	⑤	⑤	⑤	⑤	⑤	⑤	⑤
Ignition system	③	③	③	④	⑤	⑤	⑤	⑤
Manual transmission	③	③	③	④	④	④	④	⑤
- automatic	②	②	③	③	③	③	④	⑤
Rust/Paint	②	②	③	④	⑤	⑤	⑤	⑤
Steering	④	④	④	⑤	⑤	⑤	⑤	⑤
Suspension	②	③	④	⑤	⑤	⑤	⑤	⑤
Crash Safety	②	—	—	—	—	—	—	—

NISSAN

200SX

Rating: Above average; high-performance for those drivers with low-performance expectations. (1995–97). **Maintenance/Repair costs**: Average, and most repairs can be done by any garage. **Parts**: Reasonably priced, but hard to find.

Technical Data

ENGINES	Liters/CID	HP	MPG	Model Years
DOHC I-4T FI	1.6/97	115	27–35	1995–98
OHC I-4T FI	1.8/110	120	22–25	1985–86
OHC I-4 FI	2.0/120	102	23–27	1985–88
DOHC I-4 FI	2.0/121	140	23–30	1995–98
OHC V6 FI	3.0/181	160	19–23	1987–88

Strengths and weaknesses: Nissan calls this front-drive compact their sporty coupe class leader, but the 200SX is merely a Chrysler Neon fighter that has a sports car flair without the substance. The interior is unnecessarily cramped and you get only average power and handling with the base powerplant. Later models are much sportier and have more passenger room. Prices are reasonable, though, and the repair history for these cars is average.

Both engines have performed reasonably well, although the 2.0L has been the most suitable for hard-driving thrills. The clutch has been the source of some complaints, along with occasional electrical malfunctions. Rapid front brake wear and rotor damage are common problems.

Dealer service bulletins: 1995—AC system shuts off. • AC compressor leakage. • Brake noise. • Cold weather starting tips. • C-pillar finisher lifting. • Engine cranks but won't start. • Front window misalignment. • Fuel gauge not indicating full tank. • Horn activates randomly. • Squeak and rattle troubleshooting tips. • Wind noise field fix procedure. • Windshield cracking may be covered under the warranty. **1996**—Engine cranks but won't start or is hard to start. • Squeak and rattle repair.

Safety summary/recalls: **Recalls**: **1995**—On vehicles with ABS, the hydraulic actuator may malfunction, increasing the stopping distance. **1995–98**—Install upgraded windshield wiper arm linkage.

Secret Warranties/Service Tips

All models/years—DSB 006/94 gives all of the possible causes and remedies for brake vibration. • 1994 and earlier models equipped with RE4RO1A transmissions may experience repeated planetary failure due to poor cooler flow in the fin-type cooler. Apparently, cooler line flushing machines can't flush clear this type of cooler. In the past, the entire radiator would need to be replaced to upgrade the cooling system. Nissan now has a spiral cooler replacement kit (#21606-15V25) that can be used instead.

200SX Profile

	1995	1996	1997
Cost Price ($)			
Base			
Used Values ($)	13,874	14,303	14,418
Base ↑		9,000	10,000	11,000
Base ↓		8,000	9,000	10,000
Extended Warranty	N	N	N
Secret Warranty	N	N	N
Reliability	④	④	⑤
Crash Safety	—	—	⑤

240SX

Rating: Recommended (1995–97); Above Average (1989–94). Only the convertible was carried over to the '94 model year. **Maintenance/Repair costs**: Average, and most repairs can be done by any garage. **Parts**: Reasonably priced and easy to find.

Technical Data

ENGINES	Liters/CID	HP	MPG	Model Years
OHC I-4 FI	2.4/146	140	21–25	1989–90
DOHC I-4 FI	2.4/146	155	22–27	1991–98

Strengths and weaknesses: Although this rear-drive sport coupe carried a 2.4L 4-cylinder engine to differentiate it from its 2.0L predecessor, the 200SX, it still falls far short of producing high performance thrills. Its

140-hp base engine provides more than enough torque to handle most driving needs—just don't expect fast acceleration times or a comfortable ride. Handling is impressive, though, thanks to the car's independent suspension. The redesigned '95 coupe features a longer wheelbase, 15 additional horses, and optional ABS/traction control. It still provides a harsh ride and poor traction on slippery roadways. Headroom remains limited, cargo space practically nil, and the trunk is barely large enough to carry your lunch, as long as you eat light and can fit it through the small opening.

This car doesn't have any major serious shortcomings apart from a cramped interior and excessive engine noise. The few deficiencies reported concern electrical malfunctions, early AC burnout, premature clutch wear, noisy brakes that wear out quickly, exhaust system rust-out, and fit and finish deficiencies.

Dealer service bulletins: **1995**—Engine overheating and poor driveability–Code 45. • AC compressor leaks or is noisy. • Excessive brake noise. • Which windshield cracks are covered under warranty. **1996**—Engine cranks, but won't start.

Safety summary/recalls: **Recalls**: **1989–91**—Takata seatbelt replacement. **1995**—Faulty brake warning light.

Secret Warranties/Service Tips

1989—Doors that won't lock from the outside may need a door rod clip modification. • A special service campaign covers the free replacement of the engine timing belt and tensioner. It's worth a fight for a partial refund. **1989–91**—Starting difficulties can often be traced to a connector not fully seated in the ECU. **1990**—Excessive squeaking from the front brakes can be fixed by increasing the front brake pad chamfer. **All models/years**—DSB 006/94 gives all of the possible causes and remedies for brake vibration.

240SX Profile

	1990	1991	1992	1993	1994	1995	1996	1997
Cost Price ($)								
Base	15,164	15,539	16,495	16,785	25,344	19,758	20,563	20,628
Used Values ($)								
Base	6,500	7,500	8,500	9,500	13,000	11,500	13,500	14,500
Base	5,000	6,000	7,000	8,000	12,000	10,500	12,500	13,500
Extended Warranty	N	N	N	N	N	N	N	N
Secret Warranty	N	N	N	N	N	N	N	N
Reliability	③	③	③	③	④	④	⑤	⑤
Air conditioning	❷	❷	❷	③	④	④	④	④
Automatic transmission	③	③	③	③	⑤	⑤	⑤	⑤
Body integrity	❷	❷	❷	③	③	③	③	③
Braking system	❷	❷	❷	❷	❷	③	③	③
Electrical system	❷	❷	❷	❷	❷	③	③	③

Engines	④	④	④	④	④	⑤	⑤	⑤
Exhaust/Converter	❷	❷	❷	③	③	③	④	⑤
Fuel system	❷	③	③	③	④	④	⑤	⑤
Ignition system	③	③	③	③	④	④	⑤	⑤
Rust/Paint	③	③	③	③	④	④	⑤	⑤
Steering	❷	❷	③	④	④	④	⑤	⑤
Suspension	③	④	④	④	④	⑤	⑤	⑤
Crash Safety	—	⑤	⑤	❷	③	③	③	—

300ZX

Rating: Average (1990–96); Below Average (1988–89). Nissan's answer to the Corvette, this car has everything: high performance capability, a heavy chassis, complicated electronics, and average depreciation. Turbocharged '90 and later models are much faster than previous versions and better overall buys. 1996 was its last model year. **Maintenance/Repair costs**: Way higher than average, and only a Nissan dealer can repair these cars. Just replacing the air cleaner and spark plugs is a task. Turbocharger repairs can put a big dent in your wallet, as well. **Parts**: Expensive and hard to find.

Technical Data

ENGINES	Liters/CID	HP	MPG	Model Years
OHC V6 FI	3.0/181	160–165	21–25	1988–89
OHC V6T FI	3.0/181	200–205	19–23	1988–89
DOHC V6 FI	3.0/181	222	21–25	1988–89
DOHC V6T FI	3.0/181	300	17–22	1990–96

Strengths and weaknesses: Nissan's shouting high performance with this weighty, rear-drive that offers a high degree of luxury equipment along with a potent 300-hp engine. Traction is poor on slippery surfaces, however, and the rear suspension hits hard when going over speed bumps.

The complexity of all the bells and whistles on the 300ZX translates into a lot more driveability and electrical problems than you'd experience with either a Mustang or a Camaro—two cars that have their own reliability problems, but are far easier and less costly to troubleshoot and repair. The best example of this is the electrical system—long a source of recurring, hard-to-diagnose shorts. Fuel injectors are a constant problem and lead to poor engine performance. The manual transmission has been failure prone, clutches don't last very long, front and rear brakes are noisy and wear out quickly, and the aluminum wheels are easily damaged by corrosion and road hazards. The exhaust system is practically biodegradable. The glitzy digital dash with three odometers and weird spongy/stiff variable shock absorbers are more gimmicky than practical. Mediocre body assembly.

Dealer service bulletins: **1995**—Poor driveability-Code 45. • The AC compressor leaks or is noisy. • Excessive brake noise. • Particular windshield cracks are covered under warranty. **1996**—Engine cranks but won't start.

Safety summary/recalls: **Recalls**: **1979–87**—Nissan will install, at no charge, a shift interlock to prevent sudden acceleration.

Secret Warranties/Service Tips

1990—Clunking when braking in Reverse can be eliminated by installing a retainer on each front brake pad. **1990–91**—Starting difficulties can often be traced to a connector not fully seated in the Electronic Control Unit. **1991**—An automatic transmission that shifts poorly or slips out of gear can be fixed by re-torquing the band servo retainer bolts. **1992**—An oil leak from the drive pinion oil seal can be fixed by installing an upgraded seal. **All models/years**—Premature rear brake pad wear may be caused by poorly adjusted brakes or rusty rear rotors. The rear brake pad kit (#D4060-01P90) will help to correct the problem. • DSB 006/94 gives all of the possible causes and remedies for brake vibration. • 1994 and earlier models equipped with RE4RO1A transmissions may experience repeated planetary failure due to poor cooler flow in the fin-type cooler. Apparently, cooler line flushing machines can't flush clear this type of cooler. In the past, the entire radiator would need to be replaced to upgrade the cooling system. Nissan now has a spiral cooler replacement kit (#21606-15V25) that can be used instead.

300ZX Profile

	1989	1990	1991	1992	1993	1994	1995	1996
Cost Price ($)								
Base	23,309	28,960	30,175	31,490	30,445	34,080	35,399	37,845
Used Values ($)								
Base ↑		6,500	11,500	13,000	14,500	16,500	19,000	22,000	24,000
Base ↓		5,500	10,000	11,500	13,000	15,000	17,000	19,500	22,000
Extended Warranty	Y	Y	Y	Y	Y	Y	Y	Y
Secret Warranty	N	N	N	N	N	N	N	N
Reliability	②	③	③	③	③	③	④	④
Air conditioning	①	①	③	③	④	④	⑤	⑤
Body integrity	①	①	①	①	①	①	②	③
Braking system	①	①	①	①	①	①	②	②
Electrical system	①	①	①	①	②	②	③	③
Engines	③	③	③	③	③	④	④	⑤
Exhaust/Converter	①	③	③	③	④	④	④	⑤
Fuel system	②	②	③	③	③	③	④	④
Ignition system	②	②	③	③	③	③	④	④
Manual transmission	③	④	④	④	④	⑤	⑤	⑤
- automatic	②	②	③	③	③	④	④	④
Rust/Paint	②	②	③	③	③	④	⑤	⑤
Steering	③	③	③	③	④	④	⑤	⑤
Suspension	③	③	③	③	④	④	④	⑤
Crash Safety	—	—	⑤	⑤	①	—	—	—

TOYOTA

Celica

Rating: Recommended (1994–97); Above Average (1990–93); Average (1988–89). The 1996 and 1997 models are practically identical; choose the cheapest version. Keep in mind that the GT and GTS have a firmer suspension, better-equipped interior, ABS, and a more sporting feel than do other versions. All handle competently and provide the kind of sporting performance expected from a car of this class. The extra performance in the higher-line versions does come at a price, but this isn't a problem, given the high resale value and excellent reliability for which Celicas are known.

If you want to buy something comparable for less, consider the Mitsubishi Eclipse or Eagle Talon 4X4—it matches the Celica's features for thousands of dollars less. Other cars worth considering are the '96 Dodge Stealth, Ford Mustang and Probe, GM Camaro and Firebird, and Mazda Miata. **Maintenance/Repair costs**: Average, and most repairs can be done by any garage. **Parts**: Reasonably priced and easy to find.

Technical Data

ENGINES	Liters/CID	HP	MPG	Model Years
OHC I-4 FI	2.0/122	97	23–27	1986
DOHC I-4 FI	2.0/122	115	24–28	1987–89
DOHC I-4 FI	2.0/122	135	21–25	1986–89
DOHC I-4T FI	2.0/122	190	20–23	1988–89
DOHC I-4 FI	1.6/97	103	23–29	1990–93
DOHC I-4T FI	2.0/122	200	19–23	1990–93
DOHC I-4 FI	2.2/132	135	21–26	1990–93
DOHC I-4 FI	1.8/108	105–110	26–30	1994–97
DOHC I-4 FI	2.2/132	130–135	23–27	1994–97

Strengths and weaknesses: The pre-1986 Celicas weren't very sporty. Their excessive weight and soft suspension compromised handling and added a high fuel penalty. With the 1986 make-over, Celicas gained more power and much better handling—especially in the GT and GTS versions—but they're still more show than go, with limited rear passenger room.

Redesigned '94 models are full of both show and go, with more aerodynamic styling, an enhanced 1.8L that gives more pickup than the ST's 1.6L, and better fuel economy. Among the upgraded models available, smart buyers should choose a used '94 ST for its more reasonable price, smooth performance, quiet running, and high fuel economy.

All Celicas offer exceptional reliability and durability. Servicing and repair are straightforward and parts are easily found. The front-wheel drive series performs very well and hasn't presented any major problems to owners. Prices are high for Celicas in good condition, but some bargains are available with the base ST model.

Owner gripes target the excessive engine noise, limited rear seat room, and inadequate cargo space. Pre-'94 models have the most complaints regarding brakes, electrical problems, AC malfunctions, and premature exhaust wear-out. The '94 models may have a manual transmission that slips out of second gear and hard starts caused by a faulty air flow meter (#22250-74200). Areas vulnerable to early rusting include rear wheel openings, suspension components, the area surrounding the gas filler cap, door bottoms, and trunk or hatchback lids.

Safety summary/recalls: Even if you have 4X4 capability it's imperative that snow tires be fitted in order to avoid dangerous control problems on snow and ice. **Recalls: 1988–89 All-Track Turbos**—The radiator and coolant will be replaced for free by Toyota. **1990**—Campaign L03 provides for the free replacement of the instrument panel light control switch. • Faulty airbag inflator.

Secret Warranties/Service Tips

1986–89—Reduce excessive engine ping and jerking by installing an upgraded TCCS Electronic Control Unit under the emissions warranty. **1986–91**—Rattling headrests is a common problem addressed in DSB B091-010. **All models/years**—Older Toyotas with stalling problems should have the engine checked for excessive carbon buildup on the valves before any more extensive repairs are authorized. • Owner feedback and dealer service managers (who wish to remain anonymous) confirm the existence of Toyota's secret warranty, which will pay for replacing front disc brake components that wear out before 2 years/25,000 miles. • The decade-old problem of brake pulsation/vibration is fully outlined and corrective measures are detailed in DSB BR94-002, issued February 7, 1994. • To reduce front brake squeaks on ABS-equipped vehicles, ask the dealer to install new, upgraded rotors (#43517-32020).

Celica Profile

	1990	1991	1992	1993	1994	1995	1996	1997
Cost Price ($)								
Base	13,673	14,323	15,063	15,983	18,628	19,410	19,638	19,703
Used Values ($)								
Base ↑	7,000	8,000	9,500	10,500	12,500	14,500	16,500	17,500
Base ↓	6,000	7,000	8,000	9,500	11,500	13,000	15,000	16,500
Extended Warranty	N	N	N	N	N	N	N	N
Secret Warranty	N	N	N	N	Y	Y	Y	Y
Reliability	③	③	④	④	④	⑤	⑤	⑤
Air conditioning	❶	❶	❷	❷	❷	③	③	④
Body integrity	❷	❷	❷	❷	③	③	⑤	⑤
Braking system	❶	❶	❷	❷	❷	❷	③	③

Electrical system	❶	❶	❶	③	③	④	⑤	⑤
Engines	④	④	③	③	③	③	④	⑤
Exhaust/Converter	❷	❷	❷	❷	③	③	⑤	⑤
Fuel system	④	④	④	④	④	④	④	④
Ignition system	④	④	④	④	④	④	⑤	⑤
Manual transmission	③	④	④	④	④	④	⑤	⑤
- automatic	③	③	③	④	④	④	④	⑤
Rust/Paint	❷	④	④	④	④	④	④	④
Steering	④	④	④	④	④	④	⑤	⑤
Suspension	④	④	④	④	④	④	⑤	⑤
Crash Safety	❶	⑤	—	❶	—	—	—	—

Note: The low frontal crash ratings represent the inclusion of leg trauma in the overall score.

MR2

Rating: Recommended (1991–93); Above Average (1988–90); Average (1986–87). The best choice is the '93 model which had improved handling and engine performance all at a decent price. The '95 model, however, has a higher depreciation rate and less years. **Maintenance/Repair costs**: Average, but most repairs have to be done by a Toyota dealer and engine repairs can get quite expensive due to the limited access to the engine compartment. **Parts**: Reasonably priced, but not easily found.

Technical Data

ENGINES	Liters/CID	HP	MPG	Model Years
OHC I4 FI	1.6/98	115	25–30	1988–90
OHC I-4 FI	1.6/98	145	23–28	1988–90
DOHC I-4 FI	2.2/132	135	23–27	1991–95
DOHC I-4T FI	2.0/122	200	21–25	1991–95

Strengths and weaknesses: The MR2 does everything a sports car should without fuss or surprises. Except for vague steering and some front-end instability (corrected with the '93 models), handling is practically flawless. The standard 16-valve 4-cylinder motor is smooth and adequate. The supercharged and turbocharged engines, though overpriced, produce more power than even a sporty car driver would want to use. They also have a bit of turbo lag and require deft handling. The engine's placement behind the driver's seat also produces excessive noise and vibration that make long trips very uncomfortable.

In order of frequency, the most common complaints on all MR2s are the brakes, electrical glitches, and body hardware (fit and finish) deficiencies.

Safety summary/recalls: Recalls: N/A.

Secret Warranties/Service Tips

1991—Front brake squeal can be reduced by using new anti-squeal springs (#47743-32030). • Sound system interference can be eliminated by changing the alternator. **All models/years**—Toyota has a secret warranty that will pay for replacing front disc brake components that wear out before 2 years/25,000 miles. • The brake pulsation/vibration problem is fully outlined and corrective measures are detailed in DSB BR94-002, issued February 7, 1994.

MR2 Profile

	1988	1989	1991	1992	1993	1994	1995
Cost Price ($)							
Base	13,843	14,848	16,848	17,813	20,208	23,613	24,655
Used Values ($)							
Base ↑	4,000	4,500	8,500	9,500	11,000	14,500	16,500
Base ↓	3,000	3,500	7,000	8,000	9,500	13,000	15,000
Extended Warranty	Y	Y	Y	Y	Y	Y	Y
Secret Warranty	Y	Y	Y	Y	Y	Y	Y
Reliability	③	③	③	③	④	④	④
Air conditioning	②	②	③	④	⑤	⑤	⑤
Body integrity	②	②	③	③	③	③	③
Braking system	②	②	②	②	③	③	③
Electrical system	②	②	②	③	③	③	③
Engines	⑤	⑤	⑤	⑤	⑤	⑤	⑤
Exhaust/Converter	②	②	③	③	③	④	⑤
Fuel system	④	④	④	④	④	④	④
Ignition system	③	③	③	③	③	④	④
Manual transmission	③	③	③	③	③	⑤	⑤
- automatic	③	③	④	④	④	④	④
Rust/Paint	③	③	⑤	⑤	⑤	⑤	⑤
Steering	③	③	③	③	③	⑤	⑤
Suspension	③	③	③	③	③	③	③

Note: The MR2 hasn't been crash tested by NHTSA.

Supra

Rating: Above Average (1993–97); Average (1988–92). Supras are average sports cars that suffer from the Chevrolet Corvette/Nissan 300ZX affliction—they're overpriced and overweight. **Maintenance/Repair costs**: Way higher than average, and only a Toyota dealer can repair these cars. **Parts**: Expensive and frequently back-ordered.

Technical Data

ENGINES	Liters/CID	HP	MPG	Model Years
DOHC I-6 FI	3.0/180	200	16–21	1986–92
DOHC I-6T FI	2.2/135	232	15–20	1987–92

| DOHC I-6 FI | 3.0/183 | 220–225 | 16–21 | 1993–98 |
| DOHC I-6T FI | 3.0/183 | 320 | 15–19 | 1993–98 |

Strengths and weaknesses: This is a nicely styled sports car that has caught the Corvette/Nissan 300ZX malady: cumulative add-ons that drive up the car's price and weight and drive down its performance and reliability. The 6-cylinder engines are smooth and powerful. Handling is sure and precise—better than the Celica because of the independent rear suspension. The Supra has limited rear seating, fuel mileage is marginal around town, and insurance premiums are likely to be much higher than average. Owners report major engine problems, frequent rear differential replacements, electrical short circuits, AC malfunctions, and premature brake, suspension, and exhaust system wear. The engine is an oil-burner at times and cornering is often accompanied by a rear end growl. Seatbelt guides and the power antenna are failure-prone. Body deficiencies are common.

Safety summary/recalls: Recalls: N/A.

Secret Warranties/Service Tips

1981–86—Valves must be adjusted annually or serious engine damage may occur. **1984–86**—Defective catalytic converters are responsible for a rotten-egg odor. **1985–88**—Starter/ring gear clash can be corrected with an upgraded starter assembly (#28100-62011 or -62021). **1986–88**—Excessive brake squeak and groaning can be reduced by installing revised brake pads (04491-14240). **1989–90**—Cold driveability and startability is improved with a modified TCCS Electronic Control Unit. **1990–91**—A new front brake pad material is now used (#04491-14280) to improve brake pad durability. **All models/years**—Older Toyotas with stalling problems should have the engine checked for excessive carbon buildup on the valves before any more extensive repairs are authorized. • Toyota has a secret warranty that will pay for replacing front disc brake components that wear out before 2 years/25,000 miles. • The brake pulsation/vibration problem is fully outlined and corrective measures are detailed in DSB BR94-002, issued February 7, 1994.

Supra Profile

	1990	1991	1992	1993	1994	1995	1996	1997
Cost Price ($)								
Base	23,875	24,845	25,575	34,225	36,185	31,497	39,020	30,340
Used Values ($)								
Base ↑	8,500	9,500	11,000	18,000	20,000	22,000	26,000	28,000
Base ↓	7,000	8,500	9,500	16,000	18,500	20,000	24,000	26,000
Extended Warranty	N	N	N	N	N	N	N	N
Secret Warranty	Y	Y	Y	Y	Y	Y	Y	Y
Reliability	❷	③	③	③	③	③	④	④

Air conditioning	②	②	②	③	③	③	④	④
Body integrity	②	②	②	②	②	③	③	③
Braking system	②	②	②	②	②	②	②	③
Electrical system	②	②	②	②	②	②	③	③
Engines	③	③	③	③	④	④	④	⑤
Exhaust/Converter	②	②	②	②	③	③	③	④
Fuel system	②	②	②	②	③	③	④	④
Ignition system	②	③	③	④	④	④	④	⑤
Manual transmission	③	③	③	③	③	③	④	⑤
- automatic	③	③	③	③	③	③	④	⑤
Rust/Paint	②	②	②	③	④	④	④	⑤
Steering	③	③	③	③	③	③	④	⑤
Suspension	③	③	③	③	③	③	③	③

Note: The Supra hasn't been crash tested by the NHTSA.

MINIVANS

Chrysler launched the minivan concept with its 1984 Caravan/Voyager. Although poorly assembled and riddled with deficiencies, the tall, boxy vehicle was an instant success because it combined fuel efficiency, car-like maneuverability, and increased cargo/passenger space in a smartly styled "garageable" van. On the other hand, Volkswagen's minivan—replaced by the EuroVan in the early '90s—had been on sale for over 20 years and never did very well. Used mostly as a camper, it suffered from decades-old styling, poor dealer support, insufficient heating, glacial acceleration, and its reputation for being more unreliable than Chrysler's minivans.

Fortunately, while Chrysler and VW have apparently stood still from a quality improvement standpoint, the competition has caught up, and, in the case of Ford and Toyota, surpassed the two originators of the minivan concept. Vehicles produced during the past few years use more powerful engines, have better crash ratings, more safety features (airbags, etc.), more responsive road handling, better quality control, more competitive prices, greater parts availability, and offer a greater variety of powertrains.

If you must buy a minivan, remember that, much like sport-utilities, they usually fall into two categories: up-sized cars and down-sized trucks. The up-sized cars are "people movers." They're mostly FWD, handle like a car, and get great fuel economy. Chrysler's Caravan and Voyager are the best examples of this kind of minivan. GM's Astro/Safari and the Ford Aerostar, on the other hand, are down-sized trucks. Using rear-wheel drive, 6-cylinder engines, and heavier mechanical components, these minivans handle cargo as well as passengers. Towing capacity varies between 3,000 and 5,000 lbs. On the negative side, fuel economy is no match for the FWD minivans, and highway handling on rear-drives is also more truck-like.

Minivan ownership costs are quite reasonable, according to the American management consulting firm Runzheimer International, which has concluded that it costs less to operate a minivan than it does many compact cars. Still, most minivans are overpriced and motorists needing a vehicle with large cargo and passenger carrying capacity should consider a cheaper GM Vandura or Chevy Van, even if it means sacrificing some fuel economy and convenience features (they can be added by most conversion shops at competitive prices). You just can't beat the excellent forward vision and easy-to-customize interiors that these large vans provide.

Recommended

Ford Windstar (1996–97)   Nissan Quest (1994–97)
Mercury Villager (1994–97)   Toyota Previa (1992–97)
Nissan Axxess (1994–95)

1996 Windstar: A recommended buy mainly because of its superior crash-worthiness and good (not great) quality control.

Above Average

Ford Windstar (1995)   Nissan Quest (1993)
Mercury Villager (1993)   Toyota Previa (1991)
Nissan Axxess (1993)

Average

Ford Aerostar (1992–97)   Honda Odyssey/Isuzu Oasis
GM Astro, Safari (1992–97)   Mazda MPV (1996–97)
GM Lumina, Trans Sport,   Nissan Axxess (1991–92)
  Venture (1996–97)

Below Average

Chrysler Caravan, Voyager,   Mazda MPV (1989–95)
  Town & Country (1997)
GM Lumina, Trans Sport
  (1991–95)

Not Recommended

Chrysler Caravan, Voyager,   GM Lumina, Trans Sport (1990)
  Town & Country (1984–96)   Nissan Axxess (1990)
Ford Aerostar (1988–91)   Toyota LE Van (1984–90)
GM Astro, Safari (1985–91)   VW Camper, EuroVan,
                         Vanagon

1994 Caravan LE: Chrysler minivans aren't recommended due to their poor crashworthiness, chronic automatic transmission, brake failures, and paint delamination.

CHRYSLER

Caravan, Town & Country, Voyager

Rating: Below Average (1997); Not Recommended (1984–96). Major generic defects affecting the 1984–96 models make these minivans very risky buys. In spite of the poor reliability of the early versions, Chrysler minivans remained popular because Chrysler's comprehensive 7-year warranty paid for their shortcomings. But that warranty's gone and the defects remain. **Maintenance/Repair costs**: Higher than average, but any garage can repair these minivans. **Parts**: Expensive (especially transmission and ABS components, which are covered under secret warranty programs and several recall campaigns) and frequently back-ordered.

There's presently an abundance of used Chrysler minivans on the market; however, very few have any of their original warranty coverage left. Count on spending at least another $1,000 for a supplementary warranty to protect yourself from Chrysler's costly generic defects. You'd be foolish to buy one of these minivans without an extended supplementary warranty. Just ABS and transmission repairs alone could cost you $5,000. Other minivans you may wish to consider: the Ford Windstar, Mercury Villager, Nissan Quest, or Toyota Previa and Sienna.

Technical Data

ENGINES	Liters/CID	HP	MPG	Model Years
OHC I-4 2 bbl.	2.2L/135	101	17–21	1985–87
OHC I-4 2 bbl.	2.6L/156	104	15–20	1985–87
OHC I-4 FI	2.5L/153	102	17–22	1987–90
OHC I-4T FI	2.5L/153	150	15–21	1989–90

DOHC I-4T FI	2.4L/148	150	15–21	1996–98
OHC V6 FI	3.0L/181	144	16–20	1987–94
OHC V6 FI	3.0L/181	150	16–20	1996–98
OHV V6 FI	3.3L/201	150–162	15–20	1990–95
OHC I-4 FI	2.5L/153	100	18–22	1991–95
OHV V6 FI	3.3L/201	158	14–19	1996–98
OHV V6 FI	3.8L/230	162	15–19	1996–98
OHV V6 FI	3.8L/232	162	14–19	1994–95

Strengths and weaknesses: Chrysler's minivans dominate the new and used minivan market because they offer pleasing styling and lots of convenience features. They also ride and handle better than most truck-based minivans (although there's lots of room for improvement), and can carry up to seven passengers in comfort. Cargo hauling capability is more than adequate, with a 3,000-pound maximum towing range.

On the downside, these minivans pose maximum safety risks due to their poor crashworthiness and chronic mechanical failures. Worse still, owners report experiencing a host of bizarre "happenings" with their minivans, suggesting that these vehicles require the services of an exorcist rather than a mechanic (seatbelts that may strangle children, airbags that deploy when the ignition is turned on, and stalling when within radar range—see page 427).

```
NO: 18-16-96
GROUP: Vehicle Performance
DATE: May 3, 1996
SUBJECT:
Intermittent Driveability Problems When Driving Near Radar
MODELS:
1996 (NS) Town & Country/Caravan/Voyager
NOTE:
THE FLASH SECTION OF THIS BULLETIN APPLIES TO ALL VEHICLES BUILT PRIOR TO SEPTEMBER 27, 1995 (MDH 09-27-XX).
THE INSTALLATION OF THE "HARDENED" CRANK SENSOR APPLIES TO ALL VEHICLES BUILT PRIOR TO NOVEMBER 1, 1995
(MDH 11-01-XX).

SYMPTOM/CONDITION:
Some vehicles may experience intermittent driveability concerns or problems when driven in close proximity to military or
air traffic control radar installations.

DIAGNOSIS:
Using the Mopar Diagnostic System (MDS) or the Scan Tool (DRBIII) and appropriate. Diagnostic Procedure Manual, verify
that all engine systems are functioning correctly. If Diagnostic Trouble Codes (DTCs) are present, record them on the repair
order for future reference and repair as necessary. If none are found, proceed to the repair procedure.

EQUIPMENT/PARTS REQUIRED:
1    4727336    Crankshaft Position Sensor, Hardened
1    CH6000      Scan Tool (DRB III)
1    CH7035      General Purpose Interface Bus Cable (GPIB)
1    CH7000      J1962 Cable
1    4669020     Label - Authorized Software Update
1    4275086     Label - Authorized Modification

REPAIR PROCEDURE:
This bulletin involves installing a new "hardened" crankshaft position sensor and/or reprogramming (flashing) the PCM with
new software calibrations.
```

Believe it or not, your minivan's chronic stalling could be caused by airport radar. Will we soon see "Watch out for low-flying aircraft and stalling Chrysler minivans" signs posted at airports and military installations?

Powertrain problems

These minivans are way underpowered with the base 4-cylinder engine. It has a history of head gasket failures, but outshines the larger Mitsubishi 2.6L, which is guaranteed to self-destruct just as the warranty expires. The timing belt, piston rings, and valves are particular weak points on the 2.6L powerplant. The two-piece camshaft oil seals are also prone to sudden leaks. The Chrysler-built 2.5L engine is fairly dependable but sluggish, and the 3.3L V6 is the most reliable. The Mitsubishi 3.0L V6 is much more reliable than its smaller 2.6L version. But it lacks power on long climbs, has multiple fuel-injection and oil leak problems, and produces a loud piston "slapping" noise during cold starts. Cold weather presents additional problems for Chrysler minivan owners: one owner of an '89 Voyager says that dealers in his area claim that his 3.0L engine seized because of "poor cold weather oil lubrication." If this is true, it spells trouble for the many owners who have to drive in cold weather conditions and are now nearing the end of Chrysler's original warranty coverage.

Automatic transmissions are a nightmare and are unsafe (see "Safety Summary"). The disastrous Ultradrive 4-speed automatic was particularly troublesome on 1988–91 models. Then it was renamed—and continued to pile up complaints. Chrysler, stung by critics' charges that these transmissions were lemons, pledged that a free oil cooler by-pass valve would be installed on 1989–90 mini-vans to prevent transmission damage in cold temperatures. This program is outlined in Customer Satisfaction Notification #281T.

Automatic transmissions on the post-'91 versions have been known to leak, gear down to a "limp in" mode, shift noisily, and "hunt" for the proper gear—the likely cause of some of the poor gas mileage claims. These factory-related defects on recent minivans and other models are listed in DSB 18-24-95.

GROUP: Transmission
DATE: Feb. 17, 1995
SUBJECT
Delayed Transaxle
MODELS:

1993 – 1995	(AA)	Spirit/Acclaim/LeBaron Sedan
1993	(AC)	Dynasty/New Yorker/New Yorker Salon
1993	(AG)	Daytona
1993 – 1995	(AJ)	LeBaron Coupe/LeBaron Convertible
1993 – 1994	(AP)	Shadow/Shadow Convertible/Sundance
1993 – 1995	(AS)	Town & Country/Caravan/Voyager
1993	(AY)	Imperial/New Yorker Fifth Avenue
1993 – 1995	(ES)	Chrysler Voyager (European Market)
1993 – 1995	(LH)	Concorde/Intrepid/LHS/New Yorker/Vision

SYMPTOM/CONDITION:
Intermittent delayed transmission engagement at vehicle start up (garage shift) in excess of 3 seconds. The transaxle may be cold or hot.

Other possible conditions that may cause delayed transaxle engagement are a sticking or frozen PRNDL switch, or a transaxle front pump with excessive gear clearances.

PARTS REQUIRED:

AR 4659085	Valve Body, 41TE
AR 4504048	Package, Oil Filter 41TE
AR 4659084	Valve Body, 42LE
AR 4796730	Package, Oil Filter 42LE
AR 4467721	Fluid, Mopar Automatic Transmission — Type 7176

REPAIR PROCEDURE:
This bulletin involves replacing the transaxle valve body and oil filter.
1. Raise the vehicle with an appropriate hoist.
2. Clean the transaxle oil pan and mating area thoroughly, preferably with steam.
3. Remove the transaxle oil pan. Remove all sealant from the transaxle oil pan and mating area. Clean the inside of the oil pan and magnet.
4. Check the transaxle oil filter engagement and O-ring condition. Cut or poorly installed O-rings also may cause delayed garage shifts.
5. Separate the transaxle oil filter and O-ring from the valve body and discard.
6. Remove the 18 bolts attaching the valve body and separate the valve body from the transaxle and properly dispose of the transmission fluid.

This bulletin and the one that follows clearly show that Chrysler is well aware of its automatic transmissions' propensity for shuddering, delayed engagement, and eventual self-destruction.

NO: 18-24-95
GROUP: Veh. Performance
DATE: June 23, 1995
SUBJECT:
Improved Transmission Shift Quality
THIS BULLETIN SUPERSEDES TECHNICAL SERVICE BULLETIN 18-27-94 REV. A, DATED JAN. 30, 1995, WHICH SHOULD BE NOTED IN THE 1994 TECHNICAL SERVICE BULLETIN MANUAL (PUBLICATION NO.81-699-95054). THIS REVISION ADDS MODELS AND A PART NUMBER. ALL REVISIONS ARE HIGHLIGHTED WITH **ASTERISKS**.

MODELS:

1989 – 1995	(AA) Acclaim/Sprint/LeBaron Sedan
1989 – 1993	(AC) Dynasty/New Yorker/New Yorker Salon
1990 – 1993	(AG) Daytona
1990 – 1995	(AJ) LeBaron Coupe/LeBaron Convertible
1993 –1994	(AP) Sundance/Shadow/Shadow Convertible
1990 – 1991	(AQ) Chrysler TC
1989 – 1995	(AS) Caravan/Voyager/Town & Country
1990 – 1993	(AY) Imperial/New Yorker Fifth Avenue
1993 – 1995	(ES) Chrysler Voyager (European Market)
**1995	(FJ) Sebring/Avenger/Talon**
1995	(JA) Cirrus/Stratus
1993 – 1995	(LH) Concorde/Intrepid/Vision/LHS/New Yorker

NOTE:
THIS BULLETIN APPLIES TO VEHICLES EQUIPPED WITH THE 41TE OR 42LE TRANSAXLE.

SYMPTOM/CONDITION:
1992 AC. & AY VEHICLES BUILT AFTER FEB. 15, 1992 (MDH 02-15-XX). **1995 FJ VEHICLES** AND ALL OTHER 1993–1995 SUBJECT VEHICLES BUILT BEFORE OCT. 24, 1994 (MDH 10-24-XX), ARE VEHICLES EQUIPPED WITH AN ELECTRONICALLY MODULATED CONVERTOR CLUTCH (EMCC).
Vehicles that operate at speeds where EMCC usage is engaged (vehicle speeds between 34 and 41 MPH), may experience early deterioration of the transmission fluid (15,000 to 30,000 miles), exhibit a pronounced shudder during EMCC operation, harsh upshifts/downshifts, and/or harsh torque converter clutch engagements. Performing REPAIR PROCEDURE # 2, which includes updates to the Transmission Control Module (TCM) calibration and eliminates EMCC, will resolve these symptom/conditions. However, if an overheat condition is identified by the PCM or TCM, EMCC operation will be temporarily enabled.

ALL 1995 FJ VEHICLES AND ALL OTHER 1989–1995 SUBJECT VEHICLES BUILT BEFORE OCT. 24, 1994 (MDH 10-24-XX).

The TCM calibration used in the 1995 model year 41TE arid 42LE TCM is being made available for all vehicles dating back to the 1989 model year. The shift quality improvements and default issues that will be corrected by the new TCM calibration are:

1. COASTDOWN TIP-IN BUMP: Vehicle is decelerated almost to a stop (less than 8 MPH), then the driver tips back into the throttle to accelerate a noticeable bump may be felt.
2. COASTDOWN SHIFT HARSHNESS: Harsh coastdown shifts on some 4–3, 3–2 and 2–1 downshifts.
3. 1995 LH WITH 42LE TRANSAXLE — SLUGGISHNESS/LACK OF RESPONSE: On some early 1995 LH vehicles built prior to Oct. 24, 1994, a perceived lack of power or transmission responsiveness may be encountered under normal operating conditions. The transmission may not release the converter clutch as desired with increased throttle. This occurs in 4th gear from 35 MPH to 50 MPH.
4. 1989–1994 WITH 41TE & 42LE TRANSAXLES: Harsh shifts and/or vehicle shudder during 3–2 or 2–1 kickdowns at speeds less than 25 MPH.
5. 1993 WITH 41TE TRANSAXLE: Harsh 3–4 upshifts may occur, especially at highway speeds, while using the speed control.
6. 1989–1994 WITH 41TE TRANSAXLE — HARSH/DELAYED GARAGE SHIFTS: Delay is less than 2 seconds and the shift is harsh after the brief delay. NOTE: Delays greater than 2 seconds are caused by transmission hardware malfunction, i.e., valve body, pump, failed lip seals or malfunctioning PRNDL or neutral start switch.
7. 1989–1994 WITH 41TE & 42LE TRANSAXLES—POOR SHIFT QUALITY AFTER A BATTERY DISCONNECT: All transmission learned values are reset to the factory default values if battery power is lost to the TCM. The new 1995 calibration will now retain all learned values in memory after battery disconnect. However, if a transmission is rebuilt or a new transmission or TCM is installed. the Quick Learn procedure must be performed to calibrate Clutch Volume Indexes (CVI)on 1993 and later vehicles. (1992 and prior vehicle cannot be Quick Learned).

NOTE:
BEFORE PERFORMING THE QUICK LEARN PROCEDURE, THE TRANSMISSION MUST BE SHIFTED INTO OVERDRIVE (OD) WITH THE ENGINE RUNNING AND THE TRANSMISSION FLUID SET TO THE CORRECT LEVEL. THIS PROCEDURE WILL PURGE THE AIR IN THE CLUTCH CIRCUITS TO PREVENT ERRONEOUS CLUTCH VOLUME VALUES WHICH COULD CAUSE POOR INITIAL SHIFT QUALITY.
8. EARLY 1993 WITH 41TE & 42LE TRANSAXLE — INTERMITTENT SPEED CONTROL DROP OUT: The new service calibration change corrects this condition (this condition was also covered in Technical Service Bulletin 08-09-93 dated Mar. 12, 1993).
9. 1989–1993 WITH 41TE & 42LE TRANSAXLES — New fault code 35 (failure to achieve pump prime) has been added for improved diagnostic capability and fault codes 21, 22 and 24 are de-sensitized to reduce erroneous limp-in conditions.

Code 21 (OD Pressure Switch Circuit)—
Can be set in error on vehicles with a misadjusted shift cable or if the transaxle is shifted slowly from OD position to the N position. This typically happens if the operator has a tendency to teat his hand on the shift lever, or overshoots the OD gate while manually shifting from L or 3 to OD. The new software detects this maneuver and shifts the transaxle into Neutral rather than setting code a 21 fault and the subsequent limp-in conditions.

Code 22 and 24 (2-4 and L-R Pressure Switch Circuits) —
In low ambient temperatures (below 32(F or 0(C) some 1989 and 1990 model year vehicles may set this fault in error. Condensation can form and freeze in the PRNDL and/or neutral start switch and cause a delay on garage shifts. The new software prevents this fault code from being set in error and the transaxle going into the limp-in mode.

Code 24 (Low Reverse Pressure Switch Circuit)—
Can get set in error on vehicles where pump prime problems exist. The new fault code 35 (failure to achieve pump prime) has been added and does not trigger a limp-in condition.

POLICY: Reimbursable within the provisions of the warranty.

Other mechanical weaknesses in early models include the premature wearing out of front suspension components, wheel bearings, front brake discs, brake master cylinder, water pump, air conditioning unit, engine-cooling system, and manual transmission clutch. Fuel injectors on all engines have been troublesome and engine supports may be missing or not connected.

Overall fit and finish has gotten worse, not better, over the years (see "Service Tips"). Body hardware and interior trim are fragile and tend to break, warp, or fall off (door handles are a good example). After about a year's use, the Caravan and its various spin-offs become veritable rattle boxes, with poorly anchored bench seats being a major player. Finish problems can be summed up in three words: paint, paint, paint. The paint tends to discolor or delaminate after the second year. Chrysler knows about this problem and often tries to get the owner to pay half the cost of a repainting job (about $1,500 on a $3,000 job) before agreeing to the total cost if the owner stands fast, threatens small claims court action, or belongs to a consumer protection group like CLOG (Chrysler Lemon Owners Group). Moreover, minivan owners fed up with Chrysler's refusal to repaint their vehicles recently filed a class action in Washington State seeking damages for owners of 1986–97 cars, sport-utilities, minivans, and trucks (see Part 2 for the full text of the lawsuit).

Mechanical weaknesses on later models include the premature wear out of the engine tensioner pulley, motor mounts, starter motor, front brake discs and pads (the brake pad material crumbles in your hands), brake master cylinder, suspension components, exhaust system components, ball joints, wheel bearings, water pumps, fuel pumps and pump wiring harnesses, radiators, heater cores, and AC units. Fuel injectors on all engines have been troublesome, the windshield wiper washers freeze up in cold temperatures, sliding doors malfunction, engine supports may be missing or not connected, and there are frequent power steering pump leaks. Two further problems are batteries that last between 9 and 12 months, and factory-installed tires that fail prematurely (at 20,000 to 25,000 miles) and are hard to find—especially in the LT rating.

Cold weather problems abound. One owner says that her '92 Voyager's rear heater coolant tubes were so badly corroded they had to be replaced after two years at a cost of $160. Radiators and AC lines also quickly succumb to winter's wrath.

Chrysler owners unite
Chrysler's repeated attempts to blame drivers for its ABS, automatic transmission, and paint delamination problems continue to arouse consumer anger. The Internet is replete with postings relating to failures all over the world (Chrysler Problems web page: *http://www.wam.umd.edu/~gluckman/Chrysler* or *http://z.simplenet.com/cc/ fix.html*; Jeep: *http://goofball.com/badpaint/*); and Chrysler is currently the defendant in half a dozen class actions.

Furthermore, Chrysler's lack of an adequate response to owner complaints has ticked off its Canadian customers to the extent that about 600 Chrysler owners have formed Chrysler Lemon Owners Groups (CLOG) in British Columbia and New Brunswick. These groups have submitted members' names to the automaker and have succeeded in getting sizeable refunds for brake, transmission, and paint repairs. Even if you don't live in Canada, if you have had any of these problems and want "goodwill" repairs or a refund for repairs already carried out, contact CLOG Canada, file a small claims action, or ask to be part of the Washington state class action. See Part Two for more information on calculating how much you are owed from the durability chart.

Interestingly, the defects affecting Chrysler's newest minivans are similar to those failures we have seen for over a decade (see page 362). All the more reason to be skeptical of Chrysler's claims that its quality control has improved since the 1996 model was redesigned.

DSB SUMMARY	1997 CHRYSLER CARAVAN
1. MAY-97	41TE/42LE TRANSMISSION SERVICE INFORMATION
2. OCT-96	A/C ERROR STARTER, EATX, CRUISE CONTROL...
3. JUL-97	A/C EVAPORATOR ODORS
4. JUN-97	A/C SUCTION AND/OR DISCHARGE LINE SERVICE
5. FEB-97	AIR BAG WARNING LABELS
6. OCT-96	BRAKE NOISE
7. FEB-97	CHALKY RESIDUE ON BLACK PLASTIC BODY COMPONENTS
8. JAN-97	COMPASS (CMTC) AND/OR INSTRUMENT CLUSTER MALFUNCTION
9. MAR-97	COOLANT SEEPAGE AT UNDERBODY AUXILIARY REAR HEATER LINE
10. APR-97	CUSTOMER NOTIFICATION #712—PASSENGER AIR BAG SAFETY
11. JUL-97	CUSTOMER SATISFACTION NOTICE #721—CHILD SAFETY SEAT
12. SEP-96	DINGS FROM INSIDE-OUT AT SLIDING DOOR(S) LATCH AREA
13. MAY-97	ENGINE COOLANT USAGE
14. JAN-97	ERRONEOUS M L ON WITH HEX CODE S29, S2A, S2B
15. MAY-97	FRONT HVAC BLOWER MOTOR RESISTOR CONNECTOR SERVICE
16. JAN-97	FUEL TANK SERVICE
17. MAY-97	HIGH EFFORT REQUIRED TO UNLATCH REAR BENCH SEATS
18. DEC-97	HONK NOISE DURING LOW SPEED MANEUVERS
19. SEP-97	INOPERATIVE CD PLAYER/SALES CODE RAZ RADIO
20. OCT-97	INTERMITTENT MOMENTARY LOSS OF POWER ASSIST
21. NOV-96	INTERMITTENT/INOPERATIVE RADIATOR FANS
22. MAY-97	LEAK DETECTION PUMP (LDP) DEALER TEST MODE
23. SEP-97	NHTSA AUTHORIZED AIRBAG DEACTIVATION / MEDICAL NECESSITY
24. NOV-97	POOR DRIVEABILITY WITH HIGH DI FUEL
25. FEB-97	REAR BRAKE CYCLIC RUBBING NOISE
26. FEB-97	REAR BRAKE MOAN/HOWL NOISE
27. NOV-97	REMOTE KEYLESS TRANSMITTER BATTERY FAILURE
28. NOV-96	REPAIR OF FALLOUT DAMAGED PAINT
29. APR-97	SAFETY RECALL #714/MASTER CYLINDER PRIMARY PISTON
30. MAY-97	SAFETY RECALL #724 — STAMPED STEEL ROAD WHEELS
31. NOV-97	SERVICE MANUAL REVISION
32. JUN-97	SERVICE MANUAL, REVISIONS
33. MAR-97	SLIDING DOOR — POOR FIT AT REAR
34. OCT-97	THUMPING NOISE AT REAR OF VEHICLE DURING COLD OPERATIONS
35. JUN-97	TIRE & WHEEL RUNOUT
36. MAR-97	TRANSAXLE SHUDDER DURING EMCC SHIFT
37. JUN-97	TRANSMISSION FLUID AUXILIARY COOLER
38. JAN-97	UNDER BODY CREAK OR KNOCK SOUND
39. SEP-97	WATER LEAKS ONTO FLOOR FROM HVAC HOUSING
40. JUN-97	WIPERS DON'T PARK OR WIPE IN INTERMITTENT MODE

Déjà vu, all over again!

Safety summary, NHTSA complaints/probes, and recalls: Chrysler continues to downplay the seriousness of its minivan safety defects, whether in the case of ABS failures, inadvertent airbag deployments, or faulty rear latches. Owners report that cruise control units are often dysfunctional, accelerating or decelerating the vehicle without any warning, and that sudden stalling and transmission failures also create life-threatening situations. One owner of a 1993 SE equipped with a 3.3L engine calls the transmission malfunction a safety hazard: "I have experienced a transmission control module failure where the vehicle immediately dropped into second gear....This could have been tragic if it had occurred in heavy traffic." **NHTSA: 1991–93**—Seatbelts may become unhooked from the floor anchor. **1994**—

Airbags deploy when the vehicle is started. **1994–95**—Airbags and wiper motor share the same fuse; if the wiper motor fails, the airbags are deactivated. **1995**—Engine fires. • Thieves love the door lock design. • Broken spare tire suspension cable allowed tire to fall away while driving. • Right side rear door suddenly flew open when vehicle passed over a small bump. • Seatbelt buckles jam or suddenly release. • Child shoulder harness clip pulls out easily. • Roof drip rails allow water to leak inside. • Open glove box back section allows for papers to be sucked into the AC blower. • Inoperative horn. **1995–96**—Brake failures, lockup, excessive noise, and premature wear. • Airbag failed to deploy or accidentally deployed. • Injury from airbag. • Sudden acceleration, stalling. • No steering. • Seatbacks fall backward. • Fuel tank easily damaged. • Park won't hold vehicle. • Transmission failure, no Reverse, suddenly drops into low gear, delayed engagement, jumps out of gear. • Rear windows fall out or shatter. • Power window and door lock failures. • Sliding door jams, traps occupants. • Weak headlights. **1996**—When opening driver's window, face is dangerously close to airbag. • Driver's side airbag deployed when the ignition was turned on. • Child safety seat harness over-retracts, trapping children or catching their hair. • Fuel tank leaks from tank top and fuel rail. • Incorrect fuel gauge. • Fuel sloshes around (no baffle), deforms tank, and makes noise. • Fuel leaks from vapor recovery canister. • Broken steering belt tensioner caused the sudden loss of power steering and power brakes. • Wipers self-activate. • Sliding door fell off. • Faulty power door locks. • Cracked axle/drive shaft. • Cruise control drops speed and then surges to former setting. • With AC engaged, vehicle stalls, then surges forward. • Power-steering failure, excessive noise. • Vehicle was parked with gear in Park and emergency brake applied; it rolled into a lake. **ABS:** Following a sustained Internet campaign against Chrysler—led by irate car and minivan owners and buttressed by thousands of complaints registered by safety investigators on both sides of the border—the automaker announced last year that it would recall 1990–93 minivans and passenger cars in order to correct life-threatening ABS malfunctions and extend the base warranty to 10 years/100,000 miles. Chrysler's recall notice seems rather straightforward at first glance—until you look at the details, where the automaker uses "weasel" words to downplay the significance of its recall. It states that "no action is necessary," and further implies that the vehicles will be fixed only if the braking system shows a serious braking problem. This flies in the face of the recall warning, which says that at any time "the ABS function (may be) lost, and reduced power assist may be experienced during braking." In other words, drivers of these defective minivans and passenger cars (Fifth Avenue, Imperial, New Yorker, Salon, Dynasty, Monaco, and Premier) would never know when the system would fail, which would force them to push harder on the brake pedal and increase their stopping distance—as well as their chance of having serious accident injuries. Don't let Chrysler lull you into delaying the correction of this braking hazard, which can strike at any time and without any warning. If your vehicle is one of those involved, take it to your nearest dealer and demand that the ABS be corrected at Chrysler's expense. Apply the extended warranty if any malfunctions occur. **Recalls: 1984–95**—All minivans are subject to a voluntary service campaign that will fix a rear liftgate latch that may fail in a collision. Unfortunately, American government records show that fewer than half the rear latches on these minivans were replaced during the first 15 months of Chrysler's "service program." **1985**—Dealers will install a protective cover over the brake proportioning valve. • The fuel supply tube leaks on vehicles equipped with a 2.2L engine. **1986–88 passenger models**—First rear seats may detach in an accident. **1988**—Possible fuel tank leakage. **1988–89**—Notification #281T, applicable to vehicles with a trailer towing package, provides for a free oil cooler by-pass valve to prevent transmission failure in cold weather. **1989–90**—Engine valve cover gasket may leak oil, creating a fire hazard. • Notification #466 provides for a free 3.3L engine valve spring. • Safety recall #314T provides for the free installation of a reinforcing plate on the front seatbelt strap. **1990**—An incorrectly mounted proportioning valve may increase the chance of skidding. • Notification #281T extends the free oil cooler by-pass valve program to cars and 1990 minivans. **1990–93**—Transport Canada Defect Investigator, Nigel Mortimer, says that this Chrysler ABS recall calls for the installation of a new pump and seal kit, if needed. The kit comes with a lifetime warranty, while all other ABS components will henceforth be covered for 10 years/100,000 miles. **1991**—Faulty turn signal flasher. **1991 ABS**—Hydraulic fluid leakage. **1991–92**—Steering wheel cracks may cause wheel to loosen. **1991–93**—Recalled to fix two kinds of seatbelt problems: faulty buckle cover may prevent seatbelt from being fully latched; seatbelt anchor hook could become detached from the anchor. **1992**—Replace liftgate supports which may break from fatigue. • Safety recall #326T requires the replacement of all brake pedals that have been found to lack sufficient strength. • Faulty steering column shaft coupling bolts. • Improperly bent fuel tank flanges could cause a fire. • Rear liftgate struts and bolts will be replaced to prevent liftgate from falling down. **1993–94**—Possible separation of 15-inch steel wheels. **1996**—Faulty bench seat attaching bolts. • Filler tube rollover valve. • Installation of a fuel filler ground strap. • Improved retractors for child safety seats (service action) and upgraded seat module bolts (recall). **1997**—Brake master cylinder seals may be defective, allowing fluid to be drawn into the power-assist reservoir. • Wheels may have been damaged during mounting.

Secret Warranties/Service Tips

1987–88—Vehicle sag, stumble, or hesitation during initial start-up and drive-away likely requires the removal and cleaning of the throttle body bore and blade, disconnection of the EGR vacuum line, plugging of the EGR vacuum port, and replacement of the single module engine controller (SMEC). • If the manual transmission fails to engage second or third gear, consider replacing the second and third thrust washer snap ring (#6033348). **1987–89**—Erratic 3.0L engine idle speed in cold weather may require the installation of a new AIS motor. • Vehicles equipped with the 3.0L engine may experience loss of engine coolant from an external cylinder head gasket leak. Use the cylinder head gasket kit that includes an upgraded head gasket (#MD143540). **1987–92**—The heater and air conditioning system may suddenly change to the defrost mode during a low vacuum condition, which can occur during trailer towing, hill climbing, and acceleration. Install a revised vacuum check valve to correct this problem. **1987–93**—3.0L engines that burn oil or produce a smoky exhaust at idle can be fixed by installing snap rings on the exhaust valve guides and replacing all of the valve guide stems or the cylinder head. **1988–90**—Intermittent rough running at idle signals a need for a new EGR. **1988–94**—A sticking AC/heater blend door can be corrected by spraying an anti-rust penetrant into the assembly. **1989–90**—Cylinder head cover oil leaks with 2.2L and 2.5L engines are caused by poor sealing. The original cylinder head cover must be replaced with one that uses silicone sealant (RTV) instead of a gasket (DSB No. 09-17-89). • Defective valve stem seals are the likely cause of high oil consumption with 2.2L and 2.5L engines (DSB HL-49-89C). • A-604 automatic transmission clutch slippage is a common problem addressed in DSB 21-09-9. • A surge/buck at 35–55 mph with an automatic transmission can be corrected by installing driveability kit #4419447. **1989–95**—An excellent summary of Chrysler's transmission glitches and corrections over the past six years can be found in DSB 18-24-95. **1989–96**—Acceleration shudder that may be accompanied by a whine is likely the result of leakage in the transmission front pump caused by a worn pump bushing. **1990–92**—Erratic idle speeds occurring after deceleration from a steady cruising speed can be corrected by replacing the idle air control motor with a revised motor. **1990–94**—Harsh automatic shifts can be tamed by installing the following revised parts: kickdown, accumulator, reverse servo cushion springs, and the accumulator piston. • Cold start-up piston knocking noise can be eliminated by replacing the piston and connecting rod assembly (see below).

NO: 09-03-94
GROUP: Engine
DATE: Apr. 1, 1994
SUBJECT: Engine Idle Piston Noise
MODELS:

1990-1993	(AC)	Dynasty/New Yorker/Salon
1990-1994	(AS)	Caravan/Voyager/Town & Country
1990-1993	(AV)	Imperial/New Yorker Fifth Avenue
1993-1994	(LH)	Concorde/Intrepid/Vision

NOTE: THIS BULLETIN APPLIES TO VEHICLES EQUIPPED WITH THE 3.3L AND 3.8L ENGINE
SYMPTOM/CONDITION:
Cold start up piston knocking noise at idle that diminishes 3 to 5 minutes after startup. The condition is more prominent in low ambient temperatures and after the vehicle has set overnight.
Similar symptoms are described in Technical Service Bulletin 09-21-93 dated Dec. 31, 1993, "Carbon Buildup on Top of Piston". Refer to this Bulletin for additional details.
DIAGNOSIS:
Using the Mopar Diagnostic System or the Scan Tool (DRB II) with appropriate diagnostic procedure manual, verify that all engine systems are functioning as designed. If Diagnostic Trouble Codes (DTC's) are present, record them on the repair order for future reference, and repair as necessary. If no codes are present and all systems are functioning correctly, and carbon buildup on the top of the piston is not evident, proceed with the following repair.
PARTS REQUIRED:

AR	4621978	Piston & Connecting Rod Assy (use w3.3L engine)
AR	4621981	Piston & Connecting Rod Assy (use w3.8L engine)

REPAIR PROCEDURE: This repair involves installing a new coated piston and connecting rod assembly.

This engine repair should be covered by the base warranty or emissions warranty. If neither one applies, demand a pro rata refund.

• Erratic fuel gauge operation can be fixed by installing a revised sender assembly or fuel pump/sender assembly. **1991**—Loss of fuel pressure causing fuel-pump noise, erratic transmission shifting, engine power loss, or engine die-out may be due to a defective fuel pump. • An erratic idle with 2.2L and 2.5L engines can be cured by using an improved SMEC/SBEC engine controller. • Faulty power door locks may have a short circuit, need a new fuse, or require a new door latch with power door lock assembly. **1991–92**—If the engine knocks when at full operating temperature and during light to medium acceleration, it may mean that the single board engine controller (SBEC-Powertrain Control Module) needs replacing. • Engines with a rough idle and stalling following a cold start may also require a new SBEC. • The airbag warning light may continuously illuminate when the vehicle's ignition is in the ON position. This malfunction may be due to corrosion caused by water in the airbag's six-way connector. **1991–93**—Engines that stall following a cold start may need an upgraded Park/Neutral/Start switch (see below).

NO: 21-02-94
GROUP: Transmission
DATE: Feb. 18, 1994
SUBJECT: Engine Stalls Following Initial Shift From Park Or Neutral To A Forward Gear
MODELS:

1991-1994	(AA)	Spirit/Acclaim/LeBaron Sedan
1991-1993	(AC)	Dynasty/New Yorker/New Yorker Salon
1991-1993	(AG	Daytona
1991-1994	(AJ)	LeBaron Coupe/LeBaron Convertible
1992-1993	(AP)	Shadow/Shadow Convertible/Sundance
1991-1993	(AS)	Town & Country/Caravan/Voyager
1991-1993	(AV)	Imperial/New Yorker Fifth Avenue

NOTE: THIS BULLETIN APPLIES TO VEHICLES EQUIPPED WITH 41TE TRANSMISSIONS. IN ADDITION TO THE VEHICLES LISTED ABOVE, ANY 1989-1990 41TE-EQUIPPED VEHICLES THAT HAVE HAD A REPLACEMENT CONTROLLER INSTALLED THAT HAS COOLING FINS, OR IS LABELED WITH P/N 4672104, OR 4713832 ARE ALSO INCLUDED.
SYMPTOM/CONDITION: While the temperature of the transmission is -16° F (-27° C) or colder, and the transmission selector lever is placed in any forward gear position, the engine stalls. This can be the result of ice in the neutral/start switch while the Tramsmission Control Module (TCM) performs the pump prime test when the transmission temperature is -16° F (-27° C) or colder.

This bulletin involves replacing the park/neutral position switch.

SOLENOID ASSEMBLY
PARK/NEUTRAL (NEUTRAL/START) POSITION SWITCH
TRANSMISSION RANGE (PRNDL) SWITCH

1.   Replace the black park/neutral position switch (P/N 5234319). Torque the new switch to 25 ft.lbs. (34 N-m).
POLICY: Reimbursable within the provisions of the warranty.

The above DSB gives one reason why your minivan stalls when you put it in gear.

1991–94—The serpentine belt may come off the pulley after driving through snow. Install an upgraded shield, screw, and retainers. • Noisy fuel pumps need to be replaced by an upgraded pump, wiring harness, fuel tank isolators, and fuel tank straps. • Noise when shifting into Reverse or when turning is addressed in DSB 09-14-94. **1991–95**—Poor AC performance while the AC blower continues to operate is likely due to a frozen evaporator. • DSB 24-05-94 looks at all the causes of, and remedies for, poor heater performance. • If the vehicle tends to drift left, cross-switch the tire and wheel assemblies, readjust the alignment, or reposition the front cross-member. **1992**—The brake pedal may not return to its fully released position, causing the brake lights to remain illuminated. Install a pedal return kit (#4723625). • Front door forward hem separation (the door seems to sag) can be corrected by welding the inner door panel to the outer door panel along the front door forward hem. • Long crank times, a rough idle, and hesitation may be corrected by replacing the intake manifold assembly. • A vehicle that's hard to start may have a corroded ECT/sensor connector. • An oil leak in the oil filter area may be corrected by installing a special oil filter bracket gasket (#MD198554). • If the heater and ventilation system change to the defrost mode during acceleration, trailer towing, or hill climbing, the installation of a revised vacuum check valve should cure the problem. • Intermittent failure of the power door locks, chimes, wipers, gauges, and other electrical devices can be corrected by replacing defective relays with revised relays (#4713737). **1992–93**—Some 41TE transaxles may produce a buzzing noise when shifted into Reverse. This problem can be corrected by replacing the valve body assembly or valve body separator plate. • A deceleration shudder can be eliminated by replacing the power-train control module with an upgraded version. • Rough idling after a cold start with 2.2L and 2.5L engines can be corrected by installing an upgraded powertrain control module (PCM). **1992–94**—AC duct odors are addressed in DSB 24-21-93. • Poor heater performance may be the result of a misadjusted clip on the blend air door cable. **1993**—A fuel pump check valve failure can cause start-up die-out, reduced power, or erratic shifting. **1993–94**—Improved automatic shifting can be had by installing an upgraded transmission control module. • AC evaporator whistling requires the installation of upgraded AC expansion valves and gaskets. • An AC moan may be silenced by installing an AC clutch plate with a damper ring. **1993–95**—Delayed automatic transmission engagement may be due to low fluid, a stuck or frozen PRNDL switch, or a transaxle front pump with excessive ground clearances. • Harsh low-speed automatic transmission shifting, accompanied by a fluctuating digital speedometer reading, may be corrected by covering the wiring harness with aluminum wire to prevent the spark plug wires from sending false signals into the outport speed sensor wiring that connects to the TCM. • Constant upshifting/downshifting on vehicles equipped with cruise control has a variety of causes set out in DSB 08-15-95. • An exhaust that smells like rotten eggs can be corrected by installing an upgraded catalytic converter.

No: 11-03-96
GROUP: Exhaust
DATE: June 17, 1996
SUBJECT: Excessive Sulphur Odor
MODELS:
1992-1995 (AA) Acclaim/Spirit/LeBaron Sedan
1992-1993 (AC) Dynasty/New Yorker/ New Yorker Salon
1992-1993 (AG) Daytona
1992-1995 (AJ) LeBaron Coupe/LeBaron Convertible
1992-1994 (AP) Sundance/Shadow/Shadow Convertible
1993-1995 (AS) Caravan/Voyage/Town & Country
NOTE: THIS BULLETIN APPLIES TO VEHICLES EQUIPPED WITH 2.2L OR 2.5L ENGINES ONLY.
SYMPTOM/CONDITION:
New catalytic converters are now available to address customer complaints of excessive hydrogen sulfide
odor (rotten egg smell) coming from the tailpipe of their vehicles at idle. These catalysts were specially
manufactured with a revised internal coating which minimizes sulphur odor.

1	4882530	Catalytic Converter	(AS 2.5L ATX/MTX FED/CAL)
1	4882531	Catalytic Converter	(AA,AG,AP 2.2l/2.5l MTX FED/CAL) 1992-1994
1	4882532	Catalytic Converter	(AA,AC,AG,AJ,AP 2.2l/2.5l ATX FED) 1992-1995
1	4882533	Catalytic Converter	(AA,AC,AG,AJ,AP 2.2l/2.5l ATX CAL) 1992-1995
			(AA, 2.5l ATX FED) 1994)
			(AA, 2.5L FFV) 1992
1	4882534	Catalytic Converter	(AA, 2.5L FFV) 1993-1994

PARTS REQUIRED:
REPAIR PROCEDURE: This bulletin involves the replacement of the catalytic converter with a revised part.
Replace the catalytic converter following the repair procedures given in group 11 of the appropriate service
manual.
POLICY: Reimbursable within the provisions of the warranty.
TIME ALLOWANCE:
Labor Operation No: 11-50-01-91   0.7 Hrs.
FAILURE CODE: P8-New Part

If your minivan stinks, blame Chrysler, not your passengers. Repair costs
should be covered by the emissions warranty.

1994—Harsh, erratic, or delayed transmission shifts can be corrected by
replacing the throttle position sensor (TPS) with a revised part. • A creaking left B-pillar can be silenced by repositioning the metal portion of the
left B-pillar baffle. **1994–95**—Intake valve deposits are frequently the cause
of poor driveability complaints. • Intermittent no-cranks can be corrected
by modifying the battery to starter cable terminal insulator at the starter
connection. • A front suspension rapping noise heard when going over
bumps can be corrected by providing additional clearance between the
front coil springs and strut towers. **1996**—Poor engine performance near
military installations or airports is caused by radar interference. Correct by
installing a "hardened" crankshaft position sensor and/or reprogramming
(flashing) the PCM with new software calibrations. • Rear brake noise that
occurs at any time can be silenced by replacing the rear brake shoes and
rear wheel cylinders. Another possibility is the addition of rear brake shoe
springs as well.

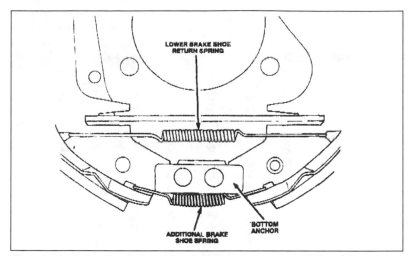

Rear brake noise should be silenced under warranty on '96 models.

• Rough idle, hesitation, or sags after the fuel tank is filled can only be corrected by the installation of a new fuel tank, says Chrysler DSB 18-28-95. The repair is covered under warranty and should take about an hour. The dealer should also give you your gas back. • Steering noise during parking lot maneuvers may be fixed by installing a new power steering gear and left side attaching bolt. • As if flying toasters weren't enough, Chrysler minivan wheel covers tend to take flight as well. (Hey, I thought that was only a Chevy Caprice problem.) Chrysler will install upgraded covers under warranty. **All models/years**—If pressed, Chrysler will pay the full cost of correcting paint defects during the first six years of ownership. The company will try to convince you that the problem is either normal or part of routine maintenance. In both cases, it's not. You'll have to show that the problem is factory related, though, by producing a DSB or a body shop confirmation that it's a Chrysler defect. • A rotten-egg odor coming from the exhaust may be the result of a malfunctioning catalytic converter. There's *plenty* of written documentation that will give you all the ammunition you need to stop Chrysler from weaseling out of its obligation to replace the catalytic converter for free under its emissions warranty. • Front brakes tend to wear out quickly on front-drive minivans. Owners say that Chrysler has paid half the cost of brake repairs for up to 2 years/25,000 miles.

Caravan, Town & Country, Voyager Profile

	1990	1991	1992	1993	1994	1995	1996	1997
Cost Price ($)								
Caravan, Voy.	11,640	12,806	13,360	14,106	14,972	16,705	18,510	19,570
G. Caravan Voy.	16,775	17,472	18,723	18,140	19,595	20,025	19,410	20,565
Town & Country	25,515	24,425	25,160	26,080	27,845	28,240	25,865	28,070
Used Values ($)								
Caravan, Voy. ↑	5,500	6,500	7,500	8,500	9,500	10,500	15,000	16,500
Caravan, Voy. ↓	4,500	5,500	6,000	7,500	8,000	9,500	14,000	15,500
G. Caravan Voy. ↑	7,500	8,500	9,500	10,500	11,500	12,500	17,500	18,500
G. Caravan Voy. ↓	6,000	7,000	8,000	9,500	10,500	11,500	16,000	17,500

Town & Country ↑	10,000	11,500	12,500	14,000	15,500	17,000	22,000	24,000
Town & Country ↓	8,500	10,000	11,000	12,500	14,000	15,500	20,000	22,000

Extended Warranty	Y	Y	Y	Y	Y	Y	Y	Y
Secret Warranty	N	Y	Y	Y	Y	Y	Y	Y

Reliability	①	①	②	②	②	②	②	③
Air conditioning	①	①	②	②	②	②	③	③
Body integrity	①	①	①	①	①	①	②	②
Braking system	①	①	①	①	①	①	①	②
Electrical system	①	①	①	①	①	①	②	③
Engines	①	①	②	②	②	③	③	③
Exhaust/Converter	②	②	②	②	③	③	③	④
Fuel system	①	①	①	②	③	③	③	④
Ignition system	②	②	②	②	②	②	③	④
Automatic transmission	①	①	①	①	①	①	①	①
Rust/Paint	①	①	①	①	①	①	①	①
Steering	③	③	③	③	③	④	④	④
Suspension	③	③	③	③	③	③	③	③
Crash Safety								
Caravan	—	—	⑤	①	①	④	—	④
Grand Caravan	—	—	—	—	—	—	③	③
Town & Country	—	—	—	—	—	—	—	④
Town & Country LX	—	—	—	—	—	—	—	③

Note: The low frontal crash ratings represent the inclusion of leg trauma in the overall score.

FORD

Aerostar

Rating: Average (1992–97); Not Recommended (1988–91). More brawn and more reliable than Chrysler's minivans. The Aerostar's last model year was 1997. **Maintenance/Repair costs**: Average, and any garage can repair an Aerostar. **Parts**: Plentiful, but costly (especially AC and electrical components).

Despite having been taken off the market, there are still plenty of used Aerostars for sale. Bargains can often be found with high-mileage leased versions. Other minivans you may wish to consider: the Ford Windstar, or GM Astro and Safari.

Technical Data

ENGINES	Liters/CID	HP	MPG	Model Years
OHC I-4 FI	2.3L/140	88	21–25	1986–87
OHV V6 2 bbl.	2.8L/171	115	17–22	1986
OHV V6 FI	3.0L/182	135–145	16–22	1986–97
OHV V6 FI	4.0L/244	152	15–21	1990–97

Strengths and weaknesses: The 1986–91 models are at the bottom of the evolutionary scale as far as quality control is concerned. However, the last five model years have shown lots of improvement. Repair costs are reasonable (except for high AC costs), but mainly because the Aerostar's myriad mechanical and body defects are covered by Ford warranty extensions (see "Secret Warranties"). The Aerostar's modern, swoopy shape belies its limited performance capabilities: the 3.0L and 4.0L engines are unreliable through the '91 model year, and the 3.0L is a sluggish performer. Older 2.3L and 2.8L engines can barely pull their own weight. The 4-speed automatic transmission often has a hard time deciding which gear to choose, and the power steering transmits almost no road feel to the driver. The ride is bouncy, handling is sloppy, and braking performance is poor. Reliability problems on all models make the Aerostar a risky buy, especially if the previous owner has been less than fastidious in maintenance and repairs.

Early models have compiled a miserable repair record. As soon as you plug one leak another leak springs up somewhere else; valve cover and rear main oil seal leaks are frequent; and leaks from the front axle vent tube often require the replacement of the front axle assembly. Even oil pans, which you wouldn't normally associate with leaks, tend to leak as a result of premature corrosion. Fuel injectors are either faulty or plugged. Other problems include expensive automatic transmission failures; electronic and electrical-system glitches; power steering, suspension, and brake defects; and premature and chronic air conditioner breakdowns involving AC condensers and compressors that tend to fail after the first three years of use. (Ford has consistently produced failure-prone AC systems in the Aerostar van since its birth in 1986; according to *Consumer Reports* their failure rate was almost three times that of other vehicles in its class.). Auto air conditioning experts refer to the problem as the "Black Death," in reference to the sludge these Ford ACs produce that leads to massive internal component failures.

A/C SYSTEMS
FORD AIR CONDITIONING SYSTEMS (CONT)
FORD FX15 COMPRESSORS

The biggest problem the Ford FX15 compressor had was that the teflon piston rings deteriorated, creating a sludge in the refrigerant oil. This sludge made its way into other parts of the A/C system. When the sludge made it through the whole A/C system, it was very difficult to flush out.

If you replace one of these compressors without cleaning the system completely, the replacement compressor won't last very long. Before Ford introduced a new refrigerant oil to combat this problem, the only real solution was to replace all of the components.

BLACK PLAGUE (BLACK DEATH)

Ford A/C systems with the FX-15 compressor may experience a failure that includes a black goo that clogs the system. The two dominant theories about what causes this are:

Theory #1— Refrigerant loss reduces oil flow, causing the oil to overheat. As the oil overheats, the system deteriorates and compressor wear accelerates, causing the metal particles to appear.

Theory #2— Black plague comes from the solder flux from the condenser mixing with the aluminum particles from the compressor.

Whatever the cause, fix the problem by flushing the evaporator and condenser. Replace the orifice tube if it has a cracked inlet screen. Replace the hoses and compressor. Then install an in-line filter, and expect to change the filter at least once afterwards.

Notice: If the black coating is severe, condenser replacement will be necessary.

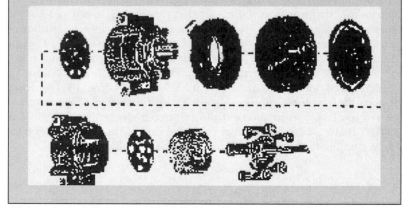

This appears to be a major Ford defect affecting most Ford models over the years, judging by what AC experts have posted on the Internet.

One AC specialist describes the problem in these terms:

> The biggest problem is the original FX-15 compressor that came with the truck and the rebuilt replacement likely another FX-15. These compressors are bad news. When they go bad they fall to pieces internally and contaminate your system. The "gook" settles in your condenser and is hard to get rid of. We sometimes end up having to

flush as many as three times, operating the system for 30 to 45 minutes between flushes and changing the orifice tube each time. This allows the heat and pressure to break loose the "gook" in the condenser. When we replace an FX-15 compressor, we will not use a remanned FX-15...they simply do not hold up. Motorcraft's FS-10/FX-15 compressors are specially sensitive to high pressures. Faulty fan clutches are one of the reasons why so many late-model Ford ('89 and newer) compressors fail. This also applies to FWD cars with weak or inoperative radiator cooling fans. FS-10 compressor design is excellent, however, something could be done about their fan clutch durability. We have noted an above normal incidence in Aerostars ('91 and up), Explorers ('91 and up), Ford Taurus, Sable (up to 1994), T-Bird/Cougar ('89 and up), and F-series ('92 and up).

A grinding/growling coming from the rear signals that the in-tank electric fuel pump is defective. Many mechanics find that the electronic engine controls are difficult to diagnose if problems arise. Routine repairs are very awkward because most components are buried under the windshield and dashboard. Windshield wipers are badly designed for winter driving. They freeze at the bottom of the windshield and wear out the wiper motor. Body hardware and integrity have earned low marks as well.

Safety summary, NHTSA complaints/probes, and recalls: **1988–90**—Cracked fuel tanks • A draft of a Jan. 20, 1993, Ford internal document lists "known incidents which are attributed to the ignition switch." It includes the 1986 Aerostar and Econoline full-sized vans. NHTSA documents show that the Aerostar has almost the highest rate of ignition switch fires of any Ford truck, second only to the 1988 Bronco. State Farm Insurance has filed an action against Ford to cover its payouts to policyholders whose Aerostars caught fire from an overheated ignition switch. • The hefty B-pillar (where the edge of the door meets the body behind the front seat) obstructs peripheral vision. • Some Aerostars don't have front seat head restraints, unless they're equipped with the optional captain's chairs, and even then the restraints sit far too low for the average person. • Owners complain that the brake master cylinder and daytime running lights module may suddenly fail, and that '90 Aerostars' rear brakes sometimes lock up in wet weather. **NHTSA: 1993–94**—NHTSA is looking at electrical malfunctions that may cause overheating and/or fires at the fuel sender assembly on fuel tanks. **Recalls: 1986**—The rear suspension separating from the axle could cause steering loss. • Recall #90S04 provides for a free fuel tank replacement. • Lumbar seat wiring could short-circuit, creating a fire hazard. **1986–87**—Possible fuel line leaks. • Captain's chair may cut into seatbelt webbing. **1986–88**—Trailer towing package taillight wires may short-circuit, creating a fire hazard. **1987–89**—The rear liftgate may fail due to defective ball studs attaching the lift cylinders to the body. **1988–91**—The ignition switch could experience an internal short circuit, creating the potential for overheating, smoke, and possibly fire in the steering column area of the vehicle. **1989–90**—Quad Bucket seat assemblies. **1990**—Ford will replace, gratis, faulty brake master cylinders. **1990–91**—Models with the A4LD automatic transmission may slip out of Park and roll as if in Neutral. **1992–94**—Vehicles may have a defective rear anti-lock brake control module. **1992–97** Aerostar (AWD)—The transmission or transfer case may crack or break. Dealers will install a new rear transfer case extension and a new aluminum rear driveshaft. **1995**—Spare tire may fracture the brake line. **1996**—Driver's door may not sustain specified load in the secondary latched position. • Certification label shows incorrect rear tire inflation pressure.

Secret Warranties/Service Tips

1986–91—3.0L engine knocking at idle may require the installation of a new, thicker thrust plate to reduce camshaft end play. • Hard cold starts, hesitation, and stalling may be caused by sludge in the throttle body and/or an idle by-pass valve. Install an idle air by-pass service kit (#F2DZ-9F939-A). **1986–94**—A speaker whine or buzz caused by the fuel pump can be stopped by installing an electronic noise RFI filter. • Rust perforations may occur in the front and/or rear lower rocker panel area(s) because the panels weren't coated with electrodeposition primer. Ford will replace the panel at no charge for up to 6 years/100,000 miles (see below).

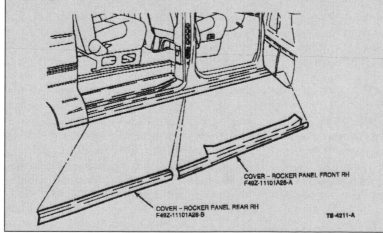

95-6-12
03/27/05
ROCKER PANEL - FRONT AND/OR REAR - RUST PERFORATION - SERVICE TIPS
LIGHT TRUCK:
1986–94 AEROSTAR
ISSUE:
Rust perforation may occur in the front and/or rear lower rocker panel area(s) on some vehicles. This may be due to the lower rocker panels having no electrodeposition primer (E-Coat) on the inside surface, for vehicles built from 1985–94.
ACTION:
Weld on lower rocker panel covers and blend to body with body filler. Paint rocker panel(s) to match the vehicle. Refer to the following procedures for service details.

COVER – ROCKER PANEL FRONT RH
F49Z-11101A26-A

COVER – ROCKER PANEL REAR RH
F49Z-11101A26-B

TB 4211-A

1987–92—Brakes that stick or bind may have corroded brake caliper slide pins. Install corrosion-resistant pins (#E8TZ-2C150-B). **1988**—Delayed Reverse engagement can be corrected by installing a new separator plate. **1989–92**—If there's a popping or clunking and floorboard vibration when braking, it's likely caused by the front brake caliper suddenly springing away from the caliper abutment and returning. Adjusting the front brake pads and knuckle clearance will correct this problem. **1989–96**—A chatter noise during sharp turns is likely due to insufficient friction modifier, or over-shimming of the clutch packs within Traction-Lock differentials. **1990**—Delayed upshift or no upshift can be corrected by installing a new #4 thrust washer. • AC compressor shaft seal leaks can be best fixed by installing a new seal (#E9SZ-19D665-A). **1990–92**—A 4.0L engine oil leak may occur around the rocker gasket because of variations in the gasket quality. Install two new rocker cover gaskets (Carrier type), along with conical spring screws. • Automatic transmission fluid leakage may be caused by a faulty or loose transfer case rear output seal. **1990–96**—Noisy power steering is likely caused by a pressure spike in the serpentine tube of the power steering cooler. **1993–95**—A squeak or chirp coming from the blower motor can be stopped by installing an upgraded blower motor with improved brush-to-commutator friction. • An automatic transmission whine heard upon light acceleration can be silenced by replacing the front and rear planetary assembly and the front and rear sun gear. • Overheating or binding rear brakes can be corrected by backing off the self-adjusters. **1995–96**—Hard starts and stalling can be corrected by installing an upgraded idle air control valve under the emissions warranty. **1995–97**—Coolant leakage from the engine block heater requires the replacement of the block heater with an upgraded one that attaches better. **1997**—Delayed transmission engagement or constant shifting may be caused by an improper torque converter apply and release schedule (reprogram the powertrain control module). **All models/years**—Press Ford for "goodwill" warranty coverage if your AC is afflicted by the "Black Death" within 5 years/50,000 miles. • Use the emissions warranty to cure rotten-egg odors caused by a defective catalytic converter. • Two components that benefit from Ford's "goodwill" warranty extensions are fuel pumps and the computer modules which govern engine, fuel injection, and transmission functions. If Ford balks at refunding your money for a faulty computer module or fuel pump, apply the emissions warranty for a full or partial refund. • Paint delamination, fading, peeling, hazing, and "microchecking": See pages 94–95 for details on claiming a refund.

Aerostar Profile

	1990	1991	1992	1993	1994	1995	1996	1997
Cost Price ($)								
Cargo	12,542	13,310	14,478	14,977	15,796	17,486	17,966	17,995
Wagon	14,487	15,466	15,881	15,682	16,302	17,895	18,375	18,405
Used Values ($)								
Cargo ↑	6,000	6,500	7,500	8,500	9,500	10,500	11,000	11,700
Cargo ↓	5,000	5,500	6,500	7,000	8,000	9,000	9,500	10,500
Wagon ↑	6,500	7,000	8,000	9,000	10,000	11,500	12,500	14,000
Wagon ↓	6,000	6,000	6,500	7,500	8,500	10,000	11,500	12,500

Extended Warranty	Y	Y	Y	Y	Y	Y	N	N
Secret Warranty	N	Y	Y	Y	Y	Y	Y	N
Reliability	①	②	②	③	③	③	③	④
Air conditioning	①	②	②	②	②	③	④	④
Body integrity	②	②	②	②	②	②	②	②
Braking system	①	①	①	①	①	③	③	③
Electrical system	①	①	①	②	③	③	③	④
Engines	①	①	②	②	③	③	④	④
Exhaust/Converter	①	①	①	②	③	④	④	⑤
Fuel system	①	③	③	④	④	④	④	④
Ignition system	②	②	③	③	④	④	⑤	⑤
Manual transmission	③	③	③	③	③	③	④	⑤
- automatic	①	②	③	③	③	③	④	④
Rust/Paint	①	①	①	①	②	②	③	③
Steering	②	②	③	③	③	④	④	④
Suspension	②	②	②	③	③	③	④	④
Crash Safety	—	—	⑤	①	①	④	④	④

Note: The low frontal crash ratings represent the inclusion of leg trauma in the overall score.

Mercury Villager, Nissan Quest

Rating: Recommended (1994–97); Above Average (1993). More car-like than most competitors, these minivans are far more reliable than the Ford Aerostar and GM minivans. The Quest is practically identical to the Mercury Villager, except for some slight styling differences and more standard equipment. By choosing a cargo van over a wagon you can save between $1,500 and $2,000. **Maintenance/Repair costs**: Higher than average; any garage can repair these minivans. **Parts**: Both Mercury and Nissan dealers carry parts and auto club surveys show that parts are less expensive than those of most other minivans in this class. The exception to this rule: broken engine exhaust manifold studs (a frequent problem), AC, and electrical components.

There are plenty of two- and three-year-old models on the market that have just come off lease; the Nissan may cost a bit more, however, because it depreciates more slowly than the Villager. Other minivans you may wish to consider: the Ford Windstar, Nissan Axxess, or Toyota Previa and Sienna.

Technical Data

ENGINES	Liters/CID	HP	MPG	Model Years
OHC V6 FI	3.0L/181	118–23	17–21	1993–98

Strengths and weaknesses: The Villager's strongest features are its impressive highway performance (as long as it's not carrying a full load) and easy, no-surprise, car-like handling. Additional assets are a 4-speed automatic transmission that's particularly smooth and quiet, and mechanical components that have been tested for years on the Maxima and other Ford vehicles. The ride on both smooth and uneven highways is comfortable, overall highway stability is above reproach, and braking performance is quite good, aided by standard ABS on the Villager that improves directional control by eliminating wheel lockup.

These fuel-thirsty minivans are heavier than the Aerostar by about 700 pounds and the 3.0L engine has only 16 additional horses to carry the extra weight. GM's 2.8L engines produce more torque than what the Villager and Quest can deliver. Precise steering makes the Villager feel more responsive at highway speeds and in emergency maneuvers than it really is. The control layout is a bit confusing.

The interior space is impressive. The Villager is nearly a foot longer and two inches wider and higher than Chrysler's short-wheelbase minivans. There's better seating for three adults in the rear than with the Caravan, middle seatbacks fold flat, and the rear seats have tracks that allow them to slide forward all the way to the front or fold flat and convert to a serving area for tailgate parties.

There have been some reports of electrical problems, premature wear of the front disc brakes, and excessive vibration. One owner of a 1993 Villager GS tells of chronic vibrations at 60 mph that can't be dampened even after frequent tire replacements and suspension retuning. Body fit and finish is below par and there's a lot of wind noise entering the interior. There have also been some reports of rusting on the inside sliding door track and panel and paint defects.

Safety summary, NHTSA complaints/probes, and recalls: 1993— Possibility of fire caused by foreign material entering the blower area. • Owners of '93 Villagers say that the driver's side wiper doesn't wash or wipe properly. **Recalls: 1993—**Defective automatic seatbelt anchor bolts. • Fuel filler hoses may leak. • Leaves or other debris can accumulate in the fresh-air intake of the heating and AC system, creating a possible fire hazard. • Master cylinder on some vans was improperly assembled or damaged during assembly, which can result in loss of braking at two wheels, causing increased pedal travel and effort and increased stopping distance. **1995—**A faulty electrical socket may cause the rear light to fail to operate. **1997—** Fuel line hoses could crack or split. **1997–98 Villager—**Faulty batteries may rupture or cause a fire.

Secret Warranties/Service Tips

1993—Harsh automatic transmission upshifts may be caused by metal contamination in the solenoid assembly. Excessive exhaust manifold noise is likely due to a broken stud. Install upgraded studs.

Classification: EM94-002
Section: Engine Mechanical
Reference: TECHNICAL BULLETIN NTB94-041
Models: See below
Date: April 14, 1994
BROKEN EXHAUST MANIFOLD STUD
APPLIED MODELS:
- Pathfinder (WD21)
- Maxima (J30 and U11)
- Truck (D21)
- 300ZX (Z31)
- 200ZX (S12)
SERVICE INFORMATION: The exhaust manifold stud has been changed for improved durability. Use the following procedure to repair vehicles that exibit excessive exhaust noise due to exhaust manifold stud breakage.
REPAIR PROCEDURE:

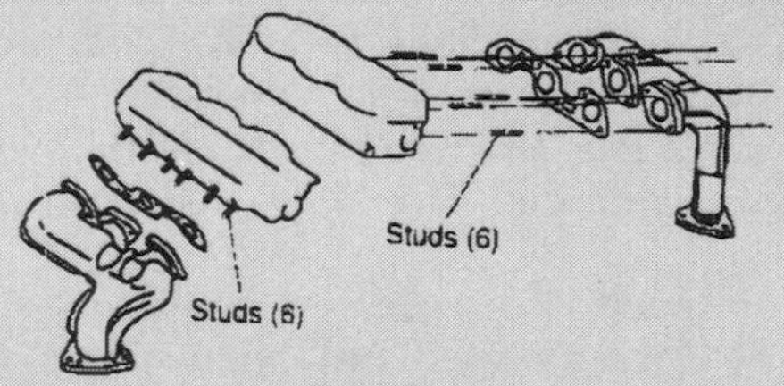

Studs (6)

Studs (6)

Figure 1

1. Remove the exhaust manifold on the side of the engine with broken stud(s). (Figure 1)
2. Replace the broken stud(s) and the front and rear studs DWI using the improved part, P/N 14065-V5003
3. Replace the exhaust manifold gasket and the exhaust manifold with new parts.
WARRANTY INFORMATION:
Please reference Section "AT-Manifolds (V6 Engine)" of the current "Nissan Flat Rate Manual" and select the appropriate right/left manifold gasket replacement OpCode with the indicated combination OpCode for the replacement of the right/left exhaust manifold stud. Use PNC 14006 and the indicated FRT's for the applicable vehicle.

Although Ford has covered this repair under an extended warranty, Nissan is harder to deal with, and denies that the problem exists or that the service bulletin above applies to owners.

• An inoperative air conditioning blower motor can be fixed by installing a new blower motor resistor. • Stalling whenever the vehicle is shifted from Park to Drive to Reverse may mean that the torque converter is stuck in the "lock-up" mode. Install an upgraded valve body assembly (#F3XY-7A100-D) and a transaxle oil pan gasket to fix the problem. • A ticking or clicking coming from the suspension strut area signals the need for an upgraded front strut spacer (#F3XY-3A120-A). • Fogging or frosting of the side windows may be caused by a misconnected C261 electrical connector. • If the liftgate light/door ajar light flickers or the vehicle won't start, the rear liftgate latch may need to be changed. • A rear suspension clunk or thump when passing over bumps is likely caused by improperly calibrated rear shock absorbers. • Install an upgraded speed control module (F3XY-9FS12-B) if the vehicle loses 3–5 mph on hills or grades with the present module. • A clicking or ticking noise when accelerating can be corrected by installing a new EGR tube with a redesigned fitting. • A shudder or vibration that occurs during the 1–2 shift can be corrected by replacing the automatic transaxle valve body with an upgraded valve body and transaxle oil pan gasket. **1993–94**—A squeak or chirp coming from the blower motor can be stopped by installing an upgraded blower motor with improved brush-to-commutator friction. • Sliding door noise may need a new service spring in the upper hinge and a readjustment of the dovetail. • The transmission may not go into Reverse and, upon checking, the fluid will be full but burnt. The rear control valve and Low/Reverse brake (plate, piston, and retainer) must be replaced under normal warranty provisions. • A rattle in either of the front doors may be caused by the door guard beam spot welds breaking loose and a campaign was conducted to repair both beams, free of charge. • Body squeaks and rattles are thoroughly discussed in DSB 04-86-94. **1993–95**—Coolant may leak from the front of the cylinder head, which may appear to be a head gasket but comes from a threaded plug in the front of the head; this must be cleaned and Teflon tape applied to the threads to prevent future leaks. • The rear wiper motor may quit or stop intermittently because water has gotten into the motor printed circuit board. • A new stabilizer bar and bushings will be installed if there is a crunching or scraping noise from the front end when going over bumps (such as speed bumps) or on highway ramps. • Replace front brake pads that cause excessive brake squeaking or groaning with upgraded pads. Ford and Nissan will cover part of the cost on a case-by-case basis.

96-5-13
02/26/96
• BRAKES - FRONT BRAKE "SQUEAL" DURING BRAKING - "GROAN" NOISE DURING GRADUAL BRAKE PEDAL RELEASE - VEHICLES BUILT THROUGH 9/18/95
• NOISE - "SQUEAL" FROM FRONT BRAKES DURING LIGHT BRAKE APPLICATION - "GROAN" NOISE DURING GRADUAL BRAKE PEDAL RELEASE - VEHICLES BUILT THROUGH 9/18/95
LIGHT TRUCK: 1993-95 VILLAGER
ISSUE: A front brake "squeal" during light brake application and/or a "groan" noise during gradual release of the brake pedal may be heard on some vehicles. This may be caused by the friction material composition of the front brake pads.
ACTION: Replace the front brake pads and machine both front rotors on the vehicle. The revised front pads are contructed of a non-asbestos organic material that was developed to reduce the possibility of front brake noise.

Ford's fix will silence front brake groans and squeals.

1993–96—A "crunch/grunt" noise from the rear suspension may be caused by rear shackle bushings that need lubrication. **1993–97**—Front door windows that bind may have the glass rubber improperly installed into the door sheet metal channel. **1994–98**—If there's a strong fuel odor in the passenger compartment when refueling, it's likely there's a missing sealer between the fuel filler opening upper flange and the fuel filler base assembly. **1995–96**—Ford has replaced at no charge 3.0L V6 engine blocks that produce excessive engine knock following a cold start.

Article No. 96-20-17
09/23/96
• ENGINE - "KNOCKING" NOISE IN LOWER ENGINE AREA - HEARD AFTER COLD SOAK
  START-UP VEHICLES BUILT FROM 5/1/95 THROUGH 2/1/96
• NOISE - "KNOCKING" IN LOWER ENGINE AREA - HEARD AFTER COLD SOAK START-UP
  VEHICLES BUILT FROM 5/1/95 THROUGH 2/1/96
LIGHT TRUCK: 1995-96 VILLAGER
This DSB is being republished in its entirety to correct the part number for the Balance Tube Gasket.
ISSUE: There may be a "knocking" noise in the lower engine area after a cold soak on start-up on some
vehicles. This may be caused by reduced oil flow to the piston during start-up causing piston slap.
ACTION: Replace the long block assembly. The connecting rods in the new long block have oil holes to
improve cold engine start-up noise. Refer to the appropriate Villager Service Manual for replacement procedures.
The noise is most audible at a cold start-up between 1200-1800 rpms. It may resemble a lower engine
knock. Perform a cylinder balance test on cylinders 2, 3, and 4. If the noise diminishes, the cause is piston
slap. Proceed with this DSB. Replace the long block assembly.
Drain all fluids from the engine core. It will be picked up by your local Ford Authorized Remanufacturer.

PART NUMBER	PART NAME
F3XZ-6007-BA	Long Block - 1995
F6XZ-600Z-BA	Long Block - 1996
F4XY-9448-A	Gasket - Right Exhaust Manifold
F4XY-9448-B	Gasket - Left Exhaust Manifold
F3XY-9H486-B	Gasket - Upper Intake Manifold
F4XY-9439-A	Gasket - Intake Manifold-To-Head
F4XY-9448-C	Gasket - Exhaust Manifold-to-Balance Tube
F3XY-5E281A	
F3XY-9A288-A	Injector Insulator
F3XY-6659-B	Gasket - Oil Pump
14039-W1500	Nut - Exhaust Manifold

1997—Hard starts or no-starts in cold temperatures or at high altitudes can be
corrected by replacing the power control module (PCM) under the emissions
warranty. • **All models/years**—If the transmission does not shift properly
until warmed up, make sure it is filled only with Nissanmatic "C" transmission fluid. • A rotten-egg odor coming from the exhaust is probably caused
by a malfunctioning catalytic converter, which is covered by Ford's original
warranty and the 5-year/50,000 mile emissions warranty. • Two components that benefit from Ford "goodwill" warranty extensions are fuel
pumps and computer modules that govern engine, fuel injection, and
transmission functions. If Ford balks at refunding your money for a faulty
computer module or fuel pump, apply the emissions warranty for a full or
partial refund. • Paint delamination, fading, peeling, hazing, and
"microchecking": See pages 94–95 for details on claiming a refund.

Mercury Villager, Nissan Quest Profile

	1993	1994	1995	1996	1997
Cost Price ($)					
Villager GS	17,401	18,325	18,995	19,940	20,540
Villager LS	22,683	22,975	24,650	25,595	27,595
Quest XE	17,895	18,909	20,229	21,304	21,699
Quest GXE	21,800	23,419	24,999	26,104	26,469
Used Values ($)					
Villager GS ↑		8,500	9,500	11,000	12,200	13,000
Villager GS ↓		7,000	8,000	9,500	10,500	12,000
Villager LS ↑		12,000	13,000	14,000	16,000	17,500
Villager LS ↓		10,000	11,500	12,500	14,500	16,000
Quest XE ↑		11,000	12,000	13,000	15,000	16,000
Quest XE ↓		9,500	10,500	12,000	13,000	15,000

Quest GXE ↑   12,000 13,000 14,500 16,500 18,000
Quest GXE ↓   10,500 12,000 13,000 15,000 16,500

Extended Warranty	N	N	N	N	N
Secret Warranty	Y	Y	Y	Y	N
Reliability	④	④	④	④	⑤
Air conditioning	③	③	④	④	⑤
Automatic transmission	④	⑤	⑤	⑤	⑤
Body integrity	❶	❷	❷	❷	③
Braking system	❷	❷	❷	③	③
Electrical system	❶	❷	❷	❷	③
Engines	⑤	⑤	❷	❷	④
Exhaust/Converter	❶	❷	③	④	⑤
Fuel system	⑤	⑤	⑤	⑤	⑤
Ignition system	⑤	⑤	⑤	⑤	⑤
Rust/Paint	④	⑤	⑤	⑤	⑤
Steering	④	⑤	⑤	⑤	⑤
Suspension	③	③	④	④	⑤
Crash Safety	❶	❶	④	④	④

Windstar

Rating: Recommended (1996–97); Above Average (1995). Combines plenty of raw power, an exceptional ride, and impressive cargo capacity. Although there was as much as $5,000 separating the entry level '96 GL from the LX when new, the difference narrows to only $1,000 for used versions. **Maintenance/Repair costs**: Average. **Parts**: Expensive and frequently back-ordered.

There won't be many used '96 Windstars on the market until next year when most two-year leases expire. Other minivans you may wish to consider: the Mercury Villager, Nissan Quest, or Toyota Previa and Sienna.

Technical Data

ENGINES	Liters/CID	HP	MPG	Model Years
OHV V6 FI	3.0L/182	150	16–22	1998
OHV V6 FI	3.8L/232	155–200	15–20	1995–98

Strengths and weaknesses: Launched as a 1995 model in March 1994, the Windstar is a front-drive minivan that looks a bit like a stretched Mercury Villager. It's longer, larger, and lower than most other minivans. It's also one of the few minivans not built on a truck platform (it uses the Taurus platform instead) and as a result has some of the car-like handling distinctions of Chrysler's minivans. It's offered in two body styles—a seven-passenger people-hauler and the less expensive basic cargo van.

The Windstar offers good assembly quality and a nice array of standard safety features. Unlike Chrysler and GM minivans, Windstars don't depend upon shims, slots, and toytabs on sheet metal to permit inexact parts to be maneuvered into a fit (akin to putting a round peg into a square hole). This ensures a quiet interior with little engine or road noise. There are some performance problems, though, like the automatic transmission that sometimes pauses before downshifting or shifts roughly into higher gear and the 3.0L engine that struggles to keep up. Owners have also reported that Windstar air conditioners aren't very durable and the 3.8L engine head gaskets need replacing after the 80,000 mile mark (covered by Ford's 98M01 secret warranty).

Safety summary, NHTSA complaints/probes, and recalls: Base models don't have head restraints for all seats and the digital dash can be confusing. **NHTSA: 1995–96**—Excessive brake fading and extended stopping distances. **1998**—Loose or missing front brake bolts could cause the wheels to lock up or cause loss of vehicle control. **Recalls: 1995**—A loose connection within the electrical power distribution box could ignite the electrical wiring under the hood. • A pinched instrument panel wire harness could cause a short circuit and start an electrical fire. • The passenger airbag may not deploy properly. • An alternator wiring short circuit could cause a fire. **1996**—Transmission may not engage; PRNDL may give a false reading. **1997**—Servo cover can leak, creating a fire hazard.

Secret Warranties/Service Tips

1995—Blower motor squeaking or chirping can be silenced by installing an upgraded blower motor. **1995–96**—Intermittent no-starts may be caused by microscopic cracks on the fuel pump relay cover located inside the Constant Control Relay Module. Install a new CCRM. • Hard starts and stalling can be corrected by installing an upgraded idle air control valve under the emissions warranty. **1995–97**—Engine block heater coolant leakage. **1995–98**—If the front end accessory drive belt (FEAD) slips during wet conditions causing a reduction in steering power assist, Ford suggests the belt be replaced. **1996–98**—Harsh automatic shifting from 1–2 may be caused by a malfunctioning electronic pressure control or the main control valves sticking in the valve body. • An intermittent Neutral condition when coming to a stop signals the need to replace the forward clutch piston and the forward clutch cylinder. • Right rear quarter panel black soot deposits can be avoided by installing an exhaust tailpipe extension under Ford's base warranty. **All models/years**—3.8L engine head gaskets that need replacing after the base warranty has expired are covered by Ford's #98M01 secret engine warranty.

Windstar Profile

	1995	1996	1997
Cost Price ($)			
GL	19,995	20,785	23,070
LX	24,080	25,340	26,195
Used Values ($)			
GL ↑	14,000	15,000	16,500
GL ↓	12,000	14,000	15,000

LX ↑	15,000	16,000	17,000
LX ↓	13,000	15,000	16,000

Extended Warranty	Y	Y	N
Secret Warranty	N	N	N
Reliability	④	④	⑤
Crash Safety	⑤	⑤	⑤

GENERAL MOTORS

Astro, Safari

Rating: Average (1992–97); Not Recommended (1985–91). These are more minitruck than minivan. **Maintenance/Repair costs**: Average; any garage can repair these rear-drive minivans. **Parts**: Plentiful and reasonably priced.

As with the Aerostar, the classified ads are jam-packed with sellers wanting to unload their Astros and Safaris simply because they've got high mileage or a small business has moved up to a larger van. Whatever the reason, you can find some real bargains if you're patient. Other choices you may wish to consider: the Ford Aerostar or a full-sized GM or Ford van.

Technical Data

ENGINES	Liters/CID	HP	MPG	Model Years
OHV I-4 FI	2.5L/151	92–96	19–23	1985–88
OHV V6 4 bbl.	4.3L/262	147	14–19	1985
OHV V6 FI	4.3L/262	165	15–20	1986–94
OHV V6 FI	4.3L/262	170–200	15–20	1991–98

Strengths and weaknesses: Introduced during the 1985 model year, these minivans are basically trucks dressed in minivan garb. Nevertheless, these spacious vans can be fitted to tow up to 6,000 pounds and carry eight people. The base 4.3L V6 gives acceptable acceleration, but the High Output variant of the same engine (first available in the '91 model) is a far better choice, particularly when it's mated to a manual gearbox. The full-time AWD versions aren't very refined, have a high failure rate, and are expensive to diagnose and repair. The 1995 models got a minor facelift, a bit more horsepower, and extended bodies.

Early versions suffer from failure-prone automatic transmissions, a poor braking system, and fragile steering components. The early base V6 provides ample power, but also produces lots of noise, consumes excessive amounts of fuel, and tends to have leaking head gaskets and failure-prone oxygen sensors. These computer-related problems often rob the engine of sufficient power to keep up in traffic. Even though the 5-speed manual transmission shifts fairly easily, the automatic takes forever to downshift on the highway. Handling isn't particularly agile on these minivans and the power steering doesn't provide the driver with enough road feel. Unloaded, the Astro provides very poor traction, the ride isn't comfortable on poor road surfaces, and interior noise is rampant. Many drivers find the driving position awkward (no left leg room) and the heating/defrosting system inadequate. Many engine components are hidden under the dashboard, making repair or maintenance awkward.

Even on more recent models, highway performance and overall reliability remain problematic. The 4-speed automatic transmissions are poorly engineered and suffer from frequent failures. Excessive rear-end clunking and clanging occurs whenever the transmission shifts or downshifts while under load. One worker at GM's Oshawa, Ontario plant, a 1993 Safari owner, wrote GM's President asking that the problem be fixed:

> Do you as CEO really know what's going on or does middle management filter out the bad news? GM's policy on warranty service is atrocious, your service representative was rude and your parts are substandard... Your bulletin 93-4A-101, "Discouraging dealers from attempting to repair driveline clunk," is weaseling out on your responsibilities to the customer.

Other owners report that the front suspension, steering components, computer modules, and catalytic converter can wear out in as little as 35,000 miles. There have also been lots of complaints about electrical, exhaust, cooling, and fuel system bugs, inadequate heating/defrosting, and axle seals wearing out every 12 to 18 months. Many owners write that they've had to endure a rotten-egg smell coming from the exhaust. Body hardware is fragile and fit and finish is the pits. One 1994 Safari owner, frustrated by chronic water leaks, replaced the rear hatch molding three times without any improvement. Squeaks and rattles are legion and hard to locate. Sliding door handles often break off and the sliding door frequently jams in cold temperatures. The hatch release for the Dutch doors occasionally doesn't work and the driver's side seat vinyl lining tears apart. Premature paint peeling/delamination and surface rust are fairly common.

Safety summary, NHTSA complaints/probes, and recalls: According to insurance industry figures, both the Astro and Safari have amassed a higher-than-average number of accident injury claims. • Owners report that 1987–88 Astros and Safaris have a quirky braking system that can cause the wheels to suddenly lock up under heavy braking, throwing the vehicle into a spin. • Seatbelts may fail to retract on 1989 versions. • One owner of a '93 Safari reports a host of safety-related failures, including brake/shift interlock failures, seatbelt retractor buttons that fall off, leaky dual brake master cylinders, and a cruise control that won't automatically reset to its previous speed. **NHTSA: 1990–91**—31 complaints of dashboard fires. **1995**—Fire ignited under the dashboard. • Headlight switch shorted out, resulting in a fire. • Driver airbag failed to deploy. • Vehicle continues to accelerate after foot is removed from accelerator. • Frequent stalling. • Erratic engine performance due to blocked catalytic converter. • Engine leaks oil. • Loose fan belts cause belt to come off, causing loss of power steering and brakes. • Frequent brake failures. • Loss of braking when going over a bump. • ABS failed to engage. • ABS suddenly engaged for no reason and then wouldn't disengage. • ABS hesitates when applied. • Defective brake calipers. • Power brake hose fell off, causing loss of power brakes. • Front brake hoses collapsed, causing sudden brake failure. • Premature front brake wear. • Power-steering lockup. • Power-steering hose fell off, causing loss of power steering. • Power-steering fluid leaks. • Vehicle jerks to one side when braking. • Front wheels lock up when turning the steering wheel to the right from a stop while in gear. • Steering stuck when turning. • Seatbelts fail to work properly. • Shoulder belt failed to restrain driver in collision. • When the middle seat is removed, the seatbelt which is attached permanently to the headliner swings freely in the passenger compartment. • There is no room to latch the seatbelt. • Passenger side seatbelt tightens up with every movement. • Seatbelt locks up unexpectedly. • Bench seatbelts are too short and cannot be adjusted. • Fresh air ventilation system allows fumes from other vehicles to enter interior compartment. • With jack almost fully extended, wheel doesn't lift off of ground. • Spare tire not safe for driving over 35 mph. • Design of horn makes it difficult to use. • Horn buttons require excessive pressure to activate them. • Driver-side window failure. • Sliding door suddenly fell off. • Faulty door hinges allow the door to fall off. • Sliding door rattles. • Front passenger door won't close. • Passenger-side door glass fell out. • Rear hatch latch release failed. • Rear hatch hydraulic rods are too weak to support hatch. • Front passenger's seat reclining mechanism failed. • Poor traction. • Parked in gear and rolled downhill. • Transmission failures. • Left rear axle seal leaks, causing lubricant to burn on brake lining. • Excessive rear-end axle noise. • Sudden wheel bearing failure. • AC clutch fell apart. • Alternator bearing failure. • Windshield wipers fail intermittently. **Recalls: 1985**—The steering gear may crack or break free, causing sudden steering loss. **1985–91**—The seatback may recline suddenly. **1989**—GM will install and relocate a new AC line under a recall campaign. **1990**—GM will repair the fuel return line fitting crimp for free. **1995**—Possible separation of control arm from the frame. • Vehicles with the L35 engine may have fuel line leakage. **1996–97**—Outboard seatbelt webbing on right rear bucket seat can separate during a crash.

Secret Warranties/Service Tips

1985–93—Vehicles equipped with a Hydramatic 4L60 transmission that buzzes when the car is in Reverse or idle may need a new oil pressure regulator valve. • A power-steering hiss can be silenced by replacing the power-steering valve assembly. **1988–92**—Hydramatic 4L60/700R4 automatic transmission may click or whine in third or fourth gear. There may also be a rattling noise coming from the rear of the transmission. Correct by installing five new fiber plates in the Low and Reverse clutch. The new plates have a different groove configuration that prevents third and fourth gear vibration. **1989–91**—THM 700-R4 automatic transmissions may exhibit a no-Reverse or delayed Reverse condition in cold weather. This problem can be corrected by replacing the piston outer seal with a long lip design. If this design is already being used and there's no improvement, change the Reverse input clutch housing. • A binding sliding door requires the replacement of the center track rolling bracket, the center track assembly, and the lower track striker/bumper assembly. **1992–94**—The PCV hose may freeze, causing oil starvation to the engine and leading to engine failure. Alaskan owners are eligible for free higher-flow calibrated PCVs under the emissions warranty. All other cold weather operators are supposed to be told of the problem and given free servicing on a case-by-case basis. **1993–94**—A faulty speedometer, inability to shift down into second gear, or a transmission stuck in second gear may all be corrected by replacing the C240 connector. • Poor cold starting can be traced to a defective fuel pump relay. **1993–95**—Malfunctioning gauges and driveability problems may be the result of a short circuit caused by the C110 connector wire rubbing against the AC accumulator pipe. • GM says that a chronic driveline clunk can't be silenced and is a characteristic of its late model vehicles. **1996–97**—Excessive engine noise can be curtailed by installing an upgraded valve stem oil seal. **1996–98**—Rough engine performance may be caused by a water contaminated oxygen sensor. **All models/years**—Defective catalytic converters that cause a rotten-egg smell will be replaced free of charge under the vehicle's emissions warranty. • Paint delamination, peeling, or fading: See page 95.

Astro, Safari Profile

	1990	1991	1992	1993	1994	1995	1996	1997
Cost Price ($)								
Cargo	12,691	14,081	14,636	15,336	15,985	18,340	19,152	19,583
CS/base	15,261	17,145	16,726	17,146	17,819	19,886	19,736	20,167
Used Values ($)								
Cargo ↑	6,000	7,000	8,000	9,000	10,500	12,000	13,000	14,000
Cargo ↓	4,500	6,000	7,000	8,000	9,000	10,500	11,500	12,500
CS/base ↑	7,000	8,000	9,000	10,000	11,500	13,000	15,000	16,500
CS/base ↓	6,000	7,000	7,500	8,500	10,000	12,000	13,500	15,000
Extended Warranty	Y	Y	Y	Y	Y	Y	Y	Y
Secret Warranty	N	Y	Y	Y	Y	Y	Y	N
Reliability	❶	❷	❷	③	③	③	③	④
Air conditioning	❷	❷	❷	③	③	③	④	④
Body integrity	❶	❶	❶	❶	❶	❶	❷	❷

Braking system	❶	❶	❶	❷	❷	❷	❷	③
Electrical system	❶	❶	❶	❶	❶	❶	③	③
Engines	❶	❷	③	④	④	④	⑤	⑤
Exhaust/Converter	❷	③	③	③	④	④	④	④
Fuel system	④	④	④	④	④	④	④	④
Ignition system	❶	❶	❷	❷	③	④	④	④
Automatic trans.	③	③	③	③	③	③	③	③
Rust/Paint	❶	❶	❶	❶	❶	❶	❷	❷
Steering	❷	③	③	③	③	④	④	④
Suspension	❷	❷	❷	③	③	④	④	④
Crash Safety	—	—	❶	❶	❶	—	③	③

Lumina APV, Silhouette, Trans Sport

Rating: Average (1996–97); Below Average (1991–95); Not Recommended (1990). The Lumina's last model year was 1996; the Trans Sport was carried over an additional model year. **Maintenance/Repair costs**: Higher than average, but any garage can repair these minivans. **Parts**: Plentiful, but costly. Plastic body panels may soon be in short supply.

There are plenty of reasonably-priced two- and three-year-old models on the market that have just come off lease. Other minivans you may wish to consider: the Ford Windstar, Mercury Villager, Nissan Axxess and Quest, or Toyota's Previa and Sienna.

Technical Data

ENGINES	Liters/CID	HP	MPG	Model Years
OHV V6 FI	3.1L/191	120	17–22	1990–95
OHV V6 FI	3.4L/207	180	18–24	1996–98
OHV V6 FI	3.8L/231	170	16–21	1992–95

Strengths and weaknesses: Although the '94s have less of a Dustbuster look, GM's plastic-bodied, front-drive minivan looks more like a swoopy station wagon than the traditional minivan (like the popular, boxy Chrysler Caravan). These vehicles use the Chevrolet Lumina platform, and therefore have more car-like handling than GM's Astro/Safari. Seating is limited to five adults on the standard models (two up front and three on a removable bench seat), but this can be increased to seven if you order optional modular seats. Seats can be folded down flat, creating additional storage space. Incidentally, be careful not to drop your keys between the windshield and the dash because you'll need a fishing rod to get them back.

The chassis and mechanical components come from GM's failure-prone W-bodies (Lumina, Regal, Cutlass Supreme, and Grand Prix), which explains why these minivans have so many of the same factory-related defects as their smaller cousins—notably, electronic module (PROM) and starter failures, short circuits, automatic transmission breakdowns, abysmal fit and finish, chronic sliding door malfunctions, and faulty rear seat latches. Other problems include a 4-speed automatic transmission that isn't as durable as the less fuel-efficient 3-speed automatic; a poorly mounted sliding door; side-door glass that pops open; squeaks, rattles, and clunks in the instrument panel cluster area and suspension; and a wind buffeting noise around the front doors. By the way, don't trust the towing limit listed in GM's owners manual. Automakers publish tow ratings that are on the optimistic side—and sometimes they even lie. Also, don't be surprised to find that the base 3.1L engine doesn't handle a full load of passenger and cargo, especially when mated to the 3-speed automatic transmission. The ideal powertrain combo would be the 4-speed automatic coupled to the optional "3800" V6 (first used on the '96 versions).

The large dent- and rust-resistant plastic panels are robot-bonded to the frame with unique new adhesives, and they absorb engine and road noise very well in addition to having an impressive record for durability. Some body shops complain, however, that the innovative panels are in short supply and that damaged panels can't be recycled. This drives up the cost of repairs and tempts insurance adjusters to simply write off repairable vehicles.

Safety summary, NHTSA complaints/probes, and recalls: Some front door-mounted seatbelts cross uncomfortably at the neck and there's a nasty blind spot on the driver's side that requires a small stick-on convex mirror to correct. • NHTSA has closed an investigation of transaxle hose separation in exchange for GM's promise to conduct a regional recall. **Recalls: 1990**—Defective modular rear seat latches. **1990–91 Trans Sport**—The upper glove box doors may not stay closed in an accident. **1993–94**—The rear seatbelt may not retract on vehicles with power sliding doors. **1995**—The throttle cable support bracket needs to be replaced in order to enable the engine to decelerate. • Steering could fail. • Brake pedal arm could fracture. **1997–98 Silhouette and Venture**—Installation of safety guards on seat-latch mechanisms.

Secret Warranties/Service Tips

1990–91—Hydramatic 4L60/700R4 automatic transmission may have no upshift or appear to be stuck in first gear. The probable cause is a worn governor gear. It would be wise to replace the retaining ring as well. **1990–92**—Vehicles with a 3T40 automatic transmission may slip in Low or Reverse gear. Correct by replacing the Low/Reverse clutch components, including the Low/Reverse release spring, clutch spring retainer, and piston snap ring. • A shudder or vibration at low speeds in vehicles equipped with a 3.1L engine may be caused by a faulty PROM electronic module. • A power-steering shudder can be corrected by replacing the power-steering return hose/pipe assembly with a revised assembly and internal tuning cable (#26030907). **1990–94**—An engine ticking at idle can be traced to rattling piston pins that must be replaced with upgraded parts. **1991 with 3.1L**

engine—Engine hesitation or stalling may require a new service calibration PROM that revises tip-in fuelling. • If the problem is reduced power, it may signal the need to replace the electronic spark control (ESC). **1991–92**—A delayed shift between Drive and Reverse is likely caused by a rolled or cut input clutch piston outer seal. **1992**—Power-steering shudder can be reduced by installing an upgraded power-steering outlet hose/pipe assembly (#260337593). **1992–93**—No Reverse gear or slipping in Reverse can be corrected by installing an upgraded Low/Rev clutch return spring and spiral retaining ring. **1992–94**—Loss of Drive or erratic shifts may be caused by an intermittent short to ground on the A or B shift solenoid, or an electrical short circuit in the transaxle. • A front-end clunking noise when driving over rough roads may require the repositioning of the diagonal radiator support braces. • A front-end engine knock troubleshooting chart is found in DSB 306001. **1993–94**—Owners who complain of automatic transmission low-speed miss, hesitation, chuggle, or skip may find relief with an improved MEMCAL module that GM developed to remedy the problem. **1993–95**—An engine coolant leak from the throttle body assembly may require an upgraded service seal kit. **1994**—Front door glass window scraping/chattering can be eliminated by relocating the front lower guide attachment. • Lazy front seatbelt retractors will be replaced free of charge. • A liftgate that fails to lock may have a loose or missing lock cylinder lock-out pin. • Manual sliding side doors that stick shut require a lock replacement. **1995**—A thud/clunk noise occurs when the fuel tank is more than three-quarters full. GM will replace the fuel tank and sender assembly. **1995–96**—Intermittent Neutral/loss of Drive at highway speeds can be fixed by replacing the control valve body assembly. **1997**—Rear brake clicking or squealing may be caused by a misadjusted park brake cable. • Brakes that don't work, drag, heat up, or wear out early may have a variety of causes, all outlined in DSB #73-50-27. • A rear suspension thud or clunk may be silenced by installing upgraded rear springs. **All models/years**—Defective catalytic converters that cause a rotten-egg smell in the interior may be replaced free of charge under the emissions warranty.

Lumina APV, Silhouette, Trans Sport Profile

	1990	1991	1992	1993	1994	1995	1996	1997
Cost Price ($)								
Lumina Cargo	13,395	14,102	14,905	15,225	16,015	16,775	18,415	—
Passenger	15,300	16,045	16,930	17,255	18,178	19,625	20,435	—
Silhouette	17,695	18,705	19,625	20,029	20,625	20,795	21,900	22,245
Trans Sport	16,300	17,609	17,585	18,049	18,279	19,965	21,595	21,049
Used Values ($)								
Cargo ↑	5,500	6,200	7,000	8,000	9,500	10,500	11,500	—
Cargo ↓	4,500	5,300	6,000	7,000	8,000	9,500	10,500	—
Passenger ↑	6,200	7,000	7,500	8,500	10,000	11,000	12,000	—
Passenger ↓	5,000	5,800	6,500	7,500	9,000	10,000	11,000	—
Silhouette ↑	7,000	7,500	8,500	9,500	11,000	12,500	13,500	17,500
Silhouette ↓	5,800	6,500	7,500	8,500	10,000	11,000	12,500	16,500
Trans Sport/SE ↑	6,500	7,500	8,000	9,000	10,500	11,500	13,500	17,500
Trans Sport/SE ↓	5,500	6,500	7,000	7,500	9,000	10,000	11,500	16,500
Extended Warranty	Y	Y	Y	Y	Y	Y	Y	Y
Secret Warranty	N	N	N	N	Y	Y	Y	N

Reliability	❶	❷	❷	③	③	③	④	④
Air conditioning	③	③	③	④	④	④	④	④
Body integrity	❶	❶	❶	❷	❷	❷	❷	③
Braking system	❶	❷	❷	❷	❷	❷	③	③
Electrical system	❶	❶	❶	❷	❷	❷	③	③
Engines	③	④	④	④	④	④	④	⑤
Exhaust/Converter	③	④	④	④	④	④	④	⑤
Fuel system	④	④	④	④	⑤	⑤	⑤	⑤
Ignition system	❶	❷	❷	③	④	⑤	⑤	⑤
Automatic transmission	❷	❷	❷	③	③	③	③	③
Rust/Paint	④	④	④	④	⑤	⑤	⑤	⑤
Steering	④	④	④	④	④	④	④	⑤
Suspension	③	③	③	④	④	④	④	④
Crash Safety	❷	—	⑤	❷	❶	④	④	④

Note: The low frontal crash ratings represent the inclusion of leg trauma in the overall score of the '93 and '94 models.

HONDA

Odyssey, Oasis

Rating: Average (1995–97). An Accord masquerading as a minivan. Consider these smartly styled, fuel-efficient vehicles as full-sized, urban station wagons rather than highway-hauling minivans. **Maintenance/Repair costs**: Higher than average, but any garage can repair these minivans. **Parts**: Limited supply and costly.

There aren't many reasonably-priced two-year-old Odysseys on the market. If you can't afford to wait, consider the Ford Windstar, Mercury Villager, Nissan Axxess and Quest, or the Toyota Previa.

Technical Data

ENGINES	Liters/CID	HP	MPG	Model Years
OHC I-4 FI	2.2L/132	140	19–24	1995–97
OHC I-4 FI	2.2L/132	140	19–24	1998

Strengths and weaknesses: One can sum up the Odyssey and Isuzu Oasis strengths and weaknesses in three words: performance, performance, and performance. You get car-like performance and handling, responsive steering and a comfortable ride, offset by slow-as-molasses-in-January acceleration with a full load, a raucous engine, and limited passenger/cargo space due to its narrow body.

The Odyssey and Oasis have proven to be more reliable and give better handling than the American rear-drive, truck-inspired minivans. But their high price on the used car market, weak 2.2L 4-cylinder engine, and small dimensions can't compete with Chrysler and Ford's newest versions. About the same size as the Nissan

Quest/Mercury Villager twins, the Odyssey and Oasis use four sedan-type doors, second row bench seating, and have a third seat that folds flat. With their four sedan-style doors and relatively compact size, these cars are more like tall station wagons.

Like the Accord, component quality and assembly are first class. Nevertheless, potential problem areas are the front brakes (premature wear and noise) and trim and accessory items that come loose, break away, or malfunction. The timing chain may also have to be replaced frequently.

Safety summary, NHTSA complaints/probes, and recalls: Horn buttons may be hard to find in an emergency. **NHTSA: 1997—** Sudden acceleration upon brake application. • Cannot secure child safety seat with the vehicle's seatbelts; too much play in rear lap belts. • Put vehicle in Drive and turned AC on. Vehicle suddenly accelerated, brakes failed, and minivan hit a brick wall. • Both front airbags failed to deploy in a head-on collision. **Recalls**: No data available.

Secret Warranties/Service Tips

1995–96—Warped wheel covers are caused primarily by bent tabs. **1996–97**—In a settlement with the Environmental Protection Agency, Honda paid fines totaling $17.1 million and extended its emissions warranty on 1.6 million 1995–97 models to 14 years or 150,000 miles. This means that costly engine components and exhaust system parts like catalytic converters will be replaced free of charge, as long as the 14-year/150,000-mile limit hasn't been exceeded. Additionally, the automaker will provide a full engine check and emissions-related repairs at 50,000 to 75,000 miles and will give free tune-ups at 75,000 to 150,000 miles. It is estimated that the free check-ups, repairs, and tune-ups will cost Honda over $250 million. The story of the settlement was first reported on page 6 of the June 15, 1998, edition of *Automotive News*.

Odyssey, Oasis Profile

	1995	1996	1997
Cost Price ($)			
LX	23,380	23,955	23,955
Used Values ($)			
LX ↑	15,500	16,500	18,500
LX ↓	14,000	15,000	17,500
Extended Warranty	N	N	N
Secret Warranty	N	Y	Y
Reliability	⑤	⑤	⑤
Crash Safety	④	④	④

MAZDA

Rating: Average (1996–97); Below Average (1989–95). The MPV is a good performer hobbled by poor reliability and servicing. **Maintenance/Repair costs**: Higher than average, but any garage can repair these minivans. **Parts**: Limited supply and costly.

There are plenty of reasonably-priced two- and three-year-old models on the market that have just come off lease. Be wary of earlier, high-mileage versions, though; they tend to deteriorate fairly rapidly after the first few years. Other minivans you may wish to consider: the Ford Windstar, Mercury Villager, Nissan Quest, or Toyota's Previa and Sienna.

Technical Data

ENGINES	Liters/CID	HP	MPG	Model Years
OHC I-4 FI	2.6L/159	121	17–23	1989–94
OHC V6 FI	3.0L/180	150–155	16–22	1989–98

Strengths and weaknesses: Handling and overall highway performance put the MPV in the top third of the minivan pack, but the poor winter handling, below average reliability of early models that are no longer under warranty, a "take it or leave it" attitude when handling warranty claims, mediocre servicing, and high fuel and parts cost make pre-'96 versions below-average buys when it comes to overall operating costs.

The 5-speed manual transmission shifts easily and has well-spaced gears, but it's relatively rare. The automatic performs fairly well but sometimes hesitates before going into gear at about 15 mph and again at 35 mph. Steering is crisp and predictable. Rear-drive setup makes for easy load carrying and trailer towing. The base 2.6L 16-valve (121-hp) 4-cylinder engine is a dog, especially when hooked up to the automatic 4-speed transmission that robs it of what little power it has. The 3.0L 6-cylinder engine, on the other hand, delivers snappy acceleration with the front-drive and slower, though acceptable acceleration with the 4X4. Says the owner of a '91 MPV:

> ...As the owner of a '91 MPV which I bought new, I agree with the vast majority of your comments—and with your overall rating. I would not buy another one.
>
>   Our problems included a windshield wiper motor that got over-loaded and went haywire early on; fragile paint that chipped off (and over which I successfully took Mazda to small claims court, settling before the trial date for the full amount of a repaint); a defective ignition that failed out of warranty; a defective steering column shifter assembly that was never properly repaired and which I wound

up repairing out of warranty; and generally terrible winter handling (we didn't have the 4X4). It has also been a terrible gas hog.

The key point I dispute with you is the assessment that, with the V6 engine, the MPV is merely adequate in power and pickup. This is the one area that really sold us on the vehicle in the first place where I beg to strongly differ.

I find the MPV's acceleration power extraordinary. Up here in the Thunder Bay area, we have many miles of crummy two-lane highway where the ability to quickly pull out and overtake is something of a safety feature; we frequently floor our MPV into Overdrive, and it takes off like a shot.

I have recently road-tested a whole slew of minivans and SUVs, and my conclusion is that the MPV really kicks butt while maintaining a solid, non-jerky, comfortable ride. Among minivans, only the Windstar with its 3.8L engine matched it. With the Explorer, only the OHC 6 equaled it (aside from the V8). The Pathfinder was no slouch either, but its fuel consumption is even worse than the MPV's. It occurs to me that the 4X4 V6 (which I have never driven) may not be as responsive as the 4X2 that I have, perhaps due to the extra weight...

Overheating and head gasket failures are commonplace with the 4-banger, and the temperature gauge warns you only when it's too late. Some cases of chronic engine knocking in cold weather with the 3.0L have been fixed by installing tighter-fitting, Teflon-coated pistons. Valve lifter problems are also common with this engine. Winter driving is compromised by the MPV's light rear end and mediocre traction, and low ground clearance means that off-road excursions shouldn't be too adventurous.

Owners report that the electronic computer module (ECU), automatic transmission driveshaft, upper shock mounts, front 4X4 drive axles and lash adjusters, AC core, and radiator fail within the first three years. Cold temperatures tend to "fry" the automatic window motor, and the paint is easily chipped and flakes off early, especially around the hood, tailgate, and front fenders. Premature brake caliper and rotor wear and excessive vibration/pulsation are chronic problem areas (repairs are needed about every 15,000 miles).

Safety summary, NHTSA complaints/probes, and recalls: **1991–93**—Liquid-vapor separator may fail, causing fuel leaks. • The front brake calipers may suddenly grab and then release, losing their efficacy, and the rear brakes may occasionally lock up in emergency situations. • Some models have head restraints and rear seatbelts that are too slack. • Lots of buffeting about by strong winds. **Recalls: 1989**—Rear brake shoes may fail. **1989–91**—Takata seatbelt replacement. **1990–91**—Rear brakes may be too aggressive when braking at low speeds, causing the rear wheels to lock up with a possible loss of vehicle control. The shoe linings on the rear brakes can change over time and increase friction, causing the rear-wheel ABS to activate prematurely.

Secret Warranties/Service Tips

1988–91—Hard shifting after cold-weather starts can be corrected by installing upgraded synchronizer rings and clutch hub assemblies. **1989–91**—Cold engine piston slapping requires replacement pistons to fix the problem. **1989–93**—AC refrigerant leaks that can't be detected using a leak detector may be caused by a failed O-ring at the block fittings. **1989–94**—Mazda has extended its emissions warranty to 11 years to cover failure of the fuel vapor separator that may allow fuel vapors to leak into the passenger compartment. **1990–92**—If parking on an incline makes your MPV impossible to start, the problem is the increased amount of play in the transmission linkage. Correct by installing an upgraded inhibitor switch and manual plate. **1992–93**—DSB 007/94 describes Mazda's upgraded head cylinder gasket. **1992–94**—A rough idle following a warm restart can be corrected by installing an upgraded two-stage fuel regulator. **All models/years**—DSB 006-94 looks into all the causes and remedies for excessive brake vibrations, and DSB 11/14/95 gives an excellent diagnostic flow chart for troubleshooting excessive engine noise. • Serious paint peeling and delaminating will be fully covered for up to six years under a Mazda secret warranty, say owners who've been compensated after refusing to accept Mazda's denial of responsibility.

MPV Profile

	1990	1991	1992	1993	1994	1995	1996	1997
Cost Price ($)								
Base	16,822	18,073	17,844	19,255	20,900	22,500	22,845	24,370
4X4	20,572	20,743	21,394	22,960	24,700	—	—	—
Used Values ($)								
Base ↑	7,000	8,000	9,000	10,000	11,000	12,500	14,500	16,500
Base ↓	6,000	6,500	7,500	8,500	9,500	11,000	13,500	15,000
4X4 ↑	9,000	7,000	11,000	12,000	13,500	—	—	—
4X4 ↓	7,500	6,500	9,000	10,500	12,000	—	—	—
Extended Warranty	Y	Y	Y	Y	Y	Y	Y	Y
Secret Warranty	Y	Y	Y	Y	Y	Y	Y	Y
Reliability	❷	❷	❷	❷	❷	❷	③	③
Air conditioning	❷	❷	❷	③	③	③	④	④
Body integrity	❷	❷	❷	❷	❷	❷	③	❷
Braking system	❶	❶	❶	❷	❷	❷	③	③
Electrical system	❶	❶	❶	❷	③	③	④	④
Engines	❷	❷	❷	❷	③	③	④	④
Exhaust/Converter	❷	❷	③	③	④	④	⑤	⑤
Fuel system	③	③	③	④	④	④	⑤	⑤
Ignition system	③	③	③	④	④	④	⑤	⑤
Automatic transmission	❷	❷	❷	③	③	③	④	④
Rust/Paint	③	③	③	③	③	③	③	④
Steering	❷	❷	③	③	④	⑤	⑤	⑤
Suspension	❷	❷	❷	❷	③	④	④	④
Crash Safety	—	—	—	—	—	—	④	④

TOYOTA

LE, Previa

Rating: Recommended (1992–97); Above Average (1991); Not Recommended (1984–90). The Previa has high-priced reliability and mediocre road performance. The Previa's last model year was 1997; it was replaced by the Sienna. **Maintenance/Repair costs**: Higher than average, and only Toyota dealers can repair these minivans, particularly when it comes to troubleshooting the supercharged 2.4L engine and All-Track. **Parts**: Limited supply, but reasonably priced. Parts for the LE are often back-ordered.

There are plenty of reasonably-priced two- and three-year-old Previas on the market that have just come off lease. Other minivans you may wish to consider: the Ford Windstar, Mercury Villager, or Nissan Quest. If you have the patience, Toyota's new Sienna is well worth the wait.

Technical Data

ENGINES	Liters/CID	HP	MPG	Model Years
OHC I-4 FI	2.2L/135	101	23–27	1988–90
DOHC I-4 FI	2.4L/149	138	20–25	1991–94
DOHC I-4 FI	2.4L/149	161	18–23	1994–97

Strengths and weaknesses: When you look at Toyota's minivan offerings, you're faced with the choice of buying an early model LE Van or the more recent Previa. The LE uses a conventional mechanical layout borrowed from the Toyota truck line. This means that, with its short wheelbase, it has an unusually high center of gravity and a tendency to tip precariously in tight turns. Add to this the brakes' tendency to lock on hard application and you have a recipe for disaster. The engine's placement under the front seats takes first prize for poor design and makes routine maintenance an all-day affair. Furthermore, the only way to go from the front of the vehicle to the rear is to get out and get back in. The LE is also extremely vulnerable to side winds flinging it about, and the short wheelbase accentuates the discomfort experienced when going over bumpy roads.

LE reliability isn't very good either, with owners reporting lots of premature fuel pump and air conditioning failures, faulty engine oil pressure sensors and cruise-control mechanisms, excessive front brake vibrations and pad and disc wear, and poorly engineered, rust-prone steering components.

The redesigned '91 Previa's performance and reliability are so much improved over its predecessor that it seems like it's almost a different vehicle. Roomier and rendered more stable thanks to its longer wheelbase, equipped with a new 2.4L engine (supercharged as of the '94 model year) and loaded with standard safety and convenience features,

1991–97 Previas are almost as driver-friendly as the Chrysler and Mazda competition. Still, it can't match Chrysler for responsive handling and a comfortable ride, and Toyota's small engine is overworked and doesn't hesitate to tell you so.

Previa owners have learned to live with excessive engine noise, poor fuel economy, premature front brake wear and excessive brake vibration and pulsation, electrical glitches, AC malfunctions, and fit and finish blemishes. Four-wheel drive models with automatic transmissions steal lots of power from the 4-cylinder powerplant.

Safety summary, NHTSA complaints/probes, and recalls: Wind buffeting makes the Previa wander and rear seat head restraints block visibility. **NHTSA: 1996**—Defective brake booster. • Brake master-cylinder failure. • Multiple ABS failures. • Poor, noisy AC compressor performance. • Windshield wipers suddenly stopped working. • Middle right bench seat lap belt is impossible to adjust due to its poor design. • Speed sensor failure. **Recalls: 1991**—Dealers will replace faulty electrical components in Fujitsu Ten radios to eliminate a fire hazard. • Premature windshield wiper failure. **1997**—Oil leakage will result in a sufficiently low oil supply to cause bearing damage to the front differential unit. This can lead to eventual seizure of the unit, increasing the risk of a crash. Dealers will install a modified air breather plug to prevent such oil loss.

Secret Warranties/Service Tips

1988–92 LE Van—In its memo to dealers, No. 89-11 issued 2/21/89, Toyota says that it will pay for the replacement of the oxygen sensor for up to 80,000 miles on all of its trucks and vans. • Transmission extension seal leaks require the installation of an upgraded seal (#24201470). **1990 Previa**—If the sliding door makes a scraping noise as it travels, it signals the need to replace the center rail with an improved part (#68303-28020). **1991**—Under a Special Service Program, Toyota has replaced at no charge the radiator, fan, and fan shroud with improved parts. • Under Special Service Program LO5, Toyota will also replace the cylinder head core plugs and gaskets with improved components. If your minivan requires these repairs, ask Toyota for a partial refund. **1992–93**—Panasonic CD players that skip or won't play were upgraded as of June '93. **1994–96**—Excessive brake vibration or pulsation can be corrected by installing upgraded front brake pads (see chart on following page).

BRAKES
BR007-97
April 18,1997
Title:
PREVIA FRONT BRAKE VIBRATION
Models:
'96 Previa
Introduction:
The front brake pad material has been changed to reduce front brake vibration on 1994 through 1996 Previas.
Production Change Information

MODEL	VIN
Front Disc/Rear Drum	JT3GKI * M * T1233508
Front Disc/Rear Disc	JT3HK2 * M * T1062569

MODEL	PREVIOUS PART NUMBER	NEW PART NUMBER	PART NAME
Front Disc /Rear Drum	04465-28150	04465-28151	Pad Kit, Brake Front
Front Disc /Rear Disc	04465-28170	04465-28171	Pad Kit, Brake Front

Parts Information

OPCODE	DESCRIPTION	TIME	OPN	T1	T2
473025A	Grind front disc rotors on-car (both sides) includes disc brake pads	2.0 (2wd) 2.1 (4wd)	04465-XXXXX	21	13
473015A	Grind front disc rotors off-car (both sides) includes disc brake pads	1.8	04465-XXXXX	21	13
473301	Front disc brake pads and/or shims (both sides) R&R	0.6	04465-XXXXX	21	13

Warranty Information
Warrantable only for 12 months or 12,500 miles from the date-of-first-use or demo date, whichever occurs first. Coverage is extended to 24 months or 18,000 miles, whichever occurs first, in the state of New York due to "Lemon Law" legislation.
NOTE:
Replacement of front brake pad kit and/or shims is limited to correction of a problem based upon customer complaint and subject to all of the provisions of Toyota Warranty Policy Bulletin POL94-18, dated October 7, 1994.

Try these upgraded pads before following the advice found in earlier bulletins listed below.

All models/years—Owner feedback confirms that front brake pads and discs will be replaced free of charge if they're prematurely worn before 2 years/25,000 miles. Improved disc brake pad kits are described in DSB BR94-004. Brake pulsation/vibration, another generic Toyota problem, is fully addressed in DSB BR94-002, "Cause and Repair of Vibration and Pulsation."

Previa Profile

	1991	1992	1993	1994	1995	1996	1997
Cost Price ($)							
Previa	17,173	19,453	21,198	24,218	24,400	26,473	26,963
Used Values ($)							
Previa ↑	10,000	11,000	12,500	14,000	15,500	18,500	20,500
Previa ↓	8,500	9,500	11,000	12,500	14,000	17,000	18,500

| Extended Warranty | Y | Y | Y | Y | Y | Y | Y |
Secret Warranty	N	Y	Y	Y	Y	Y	Y
Reliability	③	③	③	④	⑤	⑤	⑤
Air conditioning	②	②	③	③	③	④	⑤
Body integrity	③	③	③	④	⑤	⑤	⑤
Braking system	❶	❶	❷	❷	❷	❷	❷
Electrical system	❷	❷	③	③	③	❶	❶
Engines	③	③	③	④	⑤	⑤	⑤
Exhaust/Converter	③	③	④	④	⑤	⑤	⑤
Fuel system	③	③	③	④	⑤	⑤	⑤
Ignition system	❷	③	③	③	④	⑤	⑤
Automatic trans.	③	③	③	④	⑤	⑤	⑤
Rust/Paint	④	④	④	④	⑤	⑤	⑤
Steering	④	④	④	③	④	④	④
Suspension	③	③	③	③	④	④	④
Crash Safety	—	—	⑤	❶	④	④	④

VOLKSWAGEN

Camper, EuroVan, Vanagon

Rating: Not Recommended (1986–93). **Maintenance/Repair costs**: Repairs are costly and difficult to carry out. **Parts**: Expensive; there are few independent parts suppliers for other than routine maintenance items.

Relatively rare vehicles, these minivans are not very popular—though the Camper version has attracted a cult following. Prices are generally higher for Campers due to their popularity and extensive standard equipment. An extended warranty is essential. Other minivans that are likely to be more reliable are the Ford Windstar, Mercury Villager, and Quest. For camping, consider a converted, full-sized GM or Ford van.

Technical Data

ENGINES	Liters/CID	HP	MPG	Model Years
OHC I-5 FI	2.5/150	109	16–20	1992–96
OHC I-5D FI	2.4/145	77	22–26	1993–94

Strengths and weaknesses: VW minivans are ugly, grossly underpowered, give insufficient heat and are predictably unpredictable. They handle poorly and are easily flung about in crosswinds. They provide poor traction (except in the 4X4 mode) on slippery roads and take a long time to get up to cruising speed. Heating and air conditioning are inadequate. Excessive tire, wind, road, and engine noise are problems.

Overall reliability is worse than average. Both air-cooled and water-cooled engines are unreliable. The water-cooled version in particular has a tendency to form air pockets in the water jacket, resulting in engine overheating and poor heater performance. Other major problem areas are the air-conditioning and fuel systems, brakes, driveline, manual and automatic transmissions, and suspension.

The 1993 EuroVan has a more powerful engine than its predecessor, but it is still overwhelmed by the vehicle's excess weight. It is unbelievably slow to accelerate. It is not surprising, therefore, that towing is not recommended for any VW minivan—unless the van is the vehicle being towed.

Safety summary, NHTSA complaints/probes, and recalls: A 1988 Vanagon did very poorly in crash tests: the driver would have sustained fatal injuries, and the front passenger would have been severely injured. • One owner of a 1990 Camper reports that the fuel injectors may pump fuel onto the engine manifold. **Recalls**: **1986–87**—Stalling and rough running likely caused by defective fuel tank/filter. **1993**—Dealers will install a new locking bolt to secure the collapsible steering column.

Secret Warranties/Service Tips

1993—If the ABS warning light won't go out, a faulty start switch/lock is the likely culprit. • A rattling noise when accelerating may be caused by the oxygen sensor or harness pigtail contacting the heat shield. • Vehicle may start in third gear. **All models/years**—Install a new ATF strainer cover and gasket if the automatic transmission slips on turns or after stops.

Camper, EuroVan, Vanagon Profile

	1986	1987	1988	1989	1990	1991	1993
Cost Price ($)							
Vanagon	10,120	12,345	16,560	17,355	14,400	14,680	—
Camper	17,190	17,650	21,500	22,555	21,310	21,730	—
EuroVan	—	—	—	—	—	—	17,130
Used Values ($)							
Vanagon ↑	6,000	7,000	8,000	9,000	10,000	11,000	—
Vanagon ↓	5,000	6,000	7,000	7,500	8,500	9,500	—
Camper ↑	10,000	11,500	15,000	16,500	18,500	20,000	—
Camper ↓	8,500	9,500	13,000	14,500	16,500	18,000	—
EuroVan ↑	—	—	—	—	—	—	11,500
EuroVan ↓	—	—	—	—	—	—	10,000
Extended Warranty	Y	Y	Y	Y	Y	Y	Y
Secret Warranty	N	N	N	N	N	N	N
Reliability	②	②	②	②	②	③	③
Air conditioning	②	②	②	②	②	③	④
Body integrity	②	②	②	②	②	②	③

Braking system	②	②	②	②	②	②	③
Electrical system	②	②	②	②	②	②	②
Engines	②	②	②	②	②	②	③
Exhaust/Converter	②	②	②	③	③	③	⑤
Fuel system	②	②	②	②	②	②	③
Ignition system	③	③	③	③	③	④	④
Manual transmission	②	③	③	③	③	④	⑤
-automatic trans.	③	③	③	③	③	③	③
Rust/Paint	③	③	③	③	③	④	⑤
Steering	③	③	③	③	③	④	④
Suspension	③	③	③	③	④	④	④
Crash Safety	—	—	—	—	—	—	②

Appendix I
LEMON-PROOFING BEFORE YOU BUY

Now that you've chosen a vehicle that's priced right and seems to meet your needs, take some time to assess its interior, exterior, and highway performance by following the checklist below. If you're buying from a dealer, ask to take the vehicle home overnight in order to drive it over the same roads you would normally use in your daily activities. This will give you an important insight into how well the engine handles all of the convenience features, how comfortable the seats are during extended driving, and whether front and rear visibility is satisfactory without you having to double up like a pretzel. Of course, if you're buying privately, it's doubtful you will get the vehicle for an overnight test—you may have to rent a similar one from a dealer or rental agency.

Safety Check

1. Is outward visibility good in all directions? (You can't see the nose of the Lumina APV, so you'll have to park by ear.)
2. Are there large blind spots impeding vision (i.e., side pillars)?
3. Are the mirrors large enough for good side and rear views?
4. Does the rear view mirror have a glare-reducing setting?
5. Is there a rear window washer and wiper?
6. Are all instrument displays clearly visible (not washed out in sunlight) and are the controls easily reached?
7. Is the hand brake easy to reach and use?
8. Does the front seat have sufficient rearward travel to put you a safe distance away from the airbag's deployment (about a foot) and still allow you to reach the brake and accelerator pedals?
9. Are the head restraints adjustable or non-adjustable? (The latter is better if you're forgetful about setting them.)
10. Are the head restraints designed to permit rear visibility? (Some are annoyingly obtrusive.)
11. Are there rear three-point shoulder belts similar to those on the front seats? Two-point belts aren't as good. (Some older minivans don't have three-point belts anywhere.)
12. Is the seatbelt latch plate easy to find and reach?
13. Does the seatbelt fit comfortably across the chest without rubbing against the face or falling off the shoulder?
14. Do you feel too much pressure against you from the shoulder belt?
15. Does the seatbelt release easily and retract smoothly?
16. Are there child seat anchorage locations?

17. Are there automatic door locks controlled by the driver or child-proof rear door locks?
18. Do the rear windows roll only halfway down?

Exterior Check

Rust

Rust is a four-letter word that means trouble. Don't buy any used vehicle with extensive corrosion around the rear hatch, wheel wells, door bottoms, or rocker panels. Body work in these areas is usually only a temporary solution.

Cosmetic rusting (rear hatch, exhaust system, front hood) is acceptable and can even help push the price way down, as long as the chassis and other major structural members aren't affected. Bumps, bubbles, or ripples under the paint may be due to repairs resulting from an accident or premature corrosion. Don't dismiss this as a mere cosmetic problem; the entire vehicle will have to be stripped down, reprimed, and repainted.

Knock gently on the front fenders, door bottoms, rear wheel wells, and rear doors—places where rust usually occurs first. Even if these areas have been repaired with plastic, lead, metal plates, or fibreglass, once rusting starts it's difficult to stop. Use a small magnet to check which body panels have been repaired with non-metallic body fillers.

Use a flashlight to check for exhaust system and suspension component rust-out. Make sure the catalytic converter is present. In the past, many drivers removed this pollution control device in the mistaken belief that it would improve fuel economy (this was true only in the first several years that converters were used). Police can fine you for not having the converter and force you to buy one ($300–$400) before certifying your vehicle.

Accident damage

Accident repairs require a further inspection by an independent body shop in order to determine if the frame is aligned and the vehicle is tracking correctly. Frameless minivans need extensive and expensive work to straighten them out, and proper frame and body repairs can often cost more than the vehicle is worth.

Here are some tips on what you can do to avoid buying a damaged vehicle. First, ask the following questions about the vehicle's accident history:

1. Has it ever been in an accident?
2. If so, what was the damage and who fixed it?
3. Is the auto body shop that repaired the vehicle certified to do that kind of work? Is there any warranty outstanding? Can you have a copy of the work order?
4. Has the vehicle's certificate of title been labelled "salvage"? ("Salvage" means that an expert has determined that the cost

to properly repair the vehicle is more than its value. This usually happens after the vehicle has been in a serious accident.)

If the vehicle has been in an accident, you should either walk away from the sale or have it checked by a qualified auto body expert. Remember, not all salvage vehicles are bad—properly repaired ones can be a safe and sound investment if the price is low enough.

What to look for
If the vehicle has been repainted recently, check the quality of the job by inspecting the engine and trunk compartments and the inside door panels. Do it on a clear day so that you'll find any waves in the paint.

1. Check the paint—do all of the vehicle's panels match?
2. Inspect the paint for tiny bubbles. They may identify a poor priming job or premature rust.
3. Is there paint overspray or primer in the doorjambs, wheel wells, or engine compartment? These are signs that the vehicle has had body repairs.
4. Check the gaps between body panels—are they equal? Unequal gaps may indicate improper panel alignment or a bent frame.
5. Do the doors, hood, and rear hatch open and shut properly?
6. Have the bumpers been damaged or recently repaired? Check the bumper support struts for corrosion damage.
7. Test the shock absorbers by pushing hard on a corner of the vehicle. If it bounces around like a ship at sea, the shocks need replacing.
8. Look at the muffler and exhaust pipe to detect premature rust or displacement from a low-impact collision; this could channel deadly carbon monoxide into the passenger area.
9. Make sure there's a spare tire, a jack, and tools necessary for changing a flat. Can you get at the spare easily? Look for premature rusting in the side wheel wells and for water in the rear hatch channel.
10. Look at how the vehicle sits. If one side or end is higher than the other it could mean that the suspension is defective.
11. Ask the seller to turn on the headlights (low and high beams), turn signals, parking lights, emergency blinking lights, and to blow the horn. From the rear, check that the brake lights, back-up lights, turn indicators, taillights, and licence plate light all work.

Tires
Don't be concerned if the tires are worn, since retreads are inexpensive and easy to find. Look at tire wear for clues that the vehicle is out of alignment, needs suspension repairs, or has serious chassis problems. An alignment and new shocks and springs are part of

routine maintenance and are relatively inexpensive in the after-market. However, if it's a 4X4, or the MacPherson struts have to be replaced, you're looking at a $600-$800 repair bill.

Interior Check

The number of miles on the odometer isn't as important as how well the vehicle was driven and maintained. Still, high-mileage vehicles depreciate rapidly because most people consider them to be risky buys. Calculate 15,000 miles per year as average and take off about $200 for each additional 10,000 miles above this average. Be suspicious of the odometer reading. Confirm it by checking the vehicle's maintenance records.

The interior will often give you an idea of how the vehicle was used and maintained. For example, sagging rear seats and a front passenger seat in pristine condition indicate that your minivan may have been used as a mini bus. Delivery vans will have the paint on the driver's door sill rubbed down to the metal, while the passenger door sill will look like new.

What to look for

1. Watch for excessive wear of the seats, dash, accelerator, brake pedal, armrests, and roof lining.
2. Check the dash and roof lining for radio or cellular phone mounting holes (police, taxi, delivery van). Is the radio tuned to local stations?
3. Turn the steering wheel: listen for unusual noises and watch for excessive play (more than an inch).
4. Test the emergency brake with the vehicle parked on a hill.
5. Inspect the seatbelts. Is the webbing in good condition? Do the belts retract easily?
6. Make sure that door latches and locks are in good working order. If rear doors have no handles or locks, or if they've just been installed, your minivan may have been used to transport prisoners.
7. Can the seats be moved into all the positions intended by the manufacturer? Look under them to make sure that the runners are functioning as they should.
8. Can head supports be adjusted easily?
9. Peel back the rugs and check the metal floor for signs of rust or dampness.

Road Test

1. Start the vehicle and listen for unusual noises. Shift automatics into Park and manuals into Neutral with the hand brake engaged. Open the hood to check for fluid leaks. This test should be done with the engine running and be repeated ten

minutes after the engine has been shut down following the
completion of the test drive.

2. With the motor running, check out all dashboard controls:
   windshield wipers, heater and defroster, and radio.
3. If the engine stalls or races at idle, a simple adjustment may fix
   the trouble. Loud clanks or low oil pressure could mean poten-
   tially expensive repairs.
4. Check all ventilation systems. Do the rear side windows roll
   down? Are there excessive air leaks around the door handles?
5. While in Neutral, push down on the accelerator abruptly. Black
   exhaust smoke may require only a minor engine adjustment;
   blue smoke may signal major engine repairs.
6. Shift an automatic into Drive with the motor still idling. The
   vehicle should creep forward slowly without stalling or speed-
   ing. Listen for unusual noises when the transmission is
   engaged. Manual transmissions should engage as soon as the
   clutch is released. Slipping or stalling could require a new
   clutch. While driving, make absolutely sure that a four-wheel
   drive can be engaged without unusual noises or hesitation.
7. Shift an automatic transmission into Drive. While the motor is
   idling, apply the emergency brake. If the motor isn't racing and
   the brake is in good condition, the vehicle should stop.
8. Accelerate to 30 mph while slowly moving through all gears.
   Listen for transmission noises. Step lightly on the brakes; the
   response should be immediate and equal for all wheels.
9. In a deserted parking lot, test the vehicle's steering and suspension by driving in figure eights at low speeds.
10. Make sure the highway is clear of traffic and pedestrians. Drive
    at 20 mph and take both hands off the steering wheel to see
    whether the vehicle veers from one side to the other. If it does,
    the alignment or suspension could be defective, or the vehicle
    could have been in an accident.
11. Test the suspension by driving over some rough terrain.
12. Stop at the foot of a small hill and see if the truck or van can
    climb it without difficulty.
13. On an expressway, it should take no longer than twenty seconds
    for most trucks and minivans to accelerate from a standing start
    to 60 mph.
14. Drive through a tunnel with the windows open. Try to detect
    any unusual motor, exhaust, or suspension sounds.
15. After the test drive, verify the performance of the automatic
    transmission by shifting from Drive to Neutral to Reverse.
    Listen for clunking sounds during transmission engagement.

Many of these tests will undoubtedly turn up some defects, which
may be major or minor (even new trucks and vans have an average
of a half-dozen major and minor defects). Ask an independent

mechanic for an estimate and try to convince the seller to pay part of the repair bill if you buy the vehicle.

It's important to eliminate as many duds as possible through your own cursory check, since you'll later invest two hours and about $50 for a thorough mechanical inspection of your choice. Garages approved by the American Automobile Association usually do a good job. AAA-run outlet inspections run from $75 to $100 for non-members. Oil company-affiliated diagnostic clinics are recommended only if they don't do repairs. Remember, if you get a bum steer from an independent testing agency, you can get the inspection fee refunded and hold the garage or referral agency responsible for your subsequent repairs and consequential damages, like towing, missed work, a ruined vacation, etc. See Part Two for details.

Appendix II
21 BEST INTERNET GRIPE SITES

1. Chrysler Lemon Owners Group
No, you won't read about this consumer group in your owner's manual or see it displayed anywhere at your local dealership. CLOG was set up in January 1998 in Vancouver, British Columbia by over six hundred Chrysler car and minivan owners who felt their automatic transmission, brake and paint defect claims were being stonewalled by Chrysler. These groups submitted the names of irate owners to Chrysler and have succeeded in getting sizeable refunds for brake, transmission, and paint repairs.

If you have had any of these problems and want "goodwill" repairs or a refund for repairs already carried out, go through Chrysler's regular customer relations hot line. Send Chrysler copies of all your repair bills or independent garage estimates, don't accept a refusal based on the fact that you're not the first owner, and finally, don't let Chrysler turn your claim down because the repairs were carried out by an independent repair facility. See Part Two for more information on what you should ask for and what has been Chrysler's response to CLOG's demands.

If you wish to contact the co-chairs of CLOG (B.C.), contact Dean Tkatachow at tel. 604-325-0921, fax 604-325-5207; or Patricia Wong at tel. 604-657-2298, fax 604-255-1831; email *underdog@Lynx.bc.ca*.

2. Chrysler Problems (*http://www.wam.umd.edu/~gluckman/Chrysler/*)
This page is designed to be a resource for Chrysler owners who have had problems in dealing with Chrysler, including issues with peeling paint, transmission failure, the Chrysler-installed Bendix-10 ABS system, and other maladies.

3. Jeep Paint Delamination/Peeling (*http://www.goofball.com/badpaint/*)
Jeep paint and other body defects are covered. Useful links to other sites.

4. Ford Paint Delamination/Peeling (*http://www.ihs2000.com/~peel*)
Everything you should know about the cause and treatment of Ford paint delamination. Useful links to other sites.

5. Ford Contour/Mystique Gripe Site (*http://www.contour.org/FAQ/*)
Similar to the Nissan site, except that it provides a more comprehensive listing of major problems affecting the Ford Contour and Mercury Mystique.

6. Nissan Gripe Site (*http://129.22.253.156/*)
For dissatisfied owners of most Nissan vehicles, this site is particularly helpful in providing useful links to groups and government agencies who will take your complaint. It also covers in detail what it calls Nissan's "silent recall" of defective engines.

7. Sport-utility gripes, blasts, whines, and guilt trips (The Roadhog Info Trough: *http//www.suv.org*; Sport Utility Vehicle Anti-Fan Club: *http//www.howard.net/ban-suvs.html*; The Ultimate Poseur SUV Page: *http//www.poseur.4x4.org* or link from the Anti-Fan Club, above)
These anti-SUV sites believe that sport-utilities and trucks are safety and environmental hazards, in addition to being just plain annoying. You'll find lots of important info and links on the environmental and safety downsides of sport-utility, truck, and van ownership, but keep in mind that much of it is one-sided and some info is outdated. The Friends of the Earth's "Roadhog" site is a hoot to browse if only because of its Internet survey list of 22 questions and reponses that show most respondants don't care much about those policies our Corolla/Prizm-hugging activists hold dear.

8. CompuServe, America On Line Auto Forum or Consumer Forum
Here you will find owner gripes and service manager responses backed up by useful libraries.

9. Automobile News Groups
These news groups are compilations of email raves and gripes and cover all makes and models. They fall into four distinct areas: *rec.autos.makers.chrysler* (you can add any automaker's name at the end); *rec.autos.tech*; *rec.autos.driving*; and *rec.autos.misc* The following news group bulletin board is particularly helpful to owners with minivan and van problems: *http://www.he.net/~brumley/family/vanboard.html*.

10. Center for Auto Safety (*http://www.autosafety.org/*)
Consumers Union and Ralph Nader founded the Center for Auto Safety (CAS) in 1970 to provide consumers with a voice for auto safety and quality in Washington and to help lemon owners fight back across the country. CAS has a small budget but a big impact on the auto industry. It collects complaints and provides a lawyer referral service for its members.

11. NHTSA (*http://www.nhtsa.dot.gov/*)
Run by the Big Daddy of federal government auto safety regulators, the National Highway Traffic Safety Administration, this site has a comprehensive database covering owner complaints, recall campaigns, defect investigations initiated by the department, and automaker service bulletins that may be helpful. Best of all, this data is easily accessed by typing in your vehicle's year, make, and

model. Additionally, there's lots of pro and con information and updates relative to ABS, airbags, child safety seats, and frontal-side crash tests. To access the complaint data base: *http://www.nhtsa. dot.gov/cars/problems/complain/compmmy1.cfm*; for a full list of recalls per model and year: *http://www.nhtsa.dot.gov/cars/problems/recalls/ recmmy1.cfm*; a listing of repair facilities where you can get your airbag disabled: *http://www.nhtsa.dot.gov/airbags/*.

12. FTC (*http://consumer.ftc.gov/bcp/bcp.htm*)
The Federal Trade Commission is a good place to get info on false-advertising complaints, price fixing, etc., relative to automakers and suppliers who scam motorists on both sides of the border.

13. Insurance Institute for Highway Safety (*http://www.hwysafety.org*)
A dazzling site that's long on crash photos and graphs that show which vehicles are the most crashworthy. Lots of safety info that eschews the traditional "nut behind the wheel" dialectic. (Let owners deactivate their airbags if they feel at risk, and beware of driving schools: they don't make kids better drivers.)

14. Lemon-Aid Feedback (*lemonaid@earthlink.net*)
Comments and critiques are welcome, particularly if you have an experience to relate that can help other *Lemon-Aid* readers.

15. "Lemon Aid or How to Get Carmakers to Call You and Beg for Mercy" (*http://www.saabnet.com/aas/1997.W26/1344522661.2 6426.html*)
Although not affiliated with the Lemon-Aid car guides, this site contains a hilarious listing of tactics to use in getting auto manufacturers to return your calls, listen to your complaints, and give you compensation. For example, here's how you're advised to deal with the automaker's customer relations rep:

> ...This is what you should do. DENY THAT YOUR CAR HAS ANY PROBLEMS, and try to sell the car to the person who answered the phone. They will absolutely hate this. When you see that you are going nowhere with this, then ask the customer service rep to go around the office to take up a collection to pay for the car. Say outrageous things; take my word for it, they will remember your name! Alternatively, demand to know the telephone number of the rep's mother. When the rep asks you why you want his/her mother's telephone number, say you have a piece of metal to sell and you feel that his/her mother deserves it..

16. Alldata Service Bulletins (*http://www.alldata.com/consumer/ TSB/yr.html*)
Automotive recalls and technical service bulletins are listed by year, make, model and engine option . Select a year, then a manufacturer, to see a summary list of recalls and technical service bulletins for your

car or truck. The only drawback is that you can't see the contents of individual bulletins.

17. Kelley Blue Book Prices (*http://www.kbb.com/*)
Providing over 9 million free reports every month, the Kelley Blue Book site is an excellent price guide when you are ready to buy a car. It gives you the information you need to make an informed choice, whether you are buying a new or used car; selling or trading in your own car. New and used car pricing reports are free to car buying consumers.

18. Automobile Disputes (*http://photo.net/philg/litigation/automobile-disputes.html*)
Phillip Greenspun prepared this legal primer for non-lawyers who own cars, in or out of the explicit warranty, that the manufacturer refuses to repair.

19. The Lemon Aid Stand (*http://www.pond.net/~delvis/lemonlinks.html*)
Gosh, it seems like everbody's using my name these days. Nevertheless, this web site, though not affiliated with the *Lemon-Aid* guides, provides lots of useful info relative to defects, state lemon laws (listed by state), pleading your own case in court, etc. Plus, it has a comprehensive listing of other helpful sites.

20. The Consumer Law Page (*http://consumerlawpage.com/*)
This "know-your-rights" site is sponsored by the California-based Alexander Law Firm, specialists in consumer law and class actions. It contains well-researched articles of interest to consumers, hundreds of free consumer information brochures, and a resources page that provides over one thousand links to other useful sites. I find the site's manner of explaining complex legal issues in everyday terms both informative and entertaining (reading the ins and outs of the fire-prone GM pickup class action is particularly interesting). Plus, California residents can get a free legal opinion as to the merits of their claim.

21. Trujillo vs. Volvo (*http://www.law.emory.edu/1circuit/mar98/97-1792.01a.html*).
This lawsuit provides an interesting, though lengthy, dissertation on the safety hazards that airbags pose and why automakers are ultimately responsible for the injuries and deaths caused by their deployment.

Appendix III
1995–97 MODEL NHTSA
CRASH-TEST SUMMARY

The following table contains the results of the new vehicle crash test program run by the National Highway Traffic Safety Administration on 1995–97 model year cars and minivans.

NHTSA notes that while all 1997 vehicles are required to pass a 30 mph frontal crash test, government tests are conducted at 35 mph to make the differences between vehicles more apparent. Thus, all of the vehicles are crashed into a fixed barrier at a speed of 35 mph. The impact is the same as if two identical vehicles, each going 35 mph, collided head-on. Each test vehicle carries two dummies of average human size and weight, one in the driver's seat and one in the right front passenger seat. The dummies contain instruments in their heads, chests, and thighs which measure the forces and impacts that occur during the crash and could cause injury. These measures form the basis for the calculation of the star ratings for the driver and the passenger sides of the vehicle. There are two types of dummies used in these tests, the Hybrid II and Hybrid III. While NHTSA considers the dummies equally effective in measuring crash protection, Hybrid III dummies are more advanced and can provide more detailed injury data. For 1997, Hybrid III dummies were exclusively used in all tests.

NHTSA also notes that since seatbelts are now standard equipment in all vehicles, the dummies representing the driver and front-seat passenger are always belted. The test results do not apply to unbelted occupants. Airbags are used whenever they are available with a vehicle, either as standard equipment or as an option. "ND" means no data was available. "NTP" indicates that the NHTSA has no tests planned for that model.

NHTSA cautions that its data is valuable for comparison only and, in one respect, only among vehicles within the same weight class. Where the crash is between two vehicles, then the comparison is valid only for a given weight class.

Where there is a full-frontal, multi-vehicle accident involving vehicles of different weight classes, there is almost always a higher risk of injury associated with the lighter weight vehicle. However, you can use the figures comparatively when considering the safety of a vehicle involved in a full-frontal crash with an object like a tree or telephone pole (25% of all accidents are single-vehicle injury crashes).

Recent charts differ in format from early years; NHTSA researchers believe that a more basic, non-numeric rating system

481

will prove more useful to consumers than its early reports which included specific numbers for head injuries and chest injuries. Five stars (*****) is the highest rating; one (*) is the lowest. Head and chest injury data are combined into a single rating which represents the vehicle's relative level of crash protection in a head-on collision. Within each weight class:

Frontal Collision

*****	= 10% or less chance of serious injury
****	= 11%–20% chance of serious injury
***	= 21%–35% chance of serious injury
**	= 36%–45% chance of serious injury
*	= 46% or greater chance of serious injury

The 1997 reports offer both more and less information than reports for earlier years: each report now deletes the weight of each vehicle and whether the vehicle has standard driver and passenger side seatbelts, but reports whether driver and passenger side airbags are standard or available and adds whether the vehicle has standard or available anti-lock brakes and adjustable seatbelt anchors.

Note that in 1997 the NHTSA began testing vehicles as to their safety in side impact crashes. NHTSA says:

> The test configuration represents an intersection type collision with a 3,015 pound deformable barrier moving at 38.5 mph into the stationary struck vehicle. In the stationary vehicle, instrumented dummies in the driver and rear seat passenger seats register forces during the crash.

The same star ratings—one through five stars—are used for the side crashes as for the frontal crashes, but the chances of injury are different:

Side Collision

*****	= 5% or less than chance of serious injury
****	= 6%–10% chance of serious injury
***	= 11%–20% chance of serious injury
**	= 21%–25% chance of serious injury
*	= 26% or greater chance of serious injury

NHTSA further explains:

> Drivers and passengers in the side crash rating receive a one to five star rating, with five stars indicating the best performance. The side crash star ratings are assigned based in the chance of a life threatening chest injury for the driver, the front seat passenger, and the rear seat passenger. Head injury is not measured in the side crashes. For every vehicle in a severe side crash there are two vehicles in severe frontal crashes.

1995 SMALL*

Vehicle	Safety Rating driv.	pass.	Vehicle	Safety Rating driv.	pass.
Acura Integra 4d	****	***	Mazda 626	****	*****
Chev. Corsica 4d	***	**	Mitsub. Eclipse 4d	****	****
Dodge Spirit 4d	****	***	Mitsubishi Galant 4d	****	****
Ford Aspire	****	****	Nissan 240SX	***	****
Ford Escort 2d	****	****	Nissan Maxima	****	***
Ford Probe	*****	****	Olds. Achieva 2d	****	***
Geo Metro	****	****	Plymouth Neon 4d	***	***
Honda Accord	****	***	Saturn SL2 4d	****	****
Honda Civic	****	****	Subaru Legacy 4d	****	****
Honda Civic 4d	***	***	Toyota Corolla 4d	****	****
Hyundai Elantra	*	*	Toyota Tercel 4d	***	****
Hyundai Scoupe	****	****	VW Jetta 4d	***	***
Hyundai Sonata	***	****			

1995 MEDIUM

Vehicle	Safety Rating driv.	pass.	Vehicle	Safety Rating driv.	pass.
Audi A6 4d	*****	*****	Ford Taurus	****	****
BMW 325i 4d	****	****	Ford T-bird	*****	*****
Buick Century	****	****	Mazda Millenia	****	*****
Chev. Camaro	*****	*****	Mercedes C220	****	****
Chev. Monte C.	****	****	Pont. Grand Prix	****	***
Dodge Intrepid	****	****	Saab 900 4d	****	****
Dodge Stratus	***	ND	Toyota Camry 4d	****	***
Ford Contour	*****	****	VW Passat 4d	****	****
Ford Mustang	****	****	Volvo 850 4d	*****	****

*"Small" refers to minicars, sub-compacts, and compacts.

1995 FULL-SIZE

Vehicle	Safety Rating driv.	pass.	Vehicle	Safety Rating driv.	pass.
Acura Legend 4d	***	****	Infiniti J30 4d	****	****
Chevrolet			Lexus GS 300 4d	***	***
Caprice	****	**	Lincoln Town Car	*****	ND
Chrysler New			Pontiac Bonneville	*****	***
Yorker	****	****			
Ford Crown					
Victoria	****	*****			

1995 MINIVANS

Vehicle	Safety Rating driv.	pass.	Vehicle	Safety Rating driv.	pass.
Dodge Caravan	****	****	Nissan Quest	****	***
Ford Aerostar	****	***	Pontiac Trans Sport	****	***
Ford Windstar	*****	*****	Toyota Previa	****	***
Honda Odyssey	****	*****			

1996 SMALL

Vehicle	Safety Rating driv.	pass.	Vehicle	Safety Rating driv.	pass.
Acura Integra 4d	****	***	Mazda Miata	****	***
Chev. Cavalier 4d	***	***	Mazda Protegé 4d	***	ND
Chev. Corsica 4d	***	**	Mitsubishi Mirage 2d	***	***
Dodge Avenger	*****	*****	Nissan 240 SX	***	****
Dodge Neon 4d	****	****	Nissan Altima 4d	****	****
Ford Aspire 4d	****	****	Nissan Maxima	****	***
Ford Escort 2d	****	****	Nissan Sentra 4d	****	****
Ford Probe	*****	****	Pontiac Grand Am	****	****
Geo Metro 4d	****	****	Saturn SL2 4d	****	****
Honda Accord	****	***	Subaru Impreza 4d	****	****
Honda Civic 2d	****	****	Subaru Legacy 4d	****	****
Honda Civic 4d	*****	*****	Toyota Camry 2d	****	*****
Hyundai Accent	***	****	Toyota Corolla 4d	****	****
Hyundai Elantra	***	***	Toyota Tercel 4d	***	****
Hyundai Sonata	***	****	VW Jetta 4d	***	***
Mazda 626 DX 4d	****	*****			

1996 MEDIUM

Vehicle	Safety Rating driv.	pass.	Vehicle	Safety Rating driv.	pass.
Acura TL 4d	****	****	Ford Mustang	*****	*****
Audi A4 4d	****	*****	Convertible		
Audi A6 4d	*****	*****	Ford Taurus 4d	****	****
BMW 328i 4d	****	****	Ford T-bird	*****	*****
Buick Century	****	****	Lexus ES 300	*****	***
Chev. Camaro	*****	*****	Mazda Millenia	****	*****
Chevrolet			Merc-Benz C220 4d	****	****
Lumina 4d	*****	****	Pontiac G. Prix 2d	****	***
Chev. Monte C.	****	****	Saab 900 4d	****	****
Dodge Intrepid	****	****	Toyota Avalon 4d	****	*****
Dodge Stratus 4d	***	ND	Toyota Camry 4d	****	***
Ford Contour 4d	*****	****	VW Passat 4d	****	****
Ford Mustang	****	****	Volvo 850 4d	*****	****

1996 FULL-SIZE

Vehicle	Safety Rating driv.	pass.	Vehicle	Safety Rating driv.	pass.
Cadillac DeVille	***	*	Infiniti J30	****	****
Chev. Caprice	****	**	Lexus GS 300	***	***
Chrysler			Lincoln Town Car	****	*****
New Yorker	****	****	Olds. Aurora 4d	***	***
Ford Crown			Pontiac Bonneville	*****	***
Victoria	*****	*****			

1996 MINIVANS

Vehicle	Safety Rating driv.	pass.	Vehicle	Safety Rating driv.	pass.
Chevrolet Astro	***	***	Honda Odyssey	****	*****
Dodge Grand			Mazda MPV	****	****
Caravan	***	****	Mercury Villager	****	***
Ford Aerostar	****	***	Pont. Trans Sport	****	***
Ford Windstar	*****	*****	Toyota Previa	****	***

1997 SMALL

Vehicle	Safety Rating			
	driver	passenger	driver side	passenger side
Buick Skylark	*****	****	*	***
Chevrolet Cavalier	****	****	*	**
Chrysler Sebring	*****	*****	NTP	NTP
Dodge Avenger	*****	*****	NTP	NTP
Dodge Neon	****	****	NTP	NTP
Eagle Talon	****	****	NTP	NTP
Ford Aspire	****	****	NTP	NTP
Ford Escort	****	****	***	***
Ford Probe	*****	****	NTP	NTP
Geo Metro	****	****	NTP	NTP
Geo Prizm	****	****	***	***
Honda Accord	****	***	**	***
Honda Civic 2d	****	****	NTP	NTP
Honda Civic 4d	****	*****	***	***
Hyundai Accent	***	****	NTP	NTP
Hyundai Elantra	***	***	NTP	NTP
Hyundai Sonata	***	****	*	**
Infiniti I30	****	***	****	***
Mazda 626 DX	****	*****	**	***
Mazda MX6	*****	****	NTP	NTP
Mazda Miata	****	***	NTP	NTP
Mazda Protegé	**	ND	NTP	NTP
Mercury Tracer	****	****	***	***
Mitsubishi Eclipse	****	****	NTP	NTP
Mitsubishi Galant	****	****	***	***
Nissan 200SX	*****	****	NTP	NTP
Nissan 240 SX	***	****	NTP	NTP
Nissan Altima	****	****	NTP	NTP
Nissan Maxima	****	***	NTP	NTP
Nissan Sentra	****	****	NTP	NTP
Olds. Achieva	*****	****	*	***
Pont. G. Am 2d	*****	****	*	***
Pontiac Sunfire	****	****	*	**
Saturn SL2	****	****	NTP	NTP

	driver	passenger	driver side	passenger side
Subaru Impreza	****	****	NTP	NTP
Subaru Legacy	****	****	NTP	NTP
Suzuki Swift	****	****	NTP	NTP
Toyota Corolla	****	****	***	***
Toyota Paseo	****	****	NTP	NTP
Toyota Tercel	****	****	NTP	NTP
VW Golf	***	***	NTP	NTP
VW Jetta	***	***	NTP	NTP

1997 MEDIUM

Vehicle	Safety Rating			
	driver	passenger	driver side	passenger side
Acura TL	****	****	NTP	NTP
Audi A4	****	*****	NTP	NTP
Audi A6	*****	*****	NTP	NTP
BMW 328i	****	****	NTP	NTP
Buick LeSabre	****	****	NTP	NTP
Chev. Camaro	*****	*****	***	****
Chev. Lumina	*****	****	****	***
Chev. Camaro	*****	*****	***	****
Chev. Malibu	****	****	*	***
Chrys. Cirrus	***	ND	***	**
Chrys. Concorde	****	****	****	***
Chrys. Sebring Convertible	****	****	NTP	NTP
Dodge Intrepid	****	****	****	***
Dodge Stratus	***	ND	***	**
Eagle Vision	****	****	****	***
Ford Contour	*****	****	***	****
Ford Mustang Convertible	*****	*****	NTP	NTP
Ford Mustang	****	****	NTP	NTP
Ford Taurus	****	****	***	***
Ford T-bird	*****	*****	***	*
Isuzu Oasis	****	****	NTP	NTP
Mazda Millenia	****	*****	NTP	NTP
Mercedes C230	****	****	NTP	NTP
Mercury Cougar	*****	*****	***	*

Mercury Mystique	*****	****	***	****
Mercury Sable	****	****	***	***
Olds. Cutlass	****	****	*	***
Plymouth Breeze	***	ND	***	**
Pontiac Firebird	*****	*****	***	****
Pont. G. Prix 4d	****	****	NTP	NTP
Saab 900	****	****	NTP	NTP
Toyota Avalon	****	*****	NTP	NTP
Toyota Camry	****	*****	***	***
VW Passat	****	****	NTP	NTP
Volvo 850	*****	****	****	ND

1997 FULL-SIZE

Vehicle	Safety Rating			
	driver	passenger	driver side	passenger side
Cadillac DeVille	****	****	****	****
Chrysler LHS	****	****	NTP	NTP
Ford Crown Vic	*****	*****	****	****
Lexus GS 300	***	***	NTP	NTP
Lincoln Continental	****	*****	NTP	NTP
Lincoln Town Car	****	*****	NTP	NTP
Merc. G. Marquis	*****	*****	****	****
Olds. Aurora	***	***	NTP	NTP
Pont. Bonne. SSE	*****	***	NTP	NTP
Volvo 960	****	****	NTP	NTP

1997 MINIVANS

Vehicle	Safety Rating			
	driver	passenger	driver side	passenger side
Chevrolet Astro	***	***	NTP	NTP
Chevrolet Venture	****	****	NTP	NTP
Chrys. Town & C.	****	****	NTP	NTP
Chrys. Twn & C. LX	***	****	NTP	NTP
Dodge Caravan	****	****	NTP	NTP
Dodge G. Caravan	***	****	NTP	NTP
Dodge Ram Van	***	****	NTP	NTP
Ford Aerostar	****	***	NTP	NTP

Ford Windstar	*****	*****	NTP	NTP
GMC Safari	***	***	NTP	NTP
Honda Odyssey	****	****	NTP	NTP
Mazda MPV	****	****	NTP	NTP
Mercury Villager	****	***	NTP	NTP
Nissan Quest	****	***	NTP	NTP
Olds. Silhouette	****	****	NTP	NTP
Ply. G. Voyager	***	****	NTP	NTP
Ply. Voyager	****	****	NTP	NTP
Pontiac Trans Sport	****	****	NTP	NTP
Toyota Previa	****	***	NTP	NTP

Appendix IV
INDEX OF KEY DOCUMENTS

The following documents, memos, court decisions, and service bulletins aren't published in any other consumer guide. They have been put in the following index so that you can easily find and photocopy whichever document will prove helpful in your dealings with automakers, government agencies, dealers, or service managers. Most of the service bulletins outline repairs or replacements that should be done for free.

Part One

Secret Bulletins:
• Chrysler's radar stalling 3
• Ford's aluminum transmission failure...3
• GM's clunking transmission 4
• *Autoweek* clipping says GM secretly buying back trucks, minivans, and sport-utilities with faulty ABS brakes....................10
• Transport Canada study: airbag deployment may severely injure women and seniors...11
• Doorplate tells true model year...34
• Domestic vs. Asian: shocking internal service bulletin summaries compare the 1994 Ford Taurus to the 1994 Toyota Camry....38–42

Part Two

A Secret Warranties Sampler:
• Free AC odor servicing by GM, Ford and Chrysler...............58–59
• Ford Villager, Nissan Quest: free engine replacements..............60
• GM Cavalier, Sunbird: free engine head gasket repairs..............61
• Honda Civic, Accord, Prelude, Odyssey: free 14-year engine repairs (free check-ups and tune-ups to 150,000 miles) 62
• Toyota sport-utilities and pickups: free V6 engine replacements...62–63
• Estimated part durability chart 64–65
• GM's confidential "goodwill" warranty guidelines bulletin 69
Sample letters/faxes:
• Used car complaint letter/fax..72
• Secret warranty claim letter/fax 73
• Claim fact sheet..74
• Settlement form 86
Paint defects (Chrysler, Ford, GM):
• Chrysler class action: paint delamination, peeling................90–94
• GM paint delamination bulletin 95–96
• GM secret paint memo promises free repairs for 6 years......98–105

Part Three

Bulletins showing factory-related defects:
• Chrysler Neon water leaks...121
• Ford Escort fuel pumps 127
• Ford Escort windnoise 127
• GM Cavalier, Sunbird faulty engines 133
• Honda Civic water leaks 140
• Honda Civic "clunking"..141
• Mazda 323 tailpipe upgrade..150
• Nissan Sentra brake pedal "feel" kit 153
• GM Saturn cylinder heads...160
• Toyota Tercel window molding noise 170
• Chrysler Cirrus, Stratus, Breeze water leaks 198
• Chrysler Cirrus, Stratus, Breeze quieter,
  longer-wearing brake pads 199
Ford Taurus, Sable:
• Ford Taurus, Sable paint delamination 209
• Ford Taurus, Sable no-start with 3.0/3.8L engines................210
• Ford Taurus, Sable automatic transmission aluminum
  piston defect...213
• Ford Taurus, Sable automatic transmission defect..................214
• Ford Taurus, Sable harsh automatic shifting...........................215
• GM automatic transmission loss of drive................................226
• GM suspension squawk...232
• GM cold start rattle..237
• GM more durable brake pads..238
• Honda Accord front windshield windnoise 244
• Hyundai Sonata brake pulsation...247
• Toyota Camry, Avalon front brake noise..................................263
• Chrysler Concorde, Intrepid, LHS, Vision,
  New Yorker trunk leaks 282
• Ford Crown Victoria, Grand Marquis ABS malfunctions..........287
• GM Caprice, Roadmaster excessive engine noise.....................297
• Nissan Maxima noisy brakes...356
• GM Camaro, Firebird uneven rear brake pad wear 394
Chrysler minivans:
• Stalling near airports, military bases 427
• Delayed transmission engagement 428
• Reasons for poor transmission shifting 429–30
• '97 minivan bulletin summary (40 bulletins) 432
• Engine piston knocking...435
• Stalling when shifting 436
• Foul exhaust odor (rotten eggs) 438
• Rear brake noise 439
Ford Aerostar:
• Premature AC failure ("Black Death")....................................442
• Rust-perforated front and rear lower door rocker panels........444

Mercury Villager, Nissan Quest:
• Broken engine exhaust manifold studs.....................................448
• Excessive front brake squealing 449
• Lower engine knocking noise 450
Toyota Previa:
• Excessive front brake vibration 467

Appendix V
SURVEY AND BULLETIN SEARCH

Rate your vehicle

The information found in this book has been garnered from motorists' responses to surveys like the one on the following page. Your answers help us protect others from sales scams and bad products. Include any photographs (especially of paint defects), diagrams, contracts, or work orders that expose a defect or dishonest practice. If you order a bulletin summary, your survey comments will also help me to zero in on bulletins that may be useful to you.

I pull the computer bulletin summaries myself (it keeps me in touch with readers like you), and usually fax them back within a few days. Sorry, I can only process Visa cards.

Phil Edmonston

lemonaid@earthlink.net

Cut Repair Costs • Fight Fraud and Incompetence with...
Lemon-Aid's $15 Bulletin Summary

If you plan to buy a used vehicle, have just bought one, or want to know what to check before the warranty expires, you'll need a bulletin summary computer printout. Nothing gives you a stronger argument with a mechanic than pulling out a confidential bulletin (DSB) that says a failure is factory related or is covered by an extended warranty.

Fill out the request on the next page. You'll receive an exhaustive summary of the DSBs that concern your 1982–97 vehicle. (It's too early for '98 models.)

Bulletins show repair shortcuts, labor time, lists of upgraded parts, probable defects, recall campaigns, and secret warranties. As well, we'll list your vehicle's present wholesale and retail value.

Order by fax or mail. There's no difference in price, although faxing is much faster. Expect 5–10 faxed pages. You may email your request, but be sure to give a fax number or mailing address because I can only fax or mail the summary.

- **FAX** (Visa only): 954-563-2448 (24 hours a day). Replies by fax should take only a few days—unless I'm on vacation or way behind in my work. You may fax your request and have the bulletin summary mailed. That takes about a week.

- **MAIL**: Make your cheque payable to "DSB" (2805 E. Oakland Park Blvd., Suite 211, Ft. Lauderdale, FL, 33306). Allow a total of 2–3 weeks for reception and delivery.

LEMON-AID SURVEY/DSB SUMMARY REQUEST

❏ I don't need a DSB summary; my survey comments are below.
❏ Please fax ❏ mail ❏ me a DSB summary for my vehicle and
an estimate of its worth ($15 fee enclosed).
Fax #_____
VISA (ONLY) # _____
(will be used once and then destroyed)
Signature: _____

Name: _____
Address: _____
_____

MY VEHICLE'S PROFILE

Make _____ Model: _____
Year:_____Engine (liters): ____Mileage: _____

GENERAL COMMENTS
(Include a photo, diagram, or bill)

Safety: _____
Reliability: _____
_____
_____

Performance: _____
_____
_____

JOY OF OWNERSHIP
(Recommended ⑤, Above Average ④, Average ③,
Below Average ❷, Not Recommended ❶)

Overall reliability

Air conditioning	Ignition system
Automatic transmission	Rust resistance
Body integrity	Steering
Braking system	Suspension
Electrical system	**Dealer service**
Engine	**Maintenance**
Exhaust/converter	**Parts availability**
Fuel system	**Repair costs**